American Automobile Association

All-in-One
LONDON
AND
SURROUNDINGS

MILL HOUSE® ASSOCIATES

COLLIER BOOKS
MACMILLAN PUBLISHING COMPANY
NEW YORK

Mill House Publishing Ltd.
Monxton Mill, Monxton, SP11 8AW
· Hampshire, United Kingdom

Collier Books
Macmillan Publishing Company
866 Third Avenue, New York, NY 10022
Collier Macmillan Canada, Inc.

Library of Congress Cataloging-in-Publication Data
AAA all-in-one. London and surroundings / Mill House Associates.
— 1st Collier Books ed.
p. cm.
Includes index.
ISBN 0-02-035110-0
1. London (England)—Description—1981– —Guide-books. 2. London
Region (England)—Description and travel—Guide-books I. Mill
House Associates. II. Title: London and surroundings.
DA679.A33   1989   88-31588   CIP
914.21′04858—dc19

All prices quoted in this book were accurate at the time of
going to press. Sadly, prices are constantly changing. Mill
House Associates apologizes in advance for any inaccuracies
which may occur as a result of this changing world.

First Collier Books Edition 1989
Printed in the United States of America

THE ALL-IN-ONE GUIDE

This book represents a whole new way of looking at travel – one that starts from *your* point of view.

- You have your own particular interests, and you want to know where to find the facts. Until now you had to buy an armful of guidebooks – no more. **All-in-One** covers everything, from castles and museums to boat rides and golf, with the best food, hotels and hotspots en route.

- You want the best at a price you can afford – this book is just that. It's been researched by people who live in the region and know what's good value – **all-in-one** book.

- You're not a packaged tour traveler, so you want non-touristy spots and driving directions. These, too, are included: maps, road and visual references checked out for you. **All-in-one** location when you need it.

- You don't want to have to retrace your steps, so we've built in a unique BUILD-A-TOUR concept which allows you to design your own tours, **all-in-one**.

- You don't want clichés. You *do* want to know where to eat, what's a bargain, what to see when you're on the spot. So we advise you what to choose at that specific restaurant and why this particular hotel has been selected. You have it **all-in-one** and right at hand.

- In golden bygone days, route maps and books were extraneous: you had a friendly, knowledgeable guide at your elbow every step of the way. They were all-in-one experts: so is this **All-in-One** book.

  We hope you'll find it an especially helpful, amusing and comprehensive companion.

Acknowledgements

A guide is only as good as its researchers and writers. We would like to express our particular thanks to:

Research/Writers	Researchers
Judith Carter	Jean Arnell
Michael Hobbs	Penny Chambers
Bridget Jones	Penny Colston
Barry Randle	B Doyle
Emma Stanford	Daphne Hobbs
Caroline White	Dee Paterson
	Harriet Peacock
	Kelly Verstappen

In addition we would like to thank the British Tourist Authority and the English Tourist Board for their help in gathering information.

Editorial Director: Peter Verstappen
Managing Editor: Wendy Weber Verstappen
Executive Editor: Judith Carter
Art Director: Robert Mathias
Cartographers: Nicholas Skelton, Kevan Hamman, Publishing Workshop

Chief Copy Editor: Helen Norris
Copy Editors: Sonya Mills, Earnest Roth

Copy Typists: Philippa Hamblin, Caroline Mallam, Helen Stephens, Leigh Stewart

Indexer: Helen Norris

Typesetter: York House Typographic, London W7

We hope you've enjoyed this book and benefited from its recommendations. We welcome correspondence from readers. So, if we got it wrong, do set us right. Alternatively, if we've missed a 'best bet' let us know. Write to:

The Managing Editor
Mill House Associates Ltd
Monxton Mill
High Street
Monxton, near Andover
Hampshire SP11 8AW
United Kingdom

CONTENTS

HOW TO USE THIS GUIDE

This book divides into three distinct sections – London, driving tours centered on London and longer motoring tours. The out of London tours cover Southern England's most scenic routes as well as numerous attractions. The maps in each section show both the round London drives and the longer itineraries. You'll note from this that you can start an itinerary with one of the shorter journeys then link it up with one of the longer ones.

By the same token you can link day trips together to form your own two-day, three-day, four-day or even longer itinerary. You can do this by taking one of the link routes which interconnect the day tours out of London. These eliminate the need to return to the capital if you want to stay out in the country. For example, set off on Day Tour 1, Route A to Canterbury, then connect via Route C (Tour 1) with Brighton (which is also on Tour 2). From Brighton you can take Tour 2, Route B, straight back to London, or wander on via Route C to Windsor.

The link routes are designed to take you quickly from one area of outstanding appeal to another. Yet even on these we've listed a few places to stay or have a pleasant meal as well as the occasional shop or attraction which might merit a stop. Precise details of the round London tours and the links are shown on page 218.

The tours in this guide are each very different. They reflect not only the style of the different writers and researchers who went out on the road, but also the different landscapes, social and economic history of each region. We have, of course, tried to be consistent in the information available in each section of the guide, pointing out good places to stop for coffee, for a pub lunch or an overnight stay. The lack of any of these simply means that we haven't found anywhere nice enough, or of sufficient good value to recommend to you.

TOURIST INFORMATION CENTRES

You'll find one or more of these in every major town and in many smaller towns that are of interest to visitors. Staff here will answer your travel enquiries and supply you with local maps and guides along with details of opening times for places of interest in the area. The TICs also have information on what's playing at the local theaters and concert halls.

Visiting Country Houses, Castles and Gardens

We have not given exact dates of open periods, but have erred on the side of caution. Where we have 'Mar-Sept', for example, you can be sure that the property will be open to the public throughout all of March and September, but if you're traveling at the beginning of March, say, or the end of September, it's worth checking with the local Tourist Information Centre to see if there are a few open days tacked on (opening times are often tuned to the ever-changing school vacation dates).

Details of opening hours give you the times when the property is open to the public. Many of the larger houses and castles, and all of those with guided tours, have a time for last admissions, which is normally about one hour before closing time.

SHOPPING

Normal shopping hours in Britain are between 9am/9:30am and 5:00pm/6pm, Monday to Saturday. In some towns, many of the smaller shops will close for half a day, usually at 1pm on either a Wednesday or Thursday. This is called 'early closing day'. It is becoming increasingly rare, and does not usually apply to national chain stores.

We have included details of opening times for individual shops in major cities. Elsewhere, opening times are only given if they are unusual. Small shops run by one or two people, especially antique shops, often close for an hour for lunch.

Apart from London, we have not written about major national stores, such as Marks & Spencer. These, in common with the high street fashion stores like Next, are to be found in most major cities and large towns.

Many antique shops and major stores will help with tax and shipping arrangements on substantial purchases.

CREDIT CARD SYMBOLS

Plastic is a way of life. Here are our symbols for accepted credit cards:

AE = American Express
DC = Diners Card
MC = Mastercard, Access, Eurocard
V = Visa

ADDED CONFUSIONS AVOIDED

1. All telephone numbers shown include the area code from London. (The (01) beside London numbers is the code for calling London from outside the city.) While generally this code works throughout the country, this is not always the case.

If you have problems completing your call Telephone Enquiries can help – dial 192.

2. Precise closing dates for some hotels were not fixed as we went to press. So if you're coming out of season and we've indicated a closing period, best write ahead.

3. For London we've listed the nearest underground (for which read 'subway') station. The city also has a comprehensive bus route. Virtually all London hotels we recommend are on or within reasonable distance of a bus stop.

HOTELS

HOTEL CODES

Wherever possible we've tried to give you a good representative range of hotels from those that are small, family run and remarkably reasonable to more elegant and elegantly priced establishments.

For hotels we've used pound sterling symbol codes to indicate not only degree of expense but value for money. Broadly speaking the codes indicate the following prices per person based on double occupancy:

	London	Immediate Surroundings	Further Afield
£	£20-£35	£15-£30	£12.50-£25
££	£35-£45	£30-£40	£25-£30
£££	£45+	£40+	£30+

Prices are further affected by time of year and demand at the particular locale. Thus, for example, hotels in all categories tend to be more expensive in Bath than in Brighton.

HOTEL SYMBOLS

For simplicity we've used hotel symbols throughout the guide. These are as follows:

☎ = Telephone in room   ≈ = Swimming Pool
➠ = TV in room   ↗ = Golf Course
🅿 = Parking Lot   ℗ = Tennis
⑂¶ = Restaurant on premises   ◎ = Mini-bar in room
⅄ = Bar on premises

GENERAL HOTEL DOS AND DON'TS

1. Do book your first several days' worth of hotel stops before you arrive.

2. Do use the book to plan your motoring tours then call the hotels along the way a few days in advance to reserve a room. Citing a credit card number will confirm space, but you'll be charged if you don't show up and don't cancel in time.

3. Don't panic if the hotels on your route are full. Throughout the country the British Tourist Authority operates an excellent Book-A-Bed Ahead service. Operated by the Travel Information Centres you'll find identified in this guide, they will find you a room for a nominal reservation fee of £1.75.

4. Do specify which newspaper you'd like for the following morning. It will normally magically appear with breakfast. The *International Herald Tribune, USA Today* and The *Wall Street Journal* are available on the date of issue in London and selected major cities. For a good quality read we recommend *The Independent* while *Today* has great features.

5. Do leave valuables out of sight, both in the car and in your room.

SOME FURTHER HOTEL SUGGESTIONS

The Crown System

The English Tourist Board has recently introduced a grading scheme for accommodation. This ranks hotels and guest houses on a scale from one to five crowns. This rating is normally shown outside the establishment. One and two crown accommodation is fairly basic and you are not likely to enjoy a bathroom en suite. Three crowns indicates well-appointed rooms with at least one third of all bedrooms having a bath or shower and a toilet en suite, while four crowns indicates particularly comfortable accommodation with a wider range of facilities and services and, importantly from your standpoint, at least three quarters of all bedrooms have a bath or shower and a toilet en suite. Five crowns indicates luxurious accommodation while five *gold* crowns indicates accommodation on a par with any you will find in the world.

Commended Hotels

The British Tourist Authority operates an excellent Commended Scheme for hotels and guest houses with under 50 rooms, and restaurants throughout the country.

Candidate establishments are anonymously checked and, once accepted, thereafter regularly inspected.

An annual guide covers these. This includes a detailed description of each, a photograph (these range from the crystal-clear to the unintelligible) and maps to show you how to reach them.

This guide is available from BTA offices before you leave North

America. In which case it's free. That's a considerable bargain since it costs £4.25 in the United Kingdom.

Wolsey Lodges

Wolsey Lodges are private homes which welcome guests in extremely pleasant surroundings. Often your hostess will have two or three extra bedrooms as a result of children who have fled the coop. These can be quite luxurious. While you won't always have your own private bathroom you will have easy access to one and the same sort of privacy you would have staying with friends.

These houses are often of historic interest and include timber-framed Elizabethan manor houses, Georgian mansions and thatched cottages.

The grounds can also be a revelation. Many have beautiful gardens, some have croquet lawns, tennis courts, stables or swimming pools.

We have gone to great care to select hotels in this guide but these are certainly an excellent alternative. You can obtain a booklet listing all properties in detail, with colored photos, by writing to your nearest British Tourist Authority office or to Wolsey Lodges, 14 Museum Street, Ipswich, Suffolk, (tel: (0473) 214 2111).

RESTAURANTS

Again we've tried to give you a good selection from the cheap and cheerful to the terribly good. What we've bent over backwards to avoid are the terribly pretentious. We've tried to give pride of place to restaurants where the welcome is genuinely welcoming, the food, whatever the price, good value for money and where at least some excellent local dishes are available.

Credit card designations are as for hotels. Above the pub/wine bar level it's the rare restaurant that doesn't accept these.

For restaurants we've also used pound sterling symbols to indicate price levels. In general, the more £ designations the greater the choice, elegance and service level. But this isn't always the case. Some of our top choices fall in the economy category. Most restaurants post menus outside, which we applaud. Many now offer reasonable prix fixe set lunches and dinners, which we also applaud.

Broadly speaking, the codes indicate the following prices per person for a three course dinner with a glass of wine:

£   Under £12.50
££   £12.50 – £18.00
£££   £18+

GENERAL RESTAURANT DOS AND DON'TS

1. Do reserve in advance and show up five minutes early.

2. If a roast of the day (what we call a 'joint') is available on the cart (what we call a 'trolley') to be carved at the table, tip the carver 50p at the time.

3. Do check to see whether or not service is included. If so, unless it has been truly exceptional, we don't recommend a further tip.

4. Do beware of house wine when eating in pubs. It's apt to be dreadful.

5. Don't turn up your nose at Australian and Spanish wines as well as English whites. These can be excellent and reasonable.

6. Do beware of our ghastly British Sunday licensing laws. Even with the new licensing laws it's still hard to get lunch after 2:00pm, almost impossible to get a drink after 3pm.

PLANNING AHEAD

If you plan to visit a number of stately homes and historic buildings in England, it could be worth buying a **Great British Heritage Pass**, previously known as 'Open to View'. Available in the USA through travel agents ($29 for 15 days, $43 for one month) or in Britain at selected Tourist Information Centres, including the British Travel Centre, 12 Regent Street, London SW1 (£16 or £24 respectively), the pass entitles you to free admission to over 600 properties and gardens in Britain as well as half-price admission to the Tower of London. Valid from the day that you first use it. There is no pass for children.

Many of Britain's greatest houses and gardens are administered by either **English Heritage** or the **National Trust**. Membership of each organization entitles you to free admission to its properties, plus reduced price, or free admission, to special events such as concerts. Write to:

> **English Heritage**,
> Membership Department,
> PO Box 71
> Bromley
> Kent BR1 1LB

Membership costs £10 per annum, family membership £20 (2 parents, all children under 16). You can also buy membership at any English Heritage property, including Hampton Court Palace and Kensington Palace, except the Tower of London, which it also administers. Alternatively, contact Ann Webb Smith of the **American Friends of English Heritage**, 3233 Klingle Road, Washington D.C. 20008.

> **National Trust**,
> 42 Queen Anne's Gate,
> London SW1H 9AS

Membership costs £16 per annum, family membership £30 (2 parents, all children under 18). Alternatively, you can join its USA foundation: **Royal Oak Foundation Inc**, 285 West Broadway, Suite 400, New York 10013. Individual membership is $35 per annum, family $50.

EVENTS

These are some of the highlights in the British social calendar:

Glyndebourne, mid May-late August

International standard opera house on a private, country estate, where patrons traditionally picnic (very stylishly) in the grounds during the long interval. Booking form available to those on their mailing list (cost: £2); tickets are then awarded by ballot. Information on '89 season available end February/early March. Write to the Information Office, Glyndebourne Opera, Lewes, East Sussex BN8 5UU.

Royal Ascot, mid June

Four days of flat racing at Ascot when the Queen and members of the Royal family attend. The Royal Procession takes place each day at 2:30pm. More information on tickets from the Grandstand Office, Ascot Racecourse, Ascot, Berkshire SL5 7JN.

Wimbledon Lawn Tennis Championships, late June-early July

Tickets for central courts, on which the stars play, are usually hard to come by and often sold by ticket touts outside the court for premium prices. The proper route for buying tickets is by ballot form (one per person only). Apply by January 31 of the year in which you want to visit Wimbledon to: Ballot Office, All England Tennis Club, PO Box 98, London SW19 5AE (tel: (01) 946 2244). Remember there's no guarantee that you're going to get tickets so it's really whether your number comes out of the box.

Henley Royal Regatta, late June-early July

International rowing regatta. Overseas visitors are eligible to apply for tickets to the stewards' enclosures. Brochure giving details available in March. Write to The Secretary, Henley Royal Regatta, Regatta Headquarters, Henley-on-Thames, Oxon RG9 2LY.

CEREMONY OF THE KEYS, TOWER OF LONDON

The ceremony of the keys is the nightly locking of the Tower of London and begins at 9:30pm when a limited number of the public is admitted. The ceremony and the origins of the keys are explained by a Yeoman of the Guard. At precisely eight minutes to 10pm the short ceremony takes place, culminating in the sounding of the Last Post by a Yeoman. Attendance at this ceremony is strictly by 'invitation' only, but invitations can be applied for by writing to: The Resident Governor, Tower of London, London, EC3N 4AB. Although there is no charge, you must enclose an international postal coupon for the return of your tickets. This ceremony is not suitable for young children.

BRITISH TOURIST AUTHORITY OVERSEAS OFFICES

Get in touch with a BTA office when you're planning your trip. They are a valuable source of help and information.

Canada
British Tourist Authority
94 Cumberland Street
Suite 600
Toronto, Ontario M5R 3N3
Tel: (416) 925-6326
Tlx: 6104914211 BRITOURIST TOR
Fax: (416) 961 2175

USA
British Tourist Authority
40 West 57th Street
New York NY 10019
Tel: (212) 581-4700
Tlx: 237798 BRA UR
Fax: (212) 265 0649

British Tourist Authority
John Hancock Center
Suite 3320
875 North Michigan Avenue
Chicago, Illinois 60611
Tel: (312) 787-0490
Fax: (312) 787 7746

British Tourist Authority
World Trade Center
350 South Figueroa Street
Suite 450
Los Angeles, CA 90071
Tel: (213) 628-3525
Fax: (213) 687 6621

British Tourist Authority
Cedar Maple Plaza
2305 Cedar Springs Road
Dallas, Texas 75201-1814
Tel: (214) 720-4040
Tlx: 4952106
Fax: (214) 871 2665

TOURIST INFORMATION CENTRES

Tourist Information Centres (TICs) are invaluable sources of facts and help, with information from do-it-yourself walking tours to restaurant guides. Many publications (and all advice) are free. Be sure to check in at the nearest TIC office when you arrive. There are about 700 Centres throughout England. We've listed those in the major towns profiled in this book. Below are the symbols designating the London and English Tourist Board information offices or services.

London Tourist Board

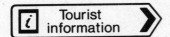

Tourist Information Centre, Victoria Station Forecourt, London SW1.

Open:
Daily 9am–8:30pm
Easter–end Oct; Mon–Sat
9am–7pm, Sun 9am–5pm
Jan–Easter and Nov–Dec

Tel: (01) 730 3488 (Mon–Sat)
Information on London and England only

English Tourist Board

Thames Tower,
Black's Road,   Hammersmith,
London W6 9EL

(written enquiries only).

In addition the **British Tourist Authority** runs the **British Travel Centre**, 12 Regent Street, London SW1 (open: Mon–Fri 9am–6:30pm Sat and Sun 10am–4pm, later in summer, personal callers only). The centre offers a comprehensive information and reservation service as well as souvenir and book shops and a Bureau de Change. For telephone enquiries call (01) 730 3400 Mon – Fri 9am–6:30pm, Sat 10am–4pm (later in summer).

Special Note: The Travel Centre is located on that portion of Regent Street which was called Lower Regent Street until about six years ago. Most cab drivers still refer to this area as Lower Regent Street – when giving directions to a cabby you may have to, too. By subway, the Centre is no distance at all from Piccadilly Circus – just 100 yards down Regent Street.

CALENDAR OF ANNUAL EVENTS

JANUARY
Early Jan..................London International Boat Show
Earls Court Exhibition Centre,
Warwick Road, London SW5

FEBRUARY
Early Feb ....Crufts Dog Show
Earls Court Exhibition Centre,
Warwick Road, London SW5

MARCH
Mar-Jan ....Shakespeare Theatre Season
Royal Shakespeare Theatre,
Stratford-upon-Avon
Early Mar.................Daily Mail Ideal Home Exhibition
Earls Court Exhibition Centre,
Warwick Road, London SW5
Mid Mar ....Cheltenham Gold Cup Meeting (horse racing),
Cheltenham Race Course, Prestbury,
Cheltenham, Gloucestershire
Late Mar..................Oxford v Cambridge University Boat Race,
Putney to Mortlake,
River Thames, London

APRIL
Late Apr..................London Marathon, London

MAY
Early May ....Badminton Horse Trials
Badminton, Avon
Mid May-mid Aug......Glyndebourne Festival Opera Season
Glyndebourne, near Lewes, East Sussex
Mid May ....Royal Windsor Horse Show
Home Park, Windsor, Berkshire
Mid May ....Devon County Show
The Showground, Exeter, Devon
Late May ....Chelsea Flower Show
Royal Hospital, Chelsea London SW3
Late May ....Festival of English Wines
Leeds Castle, Maidstone, Kent
Late May ....Wessex Craft Show
Wilton House, Wilton, Salisbury,
Wiltshire

Late May-early Jun.....	Royal Bath & West Show The Showground, Shepton Mallet, Somerset
Late May-early Jun.....	Exeter Festival Various places, Exeter, Devon
Late May-early Jun.....	Bath International Festival Various places, Bath, Avon

JUNE

Jun-Sep	Open Air Theatre Season Open Air Theatre, Regent's Park, London NW1
Jun-Sep	Kent Repertory Theatre Company Open Air Theatre Season Hever Castle, Edenbridge, Kent
Early Jun-late Aug	Royal Academy of Arts Summer Exhibition Royal Academy of Arts, Piccadilly, London W1
Early Jun.................	Rochester Dickens Festival Various places, Rochester, Kent
Early Jun.................	Beating Retreat by the Guards Massed Bands, Horse Guards Parade, Whitehall, London SW1
Early Jun.................	The Derby (horse racing) Epsom Racecourse, Epsom, Surrey
Mid Jun	Trooping the Colour – The Queen's Official Birthday Parade Horse Guards's Parade, Whitehall, London SW1
Mid Jun	International Air Fair Biggin Hill Airport, Biggin Hill, Kent
Mid Jun	Royal Cornwall Show Royal Cornwall Showground, Wadebridge, Cornwall
Mid Jun	International Balloon Fiesta Leeds Castle, Maidstone, Kent
Mid Jun	Stella Artois Grass Court Championships (tennis) The Queen's Club, Palliser Road, London W14
Mid Jun	Royal Ascot Week (horse racing) Ascot Racecourse, Ascot, Berkshire
Mid Jun-mid Jul.........	Polo: British Open Championship Cowdray Park, Midhurst, West Sussex
Late Jun-early Jul.......	Wimbledon Lawn Tennis Championships Wimbledon, London SW19
Late Jun-early Jul.......	Henley Royal Regatta Henley-on-Thames, Oxon

JULY

Early Jul ....Henley Festival of Music and the Arts
Stewards' Enclosure, Remenham, Henley-on-Thames, Oxfordshire

Early Jul ....Goodwood International Dressage Championships
Goodwood, Chichester, West Sussex

Early Jul ....British Rose Festival
Gardens of the Rose, Chiswell Green Lane, St Albans, Hertfordshire

Early-mid Jul ....Cheltenham International Festival of Music
Cheltenham, Gloucestershire

Early-mid Jul ....Chichester '89 Festivities
Various venues, Chichester, W. Sussex

Early-mid Jul ....St Albans Organ Festival
St Albans Abbey, St Albans, Hertfordshire

Mid Jul ....Kent County Show
Kent County Showground, Detling, Maidstone, Kent

Mid-late Jul ....City of London Festival
Various venues, The City, London

Mid-late Jul ....Royal Tournament
Earls Court Exhibition Centre, Warwick Road, London SW5

Mid-late Jul ....Stratford-upon-Avon Festival
Various venues, Stratford-upon Avon, Warwickshire

Late Jul...................East of England Show
East of England Showground Peterborough, Cambridgeshire

Late Jul...................Goodwood Races (horse racing)
Goodwood Racecourse, Chichester, West Sussex

Late Jul...................Country Landowner's Association Game Fair
Stratfield Saye, near Basingstoke, Hants

Late Jul-early Aug......Cowes Week (sailing)
Cowes, Isle of Wight

Late Jul-mid Aug.......Canterbury Mystery Plays
Canterbury Cathedral, Canterbury, Kent

Late Jul-mid Sep........Henry Wood Promenade Concerts 1989
Royal Albert Hall, Kensington Gore, London SW7

AUGUST

Early Aug ....Bath Guildhall Antique Fair
Guildhall, High Street, Bath, Avon

Late Aug-early Sep ....Arundel Festival
Various venues, Arundel, West Sussex

SEPTEMBER

Early Sep ....London Rose Festival
New Horticultural Hall,
Greycoat Street, London SW1

Early Sep ....Rye Festival
Various venues, Rye, East Sussex

Mid-late Sep   Chelsea Antiques Fair
Chelsea Old Town Hall, Kings Road,
Chelsea, London SW3

Late Sep-mid Oct   Cheltenham Festival of Literature
Cheltenham, Gloucestershire

OCTOBER

Early Oct ....Horse of the Year Show
Wembley Arena, Wembley, London

Mid-late Oct ....Motor Fair '89
Earls Court Exhibition Centre,
Warwick Road, London SW5

Mid Oct-early Nov .....Canterbury Festival
Various venues, Canterbury, Kent

Late Oct ....International Women's Tennis Tournament
Brighton Centre, King's Road,
Brighton, East Sussex

NOVEMBER

Early Nov................London to Brighton Veteran Car Run
Hyde Park, London to
Brighton, East Sussex

Mid Nov ....Lord Mayor's Procession and Show
The City, London

DECEMBER

Early Dec-early Jan ....Norwegian Christmas Tree Illuminations
Trafalgar Square, London WC2

Mid Dec..................National Cat Club Show Olympia,
Hammersmith Road, London W14

GLOSSARY

Here are a few explanations which may help you untangle England's architecture and our past.

GOTHIC Architecture of the medieval period featuring the pointed arch, stone vaults and huge, traceried windows

GOTHICK 18th- and early 19th-century use of what was thought to be medieval Gothic style

GOTHIC REVIVAL 19th-century interpretation of Gothic architecture which developed from the Gothick

DISSOLUTION OF THE MONASTERIES Henry VIII dissolved England's monasteries in 1536 and 1539, breaking up ancient religious orders and handing out land and property to members of his court and the aristocracy.

MAGNA CARTA Document sealed by King John in 1215, agreeing to what the barons at that time took to be the principles of government. Both barons and king were bound to maintain these. The principles included provisions which form the core of a democratic society, including the agreement that no man should be punished without fair trial.

PALLADIAN Architectural style influenced by the designs and buildings of Andreo Palladio, 16th-century Italian architect who favored harmonic proportions and symmetry. This was introduced to England by Inigo Jones (see below) early in the 17th century and revived in England early in the 18th century.

REFORMATION The break with the teachings of the Roman Catholic Church and the authority of the Pope came in England during the reign of Henry VIII. The anti-papal cause in England was rapidly fueled by Rome's refusal to grant Henry a divorce from Catherine of Aragon. Henry declared himself head of the Church in England and life for Catholics became grim (see also Dissolution of the Monasteries).

WHO'S WHO

ROBERT ADAM (1728-92) Scottish architect working for the family company who devised a neo-classical style lighter than the prevailing Palladian. Whilst retaining the Palladian balance and proportion, he added ornament and decoration. Also celebrated as an interior designer.

CAPABILITY BROWN (1716-83) Celebrated landscape gardener whose real name was Lancelot Brown: the story goes that he earned his nickname by his habit of wandering through the grounds of country houses saying 'Hmm, this shows real capabilities'. He 'improved' nature through informal, though carefully planned, parks, usually including wide stretches of lawn, clumped trees and serpentine lakes.

INIGO JONES (1573-1652) First became famous as a stage designer. He visited Italy in 1613 and brought back the Palladian style of architecture to England (see above).

WILLIAM KENT (1685-1748) Painter, furniture designer, architect and landscape gardener, for which he is best remembered. He was one of the first to eschew the formal, 17th-century garden in favor of a gentler landscape.

SIR EDWARD LUTYENS (1869-1944) Arguably architect of the last great country houses to be built in England.

HUMPHREY REPTON (1752-1818) Celebrated landscape gardener who introduced formal gardens and terraces close to the houses, in contrast with the landscaped parks beyond.

SIR JOHN SOANE (1783-1837) Notable individual architect and designer influenced by his contemporary Robert Adam (see above).

SIR CHRISTOPHER WREN (1632-1723) Remarkable and prolific architect whose first, brilliant career was as a scientist and mathematician. He rebuilt 52 of the churches destroyed by the Great Fire of London in 1666, including St Paul's Cathedral.

ARCHITECTURAL STYLES, PERIODS & MONARCHS

NORMAN (1066-1189) William the Conqueror (invaded England 1066), William II, Henry I, Stephen, Henry II

EARLY ENGLISH (1189-1307) Richard I, John (Magna Carta, see above), Henry III, Edward I

DECORATED (1307-1377) Edward II, Edward III

PERPENDICULAR (1377-1485) Richard II, Henry IV, Henry V, Henry VI, Edward IV, Edward V, Richard III

TUDOR (1485-1558) Henry VII, Henry VIII (Dissolution of the Monasteries, see above), Edward VI, Mary

ELIZABETHAN (1558-1603) Elizabeth I

JACOBEAN (1603-1625) James I

STUART (1625-1702) Charles I (Civil War), Charles II, James II, William & Mary, William III

GEORGIAN (1702-1830) Anne, George I, George II, George III, George IV

REGENCY In the last ten years of his life George III was permanently mad. His son, later George IV, became Prince Regent during that time – from 1811 to 1820, when George III died. 'Regency' has come to mean the period between 1810 and 1820.

VICTORIAN (1830-1901) William IV, Victoria

EDWARDIAN (1901-1910) Edward VII

All establishments in this guide have been anonymously checked, then selected from dozens who didn't make the grade. If standards aren't as described please write to the Editor (see acknowledgements for address).

SO YOU THOUGHT YOU SPOKE ENGLISH

GLOSSARY OF THE ENGLISH LANGUAGE

Use it with restraint, as accurate English spoken by a foreigner is regarded with deep suspicion. Don't forget if you say it right, that deprives an Englishman of his chance to correct you. And that could be the start of a conversation. So if you really want to get to know the British, use the occasional three-syllable version of Worcester. Everyone loves having their stereotypes confirmed. And remember, we're not putting you on, we really talk this way.

English	North American
Food and Drink	
Banger	Sausage. Also old car.
Bitter	Unchilled, tasty bitter ale
Caff	Café. Cheaper without the acute accent. Always spelt café, sometimes pronounced caff, sometimes in London 'cafe' to rhyme with safe.
Chips	French fries, although the sort you get with fish are usually thicker than the foreign versions. Eat with plenty of vinegar and salt.
Cooker	Stove
Crisps	Potato chips
Free house	Pub serving a variety of beers not 'tied to' (belonging to) a brewery.
Tied house	Reverse of above
French beans	String beans
Martini	Straight vermouth. If you want a Martini cocktail it's called a 'double gin with ice'.
Nosh	Food
Off licence	Retail liquor store
Other half	Either another half pint (see bitter), or spouse.
Public house	Bar
Sweet	Dessert
Sweets	Candy
Top up	Refill

Shopping

Biro	Ballpoint
Braces	Suspenders
Brolly	Umbrella
Carrier bag	Shopping bag
Chemist	Drugstore, but strictly for cosmetics and medicines.
Handbag	Purse, pocketbook
Jumper	Sweater
Mackintosh, or Mack	A raincoat. 'Got a light, mac? No I have a dark overcoat.'
Made-to-measure/Bespoke	Custom-tailored. Incidentally, watch for tailor's abbreviations added to your measurements and instructions, like '2½' BL (bandy legged). 'LDS' (left dropped shoulder) and worst of all, '3 buttons on cuff A.O.A.' – (against our advice). Cuffs, by the way are what your sleeves end in. Your trousers have 'turn ups'! Your pants are what you wear under your trousers. Choose cautious ones for your fitting, to avoid stifled snorts of mirth. The answer to 'which side do you dress?' after your inside leg measurement has been taken is not 'by the window'.
Nappy	Diaper
Off the peg	Ready made
Stockists	Suppliers
Suspenders	Garters
Vest	Undershirt

Transportation, Traffic

Bonnet	Hood
Boot	Trunk
Car Hire	Auto rental
Cul-de-sac	Dead end
Flyover	Overpass
Gallon	More than a US Gallon. About a fifth more.
Juggernaut	Ordinary truck, considered vast in Britain.
Lay-by	Off-highway parking
Lorry	Smaller truck
To motor	To drive

Motorway	Expressway
Pavement	Sidewalk
Petrol	Gasoline
Polite request	Firm order
Return	Round trip
Roundabout	Traffic circle
Self-drive	Auto rental
Subway	Below ground pedestrian passage
Tube	Subway
Underground	Subway
Van	Truck. Hertz van rental is not a Dutch painter.
Wing (car)	Fender
Zebra crossing	Pedestrian crossing

Theater

Dress Circle	First Balcony
Gallery (Gods)	Third Balcony
Stalls	Orchestra seat
Upper Circle	Second Balcony

Telephone

Directory enquiries	Information
Reverse charges	Collect call
Ring	To telephone. 'I'll give you a ring' is not a promise of marriage. 'Engaged' is a busy signal. Do not sue for breach of promise.

General Confusions

Bed-sit or bedsitter	One room apartment
Block of flats	Apartment building
Bobby	Policeman
Cheers	Bottoms up, a toast. Also goodbye.
Dicey	Problematic
Digs	Lodgings
'Drop in'	Don't drop in
Estate Agent	Realtor

First floor	Second floor
Fiver	Five pound note. There isn't a single slang expression for any one of our decimal coins, which are disparagingly referred to as p's.
Flat	Apartment
Ground floor	First floor (All the doors seem to open the wrong way. But you'll cope.)
Hairdresser – mens/ladies	Barber shop/Beauty parlor
Innit?	'n'est-ce pas?' in London
'Interesting', as in 'How interesting! Sounds fascinating	Not very interesting. I'm bored and I might scream were I not so well bred.
Keen	Eager if a person, competitive if referring to a price.
Landlady	Lady owner and manager of boarding house offering bed and breakfast. Probably owns no land at all.
Left luggage	Airport/railroad check room
Lift	Elevator
Loo	Lavatory
Look out!	Duck
Look out for	Keep an eye open for . . .
Maisonette	Duplex
Mother's ruin	Gin
Never-never	Instalment buying
Not on	Won't work. Also relates to incorrect behaviour, eg 'They've blown up the Bishop. It's just not on.'
Peckish	A bit hungry. Could probably eat a Percheron (large cart horse).
Porter	Janitor of apartment building, or man who carries your bags at airports and stations if he can't see anyone else who might give him a bigger tip.
Public convenience	Private relief
Public school	Very private school
Queue	Stand in line (please do so).
Quid	Pound note. 'Quids in' – on the profitable end of a deal.
Smashing	Great

Spend a penny	Go to the loo but only used by ladies who often have to pay 2p.
Storeys	Floors of a building, eg. 'Twenty-story sky scraper – office block.
Surgery	Doctor's/Dentist's office
Ta	Thanks
Tart	Prostitute
Tata/Tara	Good-bye
Telly	Television
Torch	Flashlight
Turf accountant	Bookie
Very/Most 'Civil'	Kind
Vet	Check out
Zed	Z

USEFUL BUT BORING INFORMATION

GREAT BRITAIN – Country Briefing

Size: 94,500 square miles

Population: 55,355,000 (mid 1987)

Capital: London

Capital population: Inner London 2,512,200
    Greater London 6,770,400

Climate: Temperate, but often unpredictable; don't forget your umbrella!

Entry Requirements
A valid passport; visas not required for US or Canadian citizens. Smallpox and cholera vaccination certificates required if you're coming from an infected area.

N.B. Pets brought into the country are subject to six months' quarantine.

Weather in Britain
No matter how many jokes you've heard about British weather, it's still going to surprise you. It will rain when you'd be enjoying a heat wave back home and you'll bask in warm sunshine when the calendar says it's early winter. Include a raincoat in your luggage, just as you would if you were visiting any north European country.

Weather in London: Lat 51°29′; Alt 149 ft

Temp (°F)	Jan	Feb	Mar	Apr	May	Jun	Jul	Aug	Sep	Oct	Nov	Dec
Av Low	35°	35°	37°	40°	45°	51°	55°	54°	51°	44°	39°	36°
Av High	44°	45°	51°	56°	63°	69°	73°	72°	67°	58°	49°	45°
Days no rain	14	15	20	16	18	19	18	18	17	17	14	15

PUBLIC HOLIDAYS

New Year's Day, Jan 1
Good Friday
Easter Monday
May Day Bank Holiday (May 1)
Spring Bank Holiday, last Monday in May
Summer Bank Holiday, last Monday in August
Christmas Day, Dec 25
Boxing Day, Dec 26

When a public holiday falls on a Sunday the following day, Monday, is taken as the Bank Holiday.

Most shops, restaurants and places of interest close for Christmas Day and Boxing Day (Dec 26) but many will also close New Year's Day or for the entire holiday period. Public transport's full service grinds to a halt the evening of December 24 to begin again on December 27.

Good Friday is a public holiday in England. While most stores are open many of the museums and stately homes close.

When a public holiday falls on Monday many museums and places of interest which normally close will be open.

All of the above indicate that it's best to check opening hours on or around Bank Holidays (British for public holidays).

BANKING HOURS AND CHANGING MONEY

Any bank will change travelers' checks and convert currency. In the larger cities banks are open Monday to Friday 9:30am-3:30pm. Some larger branches are open on Saturday mornings from 9:30am-12:30pm. Some banks have a late closing day; enquire at a large branch for details. Best to arrange to cash checks in the larger centers. Occasionally you'll find a village which only has banking facilities four mornings a week or less.

Extended opening: There's a 24-hour service at Heathrow Terminal 1, 3 and 4 for passengers.

CURRENCY

Britain used to have a currency system as splendidly eccentric as the nation itself. This featured pounds divided into twenty shillings, each of which was worth twelve pence with half pennys known as 'ha'pennies' as the smallest coin. Not content with divisions into 20s and 12s there was also something called 'a guinea' – which was twenty-one shillings. This was much favored by stores for their sales e.g. 'dresses only 7 Gns', and hotels 'weekends for only 22 Gns'.

With entry into the Common Market Britain rationalized her currency so that today we have a decimal system. This consists of pounds (£), each of which is worth 100 pence (p). Sadly, paper pounds have now been replaced by a golden colored thick small coin which resembles nothing so much as play money in a cheap board game. This is roughly half the size of the next most valuable coin, the 50 pence piece which is seven-sided, as is the 20 pence coin at half its size.

Coins, their color and approximate size are as follows:

Coin	Color/Shape	Closest Size In US Equivalent*
£1	golden, thick and round	nickel
50p	silver, seven-sided	50¢ piece
20p	silver, seven-sided	nickel
10p	silver, round	slightly larger than the US 50¢ piece
5p	silver, round	nickel
2p	copper, round	25¢ piece
1p	copper, round	penny

Paper notes are £5 (known as 'a fiver'), £10 (known as 'a tenner'), £20 and £50.

*Special note: These are size not value comparisons. The value of the pound has fluctuated between $1.40 and $1.85 over the last two years.

CREDIT CARDS

Should you lose your credit card, report it immediately on these numbers:

American Express (01) 222 9633
Diners Club (0252) 513500
MasterCard (0702) 352211
Visa (0604) 230230

POSTAL INFORMATION

There are post offices in most British towns and in some villages. Buy stamps over the counter in the post office or from machines outside larger branches. Post boxes are either rectangular boxes set in the wall or red metal cylinders standing on the pavement. In Britain post offices are open Mon-Fri 9am-5:30pm and on Saturdays 9am-12:30pm. (N.B. Many sub-post offices, whether they're in cities or villages, open mornings only on the early closing day, generally Wednesday or Thursday.)

Postal Rates

There are two rates within Britain. First class costs 19p and mail should be delivered within 24 hours. The second class rate is 14p and takes at least 48 hours, sometimes longer. A 10gm letter to the USA or Canada costs 32p, postcards cost 27p.

Poste Restante

This service is available free at any post office for only one month but proof of identity is required.

TELEPHONES

Most places in Britain have area codes. If you're calling a number check the correct area code in the front of the telephone directory. They're available in most telephone booths in hotels, pubs and similar places. Public pay phones often don't have phone number books. In this case, dial 100 to get the operator, who'll answer your questions, or dial 192 for directory enquiries outside of London. If you're checking a London number, dial 142 for London directory enquiries. Area codes can be different in different parts of the country, except for the major cities which always have the same area codes:

London	01
Birmingham	021
Edinburgh	031
Glasgow	041
Liverpool	051
Manchester	061

Using a British Pay Phone

Britain is modernizing their pay phone system to accord with the system used in the US and Canada, namely, put the coin in, get a dial tone and dial the number. However, there are still some older phones in use. Use them in this manner:

Pick up the phone and listen for a dialing tone; dial the number (the area code first if you're calling a number out of town), and then wait for the phone to be answered. When you hear a blip-blip-blip noise, push a 10p piece into the slot. Keep some more coins handy. When the first coin has been used up, the blip-blip signal will start again. You'll find directions on most public phones.

Some pay phones accept major credit cards such as American Express, Diners Club, MasterCard and Visa. Other phones accept a phone card. These cards may be purchased at post offices, British Telecom shops, or shops such as newsagents with a green notice in the window advertising this service.

AT&T USADIRECT℠ SERVICE

Hotels usually add a surcharge to long distance calls, while calling from a phone box could involve oodles of change – some of which may not be rebated.

AT&T have a better way. With the new **USADIRECT℠** service calling home has never been so easy. To make an AT&T card or collect call to the USA, simply dial 0800-80-0011 from any British phone and you will get straight through to a helpful and familiar AT&T operator back in the States.

USEFUL PHONE NUMBERS

American Embassy – Consular/Passport Affairs – (01) 499 9000

Canadian Embassy – Consular/Passport Affairs – (01) 629 9492

Directory Enquiries – 142 (London) 192 (elsewhere)

American Express (01) 930 4411

London Weather (0898) 500480 (for southeast England)

Southwest Weather (0898) 141275

Fire, Police, Ambulance 999

Operator 100

International Telegrams – 100 and ask operator for International Telegrams

Time (Speaking Clock) 123 (London)
  Directory enquiries for numbers outside London

HEALTH INSURANCE

If an American/Canadian tourist falls ill in the UK they are not covered by National Insurance as a matter of course. Insurance may be taken out with most travel agents at a nominal rate – i.e., £4.50 for 8 days and £8.00 for 31 days. This entitles a tourist to basic National Health Insurance coverage. Rates may be more favorable in North America and tourists should check before leaving home about health coverage in the UK.

If someone becomes ill without any insurance coverage they must pay for their health care while in the UK.

ELECTRICITY

The current from wall sockets is 240 volts at 50 c/s. Bring a converter with you.

TIPPING

Porters in airports and railway stations get 50p for the first piece of luggage and 25p for each additional piece. Taxi drivers expect a minimum of 10% of the fare but at least 50p.

The head porter in a hotel gets between £1 and £2; chambermaids about 50p each, waiters 10% of the bill's total (if service isn't included). Hairdressers usually get 10% of the bill's total but at least 80p.

Tipping is never necessary in a pub for drinks or bar food service.

CUSTOMS ALLOWANCES FOR RETURNING US AND CANADIAN CITIZENS

When you leave Britain you can take what you like, although certain works of art and antiques are subject to export licensing control.

Duty free allowance for US citizens is not more than 100 cigars or 200 cigarettes; liquor depends on the state you're re-entering, usual amount is 1 litre of alcohol including wine; perfume not more than .5% alcohol content. You're allowed to bring back $400 worth in gifts duty free. A formal declaration is required if you bring back more than $10,000 in cash. Restrictions on certain foods taken into the US: no meat or fish products; hard cheese to the value of $25 is allowed provided it is commercially sealed.

Duty free allowance for Canadian citizens is $300 Canadian, including tobacco allowance of 200 cigarettes plus 50 cigars plus 1kg tobacco and alcohol allowance of 40 oz. Restrictions on certain foods taken into Canada: no meat or fish products, hard cheeses are permitted, the value of which is limited by the overall $300 Canadian allowance.

USEFUL ADDRESSES IN LONDON

Airline Ticket Offices

Air Canada, 140-144 Regent Street, W1
Reservations: (01) 759 2636, Mon-Fri 8am-7pm, Sat 10 am-4pm, Sun 10am-3pm.
Flight enquiries: (01) 897 1331, 24 hours recorded information

American Airlines, 421 Oxford Street, W1
Reservations: (01) 834 5151, Mon-Fri 8am-7pm, Sat 8am-6:30pm, Sun 8:30am-5pm
Flight enquiries: same as above

British Airways, 65-75 Regent Street, W1 (near Piccadilly Circus)
Reservations: (01) 897 4000, Daily 7am-10:30pm
Flight enquiries: (01) 759 2525, 6am-11pm manned, 11pm-6am recorded information

Continental Airlines, Terminal House, 52 Grosvenor Gardens, SW1
Reservations: (0293) 776464, Mon-Fri 8am-7pm, Sat-Sun 9am-6pm
Flight enquiries: same as above

Pan American World Airways, 193 Piccadilly, W1
Reservations: (01) 409 0688, Mon-Sat 7am-10pm, Sun 7pm-9pm
Flight enquiries: (01) 725 0747, 24 hours recorded information

Trans World Airlines, 200 Piccadilly, W1
Reservations: Freephone (0800) 222 222 or (01) 439 0707, Mon-Fri 8am-8:30pm, Sat-Sun 8am-5:30pm
Flight enquiries: (01) 759 5352, 24 hours recorded information

London Airport Information
Heathrow Airport (01) 759 4321
Gatwick Airport (0293) 28822

Chemists/Drug Stores

Boots, 44-46 Regent Street, W1
Tel: (01) 734 6126

John, Bell and Croyden, 50 Wigmore Street, W1
Tel: (01) 935 5555

Underwoods, 94 Oxford Street, W1
Tel: (01) 636 4574

Churches

The American Church in London, 29 Tottenham Court Road, W1
Tel: (01) 580 2791 (Interdenominational)

The Brompton Oratory, Brompton Road, SW3
Tel: (01) 589 4811 (Catholic)

Nottinghill Methodist Church, Lancaster Road, W11
Tel: (01) 229 7728

St James's Church Piccadilly, 197 Piccadilly, W1
Tel: (01) 734 5244 (Anglican/Episcopal)

St Anne's Lutheran Church, Gresham Street, EC2
Tel: (01) 373 5566

St Paul's Church, Covent Garden, WC2
Tel: (01) 836 5221 (Anglican/Episcopal)

West End Great Synagogue, 21 Dean Street, W1
Tel: (01) 437 1873

Miscellaneous

Post Office, 24-28 William IV Street, WC2 (near Trafalgar Square)
Tel: (01) 930 9580 – Open: Mon-Sat 8am-8pm

Metropolitan Police Headquarters, New Scotland Yard, Broadway, SW1
Tel: (01) 230 1212

MOTORING MADE EASY

Touring by car is a great way to explore the real UK. Adjusting to British motoring shouldn't be a problem if you follow a few simple guidelines.

Car Rental
International car rental companies, such as Hertz, Avis and Budget, are at all major airports, such as Heathrow and Gatwick and in most major cities. See below for list of addresses.

To rent a car you'll need a passport, valid driving license and one of the major credit cards such as American Express, Visa, Diners or MasterCard. Alternatively, some companies will accept a cash deposit. Terms and conditions on this vary widely so do check when inquiring.

Many car rental companies offer better rates if you reserve before you depart for Britain so it's advisable to call them using their toll-free numbers well before you depart (some of their special packages must be booked well in advance like APEX airline fares). The key point to bear in mind is that shopping around can save you pots of money.

It's also worth looking into the airline's joint fly-drive programs. These offer low cost car rental as an add-on to the basic air fare. Indeed in the off-season airlines have been known to throw in the car at no extra cost.

Do check with airlines such as Air Canada, British Airways, Pan Am, TWA and American Airlines to see what they have to offer in the way of car rental 'bolt-ons'. Again comparative shopping pays.

Some other tips to bear in mind:
- Short term rentals, generally under one week, are way more expensive on a per day basis than longer hires. The reason? They try to capture business travelers for maximum rates.

- As a result you may be better advised to hire for a week even if you're not sure you will use the car every day.

- The more expensive rates of the major multinationals may actually be cheaper when three other factors are taken into account – the insurance premiums for personal accident insurance and collision damage waiver, gas for the car and – very importantly – how much free mileage you get. Is the first tank of gas included?

- Do insure, the complications of not doing so can cost lots of money and valuable vacation time.

- When choosing a car rental company be sure to ask how

extensive their national network is. Also ask if breakdown service by one of the automobile clubs is included.

Having your Ford Granada collapse in Penzance when the nearest repair point is Exeter is decidedly not nice.

- Once you've found exactly what you want, obtain a reservation order number to quote when picking up the car (in case of confusion) as well as written confirmation of your reservation, the length, rate and conditions.

Car Rental Offices London

Avis, 68 North Row, W1 (Marble Arch)
Tel: (01) 629 7811   Main res. no. (01) 848 8733

Budget, 50 Curzon Street, W1 (Piccadilly)
Tel: (01) 499 2521   Main res. no. freephone (0800) 181 181

Europcar, 170 Marylebone Road, NW1
Tel: (01) 487 3421   Main res. no. (01) 950 5050

Hertz, 200 Buckingham Palace Road, SW1
Tel: (01) 730 8323   Main res. no. (01) 679 1799

Travelwise, 77 Pavilion Road, SW1
Tel: (01) 235 0751

Before you start

One car's turn indicators are positioned where another model's windshield wipers are. Murphy's law predicts that in neither case do these accord with your car back home. Consequently, five quiet minutes checking out all the controls in the car rental parking lot or friend's driveway represent time amply repaid once underway. Several of the major car rental firms provide you with magazines or other instructional material which help. Special tip: inserting the key and starting the car is easy. Given various anti-theft devices (which again vary widely) removing the key can be another matter. Make sure you've mastered this minor but vital maneuver.

Many car rental companies also provide maps and these are a good idea. Much as we've tried to anticipate your every driving need with clear directions and maps, space dictates that we can't be as graphically detailed as we'd like. A map has other benefits. It shows you what's just off the route which may appeal. Finally, if you encounter roadworks a map is vital. About 2% of Britain's out-of-town road system is undergoing repair or alteration on any given day. The nearest branch of W H Smith, the nation's largest newsagent, has an excellent selection. If you're exploring a region in great detail, do look into the Ordnance Survey series which is unrivaled for detail.

Underway

The obvious difference between driving in Britain and back home is that you'll be driving on the left-hand side of the road. This is by no means as difficult as you'd think. Unless you've brought a car from the Continent (which is a genuinely bad idea) the driver's side is the right-hand side of the vehicle. You simply have to remember that the curb ('verge' to the British) is always to your left, the middle of the road to your right.

Distances are measured in miles (though some signs now show kilometers as well). Highway signs in Britain, as throughout the Common Market, are based on pictures and numbers rather than words so their meaning is crystal clear. They come in three main types: rectangles, triangles and circles. Rectangular signs inform. Triangular signs warn. Then there are the really important ones – circular signs – they command. A selection of the most important signs and their meanings are shown on the opposite page.

Speed restrictions are shown by a number on a circular sign. Generally, speed limits are 30mph in towns, villages and built up areas, 60mph on bypasses and trunk roads, and 70mph on motorways.

Thirty miles per hour is the maximum prudent speed when entering any small village. What's more, you'd not want to go any faster on some of our narrow, hedgerowed lanes. Speaking of hedgerowed lanes, when you meet another vehicle on one of these, the one heading uphill has priority over the one going down.

When you come to a traffic circle (called a 'roundabout' in Britain) vehicles already in the circle to your right have priority and you'll drive clockwise round it once you enter. When you intend to exit you need to be in the left-hand lane beforehand to do so.

When entering towns and cities watch for one-way routes and no-entry areas. White crosswalks are called zebra crossings and anyone on them has an absolute right of way. You must stop. A flashing amber light at a crossing means that you must stop if there are pedestrians on or about to enter the crosswalk.

Help While Under Way

The British Broadcasting Corporation (BBC) operates four national radio channels: Radio 4 which is basically conversations of a high order, Radio 3, which offers classical music, Radio 2 which is our 'popular' channel, and Radio 1 which you will listen to in peril to your eardrums. All four carry traffic reports on major motorways delays throughout the day. In addition, there are local BBC and regional stations which cover traffic on a more localized basis.

You can find these by scanning the dial or by referring to the entertainments sections in a local newspaper.

ROUND SIGNS COMMAND

STOP

CLOSED TO
ALL VEHICLES

NO ENTRY

NO ENTRY FOR
AUTOMOBILES

CLOSED TO
PEDESTRIANS

NO LEFT TURN

NO U-TURNS

NO PASSING

SPEED LIMIT

END OF
SPEED LIMIT

NO WAITING

GIVE PRIORITY TO
ONCOMING TRAFFIC

DIRECTION TO
FOLLOW

TRAFFIC
CIRCLE

TRIANGULAR SIGNS WARN

PRIORITY
ROAD AHEAD

DANGEROUS
BEND

RIGHT BEND

DOUBLE BEND

INTERSECTION

PEDESTRIAN
CROSSING

TRAFFIC
CIRCLE

DANGEROUS
HILL

RECTANGULAR SIGNS INFORM

PRIORITY OVER
ONCOMING TRAFFIC

END OF TWO-WAY
TRAFFIC

MOTORWAY

END OF
MOTORWAY

NO THROUGH
ROAD

GAS
STATION

HOTEL

FIRST AID
POST

CAR REPAIR

TELEPHONE

Drinking and Driving

One or two glasses of wine or a pint of beer with a meal is only human. Anything more can cause problems. This is when you're apt to forget about driving on the left, so pause and reflect before you set off. The legal limit for alcohol in the blood roughly equals three single whiskies or a pint and a half of beer; that's not very much.

The breathalyzer comes into automatic practice if you're involved in an accident, discretionary practice if you're stopped by the police.

As a foreign driver you'll be charged and fined and have all your particulars (passport number, driver's license number etc) noted. This can require a return visit to the jurisdiction where the incident took place.

Accidents

If you're unlucky enough to be involved in an accident, the procedure is standard. Exchange your names and addresses. Get the name of their insurance company. Make a note of the other fellow's license plate. Call the car rental company as soon as possible. Keep cool and make a note of exactly what happened as soon as you can so that you can file an accurate report. Take the names and addresses of witnesses. If medical assistance is required, ask someone to telephone for help. If it's a serious accident, the police should be called and the car shouldn't be moved until they arrive.

Parking

White zig-zag lines on the road, which you'll find approaching crosswalks, by bus stops and in other 'no go' areas, mean that parking is not only strictly forbidden but subject to an instant tow. Similarly, double yellow lines mean parking is strictly forbidden. These command a hefty fine and the possibility of being clamped or towed away. Single yellow lines mean you can park between specified hours – usually marked on a nearby parking sign attached to a lamppost or pole.

In London and selected other major cities you'll find resident parking areas, denoted by a white R in a blue box. These mean what they say. If you park here you're apt to be fined, clamped or otherwise inconvenienced.

If you park illegally you may return to your car to find that a traffic warden has left a ticket stating your offence and the fine involved under your wiper. The ticket will contain instructions for paying the fine.

Virtually all towns have public parking areas as well as car parks. In some car parks you pay upon departure. In others you deposit the appropriate coinage, depending upon the amount of time you wish to stay, which yields a time-stamped ticket which you display inside the car.

Motoring Organizations

There are two major motoring organizations in Britain, the Automobile Association (AA) and the Royal Automobile Club (RAC). If you rent from Hertz you automatically enjoy the benefits of the former, Britain's largest motoring organization. If you rent from Avis the privileges of the RAC are yours.

The two associations cover around 1500 roadside telephones between them so help is never far away. If you're already a member of an automobile association bring your membership card with you. The AA and RAC have reciprocal arrangements with many foreign associations, including the American Automobile Association.

Automobile Association
Head Office
P.O. Box 50
Basingstoke
Hampshire RG21 2ED
Tel: (0256) 24872 (membership),
    20123 (enquiries)

Leicester Square
Information Centre
Fanum House
5 New Coventry Street
London W1V 8HT
Tel: (01) 930 2462

Breakdown service: Countrywide freephone (0800) 88 77 66

Royal Automobile Club
Head Office
P.O. Box 700
Spectrum House
Bond Street
Bristol BS99 1RB
Tel: (0272) 73 22 01 (general
    information and routes)

Touring Services
49 Pall Mall
London SW1Y 5JG
Tel: (01) 839 7050 (touring
services other than route
information)

Breakdown service: the telephone number varies according to area. Dial directory enquiries 142 in London or 192 in all other places.

Petrol Stations

Petrol stations (gas stations) in Britain sell petrol according to a star rating which corresponds to the octane content. Our gallons are imperial gallons which means that they contain eight pints instead of six. Increasingly pumps in the UK refer only to liters, as on the continent. Each liter is worth 0.22 of a gallon.

Lead-free petrol is slowly becoming widely available. These pumps are clearly marked. Do make sure that the pump you're using is not for diesel which can cause mechanical chaos.

Some petrol stations have attendants who will clean your windscreen or check your oil. Others are self service, in which case you pay an attendant in the main building. These buildings normally sell soft drinks, snacks and cigarettes.

On Sundays and after 6pm it's sometimes difficult to find an open petrol station so bear this in mind as your fuel level drops.

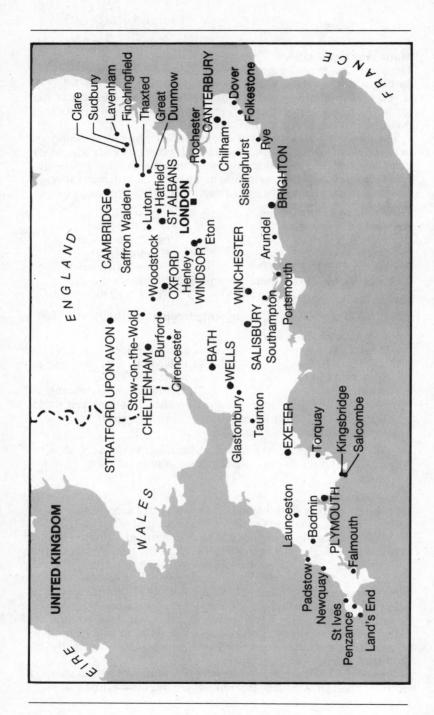

DISCOVERING GREAT BRITAIN

Many readers will have visited Great Britain before (people do have a pleasant habit of coming back for more). While even those contemplating a first visit will no doubt know a fair bit about Britain. So we won't dwell on the obvious – our shared language (although some would dispute this), the longstanding 'special relationship', our driving on the 'peculiar' side of the road, and so on. Instead, we'd like to give you a quick briefing on our country, some of the less well-known attractions it has to offer, how to save money while having an unstinted good time and, very importantly, what's special and on special offer that we cover.

First Things First

Just how big is Great Britain? From Land's End (Cornwall, bottom left) to John O'Groats (Scotland, top right) it's a touch under 700 miles. In addition, there's a delightful selection of islands top and bottom. You're never more than 75 miles from tidal water anywhere in the British Isles, which perhaps explains why we spent so much time dashing off to sea, and then renaming large parts of the New World after the Old.

First-time visitors will probably find more than enough to fill a busy fortnight (British for two weeks) just in and around the magic triangle of London, Bath and Stratford-upon-Avon. But that's only a fraction of what England has to offer. Even the English language takes on a fiercely local character, to the extent of being a second tongue in some of the more remote parts of Wales.

What's In A Village Name

Our towns and villages harbor surprises. In many cases their name is not the least amongst these. Here's a sanitized alphabetical list (yes, there is a town called The Bog) of some of the more extraordinary.

Affspuddle	Mousehole
Blubberhouses	Nasty
The Bog	Old Sodbury
Catbrain	Piddletrenthide
Daffy Green	Quarff
East Yell	Rickinghall Inferior
Follifoot	Steeple Bumstead
Great Snoring	Toot Hill
Hope Under Dinsmore	Upper Slaughter
Inkpen	Vicarage
Jump	Wootton Bassett
Knock	Yetts o'Muckart
Lower Swell	Zeals

Weather Wise

It's no good pretending we didn't invent the mackintosh (a.k.a. raincoat). Or the umbrella. Both did indeed originate in Britain, and for excellent reasons. And yes, it is equally true that we are obsessed by the weather. However, the surprising, even mildly disappointing, truth is that our weather is rather better than we like to admit. London, startlingly enough, is the driest capital in Northern Europe. We have half the rainfall of New York or Sydney. Somehow or other we seem to bask in 1,500 hours of sunshine a year. And there hasn't been a decent Dickensian fog in over twenty-five years. Maybe they'll rename the raincoat. That said, obviously the country looks its best from spring to autumn. The summer can even, on occasions, surprise you. A few years ago, we were so surprised we had to appoint a Government Minister for Drought. This was by way of a temporary appointment, however. By and large, we prefer our weather to avoid extremes of conduct, and usually it obliges.

'New' Doesn't Excite Us

We don't think new necessarily equals better – quite the opposite. Take Castle Howard, where 'Brideshead Revisited' was filmed. Admittedly, it lacks central heating, and any form of air-conditioning is purely unintentional, but Castle Howard, along with hundreds of other stately homes, castles, and country houses is faithfully preserved to depict life as it was lived *then*, not now.

What You Won't Find

This reverence for our heritage is decidedly pervasive. You won't find strips of fast-food and discount emporia outside our cities, towns and villages; billboards are also thin on the ground. Confession 1 – we couldn't afford them when they came into vogue. Confession 2 – weren't we lucky. As a consequence, you'll encounter villages of flint, stone, timber and thatch from Cornwall to Oxford with nothing to mar their stage-like settings.

The British Year

Every year follows a pleasantly predictable pattern of social and ceremonial occasions. While we cannot expect a Royal Wedding at more than decent intervals, we can rely on a jolly good State Opening of Parliament every autumn, complete with gold coach and a fair sprinkling of Crown Jewels. Plus an equally splendid annual Trooping of the Colour on the monarch's official birthday (don't you wish you had two birthdays a year?). And there would seem to be some wafer-thin excuse for ceremonial dressing-up virtually every week of the year. Burns' Night, on the 25th January, finds every self-respecting Scot donning a kilt and downing a dram or three in memory of their national poet.

London's lively Chinese population put on a cracking celebration of their New Year with a display of dancing dragons and fireworks which continues in full spate for at least a week (or so it seems), and should, by all rights, cost you the airfare to Hong Kong.

March signals the start of the Royal Shakespeare Theatre season at Stratford-upon-Avon, and the annual Oxford and Cambridge Boat Race, in which one crew gets into the lead and stays there for twenty minutes, a procession along the Thames all too rarely enlivened by a sinking. Mind you, everyone watching seems to get very emotional, but then they do tend to watch from a convenient riverside pub.

April brings you Shakespeare's birthday, thoughtfully shared with St George, England's patron saint. This would seem to be as good an excuse as any to pop up to Stratford for a spot of tea and culture. Try and fit in a visit to Blenheim Palace en route.

May blossoms into the Chelsea Flower Show, and June finds the horses charging round Epsom for the Derby, which is a race, not a hat. Then there's more of the same, but with a touch more class, at Royal Ascot in June, which gives the upper-crust a chance to wear very silly hats. This is closely followed by two weeks of bad manners masquerading as competitive tennis at Wimbledon.

Come autumn, the British love affair with the horse gets into full swing with the Horse of the Year Show in London, followed extremely slowly by the truly bizarre London to Brighton Veteran Car Run. Good grief, another year seems to have flashed by. They have the Christmas decorations up in Regent Street already.

FOR ENDURING VALUES – A Rich Slice of History

Britain has been attractive to tourists for quite some time. Going back a bit, Julius Caesar thought the place looked promising, and duly popped over the Channel without so much as a visa. His excuse was a shortage of good butlers in Rome, plus a justifiable predilection for our famous Colchester oysters. The civilizing influence of the Romans saw Wales peppered with strategic fortresses, and the Scots firmly partioned behind Hadrian's Wall. But, unfortunately for British plumbing standards, we were abandoned to our own devices after a few centuries, leaving it almost to the present day before we re-discovered the long-lost secret of getting hot water out of taps. In the interim, we were visited by Saxons, Vikings, and finally, in 1066, the French. Tourism of this nature rather fell off after that, and we settled down to a long line of extremely colorful monarchs (apart from one brief flirtation with republicanism, in the unattractive shape of Oliver Cromwell). First in the minds of most school-boys is William the Conqueror, inventor of strip cartoons in the shape of tapestries, and centralized government in the shape of the Domesday Book, certainly worth a look should you find yourself in the vicinity of the British Museum, which has neither lost its charm, nor needs a foggy day as an excuse to visit. While there, you can also check out the Magna Carta, reluctantly sealed by King John in 1215, and the nearest thing we have to a constitution.

Led by popular Scottish naturalist and spider-lover, Robert the Bruce, the Scots made several forays south before being trounced at Bannockburn, after which, rather than acknowledge an English monarch, they kept their own court. Meanwhile, the English looked to Wales and the Tudors for guidance. King Henry VIII (you can skip the other seven for now) advanced male chauvinism to a fine art in his touching pursuit of a meaningful relationship. His various wives were summarily despatched (divorced, beheaded, died, divorced, beheaded, survived), leading to his daughter, Elizabeth I of England, the 'Virgin Queen', remaining a confirmed career girl to her death. Interestingly, the state of Virginia is named after her. It was during the reign of Good Queen Bess that England achieved its first true golden era. The Scottish threat was neutralized by the beheading of scheming, romantic Mary Queen of Scots, and Sir Francis Drake gave us a circumnavigation of the globe. He also delivered an early lesson in the therapeutic nature of the game of bowls, a pursuit he declined to interrupt merely because someone claimed to have sighted the Spanish Armada. Whatever the outcome of that game, he proceeded to chase the Spanish fleet all the way back to Cadiz, a move which heralded the annual British invasion of Spanish beaches. Not to be outdone, Sir Walter Raleigh sailed away and came back with the potato, and tobacco. His subsequent execution by our first Scottish king, James Stuart, probably had nothing to do with an early-English anti-smoking lobby. Or, indeed, weight-watchers. Meanwhile, the young William Shakespeare was packing them in at The Globe Theatre.

Britain's prosperity really began to flourish in the mid-eighteenth century, with the growth of the Empire and the onset of the Industrial Revolution. The great houses built during this period can be seen all over England, sometimes at the center of a huge estate, sometimes in magnificent city architecture such as Bath. The Victorian excesses of style which followed are only recognized today as sublime examples of decorative art. Mind you, it was a period in which the Moral Majority were the majority, and showed it by putting lacy skirts on the legs of grand pianos. Other Victorian concepts, such as the God-given right to Empire, have become less fashionable as well in this century, fortunately for all concerned. In the years following the Second World War, almost all the countries in the British Empire have achieved independence, some painfully, but many less so. As was remarked at the time: 'Britain will be honored by historians more for the way she disposed of an empire than for the way she acquired it'.

LONDON

IN PRAISE OF LONDON

Where to start on London? Perhaps it's as best at the outset to destroy two monumental myths.

Myth No. 1: It Rains All the Time

New York has twice London's average rainfall. The weather's not wet, it's mild and mellow, just like Londoners.

Myth No. 2: The Food is Bad

Rubbish! Insiders think that London has the most remarkably diverse cuisine under the sun. This is, in large part, the result of the sun that never set, the British Empire. Today, in the heart of London, you can experience pure Peking cooking cheek by jowl with a restaurant which will serve you Pakistani Tandoori chicken so succulent it melts in your mouth; and, chances are, in the same block you'll encounter fine French fare and the ubiquitous American hamburger.

The only difficult dishes to find are good, hearty British fare, and we've uncovered an assortment ranging from grouse that will leave you grousing for more to Athol brose, a dessert which includes in its recipe the delightful instruction: 'Now add the bottle of whisky'!

AN OPEN CITY WITH OPEN WAYS

From the outset we believe that you'll be enchanted with our scale – it's human size. Greater London contains over 80 parks, as well as gardens galore. These are our lungs. They let us breathe. They range from majestic Kenwood, with its open-air concerts, to the Heath at Hampstead, where highwaymen roamed in days of yore.

Come to the Victoria Embankment Gardens for one of the world's great free floral displays as well as open-air concerts that will leave you humming. Rent a deckchair in St James's Park and watch the passing parade.

It's the changing of the Guard approaching Buckingham Palace. The last time we looked in, they were busy greeting the Queen with '*Hello Dolly*'.

Wander through our many mews – they'll make you muse that this must be a better way of life. Sit upright in a proper taxi, and you'll damn Detroit forever (unfortunately you'll have lots of time to do so – our traffic has become abysmal).

PEOPLE WHO CARE

Pop into a pub. They're the safety valve in the British democratic way of life. You'll soon find you're regarded as a regular and treated accordingly. You'll have to learn to translate though. Our language approaches the direct via the circuitous.

Where else but at Harrods in London could you spot a sign which says: 'Customers are kindly requested to attempt to refrain from smoking'?

WE CHERISH THE OLD AND FOSTER THE NEW

Our street markets have been going for donkey's years. For example, Bermondsey on the south bank is still an antique lover's mecca. (You'll have to get up early though – it opens at 6 o'clock for serious dealers.)

The silver vaults, double deckers, letters to *The Times*, the Old Bailey, Marks and Spencer's (known as 'Marks and Sparks'), the square mile called 'The City', where the Queen has to ask permission to call, are all British institutions.

All this plus Beefeaters, Chelsea Pensioners, the King's Road and the Albert Hall fall into the category labeled Traditional London.

But there's another London. A vibrant changing city which thrives on new ideas and people-pleasing pleasures. You knew we had pubs that date back to the original Elizabeth. But did you know that we have hundreds of wine bars which rival France's finest? You knew we were great for brollies and tartans, but did you know that cooking is one of the current rages, and culinary shops abound?

PERHAPS THE LAST OF THE TRULY CIVILIZED CITIES

In the pages which follow, we have attempted to give you an insight into all that's best in Britain's Crown Jewel. Whatever your taste, we think you'll find London provides it in full measure. We also think you'll find that London is the last of the civilized cities.

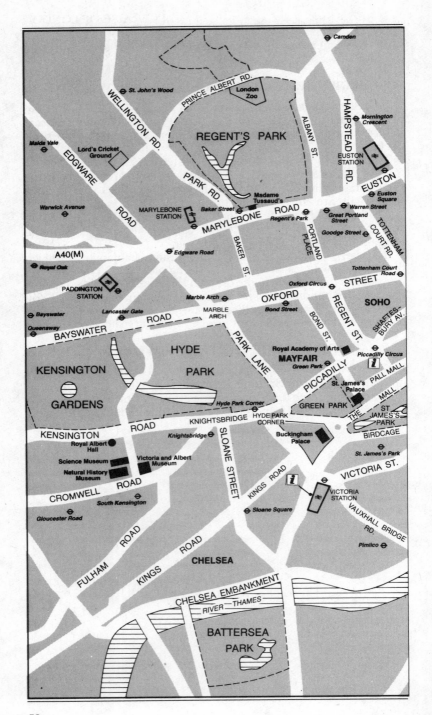

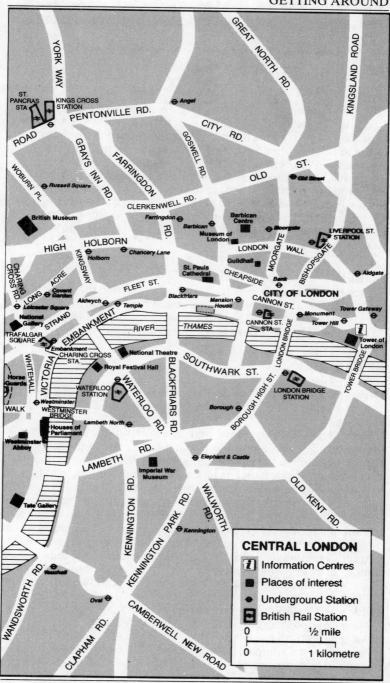

CENTRAL LONDON

- ℹ️ Information Centres
- ■ Places of interest
- • Underground Station
- 🚉 British Rail Station

0 ½ mile

0 1 kilometre

GETTING AROUND

FROM THE AIRPORT

Heathrow

Heathrow airport is approximately 16 miles from the center of London. The Piccadilly Line underground (subway) trains run from here directly into town. There's no service in the very early hours of the morning but during the day and evening the trains run frequently. What's more at £1.70 it's reasonable. London Regional Transport buses run from the airport terminals into central London, stopping at major points in the city. Taxis from the airport into town will cost around £25. Be sure to take one of the licensed cars. Check the fare first to avoid any confusion. You may find someone at the cab stand who is going your way in which case you'll be able to split the fare.

Gatwick

Trains provide a fast and frequent service from the British Rail Station at the airport into Victoria main line station. The journey time is approximately 30 minutes. Trains run frequently, the cost is £5 one way, £10 round trip (good for three months).

BY CAR

Driving into the center of London is not recommended; however, if you do have to take the car into the city certain major points are worth remembering.

Parking is a problem governed by regulations which are vigorously enforced. Breaking the parking laws results in misery. The car can be 'clamped', i.e. immobilized by a yellow contraption fixed to the wheel. If this happens instructions placed on the windscreen will direct you to the payment office. A hefty fine will secure the release of the car: if the office is closed you'll just have to wait until it opens. Even if you do escape a 'yellow dragon' you could well acquire a parking ticket and a fine. Don't park on any roads which are marked with double yellow lines at the curb. If the road is marked with a single yellow line or a dotted yellow line there'll be a notice nearby giving the times when parking is not allowed or showing the length of time for which parking is allowed. If the sign isn't visible where you happen to stop, walk around to find it – traffic wardens don't brook excuses.

Never park on zig-zag markings – they indicate the close proximity of a pedestrian crossing.

So where can you park? Find a meter and make sure you put in enough money on arrival – it is an offense to 'feed' meters later in your stay. Car parks in London are often full – you may have to queue for some time to get a space. They're always expensive. Some provide overnight parking facilities, others shut at a certain time. If you have not removed your vehicle by then, it'll be locked in. Essentially, if you have any intention of bringing a car into the center of London, find out whether your hotel has adequate parking or garaging facilities. If not, how far is the nearest public lot? Driving around London is maddening and time-wasting. Unless you're an even-tempered human compass avoid it.

BY BUS

Those famous red London buses provide an excellent means of getting around. First arm yourself with one of London Transport's invaluable bus maps available from Tourist Information Centres and underground stations. The route numbers and destinations are shown on the front and back of the vehicles. Single fares start at 50p, so it's advisable to get an unlimited travel ticket (see, **Underground** section). Bus stops are clearly marked; buses stop at all stops except those marked 'Request'. At a request stop hold out your arm to indicate to the driver that you want him to stop. If the bus is full, he'll sail on regardless.

For longer journeys out of London long-distance buses (coaches in English) leave Victoria Coach Station, Buckingham Palace Road, SW1 (tel: (01) 730 0202). The National Express bus services travel to destinations all over Britain, providing the least expensive means of public transport.

BY TRAIN

The British rail network covers the outer suburbs of London as well as the rest of Britain. Special day trip and excursion fares are a regular feature (for details enquire at travel centers at all the main stations). If you travel after 9:30am ask for a 'cheap day return' for best value.

For combined car and rail travel, enabling you to cover large distances in the comfort of the train but then allowing you to explore the more remote corners of the countryside, find out about a Britrail Pass. Available for 7, 14 or 21 days you must buy this pass in your home country prior to arrival. Passes are available from **Britrail North American Travel Information** offices at:

630 Third Avenue, New York, NY 10017 (tel: (212) 599 5400)

Suite 210, Cedar Maple Plaza, 2305 Cedar Springs, Dallas TX 75201 (tel: (214) 748 0860)

Suite 603, 800 S. Hope Street, Los Angeles CA 90017 (tel: (213) 624 8787)

94 Cumberland Street, Toronto, Ontario M5R 1A3 (tel: (416) 929 3333)

409 Glanville Street, Vancouver, B.C V6C 1T2 (tel: (604) 683 6896)

BY TAXI

The majority of London taxis are still those familiar black cabs with enough headroom to wear a topper. You can hail a cab if it shows the 'For Hire' sign lit up. The minimum fare on the meter is £1. There are surcharges for extra passengers, for journeys in the evenings, on Sundays and public holidays. You'll find that most cab drivers are incredibly knowledgeable about London. Tip 15%.

BY UNDERGROUND

London's extensive underground railway (known as 'the tube') is simple and efficient. Avoid traveling at peak times where possible (Mon-Fri 8am-9:30am, 4:30pm-6:30pm). On the easy-to-read maps each line is designated a different color; they are displayed on all platforms and in the ticket hall. You can pick up a pocket map from the ticket office at any station.

The system is divided into three fare zones: inner, outer and a-long-way-out-of-London. **The Visitor's Travel Card**, valid for 3, 4 or 7 days, allows unlimited travel on buses and the subway, plus useful discounts. A voucher for the travel card must be purchased in your home country; they're not available here. Buy the vouchers through your travel agents, or direct from British Rail overseas offices (see **By Train** for addresses). The voucher is exchanged for a ticket when you arrive in London.

Alternatively, you can buy one- or seven-day travel cards for up to three fare zones from any underground station. To obtain a seven-day ticket you'll need a passport photograph.

ON FOOT

If you're keen, well shod and the weather's good, the best way to see London is on foot. There are a few points to remember, starting with the British driving on the other side of the road. To make things easier on pedestrians, they invented the zebra crossing – broad black and white stripes with orange flashing lights at each end. While pedestrians have right of way beware – some taxis ignore this. There's also the pelican crossing – push-button traffic lights which really put you one up on the motorists.

Several companies arrange fascinating walking tours, adopting a particular area or theme such as *Shakespeare's London* or *Underworld London*, for example. Groups usually meet at an underground station; the walks last one and a half to two hours (cost around £3.00, no booking required). Details from Tourist Information Centres or:
Citisights of London (tel: (01) 739 2372)
London Walks (tel: (01) 441 8906)
The Londoner (tel: (01) 883 2656)

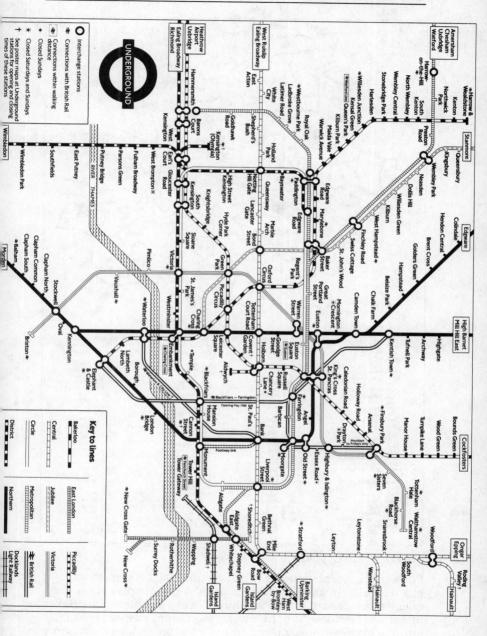

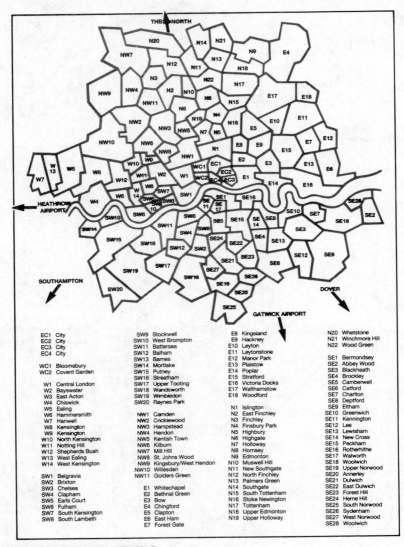

EC1	City	SW9	Stockwell	E8	Kingsland	N20	Whetstone
EC2	City	SW10	West Brompton	E9	Hackney	N21	Winchmore Hill
EC3	City	SW11	Battersea	E10	Leyton	N22	Wood Green
EC4	City	SW12	Balham	E11	Leytonstone		
		SW13	Barnes	E12	Manor Park	SE1	Bermondsey
WC1	Bloomsbury	SW14	Mortlake	E13	Plaistow	SE2	Abbey Wood
WC2	Covent Garden	SW15	Putney	E14	Poplar	SE3	Blackheath
		SW16	Streatham	E15	Stratford	SE4	Brockley
W1	Central London	SW17	Upper Tooting	E16	Victoria Docks	SE5	Camberwell
W2	Bayswater	SW18	Wandsworth	E17	Walthamstow	SE6	Catford
W3	East Acton	SW19	Wimbledon	E18	Woodford	SE7	Charlton
W4	Chiswick	SW20	Raynes Park			SE8	Deptford
W5	Ealing			N1	Islington	SE9	Eltham
W6	Hammersmith	NW1	Camden	N2	East Finchley	SE10	Greenwich
W7	Hanwell	NW2	Cricklewood	N3	Finchley	SE11	Kennington
W8	Kensington	NW3	Hampstead	N4	Finsbury Park	SE12	Lee
W9	Kensington	NW4	Hendon	N5	Highbury	SE13	Lewisham
W10	North Kensington	NW5	Kentish Town	N6	Highgate	SE14	New Cross
W11	Notting Hill	NW6	Kilburn	N7	Holloway	SE15	Peckham
W12	Shepherds Bush	NW7	Mill Hill	N8	Hornsey	SE16	Rotherhithe
W13	West Ealing	NW8	St. Johns Wood	N9	Edmonton	SE17	Walworth
W14	West Kensington	NW9	Kingsbury/West Hendon	N10	Muswell Hill	SE18	Woolwich
		NW10	Willesden	N11	New Southgate	SE19	Upper Norwood
SW1	Belgravia	NW11	Golders Green	N12	North Finchley	SE20	Annerley
SW2	Brixton			N13	Palmers Green	SE21	Dulwich
SW3	Chelsea	E1	Whitechapel	N14	Southgate	SE22	East Dulwich
SW4	Clapham	E2	Bethnal Green	N15	South Tottenham	SE23	Forest Hill
SW5	Earls Court	E3	Bow	N16	Stoke Newington	SE24	Herne Hill
SW6	Fulham	E4	Chingford	N17	Tottenham	SE25	South Norwood
SW7	South Kensington	E5	Clapton	N18	Upper Edmonton	SE26	Sydenham
SW8	South Lambeth	E6	East Ham	N19	Upper Holloway	SE27	West Norwood
		E7	Forest Gate			SE28	Woolwich

SIGHTSEEING TOURS

For a quick orientation trip round the main sights (no stops) try a
red bus ride. In good weather take the open-topped buses. Frequent tours depart from Piccadilly Circus, Marble Arch, Baker
Street and Victoria Street between 10am-5pm (they extend later
into the evenings in summer); tours last approximately one and a
half hours. There's no need to book; but, if you do make an
advance reservation, there's a discount of £1 on the price.

London Transport (tel: (01) 227 3456) also operate a choice of half and full day tours. Tickets for these trips are available from London Transport or London Tourist Board Offices; you must book in advance. **Frames Rickards**, 11 Herbrand Street, WC2 (tel: (01) 837 3111) offer excellent tours in and around London, including places like Stratford, Warwick and Windsor/Hampton Court. As do **Green Line Coaches**; their tours run from about May to September. Stop in at their enquiries desk, Eccleston Bridge, SW1 for brochures or contact the office (tel: (01) 668 7261).

ON THE WATER

A trip on the River Thames is relaxing, entertaining, and you'll get a fine view of London from a new angle. For full information on services available (in both directions) ask at an Information Centre or telephone **Riverboat Information** (tel: (01) 730 4812) or enquire at the pier. Boats going downstream to the Tower of London and Greenwich leave **Westminster Pier** and **Charing Cross Pier** at approximately twenty minute intervals between 10am-5pm. Upstream services from Westminster Pier will take you to Kew, Richmond and Hampton Court. **Catamaran Cruises** (tel: (01) 839 3572) operate trips that include lunch or dinner, plus disco cruises.

If a trip on the river doesn't appeal, then you may like to try Regent's Canal. Trips on the canal start from Little Venice. **Jason's Trips** (tel: (01) 286 3428) run one and a half hour cruises (with or without a meal). **'My Fair Lady'** (tel: (01) 485 4433) is a floating restaurant providing dinner or Sunday lunch. You'll have to book for these trips. The Regent's Canal **Waterbus** (tel: (01) 482 2550) runs hourly from 10am-5pm, starting at Little Venice and traveling via the Zoo to Camden Lock.

INFORMATION CENTERS

There's a network of Tourist Information Centres all over Britain so pick up a free list and make use of them. The knowledgeable staff are ready to help with enquiries, theater bookings and hotel reservations. In London you'll find centers at:

British Travel Centre, 13 Regent Street, W1 (tel: (01) 730 3400)
Victoria Railway Station, Forecourt, SW1 (for all London
  enquiries tel: (01) 730 3488)
Harrods (4th Floor), Knightsbridge, SW1
Selfridges Basement Arcade, Duke Street entrance, Oxford
  Street, W1
Tower of London, West Gate, EC3 (summer only)
Heathrow Terminals One, Two, Three and Underground Station

MUST SIGHTS

Changing the Guard, Buckingham Palace
Daily 11:30am – alternate days in winter
⊖ Victoria
Also at Horseguards, Whitehall
Mon-Sat 11am, Sun 10am
⊖ Charing Cross or Westminster

The new guard assembles at Wellington Barracks (or Chelsea Barracks), leaving the barracks at 11:27am and marching to the forecourt of the palace, accompanied by rousing tunes from their band. The musical tempo slows as the keys are handed over, then the old guard marches off. The guard is mounted by the five regiments of Foot of the Guards Division: the Grenadiers (formed in 1656), the Coldstreams (1659), the Scots (1642), the Irish (1902) and the Welsh Guards (founded 1915).

The ceremony is subject to cancellation in wet weather or on state occasions so check with the Tourist Information Centre (tel: (01) 730 3488) or the Palace (tel: (01) 930 4832). It's best to get there by 10:45am if you want to see the ceremony clearly (top of the Fountain – orchestra seats).

At the changing of the Queen's Life Guard in Whitehall the old guard in their splendid Household Cavalry uniforms are relieved by the new, who have ridden from Knightsbridge Barracks via The Mall and across Horse Guards Parade.

Houses of Parliament, Westminster, SW1
Tel: (01) 219 4272
Strangers' Gallery Open: Mon-Thurs 2:30pm-10pm or later,
    Fri 9:30am-3pm during sessions
⊖ Westminster

For many, this vast Victorian pseudo gothic building is the main attraction in London. It is correctly called the New Palace of Westminster because the site was a royal residence from the time of Edward the Confessor (1042-66) until 1529 when the Court moved to Whitehall. The original building survived Guy Fawkes's attempt to blow it up in 1605, but it was burnt down in 1834; only St Stephen's chapel and Westminster Hall were saved. Built by William II, the hall is famed for its hammerbeam roof of solid oak timbers. A competition for the design of the new parliamentary building was won by Sir Charles Barry and Augustus Pugin, and work started in 1836. It is huge, with some 1100 rooms, 100 staircases and two miles of passageways.

Unfortunately, for security reasons, there are no longer tours of the building; however, it is possible to listen to debates. Apply to your Embassy, which has a limited allocation of tickets. If you are unable to obtain a ticket, you can queue up at St Stephen's entrance (by Westminster Hall at the center of the building on the Parliament Square side). The best time to queue is on Friday or after 6pm in the evening.

Lloyds, Leadenhall Street, EC3
Tel: (01) 623 7100 (ext. 6210)
Open: Mon-Fri 10am-2:30pm
For groups less than six; larger groups by prior appointment only
Free admission
⊖ Bank

Until this century the biggest insurance company in the world possessed no exclusive office premises. The two massive insurance offices either side of Lime Street date from 1928 and 1957; Lloyds shipping register was opened in 1900. The history of the company is extraordinary. In 1691 Edward Lloyd moved his coffee house business from somewhere near the Tower of London to 16 Lombard Street. Here it developed into the place for merchants, shippers, bankers, agents, newsmen and underwriters to gather and do business. All this and more you can glean from Lloyds' Visitor Centre where the history of Lloyds is carefully charted. You can look down from a gallery onto the underwriting floor below and up to a towering glass atrium. Admission is free and anyone in groups of less than six is welcome to walk in off the street. For groups of six or more, write to the Visits & Lectures Section, Public Affairs Department, Lloyds of London, One Lime Street, London EC3M 7HA for an appointment.

Mansion House, Mansion House Street (facing the Bank of
    England), EC3
Free admission, donations to the Lord Mayor's Charity
    appreciated
⊖ Bank

Offical residence of the Lord Mayor of London, who holds office for one year only, Mansion House dates from 1739-52. Previous Lord Mayors remained in their own homes during their mayoralty. The architect was George Dance, the elder, who used Portland Stone for this Palladian style mansion. The interior is open only by appointment. You must write 6 months in advance, to Miss Ann Gale, Principal Diary Assistant, Mansion House, London EC4N 8BH. Tours take place Monday-Thursday at 11am and 2pm, except when Mansion House is in use for official purposes. You will be guided through the dining, or Egyptian Hall (named after an interior Vitruvius described as an Egyptian Hall and favored by the 18th century Palladian, but having nothing to do with Egypt), where giant Corinthian columns support the cornice. The niches in the walls contain Victorian statuary on subjects taken from English literature ranging from the works of Chaucer to Byron. Also on show is the plate belonging to the Corporation of London, dating from the 17th century. The Lords Mayor's chain of office is even older, dating from around 1535, and set with enameled Tudor roses, onyx and diamonds. The 16th-century Pearl Sword was purportedly presented by Elizabeth I.

The Lord Mayor is Chief Magistrate of the City; his residence contains the only British Court of Justice to be found in a house. Beneath the court are cells where the campaigner Emily Pankhurst was for a time imprisoned.

Old Bailey, Newgate Street, EC4
Tel: (01) 248 3277
Open: Mon-Fri 10:30am-1pm, 2pm-4pm
Free admission
⊖ St Paul's

Newly reconstructed in 1907, this is the third criminal court on a site close by what used to be New Gate in the old city walls. Unlike earlier courts, there is no jail attached: prisoners are brought daily to be held in one of 60 cells to await their appearance in court. The Lady of Justice, a gold figure on a green copper dome, holding scales and sword, stands 12 feet tall on the building's summit. Inside there is a majestic sweep of marble, including two halls and a grand staircase, as might befit Britain's Central Criminal Courts. Visitors are admitted to the public gallery when courts are sitting.

Royal Britain, Aldersgate Street, Barbican, EC2
Tel: (01) 588 0588
Open: Daily 9am-5:30pm
Admission: Adults £5, children £3
⊖ Barbican

This new, permanent exhibition covers a thousand years of royal history, from the myths and legends surrounding King Arthur and Boadicea to the present monarchy. Visitors pass through a series of chambers, each featuring in chronological order the different styles, social issues and events in the reigns of successive monarchs. Make this an early stop in your visit to London, because the exhibition will put into perspective everything else you'll see in historic Britain. Best of all, it's an exciting exhibition, using the very latest technology to produce sound and visual effects that bring each period vividly to life, including the execution of Mary, Queen of Scots, and the battle-weary troops in the Wars of the Roses.

St Paul's Cathedral, Ludgate Hill, EC4
Open: Mon-Fri 10am-4:15pm, Sat 11am-4:15pm (including
   Galleries, main parts of the Cathedral, crypt)
Admission to Crypt: Adults 80p, children 40p Galleries: Adults
   £1.00, children 50p American Chapel: Adults 60p, children 50p
⊖ St Paul's

(Note: The Cathedral is open daily 8am-6pm; the opportunities for
sightseeing are limited, however, and the above times are suggested.) Services are held weekdays: 8am, 12:30pm, 5pm (evensong) Sun 8am, 10:30am, 11:30am and 3:15pm (evensong).
Guided Super Tours: Mon-Sat 11am, 11:30am, 2pm, 2:30pm
Adults £3.50, children 5-16 years £1.60.

The first cathedral on this site was founded in 604 AD. The building
we see today was built between 1675 and 1708. It was designed by
Wren to replace the previous cathedral which was destroyed in the
Great Fire of London in 1666.

Inside, there are many fine monuments and rich ornamentation,
and an awe-inspiring view upwards into the richly decorated dome
which rises over 200 feet from the ground. For the energetic there
are 259 steps to climb up to the Whispering Gallery, so called
because of the acoustics which enable someone standing at one side
of the gallery to hear conversations from the opposite side 107 feet
away. The crypt is reputed to be the largest in Europe and many
famous people are buried here, including Nelson, Wellington and
Wren.

Tower of London, Tower Hill, EC3
Tel: (01) 709 0765
Open: Mon-Sat 9:30am-5pm, Sun 2pm-5pm Mar-Oct;
   Mon-Sat 9:30am-4pm Nov-Feb
Closed: Winter and spring public holidays
Admission: Adults £4.50, children 5-16 years £2.00
⊖ Tower Hill

The Tower of London was begun by William the Conqueror in 1067
with the erection of fortifications to protect the City. The White
Tower (begun 1078) is the earliest building. The royal armory was
first installed here by Henry VIII. Today you'll find a splendid
display of arms and armor on view. On the third floor you'll see four
suits of armor that were worn by Henry VII. Up until this century
the Tower was used as a prison. Its illustrious inmates have
included Thomas More, Sir Walter Raleigh and Anne Boleyn, who
was executed on Tower Green.

The magnificent Crown Jewels are on display in the Jewel House:
the Imperial State Crown is studded with 3,000 jewels; the Queen
Elizabeth Crown (made in 1937 for the Queen Mother's Coronation) is adorned with the Koh-i Noor diamond which was presented

to Queen Victoria by the East India Company.

You can't miss the Beefeaters (or Yeoman Warders as they are correctly called) in their uniforms which date from Tudor times. Each night the Tower is ceremonially locked up at 9:40pm. To view the ceremony you must apply in advance for a pass, by writing to The Resident Governor, HM Tower of London, EC3 enclosing a addressed envelope and enough international reply coupons to cover the cost of air mail. The coupons are available at US post offices.

Trafalgar Square
⊖ Charing Cross or Embankment

Nelson's Column makes this one of London's most famous landmarks. The column is 185 feet high and the statue of Nelson is just over 17 feet high (three times the man's actual height of 5 foot 9½ inches). At the base of the column notice the bronzes which were cast from captured French cannons and represent scenes from the battles of St Vincent, Aboukir, Copenhagen and Trafalgar. The splendid lions are by Landseer (better known as a painter). In the north-east corner of the square there's a fine statue of George IV, and at the top of Whitehall the statue of Charles I looks down the road towards his place of execution. The National Gallery stands proudly dominating the north of the square and towards the eastern corner there's the church of St Martin-in-the-Fields.

Trafalgar Square has long been an assembly place for political meetings and for the annual New Year celebrations. At Christmas the square is decorated with a huge tree, an annual gift from Norway as a token of thanks for help during World War II.

Westminster Abbey, Parliament Square, SW1
Tel: (01) 222 5152
Open: Daily 8am-6pm (Wed 8am-8pm), subject to services
  Royal Chapels open: Mon-Fri 9am-4:45pm; Sat 9am-2:45pm,
  3:45pm-5:45pm; last admission 45 min before closing
Admission: To Royal Chapels Adults £1.80, children 5-16 years
  40p
⊖Westminster

Guided tours are conducted by the Abbey's vergers Monday-Friday 10am, 10:30am, 11am, 2pm, 2:30pm, 3pm; Saturday 10am, 11am, 12:30pm (less frequent in winter) – at a cost of £4.00 per person. These are very comprehensive and it is advisable to book ahead in summer (tel: (01) 222 7110).

There has been a church on this site since the 7th century, but the origins of the present building date back to the 11th century. Edward the Confessor rebuilt the church and it was consecrated in 1065, just a week before he died. William I was crowned here in

1066. Since then every Coronation has taken place in the Abbey. The imposing Coronation Chair, which has been used for the occasion since 1308, is on view here. The Abbey is an architectural masterpiece which has been added to and embellished over the centuries. Henry III undertook a major rebuilding and extension program between 1220 and 1245. Influenced by the great French cathedrals at Reims and Amiens, Henry III was responsible for the Lady Chapel and the Shrine of Edward the Confessor (surrounded by the tombs of five kings and three queens). Later, in 1519, the Henry VII Chapel was completed: notice the fan-vaulted roof which is a superb example of its kind. In the North aisle you'll see the tomb of Queen Elizabeth I (who died in 1603) with the marble effigy which is considered to be a good likeness of her. Later additions include the West Towers by Wren and Hawksmoor (built in 1722-45) and repairs by Scott in the 19th century.

In addition to royalty, many other luminaries are either buried or commemorated here – such as David Livingstone and Thomas Telford, or soldiers like General Gordon (killed at Khartoum). The Poets' Corner has tombs and memorials to some great literary figures including Chaucer, Shakespeare, Dryden, Thomas Hardy and Jane Austen.

LOCAL DELIGHTS

Be Part Of An Event

There's always something exciting happening in London. Whatever the season, regardless of the weather, you'll find something going on. Major sporting events include the Royal International Horse Show, Royal Ascot, cricket at Lords, tennis at Wimbledon and Sunday polo matches at Ham near Richmond. On the second Saturday in June you can experience the pageantry of Trooping the Colour – just stand on the Mall and observe living history. Colorful local events include the Sagra fete (festival) held by the Italian community in Clerkenwell on the first Sunday after July 16th or the Notting Hill Carnival in August. On a grand scale, the Lord Mayor's Show is held on the second Saturday in November when a procession takes to the streets. Local festivals, fairs, exhibitions and musical events offer a real insight into the different areas of the city. Greenwich and Richmond both run annual festivals; the latter, in May, includes a fair on the green.

The British Travel Centre (12 Regent Street, tel: (01) 730 3400) will provide the exact dates and full details of major events. Local events are often listed in the weekly magazine *Time Out*, in *The Times* or *Independent* newspaper or in local papers.

Chelsea Physic Garden, 66 Royal Hospital Road, SW3
Tel: (01) 352 5646
Open: April 10-Oct 23, Sun and Wed 2pm-5pm
Admission: Adults £1.50, children 5-16 years £1
⊖ Sloane Square

Britain's second-oldest Botanic Garden was established by the Apothecaries Company in 1676. There are around 5,000 plants here, many of which are rare and unusual, all packed into 4 acres of ground. The fascinating herb garden has an outstanding collection of medicinal and culinary plants. It was from here that cotton seeds were sent to Georgia in 1732 to help establish a cotton industry. Nearby, the Royal Hospital designed by Wren (open Mon-Sat 10am-noon 2pm-4pm, Sun 2pm-4pm) is the home of the Chelsea Pensioners – army veterans in colorful uniforms. There is no admission fee, but if one of the pensioners shows you round a tip is called for. (See **London Walks – Royal Chelsea Ramble**.)

Covent Garden

Covent Garden, a fashionable meeting place for young Londoners, is a center for activity all through the day and evening. It once housed Britain's foremost fruit and vegetable market. The splendid old buildings remain to house museums, small fashionable shops and craft stalls. The Piazza has become an open stage for amateur performers of all types. Buskers, jugglers or clowns give impromptu performances throughout the day.

Nearby you'll see St Paul's Church designed by Inigo Jones with its fine carving and plaques commemorating actors and other famous people associated with the theater. In the portico Samuel Pepys saw the first ever Punch and Judy show given in England in 1662.

This is one of London's best areas in which to idly wander or to sit back and watch the world go by, while enjoying one of the many open air cafés, restaurants or pubs.

Highgate Cemetery, Swains Lane, Highgate, N6
Tel: (01) 340 1834
Open: Daily. Western Cemetery tours 10am-4pm (3pm Oct-Mar)
Free Admission, but donations are appreciated
⊖ Archway

A fascinating place for those who enjoy reading tombstones. In the Eastern Cemetery lie the graves of George Eliot and Karl Marx. After years of neglect, the Western Cemetery is being restored to reveal extraordinary monuments and memorial architecture, among them carved angels, animals and catacombs. (To see this area you'll have to join a guided tour.) Christina Rossetti and Michael Faraday are buried here. Outside the cemetery, Highgate village is charming with some fine architecture. A. E. Housman and the late Sir John Betjeman both lived here. For a little earthly refreshment try **The Flask,** 77 Highgate West Hill (walk up Swains Lane and left along South Grove). Built in 1767, it is a pretty pub with flowers, a cosy bar and an open fire. Dick Turpin is said to have hidden in the cellars and Hogarth frequented the bar. At lunchtime there's good bar food, sausages and sandwiches. There's also a restaurant serving traditional English food, such as roasts for lunch; children are welcome.

Kenwood, Hampstead Lane, NW3
Tel: (01) 348 1286
Open: Daily 10am-7pm Apr-Sep; until 5pm Feb, Mar, Oct; until 4pm Nov, Jan
Free admission
⊖ Archway or Golders Green then Bus 210 to Kenwood

Splendid Kenwood House was once the seat of Lord Mansfield who commissioned Robert Adam to remodel the existing house in 1764. Inside there's a fine example of Adam's work in the library which is considered to be a masterpiece, with its rich decor and impressive ceiling. In 1925 the house was bought by Lord Iveagh and he bequeathed it to the nation together with the fine art collection on display here, including works by Rembrandt, Vermeer, Gainsborough and Romney.

On Saturday evenings from June to September, popular classical music concerts are held beside the lake. Tickets are available in advance from Duke of York's Theatre, St Martin's Lane, WC2 (tel: (01) 379 5533) or at Kenwood from 6pm on the evening of the concert. The concerts provide the perfect excuse for a grand picnic. Order a hamper from Harrods, Selfridges or Fortnum and Mason. Alternatively, buy delicatessen foods and a bottle of wine and make up your own.

Linley Sambourne House, 18 Stafford Terrace, W8
Tel: (01) 994 1019
Open: Wed 10am-4pm, Sun 2pm-5pm, Mar-Oct
Admission: £1.50
θ High Street Kensington

Just off Kensington High Street, this fascinating town house offers a picture of life in the late 19th century. It was the home of Linley Sambourne (1844-1910) who was a political cartoonist for *Punch* magazine. The original Victorian furnishings decorate all three floors, along with examples of Sambourne's work and that of other cartoonists and artists of his time. He was also a book illustrator and among the titles he illustrated you'll see works of Dickens and Hans Andersen. The house is administered by the Victorian Society which was founded at a meeting here in 1958.

Live Jazz Restaurants
Enjoy an evening, or for that matter, a morning, of jazz. The following are the best-known jazz restaurants – the music usually starts about 7:30pm-8pm. Telephone the restaurant in advance to find out who's playing.

Café Italien
19 Charlotte Street, W1 (tel: (01) 636 4174)

Pizza Express
10 Dean Street, W1 (tel: (01) 439 8722)

Pizza on the Park
11 Knightsbridge, Hyde Park Corner, SW1 (tel: (01) 235 5550)

For Sunday morning jazz try the Jazz Brunch at the **Portman Inter-Continental Hotel** 22 Portman Square, W1 (tel: (01) 486 5844). It's a weekly event, so telephone first to make sure there's a table. For about £13 you'll be able to feast your ears and stomach.

Listings of events and venues can be found in *What's On* and *Time Out* magazines.

Royal Mews, Buckingham Palace Road, SW1
Tel: (01) 930 4832
Open: Wed, Thur 2pm-4pm only
Admission: Adults 40p, Children 5-16 years 20p
⊖ Victoria

Along the road from the Queen's Gallery, at the side of Buckingham Palace, the Royal Mews house magnificent, centuries-old ceremonial carriages. The star of the mews is the fabulous Gold State Coach made in 1762 at a cost of £7,661 16s 5d, which has carried every monarch on Coronation Day since 1820. There's the glass coach, bought by George V in 1910, and used at royal weddings, most recently for the marriages of the Prince and Princess of Wales, and the Duke and Duchess of York. As well as the carriages, all the other equipment for saddling the royal horses is on display – you may even see a horse.

Southwark
⊖ London Bridge

Rich in history but off the usual tourist routes, this is an area in which to discover much of Old London. **Southwark Cathedral** dates from the 13th century, but it has been greatly altered since then. As well as many fine monuments, notice the chapel dedicated to John Harvard who was born in **Borough High Street**, and whose bequest assured the continued existence of what became Harvard University. Along Borough High Street you'll pass a series of narrow streets which mark the entrance to old inns. The most famous is the **George Inn** dating from 1676, the only galleried inn in London, which serves good food. Shakespeare's plays are performed in the courtyard in summer (tel: (01) 407 2056 for details). (see **Delightful Drinking** – *City Pubs*). Walk behind Southwark Cathedral, into **Clink Street** and under the bridge to **Bankside**. Here you'll find the **Anchor**, another famous pub associated with Shakespeare and Dr Johnson. It was in this area that Shakespeare's Globe Theatre was located.

Nearby, in **St Mary Overy Dock**, you'll see the three-masted schooner *Kathleen and May* which was launched in 1900. This vessel carried cargo round the coast of Britain until 1961, and is now restored. The vessel is on view to the public (open: daily 10am-5pm; closed: Christmas Day, New Year's Day; admission: adults £1, children 5-16 years 50p). On board there's an exhibition of the history of Britain's coastal trade.

Running eastwards beyond London Bridge the old **Hay's Dock** has been covered with a glass roof and it now houses shops, pubs, cafés and restaurants. Further along you'll find the mooring place of HMS *Belfast*, a battleship preserved as a floating museum (open: daily 11am-5:50pm summer; 4:30pm winter; admission: adults £3.00, children £1.50).

On the far side of Tower Bridge you'll see the **Butler's Wharf** development, which includes shops, leisure facilities and the Conran Foundation Design Museum which is scheduled to open soon.

Speakers' Corner, Hyde Park near Marble Arch
⊖ Marble Arch

Hard by Marble Arch, erected here in 1851 on the site of famous Tyburn gallows where in centuries past literally thousands met their death, Speakers' Corner occupies a small part of Hyde Park. It was established in 1872, the government's answer to a need for a place of public assembly and debate. Here anyone may publicly say anything as long as it is not obscene, blasphemous, a breach of the peace or likely to cause one. Traditionally, the time for open debate is Sunday mornings, but people who like to pontificate can still be going strong well into the late afternoon. Heckling often provides the best entertainment.

Walk Along Regent's Canal
Stretches of the tow paths along which horses used to tow barges are open to the public. The walks are controlled by the Boroughs of Westminster, Hammersmith, Kensington, Chelsea, Ealing, Camden and Hackney.

They can be a most enjoyable way of discovering London. Ring the British Waterways Board (tel: (01) 262 6711) for further information. If you visit them at Melbury House, Melbury Terrace, NW1, you can pick up their informative map.

PARKS AND GARDENS

London's parks are well used and well kept. They're areas for recreation and relaxation, popular with local residents, business people in search of fresh air during their lunchbreak, and visitors to the city. Generally open from dawn to dusk, many of the parks have deckchairs for rent; ice cream and hot dog sellers are usually on hand in the summer months; picnickers are welcome.

Green Park
⊖ Green Park

A convenient short-cut from Buckingham Palace up to Piccadilly, Green Park lives up to its name. Green lawns are dappled with sunlight beneath shady trees, deckchairs are for hire (green canvas), with nary a flowerbed in sight. A great favorite with local office workers, on a sunny summer weekday lunchtime all you can see are prostrate bodies. This is not the aftermath of some appalling plague-infested horror movie; just the British at ease.

Hampstead Heath
⊖ Hampstead

Hampstead Heath is a real slice of open country, where highwaymen once roamed and where you can escape city life among wooded walks, ponds and open fields that stretch over 240 acres. The Heath was once the common attached to Hampstead Manor in the time of Charles II. The adjoining Parliament Hill attracts kiteflyers and those who know about the stunning views south of here to the City of London's skyline. You can easily park off the East Heath Road and find a sheltered picnic spot, often with panoramic views. The center of Hampstead village is less than 10 minutes away.

Hyde Park
⊖ Marble Arch, Knightsbridge, Lancaster Gate

The largest of the central London parks, once stocked with deer, Hyde Park was used as a royal hunting ground by Henry VIII. It extends from Bayswater Road south to Knightsbridge; from Park Lane west to Kensington Gardens. One of its main attractions is the Serpentine, a large stretch of water where you'll find row boats for hire. This is also the focus of the Serpentine Swimming Club, where members traditionally 'break the ice' for a bracing dip on Christmas Day. Rotten Row has been a fashionable showcase for horses and riders since the 18th century. Sadly, carriages have long since disappeared from the scene, while dress standards have plummeted. If you've ever felt inclined towards soap box oratory,

Speakers' Corner is a must. Located at the Marble Arch entrance to the park, every Sunday morning, speakers wise and wacky berate bemused audiences and incite themselves to riot (rarely the audience). Potential speakers should bring their own box.

Kensington Gardens
e High Street Kensington

On the west side of Hyde Park, stretching towards Kensington Palace, you'll find Kensington Gardens. Kensington Palace is the London home of the Prince and Princess of Wales, and Princess Margaret; the former State Apartments are open to the public (see **Museums**). The northern tip of the Serpentine reaches as far as the Gardens, where it's known as Longwater. Here you'll find a delightful statue of Peter Pan, J.M. Barrie's storybook hero. Nearby, the Round Pond is a traditional place for children to sail model boats, under the watchful eye of nanny. Just beside the palace is a particularly attractive sunken garden.

Kew Gardens
Tel: (01) 940 1171
e Kew Gardens
Open: Daily 9:30am-4:30pm, Sun until 5:30pm; longer hours in summer
Admission: Adults 50p, children under 10 years free

The famous Royal Botanic Gardens, covering 300 acres, contain around 50,000 different plants. They're beautifully laid out. Well annotated, and truly magnificent in the prime spring and summer flowering periods. Don't avoid a visit if the weather's bad, the gorgeous greenhouses provide shelter as well as many rare and colorful blooms. Architectural treats include the Orangery, Palm House and Pagoda. Also, Kew Palace (open daily 11am-3:30pm, Apr-Sept, admission: adults £1, children 50p), a small Jacobean mansion within the gardens. Built in 1631, also known as The Dutch House, it's where King George III was born. Although small by some standards, it was a popular royal retreat in the King's day, now beautifully restored in period style.

Regent's Park
e Regent's Park, Baker Street

This area was originally enclosed by Henry VIII in the 16th century. Three hundred years later, Regency architect John Nash proposed a plan to ring the park with elegant terraces, and build several villas in the park itself. The plan was only partially realized, his elegant terraced houses constructed only partway round. If you enter the park by Regent's Park underground station, follow Broadwalk northwards towards the zoo. At Chester Road turn left for Queen Mary's Rose Garden, one of the most spectacular displays of roses in the world. During the summer months, a season of Shakespeare's plays are performed in the Open Air Theatre on Inner Circle. Further north (by Outer Circle) you'll find the famous zoo (see **Fun For The Kids**).

Richmond Park
⊖ Richmond

The largest of the royal parks (over 2,000 acres), Richmond was enclosed by Charles I in 1637. There are several old hunting lodges dotted around the park; Princess Alexandra and her family live in one, the Royal Ballet School occupies another. Herds of deer roam the open grasslands, or shelter under ancient oak trees, eyeing passing motorists and ramblers with remarkable tolerance. The Isabella Plantation, a spectacular display of rhododendrons and azaleas in May, is well signposted from all the entrances. This pretty woodland garden with a stream running through it is a favorite spot for visitors; as is the café and tearoom at Pembroke Lodge. In summer you can sit out on the terrace and have a delicious cream tea.

St James's Park
⊖ St James's Park

London's oldest Royal park, St James's dates back to 1532. Landscaped and improved by John Nash in the 19th century, it lies south of The Mall overlooked by both Buckingham Palace and Clarence House, where the Queen Mother lives. It's one of the most attractive parks to visit with decorative flowerbeds and picturesque views of Westminster and the Houses of Parliament. Its other great attraction is the lake which has become home to a wide variety of wildfowl, native and foreign. In spring, daffodils carpet the lawns, the odd rabbit pops up and down, revelers have even been known to catch a glimpse of a wild fox.

MUSEUMS

Apsley House, Hyde Park Corner, W1
Tel: (01) 499 5676
Open: Tues-Sun 11am-4:50pm
Closed: Mon and winter public holidays, Labour Day in May
Admission: Adults £2, Children £1
⊖ Hyde Park Corner

This impressive residence which dominates Hyde Park Corner was built by Robert Adam in 1771 for Baron Apsley. The Duke of Wellington bought the house in 1817 and lived here until his death in 1852. In 1828 he commissioned Benjamin and Philip Wyatt to remodel the building and the splendid portico was added, along with the exterior facing of Bath stone. Inside the decor is quite splendid. The green, white and gold Piccadilly Drawing Room was decorated by Adam and is a fine example of his work. The vast 90 foot-long long Waterloo Gallery was designed by Wyatt in 1828. It was here that the Iron Duke held banquets on the anniversary of Waterloo Day (June 18th).

The house is filled with Wellington memorabilia – the Duke's traveling canteen, medals and so on. There is a notable art collection on display, including much which was captured during his campaigns, with works by Velasquez, Van Dyck, Rubens, Correggio, and a superb portrait of Wellington by Goya. You'll also see fine porcelain (Meissen, Sèvres), snuffboxes and a wealth of gold and silver plate.

Bethnal Green Museum of Childhood, Cambridge Heath Road, E2
Tel: (01) 980 2415
Open: Mon-Thur 10am-6pm, Sat 10am-6pm, Sun 2:30pm-6pm
Closed: Fri and public holidays
Free admission
⊖ Bethnal Green

This outpost of the Victoria and Albert Museum houses an enchanting collection of toys, dolls, puppets and models. There are some beautiful dolls' houses on display, including one from Nuremberg, dating from 1673, and one which was owned by Queen Mary, dating from 1887, furnished with all the equipment and comforts that were necessary in a mansion of the day. There is a display of wedding dresses, some dating from the 18th century, and including fabulous examples made in Spitalfields silk, which was woven in the area mainly by Huguenots who had fled from France.

British Museum, Great Russell Street, WC1
Tel: (01) 636 1555
Open: Mon-Sat 10am-5pm, Sun 2:30pm-6pm
Closed: Winter and spring public holidays
Free admission
⊖ Tottenham Court Road

One of the finest museums in the world, the British Museum was established in 1753 around the collections of antiquary and bibliophile Sir Robert Cotton and the collector of scientific books and manuscripts, Sir Hans Sloane. The present building dates from 1823 with a new wing added in 1884.

The museum's library is the nation's main copyright library. By law one copy of all UK books published must be sent here. The library contains over six million books (on 85 miles of shelving). As well as modern publications they have items such as the log book of Nelson's *Victory* and a 1623 first folio of Shakespeare's plays. There's a 4th-century manuscript of the Bible, the Codex Sinaiticus, bought by the British Government in 1933 for £100,000. The parchment was found in 1844 at St Catherine's monastery on Mt Sinai in a basket of rubbish which was just about to be burnt. Two of the four remaining copies of the Magna Carta are in the museum, together with the original seal attached in 1215.

From Babylon to the Orient, from Egypt to Medieval England, the museum has it all. Among the collection of Egyptian antiquities you'll see the famous Rosetta Stone which carries the same inscription in three alphabets: the formal Egyptian hieroglyphics, the popular demotic script, and Greek. The Greek inscription gave the key to the ancient Egyptian scripts which, till the stone was brought to England in 1802, could not be deciphered. In the Duveen Gallery you'll see some of the most famous of all the treasures – the Ancient Greek Parthenon sculptures known as the Elgin Marbles. These were being destroyed in the fighting between Turks and the Greeks in the 19th century when Lord Elgin bought them and brought them to England.

When you've absorbed as much information as you can and wondered at the awe-inspiring collections, visit the shop, which is an excellent source of gifts.

Cabinet War Rooms, Clive Steps, King Charles Street, SW1
Tel: (01) 930 6961
Open: Daily 10am-5:50pm
Closed: Public holidays in winter and spring.
Admission: Adults £2.80, children 5-16 years £1.50
⊖ Westminster

Situated underground, in the basement of the Government offices, this was where Winston Churchill, his War Cabinet and Chiefs of

Staff worked during World War II, safe from the threat of bombing. The suite of 21 rooms was in use from August 1939 until the Japanese surrender in 1945, and they retain the deep sense of urgency that prevailed. From the Transatlantic Room Churchill could speak directly to President Roosevelt; he used the Prime Minister's Room as his bedroom/office, and the Map Room was the main operations room. It was from here that Churchill made his famous radio broadcasts.

Dickens' House, 48 Doughty Street, WC1
Tel: (01) 405 2127
Open: Mon-Sat 10am-5pm
Closed: Sun and public holidays
Admission: Adults £1.50, children 5-16 years 50p
⊖ Russell Square

Charles Dickens lived in this house from 1837 to 1839, and it was here that he wrote *Oliver Twist*, *Nicholas Nickleby* and completed *Pickwick Papers*. His study, where he wrote, houses some of his furniture and there are portraits, manuscripts, letters, first editions and personal mementoes on view. The family Bible, with records of his sons and daughters, and the reading desk he used on the Reading Tours he conducted, are particularly interesting exhibits.

Geffrye Museum, Kingsland Road, E2
Tel: (01) 739 8368
Open: Tues-Sat 10am-5pm, Sun 2pm-5pm
Closed: Mon and public holidays in winter
Free admission
⊖ Liverpool Street then Bus 22, 22A, 48, 149 or 243A

This museum of domestic life is located in almshouses built by the Ironmongers Company in the 18th century and financed by a bequest from Sir Robert Geffrye who was then Lord Mayor. Domestic rooms, decorated and furnished in the style of different periods from 1600 to the 1930s, highlight the theme. On Saturdays (and during the week in school holidays) special workshops and activities are organized for children. There is no need to reserve a place for these, but do telephone for program details.

Geological Museum, Exhibition Road, SW7
Tel: (01) 589 3444
Open: Mon-Sat 10am-6pm, Sun 1pm-6pm
Closed: Winter public holidays
Admission: Mon-Fri free, Sat-Sun Adults £1, children 5-16 years 50p
⊖ South Kensington

The Geological Museum houses a definitive collection of minerals and rocks, with special displays showing the Story of the Earth, Treasures of the Earth, Britain before Man and Fossils. The geology of Britain and its natural resources are cleverly illustrated by means of maps and models. There's an amazing collection of gemstones, in cut and uncut forms. You'll even find raw Uranium 237. The museum runs lectures and film shows. On Saturdays at 2:30pm family events are arranged – film shows or talks on minerals or fossils, for example. Telephone for details of special events.

Hayward Gallery, Belvedere Road, SE1
Tel: (01) 928 3144
Open: During exhibitions Mon-Wed 10am-8pm, Thurs-Sat 10am-6pm, Sun noon-6pm
Closed: Public holidays in winter and spring
Admission: Adults £3, children 5-16 years £1.50. Reduced adult rate £1.50, all day Mon and Tues-Wed 6pm-8pm
⊖ Waterloo or Embankment and walk across Hungerford or Waterloo Bridge

Opened in 1968, this modern gallery forms part of the South Bank arts complex which includes the Royal Festival Hall, National Theatre, National Film Theatre, Queen Elizabeth Hall and Purcell Room. The gallery houses major art exhibitions, both historical and contemporary. The exhibitions change frequently and the gallery is closed between events, so telephone for details.

Imperial War Museum, Lambeth Road, SE1
Tel: (01) 735 8922
Open: Mon-Sat 10am-5:50pm, Sun 2pm-5:50pm
Closed: Public holidays in winter and spring
Free admission
⊖ Lambeth North

This large museum exhibits all facets of the wars and conflicts which have involved Britain and the Commonwealth from 1914 to the Falkland Islands campaign. The exhibits include weapons, uniforms, documents, vehicles, aircraft (including a Sopwith Camel and a Spitfire), as well as domestic and personal memorabilia such as ration books, gas masks and photographs. Well-designed display boards outline the history of conflicts and operations, and exhibitions concentrate on specific subjects relating to war, such as animals at war. Talks and film shows are also featured: telephone for details.

Kensington Palace, The Broad Walk, Kensington Gardens, W8
Tel: (01) 937 9561
Open: Mon-Sat 9am-5pm, Sun 1pm-5pm
Closed: Public holidays in winter
Admission: Adults £2.50, children 5-16 years £1.25
⊖ High Street Kensington or Queensway

Queen Mary disliked Whitehall Palace intensely, and when her husband William III bought this building in Kensington in 1689, she was eager to move. William suffered from asthma and presumably they hoped that a change of residence would alleviate his condition. He commissioned Wren to remodel the existing building and although they moved in 1690, the Palace wasn't completed until 1702. Alterations and redecoration were carried out later by William Kent. Queen Anne, George I and George II also lived here during their reigns, and Queen Victoria was born in the Palace. Today, it is still a royal residence. The Prince and Princess of Wales, Princess Margaret and the Duke and Duchess of Gloucester all have apartments here.

Inside, on view to the public, there are splendid state apartments, decoratively finished with rich carving by Grinling Gibbons, Montlake tapestries on the walls and interesting royal portraits. The suite of Victorian rooms is particularly fascinating as it contains personal mementoes of Queen Victoria – photographs, ornaments and knick-knacks. In the Council Chamber there are interesting souvenirs of the 1851 Exhibition, including a picture of the opening; and a special exhibition of Court Dress will delight those interested in fashion.

London Toy and Model Museum, 21 Craven Hill, W2
Tel: (01) 262 7905
Open: Tues-Sat 10am-5:30pm, Sun 11am-5:30pm
Closed: Mondays except public holidays
Admission: Adults £2.20, children 5-16 years 80p
⊖ Queensway or Bayswater

This wonderland collection, consisting of some 3,000 toys and models, is kept in a pair of Victorian houses. Many of the exhibits date from the 18th century, and they include dolls and dolls' houses, teddy bears (Paddington Bear has a corner all to himself), model trains, boats and cars, toy soldiers and nursery toys. There's a boating pond outside in the garden, along with electric and clockwork trains, plus a miniature train to ride on (usually steam-operated on Sundays). Special events – like model boat regattas, in June, and a Teddy Bears' Picnic, in July – are a key feature: telephone for details. There's a café to quench young thirsts and provide snacks.

London Transport Museum, Covent Garden Market, WC2
Tel: (01) 739 6344
Open: Daily 10am-6pm
Closed: Public holidays in winter
Admission: Adults £2.40, children 5-16 years £1.10
⊖ Covent Garden

Old maps, photographs, tickets and attractive, informative wall displays illustrate the development of London's complex transport system. The exhibits bring the past to life – there are horse-drawn buses, trains and trolley buses, as well as early examples of underground trains. The enthusiast can 'drive' an underground train or experiment with the controls of a London bus – an ideal place to entertain youngsters on wet days.

Museum of London, London Wall, EC2
Tel: (01) 600 3699
Open: Tues-Sat 10am-6pm, Sun 2pm-6pm
Closed: Monday and public holidays in winter
Free admission
⊖ St Paul's or Barbican (closed Sun)

A modern museum which tells the story of London. Arranged chronologically, the various periods are illustrated by means of costumes, pictures and photographs, furniture, everyday objects and display boards. The Roman period is brought vividly to life in the reconstruction of the main room of a villa, with couches, eating vessels and a realistic little mouse picking up the leftovers. The Great Fire of 1666 is illustrated by means of a diorama, complete with sounds and smoke. There are reconstructions of 19th-century shops, such as a barber's and chemist's. The ornate, original lifts from Selfridge's department store are here and by way of contrast there's the fabulous 200-year-old golden Lord Mayor's coach. It's taken out each year and used in the Lord Mayor's Show in November.

Museum of Mankind, 6 Burlington Gardens, W1
Tel: (01) 437 2224
Open: Mon-Sat 10am-5pm, Sun 2:30pm-6pm
Closed: Public holidays in winter and spring
Free admission
⊖ Green Park or Piccadilly Circus

The Museum of Mankind is the ethnography department of the British Museum, and its wide-ranging collection comprises items and information on tribal societies and cultures all over the world. Among the exhibits you'll find shadow puppets from Java, a fantastic Benin ivory mask from Africa, and bows and arrows that once belonged to American Indians. Special exhibitions highlighting particular tribes and cultures, such as those from the Solomon Islands, an Indian village or areas of Northern Canada, complement the permanent displays.

Museum of the Moving Image (MOMI), under Waterloo Bridge, behind the National Film Theatre on the South Bank, SE1
Tel: (01) 401 2636 for recorded information.
Open: Tues-Sat 10am-8pm, Sunday and public holidays 10am-6pm
Closed: Mon and Dec 24-26
Admission: Adults £3.25, children £2.50, family ticket £10 (up to 2 adults and 4 children)
⊖ Waterloo

A magical environment with over 1000 film and television extracts on show, this museum involves you in the creation of moving pictures from the crude early attempts at cinematography to the sophistication of the likes of Steven Spielberg.

In the Moving Image Workshop you'll find the world's first four-screen unit: four screen surfaces (for rear, flat, Perlux and 3-D projection). They're mounted on a traveling gantry enabling the perfect projection of different film image ratios and light intensities.

You, too, can fly like Superman.

National Army Museum, Royal Hospital Road, SW3
Tel: (01) 730 0717
Open: Mon-Sat 10am-5:30pm, Sun 2pm-5:30pm
Closed: Public holidays in winter and spring
Free admission
⊖ Sloane Square

Beginning from the year 1465, the National Army Museum outlines the development and history of the British army. The role of the colonial forces and the Indian Army are explained, and hundreds of campaigns are recorded. The museum displays a fascinating collection of uniforms, weapons and military decorations, as well as paintings (works by Reynolds and Lawrence, for example) and photographs. The skeleton of Napoleon's horse Marengo is on display, and there's a longbow from Henry VIII's ship the *Mary Rose*.

The National Gallery, Trafalgar Square, WC2
Tel: (01) 839 3321
Open: Mon-Sat 10am-6pm, Sun 2pm-6pm
Closed: Public holidays in winter and spring
Free admission
⊖ Charing Cross

Spanning the period between 1200 and 1900, the art collection housed in the National Gallery is one of the finest in the world. Over 2,000 pictures represent the major European schools as well as individual masters. You're unlikely to have time to appreciate the collection in just one visit, but you might decide to concentrate on the most famous masterpieces: Leonardo da Vinci's Madonna on the Rocks, Van Dyck's portrait of Charles I on Horseback, Goya's Duke of Wellington and Van Gogh's Sunflowers, for example.

The gallery has thoughtfully designed quiz sheets for children to maintain their interest.

The shop sells postcards, posters and pretty stationery items. Free lectures are held Tuesday-Friday at 1pm and Saturday at noon. Films are shown at 1pm on Monday. Free guided tours of six selected pictures Monday 11:30am, Monday-Friday 3pm, Saturday 2pm, 3:30pm.

National Maritime Museum, Romney Road, SE10
Tel: (01) 858 4422
Open: Mon-Sat 10am-6pm, Sun 2pm-6pm; until 5pm in winter
Closed: Public holidays in winter and spring
Admission: Adults £2.20, children 5-16 years £1.10
For details of transport to Greenwich and other attractions see
Non-Driver Escapes – Greenwich.

Britain's maritime history is vividly portrayed here at Greenwich in a building of great architectural interest. The central area was designed by Inigo Jones; known as the Queen's House, it was the first Palladian-style villa to be built in England. The West and East wings were built in 1809. There's a fine art collection, including seascapes and paintings of naval heroes and battles, by a diverse range of artists, (Turner, Canaletto and Gainsborough, for example). Model ships, figureheads, maps and navigational instruments illustrate the successes and sinkings that make up the history of this seafaring country. The uniform which Nelson wore when he was fatally wounded is on display and, by way of a peaceful contrast, there's an impressive collection of gilded royal barges to view. Special exhibitions on maritime themes are arranged: telephone for details.

National Portrait Gallery, St Martin's Place, WC2
Tel: (01) 930 1552
Open: Mon-Fri 10am-5pm, Sat 10am-6pm, Sun 2pm-6pm
Closed: Public holidays in winter and spring
Free admission except for special exhibitions (Adults £1, children 50p approximately)
⊖ Charing Cross

The idea of establishing a portrait gallery of the most eminent persons in British history was suggested in 1856 by the 5th Earl of Stanhope. The gallery duly opened in 1859, displaying just 57 portraits. It proved to be highly popular and grew rapidly, moving to its present site – the building was a gift from William Henry Alexander, a wealthy property owner – in 1896. Today there are some 8,000 portraits and 500,000 photographs to view, including a special portrait of Elizabeth I by Marcus Gheeraets the younger. Artists, literary figures (such as Keats and Byron, Beatrix Potter, Virginia Woolf), heroes and heroines have all earned their place in this gallery. Special exhibitions concentrate on contemporary photographs: telephone for details. The shop is an excellent source of gifts and postcards. Free lectures are held Tues-Fri 1:10pm, Sat 3pm.

National Postal Museum, King Edward Street, EC1
Tel: (01) 239 5420
Open: Mon-Thur 10am-4:30pm, Fri 10am-4pm
Closed: Sat, Sun and public holidays
Free admission
⊖ St Paul's

Great Britain established the first efficient postal system and introduced the idea of postage stamps to many corners of the world. Here the history of this great means of communication is outlined. The two major collections are: The Phillips Collection of Victorian Stamps and The Universal Postal Union Collection covering stamps of the world. As well as the many obscure items of postal history, there's an exhibition highlighting the creation of the famous Penny Black. Special displays relating to particular countries are featured: telephone for details.

Natural History Museum, Cromwell Road, SW7
Tel: (01) 589 6323
Open: Mon-Sat 10am-6pm, Sun 1pm-6pm
Closed: Public holidays in winter and spring.
Admission: Adults £2.00, children 5-16 years £1 (free admission
    Mon-Fri except public holidays 4:30pm-6pm)
⊖ South Kensington

The core of this vast collection was bequeathed by Sir Hans Sloane in 1753, and first exhibited in the British Museum. The collection outgrew its allotted space there, so in 1860 it was suggested that it should have its own building. Captain Frances Fowke won a competition to design the new museum but, unfortunately, he died before the work was complete and the trustees appointed Alfred Waterhouse to finish this splendid, romanesque-style London landmark (built 1873-80). Note the terra cotta moldings of plants and animals, some real others surely mythical.
    Through a series of exhibitions the museum traces the course of

evolution on our planet. The collection of botanical, entymological and zoological specimens is unrivaled, from small-scale fossils to the amazing dinosaurs, including the gigantic 85-foot-long skeleton of the Diplodocus. For those who are fascinated by sheer bulk, the Whale Hall, with its model of a Blue Whale, is an area not to be missed.

Percival David Foundation of Chinese Art, 53 Gordon Square, WC1
Tel: (01) 387 3909
Open: Mon-Fri 10:30am-5pm
Closed: Weekends and public holidays
Free admission
⊖ Russell Square

Sir Percival David, scholar and sinologist, assembled this remarkable collection of Chinese ceramics and books, presenting it to the University of London in 1950. It comprises around 1500 pieces of the Song, Yuan, Ming and Qing dynasties (10th to 18th centuries), including bowls, plates, jars and vases, all in exquisite colors with intricate designs. Clearly a must for devotees of Chinese porcelain.

Queen's Gallery, Buckingham Palace Road, SW1
Tel: (01) 930 3007
Open: Tues-Sat 10:30am-5pm, Sun 2pm-5pm
Closed: Mon, Dec 24-26 and New Year's Day
Admission: Adults £1.10, children 5-16 years 50p
⊖ Victoria

Situated to one side of Buckingham Palace, the Queen's Gallery was originally designed by Nash as a conservatory. In 1843 it was converted into a chapel, and bombed in 1940. In 1962 the building was reconstructed, part of it as a chapel and part as an art gallery. Exhibitions change regularly, and include paintings, furniture or other *objets d'art* from the extensive Royal collection of art treasures. The gallery is closed between exhibitions so check in the press or telephone the gallery before visiting.

Royal Academy, Burlington House, Piccadilly, W1
Tel: (01) 734 9052
Open: Daily 10am-6pm during exhibitions only
Closed: Christmas Day, Boxing Day, New Year's Day
Admission: Charges vary according to exhibition – Adults £3.00, children 5-16 years £2.00 approximately
⊖ Green Park or Piccadilly Circus

The Royal Academy was founded in 1768, and a statue of its first president, Sir Joshua Reynolds, stands in the courtyard. Originally housed in Pall Mall, the collection underwent several moves before resting here at splendid Burlington House. Lord Burlington bought a house on the site in 1664, one of several great houses along Piccadilly and the only one to survive. His descendents renovated and enlarged the building. The galleries and third story were added in 1869 for the Royal Academy.

The Academy is famous for its annual summer exhibition held for over 200 years, from May to August. Approximately 1300 works are shown, selected from around 10,000 pieces submitted by about 4,000 well-known and aspiring artists. As well as the summer exhibition, world-famous treasures are displayed. Telephone for details of current exhibitions. There's an excellent restaurant, (open daily 10:30am-5pm,) and a well-stocked shop selling artists' materials, art books, catalogs, scarves, bags and postcards.

Science Museum, Exhibition Road, SW7
Tel: (01) 589 3456
Open: Mon-Sat 10am-6pm, Sun 2:30pm-6pm
Closed: Public holidays in winter and spring
Admission: Charges to be introduced (about adults £2, children £1)
⊖ South Kensington

A museum to amuse all – there are tremendous models, buttons to press and keys to turn. From the earliest steam locomotive, Puffing Billy (1813), and the oldest Rolls Royce (1904) to an Apollo space capsule, the great advances of science are clearly defined in the variety of exhibits. On the third floor, the story of flight is outlined, including hot air balloons and the plane flown by Amy Johnson on her historic flight to Australia in 1903. The Wellcome Medical Museum is a recent addition, and amidst the gruesome tools of the medical trade you'll find Napoleon's silver toothbrush, Florence Nightingale's moccasins and Dr Livingston's medical chest.

On the ground floor, the Launch pad provides entertainment for children, with experiments for them to try by themselves. Like any museum visit, you'll have to decide what to see. There's far too much to absorb in one go.

Sir John Soane's Museum, 13 Lincoln's Inn Fields, WC2
Tel: (01) 405 2107
Open: Tues-Sat 10am-5pm
Closed: Sun, Mon and public holidays
Free admission
⊖ Holborn

In 1883, architect Sir John Soane arranged a private Act of Parliament to preserve his house as a museum after his death. He was an inveterate collector, and his extraordinary hoard is exactly as he left it. There are Roman and Egyptian remains, including sarcophagi (stone coffins). Soane bought the sarcophagus of Seti I, who was king of Egypt in about 1370 BC, for £2000 after the British Museum gave it a miss. He was greatly interested in the designs of other architects, and on display you'll find a book of drawings by Wren, along with some 8,000 drawings from the offices of Robert and James Adam. He acquired an art collection, including paintings by Hogarth of his famous Rake's Progress, and works by Canaletto, Turner and Reynolds.

Tate Gallery, Millbank, SW1
Tel: (01) 821 1313
Open: Mon-Sat 10am-5:50pm, Sun 2pm-5:50pm
Closed: Public holidays in winter and spring
Free admission (except for special exhibitions)
⊖ Pimlico

The Tate Gallery exhibits 16th to 20th century work by British artists. The collection is comprehensive, including works by artists such as Stubbs, Hogarth, Reynolds, Gainsborough and Constable (including his famous Flatford Mill). The Clore Gallery provides a permanent home for the Turner collection, including about 300 paintings and 19,000 works on paper, of which about 200 are on show at any time.

In addition to great British works the Tate takes over where the National Gallery left off, specializing in European art from 1900 onwards. There is a fine collection of French Impressionist paintings, and a modern collection of European artists. There are special exhibitions, for which an admission charge is made, lectures, poetry readings and daily video shows (1pm except Monday).

The Tate Gallery restaurant has an excellent reputation for English food and a well-chosen wine list. It is open for lunch only Monday-Saturday noon-3pm (tel: (01) 834 6754 to reserve). There is also a good coffee shop serving snacks and salads. In addition, the bookshop sells reproductions, postcards and quality gifts as well as books.

Theatre Museum, 1G Tavistock Street, WC2 (entrance in Russell Street)
Tel: (01) 836 7891
Open: Tues-Sun 11am-7pm
Closed: Mon and bank holidays in winter
Admission: Adults £2.25, children 5-14 years £1.25
⊖ Covent Garden

Opened in 1987, this museum houses an unrivaled collection of costumes, drawings, set designs, props, posters, programs, and all that relates to the history of the theater in Britain and Europe. Special displays are devoted to personalities, such as Jenny Lind, or to one particular aspect of the performing arts, such as the ballet or circus. Tickets for London shows are obtainable from the box office at the entrance to the museum.

Victoria and Albert Museum, Cromwell Road, SW7
Tel: (01) 589 6371
Open: Mon-Sat 10am-5:50pm, Sun 2:30pm-5:50pm
Closed: Public holidays in winter and spring
Admission: Voluntary contribution unspecified
⊖ South Kensington

The Victoria and Albert Museum has approximately seven miles of galleries filled with decorative and practical treasures from all over the world. The museum is divided into 'primary galleries', which feature a period or civilization (Tudor, Regency or India for example), and 'subject galleries' such as ironwork, tapestries or musical instruments. There are rooms furnished entirely as they were originally designed – the gorgeous Green Dining Room designed by William Morris and Philip Webb, for example. Among the highlights of the exhibits you'll see the Raphael Cartoons, a superb Constable art collection, exquisite Russian Imperial jewelry and a recent gift of American costume jewelry dating from 1940-60. The costume gallery will fascinate all who love fashion.

There are free guided tours Monday-Saturday 11am, noon, 2pm and 3pm, and talks on Sat 2:30pm. In addition, the museum runs one-day courses, and lecture sessions running over several days. Some of these are free, others are subject to fees. Telephone for an up-to-date program.

There is a new restaurant in the museum (open: Mon-Sat 10am-5pm and Sun 2:30pm-5:30pm), serving good hot and cold buffet food at lunchtimes and delicious snacks, cakes and coffee throughout the day. For books, cards and gifts visit the museum shop.

Wallace Collection, Hertford House, Manchester Square, W1
Tel: (01) 935 0687
Open: Mon-Sat 10am-5pm, Sun 2pm-5pm
Closed: Public holidays in winter and spring
Free admission
⊖ Marble Arch or Bond Street

Housed in the family's 18th-century mansion, this collection was started by the first Marquess of Hertford, who was a patron of Reynolds and added to by successive generations.

The 4th Marquess (1777 to 1842), an eccentric recluse living in Paris, acquired the majority of the art treasures. The fine 18th-century French furniture and the works by Watteau, Fragonard and Boucher were his. His illegitimate son, Sir Richard Wallace (1818-1890), inherited the treasures and contributed both armor and medieval works of art to the collection. His widow bequeathed the entire collection to the nation in 1897.

FUN FOR THE KIDS

Sightseeing with children can be ruined by bad planning. Don't try to take in too much. Remember that London is blessed with many acres of parks and open spaces right in its center. These are perfect for picnics, for a stop to feed the ducks, go boating, or just to let off steam.

All of the major restaurant chains cater for children, but so too do some of the privately owned restaurants. This fact may not be advertised, so it's always worth enquiring about children's portions. Children under the age of 14 years are not allowed in the bars of public houses. Many pubs, however, have gardens or family rooms to accommodate patrons with children in tow: ask at the bar as you enter.

Beware the ice-cream sellers at some of the major tourist attractions. It's worth asking the price before ordering, since the charges are sometimes outrageous. You may well be better off walking round the corner to the nearest newagent's shop where ices can be significantly cheaper.

Chemist's shops stock a wide range of baby food and ready-diluted baby drinks, often catering for older children too with cartons of fruit juice.

With regard to entrance fees, the term 'children' is applied to those under 14 or 16 years. On London Transport, children under five years old travel free and those under 14 years travel at a reduced price fare.

For recorded information about children's special events, telephone *Time Out* Children's London on (0077) 900123 (London callers only). The information changes twice a week during school holidays, and on Mondays only at other times. The weekly *Time Out* magazine has a section devoted to children's events in London.

If you'd like to leave the little 'uns occasionally, London has a number of excellent baby-sitting services. Those employing notably reliable staff include:

Childminders, 9 Paddington Street, W1
Tel: (01) 935 9763

Established in 1967 and still going strong with 1,500 minders on their books. Visitor's booking fee £4; hourly rates £3 (day), £2-£2.45 (evening), plus fares: minimum of 4 hours.

Universal Aunts Ltd, 250 Kings Road, SW3
Tel: (01) 351 5767

This gem of an agency will arrange to meet trains, provide a cook/housekeeper and deal effectively with almost any domestic emergency, as well as straight forward baby-sitting. Rates vary according to service, eg £3.50 per hour meeting children from plane, train, etc.

WHAT TO SEE

Guinness World of Records, The Trocadero, Piccadilly Circus, W1
Tel: (01) 439 7331
Open: Daily 10am-10pm
Closed: Christmas Day
Admission: Adults £3.50, children under 4 years free,
    5-15 years £2.00
⊖ Piccadilly Circus

Life-size models, elaborate displays and videos illustrate some of the interesting facts and records that are to be found in the *Guinness Book of Records*. The entertainment complex also includes the London Experience (an audio-visual presentation on London) as well as an holography exhibition.

HMS Belfast, off Tooley Street, SE1
Tel: (01) 407 6434
Open: Daily 11am-5:20pm, 4pm in winter
Admission: Adults £3.00, children £1.50
⊖ London Bridge

Moored across the Thames from the Tower of London, the 11,500-ton cruiser HMS *Belfast*, built in 1939, has been preserved as a floating museum. She was the last of the Royal Navy's big-gun ships and went out of service in 1963. You can wander all over the ship, into the boiler rooms, onto the bridge or into the galley.

London Zoo, Regent's Park, NW1
Tel: (01) 722 3333
Open: Daily 9am-6pm (10am-4pm Nov-Mar)
Admission: Adults £3.90, children 5-15 years £2.00
⊖ Baker Street, then 74 bus, or   ⊖ Camden Town and then 74
    bus, or 200 Waterbus from Little Venice (for details of
    Waterbus see **Getting Around** page 57)

One of the most popular attractions in London, the zoo has been welcoming visitors since 1828. When it first opened, gentlemen were required to leave their whips at the gate and, although ladies were allowed to keep their parasols, they were forbidden to poke them into the cages. This was one of the first public zoos in the world, with the first aquarium (1853) and the first insect house (1881). Over the years, the site has expanded and the animals' accommodation has been greatly improved and updated. Apart from offering the public an opportunity to view animals they would otherwise never see, the Royal Zoological Society (who are responsible for the zoo) study the animals in captivity, and carry out research into conservation. The zoo has a highly successful breeding program and the majority of the animals on view are bred here or at Whipsnade Zoo (near Luton in Bedfordshire). Allow plenty of time for your visit because there are over 8,000 animals to see. The Charles Clore Pavilion for small mammals has a special Moonlight World section which offers a fascinating insight into the lives of nocturnal animals.

Feeding times are posted by the entrance so make a note of these as you go in. There are restaurants and cafés for meals, snacks or drinks, or take a picnic and sit on one of the many wooden benches.

Madame Tussauds, Marylebone Road, NW1
Tel: (01) 935 6861
Open: Mon-Fri 10am-5:30pm, Sat-Sun 9:30am-5:30pm
Closed: Christmas Day
Admission: Adults £4.50, children 5-15 years £2.95
⊖ Baker Street

Madame Tussaud, born in France in 1761, was introduced to the art of molding wax by her uncle who owned a waxworks museum in Paris. During the French Revolution she made death masks of the victims of the guillotine – Robespierre, Louis XIV and Marie Antoinette – which are on display in the Chamber of Horrors. She and her family brought her inheritance of waxworks to England in 1802 and traveled the country. In 1835 the waxworks were given their present, permanent home. The displays include royalty and politicians, historical figures, and stars of screen, music and sport. Among the latest additions you'll see Grace Jones, Sylvester Stallone and Boris Becker. The oldest figure (dating from 1765) is that of Madame Du Barry – if you look carefully, she appears to be breathing. The Battle of Trafalgar display is one of the most exciting areas, with the gun deck of Nelson's ship *Victory*, the roar of the cannons and swirling smoke. Before you leave take a careful look at the museum guards – are they real?
(Note: London Transport offer a combined sightseeing tour and Madame Tussaud's tickets: Adults £8.50, children 5-16 years £5.50, the tickets save joining the long queues, tel: (01) 227 3456 for details.)

Museums

Most museums have exhibits that will particularly interest the youngsters. Giant dinosaur skeletons at the **Natural History Museum**, mummies at the **British Museum** or Queen Victoria's spectacular doll's house at **Kensington Palace** are sure to amaze. If your child wants to get into the act go to the **Science Museum** which has an exhibit known as the Launch Pad with a range of exciting experiments including a robot that can be operated, a crane to maneuver and a water-course to alter. (See **Museums** for details.)

Planetarium, Marylebone Road, NW1
Tel: (01) 486 1121
Open: Mon-Fri 10am-5:30pm, Sat-Sun 9:30am-5:30pm
      Shows every 40 minutes starting 10.20am
Admission: Planetarium only: Adult £2.50, children £1.50
   combined Planetarium & Madame Tussauds: Adults £4.80,
   children £3.55
⊖ Baker Street

Stellar attractions at all times. It's right next to Madame Tussauds.
Together they make up a handy half-day outing.

Pollock's Toy Museum, 1 Scala Street, W1
Tel: (01) 636 3452
Open: Mon-Sat 10am-5pm
Admission: Adults 80p, children 40p
⊖ Goodge Street

Benjamin Pollock made toy theaters and published toy theater
sheets, sold for 'a penny plain and tuppence colored' in Victorian
times. The museum displays charming toy theaters, all beautifully
decorated. There are old peep shows and optical toys, antique dolls
and a collection of toy animals and models. You can buy cardboard
replicas of the theaters.

Regent's Canal

London Waterbus Company Tel: (01) 482 2550
Little Venice to Camden Lock daily on the hour 10am-5pm
   Apr-Oct; Sat-Sun only 10:30am, noon, 1:30pm and 3pm
   Oct-Mar
Admission: Adults £2.65, children £1.60 round trip

Jason's Trip Tel: (01) 286 3428
Little Venice to Camden Lock daily 10:30am, 12:30pm, 2:30pm,
   4:30pm June-Aug; daily 12:30pm, 2:30pm Apr, May, Sept and
   until early Oct
Admission: Adults £2.75, children £1.50 round trip; meals
   available from £2.50

The Regent's Canal, opened in 1820, runs from the Grand Junction
Canal at Paddington Basin to the River Thames at Limehouse. En
route it travels through tunnels under Edgware Road and 12 locks,
and is crossed by 40 bridges. Today you can enjoy a pleasure trip
through the Maida Hill tunnel where the crews used to have to 'leg'
their craft along (lying flat they pushed against the tunnel roof with
clogged feet) while the horses which towed the boats were
unhitched and led along the towpath. The canal takes you through
Regent's Park to the zoo.

London Waterbuses offer combined tickets with zoo entrance – one way journey plus entrance adults £5.25, children 5-16 years £2.90, and along to Camden Lock. Take a look at the market (see **Markets**) and catch a later boat back.

Tower Bridge
Tel: (01) 403 3761
Open: Daily 10am-5:45pm summer, until 4:45pm winter
Admission: Adults £2.00, children £1.00
⊖ Tower Bridge

The then Prince of Wales laid the first stone for Tower Bridge in 1881; it was opened three years later. From the walkways on this historic bridge you'll have a spectacular view of London. They are reached by means of passenger lifts. There's an exhibition of the hydraulic machinery which operated the bridge before it was modernized to open and close by electricity.

CHILDREN'S THEATER

The following theaters offer live entertainment in the form of plays, performing clowns, puppet shows, magic shows or musicals. The performances are usually staged on Saturdays and/or Sundays with weekday events limited to school holidays. The age range for audiences varies with each show, so check before booking.

Little Angel (Marionette) Theatre, 14 Dagmar Passage, Cross Street, N1
Tel: (01) 226 1787
⊖ Angel

Long established and very popular, this puppet theater presents a variety of charming and colorful productions of a very high standard. The performances vary, but some are suitable for three-year-olds upwards. Times of performances also vary, so telephone to see what's on, then reserve in advance.

Lyric Theatre, Hammersmith, King Street, W6
Tel: (01) 741 2311
⊖ Hammersmith

Children's shows are performed on Saturdays (usually 11am) and on Sundays at noon. There is a different show each week – puppets, a play or a magic show – and performances last about 50 minutes. Downstairs there is a bar and counter-service restaurant where jazz musicians provide background entertainment. Suitable for ages three up. There's usually no need to reserve but you should ring to check the times of performances, then turn up in good time.

Polka Children's Theatre, 240 The Broadway, Wimbledon, SW19
Tel: (01) 543 4888
⊖ Wimbledon

Away from the center, this theater was opened in 1979 by the Queen Mother. It is dedicated to Charlie Chaplin, and the repertoire includes mime, puppet theater, clowning and general children's theater. The productions are geared towards different age ranges and this is a popular theater with local children – so do telephone to reserve tickets. The tickets will be held until 30 minutes before the performance. There are indoor and garden play areas and a small museum of toys and dolls. The café is planned with children in mind and delicious homemade cakes and snacks are served.

Unicorn Theatre for Children, 6 Great Newport Street, WC2
Tel: (01) 836 3334 (box office); (01) 379 3280 (workshops)
⊖ Leicester Square
Admission: Performances £2.50-£4.50; workshops, morning session £4, all day £8

One of our favorite places to entertain children. This excellent theater offers four major productions per year plus about ten one or two week stints by traveling companies. Recent shows have included *Pinocchio, The Red Chair* and *Meg and Mog*.

In addition Unicorn offers workshops for children over five where they can perfect their skills in magic, drama, dance, arts and crafts and circus. Reservations required.

FILMS

ICA Children's Cinema Club, Nash House, The Mall, SW1
Tel: (01) 930 3647
⊖ Charing Cross

Don't hesitate because this organization is a club – you can join the ICA Cinema Club for one day (about 75p). On Saturdays and Sundays the program offers full length films which will appeal to children. Disney films and musicals are just two examples of the type of shows on offer.

National Film Theatre, South Bank, SE1
Tel: (01) 928 3232
⊖ Waterloo

Seasons of films for youngsters are run on Sundays or, sometimes, on selected weekdays. The variety is good – from adventure movies to Disney films. The South Bank complex which houses the film theater has several good places to eat.

LONDON WALKS

BLOOMSBURY AND THE BRITISH MUSEUM

Our walk begins at **Russell Square** underground station.

1. Turn right and walk along **Bernard Street** to **Brunswick Square**. The expanse of parkland beyond the square is known as Coram's Fields, after Captain Thomas Coram who established a Foundling Hospital nearby in 1739. The original building has gone, but the **Thomas Coram Foundation** can be seen at 40 Brunswick Square (open: Mon-Fri 10am-4pm, subject to change depending on internal meetings). The Foundation has a collection of mementoes, including paintings by such artists as Hogarth (who was a patron), Reynolds and Gainsborough, and music scores by Handel who raised £7,000 for the hospital by performing the *Messiah*. Other famed inhabitants of the area include E M Forster who lived here between 1929 and 1939. In Jane Austen's *Emma* the square was mentioned by Isabella who praised it with the words, 'Our part of London is so very superior to most others . . . We are so very airy'.

2. On the western corner of the square you'll see the **Brunswick Centre**, housing shops, restaurants and a cinema. Walk through the center and onto **Coram Street** (where Thackeray, who wrote *Vanity Fair*, once lived). If you feel the need for refreshment, the **Friend in Hand** pub in **Herbrand Street** provides sandwiches. At **Woburn Place** turn right, cross the road and turn left into **Tavistock Square**. Much of this square has been rebuilt since it was originally laid out in 1803, although the western side has been preserved since 1826. Leonard and Virginia Woolf lived at No 52 from 1924 to 39. Today, on the north side of the square you'll find the **Jewish Museum** (open: Tues-Fri 10am-4pm summer; Sun and Fri 10am-12:45pm winter; closed: Mon, Sat, public and Jewish holidays), housing a collection of Jewish antiquities and a history of Judaism. In the park itself there's a statue of Mahatma Gandhi.

3. Continue on into **Gordon Square**. On your right at No 53, you'll find the **Percival David Foundation of Chinese Art** (open: Mon-Fri 10:30am-5pm, see **Museums**), which houses a superb collection of Chinese ceramics. Gordon Square was laid out in the 1820s by Thomas Cubitt (who did not live to fulfill the task. The work was finished over a period of some 40 years according to his plans). Today most of the buildings house departments of London University. Lytton Strachey, famed biographer and

essayist, lived at No 51 and probably wrote *Queen Victoria* here. Bertrand Russell lived at No 57 from 1918 to 19 and Vanessa and Clive Bell occupied No 46.

4. On your left is **Woburn Square** and the **Courtauld Institute Galleries** (open: Mon-Sat 10am-5pm, Sun 2pm-5pm), which exhibit the major art bequests made to the University of London. These include the unrivaled private collection assembled by Samuel Courtauld of impressionist painting, with works by Manet, Degas, Bonnard, Gauguin, van Gogh, Seurat and Cézanne.

5. Continue westwards as the street turns left, then cross **Torrington Square** and walk along into **Torrington Place**. Turn left and walk down to the bottom of **Malet Street**. There, on your left, you'll pass the **Royal Academy of Dramatic Art** (RADA) and the **University of London**. Turn right into **Montague Place**, cross Gower Street and take a stroll round **Bedford Square**. This is the only complete example of a Georgian Square in the area. The buildings, constructed between 1775 and 1780, have fine wrought iron embellishments. Sir Johnston Forbes-Robertson, actor, lived at No 22 from 1888 to 1937, and Anthony Hope, novelist, lived at No 41. Today the majority of the buildings are occupied by architects' and publishers' offices.

6. From the square, turn right along **Bloomsbury Street**, then cross over and walk into **Great Russell Street**. On the corner of Museum Street you'll notice the **Museum Tavern** – a pleasant stop-off point for a drink – or if you're feeling hungry there's a **Pizza Express** restaurant in **Coptic Street**, on your right.

7. Refreshed and restored, you are now in just the right location to visit the **British Museum**. The entrance is in Great Russell Street (open: Mon-Sat 10am-5pm, Sun 2:30pm-6pm, see **Museums**).

   If you are interested in buying antique prints, take a look at some of the shops in Museum Street; for example, **The Print Room** at No 37, on the left, offers a very good selection.

8. From the British Museum, turn right along **Great Russell Street**, crossing Bloomsbury Street and continue to **Tottenham Court Road**. Turn left for **Tottenham Court Road** underground station.

BUCKINGHAM PALACE TO WESTMINSTER

1. **Victoria** underground station is the starting point for our walk. From the station forecourt turn left and at the corner turn right into **Buckingham Palace Road**. Follow the road all the way up to the Palace. Cross over to the left-hand side of the road at one

of the pedestrian crossings.

You may notice that many of the streets include the name 'Grosvenor' in them. The Grosvenor family (Duke of Westminster) own large tracts of extremely valuable land around here and in Mayfair. Cross **Lower Grosvenor Place** and you come to the walls which surround the grounds of Buckingham Palace. On your left you'll see:

2. **The Royal Mews** (open: Wed and Thurs 2pm-4pm). The mews house the fabulous state carriages and the royal horses (see **Local Delights**).

3. Continue along the road to a pathway leading to the **Queen's Gallery** (open: Tues-Sat 10:30am-5pm, Sun 2pm-5pm, see **Museums**). Special exhibitions of paintings, porcelain or other treasures selected from the fabulous Royal Collection are on display here. These change frequently.

4. Follow the road round to the left, to the **Buckingham Palace forecourt**. (To see the changing of the guard be here at 11:30am, see **Must Sights**.) George III bought the original house from the Duke of Buckingham in 1762, but it was not until 1837, when Queen Victoria moved in, that it became the London residence of the sovereign. During the intervening years, it was virtually rebuilt. If you see the Royal Standard flying, the Queen is in residence.

The **Queen Victoria Memorial**, standing directly in front of the Palace, was unveiled in 1911. The figure of the Queen was carved from one block of marble.

5. With the Palace behind you, work your way round to the south side of **The Mall** and walk along it.

On your left, across the park, are Lancaster House, Clarence House (home of the Queen Mother) and **St James's Palace**. Stop at the furthest edge of St James's Palace, by Marlborough Road, to appreciate the view back to the Palace.

6. Facing the palace, turn left into **St James's Park**. This is the oldest of London's royal parks, dating from 1532. James I established a menagerie here. It was extended by Charles II who enlarged the aviaries along the south side (hence the name Birdcage Walk). Up until 1828 only the Royal Family and the Hereditary Grand Falconer were allowed to drive along it. The delightful park is well-known for the pelicans and wildfowl on the lake.

Walk straight across the Park, over the bridge, and come into **Birdcage Walk** opposite Queen Anne's Gate.

7. To the right are the **Wellington Barracks** for the five regiments of Foot Guards who guard Buckingham Palace. There is a military museum here (open: Mon-Sat 10am-4pm). Cross Bird-

cage Walk and walk up **Queen Anne's Gate**. The fine houses are mainly 18th century (Nos 6-12 date from the 1830s) and the statue is of Queen Anne. Past inhabitants include Lord Palmerston (born at No 20) and James Mill (No 40), whose son John Stuart Mill lived here with him for some time. Turn left, continuing along Queen Anne's Gate, then turn right into **Dartmouth Street**.

8. The **Two Chairmen** pub is a friendly venue for refreshment, including good bar food.

   From the pub turn right into **Old Queen Street** which leads into **Storey's Gate**, where you turn right. On your right is the Methodist Central Hall, which is a venue for concerts. Cross **Tothill Street** and **Victoria Street** and you find yourself standing before **Westminster Abbey** (see **Must Sights**).

9. Facing the Houses of Parliament, on the far side of the square you'll see **St Margaret's Church** which has some fine examples of stained glass.

10. Cross **Whitehall** and walk over to the **Houses of Parliament**. If you want to hear a debate, queue up at the St Stephen's entrance, Mon-Thurs from 2:30pm, Fri from 9:30am, when Parliament is in session (see **Must Sights**). You'll approach **Westminster** underground station which is where our walk ends.

THE CITY – MONEY, MUSEUMS, MUSICIANS AND MORE

Start the walk from **Bank** underground station, taking the arrowed Mansion House exit, which brings you out alongside the building.

1. **Mansion House**, EC4 (tel: (01) 626 2500; tours Tues-Thur, 11am and 2pm for parties of 15, by written application only; free admission; book well in advance (see **Must Sights**). The official residence of the Lord Mayor of London, this imposing Palladian building was designed by George Dance and built in 1739-52. 'Oohing' and 'aahing' come naturally if you get a chance to see the sumptuous **Banqueting Hall** (Egyptian Room). The **Plate Room** is also shown on the tour. The only Court of Justice in Britain to be found in a private house is here; below it are cells where Emmeline Pankhurst was held.

2. With the façade of Mansion House behind you, turn right, go to the corner of **King William Street** and look along it. You can see the top of the massive column – punctuated by a gilt urn – that forms the **Monument**, built in 1671-77 to commemorate the Great Fire of 1666. It is 202 feet high and 202 feet from Pudding Lane, where the Fire started. If you're feeling particularly sprightly, you could always nip along and climb the Monument's 311 steps to a breathtaking view.

3. Cross **King William Street**, then that legendary street of bankers, **Lombard Street**, and pause at **Cornhill**. The large building over on the right with the equestrian statue of the Duke of Wellington in front of it is the **Royal Exchange**. It was founded in 1565 by Sir Thomas Gresham as an exchange where merchant brokers could conduct their business. The present building dates from 1844.

4. Directly ahead of you is the vast bulk of the 'old Lady of Threadneedle Street' (so called because Sheridan referred to it in the House of Commons in 1797 as 'an elderly lady in the city of great credit and long standing'), the **Bank of England**. The old Lady's vast girdle of windowless masonry protects the vaults which hold the country's gold reserves, in a building dating mainly from the 1920s and 30s, when Sir John Soane's original structure was virtually rebuilt. You can visit parts of the building (open: Mon-Fri 10am-6pm). Admission is free and you'll find the entrance just off Threadneedle Street in Bartholomew Lane.

5. Walk up **Threadneedle Street** and turn left into **Old Broad Street** and you'll see the **Stock Exchange** on the left (Visitors Gallery open Mon-Fri 9:45am-5pm; free admission). A talk and a film put you in the picture. Since the City's 1986 Big Bang, trading no longer takes place on the floor, so milling dealers are not in view below.

6. Turn left out of the Visitors Gallery, and left again into **Throgmorton Street** – pausing at this point to look to your right and marvel at the slender, pin-striped NatWest tower – which becomes **Lothbury** before it meets **Princes Street**. Cross to the other side of Princes Street and dodge into the alleyway on the left for a sight of the exterior of **Grocers' Hall**, one of the City Livery Companies (derived from the medieval trade and craft guilds) with an impressive coat of arms above the door.

7. At the top of Princes Street, turn left into **Gresham Street**. Cross over and continue until you come to the church of **St Lawrence Jewry** on the right, built originally by Wren after the Great Fire, but virtually destroyed by an incendiary bomb during World War II. Lunchtime piano and organ recitals are given here. Behind the church is **Guildhall**. (Great Hall open: Mon-Sat 9am-5pm, Sun 2pm-5pm except when closed for functions. Admission is free and guided tours are by arrangement: tel (01) 606 3030.) The City's governing body, the Corporation of London, meets in this splendid building, with a façade by George Dance (1789) and a medieval porch and Great Hall.

8. Continue walking along Gresham Street, crossing over to peer

through the doorway of the **Wax Chandlers' Hall**, before turning left into **Foster Lane** to admire the exuberant **Goldsmiths' Hall**. (Tours take place at 1pm on certain dates. Telephone City of London Information Centre, (01) 606 3030, to make an advance booking and to ask about tours of other City Livery Company Halls.) Built in 1835 by Hardwick, the Hall hosts fabulous jewelry exhibitions from time to time.

9. Walk to the top of Gresham Street and turn right into **St Martin's-le-Grand**, which soon becomes **Aldersgate Street**. Cross over and follow directions to the **Museum of London**, in London Wall, (open Tues-Sat 10am-6pm, Sun 2pm-6pm; free admission). This fascinating musuem traces history of London from its earliest beginnings. Don't miss the Great Fire audio-visual experience: step into a darkened room and listen to Samuel Pepys' eye-witness account of the Great Fire as the sky reddens and the conflagration grows over a model of the City.

    If you want to eat and drink, go down the stairs to the left as you come out of the museum, to the restaurant (open: Tues-Sat 10am-5pm, Sun 12 noon-5pm), serving hot and cold food, gâteaux and sometimes cream teas – a godsend at the weekend when the City pubs are closed. (See **Museums**.)

10. Retrace your steps and just before you come to the church of **St Botolph,** Aldersgate (there is a fine roof inside) turn right into **Little Britain**. On your left is the churchyard, laid out as a garden and known as Postman's Park because it is near the General Post Office. Examine the monument to heroic men and women, created by the painter G.F. Watts in 1887, consisting of plaques commemorating such deeds as: 'Daniel Pemberton, aged 61, foreman LSWR, surprised by a train when gauging the line, hurled his mate out of the track, saving his life at the cost of his own'. The bronze statue on the south side is Minotaur by Michael Ayrton.

11. Follow Little Britain as it turns to the right. On your left is the vast bulk of **St Bartholomew's Hospital**, the oldest hospital in London, founded in 1123 by Rahere, a courtier turned Augustinian monk, who, after suffering an attack of malarial fever on a pilgrimage to Rome, vowed to found a hospital in London upon his return.

12. As you come out into **West Smithfield** at the end of Little Britain, you'll see a fine, half-timbered gatehouse on the right (16th century, restored in 1932). Pass under the gatehouse and walk along the path to London's oldest church, **St Bartholomew the Great**. It was part of the Priory and Hospital founded by Rahere (whose tomb is here) in 1123. Perpendicular and 19th-century additions were made, but the interior's powerful impression is made chiefly by the beautiful Norman arcades

and galleries. During the 17th and 18th centuries the church fell into disrepair and was used for a variety of things – there was a blacksmith's forge in the north transept, a printer's workshop in the Lady Chapel. (Benjamin Franklin worked here in 1725.) In 1863-96, the church was restored.

As you emerge from the church into West Smithfield, to your right you can see **Smithfield**, London's wholesale meat market (see **Markets**). It opens very early in the morning and is not a sight for the squeamish at this time. Be sure to turn right and right again into **Cloth Fair** to admire fine examples of 17th-century houses, Nos 41 and 42 and of 18th-century houses, Nos 43 and 45, before continuing to walk round **West Smithfield** until you come to the **Bishop's Finger** at No 9-10 – that is if you're in need of refreshment. It's a pub with a split personality; it's also known as The Rutland after a restaurant that used to be upstairs. Popular with doctors, lawyers and meat market traders, it serves wonderful pub fare, including salads and a dish or two of the day, such as steak and kidney pie and lasagne. City pubs such as this are closed on Saturday and Sunday.

13. Turn right out of the pub and walk along **Giltspur Street**, a continuation of West Smithfield on this side. When you come to **Cock Lane** on the right, look up to see the gilt figure of the Fat Boy, his arms clasped about him, reputed to mark the place where the Great Fire stopped.

14. Carry on walking along Giltspur Street and turn right into **Holborn Viaduct** to visit **St Sepulchre's Church**, originally built in the 15th century, restored after the Fire and again in the 19th century. It is known as the musicians' church and contains windows dedicated to the singer Dame Nellie Melba and the ashes of Sir Henry Wood, founder of the famous Promenade concerts. Take a look at the kneelers, beautifully worked with musical themes. There is also a commemoration of Captain John Smith, governor of Virginia, who died in 1631 and is buried here. More lugubriously, the church's graveyard was raided by body snatchers for St Bartholomew's Hospital in the 18th century. The Execution Bell, preserved in the church, was rung outside condemned prisoners' cells at Newgate to rouse them to repentance – in the unlikely event that they had dropped off to sleep on the eve of their execution.

15. Retrace your steps to Giltspur Street and cross over to **Newgate Street**. On your right, where Newgate Prison once stood, is the Central Criminal Court, the **Old Bailey** (with the gilt figure of Justice on top), site of many famous and infamous trials. The present building dates from 1907 (see **Must Sights**). Cross Newgate Street and walk along **Old Bailey**, turning left at the

end into **Ludgate Hill**, which soon opens out before the majestic entrance to Wren's **St Paul's Cathedral** (built in 1675-1710), an architecturally celebratory note on which to end the walk. Stalls by Grinling Gibbons, paintings by Thornhill and ironwork by Tijou are among the treasures inside. If you didn't climb the Monument at the start of the walk, you may wish to join the huffing and puffing chorus up to the Whispering Gallery inside the superb dome, or even to climb as far as the Golden Gallery at the top of the dome (see **Must Sights**). **St Paul's** underground station is close by.

FOUR PALACE PROMENADE

Starting from **Westminster** underground station, you'll see:

1. The **Houses of Parliament** opposite (the new Palace of Westminster). Until 1529, when Henry VIII moved to Whitehall Palace, the Palace of Westminster was a royal home. The present building dates mainly from 1840 to 68, when the Houses of Parliament were rebuilt to a design by Charles Barry and Augustus Pagin. Turn right and follow **Bridge Street** to the corner of **Whitehall**.

   On **Parliament Square** the statues are of Churchill, Smuts, Palmerston, Disraeli, Peel, Canning and Abraham Lincoln. Looking up the street, past the Parliament buildings, on the right hand side of the road you'll see **St Margaret's Church**. (Westminster Abbey lies behind the church.) Built in 1504-23 and restored by Gilbert Scott, St Margaret's is the House of Commons Church. Samuel Pepys, John Milton and Winston Churchill were all married here. Inside you'll find fine stained glass – a 16th-century east window and the west window which was presented by the USA to commemorate Sir Walter Raleigh.

2. Turn right and head up **Whitehall**, which takes its name from the Palace which once stood here. It was virtually destroyed by fire in 1698 and never rebuilt. Government buildings line Whitehall, and in **King Charles Street**, the first turning on your left, you'll see the **Cabinet War Rooms**. There Churchill and his war-time cabinet operated from underground rooms (see **Museums**).

3. The **Cenotaph** stands in the center of the street, commemorating the dead of two World Wars. The annual Remembrance service is held here on the second Sunday in November.

4. Past the Cenotaph, across the street, you'll see **Downing Street**, the official residence of the Prime Minister since 1732 (at No 10). The Chancellor of the Exchequer occupies No 11. It's useful to have your banker as a neighbor.

Continue along Whitehall towards **Trafalgar Square**. Just before Horseguards Avenue on your right you'll see:

5. **The Banqueting House**. Built in 1619 by Inigo Jones (open: Tues-Sat 10am-5pm, Sun 2pm-5pm), it's well worth visiting, if only to see the fabulous painted ceiling which Charles I commissioned from Rubens in 1629. It was from here, just 20 years later, that Charles I stepped through a window onto the scaffold to face his executioner.

6. Further along, on the opposite side of the street you'll be able to watch the changing of the guard at **Horseguards** (Guards change Mon-Sat 11am, Sun 10am; see **Must Sights**). The parade ground behind the building was once the tiltyard for Whitehall Palace. On the second Saturday in June it is the setting for the annual Trooping the Colour ceremony.

7. As you continue along Whitehall you'll see the **Silver Cross,** a pub with a splendidly ornate plaster ceiling, embellished with grapes and hops. Right at the top of Whitehall is the powerful equestrian statue of Charles I.

8. **Trafalgar Square** is the unmistakable London landmark where Nelson stands on his column, in commemoration of his victory at Trafalgar in 1805. The column is 185 feet high, and the statue is three times lifesize. The imposing lions at its base are by Landseer (see **Must Sights**). To your left you'll see **Admiralty Arch**, built in 1911.

9. Cross the square to the fine church of **St Martin-in-the-Fields**, completed in 1726, and now a well-known venue for lunchtime concerts. Francis Bacon and Charles II were both christened in this church. Nell Gwyn, Thomas Chippendale and Sir Joshua Reynolds are buried here.

10. Turn right out of the church and cross the street to the bottom of **Charing Cross Road**. By the Edith Cavell monument you'll see the **National Portrait Gallery** (see **Museums**). If you want to pass this up turn right and cross the street to walk along the north side of **Trafalgar Square**.

11. Pass the **National Gallery**, which houses a magnificent art collection (see **Museums**), and walk along to the northwest corner of the square to **Pall Mall East**. Cross the Haymarket and walk along **Pall Mall**. Just beyond New Zealand House, on your right you'll see the **Royal Opera Arcade** – a genuine Regency arcade filled with elegant shops.

12. Further along Pall Mall, the memorial in Waterloo Place commemorates the Crimean War, and to your left you'll see a statue of Edward VII. On your left is **Marlborough House** (designed by Wren), famous as the center of fashionable

society when inhabited by Edward, Prince of Wales.

13. Down **Marlborough Road** to your left you'll notice the **Queen's Chapel** built by Inigo Jones in 1625. The beautiful interior is only open for services (Sun 10:45am Easter-July), when you'll find the choir boys in Tudor scarlet and gold robes.

14. Cross Pall Mall and go up the tiny **Crown Passage** to find the **Red Lion** pub, a cosy place for refreshment.

15. You can't miss the splendid, turreted **St James's Palace**. Built by Henry VIII, it was the sovereign's London residence until 1837 when Queen Victoria moved to Buckingham Palace. The accession of a new sovereign is still proclaimed here from the balcony in **Friary Court**, and foreign ambassadors are still accredited to the Court of St James's. The guard changes in the Court at 11am daily.

16. Past the guards and the Gatehouse turn left into **Ambassadors' Court**. Here you'll find the **Chapel Royal**, built by Henry VIII. The ceiling is attributed to Holbein, and it was here that William and Mary, Queen Anne and Queen Victoria were married. Charles I took Communion in this chapel on the morning of his execution. It is only open for services (Sun 8:30am and 11:15am Oct-Easter).

17. Walk through the **Stable Yard** past Lancaster House. To the left you'll see **Clarence House**, home of the Queen Mother. Walk straight on, passing Clarence House on your left and through a gateway into **Green Park**.

18. Through the trees you'll catch sight of the fourth palace on our walk – **Buckingham Palace**, the London home and offices of Queen Elizabeth II. Built originally in 1703, but added to and altered over the years, the main façade we see today was refaced in 1913. Turn right and walk up **Queen's Walk** to **Green Park** underground station. Alternatively, if you have the energy, cross the park to **Buckingham Palace**, and walk along **Buckingham Palace Road** to **Victoria** underground station. Taking this route you'll pass the **Queen's Gallery** (see **Museums**) and the **Royal Mews** (see **Local Delights**).

LEGAL AND LITERARY LONDON

1. We commence our walk from **Holborn** underground station. Turn left and walk down **Kingsway**. Turn left into **Remnant Street** and walk along into **Lincoln's Inn Fields**, a lovely square of fine architecture. Turn right and walk along the side of the square to **Portsmouth Street** where you'll find premises which claim to be Dickens's Old Curiosity Shop.

2. Retrace your steps to the north corner of the square and turn right to walk along the northern edge. On the left you'll see **Sir John Soane's Museum** (see **Museums**). He was an avid collector and the house is filled with his acquisitions.

3. Turn left out of the museum and walk along the square, then turn right along the eastern side and you come to **Lincoln's Inn**. This is one of the few great Inns of Court (the others being the Inner Temple, Middle Temple and Gray's Inn). The term 'Inns' was applied because they originally provided accommodation for lawyers and their students. Enter Lincoln's Inn through an archway in **Serle Street**.

    The buildings here are beautiful, some dating from as far back as the 15th century. Charles Dickens was once employed as a solicitor's clerk in the New Square, and John Donne gave the first sermon in the Chapel here.

4. Walk out of the splendid gatehouse (which dates from 1518) into **Chancery Lane**, and turn right. On the opposite side of the road you'll see the **London Silver Vaults** (see **Antiques**).

5. For a light lunch turn right into **Carey Street** where you'll find The **Seven Stars** – one of the smallest pubs in London.

6. Continuing along Chancery Lane, cross the street and you'll come to the **Public Records Office** (open: Mon-Fri 10am-5pm), where there's a museum. Fascinating documents are used to illustrate particular themes – trade and industry, colonies and diplomacy, for example. You'll find the death duty account of William Wordsworth, a plan of the Battle of Waterloo, a description of Virginia dating from 1583, or the record of Sir Walter Raleigh's treason trial.

7. Turn left out of the Public Records Office, walk down Chancery Lane and into **Fleet Street**, turning left. Once the street where all the main newspapers were printed, it is still home for many publications. There are plenty of pubs around here: try the **Cock Tavern** at No 22, which serves bar food and has a restaurant, opposite the **Printers' Pie** at No 60, the famous **Olde Cheshire Cheese** in Wine Office Court further along (see **Delightful Drinking** – *City Pubs*) or, on the other side of the street at No 47, the popular **El Vino's.**

8. Walk along Fleet Street passing the Royal Courts of Justice, visible on your right, and you come to **St Dunstan's Church** on the left. Standing on the site of an earlier church, it contains a fine communion rail by Grinling Gibbons, retained from the original building, and a clock which dates from the 17th century.

9. Walk along Fleet Street until you reach the alleyway at **John-**

son's Court and follow it to **Dr Johnson's House** (open Mon-Sat 11am-5:30pm). Dr Johnson lived, and wrote his dictionary here between 1749 and 1759. Prints and a collection of memorabilia are on display. Return to Fleet Street.

10. Cross the Street and work your way westwards back along Fleet Street. Just beyond the Cock Tavern, at No 22 you'll find the splendid **Prince Henry's Room** which dates from 1610. The upstairs room (open Mon-Sat 1:45pm-5pm, Sat until 4pm), has a fine example of a Jacobean ceiling and mementoes of Samuel Pepys who was born nearby.

11. Pass through the gateway outside Prince Henry's Room into the **Temple**. This area was occupied by the Knights Templar, who founded a monastery here in the 12th century. Henry VIII suppressed the order and appropriated their property, which was leased to lawyers in the 14th century. They have been here ever since. James I presented them with the freehold in 1608. The round-naved **Temple Church** was completed in 1185, modeled on the Church of the Holy Sepulchre in Jerusalem. It was badly damaged during World War II, but has been restored. On the stone floor are 10th- to 13th-century effigies of knights.

12. Leave the Church and cross Middle Temple Lane to reach **Middle Temple Hall** in **Fountain Court**. The great hall is Elizabethan with fine carving and paneling and a spectacular double hammerbeam roof. The 16th-century carved screen was painstakingly reconstructed after the World War II Blitz.

13. Re-emerging into Fountain Court which figures in Dickens's *Martin Chuzzlewit*, turn right into **Middle Temple Lane**. This leads down to **Victoria Embankment**. Turn right and walk along to **Temple** underground station where our walk ends.

NOTTING HILL TO SOUTH KENSINGTON

Start from **Notting Hill** underground station

1. Leave the station on the south side of **Notting Hill Gate** and turn right into **Kensington Church Street**. There are antique shops and art galleries on either side, and in the pretty little side streets leading off both to the left and right.

2. For a drink and a bite to eat, turn right along **Sheffield Terrace** (G.K. Chesterton was born at No 32) and then left into **Campden Hill Road**. The **Windsor Castle** pub serves good food, and on a fine day you can sit outside in the shady garden. Return to Kensington Church Street, turn right and continue until it meets **Kensington High Street**.

3. Cross the High Street, turn right and then first left into **Derry Street** which will bring you into **Kensington Square**. This, one of London's oldest squares, contains many fine houses built between the 17th and 19th centuries. Many famous people have lived here: Talleyrand at No 12 (1792-94), John Stuart Mill at No 18 (1837-1851) and Mrs Patrick Campbell at No 33 (1890-1915).

4. Return to Kensington High Street and cross to the other side. Turn right and walk along until you reach **Palace Gate** to **Kensington Gardens**. The public entrance to **Kensington Palace** (see **Museums**) is off the **Broad Walk** which runs the length of Kensington Gardens, from Palace Gate in the south to Black Lion Gate in the north. Opposite the palace is the **Round Pond**, where model boats habitually disturb the peace of the resident Canadian geese and ducks. A notice directs the owners of stranded boats to park keepers for assistance.

5. Retrace your steps along Broad Walk and turn left just before Palace Gate into the **Flower Walk**. This will lead you to the **Albert Memorial**.

    This splendid edifice, with its 14-foot-high figure of Prince Albert, was completed in 1872. It epitomizes Victorian taste and sentiment, a neo-Gothic spire of 175 feet, heavily ornamented with mosaics, pinnacles and a cross. Around the statue of Queen Victoria's beloved Albert are allegorical statues and a frieze of 169 named portraits, figures of architects, artists, poets and composers. Its designer, George Gilbert Scott, was knighted by Queen Victoria soon after its completion.

6. Opposite you can't fail to notice the huge **Royal Albert Hall** – nearly a quarter of a mile in circumference, it was built between 1868 and 1870. Since 1941, when the Queen's Hall was bombed, it has hosted the very popular Henry Wood Promenade Concerts which run from July to September. There are other concerts and events held during the year and boxing matches have been staged here since 1919 (tel: (01) 589 8212/ 9465 box office).

7. Cross the road to the Royal Albert Hall and walk left and then turn first right into **Exhibition Road**. The **Royal Geographical Society**, founded in 1830 is on the corner. The building was designed by Norman Shaw in 1874. Notice the statues of Livingstone and Scott along its outer wall. The Society has sponsored many major expeditions, and it continues to assist geographical expeditions today.

8. Exhibition Road is named after the Great Exhibition of 1851, held in Hyde Park, where Joseph Paxton's ill-fated Crystal Palace was erected.

Down to your right, in **Prince Consort Road**, you'll find the **Royal College of Music** whose former students include Vaughan Williams and Benjamin Britten. Singer Jenny Lind taught here.

9. A little further along on the left you'll see **Prince's Gate** whose former residents include Joseph Kennedy. He resided at No 14 with his family during his term as American Ambassador (1937-40). In 1928, Field Marshal Earl Haigh lived at No 21, and Joseph Chamberlain was resident at No 72 between 1880-1882. Frederick Legland, one-time owner of No 49, commissioned Whistler to decorate his dining room. A reconstruction of this room – a riot of color, known as the Peacock Dining room – is on view today at the Freer Gallery in Washington.

10. The **Science Museum** is on your right, the **Natural History Museum** is a little further west on Cromwell Road and on your left you'll see the **Victoria and Albert Museum**.

    For refreshment try the Victoria and Albert Museum restaurant or, at the end of Exhibition Road, you'll find the **Daquise** – a good coffee and pastries shop which also serves a variety of Eastern European culinary specialties and fresh salads.

ROYAL CHELSEA RAMBLE

Starting from **Sloane Square** underground (subway) station

1. Turn left, cross **Sloane Gardens** and turn left down **Lower Sloane Street**, walking along the far side of the street. On your right you'll see the **Duke of York's Headquarters**, barracks and headquarters of various army units. At the junction, turn right into **Royal Hospital Road**.

2. Walk to the splendid Wren buildings of the **Royal Hospital** (open: Mon-Sat 10am-noon, 2pm-4pm, Sun 2pm-4pm), built with the intention of housing army pensioners, which it still does. The Chelsea Pensioners, as they are known, wear distinctive scarlet uniforms. Down to the left is the museum which illustrates the history of the hospital and contains Wellington memorabilia. The Pensioners are often willing to guide visitors round the hospital for a small gratuity. The **Great Hall** houses a fine mural of King Charles II on horseback (notice also the old leather beer jugs); the beautiful paneled **Chapel** is also worth seeing. The annual Chelsea Flower Show is held each May in the grounds of the hospital.

3. Continue along Royal Hospital Road, crossing **West Road** to the **National Army Museum** (see **Museums**). Displays, uniforms, weapons and memorabilia outline the history of the British Army. From the museum continue along the road,

crossing elegant **Tite Street**, which has many artistic associations: Oscar Wilde lived at No 34, John Singer Sargent at No 31, Augustus John at No 33, and James McNeill Whistler at No 35. **Foxtrot Oscar,** a popular restaurant in Tite Street, offers delicious food at reasonable prices.

4. Turn left into **Swan Walk** where you'll find the **Chelsea Physic Garden** (open: Sun and Wed, 2pm-5pm Apr-Oct, see **Local Delights**). This fascinating botanic garden – the second oldest in the country – was founded in 1673, and contains around 5,000 plants, some of which are very rare.

5. Walk back to Royal Hospital Road and follow it until the road turns slightly to the right and becomes **Cheyne Walk**. Just by the **Embankment**, to your left is a fine Norman Shaw house dating from 1876. Along Cheyne Walk notice the beautiful houses that date from about 1765. George Eliot lived – and died – at No 4. Number 16 (called the Queen's House), once occupied by Dante Gabriel Rossetti, was a popular meeting place for the Pre-Raphaelites. Notice a plaque outside No 23, to commemorate Henry VIII's Manor House which was located between Nos 19 and 26. Katharine Parr lived here after Henry's death, and Ann of Cleves died here in 1556. From this eminent residential area cross **Oakley Street** and turn right into **Cheyne Row**.

6. If you're in need of refreshment, take the next right into **Lawrence Street** where you will find the **Cross Keys** pub. In Cheyne Row you'll see **Carlyle's House** (open: Wed-Sun 11am-5pm Apr-Oct; admission £1.60). Writer Thomas Carlyle and his wife Jane lived in the 18th-century house at No 5 from 1834 until his death in 1881. The family's books and furniture are still in the house, much as they left them. Some of the rooms still don't have electricity.

7. Continue along Cheyne Row. You'll see a plaque on No 10, commemorating Margaret Dawson who pioneered the idea of policewomen. The street turns to the right but go straight on into **Glebe Place**. Walk along it until you join the **King's Road**. Turn right and head for **Sloane Square**.

    The original King's Road was a pathway used by Charles II when he visited his mistress, Nell Gwyn, who lived in Fulham. It remained a private 'King's Road' only used by those who had a special pass until 1830. Since the 1960s it has become famous as a fashion center. At No 120 King's Road a certain Thomas Crapper once ran a company which was famous for its water closets (toilets).

    Before you reach Sloane Square you'll pass the other side of the Duke of York's headquarters. The walk ends at the **Sloane Square** underground station.

A TASTE OF THEATRICAL LONDON

1. Our walk begins at **Embankment** underground station. Walk up **Villiers Street** and turn right into **John Adam Street**. Down to your right is **Buckingham Street** which contains some fine 17th- and 18th-century houses. The Royal Society of Arts at No 8 was built in 1772-1774 by Adam. At the far end of John Adam Street, to your right you'll find the **Adelphi Terrace**: the four Adam brothers built a wonderful terrace of twenty-four houses on this site in the 1770s. The name Adelphi is taken from the Greek word meaning brothers. Sadly it was demolished in 1937 and only a few of their buildings remain. David Garrick, George Bernard Shaw and Richard d'Oyly Carte all lived here.

2. Turn left into **Adam Street**, then right along the **Strand**. On the opposite side of the road you'll see the **Adelphi Theatre**, opened in 1806 but rebuilt since then. It was the first theater in England to have a sinking stage (installed in 1834).

   A little further along, also on the left, is the **Vaudeville Theatre** built in 1870 and reconstructed in 1925. It was here that Henry Irving became famous for his performance in James Albery's *Two Roses* in 1870. The first performances in England of Ibsen's *Rosnersholm* and *Hedda Gabler* were given here in 1897.

3. Pass the **Savoy Hotel** on your right, so named because the land was granted by Henry III to his wife's uncle, Peter of Savoy. In the 14th century it was the site of a palace which fell into disrepair; in 1510-15 a hospital was founded here. The **Queen's Chapel** of the Savoy dates from this period, although it has been largely rebuilt.

   The **Savoy Theatre**, opened in 1881, was financed by Richard d'Oyly Carte as a stage for Gilbert and Sullivan operas. By 1890 their disagreements led to the theater being leased by Henry Irving. In 1929 it was totally reconstructed. D'Oyly Carte opened the famous Savoy Hotel in 1889, appointing César Ritz as its manager and the famous Auguste Escoffier as its chef. The hotel was – and still is – a luxurious establishment. Caruso sang here, Sarah Bernhardt nearly died here and Henry Irving did die in residence.

4. Cross the **Strand** at one of the pedestrian crossings and walk eastwards across **Wellington Street**, then turn left into **Catherine Street**. To your right, by the far side of the bridge, notice imposing **Somerset House** designed by Sir William Chambers and erected in 1777-1790. National birth, marriage and death records were stored here until recent years, when they were transferred to nearby St Catherine's House. A series of rooms within Somerset House exhibiting a fine collection of Impressionist art will be opened to the public shortly.

5. Next you'll come to one of London's most famous theaters, The **Theatre Royal** in **Drury Lane**. The first theater on this site was built in 1663 and it was here that Nell Gwyn made her debut in 1665 in Dryden's *Indian Queen*. It has been rebuilt several times since then. In 1742 David Garrick made his debut here. He was manager of the theater between 1747 and 1776, then Richard Brinsley Sheridan took over – the year 1777 saw the first production of his *School for Scandal*. The present building, designed by Wyatt, dates from 1812. Kean, Henry Irving and Ellen Terry all performed here. In recent years, many well-known musicals have been staged in Drury Lane including *The King and I*, *Hello Dolly* and in 1958 *My Fair Lady* which ran for over 2,000 performances. The skeleton of a man who had been stabbed here was found behind the left Circle wall in the 19th century. His ghost is said to haunt the theater.

6. Walk on towards **Russell Street**, then turn left towards **Covent Garden**. Down to your left is the site of **The Lyceum Theatre** which was closed in 1939. In 1802 Madame Tussaud held her first exhibition of waxworks in the original building. The building was destroyed by fire in 1834. Henry Irving was manager from 1878 to 1899 and Ellen Terry played in many of his productions. The theater was closed in 1902 and demolished, apart from the walls and portico, reopening as a music hall in 1904.

7. Cross **Wellington Street** and turn left to find the **Theatre Museum** (open: Tues-Sun 11am-7pm, admission £2.25, see **Museums**). Before you visit you may want to refresh your spirit with a little food, wine, or a cup of coffee. **Covent Garden** is full of coffee bars, wine bars and pubs, and the museum has a café/wine bar. Alternatively, sit outside the **Punch and Judy** pub in Covent Garden.

    In **James Street** there's the **Nag's Head** pub (turn left from the museum, then right at Covent Garden and right round the Square to the first turning on the right).

8. From the Theatre Museum turn left and walk through the **Covent Garden Piazza**. At Unit 44 of the Market you'll find **Pollock's Toy Theatre** shop.

9. At the western edge of the market place you'll find **St Paul's Church**, built in 1633 by Inigo Jones and restored in 1871. The portico of the church features in the opening scene of George Bernard Shaw's *Pygmalion*. J.M.W. Turner was baptized here in 1775, and many famous people are buried here, including Grinling Gibbons (1721), Ellen Terry (1928), Thomas Arne (1778) (who composed 'Rule Britannia'); you'll also notice plaques commemorating actors and theater people.

10. Retrace your steps through the market to the top of **Russell Street** and turn left into **Bow Street**. The police station is on the right. In the 18th century Henry Fielding, magistrate as well as novelist, had a house and court on the site of the police station. He and his half-brother, John, established what came to be known as the Bow Street Runners in an attempt to catch the thieves who were rife in this area. David Garrick lived here between 1742 and 1744.

11. Pass the **Royal Opera House** where there has been a theater since 1732. Here, in 1773, the première of Goldsmith's *She Stoops to Conquer* was performed, and in 1775 the first performance of Sheridan's *The Rivals*. However, the theater and its successor burned down, and the present building by G.M. Barry dates from 1858. Under the portico there is a frieze by Flaxman, salvaged from the previous building.

   Many operas have had their English premières here – Verdi's *Rigoletto* (1855), *Aida* (1876), *Tosca* (1900), Wagner's *The Ring* conducted by Mahler (1892). Many great singers have performed on this stage – Adelina Patti (who made her debut in *La Sonnanbula* in 1861), Nellie Melba, Caruso, Tito Gobbi, Joan Sutherland and Maria Callas, to name but a few. In 1946 the Royal Ballet was formed from the Sadler's Wells Company and others.

12. From the Opera House, turn left into **Floral Street**, then right into **James Street**. Cross **Long Acre** into **Neal Street**. Cross **Shelton Street** and turn diagonally left into **Earlham Street**. At 21 Earlham Street you'll find **Theatre 200**, a fascinating theatrical costume shop.

13. Turn left into **Monmouth Street** past the **Cambridge Theatre** on your left. It was built in 1930 and Audrey Hepburn participated in a revue here in 1950. Turn right into **West Street**, where Agatha Christie's *The Mousetrap* opened at the Ambassadors in 1952. It transferred next door to **St Martin's Theatre** and is still running.

14. Cross **Long Acre** and the street becomes **St Martin's Lane**. To your left you'll see **Garrick Street** where at No 15 the **Garrick Club** is housed. Founded in 1831, its members included Dickens and Thackeray.

15. The **Albery Theatre** (1903), on the right, staged the first London production of Shaw's *St Joan* in 1924, with Sybil Thorndike. A little further down the road on the same side, there's the **Duke of York's Theatre**. Built in 1892, it was the first theater in St Martin's Lane.

16. On the left you'll see the **Coliseum**, built in 1904 as a stage for variety shows. The decor was quite splendid for its era and it

was the first theater in England to have a revolving stage. Many greats, including Sarah Bernhardt, Edith Evans and Lillie Langtry, performed here. In 1968 it became the home of the English National Opera (formerly Sadler's Wells Company), where the productions are sung in English.

17. At the bottom of St Martin's Lane, cross the road to the **National Portrait Gallery** (notice the statue of Sir Henry Irving, 1910). If you have the energy, the National Portrait Gallery (open: Mon-Fri; 10am-5pm, Sat 10am-6pm, Sun 2pm-6pm; see **Musuems**) displays portraits of many of the theatrical characters we have come across on the walk. Just up the road, in **Leicester Square**, you'll find a statue of Charlie Chaplin, unveiled in 1981. **Charing Cross** underground station is the end of the theater walk.

NON-DRIVING ESCAPES

GREENWICH

Directions;

Boat from Westminster or Charing Cross Piers, 10:30am (Westminster) 10am (Charing Cross)
British Rail (train) from Charing Cross to Maze Hill
Bus 188 from the front of Waterloo train station to Greenwich
Docklands Light Railway from Tower Hill to its terminus at Island Gardens, then walk under the River Thames by the footway tunnel to Greenwich

Of these four possible routes, the boat trip and the Docklands Light Railway journey are the most interesting. Both will bring you to **Greenwich Pier** where the **Cutty Sark** stands high in its dry dock (open: Mon–Sat 10am–6pm, Sun noon–6pm, winter closing an hour earlier; admission: adults £1.20, children 5–16 years, 60p). Launched in 1689, she was the fastest clipper of her time, bringing first tea from China and later wool from Australia. On board are papers, charts, mementoes and models illustrating the history of the clipper trade and the Cutty Sark's own story, plus a colorful collection of ships' figureheads. Just a few paces away from the clipper, you'll find the tiny **Gypsy Moth IV** (open: Easter–Sep, times as Cutty Sark; admission: adults 20p, children 10p) in which Sir Francis Chichester, in 1966–1967, achieved the fastest single-handed circumnavigation of the world.

By now you'll have some idea that Greenwich is distinctly nautical. It has also been a hot favorite with royalty. King Alfred, Henry VIII, Mary I and Elizabeth I were all born in Greenwich. Henry VIII much enlarged the old Tudor palace at Greenwich. All that remains of several centuries of royal residence lies within the **National Maritime Museum** (see below). In 1665 Charles II instructed John Webb to build a new King's House here beside the river, but the king died when only one of three planned blocks had been built. The **Royal Naval College**, immediately on your left as you leave the Pier, occupies the site of the royal palaces. The college, where naval officers still train, moved here in 1873, taking over the 17th- and 18th-century buildings of the **Royal Naval Hospital**. The magnificent buildings are largely the work of Wren. Only two of them are open to the public: the **Chapel** and **Painted Hall**, begun by Sir James Thornhill in 1708 (open: daily except Thur 2:30–5:30pm; free admission). Admiral Nelson lay in state beneath the sumptuously painted ceiling of the Painted Hall after he was killed at the Battle of Trafalgar in 1805. The Chapel, built by Wren, was restored after a fire in 1779.

Leaving the Royal Naval College, turn left and continue along **King William Walk**. Cross **Romney Road** and turn left along it, which brings you in a matter of minutes to the **National Maritime Museum** (open: Mon–Sat 10am–6pm, Sun 2–6pm; closed: 5pm in winter; admission: adults £2.20, children £1.10, charge includes admission to the **Old Royal Observatory**. See **Museums** for details of the Maritime Museum). At the center of the museum complex stands the **Queen's House**, the first Palladian villa to be built in England. The entrance hall is a perfect 40-foot cube, encircled by a gallery and covered by a ceiling whose pattern is repeated in the black and white marble floor. The rest of the building is equally impressive. Most of it is the work of Inigo Jones who was commissioned by James I to build a house for his queen, Anne of Denmark. Work stopped on the death of Anne and continued only when Charles I offered the house to his queen, Henrietta Maria, whose name and date, 1635, you can see on the north front.

From the museum, take the path through **Greenwich Park** up to the top of the hill to the **Old Royal Observatory** (open: as National Maritime Museum). Designed by Sir Christopher Wren (who was also a key figure in deciding on its site), the observatory has humble origins and was built from bricks that were available from Tilbury Fort, from wood, iron and lead rescued from a demolished gatehouse in the Tower of London, and £500 that was contributed by the King. Since this charitable beginning, the observatory has been greatly extended, the 'new observatory' was added in 1749 to house new instruments and further additions and improvements were made in 1813, 1833–36, 1848 and 1857. Between 1948 and 1957, the observatory's work was moved to a new sight in Herstmonceux Castle in Sussex, and in 1953 the **Octagon Room** was opened as a museum. Here you can see where Flamstead, first and one of the greatest of the Astronomers Royal, made his observations in the 17th century. Gradually the maps and observations made from Greenwich for 'the finding out of the longitude of places for perfecting navigation and astronomy' gained widespread use, until all the world's charts were based on the Greenwich meridian. Now you can stand with feet straddling the meridian line, one foot in the east, the other in the west. The 24-hour clock set in the gatepost of the observatory (also known as Flamstead House) shows **Greenwich Mean Time**, which the world takes as zero in international time.

In **Greenwich High Road**, at weekends, you'll find craft and antiques stalls in the market. Greenwich has plenty of pubs and good places to eat. Just along the road from the entrance to the Maritime Museum on your right you could try the **Plume of Feathers**, 19 Park Vista (see **Delightful Drinking – *Outer London Pubs***). Right down by the water you'll find the **Yacht Tavern** and the **Trafalgar Tavern**, both with balconies overlooking the river. If you'd prefer a wine bar, try **Doug's Wine Vaults**, 165 Greenwich High Road (on your left past the Martime Museum). It's a pleasant wine bar offering a selection of delicious salads and hot special dishes of the day.

Return to **Greenwich Pier** via **Greenwich Church Street**, at the museum end of the **High Road**.

HAMPSTEAD ⊖ Hampstead

Although Hampstead is relatively close to the center of London, the area retains a village atmosphere. It has long been a popular residential area for artists and literary lights, among them Constable, Keats, H.G. Wells, Anna Pavlova and Sigmund Freud. From the underground station cross the road and walk along **Heath Street** (to your left). Turn right into **Church Row** – a fine terrace of houses dating from 1720 – pass No 17 where H.G. Wells once lived and turn right by St John's Church into **Holly Walk**. **St Mary's Church**, a little way up on the right, was founded by the Abbé Morel, a refugee from the French Revolution, who came to Hampstead in 1796. It was one of the earliest Roman Catholic churches to be built in London. Follow the road to the junction then take the right fork into **Hampstead Grove**. On your right is the house where Romney, the painter, lived. A little way along, on your left, you'll reach the fine iron gates of Fenton House – they were designed by Jean Tijou Culo who was responsible for work in St Paul's Cathedral.

Delightful **Fenton House** (open: Sat–Sun 2pm–6pm Mar; Sat–Wed 11am–6pm Apr–Oct; admission: adults £2, Mon, Tues £1.60; children £1, Mon, Tues 80p) was built in 1693 and bought a century later by merchant Philip Fenton. The drawing room on the first floor is furnished as it was in the early 19th century, showing how wealthy, but not aristocratic, people then lived. The house contains two major collections – one of English, German and French 18th-century porcelain and the other the Benton-Fletcher collection of **early keyboard instruments** dating from the early 17th century.

Just beyond the house, turn left into **Admiral's Walk** where you'll see the distinctive nautical **Admiral's House**, built in the early 18th century by colorful Admiral Matthew Burton. Sir George Gilbert Scott, designer of the Albert Memorial and many 19th-century churches, later lived here. The adjoining **Grove Lodge** is probably older, and was the home of Galsworthy, who wrote most of his *Forsyte Saga* here. Turn right into **Lower Terrace**, Constable lived at No 2 (1821–5). This road takes you to **Whitestone Pond**, so called because the milestone here tells us that we are 4½ miles and 29 yards from Holborn Bars. Once the coach horses that had toiled up the hills on either side would stop here to cool and rest, but now the only feet you'll see in the pond belong to model boat sailors, young and old. At 437 feet above sea level, this is London's highest point.

Directly ahead of you is **Jack Straw's Castle**. A white weather-board inn first mentioned in local records in 1713. The inn was rebuilt in 1962–4 and is a favorite watering hole (and eating house: try the Castle Carving Room) of both local residents and visitors. (See **Delightful Drinking – *Outer London Pubs*.**) Jack Straw was one of the leaders in the Peasant's Revolt of 1381. It is said that he hid here after the collapse of the rebellion, but was eventually captured and executed.

If you're feeling energetic, now is the time to strike out across Hampstead Heath towards **Kenwood House**. Take the road directly opposite Jack Straw's Castle, **Spaniards Road**. Shortly on your right, opposite Heath House, there's a **grass track** which will lead you across the heath and through the small wooded area south of Kenwood. This brings you to the grounds of Kenwood House itself. The way is not marked, and if you have no map and/or a rotten sense of direction you will have to rely on the advice of fellow walkers. It is, however, considerably more delightful than following busy Spaniards Road, which is the sensible route for the unadventurous. Compensation for this comes in the form of the **Spaniards Inn** which stands opposite a toll house just before you reach the high walls of Kenwood's grounds. The Spaniards Inn is said to stand on the site of a 17th-century Spanish ambassador's residence.

Kenwood House is a ¾ mile walk from Whitestone Pond, and worth the effort. A fine, country mansion enlarged and embellished by Robert Adam in 1764, with paintings by Rembrandt, Vermeer, Frans Hals, Gainsborough, Reynolds and Turner. On summer evenings concerts are held in the grounds of Kenwood House, the orchestra occupying a white dome beyond the lake – the effect is quite magical once dusk has fallen (see **Local Delights**).

If you don't want to make the detour to Kenwood House, cross the road from Whitestone Pond and walk along **East Heath Road**. Shortly on your left you will see the curiously named road, the **Vale of Health**. Turn down this and follow the road until you come to a cluster of late 18th- and early 19th-century cottages grouped, together with a few Victorian townhouses, around the edge of a large pond. Until 1677 the vale was all marsh. The origins of its name are unknown, but cynics might enjoy the tale that when the malaria-infested swamp was drained and building began, the 'Vale of Health' was a bid to attract residents. Despite one or two modern houses, the Vale feels very much like a rural outpost and has attracted D.H. Lawrence, Edgar Wallace, and Compton Macken-zie, all of whom lived here at one time.

Either retrace your steps to the top of the Vale of Health and turn left into **East Heath Road**, or skirt the pond until you come to a

gravel and sand path. Turn right onto this, which will also take you to East Heath Road where you turn left. Continue along this road, with the heath on your left and turn right into **Keats Grove** shortly after the main road becomes **South End Road**.

This takes you to **Keats House** (open: Mon–Sat 10am–1pm, 2pm–6pm; Sun 2pm–6pm; free admission), a small Regency house built in 1815–16. Turning into the garden, it is as if time has stood still: there is a plum tree, the successor to the one under which 'Ode to a Nightingale' was written. Inside the small rooms display furniture and furnishings of the period when the poet lived here for only two brief years before his untimely death. The house was originally a pair, with Fanny Brawne and her mother occupying one and Keats the other. The two fell in love, but Keats died before they could marry. Letters, mementoes and books displayed in the house tell some of the tale.

Continue along Keats Grove then turn right into **Downshire Hill** and left into **Willow Road**. The **Freemasons Arms** pub has a very pleasant garden and tasty lunchtime food. Take the right fork into **Christchurch Hill** and pause at **Well Walk**. In the early 18th century this was a fashionable spa: a Victorian fountain now stands where the spring flowed. The original pump room and assembly rooms were demolished in 1882. John Constable lived at No 40, D.H. Lawrence at No 32 and J.B. Priestly at No 27.

Bear left along **Flask Walk** and you'll return to the **Flask** public house near the starting point of our visit, or have a refreshing cup of tea or coffee at **Louis Patisserie**, 32 Heath Street (open: daily: 9:30am–6pm) with its choice of luscious cakes and pastries (see **Teas and Snacks**).

THE PERFORMING ARTS

THEATERS AND CONCERTS

London's range of theaters and concert halls, coupled with the quality of the performances, make it a world-famous center for entertainment. Whether you concentrate on the West End – those theaters within walking distance of Piccadilly – or move away from London's equivalent of Broadway, you will find plenty of variety, from chamber music to grand opera, from extravagant mainstream productions to off-beat presentations. Similarly, you'll find that the prices differ according to the type of entertainment, from inexpensive tickets costing around £5 to grand seats at Covent Garden Opera for nearer £70.

To plan ahead, find out what's playing by contacting the British Tourist Authority in your own country (see **Planning Ahead**). When you're in London the Tourist Information Centres offer information on all the current performances. Alternatively, buy *What's On* or *Time Out* magazines, the *Evening Standard* or any quality daily national newspaper.

HOW TO OBTAIN THEATER TICKETS

Box offices usually open at 10am and you can either go in to select and pay for a seat, or telephone and reserve tickets by credit card. There are ticket agencies all over town including those in large stores – Selfridges or Harrods, for example – and hotels. These agencies usually charge a commission in addition to the cost of the ticket. The best known of these are:

Premier Box Office
188 Shaftesbury Avenue, WC2 (tel: (01) 240 2245) and at
16 Bridge Street, SW1 (tel: (01) 930 0292)

Keith Prowse
Tel: (01) 741 9999 (9am–10pm)
Including branches in many hotels and at:
5 Grosvenor Street, W1; 173 Kensington High Street, W8;
93 Knightsbridge, SW1; 14 Oxford Street, W1; 44 Shaftesbury Avenue, W1

First Call
Tel: (01) 240 7200 (24 hours)

The best place for same-day ticket bargains is the **Society of West End Theatres' ticket booth** on the corner of Leicester Square. Open noon-2pm for matinées, 2:30pm-6:30pm for evening performances, they sell same-day tickets for about half-price. However, you are unlikely to find tickets for the top shows here. Tickets for most fringe theater performances (outside the West End) are available from **Fringe Box Office**, Duke of York's Theatre, St Martin's Lane, WC2 (tel: (01) 379 6002 for credit card bookings).

If you are planning your trip, and you know that there is one show you'd love to see, then do reserve well in advance. You can do so through **Edwards and Edwards** (One Times Square Plaza, New York City, (tel: (212) 944 0290)). Remember – most of the West End hits are booked up months in advance. If you haven't reserved, you may be able to get returned tickets at the theater box office but beware of ticket touts outside the big theaters who charge outrageous prices.

WHAT TO DO ABOUT EATING

Most theater performances and concerts start at 7:30pm or 8pm and finish at 10:15pm or 10:30pm. If you want to eat before the performance, then why not have a light meal at a wine bar, at about 6pm? Most wine bars open at 5:30pm to serve theater goers and office workers looking for a little refreshment before commuting out to the suburbs. After the show you can quench your thirst in a nearby pub. The following establishments are conveniently located for the major theaters.

ROYAL NATIONAL THEATRE, South Bank, SE1
Tel: (01) 928 2033 (reservation for Ovation Restaurant)
Credit Cards: AE, DC, MC, V

The National Theatre has its own, good-quality buffet, providing hot dishes, salads or light meals and wine by the glass or bottle plus the more formal Ovation Restaurant.

THEATERLAND: Shaftesbury Avenue, St Martin's Lane, Covent Garden

Blake's Wine and Food Bar, 34 Wellington Street, WC2
Tel: (01) 836 5298   ⊖ Covent Garden
Open: Mon-Sat 11:30am-11pm, Sun 11:30am-10:30pm
Credit cards: AE, DC, MC, V

This busy wine bar serves good salads as well as hot dishes (casseroles, pies and lasagne, for example).

Café Fish des Amis du Vin, 39 Panton Street, SW1
Tel: (01) 839 4880   ⊖ Piccadilly Circus or Leicester Square
Open: Mon-Sat 11:30am-11:30pm, Sun noon-3pm
Credit cards: AE, DC, MC, V

Specializing in various types of fresh fish, well cooked by a variety of methods, this is the place for anyone who loves seafood.

Café Pelican, 45 St Martin's Lane, WC2
Tel: (01) 379 0309　⊖ Leicester Square
Open: Daily 11am-2pm
Credit cards: AE, DC, MC, V

A pleasant café/brasserie that serves snacks all day and excellent French-style food at lunchtime and in the evening. This is one of the few places that you'll find open very late.

Cork and Bottle, 44 Cranbourn Street, WC2
Tel: (01) 734 7807　⊖ Leicester Square
Open: Mon-Sat 11am-3pm, 5:30pm-11pm, Sun noon-2pm, 7pm-10:30pm
Credit cards: AE, DC, MC, V

This popular wine bar offers a varied selection of hot specials on a daily basis and also provides imaginative salads.

Fino's Wine Cellar, 104 Charing Cross Road, WC2
Tel: (01) 836 1077　⊖ Leicester Square or Tottenham Court Road
Open: Mon-Sat 11:30am-3pm, 5:30pm-11pm
Credit cards: AE, DC, MC, V

Long established and extremely popular, so aim to get to this one early. Culinary refreshments range from sandwiches and salads (including a delicious seafood salad) to tempting hot dishes (pasta specials and moussaka, for example). There are irresistible gâteaux, if you feel like a dessert.
Also at 19 Swallow Street, W1, Tel: (01) 734 2049.

ROYAL ALBERT HALL

Daquise, 20 Thurloe Street, SW7
Tel: (01) 589 6117　⊖ South Kensington
Open: 10am-7pm
No credit cards

A well-established restaurant that specializes in Eastern European food – meatballs, goulash, stuffed cabbage leaves. Good if you're feeling ravenous after a long day's sightseeing, but there are also lighter salads if you don't want to overindulge.

Wine Gallery, 232 Brompton Road, SW3
Tel: (01) 584 3493　　⊖ Knightsbridge or South Kensington
Open: Mon-Fri noon-3pm, 7pm-midnight
Credit cards: MC, V

This is the ideal venue for a weekday, post-concert meal – it's a pleasantly decorated wine bar that offers tempting light meals along with hot dish specials of the day.

CONCERTS

As well as providing venues for several resident orchestras, London often plays host to world-famous orchestras, soloists and visiting musicians. In addition to performances at the major concert halls listed below, extremely good concerts and recitals by well-known choirs as well as small orchestras are held in the city churches. You'll find such events at: **St John's**, Smith Square, SW1 (tel: (01) 222 1061) and **St Martin-in-The-Fields**, Trafalgar Square, WC2 (tel: (01) 839 1930).

　London does have occasional lovely summer evenings. Then make the most of the summer season of concerts in the grounds of **Kenwood House** in Hampstead, (tel: (01) 928 3191). If you do go, celebrate the evening in style and take a picnic from Harrods or Fortnums with perhaps a bottle of champagne to savor as the music soars.

CONCERT HALLS

Barbican Centre, Silk Street, EC2
Tel: (01) 628 8795　　⊖ Barbican

This new center for arts and conferences was opened in 1982 by Her Majesty the Queen. It covers 20 acres, on ten levels, providing an art gallery, three cinemas and the concert hall. The home of the London Symphony Orchestra, it is worth a visit even if you are not attending a particular performance. Musicians and artists of all schools are encouraged to perform and exhibit here.

Royal Albert Hall, Kensington Gore, SW7
Tel: (01) 589 8212　　⊖ South Kensington

Since 1941, from July to September the Royal Albert Hall has been the venue for the famous season of Sir Henry Wood's Promenade concerts (the 'proms'). For these annual musical extravaganzas, you queue on the evening of the concert for arena tickets (take a sandwich to keep hunger pangs at bay). The arena does not have seats, so head for the sides where at least there is a wall to lean against. If you would prefer to listen to the proms in comfort, tickets are available for seats in the rest of the hall. Apart from the season of proms concerts, other concerts are held here throughout the year.

South Bank, SE1
Tel: (01) 928 3191   ⊖ Waterloo

Within the South Bank complex, you'll find the **Purcell Room** and **Queen Elizabeth Hall**, both popular venues for recitals and chamber music, and the **Royal Festival Hall** which is the setting for orchestral concerts.

Wigmore Hall, 36 Wigmore Street, W1
Tel: (01) 935 2141   ⊖ Bond Street or Oxford Circus

This concert hall was built in 1901 by Friedrich Bechstein, a German piano manufacturer who had showrooms in Wigmore Street. The hall was taken over during the First World War, sold and reopened under its present name. It's now well-known for the caliber of its chamber music and recitals.

OPERA AND BALLET

London has two major opera houses:

Royal Opera House, Covent Garden, WC2
Tel: (01) 240 1066/240 1911   ⊖ Covent Garden

Productions here are among the finest in the world, providing a stage for leading international artists, among them Placido Domingo, Kiri te Kanawa and Helga Dernesch. The repertoire includes the great classics like *Don Giovanni* or *Fidelio*, as well as modern, more experimental works, all performed in their original tongue. Tickets for the Royal Opera House may be difficult to obtain – best to order them from home.

London Coliseum, St Martin's Lane, WC2
Tel: (01) 836 3161   ⊖ Leicester Square or Charing Cross

The home of the English National Opera, performances here are all in English. Again the standard is international and the operas range from favorites like *The Magic Flute* and *Cosi Fan Tutté* to modern works. You'll find that it's easier to get tickets and they are less expensive than those for Covent Garden.

Two major ballet companies perform in London. The **Royal Ballet** can be seen at the Royal Opera House, Covent Garden, presenting the great classics (*Giselle*, *Swan Lake* and so on) and certain modern, shorter performances. You'll find that tickets for the ballet are more readily available than for the opera (particularly for matinées).

The **Ballet Rambert** company is more innovative in the style of performances and often presents modern works. They usually perform at Sadler's Wells Theatre, Rosebery Avenue, EC1 (tel: (01) 278 8916). Visiting dance and opera companies also perform at Sadler's Wells.

ROCK CONCERTS

The big names in the rock world usually perform at:

Hammersmith Odeon, Queen Caroline Street, W6 (tel: (01) 748 4081), or at the **Wembley Arena**, Empire Way, Wembley, Middlesex (tel: (01) 902 1234). Occasionally you may find a rock concert planned at the Royal Albert Hall.

THEATERS

The majority of major London theaters are situated around the Piccadilly, Shaftesbury Avenue, St Martin's Lane and Covent Garden area. Convenient for those staying in central London, the West End theaters are serviced by nearby underground stations so if you're in a hotel away from the center you will still be able to travel to the theater easily. The main theaters, with their telephone numbers, are listed below.

Adelphi, Strand, WC2
Tel: (01) 836 7611   ⊖ Aldwych

Albery, St Martin's Lane, WC2
Tel: (01) 867 1115   ⊖ Leicester Square

Aldwych, The Aldwych, WC2
Tel: (01) 836 6404   ⊖ Aldwych

Ambassadors, West Street, WC2
Tel: (01) 836 6111   ⊖ Leicester Square

Apollo, Shaftesbury Avenue, W1
Tel: (01) 437 2663   ⊖ Piccadilly Circus

Apollo Victoria, Wilton Road, SW1
Tel: (01) 828 8665   ⊖ Victoria

Comedy Theatre, Panton Street, SW1
Tel: (01) 930 2578   ⊖ Piccadilly Circus or Leicester Square

Criterion, Piccadilly Circus, W1
Tel: (01) 867 1117   ⊖ Piccadilly Circus

Duke of York's, St Martin's Lane, WC2
Tel: (01) 836 5122   ⊖ Leicester Square

Fortune Theatre, Russell Street, WC2
Tel: (01) 836 2238   ⊖ Covent Garden

Globe Theatre, Shaftesbury Avenue, W1
Tel: (01) 437 3667   ⊖ Piccadilly Circus

Her Majesty's, Haymarket, SW1
Tel: (01) 839 2244   ⊖ Piccadilly Circus

London Palladium, Argyll Street, W1
Tel: (01) 437 7373   ⊖ Oxford Circus

Lyric, Shaftesbury Avenue, W1
Tel: (01) 437 3686   ⊖ Leicester Square

Royal National Theatre, South Bank, SE1
Tel: (01) 928 2252 (box office), (01) 928 8126 (recorded booking
   information)   ⊖ Waterloo

The National Theatre complex is made up of three separate
theaters: the **Olivier**, **Lyttleton**, and **Cottesloe** (the latter being the
smallest and seating just 400). This arrangement allows for a broad
range of work to be performed from high-brow drama and Shakespeare to light-hearted plays by Alan Ayckbourn. The small theater
is used for experimental plays and slightly off-beat presentations.

New London, Drury Lane, WC2
Tel: (01) 405 0072   ⊖ Covent Garden

Old Vic, Waterloo Road, SE1
Tel: (01) 928 7616   ⊖ Waterloo

Palace Theatre, Shaftesbury Avenue, W1
Tel: (01) 434 0909   ⊖ Leicester Square

Prince Edward, Old Compton Street, W1
Tel: (01) 734 8951   ⊖ Leicester Square

Prince of Wales, Coventry Street, W1
Tel: (01) 839 5989   ⊖ Leicester Square

Piccadilly Theatre, Denman Street, W1
Tel: (01) 867 1118   ⊖ Piccadilly Circus

Queen's Theatre, Shaftesbury Avenue, W1
Tel: (01) 734 1166   ⊖ Leicester Square

Royal Court, Sloane Square, SW1
Tel: (01) 730 1745   ⊖ Sloane Square

Royal Shakespeare Company, Barbican, EC2
Tel: (01) 638 8891   ⊖ Barbican

Within the complex there is the small Pit theater which accommodates smaller Shakespearean productions as well as new or experimental plays.

Savoy Theatre, Strand, WC2
Tel: (01) 836 8888   ⊖ Charing Cross

St Martin's, West Street, Cambridge Circus, WC2
Tel: (01) 836 1443   ⊖ Leicester Square

Shaftesbury Theatre, Shaftesbury Avenue, WC2
Tel: (01) 379 5399   ⊖ Holborn

Strand, Aldwych, WC2
Tel: (01) 836 2660   ⊖ Aldwych

Theatre Royal, Drury Lane, Catherine Street, WC2
Tel: (01) 836 8108   ⊖ Aldwych or Covent Garden

There has been a theater on this site since 1662, and it was here that Nell Gwyn made her debut in 1665. Garrick and Sheridan were both responsible for the management of the theater and for the fact that it flourished.

Theatre Royal, Haymarket, SW1
Tel: (01) 930 9832   ⊖ Piccadilly Circus

This beautiful well-preserved theater was designed by John Nash in 1821. The interior has been carefully updated to retain an air of elegance.

Vaudeville, The Strand, WC2
Tel: (01) 836 9987   ⊖ Charing Cross

Wyndhams, Charing Cross Road, WC2
Tel: (01) 867 1116   ⊖ Leicester Square

FRINGE THEATERS

In addition, and by way of contrast, to the big West End establishments, London has several fringe theaters. They're less formal, the tickets are easier to obtain (see **How to Obtain Theater Tickets** earlier in this section) and these smaller venues allow room for budding artistes to exercise their talents. The performances are not necessarily weird or controversial – although it is in these houses that you may find the occasional piece of eccentricity – they can be Shakespearean as well as new styles by up-and-coming playwrights, who may be the famous names of the future.

The best known theaters are:

Arts Theatre, 67 Great Newport Street, WC2
Tel: (01) 836 2132   ⊖ Leicester Square

Donmar Warehouse, 41 Earlham Street, WC2
Tel: (01) 240 8320   ⊖ Covent Garden

Lyric Studio, King Street, W6 (Hammersmith)
Tel: (01) 741 2311   ⊖ Hammersmith

Riverside Studios, Crisp Road, W6 (Hammersmith)
Tel: (01) 748 3354   ⊖ Hammersmith

Theatre Upstairs, Royal Court, Sloane Square, SW1
Tel: (01) 730 2554   ⊖ Sloane Square

Young Vic, 66 The Cut, London SE1
Tel: (01) 928 6363   ⊖ Waterloo

SHOP IT UP

You'll find with a little effort, that London is laden with great shopping bargains. For example, the French actually come over for the day to outfit their children (and themselves) before school reopens.

British tailoring is still justly renowned for the caliber of the workmanship and the quality of the fabrics. You'll find it at its best in **Savile Row, Jermyn Street,** and in such major department stores as Harrods.

Stunning boutiques are clustered along and around **Bond Street, Sloane Street** and **Beauchamp Place. Knightsbridge** is home to The **Scotch House, Harvey Nichols** and a myriad of boutiques, shoe shops and jewelry stores. The jewel in the crown of Brompton Road is **Harrods**, the ultimate department store.

If you're a serious collector of expensive antiques you could spend a whole vacation browsing through the hundreds of specialized shops London contains, and you'd be mad to miss hitting **Bermondsey Market** (New Caledonian Market) early of a Friday morning.

Books abound in the **Charing Cross Road** and around the British Museum in **Bloomsbury**. This area also has some of our best antique print shops.

For quality souvenirs and fine crafts, the **Design Centre**, down from Piccadilly, is a good starting point to see what's available and find out more about your special interest.

Whatever your interest, in the pages that follow we've attempted to give you our best bets. Happy hunting!

Shopping hours
As a general guideline stores are open from 9 or 9:30am until 5 or 5:30pm. The Oxford Street area stays open a bit later on Thursdays until 7:30 or 8pm.

Knightsbridge and the King's Road stay open late on Wednesday evenings (until about 7pm with some shops staying open until 8pm).

Very exclusive specialist shops tend to open for shorter periods generally 10am-5pm, with no late opening and are closed all day or from 1pm on Saturday.

Value Added Tax
Britain has a 15% Value Added Tax (VAT) which you can avoid on goods you're taking home by using the **Over-The-Counter Scheme** for visitors from outside the European Community. To qualify you must complete a customs form and show your passport at the time of purchase.

You're then free to take the goods but you must take them out of the country within three months. Upon your departure show your customs form plus the goods (pack them in your hand luggage) to the Customs Officer at the desk in the departure lounge. He will then validate the form, return it to the store of purchase which will then send you a cheque for the VAT amount. Stores also operate a scheme for goods sent to your home. However, be warned, the refund will probably just about equal the postage.

Most large shops and department stores operate a VAT refund scheme. However, you may find that some establishments have chosen not to offer this facility or that they operate it only on purchases above a certain amount, £50 or £100 for instance.

Comparative Tables of Clothing Sizes

These charts should make your shopping easier but there is no substitute for trying on a garment. Each designer and manufacturer has its own slightly idiosyncratic concept of size.

Comparative Table of Clothing Sizes

MEN'S CLOTHING
Suits

USA	34	36	38	40	42	44	46	48
UK	34	36	38	40	42	44	46	48
European	44	46	48	50	52	54	56	58

Shirts

USA	14½	15	15½	16	16½	17	17½	18
UK	14½	15	15½	16	16½	17	17½	18
European	37	38	39	41	42	43	44	45

Shoes

USA	7	8	9	10	11	12	13
UK	6	7	8	9	10	11	12
European	39½	41	42	43	44½	46	47

WOMEN'S CLOTHING
Dresses

USA	8	10	12	14	16	18
UK	10	12	14	16	18	20
European	38	40	42	44	46	48

Cardigans, Sweaters, Blouses

USA	8	10	12	14	16	18
UK	32	34	36	38	40	42
European	38	40	42	44	46	48

Shoes

USA	4½	5	5½	6	6½	7	7½	8	8½
UK	3	3½	4	4½	5	5½	6	6½	7
European	35½	36	36½	37	37½	38	38½	39	39½

CHILDREN'S CLOTHING CHART

Dresses and Coats (knitwear one size larger)

USA	3	4	5	6	6X
UK	18	20	22	24	26
European	98	104	110	116	122

For older children, sizes generally correspond with their age.

Shoes

USA	8	9	10	11	12	13	1	2	3	4½	5½	6½
UK	7	8	9	10	11	12	13	1	2	3	4	5½
European	24	25	27	28	29	30	32	33	34	36	37	38½

Gift Wrapping and Packing – the easy way

The Packing Shop, 19 George Street
Tel: (01) 486 0102
Open: Mon-Fri 9am-6pm, Sat 9:30am-3:30pm
Credit cards: AE, DC, MC, V
⊖ Marble Arch or Bond Street

You've found the perfect set of matched antique teapots but the prospect of holding them in your lap all the way to JFK fills you with gloom. That crystal candlestick is the perfect wedding gift for cousin Catherine but who's going to gift wrap it and get it to the church on time and in one piece?

Life is a series of cruel choices – never more so than when shopping overseas. The headaches of getting things home can cause you to give them a miss, then quietly repent for years thereafter.

The Packing Shop makes these problems a thing of the past. Using the latest techniques, such as injecting foam around your objects, they'll guarantee to deliver all your purchases in pristine condition all over the world. Indeed using Federal Express they'll guarantee US delivery in forty eight hours. They'll quote over the phone and pick up at your hotel (or at the shop) and they're happy to gift wrap for you from their beautiful assortment of papers including some marblized ones we really adore.

UNDER ONE ROOF – DEPARTMENT STORES

Burberrys, 18-22 Haymarket, SW1
Tel: (01) 930 3343
Open: Mon-Sat 9am-5:30pm, Thur until 7pm
⊖ Piccadilly Circus   Credit cards: AE, DC, MC, V

Burberrys have been making weatherproofs since 1856 and they have been on sale at this store since 1912. Their classic trench coats are expensive, but at sale times the price reductions are significant. Accessories – hats, scarves and umbrellas – in the distinctive Burberry plaid make great gifts for oneself as well as friends. On the lower ground floor there's a Church's shoe department. If you have an old Burberry which needs smartening up, the store offers an excellent cleaning and renovation service.

Dickins and Jones, 224 Regent Street, W1
Tel: (01) 734 7070
Open: Mon-Sat 9:30am-6pm, Thur 9:30am-7:30pm
⊖ Oxford Circus   Credit cards: AE, DC, MC, V

This member of the House of Fraser group of stores provides a wide variety of choice for the fashion conscious man or woman. Departments cover Alexon, Viyella, Jaeger and other classics plus designs from younger talent too – Nicol Farhi, Wendy Dagworthy and Karl Lagerfeld are all represented. Good selection of accessories.

Fortnum and Mason, 181 Piccadilly, W1
Tel: (01) 734 8040
Open: Mon-Fri 9am-5:30pm, Sat 9am-5pm
⊖ Green Park   Credit cards: AE, DC, MC, V

One of the oldest, and finest, purveyors of fine foods, Fortnum and Mason has been introducing exotic and specialty culinary items to the British for over 250 years. During the Crimean War Queen Victoria sent Florence Nightingale a consignment of beef tea from Fortnum and Mason. Today the store also sells superb furnishings and clothes, but it is still renowned for its contribution to the best of British kitchens. You'll find a variety of fine food gifts, and if you want to indulge in the ultimate picnic, buy your hamper here. The Fountain Restaurant on the ground floor, street entrance from Jermyn Street, will enchant your children with its Soda Fountain serving the very best ice cream sodas and sundaes (open until 11:30pm, see **Restaurants – *West End***).

Harrods, Knightsbridge, SW1
Tel: (01) 730 1234
Open: Mon-Sat 9am-6pm, Wed 9:30am-7pm
⊖ Knightsbridge   Credit cards: AE, DC, MC, V

The ultimate department store and London institution. The store's motto is *Omnia Omnibus Ubique* (everything for everyone, everywhere). Its reputation as such stands unblemished: answering a midnight order by telephone, Harrods even managed to secure a baby elephant as a gift for the then Governor of California, Ronald Reagan. Today's building dates from 1884 after a fire gutted the original grocery store. There are extensive fashion departments, from top designer clothes to bright sports wear, and comprehensive china and glass departments. Most spectacular of all are the food halls where meat, poultry, fish, cheese, fruit and vegetables, groceries and delicacies are temptingly displayed. The food halls are worth a visit in themselves, if only for the Victorian mosaic friezes in the Meat Hall.

Harvey Nichols, Knightsbridge, SW1
Tel: (01) 235 5000
Open: Mon-Fri 10am-8pm, Sat 10am-6pm
⊖ Knightsbridge   Credit cards: AE, DC, MC, V

Quieter and more restrained than Harrods, this elegant store specializes in high quality fashion and accessories for men, women, and, to a lesser extent, children. Top designers sell here, and the range of handbags and leather goods is excellent. There's a good kitchen shop and a small china and glasswear department. The hungry and weary will find two restaurants and a coffee shop. Great bargains are on offer at sale times in January and July.

Peter Jones, Sloane Square, SW1
Tel: (01) 730 3434
Open: Mon-Sat 9am-5:30pm, Thur 9am-7pm
⊖ Sloane Square   Credit cards: Store card only

Peter Jones is the up-market department store in the John Lewis ('never knowingly undersold') Group. It carries classic clothes and accessories for women and children but is most noted for its good value well-designed home furnishings and accessories.

Liberty, 210-220 Regent Street, W1
Tel: (01) 734 1234
Open: Mon-Sat 9:30am-6pm, Thur until 7:30pm
⊖ Oxford Circus   Credit cards: AE, DC, MC, V

Begun by Arthur Lasenby Liberty, who came from a family of drapers in Chesham, Buckinghamshire, the store originated in East India House, 218a Regent Street. Liberty concentrated on selling fine silks, later expanding the business by importing oriental goods – fans, Japanese goods and a wide range of household items of Oriental style. By 1925 two main Liberty buildings combined contrasting architectural styles in housing the highly successful business. From early days Liberty has had its own printing facilities for silk fabrics. It is for its own distinctive designs and softly shaded fabrics that the store has won great fame. Today you'll find that Liberty sells all household items plus clothing, fabrics, jewelry and gifts. In the basement there's a broad range of Eastern goods, some at competitive prices. This is a great place to browse, the building itself is as charming as the merchandise.

Lillywhites, Piccadilly Circus, SW1
Tel: (01) 930 3181
Open: Mon-Sat 9:30am-6pm, Tues 9:45am-6pm, Thur
    9:30am-7pm
⊖ Piccadilly Circus   Credit cards: AE, DC, MC, V

This department store is well-known for its sporting equipment and clothing for adults and children. They cater for the vast majority of sporting pursuits and stock all the top international names as well as own-label goods. Particularly good selection of skiwear and equipment.

Marks & Spencer, Oxford Street, W1
Tel: (01) 935 7954
Open: Mon-Fri 9am-8pm, Sat until 6pm
⊖ Marble Arch   Credit cards: Store card only

A country-wide chain concentrating primarily on providing the best quality clothing, food and furnishings at affordable prices. Of the three branches on Oxford Street the Marble Arch store (next to Selfridges) is the fashion leader and sells much the widest range of goods. Best buys: men's sweaters and women's lingerie, stockings and tights. Only some stores have dressing rooms but Marks & Spencer operates a cash refund policy if you bring goods back with a receipt. The food halls have a tempting selection of sandwiches, salads and other ready-to-eat food. Great for picnics.

Selfridges, 400 Oxford Street, W1
Tel: (01) 624 1234
Open: Mon-Sat 9am-5:30pm, Thur until 7pm
⊖ Marble Arch or Bond Street   Credit cards: AE, DC, MC, V

Oxford Street's best known store was begun by Chicagoan Harry Gordon Selfridge, opening its doors in 1909. Today it's noted for its wide selection of designer and moderately priced clothes for men and women. Miss Selfridge is one of the trendier young boutiques while the china, glass and housewares departments offer good value. The Food Hall has taste-tempting items in their delicatessen which can be combined with a real bagel from the bakery.

Scotch House, 2 Brompton Road, SW1
Tel: (01) 581 2151
Open: Mon-Sat 9am-6pm, Wed 9am-7pm
⊖ Knightsbridge   Credit cards: AE, DC, MC, V

A popular haunt for visitors to London, this is the place to buy authentic Scottish tartans and knitwear. There's a vast range of kilts (including children's kilts), hats, scarves, ties, etc, in a wide assortment of plaids. Shetland, lambswool, and cashmere sweaters are available in many colors, and there are beautiful traditional Aran knits along with distinctive Argyle socks. The Scotch House also has branches at 84 and 191 Regent Street, W1.

Simpson, 203 Piccadilly, W1
Tel: (01) 734 2002
Open: Mon-Sat 9am-5pm, Thur until 7pm
⊖ Piccadilly Circus   Credit cards: AE, DC, MC, V

When Alexander Simpson bought the site of the old geological museum in Piccadilly and built a stylish, menswear department store, he was to bring respectability to the ready-to-wear suit. The building is now listed (protected from change by law) but the stock has expanded to serve not only the suave man about town, but ladies too. Well-known for its DAKS suits and tweeds, it also sells casual clothes and swimwear. Everything, including the accessories, is of high quality. This is reflected in the prices.

MARKETS, ANTIQUE AND OTHERWISE

Billingsgate, Lower Thames Street, EC3
Trading begins about 5:30am Mon-Sat
⊖ Monument

Both wet fish (non-shellfish) and shellfish abound – some weird and wonderful varieties. The market operates on Sundays but only for shellfish.

Camden Lock, Commercial Place, Camden High Street, NW1
Open: Sat and Sun 8am-6pm
⊖ Camden Town or Chalk Farm

Camden Lock is a great place to wander around. There are permanent shops and workshops where you can see craftspeople at work. At weekends, the place is crowded with market stalls selling an assortment of craft goods – baskets, jewelry, clothing, pottery etc. The area is well-served with inviting cafés and restaurants. Most of the shops are closed on Sunday.

Camden Passage, Upper Street, N1
Open: Wed and Sat 8:30am-3pm
⊖ Angel

This whole area is a treasure trove for antiques and all things old.
From vast dining tables to tiny thimbles, you'll find a fantastic array
of items. The permanent shops are open during the week; in
addition, on Wednesdays and Saturdays, there are market stalls in
the street. The market is the place for small bits and pieces,
including jewelry, cutlery, books and so on. The quality of the
goods varies, but there are still bargains to be found (see **Antiques –
Mall Antiques Arcade**).

Church Street Market, Church Street, NW8
Open: Mon-Sat 9am-4:30pm
⊖ Edgware Road

Although the market is open during the week for general produce,
the best days are Fridays and Saturdays when the number of stalls
increases dramatically. Fruit, vegetables, clothing and hardware
stalls are interspersed with those selling linen, toys, crafts and
books. Towards the Lisson Grove end of the market there are stalls
offering antiques and bric-a-brac. Nearby, **Alfie's** is one of the main
antique markets to visit (see **Antiques**).

Covent Garden Market, The Piazza, Covent Garden, WC2
Open: Mon 9am-5pm (Antiques), Tues-Sat 9am-5pm (Crafts)
⊖ Covent Garden

The original wholesale fruit and vegetable market, for which
Covent Garden was famous, has moved across the river to a new
site in Vauxhall.
   The old premises at Covent Garden have been renovated and the
new Piazza is lined with permanent shops including high quality
clothes shops, kitchen suppliers and gift shops. A craft market is
held in and around the square with stalls specializing in fine crafts –
hand-painted silk, handmade jewelry, gorgeous hand-knits, jolly
wooden toys and fine pottery. On Mondays you'll find stalls selling
small antiques, such as jewelry and silverware.

Jubilee Market, Jubilee Hall, The Piazza, Covent Garden, WC2
Open: Mon 7am-5pm (Antiques), Tues-Fri 9am-5pm (General),
   Sat and Sun 9am-5pm (Crafts)
⊖ Covent Garden

A stone's throw from the Covent Garden Piazza, the Jubilee
Market sells general goods – household items, lots of clothes,
records and tapes from Tuesday to Friday. Saturday and Sunday
offer a tantalising array of hand-made goods – many Londoners
come here at weekends to look for original and decorative gifts.

Monday is antiques day when you'll find a wide variety of stalls offering all sorts of treasures. For bargains, and to see the dealers in action, you'll have to arrive early in the day – 7:30am to 8:30am.

Leadenhall Market, off Gracechurch Street, EC3
Open: Mon-Fri 9am-5pm approx
⊖ Bank

There is reputed to have been a market here since Roman times, and certainly since the 14th century. The name is taken from a 14th-century mansion which had a lead roof. The market was burned down in the Great Fire of London, and rebuilt to provide three trading areas: for meat; poultry, game and fish; grain and dairy products. The present structure, a magnificent iron and glass arcade, was built in 1881 and provides the setting for today's sale of fruit and vegetables, game and poultry. It's certainly worth a visit, if only to savor the lively atmosphere of a Victorian market hall.

Leather Lane, Leather Lane, EC1
Open: Mon-Fri 10am-2:30pm
⊖ Chancery Lane

A traditional, London market, noisy, busy and full of local color. In the 19th century this was described as an undesirable area – dirty and a favorite haunt for thieves. Today you'll find a general market selling a wide variety of goods – fruit, vegetables, plants, and clothing. You may well pick up some inexpensive woolen sweaters here.

New Caledonian Market, Bermondsey Square, SE1
Open: Fri 6am-2:30pm
⊖ London Bridge

This is where the antiques dealers come to replenish their stock, and the serious bargain hunter must get here early in the morning to secure a good catch. In fact, it is amazing how many people do find good bargains. Expect to haggle over the price. The selection of goods on offer is staggeringly broad: mostly small pieces, including lots of jewelry (much of it Victorian), silver, china and small collectable objects.

Petticoat Lane, Middlesex Street, E1
Open: Sun 9am-2pm
⊖ Aldgate, Aldgate East or Liverpool Street

Arguably London's most colorful street market. Stall after stall sells new clothes and accessories, some at rock-bottom prices, some overpriced. This is the place to buy chain-store clothes that are slight second quality – they have their labels removed and prices reduced. The quality of all goods varies enormously, so inspect everything carefully before buying. The side streets are filled with stalls, too – Cutler Street specializes in jewelry and antiques, Wentworth Street in clothing and general goods. Petticoat Lane gets very crowded and it does, sadly, have a long-standing reputation as a prime ground for pick-pockets, so look after your purse or wallet.

Portobello Road, Portobello Road, W11
Open: Mon-Sat 8am-4pm, Thur until 1pm, Sat until 6pm
⊖ Notting Hill Gate

This lively market is open during the week for fruit and vegetables, but Saturday is the day to go, when Portobello Road is packed with stalls. The 'posh' end, near Notting Hill, has all the famous antique stalls. Here you can browse over quantities of jewelry, cutlery and every conceivable *objet d'art*. Investigate the little antique shops all along the street. After the antique stalls the market becomes the territory of fruit and vegetable traders before reaching stalls selling secondhand clothing and very cheap goods.

Smithfield, off Farringdon Street, EC1
⊖ Farringdon or Barbican
Open: Mon-Fri 5am-9am

A cattle market in the 14th century, now the distribution center for London's meat trade, these venerable halls are alive with activity in the very early morning

AUCTION HOUSES

Many of London's auction houses are known throughout the world. Old Masters, famous Impressionist paintings, sculpture and Chinese porcelain are all in a day's work. However, it is quite possible to acquire desirable objects at affordable prices. Collectors may even find the occasional bargain.

If you have a particular interest it's worth looking for specialist sales. Dates and times of sales are advertised in newspapers – *The Daily Telegraph* on Mondays or *The Times* on Tuesdays. The trade bible is The *Antiques Trade Gazette*, available from the newspaper stand by Sotheby's New Bond Street. It lists countrywide auctions, antique fairs, markets, shippers and restorers, plus reports on what items have been fetching at auction. Alternatively, telephone the auction houses direct for details of sales, viewing times, plus after-sales arrangements such as foreign payments, tax exemption and transportation. None of the houses listed accepts credit cards; occasionally they will consider dollar checks. Remember, in addition to your bid the auction house will charge a buyer's premium of 10% or more.

Auctions are fun. They can be a great source of real bargains, but take time to view the lot you wish to purchase. Make sure it's in good condition. Set your maximum price and stick to it – you may lose your bid, but you won't lose your shirt.

Bonhams, Montpelier Street, SW7
Tel: (01) 584 9161
Open: Mon 8:45am-8pm, Tues-Fri 8:45am-6pm
⊖ Knightsbridge

This is the smallest of the major London auction houses. Bonhams holds regular sales of paintings, furniture and *objets d'art*, as well as specialty sales.

Christie, Manson and Woods, 8 King Street, SW1
Tel: (01) 839 9060
Open: Mon-Fri 9am-4:45pm
⊖ Green Park

Founded in 1766, Christie's have two London salerooms, and many others around the world. Here they hold several hundred auctions each year, including regular sales of pictures, furniture and silver. At **Christie's South Kensington**, 85 Old Brompton Road, SW7 (tel: (01) 581 7611), they specialize in collectors' items and ephemera.

Phillips, 7 Blenheim Street, W1
Tel: (01) 629 6602
Open: Mon-Sat 8:30am-5pm, Sat until noon
⊖ Bond Street or Oxford Circus

This is the main saleroom hosting regular sales of art and collectors' items during the week, also on Saturday mornings. The **Phillips Marylebone Room**, Lisson Grove NW8 (tel: (01) 723 2647) holds sales of paintings and prints on Fridays; **Phillips West 2**, 10 Salem Road, W2 (tel: (01) 221 5303) auctions lesser quality furniture on Thursdays.

Sotheby's, 34-35 New Bond Street, W1
Tel: (01) 493 8080
Open: Mon-Fri 9am-4:30pm
⊖ Green Park or Piccadilly Circus

Founded in 1744, this is the oldest of the four big auction houses. They hold regular sales of art, furniture, silver, porcelain and other collectors' items. Specialty sales cover anything from pop memorabilia to vintage cars.

ANTIQUES

Alfie's Antique Market, 13-25 Church Street, NW8
Tel: (01) 723 6066
Open: Tues-Sat 10am-6pm
⊖ Edgware Road   Credit cards: Stalls vary

A good place to browse and pick up the occasional bargain. Over 200 stalls and showrooms offer everything from furniture to post-cards. (See **Markets – Church Street Market**.)

Antiquarius, 135-141 King's Road, SW3
Tel: (01) 351 5353
Open: Mon-Sat 10am-6pm
⊖ Sloane Square   Credit cards: Stalls vary

Approximately 200 stalls make this a paradise for browsers and buyers alike. Many dealers specialize in easily portable goods like jewelry, antique clothing, china or prints while others have a more general stock. All periods are covered, from genuine antiquities up to the 1960s. A café offers light refreshments.

Arthur Middleton, 12 New Row, WC2
Tel: (01) 836 7042
Open: Mon-Fri 9:30am-6pm
⊖ Leicester Square   Credit cards: AE, DC, MC, V

A visit here is an absolute must for serious collectors of antique scientific instruments. One of the leading dealers in this field, the collection of quality telescopes, compasses, medical and astronomical instruments of the 18th and 19th centuries is outstanding.

Belinda Coote Antiques, 29 Holland Street, W8
Tel: (01) 937 3924
Open: Mon-Sat 10am-6pm, Sat until 1pm
⊖ High Street Kensington   Credit cards: V

A delightful shop offering a wide selection of 19th-century pottery and porcelain, items of furniture, papier mâché and decorative objects. Mason's Ironstone china and beautifully-worked repro-duction French tapestries are a specialty.

Bond Street Antiques Centre, 124 Bond Street, W1
Tel: (01) 351 1145
Open: Mon-Sat 10am-5:45pm, Sat until 4pm
Bond Street Silver Galleries, 111-112 New Bond Street, W1
Tel: (01) 493 6180
Open: Mon-Fri 9am-5pm
⊖ Green Park or Piccadilly Circus   Credit cards: Stalls vary

Two establishments that are so close, we list them together. The

Antique Centre houses around 25 leading dealers whose stock is all very high quality, including porcelain, jewelry, miniatures and other collectables. The **Silver Galleries** are divided into three floors displaying all types of silver.

Button Queen, 19 Marylebone Lane, W1
Tel: (01) 935 1505
Open: Mon-Sat 10am-6pm, Sat until 1:30pm
✆ Bond Street   No credit cards

A fascinating shop offering an astonishing selection of antique buttons. Old pearl, wood, horn and glass buttons can be found as well as new ones. A great place to browse and pick up a few unusual gifts or souvenirs.

Chelsea Antique Market, 245-253 King's Road, SW3
Tel: (01) 352 5689
Open: Mon-Sat 10am-6pm
✆ Sloane Square   Credit cards: Stalls vary

Around 100 stallholders offer a wealth of items, many of them small. Here you'll find jewelry, antiquarian books, prints and old phonographs all at reasonable prices, plus a pleasant café serving light snacks.

Chenil Galleries, 181-183 King's Road, SW3
Tel: (01) 351 5353
Open: Mon-Sat 10am-6pm
✆ Sloane Square   Credit cards: Stalls vary

A cut above the average antique market, these galleries house about 45 dealers offering a wide range of antique silver, jewelry, 17th- to 18th-century paintings and collectables. There's a particular bias towards Art Nouveau and Art Deco items.

Editions Graphiques, 3 Clifford Street, W1
Tel: (01) 734 3944
Open: Mon-Sat 10am-6pm, Sat until 2pm
✆ Green Park or Piccadilly Circus   Credit cards: AE, DC, MC, V

This is the place to come for the very best in Art Nouveau and Art Deco. On display you'll find a superb collection of graphics and paintings as well as jewelry, bronzes and glass.

Gray's Antique Market and Gray's Mews, 58 Davies Street & 1-7 Davies Mews, W1
Tel: (01) 629 7034
Open: Mon-Fri 10am-6pm
✆ Bond Street   Credit cards: Stalls vary

Two neighboring antique markets conveniently located just off Oxford Street. Between the two you'll find a large number of stalls offering a diverse range of items with great strength in jewelry, silver, militaria, toys and Oriental arts.

Grosvenor Prints, 28 Shelton Street, WC2
Tel: (01) 836 1979
Open: Mon-Sat 10am-6pm, Sat until 1pm
⊖ Covent Garden   Credit cards: AE, MC, V

These London specialists in antiquarian prints offer a vast stock. The interest range is broad, from natural history prints to architectural subjects; prices are equally varied, catering for the person who seeks a quality print to display as well as for the investor.

W.R. Harvey & Co. (Antiques) Ltd, 5 Old Bond Street, W1
Tel: (01) 499 8385
Open: Mon-Sat 10am-5:30pm, Sat until 2pm
⊖ Green Park or Piccadilly Circus   Credit cards: AE, DC, MC, V

The beautifully-decorated showrooms of this well-respected, long established company reflect the quality of their merchandise. Fine 18th- and 19th-century furniture, clocks, barometers and other *objets d'art* are on sale.

G. Heywood Hill, 10 Curzon Street, W1
Tel: (01) 629 0647
Open: Mon-Sat 9:30am-5:30pm, Sat until 12:30pm
⊖ Green Park   No credit cards

Highly respected amongst the literati, the Arts are the specialist field of this well-known antiquarian bookseller. The quality stock comprises thousands of books; staff are informed and helpful.

Howard Phillips, 11A Henrietta Place, W1
Tel: (01) 580 9844
Open: Mon-Fri 10:15am-5:15pm
⊖ Bond Street or Oxford Circus   No credit cards

This exquisite glassware shop (not recommended for children) offers items from earliest times up to 1830. Although the rarest pieces cost thousands, you can find plenty of beautiful items for around £50.

Jean Sewell (Antiques) Ltd, 3 Campden Street, Kensington
  Church Street, W8
Tel: (01) 727 3122
Open: Mon-Sat 10am-5:30pm
⊖ Notting Hill Gate   No credit cards

A shop of particular interest to collectors of fine porcelain. There's a good stock of 18th- and 19th-century tableware (their specialty), complemented by many other charming and decorative individual items.

Jack Casimir, The Brass Shop, 23 Pembridge Road, W11
Tel: (01) 727 8643
Open: Mon-Sat 10am-5pm
⊖ Notting Hill Gate   Credit cards: AE, DC, MC, V

As its name implies, this shop deals in metalware. Antique copper pans and utensils, pewter tankards and other treasures rub shoulders with a wide selection of antique brassware.

London Silver Vaults, Chancery House, 53 Chancery Lane, WC2
Tel: (01) 242 3844
Open: Mon-Sat 9am-5:30pm, Sat until 12:30pm
⊖ Chancery Lane   Credit cards: Dealers vary

The London Silver Vaults are strong rooms rented to dealers who sell antiques, secondhand valuables and new items of silver and silver plate. You'll find anything here, from a single teaspoon to a solid silver dinner service.

Maggs Brothers Ltd, 50 Berkeley Square, W1
Tel: (01) 493 7160
Open: Mon-Fri 9:30am-5pm
⊖ Green Park   Credit cards: MC, V

Founded in 1857, this is an antiquarian bookstore par excellence. They specialize in travel, manuscripts, autographs and the Orient. Good for lengthy browsing; some may find the atmosphere daunting, however.

Mall Antiques Arcade, 359 Upper Street, Camden Passage, N1
Tel: (01) 359 0825
Open: Tues-Fri 10am-5pm, Wed from 7:30am, Sat 9am-6pm
and
Georgian Village Antique Centre, 30 Islington Green, N1
Tel: (01) 226 1571
Open: Wed 10am-4pm, Sat 7am-5pm
⊖ Angel   Credit cards: Stalls vary

An area warranted to delight antiques hunters of any persuasion. Specialist and general dealers cover the whole spectrum of antiques, both in terms of stock and prices. Furniture, china, prints, jewelry, bric-a-brac and clothes (see **Markets – Camden Passage**).

Mallet and Son (Antiques) Ltd, 40 New Bond Street, W1
Tel: (01) 499 7411
Open: Mon-Fri 9:15am-5:15pm
⊖ Green Park or Piccadilly Circus   No credit cards

One of the best-known specialty shops selling English furniture and pictures dating from around 1660 to 1835. They stock only the very best examples; prices match the quality. Antiques are attractively displayed in model rooms.

Map House, 54 Beauchamp Place, SW3
Tel: (01) 589 4325
Open: Mon-Fri 9:30am-5:45pm, Sat 10:30am-5pm
⊖ Knightsbridge   Credit cards: AE, MC, V

Specialists in antiquarian maps, some very rare, many delightfully eccentric and imaginatively decorated. They do not stock modern maps. A good selection of 18th- and 19th-century prints are also stocked.

Roger's Antiques Gallery, 65 Portobello Road, W11
Tel: (01) 351 5353
Open: Sat 7am-5pm only
⊖ Notting Hill Gate   Credit cards: Stalls vary

Famous for its early morning market, Portobello Road is also strung with many galleries and antique shops. Decorative and collectable items are available here in all shapes, sizes and price ranges from Georgian silver teaspoons and Victoriana, to 60s kitsch. Great atmosphere; dress down and bargain. (See **Markets**.)

Stanley Gibbons, 399 Strand, WC2
Tel: (01) 836 8444
Open: Mon 10am-6pm, Tues-Fri 9am-5:30pm, Sat 10am-1pm
⊖ Charing Cross Road or Aldwych   Credit cards: AE, DC, MC, V

Stanley Gibbons is a philatelist's mecca. The shop's comprehensive stock encompasses everything from rare items of great philatelic interest to inexpensive stamps for the junior collector. Accessories and catalogues of every kind are available here, from a packet of stamp hinges to fine, leather-bound albums and specialty items of equipment. A number of general auctions and specialist sales are held throughout the year. Telephone for information, details of auctions, viewing or for help with placing bids; enquiries are welcome.

Spink and Son, 5 King Street, SW1
Tel: (01) 930 7888
Open: Mon-Fri 9:30am-5:30pm
⊖ Green Park   Credit cards: MC, V

World famous dealers in coins, bank notes and medals, offering only the finest and rarest stock, so consequently prices are high. They also deal in silverware, jewelry, English paintings and prints, plus Eastern art.

The Witch Ball, 2 Cecil Court
Tel: (01) 836 2922
Open: Mon-Sat 10am-6pm
⊖ Leicester Square   Credit cards: AE, DC, MC, V

If you love the performing arts or have a passion for antique posters The Witch Ball will keep you occupied for hours on end. This small shop specializes in antiquarian prints that relate to the theater, opera, music and dance. They stock everything from old sheet music to Paris jazz posters from the twenties. Staff are both helpful and very knowledgeable. They also mail periodic stock lists that make for great reading. Cecil Court, with its numerous antiquarian book and print shops is well worth a visit in its own right.

BOOKS AND MAPS

Automobile Association, Fanum House, 5 New Coventry St W1
Tel: (01) 930 2462
Open: Mon-Sat 9am-5pm, Tues from 9:30am, Sat until noon
⊖ Leicester Square   Credit cards: MC, V

At the AA shop you'll find a good selection of maps and motorists' guides for Britain and Europe, both published by the AA and other organizations. Also on sale are useful bits and pieces for drivers: torches, first aid kits, driving gloves, etc.

Bell, Book & Radmall Ltd, 4 Cecil Court, WC2
Tel: (01) 836 8222
Open: Mon-Fri 10am-5:30pm
⊖ Leicester Square   Credit cards: AE, DC, MC, V

Closeted in the quiet of this cosy shop, right in the heart of noisy London, you'll chance upon English and American first editions dating as far back as 1880 – from Fitzgerald and Hemingway to Joyce, and decorative volumes of poetry.

Books Etc, 120 Charing Cross Road, WC2
Tel: (01) 379 6838
Open: Mon-Sat 9:30am-8pm
⊖ Tottenham Court Road   Credit cards: AE, DC, MC, V

If you're short of reading matter, this excellent store sells all the best sellers and new titles. Other branches at 66-74 Victoria Street, SW1 and 222 Tottenham Court Road, W1.

Cinema Bookshop, 13-14 Great Russell Street, WC1
Tel: (01) 637 0206
Open: Mon-Sat 10:30am-5:30pm
⊖ Tottenham Court Road   Credit cards: MC, V

A comprehensive collection of titles relating to the cinema – biographies, criticisms and historical aspects are all well represented.

Dillons, 82 Gower Street, WC1
Tel: (01) 636 1577
Open: Mon-Sat 9am-5:30pm
⊖ Goodge Street   Credit cards: MC, V

A well-worn trail for the students at London University, Dillons is renowned for its comprehensive selection of academic tomes. Five floors of books, tracts and manuals on a huge range of topics which include fiction, gardening, cookery, art and other subjects not necessarily covered by the university syllabus.

Dillons Arts Bookshop, 8 Long Acre, WC2
Tel: (01) 836 1359
Open: Daily 10am-8pm, Sun from noon
⊖ Covent Garden or Leicester Square   Credit cards: MC, V

Here you'll find an extensive stock of books on all aspects of the arts, including architecture, theater and music. They also offer exhibition catalogs, posters and an excellent selection of art postcards.

Edward Stanford, 12-14 Long Acre, WC2
Tel: (01) 836 1321
Open: Mon-Sat 9am-6pm, Sat 10am-5pm
⊖ Covent Garden or Leicester Square   Credit cards: MC, V

Reputed to stock the largest collection of maps, charts, guides and travel books in the world. Sherlock Holmes sent Watson to Stanfords for a map before embarking on the trail of 'The Hound of the Baskervilles'. Specialist maps and charts for geologists, yachtsmen and mountaineers are a feature. Guide books for 'the rest of the world' upstairs; Ordnance Survey maps, village guides, flower books, road maps and nautical charts to Great Britain downstairs.

Forbidden Planet, 71 New Oxford Street, W1
Tel: (01) 836 4179
Open: Mon-Sat 10am-6pm, Thur-Fri until 7pm
⊖ Tottenham Court Road   Credit cards: AE, MC, V

A bookshop which modestly describes itself as 'the biggest comics
and science fiction mega store in the known universe'. If you're a
devotee of this particular genre, beam in for a staggering choice of
books.

Foyles, 119 Charing Cross Road, WC2
Tel: (01) 437 5660
Open: Mon-Sat 9am-6pm, Thur until 7pm
⊖ Leicester Square   No credit cards

Something of a British literary institution, this fascinating store
offers one of the most comprehensive stocks of books in print. The
premises ramble over a vast area with endless corners and sub-
sections. It's a great place to browse, but if you're trying to find a
particular title seek the advice of the helpful staff.

French's Theatre Bookshop, 52 Fitzroy Street, W1
Tel: (01) 387 9373
Open: Mon-Fri 9:30am-5:30pm
⊖ Warren Street or Goodge Street   Credit cards: AE, DC, MC, V

Established 150 years ago, French's comprehensive stock covers all
aspects of the dramatic arts. The unbelievable selection of play
scripts available is overwhelming, and the staff are extremely
knowledgeable.

Grant and Cutler, 55 Great Marlborough Street, W1
Tel: (01) 734 2012
Open: Mon-Sat 9am-5:30pm, Sat until 1pm
⊖ Oxford Circus   No credit cards

This shop has been selling new and secondhand European literature for over half a century. All the major European languages are
catered for, plus numerous books in translation, many of them
quite obscure.

Hatchards, 187-188 Piccadilly, W1
Tel: (01) 437 3924
Open: Mon-Sat 9am-5:30pm, Thur until 7pm, Sat until 5pm
⊖ Green Park   Credit cards: AE, MC, V

Behind the 18th-century façade you'll find a bookworm's paradise,
with a stock of hardbacks and paperbacks covering almost every
subject. There's a good children's section, an excellent travel
section, and a selection of rare editions for collectors. Another

store can be found at 150-152 King's Road, SW3.

Penguin Bookshop, 10 The Piazza, Covent Garden Market, WC2
Tel: (01) 379 7650
Open: Mon-Sat 10am-8pm
ϴ Covent Garden   Credit cards: AE, DC, MC, V

Major British paperback publishers, Penguin offer an enormous stock covering all their current titles. Crime to classics, politics to poetry. In addition, there's a good selection of books from other publishers. Also at 157 King's Road, SW3.

Puffin Bookshop, 1 The Piazza, Covent Garden Market, WC2
Tel: (01) 379 6465
Open: Mon-Sat 10am-8pm
ϴ Covent Garden   Credit cards: AE, MC, V

Penguin's junior division, especially for children, this excellent store sells a terrific range of books for all ages, plus story cassettes. There's even a reading corner for those who can't wait to get the books home.

Silver Moon Women's Bookshop, 68 Charing Cross Road, WC2
Tel: (01) 836 7906
Open: Mon-Sat 10:30am-6:30pm
ϴ Leicester Square   Credit cards: MC, V

In the region of 6,000 books by and about women. The stock includes many titles from Virago, publishers of 'serious' women writers, among them Willa Cather, Rosamund Lehmann and Nancy Mitford.

W.H. Smith, Sloane Square, SW1
Tel: (01) 730 0351
Open: Mon-Sat 9am-6:30pm, Sat until 6pm
ϴ Sloane Square   Credit cards: MC, V

One of the largest branches of this countrywide chain of news-agents, stationers and booksellers. Here you'll find a good selection of magazines, paperbacks and general interest books. The stock satisfies basic travels needs, offering the major guides and maps for both Britain and Europe.

Waterstone's, 121-125 Charing Cross Road, WC2
Tel: (01) 434 4291
Open: Mon-Fri 9:30am-7pm, Sat 10:30am-7pm
ϴ Leicester Square   Credit cards: AE, MC, V

A large, pleasant bookstore with a welcoming atmosphere, friendly young staff and a vast choice of volumes to suit every taste. Other branches at 193 Kensington High Street, W8, and 99-101 Old Brompton Road, SW7.

GIFTS 'N' THINGS

China, Pottery and Glass

Chinacraft, 1 & 3 Beauchamp Place, SW3
Tel: (01) 225 0349
Open: Mon-Sat 9am-6pm, Wed until 7pm
⊖ Knightsbridge   Credit cards: AE, DC, MC, V

One of a chain of stores specializing in all the best makes of fine English china. Whether you want a whole dinner service or a small gift, there is an excellent selection of items, and the staff are extremely helpful. Further branches are to be found at 499 Oxford Street, W1 and 130 New Bond Street, W1.

Craftsmen Potters Shop, 7 Marshall Street, W1
Tel: (01) 437 7605
Open: Mon-Sat 10am-5:30pm
⊖ Oxford Circus   Credit cards: AE, DC, MC, V

A good selection of hand-crafted pottery from Britain's best. You'll find inexpensive small dishes and mugs, a wide range of middle-priced items, plus enormous pieces priced up to £1,000.

Gered, 173-174 Piccadilly, W1
Tel: (01) 629 2614
Open: Mon-Sat 9am-6pm, Sat until 4pm
⊖ Hyde Park Corner or Green Park   Credit cards: AE, DC, MC, V

Decorative plates and vases, cufflinks and brooches, in fine blue and white Jasperware, conjure up that instantly recognizable Wedgwood style. Also, exquisite bone china in a variety of patterns, and adorable Beatrix Potter figurines and place settings for children.

The Irish Shop, 11 Duke Street, W1
Tel: (01) 935 1366
Open: Mon-Sat 9:30am-5:30pm
⊖ Bond Street   Credit cards: AE, DC, MC, V

Excellent collection of Irish goods. Stop here for Belleck china, Waterford crystal or the indestructible Aran sweaters.

Reject China Shop, 33-35 Beauchamp Place, SW3
Tel: (01) 581 0737
Open: Mon-Sat 9am-6pm
⊖ Knightsbridge   Credit cards: AE, DC, MC, V

Well known in London as the first stop for discount china. The stock includes first quality china at reduced prices and cheap 'seconds'. Although not all ranges are comprehensive most of the big names in china – and glass – are here. You'll find a branch at 134 Regent Street, W1.

Thomas Goode & Co. Ltd., 18 South Audley Street, W1
Tel: (01) 499 2823
Open Mon-Fri 9am-5pm, Sat until 1pm
⊖ Bond Street   Credit cards: AE, DC, MC, V

All the well-known makes of English bone china and crystal, plus antique china, glass and papier mâché departments, for the best of all worlds in china and glass under one roof.

Heavenly Scents

The Body Shop, 203 Kensington High Street, W8
Tel: (01) 937 1890
Open: Mon-Sat 9:30am-6:30pm, Thur until 7pm
⊖ High Street Kensington   Credit cards: AE, MC, V

The brain child of Anita Roddick, Body Shops have sprung up all over Britain. They now number 87. Ms Roddick's philosophy is simple: to use the purest, natural ingredients to nourish and restore the hair and skin. None of her products are tested on animals. Soothing creams, excellent range of haircare items, gorgeous smelling soaps particularly the apple scented ones. If your feet are weary buy the peppermint foot cream and massage it in – heaven. Also at 13 The Market, Covent Garden, WC2 and 54 King's Road, SW3.

Culpeper, 21 Bruton Street, W1
Tel: (01) 629 4559
Open: Mon-Fri 9:30am-6pm, Sat 10am-5pm
⊖ Green Park   Credit cards: AE, MC, V

Appropriately, Culpeper takes its name from the 17th-century herbalist because this small shop is a treasure trove of herbs (medicinal and culinary), spices and wonderful smelling bath oils, soaps, talcum powders and potpourri, not to mention their mustards, vinegars and honey. Our favorite: stephanotis scented toilet water. Also at No 8, The Market, Covent Garden, WC2.

Floris, 89 Jermyn Street, SW1
Tel: (01) 930 2885
Open: Mon-Sat 9:30am-5:30pm, Sat until 4pm
⊖ Green Park   Credit cards: AE, DC, MC, V

Located at No 89 since the 1730s, Floris is a heaven sent (sic) opportunity to find that little something. Fragrant soaps embossed with the Royal Warrant, scent, pot pourri, Lalique scent bottles – even a Floris decanter for true sybarites!

Penhaligon's, 41 Wellington Street, WC2
Tel: (01) 836 2150
Open: Mon-Sat 10am-6pm, Sat until 5pm
❸ Aldwych or Covent Garden   Credit cards: AE, MC, V

Penhaligon's specialize in their own make of fragrances, including fine soaps for men and women, perfumes and other scented products. The smell of the shop is heady and everything is beautifully packaged. There's a sister shop at 55 Burlington Arcade, W1.

The Good Life

Alfred Dunhill, 30 Duke Street, SW1
Tel: (01) 499 9566
Open: Mon-Sat 9:30am-6pm, Sat until 5:30pm
❸ Green Park or Piccadilly Circus   Credit cards: AE, DC, MC, V

Ancestral home of James Bond's Dunhill lighter, where pipe smokers can concoct their own mixture, and cigar buffs are humored in the Humidor. Lots of great gift ideas and sportswear, or you can weigh up the light-weight luggage collection. Another branch at 60-61 Burlington Arcade, W1.

Bendicks (Mayfair) Ltd, 55 Wigmore Street, W1
Tel: (01) 935 7272
Open: Mon-Fri 9am-5:30pm
❸ Bond Street   Credit cards: V

Famous for their bittermints in plain chocolate. Handmade confectionery and chocolates in presentation boxes or in Wedgwood, Coalport or Dresden containers. A stunning gift for your hostess.

Berry Bros & Rudd Ltd, 3 St James's Street, W1
Tel: (01) 839 9033
Open: Mon-Fri 9.30am to 5pm
❸ Green Park   Credit cards: DC, MC, V

If you're dedicated to Lord Byron, hail from Texas or have a serious interest in wines and spirits, this is a best bet. This family firm has been around for close to 300 hundred years and set up shop in its present location way back in 1731. The old Georgian shop front leads into handsome, wood paneled rooms lined with ancient wine bottles and portraits of famous customers. The room is dominated by a set of huge scales which until recent times were used by customers such as Byron to check their weight. During Texas's brief independence (you thought that had never changed) their embassy legation had offices on the premises.

Today this Royal Warrant holder (and owner of Cutty Sark scotch) offers a dazzling array of wine, liquors and other drinks. Their house red, at under £3 a bottle, is excellent. Their knowledge and friendly service are first rate.

Charbonnel et Walker, 28 Old Bond Street, W1
Tel: (01) 491 0939
Open: Mon-Fri 9am-4pm, Sat 10am-4pm
⊖ Green Park or Piccadilly Circus
Credit cards: AE, DC, MC, V

Marvelous presentation boxes – you can get personal messages spelt out in gold-foil covered chocolates. Also theater boxes.

Davidoff of London, 35 St James's Street, SW1
Tel: (01) 930 3079
Open: Mon-Sat 9am-6pm
⊖ Green Park   Credit cards: AE, DC, MC, V

Here's heaven on earth for the connoisseur of Havana cigars. He'll discover a truly magnificent variety – from the prince of cigars, the Davidoff Dom Perignon, to Montecristo, Romeo Y Julieta, Upmann, Punch and Bolivar.

Desmond Sautter Ltd, 106 Mount Street, W1
Tel: (01) 499 4866
Open: Mon-Fri 9am-6pm, Sat until 4pm
⊖ Bond Street   Credit cards: AE, DC, MC, V

Mr Sautter specializes in the finest Havana cigars, but has extended his concern to accommodate a veritable emporium of smoking necessaries – the exclusive Sautter silver cigar cutter, Dunhill and Ashton pipes and Meerschaums, antique and modern, are a few of the delights in store.

Paxton and Whitfield, 93 Jermyn Street, SW1
Tel:(01) 930 0259
Open: Mon-Fri 8:30am-6pm, Sat 9am-4pm
⊖ Green Park   Credit cards: AE, MC, V

A famous, old-fashioned, cheese shop, offering in the region of 300 varieties of British and Continental cheeses, some of them very rare. The expert staff will be happy to advise you.

R. Twining & Co., 216 Strand, WC2
Tel: (01) 353 3511
Open: Mon-Fri 9:30am-5pm
⊖ Charing Cross or Aldwych   No credit cards

The tea people: here you'll find lots of blends available loose, in tea bags or ready gift-packaged in attractive caddies. Visit the little museum at the back of the shop.

W.H. Whittard & Co., 111 Fulham Road, SW3
Tel: (01) 589 4261
Open: Mon-Fri 8am-5pm, Sat 9am-1pm
⊖ South Kensington   Credit cards: AE, DC, MC, V

Immense range of Indian, China and Ceylon regular, scented and green teas. About 50 different kinds to choose from, with tasting samples at 5p so that you can experiment. Also freshly roasted coffee, and tea and coffee accessories.

Anything Goes

Anything Left-Handed, 65 Beak Street, W1
Tel: (01) 437 3910
Open: Mon-Fri 10:30am-5pm, Sat 10am-2pm
⊖ Piccadilly Circus or Oxford Circus   No credit cards

This shop is the perfect place to find a gift for a left-handed friend. Just about all the domestic tools normally manufactured for the right-handed have their counterparts here, including scissors, potato peelers, pens and can openers.

Asprey, 165-169 New Bond Street, W1
Tel: (01) 493 6767
Open: Mon-Sat 9am-5:30pm, Sat until 1pm
⊖ Green Park or Piccadilly Circus   Credit cards: AE, DC, MC, V

This must be one of the grandest gift shops in the world. The name is exclusive (and so are the prices), the establishment sumptuous and hushed, offering an extensive array of high-class gifts that includes leather goods, pens, umbrellas and silverware.
(See also **Jewelry**.)

Captain O.M. Watts, 45 Albemarle Street, W1
Tel: (01) 493 4633
Open: Mon-Sat 9am-6pm, Thur until 7pm, Sat until 5pm
⊖ Green Park   Credit cards: AE, DC, MC, V

If you're nautical, be sure to drop anchor here. Since 1928 O.M. Watts has been the mecca for those in search of marine equipment, be it a batten, beacon, book or bunsen stove. Even if the mere thought of taking to the water makes you seasick there's much to intrigue ranging from stylish slickers to delightful brass fittings and hilarious mottos. While here be sure to pick up a copy of their nifty catalog.

The Counter Spy Shop, 62 South Audley Street, W1
Tel: (01) 408 0287
Open: Mon-Fri 9:30am-5:30pm
⊖ Hyde Park Corner or Green Park   Credit cards: AE, MC, V

Ever wondered what James Bond's 'Q' did when he retired? He set up a small shop in South Audley Street! Cigarette lighter cameras, debugging devices, leather-bound surveillance equipment for your bookshelf, and pocketbook recording systems for cautious customers.

Czech & Speake Ltd, 39c Jermyn Street, SW1
Tel: (01) 439 0216
pen: Mon-Fri 9am-6pm, Sat 10am-5pm
⊖ Green Park   Credit cards: AE, DC, MC, V

Elegant Victorian bathroom furnishings and solid brass fittings are lovingly reproduced (and sold) in order to provide the proper setting for Czech & Speake's glorious bath oils and soaps – fragrant rosemary and thyme, mimosa, and exotic frankincense and myrrh.

David Mellor, 4 Sloane Square, SW1
Tel: (01) 730 4259
Open: Mon-Sat 9:30am-5:30pm
⊖Sloane Square   Credit cards: MC

This is the perfect place to find a present for an enthusiastic cook. The range of cooking ware in stock is comprehensive, from knives and gadgets to baking tins, molds and specialty equipment. You'll also find their own design of stylish cutlery. There's a sister shop at 26 James Street, WC2.

Design Centre, 28 Haymarket, SW1
Tel: (01) 839 8000
Open: Mon-Tues 10am-6pm, Wed-Sat   10am-8pm, Sun
   1pm-6pm
⊖ Piccadilly Circus   Credit cards: AE, MC, V

Promotes the best in British domestic design, with two floors of fascinating showrooms. You can consult the index of best-designed products. Goods approved by the Centre carry its distinctive mark, a black and white tag, wherever they are sold. Have a look at the imaginative, well-made souvenirs and gifts.

General Trading Company, 144 Sloane Street, SW1
Tel: (01) 730 0411
Open: Mon-Sat 9am-5:30pm, Wed until 7pm, Sat until 2pm
⊖ Sloane Square   Credit cards: AE, DC, MC, V

The GTC (as it is affectionately known to afficienados) is the official gift supplier to the Sloane set – crystal from Waterford, glass from Dartington, and china from Portmeirion compete with novelties from the Orient, toys, and authentic Sloane teddy bears.

Halcyon Days, 14 Brook Street, W1
Tel: (01) 629 8811
Open: Mon-Fri 9:15am-5:30pm, Sat 9:30am-4:30pm
⊖ Bond Street   Credit cards: AE, DC, MC, V

A captivating selection of antique and reproduction English enameled boxes which make the perfect gift or souvenir. Sporting and commemorative themes are popular, as are exquisite copies of traditional designs, or you can commission your own personalized message.

Heals, 196 Tottenham Court Road, W1
Tel: (01) 636 1666
Open: Mon 10am-6pm, Tues-Fri 9:30am-6pm, Thur until 7:30pm, Sat 9am-6pm
⊖ Goodge Street   Credit cards: AE, DC, MC, V

A large store famous for its quality contemporary furniture, furnishings and home accessories. This is a great place to browse: it's packed with practical and pretty gifts to suit every pocket.

House of Hardy, 61 Pall Mall, SW1
Tel: (01) 839 5515
Open: Mon-Fri 9am-5pm, Thur until 6pm, Sat until 4pm
⊖ Green Park or Piccadilly Circus   Credit cards: AE, DC, MC, V

Hardy's reputation as top class manufacturers of fishing tackle, and country clothing, is unbeatable. Their rods and reels are renowned worldwide, from the compact 'Smuggler' rod (which fits into a briefcase), to the sturdy 130lb Zane Grey Big Game Reel.

Naturally British, 13 New Row, WC2
Tel: (01) 240 0551
Open: Mon-Sat 10:30am-6:45pm
⊖ Leicester Square   Credit cards: AE, DC, MC, V

A marvelous source of take-home gifts. You'll find the best of British here: traditional pottery, woodcraft, jams and jewelry, all cleverly displayed.

Paperchase, 213 Tottenham Court Road, W1
Tel: (01) 580 8496
Open: Mon-Sat 9am-6pm, Thur until 7pm
⊖ Goodge Street   Credit cards: MC, V

You'll find all things paper in this clever, colorful store. Choose from a fantastic array of wrapping papers, writing paper, notebooks, address books, pens, pencils and everything to do with stationery.

The V & A Museum Gift Shop, Victoria and Albert Museum,
    Cromwell Road, SW7
Tel: (01) 589 6371
Open: Mon-Sat 10am-5:50pm, Sun 2:30pm-5:30pm
⊖ South Kensington   Credit cards: AE, MC, V

This gift shop has an outstanding selection of postcards and a host of high quality, unusual gifts, including reproductions of pieces in the museum and facsimile engravings. The craft shop features the work of Britain's finest craftsmen.

KID'S STUFF

Of the major stores we've profiled, Harrods, John Lewis, Marks and Spencer and Selfridges have extensive ranges of children's wear, all of good quality and in a variety of price ranges. The Scotch House sells super miniature kilts and knitwear while Laura Ashley dresses children nostalgically in cotton and corduroy prints. Harrods' toy department offers an enormous variety of items for all ages. Selfridges and John Lewis also have good toy departments.

Clothing

British Home Stores, 252-258 Oxford Street, W1
Tel: (01) 629 2011
Open: Mon-Sat 9am-6pm, Wed from 9:30am, Thur until 8pm
⊖ Oxford Circus   Credit cards: MC, V

A large chain of stores (comparable with Marks & Spencer) offering good value clothes for all the family. Simple designs and bright colors make the children's range attractive and practical, including tracksuits, trousers, shirts and sweatshirts as well as dresses and underwear. Also at 101 Kensington High Street, W8.

Clothkits, 39 Neal Street, WC2
Tel: (01) 240 7826
Open: Mon-Sat 9:30am-6pm
⊖ Covent Garden   Credit cards: MC, V

A chain of stores specializing in cut out, ready-to-sew kits for children's and adults' clothes. Basic designs, a limited range of prints and colors, and good quality fabric have made the whole concept very popular. As well as the kits, ready-made garments and complementary accessories (T-shirts, socks etc.) are also available.

Hennes, 123B Kensington High Street, W8
Tel: (01) 937 3329
Open: Mon-Fri 10am-6:30pm, Thur until 7pm, Sat 9:30am-6pm
⊖ High Street Kensington   Credit cards: AE, DC, MC, V

A great place to buy inexpensive, practical, casual clothes. From long-sleeved T-shirts and velour dungarees for babies and toddlers to bright sweat shirts or tracksuits for older children. An excellent shop for fashion-conscious teenagers. There's also an adults' department packed with trendy outfits. Another London branch at 481 Oxford Street, W1.

Mothercare, 461 Oxford Street, W1
Tel: (01) 622 6621
Open: Mon-Sat 9:30am-6pm
⊖ Marble Arch   Credit cards: MC, V

Good for inexpensive everyday clothes and essential baby equipment, from pre-natal necessities and maternity clothes to styles for early teens. Mothercare's bold, primary colors please the fashion-conscious child, and their inexpensive Wellington boots are useful for wet-footed young sightseers. Other central London branches include those at 120 Kensington High Street, W8 and 129 Victoria Street, SW1.

012 Benetton, 131 Kensington High Street, W8
Tel: (01) 937 2960
Open: Mon-Sat 10am-6:15pm, Thur until 7:15pm, Sat until 6:30pm
⊖ High Street Kensington   Credit cards: AE, MC, V

A chain of modern, lively stores offering jolly, bright sweaters, sweat shirts and corduroy clothes. Originally catering for adults; stylish mini versions are now available for children.

Pollyanna, 811 Fulham Road, SW6
Tel: (01) 731 0673
Open: Mon-Sat 9:30am-5:30pm
⊖ Parsons Green   Credit cards: MC, V

Well-known continental labels (Absorba and Tutta, for example) and traditional British clothes (Puffa jackets and duffel coats) for 0-10 year olds. As well as the stylish day-to-day wear there's a range of beautiful David Charles party frocks. The clothes are expensive, but they make very special gifts. Startrite shoe boutique downstairs.

The White House, 51/52 Bond Street, W1
Tel: (01) 629 3521
Open: Mon-Sat 9am-5:30pm, Sat until 1pm
⊖ Green Park or Piccadilly Circus   Credit cards: AE, DC, MC, V

A long-established high-class children's outfitter, the White House is famed for clothing royal babies and children in beautifully-made outfits in traditional styles. You may be side-tracked by their superlative linens and lingerie.

Toys and Games

Hamleys, 188-196 Regent Street, W1
Tel: (01) 734 3161
Open: Mon-Sat 9:30am-6pm, Thur until 8pm
⊖ Oxford Circus or Piccadilly Circus   Credit cards: AE, DC, MC, V

Six floors filled with every conceivable toy or game make this 'the finest toy shop in the world'. From traditional entertainment for youngsters and the latest juvenile fad to models of London buses and taxis, you'll find something to suit every child and every pocket in this store.

Beatties, 202 High Holborn, WC1
Tel: (01) 405 6285
Open: Mon 10am-6pm, Tues-Sat 9am-6pm
⊖ Holborn   Credit cards: AE, DC, MC, V

One of the best model shops in London, Beatties offers a huge selection of cars (from cheap Matchbox toys to expensive Solido), model kits, and a fantastic range of electric train sets with all the necessary accessories. In addition, the store stocks popular makes of toys and dolls (Barbie, Fisher Price, Playmobil etc.).

Davenports Magic Shop, 7 Charing Cross Underground Shopping
   Arcade, Strand, WC2
Tel: (01) 836 0408
Open: Mon-Sat 9:30am-5:30pm, Sat until 4:30pm
⊖ Charing Cross   No credit cards

A long-established shop providing the key to success for aspiring and established magicians. As well as all the necessary equipment and accessories for performing magic, they also stock a wonderful selection of practical jokes and amateur tricks.

Early Learning Centre, 225 Kensington High Street, W8
Tel: (01) 937 0419
Open: Mon-Sat 9am-6pm
⊖ High Street Kensington   Credit cards: MC, V

An innovative chain of shops specializing in sturdy, educational toys for younger children. Colorful, exciting products prove that early learning can be fun. The range includes chunky puzzles, drawing equipment, bricks and wooden toys. Slightly more complicated, yet still almost unbreakable, items like microscopes are available for 5 to 8 year olds. The shop has a play area.

Eric Snook, 32 The Market, Covent Garden Piazza, WC2
Tel: (01) 379 7681
Open: Mon 1pm-6pm, Tues-Sat 10am-6pm, Sun 11am-6pm
ϴ Covent Garden   Credit cards: AE, MC, V

This shop sells craftsman-produced wooden toys and beautifully made soft toys. Bright and sturdy or soft and cuddly, the items are all top quality and perfect for children of all ages.

Just Games, 62 Brewer Street, W1
Tel: (01) 734 6124
Open: Mon-Sat 10am-6pm, Thur until 7pm
ϴ Piccadilly Circus   Credit cards: MC, V

Today an increasing number of games are aimed at the adult market, so this shop is interesting for parents as well as children. The stock of games and puzzles includes plenty of traditional ones (solitaire, backgammon, Monopoly etc) as well as the latest sources of entertainment.

The Kite Store, 69 Neal Street, WC2
Tel: (01) 836 1666
Open: Mon-Fri 10am-6pm, Sat 10:30am-5pm
ϴ Covent Garden   Credit cards: AE, MC, V

This store is reputed to have the best selection of kites in the world. The range is mind-boggling – from simple, inexpensive fliers to sophisticated examples of aerodynamics for true enthusiasts. They also offer a selection of boomerangs and frisbees.

Paddington and Friends, 22 Crawford Place, W1
Tel: (01) 262 1866
Open: Mon-Sat 10am-5pm
ϴ Edgware Road   Credit cards: AE, DC, MC, V

A little shop to delight devotees of the bear from Darkest Peru. You'll find T-shirts, pyjamas, dishes, stationery and a variety of other goods all bearing his inimitable portrait.

Pollock's Toy Theatres, 1 Scala Street, W1
Tel: (01) 636 3452
Open: Mon-Sat 10am-5pm
ϴ Goodge Street   Credit cards: AE, MC, V

Robert Louis Stevenson wrote 'If you have art, folly or the bright eyes of children, speed to Pollock's'. Their enchanting cardboard toy theaters have been delighting children for years and make an unusual gift. You can also choose from among other charming toys and puzzles. The museum displays a fascinating collection of theaters and toys (see **Fun For The Kids** – *Museums*). You'll find another branch in Unit 44, The Market, Covent Garden, WC2.

MENSWEAR

Aquascutum, 100 Regent Street, W1
Tel: (01) 734 6090
Open: Mon-Sat 9am-6pm, Thur until 7pm
⊖ Piccadilly Circus or Oxford Circus   Credit cards: AE, DC, MC, V

Like Burberry, the Aquascutum name is associated with raincoats, but you'll also find the highest quality suits, jackets and slacks in traditional British weaves and styles – herringbone tweeds, Prince of Wales check, classic blazers are but a few. There's a women's department too.

Austin Reed, 103-113 Regent Street, W1
Tel: (01) 734 6789
Open: Mon-Sat 9am-5:30pm, Tues 9:30am-5:30pm, Thur until 8pm
⊖ Piccadilly Circus or Oxford Circus   Credit cards: AE, DC, MC, V

A popular shop with a huge selection of ready-to-wear suits, trousers and shirts by all the top names. Their Cue Shop stocks styles for younger men. If you're short on shopping time this is a good place to find top quality menswear to suit a broad range of tastes.

Blazer, 36 Long Acre, WC2
Tel: (01) 379 6258
Open: Mon-Sat 10am-6:30pm, Thur until 8pm
⊖ Covent Garden or Leicester Square Credit cards: AE, DC, MC, V

The theme here is traditional English style. Cavalry twill trousers, blazers and raincoats, as well as more formal wear, all at prices that are reasonable for the quality. A good range of accessories too, to complete the look.

Burstow & Logsdail, 8a Sackville Street, W1
Tel: (01) 437 1651
Open: Mon-Sat 9am-5pm, Sat until noon
⊖ Piccadilly Circus   Credit cards: AE, DC, MC, V

David Hicks, once voted Britain's best dressed man, has his suits made here – surely that is recommendation enough! Using only the finest cloth, each suit is classically styled and individually cut for a clientele which includes royalty, diplomats and top businessmen.

Gieves and Hawkes, 1 Savile Row, W1
Tel: (01) 434 2001
Open Mon-Sat 9am-5:30pm, Sat until 1pm
⊖ Piccadilly Circus   Credit cards: AE, DC, MC, V

The unbeatable combination of Gieves, the military outfitters, and Hawkes, the gentlemen's tailors, has resulted in a clutch of no less than seven Royal Warrants. Past patrons include both Lord Nelson and the Duke of Wellington. In the relaxed atmosphere of a country house library, you can browse through a selection of superior quality men's clothing, from superbly tailored suits and coats to classic double-cuff shirts and fine woolens. Finishing touches include gold fob watches and monogrammed luggage.

Hilditch and Key, 73 & 87 Jermyn Street, W1
Tel: (01) 734 4707
Open: Mon-Sat 9:30am-6pm, Thur until 7pm, Sat until 5:30pm
⊖ Green Park   Credit cards: AE, MC, V

Famous shirtmakers who offer a custom service as well as a range of ready-to-wear shirts. They also have a shoe department, and a comprehensive range of accessories.

Jaeger, 200-206 Regent Street, W1
Tel: (01) 734 8211
Open: Mon-Sat 9:30am-6pm, Wed and Thur until 8pm
⊖ Oxford Circus   Credit cards: AE, DC, MC, V

Well-cut, classic suits of undeniable quality are the trademark of Jaeger clothes for men. In addition there's a good choice of beautiful sweaters in subtle colors, and excellent casual wear.

Moss Bros, 88 Regent Street, W1
Tel: (01) 494 0665
Open: Mon 8:30am-7pm, Tues-Sat 9am-7pm, Thur until 8pm,
       Sat until 6pm
⊖ Piccadilly Circus   Credit cards: AE, DC, MC, V

Best known to Londoners as the place to hire dinner jackets, this store has a lot to offer with a good selection of formal and casual wear manufactured by all the top classic names, Jaeger and Aquascutum, for example.

Next For Men, 13-15 King's Road, SW3
Tel: (01) 730 7673
Open: Mon-Sat 9am-6pm, Wed until 7pm
⊖ Sloane Square   Credit cards: AE, DC, MC, V

A popular chain selling good quality business and leisure wear. Aimed at the younger man, the styles are classic, the prices reasonable, the selection comprehensive. Branches all over London, including 62 South Molton Street, W1 and 137 Kensington High Street, W8.

Paul Smith, 41-44 Floral Street, WC2
Tel: (01) 379 7133
Open: Mon-Sat 10am-6pm, Thur until 7pm, Sat until 6:30pm
⊖ Covent Garden   Credit cards: AE, DC, MC, V

Highly respected designer of stylish 80s menswear. The conservative look is peppered with a strong element of fun in eye-catching ties, scarves and other accessories to complement well-cut trousers and jackets.

Review, 326 Oxford Street, W1
Tel: (01) 491 7141
Open: Mon-Sat 9am-7pm, Sat until 6pm
⊖ Bond Street or Oxford Circus   Credit cards: AE, DC, MC, V

Classic styles, coordinated separates and realistic prices sum up the stock of this high-street store, catering to the youthful professional man. Casual clothes are particularly good.

Savoy Taylors Guild, 93 Strand, WC2
Tel: (01) 836 7261
Open: Mon-Sat 9am-6pm, Thur until 7pm
⊖ Knightsbridge   Credit cards: AE, DC, MC, V

The Savoy Taylors Guild offers an excellent selection of quality ready-to-wear menswear by the big name designers. The prices are reasonable (at sale time you can pick up a real bargain) and the staff helpful. Other London locations: 164 New Bond Street, W1 and Hans Crescent, SW1 (opposite door 5 of Harrods).

A. Sulka, 19 Old Bond Street, W1
Tel: (01) 493 4468
Open: Mon-Fri 9:30am-6pm, Sat until 5pm
⊖ Green Park or Piccadilly Circus   Credit cards: AE, DC, MC, V

Ninety years ago Amos Sulka undertook to serve 'a group of gentlemen who have the taste to enjoy only the best'. With mother-of-pearl buttoned shirts, 55 inch ties and hand-stitched smoking jackets, the survival of that tradition is secure.

Tommy Nutter, 19 Savile Row, W1
Tel: (01) 734 0831
Open: Mon-Sat 9am-6pm
⊖ Piccadilly Circus   Credit cards: AE, DC, MC, V

The youngest tailor in Savile Row, Tommy Nutter designs stylish suits for the modern man. His customers include Ringo Starr and Elton John – but not all his work is outrageous. Neither are his prices . . . and there's a good choice of shirts.

Turnbull and Asser, 71/72 Jermyn Street, SW1
Tel: (01) 839 5133
Open: Mon-Sat 9am-5:30pm, Sat until 4:30pm
⊖ Green Park   Credit cards: AE, DC, MC, V

World-famous shirtmakers. This is traditional shopping at its best: elegant surroundings and helpful staff. Ready-to-wear shirts are available, as well as a custom service; and there's an excellent selection of bow ties and brightly colored suspenders.

Vincci, 60 Jermyn Street, SW1
Tel: (01) 629 0407
Open: Mon-Sat 9am-6pm
⊖ Green Park   Credit cards: AE, DC, MC, V

Vincci undertakes to outfit a gentleman Italian style, from his underwear to his leather jacket, in premises on both sides of Jermyn Street – right for top quality shirts and handmade suits, left for a range of casual clothes.

Woodhouse, 138 Long Acre, WC2
Tel: (01) 240 2008
Open: Mon-Fri 10am-7pm, Thur until 7:30pm, Sat 9:30am-7pm
⊖ Covent Garden or Leicester Square
Credit cards: AE, DC, MC, V

A friendly shop catering for sophisticated, fashion-conscious younger men. The stock includes classic menswear from Europe's top designers (Giorgio Armani, for example) and excellent quality suits under their own label at more affordable prices. Their range of shirts in subtle colors is really eye-catching.

WOMENSWEAR

Brown's, 23 South Molton Street, W1
Tel: (01) 491 7833
Open: Mon-Sat 10am-6pm, Thur until 7pm
⊖ Bond Street   Credit cards: AE, DC, MC, V

One of the most extensive collections of top young British designers in London, with quite a few European brethren thrown in for good measure. Edited highlights: Jasper Conran; Jean-Paul Gaulthier; Rifat Ozbek; Sonia Rykiel; Comme des Garçons; Workers for Freedom.

Caroline Charles, 11 Beauchamp Place, SW3
Tel: (01) 589 5850
Open: Mon-Sat 9:30am-5:30pm, Wed until 6:30pm, Sat
  10am-5pm
☞ Knightsbridge Credit cards: AE, DC, MC, V

Caroline Charles's boutique is one of the most friendly and inviting in London. Classic clothes for the races or the dance floor are transformed into spectacular 'originals' by her inventive flair for mixing fabrics and flattering outlines which suit everyone.

The Chelsea Design Company, 65 Sydney Street, SW3
Tel: (01) 352 4626
Open: Mon-Sat 10am-6pm
☞ South Kensington Credit cards: AE, DC, MC, V

A relatively new arrival on the London fashion scene, French-born Catherine Walker has taken it by storm. Her ravishing, bias-cut evening dresses are, quite simply, divine; and there's a distinctive repertoire of sophisticated day dresses and severely tailored suits.

Constant Sale Shop, 50 South Molton Street
Tel: (01) 629 0827
Open: Mon-Sat 10am-6pm, Wed until 7pm
☞ Bond Street Credit cards: AE, DC, MC, V

International couturier and designer clothes at discount prices. Alistair Blair, Ungaro, Valentino and Armani are just some of the labels sold here. If you've always wanted to extend your wardrobe with top designs, but never felt able to meet the high prices, this is the store.

Country Casuals, 146 Regent Street, W1
Tel: (01) 734 1727
Open: Mon-Sat 9:30am-6pm, Thur until 7pm
☞ Oxford Circus Credit cards: AE, DC, MC, V

A chain offering smart, classic styles at reasonable prices. The stock extends beyond casual clothes to well-finished suits but separates in subtle seasonal colors are their strength.

Emanuel, 10 Beauchamp Place, SW3
Tel: (01) 584 4997
Open: Mon-Sat 10am-6pm, Wed until 8pm
☞ Knightsbridge Credit cards: AE, MC, V

Behind a theatrically draped façade, the Emanuels' boutique is filled with a glorious selection of fairytale evening dresses and ready-to-wear frocks. Favorites of the Princess of Wales, the Emanuels will also design couture clothes especially for you.

Fenwick of Bond Street, 63 New Bond Street, W1
Tel: (01) 629 9161
Open: Mon-Sat 9:30am-6pm, Thur until 7:30pm
⊖ Green Park or Piccadilly Circus   Credit cards: AE, MC, V

Sophisticated, small department store offering an excellent selection of top British and European label fashions. They sell a superb range of accessories, and their lingerie department is exceptional.

Hyper Hyper, 26-40 Kensington High Street, W8
Tel: (01) 937 6964
Open: Mon-Sat 10am-6pm
⊖ High Street Kensington   Credit cards: varies from stall to stall

A showcase for young British designers who can't yet afford their own stores. Individual stalls highlight the look of the eighties, and the young clientele appreciate the innovative styles. A great place for browsing and updating your ideas on clothes.

Jaeger, 200-206 Regent Street, W1
Tel: (01) 734 8211
Open: Mon-Sat 9:30am-6pm, Wed & Thur until 8pm
⊖ Oxford Circus   Credit cards: AE, DC, MC, V

The house of Jaeger is associated with top-quality, sophisticated, classic clothes. Here you'll find the whole range of coats, coordinates and leisure wear on display with rich colors and eye-catching designs. Some other London branches: 184 Kensington High Street, W8; 163 Sloane Street, W1; and 145 King's Road, SW3.

Janet Reger, 2 Beauchamp Place, SW3
Tel: (01) 584 9360
Open: Mon-Sat 10am-6pm, Sat until 5pm
⊖ Knightsbridge   Credit cards: AE, DC, MC, V

Small, but sensational collection of gorgeous silk and lace lingerie – frothy, feminine confections in peach and cream vie with the vamp in you, already captivated by voluptuous black satin. Heavenly nightdresses, teddies, French knickers and delicate camisoles for pure indulgence.

Key Largo, 2 Bow Street, WC2
Tel: (01) 240 7599
Open: Mon-Sat 10am-7pm
⊖ Covent Garden   Credit cards: AE, DC, MC, V

Key Largo is famous for sweaters emblazoned with cartoon characters and motifs, which the Princess of Wales has been seen wearing. Huge selection of ready-made sweaters but the shop will also create a garment to your own design. The sweaters are unisex, so they're also ideal for an adventurous man.

Laura Ashley, 256-258 Regent Street, W1
Tel: (01) 734 5824
Open: Mon-Fri 9:30am-6pm, Thur until 7pm, Sat 9am-6pm
⊖ Oxford Circus   Credit cards: AE, MC, V

Noted for floral prints, pastel colors and feminine styles, Laura Ashley stores are extending their range with striking fabrics in bright colors. Knitwear, bold T-shirts, stylish suits, beautiful evening dresses and rich velvets complete the new image. You may well find prices here less expensive than in the USA. London branches include those at 7-9 Harriet Street, SW1 and 35-36 Bow Street, WC2.

Long Tall Sally, 21-25 Chiltern Street, W1
Tel: (01) 487 3370
Open: Mon-Fri 9:30am-5:30pm, Thur until 7pm, Sat 9:30am-4pm
⊖ Baker Street   Credit cards: AE, DC, MC, V

As implied by the name, a shop catering for tall ladies. The stock covers designer label outfits as well as everyday clothes of classic and more modish designs. From neat suits to vivid tracksuits, there are clothes for every occasion.

Next, 54-60 Kensington High Street, W8
Tel: (01) 938 4211
Open: Mon 10am-6pm, Tues-Sat 9:30am-6pm, Thur until 8pm, Fri
        until 6:30pm
⊖ High Street Kensington   Credit cards: AE, DC, MC, V

A country-wide chain offering a selected range of stylish clothes at very affordable prices. Coordinated outfits for work and leisure. Next for Men and Next Collection (men and women's clothing plus home furnishings) shops are part of the group. London branches include 33 Brompton Road, SW1, and 327 Oxford Street, W1.

Scottish Merchant, 16 New Row, WC2
Tel: (01) 836 2207
Open: Mon-Sat 10:30am-6:30pm, Thur until 7pm, Sat until
        5:30pm
⊖ Leicester Square   Credit cards: AE, MC, V

A shop full of temptation if you're fond of traditional British knitwear – Aran, Guernsey and Fair Isle, for example. Beautiful hand-knitted woolen gloves and scarves make an excellent alternative purchase instead of sweaters. Knitwear for men as well.

The Thayer Street Shop, 5 Thayer Street, W1
Tel: (01) 487 3232
Open: Mon-Sat 10am-6pm
⊖ Bond Street   Credit cards: AE, DC, MC, V

The Thayer Street Shop at No 5 stocks some of the best French and Italian design. Escada, Guy Laroche, Krizia Poi and Crisca all prove beyond a doubt that classic clothes need not be boring.

The Viyella Shop, 20 Brook Street, W1
Tel: (01) 629 9331
Open: Mon-Sat 9:30am-5:30pm, Thur until 7pm
⊖ Bond Street or Oxford Circus   Credit cards: AE, DC, MC, V

A good range of fine quality, timeless clothes. Simple designs, subtle colors and the classic coordinated look are the hallmark of Viyella stores.

Whistles, 12/14 St Christopher's Place, W1
Tel: (01) 487 4484
Open: Mon-Sat 10am-6pm, Thur until 7pm
⊖ Bond Street   Credit cards: AE, DC, MC, V

Very popular amongst London's ultra-fashionable, this lovely shop is full of top-quality clothes and accessories by new designers as well as established names. A range of own-label styles is also on display. Branches at 14 Beauchamp Place, SW3, and 1 Thayer Street, W1.

Woodhouse, 4 South Molton Street, W1
Tel: (01) 493 1524
Open: Mon-Sat 10am-6:15pm, Thur until 7:15pm
⊖ Bond Street   Credit cards: AE, DC, MC, V

Woodhouse specializes in practical clothes in streamlined, classic styles for the younger professional woman. Excellent quality, well-cut suits in a variety of fabrics are a key feature. In addition, there's a range of stunning evening wear.

Zandra Rhodes, 14a Grafton Street, W1
Tel: (01) 499 6695   Open: Mon-Sat 9:30am-6pm, Sat until 5pm
⊖ Green Park or Piccadilly Circus   Credit cards: AE, DC, MC, V

The soft-lit interior is a veritable Aladdin's Cave of dazzling, bejeweled and bugled evening dresses; over-printed denim for the day; sequinned sweatshirts for the aspiring, as well as a small collection of accessories, and glitzy Andrew Logan jewelry.

ACCESSORIES

Shoes

Anello and Davide, 35 Drury Lane, WC2
Tel: (01) 836 1983
Open: Mon-Fri 9am-5:30pm, Sat 9am-4pm
⊖ Covent Garden or Holborn   Credit cards: MC, V

Situated in the heart of theaterland, this company is famous for its ballet slippers and theatrical shoes. It also sells comfortable women's court and one-strap shoes in a dazzling array of colors, made in satin or leather. There is also a selection of men's shoes and slippers.

Church's, 163 New Bond Street, W1
Tel: (01) 499 9449
Open: Mon-Sat 9am-5:30pm, Thur until 7pm, Sat until 4:30pm
⊖ Green Park or Piccadilly Circus   Credit cards: AE, DC, MC, V

Church's shoes have an international reputation for quality and distinction. Their classic styles are not cheap, but they last for years. Church's operate a repair service for shoes purchased here. Conservative women's styles available from Church's, 143 Brompton Road, SW3.

Giorgio Ferrari, 124 King's Road, SW3
Tel: (01) 589 5083
Open: Mon-Sat 9:30am-6:30pm, Wed until 7pm
⊖ Sloane Square   Credit cards: AE, DC, MC, V

With three shops in central London – others are in Covent Garden and Hampstead – Italian shoes by Giorgio Ferrari are clearly a winner. For both men and women these well-made, solidly comfortable shoes are highly fashionable and stylish without being outrageous.

Gucci, 27 Old Bond Street, W1
Tel: (01) 629 2716
Open: Mon-Fri 9am-5:30pm, Sat 9am-5pm
⊖ Green Park or Piccadilly Circus   Credit cards: AE, DC, MC, V

A shop which needs little introduction – stop off here for shoes, bags, and all accessories which carry this prestigious name.

John Lobb Ltd, 9 St James's Street, SW1
Tel: (01) 930 3664
Open: Mon-Fri 9am-5:30pm, Sat until 1pm
⊖ Green Park   Credit cards: AE, MC, V

This bespoke (custom-made) shoe and bootmaker numbers

amongst its customers the Queen, Prince Philip and the Prince of Wales. Each customer's feet are measured for custom-made lasts from which the final footwear is made on the premises (it takes up to 9 months to do so). Justifiably famous for craftsmanship, Lobb shoes can last a lifetime. That's appropriate because it just might take that amount of time to pay the tab.

Kurt Geiger, 95 New Bond Street, W1
Tel: (01) 499 2707
Open: Mon-Fri 9:30am-6pm, Thur until 7pm, Sat until 5:30pm
⊖ Green Park or Piccadilly Circus   Credit cards: AE, DC, MC, V

Providing a generous forum for other designers – Enzo, Raphael and Bruno Magli – Kurt Geiger is at the top of the women's luxury footwear business. Alongside an excellent range of boots there are elegant shoes and matching handbags.

McAfee Shoes, 17-18 Old Bond Street, W1
Tel: (01) 499 7343
Open: Mon-Sat 9am-6pm, Thur until 7pm
⊖ Green Park or Piccadilly Circus   Credit cards: AE, DC, MC, V

Beautifully made shoes for men and women with classic styling: brogues, loafers and courts. They also offer a bespoke (custom-made) service. You'll find branches at 35 Brompton Road, SW3 and 73 Knightsbridge, SW1.

Maud Frizon, 31 Old Bond Street, W1
Tel: (01) 493 5988
Open: Mon-Sat 10am-6pm
⊖ Green Park or Piccadilly Circus   Credit cards: AE, DC, MC, V

Maud Frizon's contemporary and imaginative footwear for men and women is designed to incite comment. Thigh-length black suede boots to dainty dancing pumps; the range has been extended to include leather accessories, silk ties and designer sunglasses.

Manolo Blahnik, 49-51 Old Church Street, SW3
Tel: (01) 352 8622
Open: Mon-Fri 10am-6pm, Sat 10:30am-5:30pm
⊖ South Kensington   Credit cards: AE, MC, V

Shoemaking is in Manolo Blahnik's blood, but it is unlikely the first Blahnik cobbler (200 years ago) foresaw the dizzy heights Manolo would aspire to: witty, outrageous, subtle, but never dreary, his highly individual creations attract a world-famous clientele.

Wildsmith & Co., 15 Prince's Arcade, SW1
Tel: (01) 437 4289
Open: Mon-Fri 9am-5:30pm, Sat 9:30am-2pm
⊖ Green Park or Piccadilly Circus   Credit cards: AE, DC, MC, V

Founded in 1847, as military bookmakers, this family firm justly prides itself on having manufactured the first slip-on shoe in London, and on their comfortable 'Wildsmith Country House' shoe. Ready-made or bespoke (custom-made), every shoe is created by hand.

Leather Goods and Scarves

Gold-Pfeil, 107 Jermyn Street, SW1
Tel: (01) 839 3315
Open: Mon-Sat 10am-6pm
Θ Green Park   Credit cards: AE, DC, MC, V

Established in 1856 this German company manufactures hand-crafted leather accessories and travel goods, producing 285 co-ordinated items in three main color ranges. Gold-Pfeil have been using the same quality leathers and designs since the 1920s – a godsend for collecting and matching.

Hermès, 155 New Bond Street, W1
Tel: (01) 499 8856
Open: Mon-Fri 9:30am-6pm, Sat 10am-5pm
Θ Green Park or Piccadilly Circus   Credit cards: AE, DC, MC, V

Here you'll find the silk scarves, bags and accessories which all bear this exclusive label. Need we say more? Also at 179 Sloane Street, SW1.

The Mulberry Company, 11 Gees Court, St Christopher's Place, W1
Tel: (01) 493 2546
Open: Mon-Sat 10am-6pm, Thur until 7pm
Θ Bond Street   Credit cards: AE, DC, MC, V

A name which is often featured on the fashion pages of the best magazines, this store offers very distinctive, very English, beautifully made bags and belts. The bags come in all sizes and the belts are available in fine leather or in fabric with a leather trim.

Hats

Frederick Fox, 87-91 New Bond Street, W1
Tel: (01) 629 5705/6
Open: By appointment only
Θ Green Park or Piccadilly Circus   Credit cards: AE, DC, MC, V

Frederick Fox, Royal Milliner to seven members of the Royal family and the genius behind countless splendid Ascot and wedding confections, has a world-wide clientele who enjoy his unerring innovative instinct, his penchant for veils and his personal service. Appointments essential.

Herbert Johnson, 30 New Bond Street, W1
Tel: (01) 408 1174
Open: Mon-Fri 9:15am-5:30pm, Sat 9:30am-4pm
⊖ Green Park or Piccadilly Circus   Credit cards: AE, DC, MC, V

Need a racing felt for Cheltenham? A panama for Antibes – or Brighton? A boater for that punting picnic on Isis? Then get thee hence to Herbert Johnson, hatter to the good and the great; men, women and the military, since 1889.

James Lock, 6 St James's Street, SW1
Tel: (01) 930 874
Open: Mon-Fri 9am-5pm, Sat 9:30am-12:30pm
⊖ Green Park   Credit cards: AE, DC, MC, V

The first bowler hat was commissioned by James Lock and Co Ltd in 1850 for William Coke. This hard-domed hat was requested as suitable wear for his gamekeepers when they chased poachers off the estate. It was from here that Lord Nelson was provided with a hat with a built-in eye shade, and the Duke of Wellington with the plumed hat which he wore at Waterloo. Today you'll find a broad range of hats and caps.

Sweaters and Knitwear

Edina Ronay, 141 Kings Road, SW3
Tel: (01) 352 1085
Open: Mon-Fri 10am-6pm, Wed until 7pm, Sat 11am-6pm
⊖ Sloane Square   Credit cards: AE, DC, MC, V

The atmosphere is as warm and cosy as one of Edina Ronay's gorgeous winter woolies. And her knitwear range extends far beyond the traditional Shetland and Fair Isle patterns to include summer cottons and sophisticated creations in silk, angora and cashmere.

N. Peal, 37-40 Burlington Arcade, W1
Tel: (01) 493 5378
Open: Mon-Sat 9am-5:30pm, Sat until 4:30pm
⊖ Green Park or Piccadilly Circus   Credit cards: AE, DC, MC, V

You could drown in blissful cashmere at N. Peal, surrounded by waves of spring pastels, rich autumn hues, and festive electric pink magically transformed into pullovers, wraps, and suits. Also visit the Man's Shop at No 54 for exclusive country-style woolens.

Shirin Cashmere, 51 Beauchamp Place, SW3
Tel: (01) 581 1936
Open: Mon-Fri 10am-6pm, Wed until 7pm, Sat 10:30am-6pm
⊖ Knightsbridge   Credit cards: AE, DC, MC, V

London is the place to buy cashmere, and Shirin is the place for high-fashion cashmere. Decadent head-bands with feathers; rhinestone bespotted hip sashes; lively striped jersey dresses and beautiful evening clothes are all fashioned from luxurious cashmere.

Westaway and Westaway, 62-65 Great Russell Street, WC1
Tel: (01) 405 4479
Open: Mon-Sat 9am-5:30pm
⊖ Tottenham Court Road Credit cards: AE, DC, MC, V

Westaway and Westaway specialize in sweaters for all the family. You can select from Scottish handknits, Shetlands, lambswool jumpers and cashmere knits in a rainbow of colors, a variety of sizes and styles. The prices are very reasonable indeed.

Umbrellas and Other Things

Geo. F. Trumper, 9 Curzon Street, W1
Tel: (01) 499 1850
Open: Mon-Sat 9am-5pm, Sat until 12:30pm
⊖ Green Park Credit cards: AE, DC, MC, V

Praised by Evelyn Waugh, Trumper's is the essence of the traditional barber-perfumer. You'll find a range of badger-hair shaving brushes, razors, colognes created for Lord Astor and other famous 19th-century figures, even mustache wax.

James Smith and Sons, 53 New Oxford Street, WC1
Tel: (01) 836 4731
Open: Mon-Fri 9:30am-5:30pm
⊖ Tottenham Court Road No credit cards

Founded in 1830, this is the oldest umbrella and walking stick shop in Europe in typically Victorian premises. Custom-made handles, malacca canes, silver-topped ebony canes and stage props such as sword-sticks.

The Sock Shop, 89 Oxford Street, W1
Tel: (01) 437 1030
Open: Mon-Fri 8:30am-7pm, Thur until 7:30pm, Sat 8:45am-7pm
Credit cards: AE, DC, MC, V
⊖ Oxford Circus or Tottenham Court Road

Cheery socks can make fun gifts and in this store (part of a chain) you'll find an amazing choice. There are around 2,000 different types – striped socks, dotty socks, socks with toes, socks with days and dates. These shops also sell tights and stockings, patterned and plain. Branches of The Sock Shop can be found in most major shopping streets and at some main railway stations.

Swaine Adeney Brigg, 185 Piccadilly, W1
Tel: (01) 734 4277   Open: Mon-Sat 9am-5:30pm, Thur until
  7pm, Sat until 5pm
⊖ Green Park ·   Credit cards: AE, DC, MC, V

Renowned as makers of umbrellas, riding whips and walking sticks
to the elite. The range of umbrellas is astonishing, with different
types of handles, a variety of fabrics, and a spectrum of colors. In
addition, you'll find a comprehensive range of equipment for riding
and hunting, from waistcoats and boots to the essential hip flask.

ALL THAT GLITTERS – JEWELRY

Annabel Jones, 52 Beauchamp Place, SW3
Tel: (01) 589 3215
Open: Mon-Fri 10am-5:30pm
⊖ Knightsbridge   Credit cards: AE, DC, MC, V

Treasures from the past and present abound in this delightful shop
in the heart of fashionable Knightsbridge. Their exclusive modern
designs complement their collection of fine antique and period
jewelry. Antique silver and Old Sheffield plate.

Anne Bloom, 10a New Bond Street, W1
Tel: (01) 491 1213
Open: Mon-Fri 9am-5:30pm
⊖ Green Park or Piccadilly Circus   Credit cards: AE, DC, MC, V

Anne Bloom's collection of period jewelry dates from 1840 to 1940.
Her success is due to her exquisite taste in design and practiced eye
for quality. She also always has a unique collection of period silver
photograph frames and mirrors.

Argenta Gallery, 82 Fulham Road, SW3
Tel: (01) 584 3119
Open: Mon-Sat 9:30am-5:30pm, Sat until 5pm
⊖ South Kensington   Credit cards: AE, DC, MC, V

There are literally thousands of items on view at this magnificent
gallery. It specializes in contemporary jewelry in various mediums
including silver, gold, steel and wood. A wonderful place to
browse.

Armour-Winston, 43 Burlington Arcade, SW1
Tel: (01) 493 8937
Open: Mon-Fri 9am-5:30pm
⊖ Green Park or Piccadilly Circus   Credit cards: AE, V

For those who fancy their jewelry a touch on the wild side, Armour-
Winston have a great selection of jewel-encrusted animal motifs

from dragonflies to frogs. Also, attractive jade and turquoise pins, antique pocket watches, and much more.

Asprey, 165-169 New Bond Street, W1
Tel: (01) 493 6767
Open: Mon-Sat 9am-5:30pm, Sat until 1pm
⊖ Green Park or Piccadilly Circus   Credit cards: AE, DC, MC, V

If a word could embody a whole store luxury would be it for Asprey. Both the antique and modern pieces are of superb quality. Prices to match.

Bentley and Co., 65 New Bond Street, W1
Tel: (01) 629 0325
Open: Mon-Fri 10am-5pm
⊖ Green Park or Piccadilly Circus   Credit cards: AE, DC, MC, V

Antique jewelers and silversmiths specializing in old Russian jewelry and objects – enameled and encrusted with precious stones in the best traditions of Imperial Russia.

Butler and Wilson, 189 Fulham Road, SW3
Tel: (01) 352 3045
Open: Mon-Sat 10am-6pm
⊖ Gloucester Road   Credit cards: AE, MC, V

The best place for genuine and reproduction art deco and art nouveau pieces. They have a sparkling array of pins, brooches and bracelets, as well as attractive photograph frames and boxes. The staff are helpful and courteous.

Cartier, 175 New Bond Street, W1
Tel: (01) 493 6962
Open: Mon-Fri 9:30am-5:15pm, Sat 10am-3:45pm
⊖ Green Park or Piccadilly Circus   Credit cards: AE, DC, MC, V

Started in Paris during France's Second Empire, today Cartier is a worldwide institution and commands worldly prices for its well-made, brilliantly branded products. If emulation is the sincerest form of flattery Cartier's tank watch is probably the world's most illicitly copied luxury item. Indeed at times they've used real tanks to crush thousands of poorly made knock-offs. This British outpost has it all from stunning jewelry and timepieces through lighters, writing instruments, leathergoods, scarves and decidedly upmarket desk adornments. Staff are exceedingly knowledgeable, surroundings suitably deluxe.

Cobra and Bellamy, 149 Sloane Street, SW1
Tel: (01) 730 2823
Open: Mon-Sat 10:30am-6pm
⊖ Knightsbridge   Credit cards: AE, DC, MC, V

Specialists in costume jewelry, with most of the pieces dating from
the 1920s onward. Their eye-catching contemporary designs in
silver frequently feature in top fashion magazines. Don't miss this
one.

Collingwood, 46 Conduit Street, W1
Tel: (01) 734 2656
Open: Mon-Sat 10am-5pm, Sat until 4pm
⊖ Green Park or Oxford Circus   Credit cards: AE, DC, MC, V

Collingwood holds Royal Warrants from both the Queen Mother
and the Queen. Here you can choose from a magnificent selection
of antique and modern jewelry of traditional design.

Contemporary Applied Arts, 43 Earlham Street, WC2
Tel: (01) 836 6993
Open: Mon-Fri 10am-5pm, Sat 11am-5pm
⊖ Covent Garden   Credit cards: AE, MC, V

Unusual, experimental contemporary designs are the key feature
of their stock which includes furniture and other artefacts as well as
jewelry. Designs are in gold and silver plus the more original
acrylic, tin or wood. Prices range from modest to pricey.

Demas, 31 Burlington Arcade, W1
Tel: (01) 493 9496
Open: Mon-Sat 10:30am-4:45pm, Sat until 12:30pm
⊖ Green Park   Credit cards: MC,V

A treasure trove of Victorian and some Georgian jewelry. Good for
semi-expensive gifts – perhaps a garnet brooch or turquoise earrings, but remember to get certified receipts stating the age and
value of the piece or you could get clobbered in Customs.

Detail, 49 Endell Street, WC2
Tel: (01) 379 6940
Open: Mon-Sat 11am-7pm, Sat until 6pm
⊖ Covent Garden   Credit cards: AE, MC, V

A bright, cheerful shop where you'll find inexpensive (but not tatty)
fun costume jewelry. There are jolly little airplane brooches,
bangles in masses of colors, big hoop earrings and a great deal
more. If you're looking for a clever gift for a teenager, this is a good
bet.

Dibdin & Co. Ltd, 189 Sloane Street, SW1
Tel: (01) 235 7730
Open: Mon-Fri 9:30am-5pm
⊖ Sloane Square or Knightsbridge   Credit cards: AE, MC, V

First established by Mrs G.M. Dibdin in 1831, during the reign of
William IV, this illustrious firm of jewelers and silversmiths still
offers the customer a friendly service as well as an excellent
selection of antique and secondhand jewelry, silver and Old Sheffield plate.

Ebel Boutique, 179 New Bond Street, W1
Tel: (01) 408 0321
Open: Mon-Fri 9:30am-5:30pm, Sat 10am-4:30pm
⊖ Green Park or Piccadilly Circus   Credit cards: AE, DC, MC, V

The Swiss have long been regarded as the greatest watchmakers in
the world, and the Ebel sports watch is further proof of their
supremacy. A masterpiece of design and technology, it is a formid-
able acquisition – but then, the time is right . . .

Electrum Gallery, 21 South Molton Street, W1
Tel: (01) 629 6325
Open: Mon-Sat 10am-6pm, Sat until 1pm
⊖ Bond Street   Credit cards: AE, DC, MC, V

A well-known gallery which exhibits and sells the work of top
international, contemporary jewelry designers. Much of the jewelry is expensive, but you'll also find many samples of original work
at very affordable prices, some of them under £20. Commissions for
special pieces are also undertaken here. A must to visit.

Elizabeth Gage, 20 Albemarle Street, W1
Tel: (01) 499 2879
Open: Mon-Fri 10am-5:15pm
⊖ Green Park   Credit cards: AE, DC, MC, V

Elizabeth Gage combines precious stones, bright enamels and rare
artefacts with 18 karat gold, creating evocative and sensational
jewels, inspired by the ancient, yet perfectly contemporary. She
also designs especially for clients, and sells exclusively through her
Mayfair shop.

Garrard, 112 Regent Street, W1
Tel: (01) 734 7020
Open: Mon-Fri 9am-5:30pm, Sat 9:30am-5pm
⊖ Piccadilly Circus   Credit cards: AE, DC, MC, V

These are the Crown Jewelers. The company was founded in 1720
and has enjoyed royal custom ever since. There's an impressive

selection of antique and modern jewelry, plus antique silverware, cutlery, clocks, watches and other gifts.

The Golden Past, 6 Brook Street, W1
Tel: (01) 493 6422
Open: Mon-Fri 10am-5pm
⊖ Bond Street   Credit cards: AE, DC, MC, V

A friendly, old-fashioned shop crammed with all manner of trinkets and jewelry, ideal for easily affordable presents. There's an enchanting blend of antiques and modern pieces – Victorian lockets, earrings and snuff boxes: or gold watch chains ripe for a lorgnette.

Holmes Jewellers Ltd, 29 Old Bond Street, W1
Tel: (01) 493 1396
Open: Mon-Sat 9am-5:30pm, Sat until 1pm
⊖ Green Park or Piccadilly Circus   Credit cards: AE, DC, MC, V

This shop has a good selection of antique, secondhand and some modern jewelry and silverware. They also have a branch in Burlington Arcade which is open until 4:30pm on Saturdays.

Liberty, Regent Street, W1
Tel: (01) 734 1234
Open: Mon-Sat 9:30am-6pm, Thur until 8pm
⊖ Oxford Circus   Credit cards: AE, DC, MC, V

Liberty is an excellent source of antique jewelry as well as contemporary pieces. The majority of its antique stock is Victorian with quite a number of pieces in jet and cut steel. The modern jewelry is equally stunning with many ethnic chokers and beads.

Richard Ogden, 28 Burlington Arcade, W1
Tel: (01) 493 9136
Open: Mon-Sat 9:30am-5:15pm, Sat until 4pm
⊖ Green Park   Credit cards: DC, MC, V

A lovely little shop with a sparkling array of antique and secondhand jewelry. Much of their stock is Victorian, all of it of high quality. Their modern jewelry is all in very traditional designs.

S.J. Phillips Ltd, 139 New Bond Street, W1
Tel: (01) 629 6261
Open: Mon-Fri 10am-5pm
⊖ Green Park or Piccadilly Circus   Credit cards: AE, DC, MC, V

A highly regarded shop with a superb selection of antique jewelry (mainly Victorian but some older pieces too). They have an interesting collection of Victorian cut-steel jewelry, pretty silver pieces, porcelain, snuff boxes and scent bottles.

RESTAURANTS

Price Categories
Sterling sign indicates price level per person for a three course meal with a glass of house wine.

£	Under £12.50
£££	£12.50 – £18.00
£££	£18+

Bayswater & Kensington

The Ark, 122 Palace Gardens Terrace, W8 ££
Tel: (01) 229 4024   ⊖ Notting Hill Gate
Open: Daily noon-3pm, 6:30pm-11:15pm
Closed: Sunday lunch, Christmas & Easter
Credit cards: AE, MC, V

A relaxed, pine-paneled bistro-style eating house with extremely cozy seating arrangements and a slightly Bohemian air, the Ark has been going for years. It still provides good, solid French provincial-style dishes from a blackboard menu at eminently reasonable prices. Warming home-made soups, garlicky mushrooms, rack of lamb and braised kidneys are all popular. Note that you can even visit for Sunday dinner.

Julie's Bar, 137 Portland Road, W11 £
Tel: (01) 727 7985   ⊖ Holland Park
Open: Mon-Sat 11am-midnight, Sun noon-3pm, 7pm-10:30pm
Credit cards: AE, DC, MC, V   No credit cards in Wine Bar

A long-time local favorite, Julie's is both a wine bar and a restaurant. Downstairs the narrow, wood-paneled bar is a jovial spot with bare tables, old church pews and a supercilious feline or two making the best of limited space. Upstairs, a relaxed jumble of sofas and chairs group around tables overlooking a pretty garden. The bistro-style menu features a tasty selection of starters including home-made soups, prawns and mayonnaise with black bread; good rack of lamb or steak and kidney pie for main course; the ubiquitous cheesecake and some pleasant sorbets follow on.

Kalamaras, 76-78 Inverness Mews, W2 ££
Tel: (01) 727 9122   ⊖ Bayswater
Open: Mon-Sat 7pm-midnight only   Closed: Sun
Credit cards: AE, DC, MC, V

Popular, informal Greek restaurant with just the right atmosphere in which to enjoy genuine Greek cooking. Get a range of delicious tangy dips to start before moving on to succulent grilled lamb and crisp, flavorsome filo pastries. Great salads weighed down with black olives and feta cheese; order a bottle of Greek wine to accompany your meal.

Launceston Place Restaurant, 1A Launceston Place, W8   **££**
Tel: (01) 937 6912   ⊖ Gloucester Road
Open: Mon-Fri 12:30pm-3pm, 7:30pm-11pm; Sat 7:30pm-11pm,
    Sun noon-3pm   Closed: Sat lunch, Sun dinner
Credit cards: MC, V

Perched on the corner of one of Kensington's most attractive residential streets, this intimate restaurant is a real winner. The food is nouvelle cuisine at its best, beautifully cooked and artfully presented. This holds true from unusual starters, such as ravioli filled with wild mushrooms with tomato butter or goats cheese with fried quail eggs in an oakleaf salad with hazelnut dressing, to delectable main courses, such as fricassee of sole with langoustines. Given the quality on offer, their set prices lunches (£9.50) and dinners (£11.50) are more than reasonable. So is the eminently drinkable house wine at under £7 a bottle. Divided into two tiny rooms, the walls are full of lovely mirrors and fine water colors (we like the busty maiden just inside the door). Service is attentive, knowledgeable and friendly. Reserving ahead for dinner is essential.

Leiths, 92 Kensington Park Road, W11   **£££**
Tel: (01) 229 4481   ⊖ Notting Hill Gate
Open: Daily 7:30pm-11:30pm – dinner only
Closed: Over Christmas
Credit cards: AE, DC, MC, V

Entered via a side courtyard this attractive converted townhouse now serves some of the best food in town. Owned by well-known cookery expert Prue Leith, the menu reflects her personality – dishes are straightforward yet exquisitely turned out with emphasis on the best fresh ingredients (much of the produce is grown on her own farm). To complement such fine cuisine there's a well balanced wine list. The modern decor is as classic as the cooking. Service is prompt without being servile.

192 Kensington Park Road Wine Bar/Restaurant, W11   **£**
Tel: (01) 229 0482   ⊖ Notting Hill Gate or Ladbroke Grove
Open: Mon-Sat 12:30pm-2:30pm, 5:30pm-11pm; Sun 1pm-3:30pm
Credit cards: AE, MC, V

If 'My Beautiful Launderette' had been filmed in France 192's wall to ceiling art moderne exterior would be a suitable setting. As its name implies it's unpretentious both in terms of the food – outstanding charcuterie and salads, great boundin and roasted quail –

and the staff who are friendly, super casual in an 'I'm really an actress resting between rolls' sort-of-way. At ground floor level the wine bar dominates what could easily be a truly Parisian corner café. Downstairs the mood is candlelit, crowded, rather less jolly and service can be slow. This Notting Hill locale has recently become gentrified with several interesting print and antique shops in the neighbourhood as well as two outstanding specialized bookstores – the **Cook's Bookshop** at 4 Blenheim Crescent and the **Travel Bookshop** at 13 Blenheim Crescent.

Veronica's, 3 Hereford Road, W2   ££
Tel: (01) 221 1452   ⊖ Bayswater
Open: Mon-Fri noon-3pm, 7pm-midnight, Sat 7:30pm-midnight
Closed: Sat lunch, Sun, Dec 26-27
Credit cards: AE, DC, MC, V

'English cuisine' is a phrase likely to induce shrieks of mirth in gourmet circles, but a trip to Veronica's would swiftly sort out the sheep from the goats, the duck from the salmon. In a deliciously pretty, matchbox-sized restaurant, Veronica Shaw balances carefully-researched traditional recipes with her own innovative touches. The generous menu changes monthly and features a strong seasonal flavor. There are summer salads with flowers; warming winter Fisherman's Pie with sole, haddock, mussels and Dublin Bay prawns; five different vegetables materialize at your elbow on a sideplate. After a rare selection of tempting fruity desserts (mango mousse, rhubarb crumble, plus a notable chocolate mousse), or a Best-of-British canter round the cheeseboard, you can wind off the evening with an elegant glass of *Beaume de Venise*.

Chelsea & Victoria

Ciboure, 21 Eccleston Street, SW1   £££
Tel: (01) 730 2505   ⊖ Victoria
Open: Mon-Sat noon-2:30pm, 7pm-11:15pm
Closed: Sat lunch, Sun, 2 wks Aug
Credit cards: AE, DC, MC, V

Small, attractively decorated restaurant serving classic French-style cuisine from a selection of imaginative dishes. The meals are prepared with care and well presented. Try a courgette and carrot soup or herby noisettes of lamb, for example. The dessert course is worth waiting for.

Como Lario, 22 Holbein Place, SW1   **££**
Tel: (01) 730 2954   ⊖ Sloane Square
Open: Mon-Sat 12:30pm-2:30pm, 6:30pm-11:30pm   Closed: Sun
No credit cards

A lively trattoria that attracts a number of faithful, regular customers. Excellent pasta dishes and favorite Italian specialties such as *piccata alla marsala* feature on the menu. They do a delicious *zabaglione* for dessert too. Standards are high; you'll find the service cheerful and attentive.

Ebury Wine Bar, 139 Ebury Street, SW1   **£**
Tel: (01) 730 5447   ⊖ Victoria
Open: Mon-Sat noon-2:45pm, 6pm-10:30pm, Sun noon-2:30pm,
   6pm-10pm
Credit cards: AE, DC, MC, V

A pleasant, popular wine bar that serves an extensive range of excellent bistro-type dishes. Soups, terrines, quiches; fresh salads and good value hot dishes are well presented and tasty. The daily dishes are reasonable as is the traditional Sunday lunch with roast beef, Yorkshire pudding and at least two vegetables. There is a small minimum charge.

Gran Paradiso, 52 Wilton Road, SW1   **££**
Tel: (01) 828 5818   ⊖ Victoria
Open: Mon-Fri noon-2:15pm, 6pm-11:15pm, Sat 6pm-11pm
Closed: Sat lunch, Sun, last 2 wks Aug
Credit cards: AE, DC, MC, V

This cheerful Italian restaurant could best be described as haphazard – boars's heads and deer antlers, old clocks, genuinely dreadful oil paintings and ceiling fans plus greenery galore. This is not your average tony trat. But the surroundings, as well as the staff, give you a cheery sense of anticipation. This is entirely justified for the food is first rate. Their *funghi di pratto fritto* (large mushrooms that are deep-fried) is a great starter. Their quail sublime, their *nodino di vitello* (a veal chop grilled with herbs) scrumptious. The Italian house red at under £5 is eminently drinkable. Close to Victoria station, so convenient if you're in the neighborhood to take in a show.

La Famiglia, 7 Langton Street, SW10   **££**
Tel: (01) 351 0761   ⊖ Sloane Square (a longish walk)
Open: Daily 12:30pm-2:45pm, 7pm-11:45pm
Credit cards: AE, DC, MC, V

Casual, pretty restaurant that's always busy; queues form at the bar in the evening. You must book ahead (English for reserve) to be sure of a table – try and get one on the patio in summer. The menu offers plenty of choice, fresh pasta, good salads and soups, plus a variety of more sophisticated dishes and Italian wines.

La Tante Claire, 68-69 Royal Hospital Road, SW3   **£££**
Tel: (01) 352 6045   ⊖ Sloane Square
Open: Mon-Fri 12:30pm-2pm, 7pm-11pm Closed: Sat-Sun, over
    Easter & Christmas, 3 wks Aug-Sept
Credit cards: AE, DC, MC, V

This highly-acclaimed restaurant serves immaculate French cuisine amidst delightfully elegant, spacious surroundings. The light, imaginative menu rates with the best in London – creative, assured and blissfully free of fussy conceits. Needless to say, the service is equally refined and unpretentious creating a stylish, sophisticated but relaxed atmosphere which has proven hugely popular. Reserve ahead.

Tate Gallery Restaurant, Millbank, SW1   **£**
Tel: (01) 834 6754   ⊖ Pimlico
Open: Mon-Sat noon-3pm   Closed: Sun
No credit cards

The perfect stop-off if you've been gallery-viewing, this basement restaurant serves good English food and a selection of English cheeses. The Rex Whistler mural which decorates the restaurant makes an appropriately artistic setting for lunch. Good wine list.

Villa Estense, 642 King's Road, SW6   **£**
Tel: (01) 731 4247   ⊖ Sloane Square
Open: Daily 12:30pm-2:30pm, 7pm-11:30pm, Sat-Sun until 3pm
Closed: Sun dinner
Credit cards: AE, MC, V

Popular, inexpensive, friendly and (surprise, surprise) Italian – an old favorite with the Chelsea Set. Here you'll choose from a terrific variety of different pastas and pizza; salads and meat dishes also feature on the menu. Afterwards, you may like to toy with an iced dessert.

City

Blooms, 90 Whitechapel High Street, E1   **£**
Tel: (01) 247 6001   ⊖ Aldgate East
Open: Sun-Fri 11:30am-9:30pm, Fri until 3pm
Closed: Sat, Jewish holidays
Credit cards: MC, V

London's best known kosher restaurant, with a sister establishment at 130 Golders Green Road, NW1 (tel: (01) 455 3033). Between the two, business has been going on for over fifty years and little has changed. The menu offers classic favorites from chopped liver to tasty gefilte fish, traditional salt beef and wonderful latkes (grated potato cakes). If you've spent a morning battling your way through the crowds at Petticoat Lane Market, this is just the place to revive your flagging sense of humor with a large slice of kosher wise-cracking from the incorrigible staff.

North London

Fredericks, Camden Passage, N1   **£££**
Tel: (01) 359 2888   ► Angel
Open: Mon-Sat noon-2:30pm, 7pm-11:30pm
Closed: Sun, over Christmas
Credit cards: AE, DC, MC, V

A little off the beaten track, but an ideal place to take a break from exploring the many antique shops which fill the street. Good French cooking in light and airy surroundings – on a sunny day you'll be able to relax in the delightful conservatory or wall garden.

South Kensington & Knightsbridge

L'Artiste Affamé, 243 Old Brompton Road, SW5   **££**
Tel: (01) 373 1659   ► Earls Court
Open: Mon-Sat 12:30pm-2:30pm, 6:30pm-11:15pm   Closed: Sun
Credit cards: AE, DC, MC, V

A bustling popular French restaurant with a tiny terrace and an interesting menu incorporating several daily specials. The *Carré d'Agneau* is a house specialty; good cheeses and a tempting array of desserts.

Chanterelle, 119 Old Brompton Road, SW7   **£**
Tel: (01) 373 5522   ► South Kensington
Open: Daily noon-2:30pm, 7pm-11:30pm
Credit cards: AE, DC, MC, V

A pleasant and attractive Anglo-French restaurant. The fixed price menu changes daily and presents a good choice of well-cooked dishes. Chanterelle is a particularly useful stop-off for lunch when the menu offers excellent value for money.

Luba's Bistro, 6 Yeoman's Row, SW3   **£**
Tel: (01) 589 2950   ► South Kensington
Open: Mon-Sat 6pm-midnight only   Closed: Sun
Credit cards: AE, MC

A small, cheery and long-established Russian restaurant without a license, so take your own wine and be prepared to share one of the long tables with other diners. Traditional Eastern European-style food is the order of the day; generous portions, lots of dumplings and favorite starters include a wonderful borscht and excellent piroshki. Very popular so get here early.

Motcomb Street Wine Bar and Restaurant, 26 Motcombe Street, London SW1   £
Tel: (01) 235 6382   ⊖ Knightsbridge
Open: Mon-Sat noon-3pm, 5:30pm-11pm
Credit cards: AE, DC, MC, V

It's appropriate that this friendly wine bar should be named after the street where it nestles. Both are intimate, largely unknown – even to Londoners – and well worth exploring.

The downstairs restaurant's pleasant enough but it's the upstairs wine bar at lunch that really rates the raves – seafood salads, such as shellfish and pasta, are scrumptious. So are their regular luncheon specials (if it's Tuesday it must be stir fried chicken and rice). On any given day there are over fifteen main dishes to choose from plus excellent starters. The wine list is well balanced with many vintages available by the generous glass. The decor is eclectic; boaters and ancient tennis racquets over the bar, oil paintings of rabbits, an elegant thirties gent with his dog and so on. As befits a well kept secret the Knightsbridge clientele all seem to know one another and banter with the friendly staff.

Noojahan, 2A Bina Gardens, SW5   £
Tel: (01) 373 6522   ⊖ Gloucester Road
Open: Mon-Sat noon-2:45pm, 6pm-11:45pm, Sun noon-2:30pm, 6pm-11:30pm
Credit cards: AE, DC, MC, V

A well-established, friendly Indian restaurant. The menu includes delicious tandoori dishes and a wide range of curries in varying strengths. The waiters are helpful and provide attentive service.

Poissonerie de l'Avenue, 82 Sloane Avenue, SW3   ££
Tel: (01) 589 2457   ⊖ South Kensington
Open: Mon-Sat noon-3pm, 7pm-11:45pm   Closed: Sun
Credit cards: AE, DC, MC, V

Jolly French seafood restaurant with seascapes decorating the walls to add a nautical air. Shellfish and a variety of other seafood are well prepared and served with typical Gallic aplomb in a pleasantly relaxed atmosphere.

Salloos, 62 Kinnerton Street, SW1   £££
Tel: (01) 235 4444   ⊖ Knightsbridge
Open: Mon-Sat noon-2:30pm, 7pm-11:30pm   Closed: Sun
Credit cards: AE, DC, MC, V

An elegant, well-established Pakistani restaurant. Specialties include diced chicken with ginger and traditional tandoori dishes as well as curries and kebabs. The surroundings are smart and comfortable, the service is courteous.

San Frediano, 62 Fulham Road, SW3   £££
Tel: (01) 584 8375   ⊖ South Kensington
Open: Mon-Sat 12:30pm-2:30pm, 7:15pm-11:15pm   Closed: Sun
Credit cards: DC, MC, V

Try to reserve ahead if you plan to pay a visit to this popular Italian restaurant. There is a good choice of dishes, including pasta, plenty of seafood and fresh salads. Also daily specials which come highly recommended. The friendly, informal atmosphere ensures a devoted clientele. Children are welcomed rather than tolerated.

West End

Ajimura, 51-53 Shelton Street, W1   ££
Tel: (01) 240 0178   ⊖ Covent Garden
Open: Daily noon-3pm, 6pm-11pm, Sun until 10:30pm
Closed: Sat and Sun lunch
Credit cards: AE, DC, MC, V

Japanese restaurants in London can be very expensive. This is an exception. The restaurant is unpretentious, the service efficient and, most important, the food excellent. There's a mesmerical sushi bar for light snacks or settle down at the plain wooden tables for a first-rate meal.

Au Jardin des Gourmets, 5 Greek Street, W1   £££
Tel: (01) 437 1816   ⊖ Leicester Square
Open: Mon-Sat 12:15pm-2:30pm, 6:30pm-11:30pm
Closed: Sun, over Easter
Credit cards: AE, DC, MC, V

A perennial favorite with many, this restaurant specializes in French cuisine. The menu includes classics such as onion soup and *sole meunière* but there are also slightly unusual dishes for those who prefer food that's a bit different. Good cooking, friendly service and a pleasant ambience.

Aunties, 126 Cleveland Street, W1   ££
Tel: (01) 387 3226   ⊖ Goodge Street
Open: Mon-Sat noon-2:45pm, 6pm-10:45pm
Closed: Sat lunch, Christmas, 2 wks Aug
Credit cards: AE, DC, MC, V

Intimate English restaurant which offers an interesting menu of carefully prepared old-fashioned British dishes. You'll need to work up quite an appetite before tackling the generous portions –

magnificent roasts, seasonal specials and the pastry on savory pies melts in your mouth. For dessert you can sample a fine rendering of that nursery stalwart bread and butter pudding (a firm favorite with Prince Charles).

Bentleys, 11-15 Swallow Street, W1   ££token£
Tel: (01) 734 4756   ⊖ Piccadilly
Open: Mon-Sat noon-3pm, 6pm-11pm   Closed: Sun
Credit cards: AE, DC, MC, V

There's a club-like atmosphere about this very traditional seafood restaurant. Renowned for oysters but also a good choice of other well-cooked dishes, from simple grilled fish or perfect fish cakes to richly sauced specialties. The service is attentive.

Boulestin, 1A Henrietta Street, WC2   £££
Tel: (01) 836 7061   ⊖ Covent Garden
Open: Mon-Sat 12:30pm-2:30pm, 7:30pm-11:15pm
Closed: Sat lunch, Sun, over Christmas, Aug
Credit cards: AE, DC, MC, V

You'll have to reserve ahead for this well-known (and pricey) London restaurant situated right in the center of Covent Garden. Chef Kevin Kennedy is renowned for his high standards as you'll discover. The cooking is French-style and the combinations of ingredients imaginative, creating an inspired menu. The cheese-board is excellent; the desserts are similarly well-chosen and tempting. Service is polite and efficient.

Chez Solange, 35 Cranbourn Street, WC2   ££
Tel: (01) 836 5886   ⊖ Leicester Square
Open: Mon-Sat noon-2:30pm, 6pm-11pm   Closed: Sun
Credit cards: AE, DC, MC, V

A busy restaurant on two levels; long-established, filled with atmosphere and popular with theater-goers. Good French-provincial style dishes are full of flavor, and you can follow a robust main course with one of the simple desserts.

Chicago Pizza Pie Factory, 17 Hanover Square, W1   £
Tel: (01) 629 2669   ⊖ Oxford Circus
Open: Daily 11:45am-11:30pm, Sun until 10:30pm
No credit cards

Those wonderful deep dish pizzas are the specialty, always freshly cooked to order. Stuffed mushrooms, garlic bread and crunchy salads also feature on the menu. It does get very busy so you may have to queue for a table.

Connaught Hotel Restaurant, Carlos Place, W1   **£££**
Tel: (01) 499 7070   ⊖ Bond Street
Open: Daily 12:30pm-2:30pm, 6:30pm-10:15pm
Credit cards: MC

You can expect to dine in grand style at this mahogany-paneled restaurant. The menu is French, with traditional British specialties served at lunchtime. Remember to save room for the splendid desserts. The service is formal, the setting is spacious and very traditional.

Cranks, 8 Marshall Street, W1   **£**
Tel: (01) 437 9431   ⊖ Oxford Circus
Open: Daily for snacks 8am-7pm, dinner 6:30pm-11pm
Credit cards: AE, DC, MC, V

A well-known health food restaurant (part of a small chain) that serves tasty, wholesome fare. The emphasis is 'wholemeal' and 'healthy' providing a choice of salads, imaginative hot and cold vegetarian dishes and wholefood snacks. This is a self-service restaurant although you can wine and dine by candlelight in the evenings. It's also ideal for a satisfying light lunch.

Efes Kebab House, 80 Great Titchfield Street, W1   **£**
Tel: (01) 836 1953   ⊖ Oxford Street
Open: Mon-Sat noon-11:30pm   Closed: Sun
Credit cards: AE, MC, V

Book ahead, and once seated you'll be able to watch your kebabs being cooked on the charcoal grill. There are almost 20 different varieties to choose from. Other house specialties include succulent spit-roasted lamb and chicken with a tangy walnut sauce plus a variety of tempting Turkish vegetable dishes. Finish off with strong Turkish coffee.

Food for Thought, 31 Neal Street, WC2   **£**
Tel: (01) 836 0239   ⊖ Covent Garden
Open: Mon-Fri noon-8pm   Closed: Sat-Sun
No credit cards

This simply decorated wholefood and vegetarian restaurant in Covent Garden gets very busy at lunchtime. They serve excellent, and often unusual, salads, quiches and a couple of wholesome hot dishes of the day. A good place for an inexpensive, tasty lunch.

Fountain Restaurant, Fortnum and Mason, 181 Piccadilly, W1   **£**
Tel: (01) 836 0239   ⊖ Piccadilly Circus
Open: Mon-Sat 9:30am-11:15pm   Closed: Sun
Credit cards: AE, DC, MC, V

Deliciously refined tearoom/restaurant on the mezzanine level of London's famous Fortnum and Mason store. Lunch, tea and light evening meals are all available with a choice of good salads, sandwiches, grills and savory *vol-au-vents*. You could indulge in an ice cream soda from a vast range of flavors, or sample cakes and pastries which are out of this world. Charming old-fashioned service, and a good opportunity to explore the fabulous food hall renowned for its picnic hampers which are still a regular feature at British sporting events. Street entrace from Jermyn Street.

Fung Shing, 15 Lisle Street, WC2   ££
Tel: (01) 437 1539   ⊖ Leicester Square
Open: Daily noon-11:45pm
Credit cards: AE, DC, MC, V

Situated in the heart of London's Chinatown, you'll find this attractive restaurant is a good place in which to sample authentic Cantonese cooking. There's an extensive menu offering favorite dishes as well as unusual ones – the won ton soup is a masterpiece.

Le Gavroche, 43 Upper Brook Street, W1   £££
Tel: (01) 408 0881   ⊖ Marble Arch
Open: Mon-Fri noon-2pm, 7pm-11pm
Closed: Sat, Sun, over Christmas
Credit cards: AE, DC, MC, V

Owned by the famous Roux brothers, this handsome, yet comfortable, restaurant sets high standards of cuisine in the French style. The talented chef (Steven Doherty) presents inspired combinations of fresh ingredients with complementary sauces and the desserts are perfect. The service is all that it should be at such a fine restaurant. Reserve ahead if you want to experience this gastronomic celebration.

Gay Hussar, 2 Greek Street, W1   £££
Tel: (01) 437 0973   ⊖ Leicester Square
Open: Mon-Sat 12:30pm-2pm, 5:30pm-10:30pm   Closed: Sun
No credit cards

An institution, if not a legend, this small friendly Hungarian restaurant has tremendous warmth and character. The food is rich, full of flavor and generously distributed. Classic dishes include goulash and stuffed cabbage. You'll find a good selection of Hungarian wines to complement the menu.

Hard Rock Cafe, 150 Old Park Lane, W1　　　　　£
Tel: (01) 629 0382　　⊖ Hyde Park Corner
Open: Daily noon-12:30am, Fri and Sat until 1am
No credit cards

To the young at heart the Hard Rock is as important a London landmark as Nelson's column and Madame Tussaud's. So, beware there can be queues even between main meal times. However, turnover is fast, so you won't wait long. Loud music, walls papered with rock memorabilia and good fast food with plenty of American-style burgers, ribs and huge sandwiches. Select your own salad from the salad bar.

Inigo Jones, 14 Garrick Street, WC2　　　　　£££
Tel: (01) 836 6456/3223　　⊖ Leicester Square
Open: Mon-Sat noon-2:30pm, 5:30pm-11:30pm
Closed: Sat lunch, Sun
Credit cards: AE, DC, MC, V

Right in the heart of Covent Garden this restaurant, run by Paul Gayler, will delight the gourmet visitor. The menu offers imaginative dishes that exercise flair in their creation as well as in the presentation. The fine food is perfectly complemented by the excellent service. There are set menus for both lunch and dinner and the house wine is good value for money.

Joe Allen, 13 Exeter Street, WC2　　　　　£
Tel: (01) 838 0651　　⊖ Covent Garden
Open: Daily noon-1am, Sun to midnight only
No credit cards

If you're feeling homesick for good old-fashioned American food, Joe Allen's can help. Burgers, ribs, chilli and great salads are all served in this bustling, friendly restaurant. It is very popular, so you're well advised to reserve in advance. A good place for a late-night, after theater meal.

Justin de Blank, 54 Duke Street, W1　　　　　£
Tel: (01) 629 3174　　⊖ Piccadilly Circus
Open: Mon-Sat 8:30am-3:30pm, 4:30pm-9pm
Closed: Sat dinner, Sun
Credit cards: MC, V

You'll probably spot a few of Justin de Blank's delivery vans beetling around between smart, central London addresses carrying a delicious cargo of freshly baked bread, pies and flans. To prove that it can be done, he has opened a number of good value cafés serving crisp, fresh salads, good pâtés, tempting hot dishes, fresh bread and the aforementioned pies (from their own bakery). Good for lunch or an early evening supper, while the shops offer a wonderful selection of picnic food, ideas for quick meals plus delicatessen items.

Langan's Brasserie, Stratton Street, W1   **£££**
Tel: (01) 493 6437   ⊖ Green Park
Open: Mon-Sat 12:30pm-2:45pm, 7pm-11:45pm, Sat 8pm-12:45pm
Closed: Sat lunch, Sun
Credit cards: AE, DC, MC, V

This ever-fashionable brasserie which numbers Michael Caine amongst its owners is always busy, so it's imperative you reserve ahead if you want to be sure of a table. The food is good and the menu offers plenty of variety, ranging from perfectly executed, simple cuisine to complicated specialties *en croûte* dressed with fine sauces. A wide selection of desserts plus a fine cheeseboard ensures a high standard is maintained throughout the meal. A place to watch and be watched with a liberal smattering of recognizable faces to entertain you if the service is stretched by sheer numbers.

Martin's Restaurant, 239 Baker Street, NW1   **££**
Tel: (01) 935 3130   ⊖ Baker Street
Open: Mon-Fri noon-3pm, 6pm-11pm, Sat 7pm-11pm
      Sun 12:30pm, 7pm-10:30pm
Credit cards: AE, DC, MC, V

Located at the very top of Baker Street, this relatively new restaurant has already won a coveted Restaurant of the Year award. One enters through a small, rather austere, modern bar and beyond there is the medium-sized dining room with its peach colored walls and two chandeliers nestling in the vaulted skylight. The food is as understated and tasteful as the surroundings. We particularly recommend the Wild Duck and Lamb Navarin. The wine list is excellent with some reasonable half bottles. Service is prompt and pleasant.

Neal Street Restaurant, 26 Neal Street, WC2   **£££**
Tel: (01) 836 8368   ⊖ Covent Garden
Open: Mon-Fri 12:30pm-2:30pm, 7:30pm-11pm
Closed: Sat-Sun, Christmas period
Credit cards: AE, DC, MC, V

Owned and managed by Antonio Carluccio, this smart, modern restaurant in Covent Garden is both chic and popular. There's a distinctly Italian influence pervading the menu with dishes that include a hearty *bollito misto* and various pasta specialties. You'll have to book ahead to sample the delights of this imaginative cuisine and the attentive service.

Il Passetto, 230 Shaftesbury Avenue, WC2   **££**
Tel: (01) 836 9391   ⊖ Piccadilly Circus
Open: Mon-Sat noon-3pm, 6pm-11:30pm   Closed: Sat lunch, Sun
Credit cards: AE, DC, MC, V

A friendly trattoria with a jolly atmosphere and a reliable standard of cooking. Good pasta and familiar Italian-style main dishes (especially veal) are well prepared. It's a good place for a pre-theater meal. Children are welcome.

Pizza Express, 30 Coptic Street, WC1   **£**
Tel: (01) 636 3232   ⊖ Tottenham Court Road
Open: Daily noon-midnight
Credit cards: AE, DC, MC, V

One of a chain of cheap, reliable, no-fuss pizzerias found all over London, Pizza Express offers a simple menu with a few salads, crunchy potato skins with sour cream and a range of pizza toppings. There are sometimes special lunchtime offers worth sampling and it's a good place to bring children. Generally, the restaurants are busy, bright and provide a reliable standard – if you want to play havoc with your digestion the branch in Gloucester Road has a disco in the basement. Other central branches include 10 Dean Street, W1; 15 Gloucester Road, SW7; 154 Victoria Street, SW1; 11 Knightsbridge, Hyde Park Corner, SW1. Dean Street and Knightsbridge restaurants have live jazz during the evenings (see **Local Delights**).

Poons, 4 Leicester Street, WC2   **£**
Tel: (01) 437 1528   ⊖ Leicester Square
Open: Mon-Sat noon-11:30pm   Closed: Sun
No credit cards

At Poons in Leicester Street you'll enjoy Cantonese cooking at its best for a very small financial investment. The menu is extensive; one of the house specialties is wind-dried foods (duck and sausage). These are combined with other ingredients or served on an individual platter – look for them on the menu, they're worth trying. Also, the stuffed crab's claws. The restaurant is very busy so do reserve ahead for the evening. (You may well have to wait for your table, even if you've reserved.) There are two other Poons restaurants nearby; one, sophisticated (and expensive), at 41 King Street, WC2; the other just around the corner from Leicester Street (turning right into Lisle Street) with tiny, oil-cloth covered tables, which attracts many of the local Chinese community.

Rules, 35 Maiden Lane, WC2 £££
Tel: (01) 836 5314 ☉ Covent Garden
Open: Mon-Fri 12:15pm-2:30pm, 6pm-11:30pm, Sat 6:15pm-
  10:45pm   Closed: Sat lunch, Sun
Credit cards: AE, DC, MC, V

A traditional, English restaurant that has been known to slay the
hunger pangs of such famous figures as Dickens, H.G. Wells, the
Prince of Wales (later Edward VII) and Lillie Langtry. Both the
atmosphere and the food is very British so come prepared to tuck
into hearty roasts, game in season and inexcusably calorific old
favorites like treacle tart and fruit crumble with lashings of double
cream.

Saigon, 45 Frith Street, W1 ££
Tel: (01) 437 7109 ☉ Tottenham Court Road
Open: Mon-Sat noon-11:30pm   Closed: Sun
Credit cards: AE, DC, MC, V

If you're looking for a slightly different culinary experience, this is
where you'll find excellent Vietnamese food served in pleasant
surroundings. Dishes are spiced and herby, unusual and delicious –
try the barbequed beef.

Wheelers, 19 Old Compton Street, W1 £££
Tel: (01) 437 2706 ☉ Leicester Square
Open: Mon-Sat 12:30pm-2:30pm, 6pm-10:45pm   Closed: Sun
Credit cards: AE, DC, MC, V

Originally founded by an oyster wholesaler, this famous seafood
restaurant continues to serve first class oysters as well as other fish
dishes. For a real treat sample the Dover sole. An old-fashioned
ambience and excellent service combine to create a reassuring
atmosphere. Other Wheelers Restaurants at 12A Duke of York
Street, W1 (tel: (01) 930 2460) and 33C King's Road, SW3 (tel: (01)
730 3023).

Wiltons, 55 Jermyn Street, SW1 £££
Tel: (01) 629 9955 ☉ Piccadilly Circus
Open: Mon-Sat 12:30pm-2:30pm, 6:30pm-10:30pm
Closed: Sat lunch, Sun, 3 wks Jul-Aug
Credit cards: AE, DC, MC, V

Wiltons offers traditional English atmosphere with very good English food. The restaurant is famous for its oysters – served plain, or
steamed to perfection. Excellent fish and game dishes (when in
season) along with a selection of favorite desserts and tasty savories
complete the menu.

TEAS AND SNACKS

Harrods Georgian Restaurant and Terrace, Knightsbridge, SW1
Tel: (01) 730 1234 ⊖ Knightsbridge
Open: Mon-Sat 3:45pm-5:30pm (restaurant), 3:30pm-5:30pm
(tearooms) Closed: Sun
Credit cards: AE, DC, MC, V

You can make the Harrods' set tea your main meal of the day, so take a frugal lunch or you'll never have room for this culinary treat. The chances are you won't be eating a vast dinner later either. It's the perfect place to refuel if your morning's shopping trip extended through lunch, starting off with a magnificent array of sandwiches from dainty cucumber to fishy pastes and strawberry jam (not mixed). This is followed by an irresistible selection of cream cakes and pastries. A very popular haunt with tea lovers, so do get here early.

Louis Patisserie, 32 Heath Street, Hampstead, NW3
Tel: (01) 435 9908 ⊖ Hampstead
Open: Daily 9:30am-6pm
No credit cards

Slightly out of the way, but worthy of a visit if your plans bring you up to Hampstead. Tea or coffee are served with a variety of confections from fine French-style fruit tarts to perfect macaroons; plus cakes and buns served with lashings of whipped cream topped with chopped nuts.

Methuselah's, 29 Victoria Street, SW1
Tel: (01) 222 3550 ⊖ Victoria
Open: Mon-Fri 9am-11pm Wine Bar: 11am-3pm, 5:30pm-11pm
Closed: Sat-Sun
Credit cards: AE, DC, MC, V

Conveniently situated just up the road from Westminster Abbey, Methuselah's offers a choice of refreshments. For a snack or light meal you can select coffee and croissants, soup and sandwiches or tea and cakes upstairs. If you feel a full recovery necessitates something a little stronger then downstairs you'll find the wine bar selling wine by the glass or bottle plus a range of savory cold platters, quiche and cheese. No children.

Muffin Man, 12 Wrights Lane, W8
Tel: (01) 937 6652 ⊖ High Street Kensington
Open: Mon-Sat 8:15am-5:45pm Closed: Sun
No credit cards

Traditionally the muffin man roamed the streets of London selling hot, fresh, yeasty muffins on cold winter afternoons. If you're roaming Kensington High Street, take note. The selection of snacks and light meals on sale here is more varied – home-made soup if the weather is cool, fresh salads and an interesting selection of sandwiches. To accompany tea or coffee breaks there's a range of biscuits, cakes or buttered scones.

Patisserie Valerie, 44 Old Compton Street, W1
Tel: (01) 437 3466　 ⊖ Leicester Square
Open: Mon-Sat 8:30am-7pm　 Closed: Sun
No credit cards

A well-established popular patisserie that seduces the passer-by with a luscious window full of cream-filled cakes, rich rum babas and delicate florentine biscuits all baked on the premises. If you're making the most of your holiday abandon yourself to the dictates of your heart (or stomach) and indulge.

Pirroni's, 116 Tottenham Court Road, W1
Tel: (01) 387 6324　 ⊖ Tottenham Court Road
Open: Mon-Sat 8am-10pm　 Closed: Sun
Credit cards: AE, DC, MC, V

From breakfast to dinner, from a bowl of soup to a tempting pasta supper – the menu provides anything from snacks to a substantial meal and pastries to fill in the gaps. The atmosphere is friendly, very Italian and it's a good place to bring the children.

Richoux, 86 Brompton road, SW3
Tel: (01) 584 8300　 ⊖ Knightsbridge
Open: Daily 9am-7pm, Wed until 8pm, Sun 10am-7pm
Credit cards: AE, MC, V

One of a chain of coffee houses, Richoux serves sandwiches and snacks throughout the day, salads and hot dishes for lunch and from early evening onwards. At teatime you'll be tempted by fresh cream teas or an array of cakes and pastries. The setting is restful, stylish with waitresses in pretty floral frocks and mob caps. Good for relaxing after a long session in the museums or shopping. Also at 172 Piccadilly, W1, and 41a South Audley Street, W1 (open: daily 8:30am-11:30pm, Sat 9am-midnight, Sun 10am-11:30pm).

The Ritz, Piccadilly, W1
Tel: (01) 493 8181　 ⊖ Green Park
Open: Tea served daily 3:30pm-5:30pm
Credit cards: AE, DC, MC, V

For a profoundly British experience tea at The Ritz is hard to beat.

Ensconced in the elegant salon, lit by splendid chandeliers, the ritual unfolds with effortless precision. Pots of tea accompanied by milk and transparent slivers of lemon. Sandwiches, wafer thin and freshly prepared. A myriad of scones, cakes and pastries. Remember, you're not allowed to indulge in the sweet specialties until all the sandwiches are eaten. You'll have to reserve a table beforehand. Dress for the occasion.

The Savoy, The Strand, WC2
Tel: (01) 836 4343   ⊖ Charing Cross
Open: Daily 9am-11pm
Credit cards: AE, DC, MC, V

Another perfect place to partake in the traditional British pursuit of afternoon tea. Revive flagging energy with a few delicate sips of smoky lapsang or Earl Grey tea. Nibble on a sandwich or a delicious crumbly pastry served with impeccable style by a flock of attentive waiters. Enjoy the magnificent surroundings and listen to the pianist tinkling away in the background. Light meals and snacks are available throughout the day.

Slenders, 41 Cathedral Place, Paternoster Square, EC4
Tel: (01) 236 5974   ⊖ St Paul's
Open: Mon-Fri 7:30am-6:15pm   Closed: Sat-Sun
No credit cards

Right by St Paul's Cathedral, this conveniently situated establishment is ideal for a light lunch or snack. If you intend to start early on your busy itinerary breakfast here is delicious. Slenders serves delicious vegetarian food, salads and a good choice of filled rolls. Imaginative cakes, plus a selection of fruit teas or herbal drinks are also on offer.

Victoria and Albert Museum Restaurant, Cromwell Road, SW7
Tel: (01) 581 2159   ⊖ South Kensington
Open: Mon-Sat 10am-5pm, Sun 2:30pm-5:30pm
No credit cards

A new restaurant that makes a useful addition to the museum. Croissants and cakes are served in the morning and at teatime; the lunch menu includes a variety of light snacks and sandwiches, good salads or hot dishes. The food is good, the ambience pleasant, the establishment a welcome addition to the scene given its convenient location.

DELIGHTFUL DRINKING – PUBS

The pub is a hallowed British institution. Here are a few tips to make your drinking more enjoyable.

1. Serving is by strict order. So wait your turn in patience.
2. Tipping at the bar is absolutely out. You can tip 10% to 15% if waited on at table.
3. Ice, soda and water are normally found on the bar. You serve yourself. If no ice is there, ask when you order.
4. British measures are smaller than a North American or European shot (at 1/6th of a gill about 16% less) so if you like your poison strong best ask for a double.
5. Ask for a martini and guess what? That's what you'll get – straight Martini vermouth. Rule of Thumb – pubs are for straightforward drinking so avoid fancy or complex drinks on two grounds:
   a. They probably don't know how to make them – though they'll try and you'll suffer.
   b. You'll disrupt the whole place.

Thankfully, pub hours have been extended so some are now open all afternoon. This is at the landlord's option. In high traffic downtown areas you should easily find an open pub while most country pubs remain closed in the afternoon. Pubs generally open at 11:30am and can now keep their doors open until 11:00pm, Monday through Saturday. Sundays are a different story with hours from noon until 3pm and 7pm until 10:30pm.

Measures
Draught beer comes in two measures: ½ pint (about ¼ of a liter) and pint (about ½ a liter.)

All Sorts of Beer
Bitter – The most common British drink (it takes three to grow on you) is clear yellowish-brown beer with the hops rampant. There are three varieties: Ordinary – most commonly drunk; Special or Best – as the cloudiness goes away the price goes up; and Keg – which is, unlike the others, under pressure. Lamentably, Ordinary – which is hand drawn from those handsome brass pulls you'll note, is on the way out.

Even more lamentably, the aluminum barrel is rapidly taking over from the old wooden kegs, with a corresponding loss in taste.
Lager – This is the light Continental type beer served cold. It comes in over twenty varieties (Harp being notably good) and depending on pub and brand comes from the keg or bottle.
Ale (Also called **'A Mild'**) – Reddish-brown in color, it's weaker than Bitter and sweeter.

Export Ale – Like the above but bottled and stronger.

Guinness – A unique chocolate-brown malt drink. This stout has a head of glowing creamy foam that holds up, down to the last sip. Matter of fact, you can carve your initials in the foam and still find it there when you've bottomed up. Handy in a crowd! But enough of talking about drink – as the British would say, 'get on with it'. It's the only way to learn – and fun to boot.

CENTRAL LONDON

Bayswater and Kensington

Scarsdale Arms, 23 Edwardes Square, W8
⊖ High Street Kensington

This popular pub lies at the corner of an elegant, leafy 19th-century square off Kensington High Street. The attractive, old-fashioned interior has bare boards on the floor and a central bar, while outside there's a terrace, with wooden tables and benches decorated with flowers in summer. The pub can get very busy in the evenings. Good bar food available throughout the week except Sunday.

Swan, 66 Bayswater Road, W2
⊖ Queensgate

The main attraction of this pub is the terrace which looks out across the busy Bayswater Road to the welcome greenery of Kensington Gardens. The bar food includes salads, sausages, home-made casseroles and pies.

Victoria, 10 Strathearn Place, W2
⊖ Lancaster Gate

Down a small street off the Bayswater Road, this is a great place for a drink or a snack. Decorated in Dickensian style, there are prints on the walls, cozy seating alcoves and a replica of The Old Curiosity Shop. If it is open, do go and have a look at the upstairs bar which is a replica of the Old Gaiety Theatre bar; it's splendidly plush and ornate. A good choice of food is served Monday through Saturday, no food Sunday.

Windsor Castle, 114 Campden Hill Road, W8
⊖ High Street Kensington

A smart young people's pub in a charming 18th-century building, just off Kensington High Street. The traditional interior is wood paneled and there's a pretty, shady garden with tables and chairs at the back. Bar food is served all week except Sunday. The Windsor Castle gets very crowded in the evening and at weekends, so try a lunchtime or an early evening visit.

Bloomsbury

The Lamb, 94 Lamb's Conduit Street, WC1
⊖ Russell Square

The green-tiled exterior and careful sign-writing are the first indication that The Lamb is something special. Once inside, the most striking feature is the line of mahogany and cut-glass snob-screens over the semi-circular bar. You have to peer through the gaps to order your drink. Other points of interest are the round tables, supported by baroque iron tripods, with brass railings to stop your glass falling off; some surviving (but not functioning) gas lamps; two galleries of postcard-sized portraits of Edwardian theater performers; and various old stone wine and spirit jars. As well as the wonderful atmosphere, the beer is good and the food delicious.

Museum Tavern, Museum Street, WC1
⊖ Tottenham Court Road

Splendid, Victorian-style pub right outside the British Museum. It's rumored that Karl Marx drank here while he was in London composing *Das Kapital*. Popular with visitors, local workers or as a meeting place for small groups and organizations, the pub offers a choice of bar food and a worthy selection of real ales. On Sunday you can sit down to a proper roast lunch; cream teas are served in the afternoon Monday through Saturday.

Chelsea and Victoria

Bag O'Nails, 6 Buckingham Palace Road, SW1
⊖ Victoria

Very convenient for Buckingham Palace (but you're unlikely to find the Royals out for a quick drink), this is a good stopping-off point if you're planning to visit the Royal Mews. There's an attractive, spacious bar offering comfortable seats and a selection of snacks, salads and hot dishes available at lunchtime.

Cross Keys, 2 Lawrence Street, SW3
⊖ Sloane Square

A side-street pub in a pleasant residential area close to Chelsea Embankment. The Cross Keys is built in the form of a classic coaching inn, with an entrance up a covered alley and a handsome staircase to your left as you enter. There are a number of nooks and corners furnished with wooden benches and high-backed chairs, plus a pretty flower bedecked patio for sunny days. Good salads, sandwiches and home-cooked daily specials Monday through Saturday.

Henry J. Bean's, 195-197 King's Road, SW3
● Sloane Square

If you've had enough of English beer, and hanker for familiar surroundings, Henry J. Bean's is an American-style saloon, stylishly furnished with wooden tables and decorated with photographs of Hollywood stars on the walls. You'll find salads, burgers and ribs for main courses, with brownies, ice cream and pecan pie to follow. American beer and wine are on sale plus cocktails. This bar is particularly popular with the young.

Orange Brewery, 37 Pimlico Road, SW1
● Sloane Square

Photographs and Victoriana decorate the walls of this friendly local pub which brews real ale on the premises. Available in three strengths, all fairly heady, the beer is an ideal accompaniment to the hot meat pies served at the counter. If pies are not your favorite thing, there are plenty of alternative bar snacks, including delicious hot roast beef sandwiches.

Westminster Arms, 9 Storey's Gate, SW1
● Westminster

A stone's throw from the Houses of Parliament and Westminster Abbey, this is popular with MPs and the odd Whitehall mandarin (senior civil servants). There's a wide choice of excellent beers and a selection of home-cooked food. Downstairs you'll find a wine bar (closed Sunday evenings).

City

Black Friar, 174 Queen Victoria Street, EC4
● Blackfriars

You'll find a lunchtime menu and snacks available in the evening at the Black Friar but your main reason for coming here is to appreciate the architecture. In 1905 famed sculptor Henry Poole collaborated with architect H. Fuller Clark to transform this wedge-shaped corner building into an art nouveau fantasy. Today it incorporates ornate mirrors, pink marble, gleaming mosaics and hand-beaten copper bas reliefs of Chaucerian-style clergymen sporting knowing grins and vast paunches. Their theme was inspired by the building's ancient historical associations: it stands on the site of the City's 13th-century Dominican priory (the Dominicans were known as 'the Black Friars'). The outside walls boast mosaics and carvings of jolly monks fishing, eating, drinking and laughing. The remarkable interior, with its polished stone, alabaster and marble walls, has a large, curving bar dominated by three huge copper bas reliefs; low marble archways open into the orange-lit saloon known as the Jewel Bar. Its low, barrel-vaulted ceiling is a masterpiece of gold, white and black mosaic, encircled by bronze reliefs of busy friars and mottos such as 'Don't advertise, tell a gossip'. Little devils perch on the cornices, while here and there a frog attacks a mouse, a snake poses with a sword in its mouth and, in a recess at one end, a happily snoozing monk is surrounded by fairies with mother-of-pearl wings. Don't miss the splendidly wrought copper lamp brackets, the wooden wall clock with two musical monkeys, the stained-glass window depicting a benevolent friar in a sunlit garden, or the huge bronze-canopied fireplace with firedogs topped with devils and toads.

Cittie of Yorke, 22 High Holborn, WC1
⊖ Holborn

Popular with legal eagles from the nearby Law Courts, this unusual pub has a high raftered roof and the longest bar counter in Britain. Seating space is provided in small carved wooden cubicles. Do note the unusual three-cornered stove which has fire grates on all sides. The food is not at all antique – good, fresh and varied: Ploughman's lunches and salads, substantial dishes like grilled trout or steaks. Closed on Sundays; no food on Saturday evenings.

The George, 77 Borough High Street, SE1
⊖ London Bridge

Crossing London Bridge to the south side of the river may seem a bit like entering no-man's-land, but pub enthusiasts should keep going. A pub of great character, The George was a 17th-century coaching inn. In a cobbled courtyard, it is now the only galleried pub in London. Two upper galleries have wooden balconies with latticed windows. Inside there are wooden beams, paneling and open fires in winter. In addition to the bar (serving snacks) there's a wine bar and restaurant (tel: (01) 407 2056). In summer you may witness a display of traditional Morris dancing in the courtyard.

Magpie and Stump, 18 Old Bailey, EC4
⊖ St Paul's

Closed at the weekend, this pub is popular with the legal profession and others who have cause to visit The Old Bailey. It stands directly opposite this famous seat of British justice, once the site of the notorious Newgate Prison. At one time you would have been able to rent an upstairs room in this establishment to view the public hangings which took place outside the prison walls between 1783 and 1868. You'll find a good lunchtime menu should you need more than a drink.

Princess Louise, 208 High Holborn, WC1
⊖ Holborn

This pub is a real architectural treat, boasting a fine exterior with marble pillars and a large bay window. Inside there are more columns, the walls are covered with magnificent tiles in a floral pattern, alternating with fine cut-glass mirrors, to create an unusual and richly ornate effect. Don't miss the stained-glass window at the end of the left-hand side of the bar. Roomy and comfortable so you can fully enjoy your beer, or perhaps a glass of sherry from the wood. Snacks are available downstairs throughout the week; meals in the upstairs dining room Monday through Friday and Saturday lunch. Live jazz Saturday and Sunday evenings.

Ye Olde Cheshire Cheese, Wine Office Court, off 145 Fleet Street, EC4
⊖ Blackfriars

If you decide to pay just one visit to a pub in London, this should be it. The old, oak-beamed building has been standing since the 17th century, offering hospitality to a long line of celebrated visitors listed at the entrance. Among them you'll find Charles Dickens, Arthur Conan Doyle, and the French literary lion Voltaire. Not only was Ye Olde Cheshire Cheese famed for its convivial atmosphere and ales, but also for its fine puddings which would weigh anything from 50-80lb and conceal a filling of steak, kidney and oysters; mushrooms and spices; or even larks. Today the puddings might not be as large but they are still on offer in the restaurant which specializes in the very best of traditional British cooking. The bar, with its sawdust-coated floor, open fire, wooden benches and tables, serves snacks. Reserve ahead for the restaurant (tel: (01) 353 6170).

Ye Olde Mitre Tavern, Ely Place, EC1
⊖ Chancery Lane

The original tavern was built in the 16th century to house the Bishop of Ely's servants while he stayed at his town house in the square. Although the present building is of more recent construction, it has managed to retain a reassuringly old-fashioned atmosphere with wooden paneling and exposed beams. The pub is closed on Saturday and Sunday, but during the week you'll be able to sample various tasty bar snacks as well as the beer.

North London

King's Head, 115 Upper Street, Islington, N1
⊖ Angel

Antiques buffs who find themselves exploring Camden Passage

may like to visit this rather extraordinary pub, but be prepared for a few surprises. The lofty, wooden-floored bar is decorated with theater memorabilia and the interest extends beyond the displaying of posters. At the back of the premises there's a small theater where plays are performed twice a week. Many productions which started life in this humble setting have proved successful. Some have transferred to Broadway. (For information about performances tel: (01) 226 1916.) The bar serves food – snacks or dinner – and combined theater/dinner tickets are for sale. Later in the evenings musicians provide live entertainment in the bar. Now for the real catch, the pub has refused to convert to decimal currency. It's not actually as confusing as it sounds – just remember that twenty shillings (20/-) are equivalent to one pound (£1.00) and one shilling (1/-) is worth 5 pence (5p) – good luck.

Riverside

Anchor, 1 Bankside, Southwark, SE1
⊖ London Bridge

You're sure to appreciate the superb views from this historic inn which looks across the Thames to St Paul's Cathedral. Full of atmosphere, the building is a mixture of the original structure and bars which date from around 1750. There's a good choice of bar food – salads, ploughman's lunches and hot dishes – also a restaurant (tel: (01) 407 1577). In summer you can sit outside watching the river go by. The Anchor does get very busy, so try to be there early. Children are welcomed in the dining area.

Bull's Head, 15 Strand on the Green, Chiswick, W4
⊖ Kew Gardens

A good place to revive the spirits if you've spent the day discovering Kew Gardens. Beside a quiet stretch of the river, it can be reached by walking down the Strand on the Green footpath to the right on the north side of Kew Bridge. The pub dates from the 17th century; during the civil war the site was used by Oliver Cromwell as his headquarters on more than one occasion. You'll find a good selection of beers on offer; food is available at lunchtimes only. Typical pub dishes include salads, shepherd's pie and lasagne. Children are allowed in the eating area.

Nearby is **The City Barge**, a cosy riverside pub, which fills up on sunny days when the clientele spill out to watch the river life go by. The bar provides tasty light meals and snacks, plus there's a pretty restaurant (tel: (01) 994 2148).

Dickens Inn, St Katharine's Way, E1
⊖ Tower Hill

Just beyond the Tower of London you'll find this popular pub which commands a prime spot overlooking the marina at St Katharine's Dock. Although modern, the interior has been cleverly designed with old-fashioned beams and open brickwork. When the weather's good the real delight is to sit outside on the waterside terrace. You'll be able to sample a good choice of traditional English fare – cockles and mussels or bangers and mash (sausages and mashed potatoes) for example. There is an attractive restaurant with a balcony for sunny afternoons where children are welcome (tel: (01) 488 9936).

Dove, 19 Upper Mall, Hammersmith, W6
⊖ Hammersmith

This pretty, old-fashioned pub has an attractive terrace which overlooks the river. Beamed ceiling, wooden farmhouse-type chairs and old prints of the river create a splendid atmosphere. Like most of the popular river pubs you'll find that it gets very busy – so arrive early if you want a comfortable seat. The food (lunchtime only) is plentiful and good – salads and quiches or hot dishes like shepherd's or chicken pie.

King's Head and Eight Bells, 50 Cheyne Walk, SW3
⊖ Sloane Square

Just near enough to the river to qualify for inclusion in this section, this friendly Chelsea pub is separated from the Thames by attractive gardens. Popular with locals, it's a pleasant pub in which to relax with a drink or a good place to sample bar food. The menu offers a varied selection of light meals and snacks, and the seafood platter is worthy of a mention.

Prospect of Whitby, 57 Wapping Wall, E1
⊖ Wapping

This is probably London's most celebrated riverside pub. It's not just the fine views that make a visit worthwhile (although the location did inspire both Turner and Whistler to put brush to canvas); the building is full of character, with beamed ceilings and flagstone floors. As with many of the best London pubs, the choice of food is good and you'll be entertained with live music in the evenings (a plus or minus point, depending on your taste). It is a popular tourist stop so don't expect to find a group of locals at the bar. Children are welcomed in certain areas.

South Kensington and Knightsbridge

Admiral Codrington, 17 Mossop Street, SW3
⊖ South Kensington

A pretty Victorian pub with an airy conservatory that's convenient and popular with the Sloane Ranger Set. A good choice of food is served – from soups and sandwiches to pies and grills and the standard is generally high. (No bar food Saturday or Sunday evenings.)

Bunch of Grapes, 207 Brompton Road, SW3
⊖ South Kensington

From the museums of South Kensington turn left and walk along the road towards Knightsbridge to find this comfortable Victorian pub with plenty of polished wood and glass. Good for a lunchtime snack or a light, home-cooked meal.

King George IV, 44 Montpelier Square, SW7
⊖ Knightsbridge

Away from the bustle of Knightsbridge in one of London's prettiest squares, this friendly Georgian pub is a good location for a quiet drink. You can sit outside or inside, where there's a pleasant, comfortable bar area and a good choice of freshly-cut sandwiches, salads and light dishes available at lunchtime.

West End

Grenadier, 18 Wilton Row, SW1
⊖ Hyde Park Corner

Once used by the Duke of Wellington's officers as their mess, the Grenadier is now famed for its heart-starting Bloody Marys. In fact, if you visit the pub just before Sunday lunch you'll find the majority of the clientele sipping away at this revitalizing brew. The bar is decorated with military memorabilia – prints of guardsmen, antique arms and the Duke of Wellington himself in portrait form. There's also a restaurant where you can dine by candlelight (tel: (01) 235 3074).

Lamb and Flag, Rose Street, WC2
⊖ Leicester Square

Tucked down an alleyway off Garrick Street, in Covent Garden, this is a particularly charming pub. Low ceilings and an open fire in winter make it a cosy and welcoming retreat on a wet day. The lunchtime menu is renowned for its superb selection of English cheeses which are served with fresh crusty bread, plus a choice of cold snacks, such as home-made pâté, and hot dishes available Monday through Friday only.

Nag's Head, 10 James Street, WC2
⊖ Covent Garden

A comfortable, richly-decorated pub right by the Royal Opera

House. It does get busy before opera performances begin, and afterwards if the show is short. Good bar food.

Opera, 23 Catherine Street, WC2
⊖ Aldwych or Covent Garden

Right near the Theatre Royal, Drury Lane, which provides the inspiration for the decor – an eclectic mixture of old opera playbills, photographs and other memorabilia line the walls. It's a good place for a pre-theater drink or meeting up with friends. The limited selection of bar food is not recommended.

Red Lion, Crown Passage, SW1
⊖ Green Park

A friendly pub in a narrow alley off Pall Mall, opposite St James's Palace. This is a good place to taste another old-fashioned specialty – Scotch eggs. The Scots are renowned for their breakfasts when these deep-fried savories can be served first thing in the morning along with smoked fish, kidneys, lamb chops and tomatoes (in between porridge and toast with Dundee marmalade). Here you'll find Scotch eggs included on the lunch menu – they're good ones: hard-boiled eggs encased in a savory coat of sausagemeat and herbs, all coated in crisp-cooked breadcrumbs. The Red Lion is a popular pub with local office workers so it gets busy at lunchtime (closed Sunday).

Red Lion, 2 Duke of York Street, SW1
⊖ Piccadilly Circus

A tiny, pretty Victorian pub off Jermyn Street, with a wood paneled bar decorated with splendid old mirrors. At lunchtime, along with other snacks, they serve a good cheese pie but try to get in for an early lunch or before the office workers escape for the evening since space is at a premium.

Red Lion, Kingly Street, W1
⊖ Oxford Circus

A good pub to visit if you've been shopping in Regent Street. It's conveniently close to Liberty and the ideal place to take the weight off your feet after pounding the pavement amidst swirling crowds. There are two bars, both comfortable and welcoming; each serves a lunchtime selection of sandwiches or rolls, with hot dishes prepared each day (Monday through Saturday).

Sherlock Holmes, 10 Northumberland Street, WC2
⊖ Charing Cross

Take along a Sherlock Holmes story if you want to relax for the evening in this unusual pub. Upstairs you'll find a reconstruction of part of Holmes's sitting room at 221b Baker Street, plus pipes, assorted memorabilia and photographs of actors who've played the role of the fictional sleuth on stage and screen. There's a good selection of food on offer, from snacks to more substantial dishes.

OUTER LONDON

Greenwich

Plume of Feathers, 19 Park Vista, SE10
British Rail: Maze Hill

Just the place to quench your thirst after a tour of the National Maritime Museum. This very pretty pub overlooks the park up towards the old Observatory. It's popular with locals as well as visitors (a good sign) and you'll be able to sample typical pub food as well as having a drink.

Trafalgar Tavern, Park Row, SE10
British Rail: Maze Hill

Famous for its mention in Dickens's *Our Mutual Friend*, (the author was a frequent visitor with his literary companion, Thackeray), this splendid building was erected in 1837. Its cast-iron balconies overlook the river and you'll be able to sample traditional British cooking in the restaurant or good pub snacks at the bar.

Yacht Tavern, 5 Crane Street, SE10
British Rail: Maze Hill

Beyond the Trafalgar Tavern you'll find this friendly 17th-century inn, in a narrow old street which runs parallel to the river. Good views, cheerful and friendly atmosphere plus lunchtime bar food and a selection of freshly-cut sandwiches with a wide variety of fillings.

Hampstead

Holly Bush, Holly Mount, NW3
⊖ Hampstead

Tucked in a little alleyway off the main street this pub was built in 1802. Two cozy bars with partitioned alcoves for those who want to relax in privacy; the walls are hung with prints, advertisements, plates and real gas lamps are still in place. Snacks and 'dishes of the day' are served both at lunchtime and in the evening (except Monday and Sunday).

Jack Straw's Castle, North End Way, NW3
⊖ Hampstead

This white weather-board inn is perched in an enviable position at the top of Hampstead Heath. Its name is said to derive from the time of the Peasant Revolt (1381), when supporters of ring leader Jack Straw were alleged to have met here before going off to join their leader in Highbury. The original inn has long gone and the present building was rebuilt in the 1960s. It's a spacious pub with bar snacks, a garden and a dining room.

Spaniards, Spaniards Lane, NW3
⊖ Hampstead

Built in 1585, the pub has retained its paneled walls, open fires and antique seating. In 1780, during the Gordon Riots, the mob are said to have stopped off here en route to Kenwood to burn down the home of Lord Mansfield. The quick-thinking host ensured that his revengeful clientele were well served with ale – so much so that they were still swigging the brew when the military arrived to spoil their plot. Today you'll be able to relax and contemplate history as you partake of a drink and a snack (sandwiches, rolls and hot British sausages) or a hot meal.

Richmond

Orange Tree, 45 Kew Road (opposite Richmond Station)
⊖ Richmond

A big friendly pub with a lively atmosphere. Prints on the walls and comfortable seating. The upstairs bar serves a good selection of sandwiches and snacks. Downstairs you'll find a second bar offering more substantial meals such as curry, delicious warming casseroles, game pies and wonderful desserts (open lunch and dinner except Sunday evening). The Orange Tree is also famous for its pub theater which puts on a variety of shows both classic and modern in intimate surroundings (tel: (01) 940 3633).

White Cross, Cholmondeley (pronounced 'Chumley', just to confuse) Walk (by the river)
⊖ Richmond

On sunny Sundays the lunchtime clientele overflow off the terrace onto the riverside walkway where you'll find a comfortable perch on the low walls or the steps leading down to the water. During the week there are fewer people to compete with for a table and shorter queues for food, which is good, fresh, and fairly typical. Salads, ploughman's, one or two hot dishes and the inevitable sausages.

HOTELS

Price Categories

Sterling sign indicates price level per person sharing a double room.

£   £20 – £35
££   £35 – £45
£££ £45+

Bayswater and Kensington

Colonnade Hotel, 2 Warrington Crescent, W9   ££
Tel: (01) 289 2167   ⊖ Warwick Avenue
Amenities: ☎, 💻, 🅿, 🍴, 🍷   Credit cards: AE, DC, MC, V

Located near Little Venice, the hotel has been converted from a fine Georgian house with its own garden. Although the hotel is small, most rooms have private facilities, some have four-poster beds and there are a few spacious suites which feature whirlpool baths.

Hilton International, 179 Holland Park Avenue, W11 £££
Tel: (01) 603 3355   ⊖ Shepherd's Bush
Amenities: ☎, 💻, 🅿, 🍴, 🍷, ◎   Credit cards: AE, DC, MC

A stylish, modern and efficient hotel at the Shepherd's Bush end of Holland Park Avenue. In an attractive tree-lined residential area, you're in easy striking distance of Kensington and the antique shops of Portobello Road. Spacious, light public rooms and comfortable air-conditioned bedrooms provide a welcome oasis after a hard day's sightseeing. The rooms feature thoughtful additions such as tea and coffee making facilities and quality toiletries.

Kensington Close Hotel, Wrights Lane, W8   ££
Tel: (01) 937 8170   ⊖ High Street Kensington
Amenities: ☎, 💻, 🅿, 🍴, 🍷, ≈   Credit cards: AE, DC, MC, V

A large, stylish hotel just off Kensington High Street, which offers good facilities including an indoor swimming pool, squash courts and a gymnasium. For less energetic guests, there's an open plan lounge, coffee bar and restaurant or a leafy patio garden. All rooms are comfortable and well appointed.

Leinster Towers Hotel, 25-31 Leinster Gardens, W2   ££
Tel: (01) 262 4591   ⊖ Queensway
Amenities: ☎, 💻, 🍷   Credit cards: AE, DC, MC, V

An unpretentious, pleasant hotel in the Bayswater area. The

interior is light and attractive with a bright entrance hall-lounge and cozy bar. All rooms have simple furnishings and private facilities. Meals are provided by arrangement, but you're close to plenty of restaurants small, large, expensive and moderate.

Lindon House Hotel, 4 Sussex Place, W2 £
Tel: (01) 723 9853 ⊖ Paddington
No special amenities   No credit cards

A friendly hotel providing very reasonable 'bed and breakfast' accommodation in Bayswater, conveniently close to Marble Arch. Families with children are welcome here.

London Embassy Hotel, 150 Bayswater Road, W2   £££
Tel: (01) 229 1212 ⊖ Lancaster Gate
Amenities: ☎, ⌨, 🅿, 🍴, 🍷   Credit cards: AE, DC, MC, V

A modern, comfortable hotel which overlooks Kensington Gardens. Public rooms include a chic bar which extends onto an attractive patio during summer and a comfortable lounge. Bedrooms are practical and pretty with tea making facilities and well-equipped bathrooms. Efficient service and a pleasant ambience.

Mornington Hotel, 12 Lancaster Gate, W2   ££
Tel: (01) 262 7361 ⊖ Lancaster Gate
Amenities: ☎, ⌨, 🍴, 🍷   Credit cards: AE, DC, MC, V
Closed: Over Christmas

A Swedish-owned establishment which perhaps accounts for the excellent service and the sauna. Close to Marble Arch and Hyde Park, you'll find attractive public rooms and a welcoming bar lined with bookcases. All rooms have private, well-equipped bathrooms and pleasant decor.

Whites Hotel, Lancaster Gate, W2   £££
Tel: (01) 262 2711 ⊖ Lancaster Gate
Amenities: ☎, ⌨, 🅿, 🍴, 🍷, ◎   Credit cards: AE, DC, MC, V

The hotel boasts a magnificent façade overlooking Kensington Gardens and Hyde Park. Inside, brilliant chandeliers and sumptuous furnishings create an impression of unquestionable luxury. The bedrooms are decorated in a similar vein; many have balconies, chandeliers, antiques, room safes and marbled bathrooms. You can even reserve a four-poster bed.

Bloomsbury

Arran House Hotel, 77 Gower Street, WC1   £
Tel: (01) 636 2186 ⊖ Euston
No special amenities   No credit cards

204

A small family-run establishment providing modest accommodation and breakfast in Bloomsbury. The friendly owner ensures that all the rooms (some with TV) are clean and tidy.

Crichton Hotel, 36 Bedford Place, WC1   £
Tel: (01) 637 3955   ⊖ Russell Square
Amenities: ☎, ⬛, ♿   Credit cards: AE, DC, MC, V

A welcoming 'bed and breakfast' establishment situated in a quiet location close to the British Museum. Clean, with a good standard of furnishings and fittings, this recently redecorated hotel is well run and the staff are both friendly and efficient.

Harlingford Hotel, 61-63 Cartwright Gardens, WC1   £
Tel: (01) 387 1551   ⊖ Russell Square
Amenities: ⬛   Credit cards: MC, V

A friendly, well-run family concern, this 'bed and breakfast' establishment provides simple accommodation in a residential area just north of Bloomsbury.

Lonsdale Hotel, 9-10 Bedford Place, WC1   £
Tel: (01) 636 1812   ⊖ Russell Square
No special amenities   No credit cards

Located in a quiet street in Bloomsbury, this simple 'bed and breakfast' hotel offers good value for money. Although small, there is a comfortable television lounge and breakfast room. No private facilities. Friendly service.

Russell Hotel, Russell Square, WC1   ££
Tel: (01) 837 6470   ⊖ Russell Square
Amenities: ☎, ⬛, ⬛, ♿, ◎   Credit cards: AE, DC, MC, V

A large Victorian hotel, recently smartened up but still retaining its grandeur in many of the original features. All bedrooms are pleasantly decorated and equipped with private showers or bathrooms. There are two bars, one formal, the second more pub-like.

Chelsea and Victoria

Alison House Hotel, 82 Ebury Street, SW1   £
Tel: (01) 730 9529   ⊖ Victoria
Amenities: ⬛   No credit cards   Closed: Jan

A simple, small hotel close to Victoria, which provides neat, comfortable bedrooms with shared facilities. The proprietor is eager to ensure that all guests have a pleasant visit and the result is a clean, cheerful and homey establishment.

Berkeley, Wilton Place, SW1   **£££**
Tel: (01) 235 6000   ⊖ Victoria
Amenities: ☎, 🖵, 🅿, 🍴, 🍸, ≈≈   Credit cards: AE, DC, MC, V

The exterior of this hotel is not impressive but the inside is dignified
and elegant. Many fine features adorn the public areas including
the Lutyens paneling and a splendid chandelier. There are two bars
(one overlooks the roof-top pool), a restaurant that is essentially
French in style and the less formal Buttery. The attractive rooms
have bathrooms luxuriously fitted with large baths and marbled
floors. Other facilities include a sauna, solarium, keep-fit equipment, beauty salon, hairdressers and a cinema.

Chesham House Hotel, 64-66 Ebury Street, SW1   **£**
Tel: (01) 730 8513   ⊖ Victoria
Amenities: 🖵   Credit cards: AE, DC, V
Closed: Over Christmas

Located in a terrace of townhouses near Victoria, this is a bright,
tidy but simple 'bed and breakfast' establishment. Rooms do not
have private baths but they are all very well kept; trouser presses
and hair dryers are available.

Collin House Hotel, 104 Ebury Street, SW1   **£**
Tel: (01) 730 8030   ⊖ Victoria
No special amenities   No credit cards

A simply furnished, cozy 'bed and breakfast' establishment in a
useful location between Victoria and Sloane Square. The owners
are friendly, helpful and wonderfully house-proud.

Eden House Hotel, 111 Old Church Street, SW3   **£**
Tel: (01) 352 3403   ⊖ Sloane Square
No special amenities   Credit cards: AE, DC, MC, V

Homey and very friendly, this small well-established Edwardian
hotel in Chelsea welcomes children so it's popular with families.

Elizabeth Hotel, 37 Eccleston Square, SW1   **£**
Tel: (01) 828 6812   ⊖ Victoria
No special amenities   No credit cards

A good family hotel (family rooms available) offering pleasantly
comfortable accommodation near Victoria. Public rooms include a
television lounge and breakfast room. Three rooms have private
facilities, the others make use of public bathrooms.

Wilbraham Hotel, 1 Wilbraham Place, SW1   **££**
Tel: (01) 730 8296   ⊖ Sloane Square
Amenities: ☎ 🖵   No credit cards

A modest, traditional hotel close to Sloane Square, the Wilbraham maintains a high level of service as well as reasonable prices for the area. Simply furnished rooms, most with bath or shower and television; pleasantly old-fashioned public rooms. Breakfast is served in your room, but other meals can be ordered by arrangement.

Willett Hotel, 32 Sloane Gardens, SW1
Tel: (01) 824 8415   ⊖ Sloane Square
Amenities: ☎, 🖳, 🅿   No credit cards

A small well-kept hotel in Chelsea with an enthusiastic and friendly owner. Most rooms have private facilities and all are well-equipped with tea-makers and hair dryers. There's a garden; laundry service is available.

City

Tower Thistle Hotel, St Katharine's Way, E1   £££
Tel: (01) 481 2575   ⊖ Tower Hill
Amenities: ☎, 🖳, 🅿, 🍴, ♈   Credit cards: DC, MC, V

Close to the City, the financial district of London, the massive, modern Tower Thistle enjoys all the comforts expected of a recently-built hotel. The main attraction is its superb location – overlooking the River and Tower Bridge to one side, St Katharine's Dock with its restored warehouses and historic ships collection to the other. Bedrooms, which include non-smoking rooms, offer a wealth of accessories from hair dryers to trouser presses and radio-alarms plus quality toiletries in the bathrooms. In addition 22 luxury penthouse suites occupy the top of the hotel.

South Kensington and Knightsbridge

Alexander Hotel, 9 Sumner Place, SW7   ££
Tel: (01) 581 1591   ⊖ South Kensington
Amenities: ☎, 🖳, 🍴, ♈   Credit cards: AE, DC, MC, V

Delightfully situated in an attractive 19th-century town house near South Kensington station, the hotel is pleasantly quiet and central. Visitors will enjoy the garden in summer. The rooms are most attractive and comfortable with well-designed bathrooms.

Basil Street Hotel, 8 Basil Street, SW3   £££
Tel: (01) 581 3311   ⊖ Knightsbridge
Amenities: ☎, 🖳, 🍴, ♈   Credit cards: AE, DC, MC, V

A charming Edwardian hotel that retains much of its original atmosphere. Tastefully furnished, featuring antiques throughout and fresh flowers that brighten the rooms, the Basil Street Hotel is quiet and comfortable. The staff are helpful and courteous, plus there's a coffee shop and wine bar as well as a peaceful dining room.

Beaufort Hotel, 33 Beaufort Gardens, SW3   £££
Tel: (01) 584 5252   ⊖ Knightsbridge
Amenities: ☎, ⌨   Credit cards: AE, DC, MC, V

A comfortable, elegantly decorated hotel with original water colors adorning the walls and well-furnished bedrooms. There's a lounge but no other public rooms. High quality continental breakfasts are served in guests' rooms but no other meals are available. Personal touches, like chocolates, maps and good toiletries, are in every room.

Capital Hotel, 22-24 Basil Street, SW3   £££
Tel: (01) 587 5171   ⊖ Knightsbridge
Amenities: ☎, ⌨, 🅿, ⑪, ⦵   Credit cards: AE, DC, MC, V

A small, modern, sophisticated hotel close to Harrods that achieves a high standard. The decor, furnishings and paintings used throughout the hotel are carefully designed, making use of charming fabrics in muted colors. Bedrooms and bathrooms are well equipped, service is excellent. The restaurant is elegant and offers a high standard of French cuisine.

Ebury Court, 26 Ebury Street, SW1   ££
Tel: (01) 730 8147   ⊖ Victoria
Amenities: ☎, ⑪, ⦵   Credit cards: MC, V

This charming, traditional hotel is conveniently situated near Victoria and very popular. Quite small and family run, it is a welcoming, friendly establishment. The rooms are attractively furnished, a small number have private bathrooms. All bathrooms (private and public) are well maintained and accessible. There's a lounge for the use of guests and a club bar with an outdoor terrace (guests can become temporary members). The home-cooking in the basement restaurant is highly recommended.

Eden Plaza Hotel, 68 Queen's Gate, SW7   £
Tel: (01) 370 6111   ⊖ Gloucester Road
Amenities: ☎, ⌨, ⦵   Credit cards: AE, DC, MC, V

Very good value hotel in South Kensington with simple rooms, all with shower (six have baths). This small establishment achieves a high standard for its size, offering a sauna, solarium and coffee shop. The lounge and other public areas have all been well updated, the decor is pleasant, and the staff most helpful.

Hyatt Carlton Tower, 2 Cadogan Place, SW1   £££
Tel: (01) 235 5411   ⊖ Knightsbridge
Amenities: ☎, ⌨, 🅿, ⑪, ⦵, ⚲   Credit cards: AE, DC, MC, V

An impressive, luxury hotel which offers comfort and excellent service throughout. One of its attractive features is the new leisure complex which provides keep-fit equipment, sauna, steam bath, solarium and tennis courts. There is a garden and in-house movies.

Lowndes Thistle, 21 Lowndes Street, SW1   **£££**
Tel: (01) 236 6020   ⊖ Knightsbridge
Amenities: ☎, ⌨, **P**, ⑂⑂, ⚲   Credit cards: AE, DC, MC, V

A great deal of care has been taken to beautify this modern hotel close to Knightsbridge, and it's been a great success. Chandeliers in the lounge, a gorgeous *chinoiserie* bar and bedrooms tastefully decorated with pretty fabrics and Regency-style furniture. Excellent facilities include wall safes (check when you reserve) and marbled bathrooms with telephone extensions. Charming service from a well-trained, personable staff.

Number Sixteen, 16 Sumner Place, SW7   **££**
Tel: (01) 589 5232   ⊖ South Kensington
Amenities: ☎   Credit cards: AE, DC, MC, V

Converted from a row of Victorian terraced houses, this is a delightful hotel a short distance from the Victoria and Albert Museum in South Kensington. Beautifully furnished with antiques and flowers, it is full of character with a conservatory as well as a pretty garden. Most rooms have private facilities and there's a good continental breakfast to set you up for the day. Other meals are available by arrangement.

Swallow International Hotel, 147 Cromwell Road, SW5   **£££**
Tel: (01) 370 4200   ⊖ Gloucester Road
Amenities: ☎, ⌨, **P**, ⑂⑂, ⚲   Credit cards: AE, DC, MC, V

Formerly the London International Hotel, this large modern establishment is sufficiently central to attract many businessmen and tour groups. All rooms have private facilities, plus, there's a popular bar and coffee shop. However, the sheer volume of traffic means service can be rather impersonal.

Terstan Hotel, 29 Nevern Square, SW5   **£**
Tel: (01) 373 5368   ⊖ Earls Court
Amenities: ⌨, ⚲   Credit cards: MC, V

Situated in a quiet position overlooking a leafy square, a good deal of money and effort has been put into modernizing this family-run hotel. There's a comfortable lounge, breakfast room and games room with a pool table. Many rooms have private facilities; all are bright and cheerful. Earl's Court underground station is within easy walking distance.

Brown's Hotel, Dover Street, W1 £££
Tel: (01) 493 6020   ⊖ Green Park
Amenities: ☎, ⌨, ⌇, ⌇, ◎   Credit cards: AE, DC, MC, V

A traditional-style British hotel that's a favorite with many regular
visitors. Theodore Roosevelt was married here, Kipling penned
stories and Alexander Bell made the first telephone call from
Brown's. Fine decor, charming flower arrangements and comfortable furnishings all contribute to the country-house atmosphere.
Bedrooms are all well updated with fully equipped bathrooms.
Excellent service.

Bryanston Court Hotel, 56 Great Cumberland Place, W1 ££
Tel: (01) 262 3141   ⊖ Marble Arch
Amenities: ☎, ⌨, ⌇, ⌇   Credit cards: AE, DC, MC, V

A small, family run hotel in a central location. It has recently been
redecorated and the bedrooms are smart and modern, all with their
own bath or shower. The staff are friendly and efficient.

Cavendish, Jermyn Street, SW1 £££
Tel: (01) 930 2111   ⊖ Piccadilly Circus
Amenities: ☎, ⌨, P, ⌇, ⌇, ◎   Credit cards: AE, DC, MC, V

A modern comfortable hotel replacing the original Cavendish
Hotel. There are two bars: the comfortable lounge bar on the
ground floor which is named after the famous Rosa Lewis (model
for the *Duchess of Duke Street*). She bought and ran the original
hotel in 1904. The second bar is located on the first floor along with
a coffee shop and lounge. All rooms are pleasantly appointed and
facilities include hair dryers and trouser presses. Service is efficient.

Claridges, Brook Street, W1 £££
Tel: (01) 629 8860   ⊖ Bond Street
Amenities: ☎, ⌨, ⌇, ⌇   Credit cards: AE, DC, MC, V

Claridges is one of London's landmarks and the rich, royal and
famous have been gracing this hotel for decades. The hotel is in
every way quite luxurious – from the style and standard of the decor
to the attentive service offered throughout. Drinks are served in the
lounge, there is a relaxing reading room and two restaurants: the
famous **Claridge's Restaurant** which offers classic French cuisine or
The Causerie which has a broader menu.

The Connaught, Carlos Place, W1 £££
Tel: (01) 499 7070   ⊖ Bond Street
Amenities: ☎, ⌨, ⌇, ⌇   Credit cards: MC
The Connaught has a reputation for luxury and discretion. Right in

the heart of Mayfair, the hotel is sumptuously decorated with antique furniture. Fresh flowers decorate public areas and bedrooms, and the bathrooms are equipped with fine toiletries. The hotel is small by London standards and the service is impeccable, creating a friendly atmosphere.

Cumberland, Marble Arch, W1   **£££**
Tel: (01) 262 1234   ⊖ Marble Arch
Amenities: ☎, ⌨, 🅿, 🍴, ♈, ◎   Credit cards: AE, DC, MC, V

With nearly 900 rooms, this smart hotel is conveniently located close to the shops of Oxford Street and very popular. The staff are efficient and helpful, reflecting the general style of the hotel which is modern and comfortable. Smart bathrooms adjoin well-decorated bedrooms. Other facilities on offer include a sauna and beauty parlor. Also the **Wyvern Restaurant** with a good classic menu served in pleasant surroundings.

Dukes Hotel, 35 St James's Place, SW1   **£££**
Tel: (01) 491 4840   ⊖ Green Park
Amenities: ☎, ⌨, 🍴, ♈   Credit cards: AE, DC, MC, V

Dukes Hotel is tucked away in a peaceful cul-de-sac off St James's Street, free from the bustle of the main tourist areas. The public areas are all tastefully furnished, decorated with fresh flowers and very relaxing. The bedrooms are all stylish and comfortable, well equipped with thoughtful extras like nice toiletries and bath robes.

Edward Lear Hotel, 28/30 Seymour Street, W1   **££**
Tel: (01) 402 5401   ⊖ Marble Arch
Amenities: ☎, ⌨   Credit cards: V

Named after Edward Lear, the artist and writer famous for his nonsense verse, part of the hotel occupies Lear's house at No 30. Family run, the hotel provides a friendly and personal service. Well-equipped, pleasant rooms all have color T.V.

Hilton On Park Lane, 22 Park Lane, W1   **£££**
Tel: (01) 490 8000   ⊖ Hyde Park Corner
Amenities: ☎, ⌨, 🍴, ♈   Credit cards: AE, DC, MC, V

This tall, modern landmark on Park Lane is cool and elegant inside, with crystal chandeliers and marble floors. Bedrooms are impressively furnished in pleasing color schemes, the bathrooms are well equipped and the service is efficient throughout. Within the hotel there are several bars and restaurants. From the top of the hotel there are spectacular views of London.

Holiday Inn (Mayfair), 3 Berkeley Street, W1   **£££**
Tel: (01) 493 8282   ⊖ Green Park
Amenities: ☎, 🖥, 🅿, 🍴, 🍸, ◎   Credit cards: AE, DC, MC, V

Ideally situated for visitors who want to make the most of London's
shopping and nightlife facilities, this modern hotel is attractively
furnished throughout with a smart bar and restaurant. Bedrooms
are spacious with well-equipped bathrooms. The reliable Holiday
Inn chain also has hotels at Marble Arch (134 George Street, W1,
tel: (01) 723 1277), and Swiss Cottage (128 King Henry's Road,
NW3, tel: (01) 722 7711).

Inn on the Park, Hamilton Place, Park Lane, W1   **£££**
Tel: (01) 499 0888   ⊖ Hyde Park Corner
Amenities: ☎, 🖥, 🅿, 🍴, 🍸, ◎   Credit cards: AE, DC, MC, V

Centrally located, this modern hotel maintains high standards of
luxury and service. The public rooms are beautifully decorated and
elegantly furnished, while the bedrooms have king-size beds.
Extras like mini-bars and hair dryers feature in the rooms, bathrooms are luxurious. To complement the stylish, luxurious surroundings, the staff are helpful, friendly and efficient. The **Four
Seasons Restaurant** achieves the same high standard as the rest of
the hotel providing plenty of culinary variety, from simple roasts to
specialties like sea bass with prawns and fennel.

Mostyn Hotel, Bryanston Street, W1   **£££**
Tel: (01) 935 2361   ⊖ Marble Arch
Amenities: ☎, 🖥, 🅿, 🍴, 🍸   Credit cards: AE, DC, MC, V

A comfortable hotel converted from four period houses a stone's
throw from Marble Arch, the Mostyn has been carefully and
tastefuly refitted and furbished. Plants and flowers create a bright,
spacious atmosphere in the public rooms; the bedrooms are equally
attractive and comfortable. Polite and obliging staff.

Mountbatten Hotel, Seven Dials, WC2   **£££**
Tel: (01) 836 4300   ⊖ Covent Garden
Amenities: ☎, 🖥, 🍴, 🍸   Credit cards: AE, DC, MC, V

A new hotel named after Lord Mountbatten, close to the Covent
Garden market. Paintings and other memorabilia are displayed in
the attractive Broadlands lounge and Burma bar. Smart, efficient
and luxurious throughout, the hotel features seven sumptuous
suites (each with a whirlpool bath) amongst its 125 rooms, all of
which are well equipped with luxurious Italian marble bathrooms.

The Ritz, Piccadilly, W1   **£££**
Tel: (01) 493 8181   ⊖ Green Park
Amenities: ☎, 🖥, 🅿, 🍴, 🍸   Credit cards: AE, DC, MC, V

First opened in 1906, the hotel has recently undergone a major refurbishment. Chandeliers, thick carpets and superb furnishings create the splendid surroundings that are so famous. All bedrooms are luxurious but if you feel inclined to spend a little extra you may stay in one of 22 opulent rooms, recently refurbished with silk curtains, marble fireplaces acquired from French châteaux, pickled pine furniture and gold-plated fittings in the accompanying marble bathrooms. The service will make guests feel thoroughly pampered.

Royal Trafalgar Thistle, Whitcomb Street, WC2   **£££**
Tel: (01) 930 4477   ⊖ Charing Cross
Amenities: ☎, ☐, ᵼᵼ, ⴹ   Credit cards: AE, DC, MC, V

This efficient, modern hotel, a pigeon step from Trafalgar Square, is popular with business people and tourists alike. There's a cheerful brasserie and nautical bar as well as the comfortable public lounge. All bedrooms are attractively furnished with private bathrooms of a high standard.

Savoy, Strand, WC2   **£££**
Tel: (01) 836 4343   ⊖ Charing Cross
Amenities: ☎, ☐, 🅿 ᵼᵼ, ⴹ   Credit cards: AE, DC, MC, V

A grand hotel in the old style, sumptuously decorated with ornate moldings, lashings of gilt and antique furniture. There are a number of suites which overlook the Thames offering marvelous views, and although some of the rooms are smaller than others, all are luxuriously appointed. If you don't get the view from your room, then have a drink or afternoon tea in the Thames Lounge, or sample the fabled hospitality of the American Bar. The service is impeccable throughout the hotel, and you're conveniently placed for London's theaterland with the delicious pocket-sized Savoy Theatre right outside the main entrance.

Waldorf Hotel, Aldwych, WC2   **£££**
Tel: (01) 836 2400   ⊖ Aldwych or Temple
Amenities: ☎, ☐, ᵼᵼ, ⴹ   Credit cards: AE, DC, MC, V

A large, elegant Edwardian hotel furnished with chandeliers and thick carpets. Well placed for theaterland and the Royal Opera House at Covent Garden. In the Palm Court lounge guests can participate in a tea dance – surprisingly popular revival of a genteel pastime. Stylish bedrooms and bathrooms are all well equipped and comfortable. Try to avoid rooms at the front of the hotel, traffic noise can be a problem.

NIGHTSPOTS

Barbarella, 428 Fulham Road, SW6
Tel: (01) 385 9434   ⊖ Fulham Broadway
Barbarella 2, 43 Thurloe Street, SW7
Tel: (01) 584 2000   ⊖ South Kensington
Open: Mon-Sat 7:30pm-3am (last orders 1am)
Credit cards: AE, DC, MC, V

The well-established Fulham Road venue was such a success that the genial Morelli brothers opened Number 2 recently. Popular with clients of all ages, these two nightspots provide a sophisticated, fun evening out at a reasonable price. The decor is plush and unusual, the atmosphere lively but not overpowering, the excellent Italian cuisine really delicious and there's dancing until the early hours – all the ingredients for a good evening. Must reserve.

Hilton Hotel Roof Restaurant, 22 Park Lane, W1
Tel: (01) 493 8000   ⊖ Hyde Park Corner
Open: Mon-Sat 7:30pm-1:30am
Credit cards: AE, DC, MC, V

Right up on the 28th floor of the Hilton Hotel, this is literally a top spot. If possible, reserve a table by the window because the view is stupendous. Excellent restaurant with a wide choice: try the Cornish lobster salad which is delicately flavored and a real treat. Dancing to live bands completes an enjoyable night out.

Hippodrome Centre, corner Charing Cross Road and Cranbourn
  Street, WC2
Tel: (01) 437 4311   ⊖ Leicester Square
Open: Mon-Sat 9pm-4am
Credit cards: AE, DC, MC, V

This amazing creation of nightlife supremo Peter Stringfellow is one of the really hot spots in London. The decor is spectacular to say the least, with every conceivable electrical wizardry – laser shows, video screens, the lot. Style is paramount and it's the place to go amongst London's most fashionable young. Bars, fast food and full restaurant. Live music most nights plus disco until 3:30am – all the razzmatazz you could wish for.

Rock Garden, 6-7 The Piazza, Covent Garden, WC2
Tel: (01) 240 3961   ⊖ Covent Garden
Open: Mon-Sat 8:45pm-2am, Sun 7:30pm-midnight
Credit cards: (Restaurant) MC, V

If rock music is your scene, this is the acknowledged venue. The upstairs restaurant serves juicy hamburgers, ribs, salads, etc; the real action is below. Up to three bands can play during the evening; admission prices vary according to their status. Few top names, although occasional 'surprise guests' have elevated an evening out into a night to remember. Great atmosphere, plus bands on Sundays.

Ronnie Scott's, 47 Frith Street, W1
Tel: (01) 439 0747   ⊖ Tottenham Court Road
Open: Mon-Sat 8:30pm-3am
Credit cards: AE, DC, MC, V

London's major jazz venue with a reputation for attracting all the top international names from trad to crossover. 'Main room' concerts generally begin around 8:30pm; upstairs there's a dark crowded disco (11pm-3am) which occasionally fronts struggling bands. There's a fairly standard restaurant downstairs, service is not great and Scott is known to berate his audience when they're not reacting to his satisfaction. However, you won't question the quality of the artistes; prices vary. Enthusiastic audiences welcome.

Savoy Hotel Restaurant, Strand, WC2
Tel: (01) 836 4343   ⊖ Charing Cross
Open: Mon-Sat 12:30pm-2:30pm, 7:30pm-11:30pm,
        Sun 12:30pm-2pm, 7pm-10:30pm
Credit cards: AE, DC, MC, V

Long regarded as one of the smartest places to celebrate a night out. Revel in the glorious decor, gracious and sophisticated atmosphere, then try not to be a glutton when dinner is served. Anton Edelmann, in the kitchen, has become a substantial star in London's culinary firmament. He appeals to all tastes with a broadbased menu including excellent roasts or more elaborate dishes with irresistible desserts to follow. The cabaret starts at 11:30pm and invariably features top international singers. Afterwards, there's more dancing to live bands. Jacket and tie obligatory.

Stringfellows, 16/19 St Martin's Lane, WC2
Tel: (01) 240 5534   ⊖ Leicester Square
Open: Mon-Sat Restaurant 8pm-1.30am, Disco 11pm-3am
Credit cards: AE, DC, MC, V

This, the first of Peter Stringfellows's creations (see also Hippodrome Centre) is one of the places to be seen in London. It's chic, popular and smart; striking decor with a spectacular mirrored dance floor. The cocktail bar is renowned for its exotic (read expensive) concoctions. A French à la carte restaurant serves carefully prepared, beautifully presented nouvelle cuisine dishes. Definitely a place for the *doré* (though not necessarily the *jeunesse*), if you can get in (telephone to check).

Tiddy Dols, 2 Hertford Street, W1
Tel: (01) 499 2357   ⊖ Hyde Park Corner
Open: Daily 6pm-11:30pm (last orders)
Credit cards: AE, MC, V

The atmosphere and entertainment in this pretty 18th-century house is unmistakably British. Attractive antique tables and chairs, hand-painted caricatures on the walls set the scene for strolling Elizabethan players and a live pianist. Tiddy Dols prides itself on its food which is described as 'English with a French touch' and is complemented by English wines which feature on the list. An unusual night out at reasonable cost and in good taste.

Valbonne, 62 Kingly Street, W1
Tel: (01) 439 7242   ⊖ Oxford Circus
Open: Mon-Sat 9pm-3:30am
Credit cards: AE, DC, MC, V

Popular disco located behind Regent Street. Stylish decor and a lively clientele make for a bright night out on the town. Should you decide to make a whole evening (or night) of it, the restaurant offers an à la carte menu of international cuisine (steaks, chicken dishes, etc.), to enjoy.

Xenon, 196 Piccadilly, W1
Tel: (01) 734 9344   ⊖ Piccadilly Circus
Open: Daily 9pm-3:30am
Credit cards: AE, DC, MC, V

This smart, lively nightclub-cum-disco features its own energetic dance troupe which performs as part of the cabaret. The show varies from magic or mime to jugglers or tumblers but it's always entertaining. There are three bars (including a piano bar), spectacular light and water shows. Truly international menu featuring Japanese and Italian dishes. Xenon describes itself as a '20s-style club'; dress smart.

SHORT TOURS
AROUND
LONDON

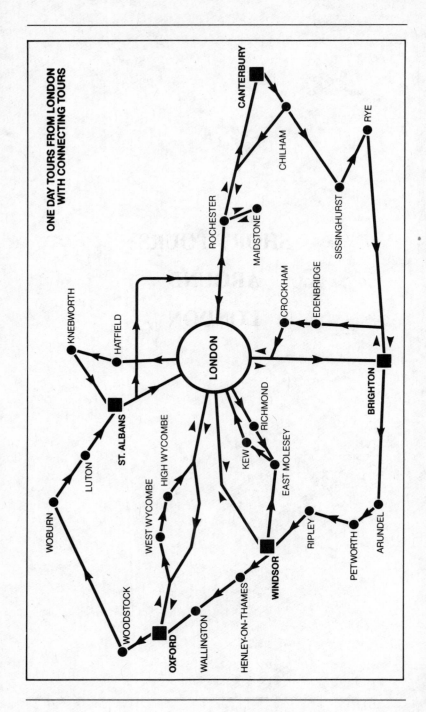

ONE DAY TOURS FROM LONDON WITH CONNECTING TOURS

DIRECT ROUTES FROM LONDON

For those readers who wish to do only a portion of a tour, you can take one of these direct routes from London to the starting point of your choice.

London to	Route	Approx Mileage
Bath	M4 to A46	117
Brighton	A23 to M23 to A23	54
Cambridge	M11 to A10	61
Canterbury	A2 to M2 to A2	61
Cheltenham	A40 to M40 to A40	97
Exeter	M4 to M5	199
Glastonbury	M3 to A303 to A36 to A361	129
Oxford	M40	56
Penzance	M4 to M5 to A30	312
Plymouth	M4 to M5 to A38	244
Rochester	A2	32
St Albans	M1/A1	23
Salisbury	M3 to A303 to A343 to A30	85
Stratford-upon-Avon	M40 to A40 to A34	95
Taunton	M4 to M5 to A358	169
Wells	M3 to A303 to A36 to A361 to A371	125
Winchester	M3	65
Windsor	M4	25

In all cases these are major roads and clearly signposted at appropriate exits, traffic circles and other junctions. Having said that, having a map along is a good idea. Most car rental companies provide these. If not, virtually all petrol stations sell road atlases and maps.

TOUR 1: KENT, CANTERBURY AND THE COAST

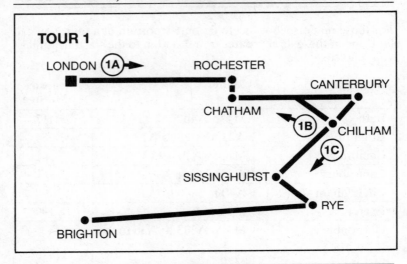

Route A: LONDON TO CANTERBURY Visiting Rochester
(about 65 miles)

LONDON TO ROCHESTER   (about 32 miles)

*Your tour begins as you cross **Tower Bridge** from the City of London. At traffic lights 200 yards past the bridge turn left into **Tooley Street** (**A200**), follow the road as it widens into **Jamaica Road** and continue over a traffic circle.*

*At the next traffic circle take the right lane, then turn right and take the third exit into **Lower Road**. Follow Lower Road, passing Surrey Docks underground station on your right, move to the center lane and go straight over the next traffic light. Go straight ahead as the road develops into **Evelyn Street** (**A200**), then **Creek Road**, where you'll cross a bridge over Deptford Creek – hence the name. Soon after the bridge you'll see **Greenwich** (see page 110) town center straight ahead.*

*Approach the Greenwich one-way system in the right lane. Drive on following signs to Greenwich town center, passing the ship **Cutty Sark** on your left. At the traffic lights opposite the **Royal Naval College** turn right, then follow the one-way system, taking the right-hand road signposted to **Deptford** (**A206**). On a Saturday you'll pass a small antiques market on your left. At the next traffic light turn left into **Blackheath Road** (**A2**) and continue to Blackheath Hill, passing the Greenwich Magistrates Court on your left. The road now* becomes **Shooters Hill Road**, *taking you across* **Blackheath Common** *with the top of the Greenwich Observatory visible on your left. Continue straight ahead at the next traffic circle, driving on through two traffic lights, over a second larger traffic circle with the Sun in the Sands pub on the corner, and then onto the* **A207**. *From the brow of Shooters Hill Road, 6 miles from Greenwich, drive across* **Eltham Common**. *From here, if the weather is kind, you'll get a clear view over the Welling and Bexley roof tops toward Rochester.*

Descend the hill, drive under a railroad bridge, take the right lane as you approach a traffic light and cross into **Welling High Street**. *At its far end continue straight on, past the traffic light and a small traffic circle. Drive on through* **Bexleyheath**, *over two traffic lights. Keep right as you approach a second light by a Victorian clock tower. Go through yet another traffic light, (by the Duke of Edinburgh pub), following signs for* **Crayford (A207)**. *Cross a small traffic circle and you may note that the road you've been following, apart from the occasional one-way system, is* **Watling Street**, *the course of an old Roman road, one of their first routes from the Kent coast.*

Three miles on you'll reach **Crayford**. *Move into the right lane as you enter the town and follow the signs for* **Dartford (A226)**. *Another 2 miles takes you into* **Dartford**. *Keep right around the one-way system, following signs for the* **A226**. *Turn right at a large traffic circle, then move immediately into the left lane to turn left at a traffic light for* **Dartford Tunnel/Gravesend (A226)**. *Drive up the hill about ³⁄₄ mile and at the top, where the road curves to the left, turn sharp right, following signs for* **Longfield (B255)**. *This takes you over the highway, past Watling Street Cemetery on your right.*

Go straight on for a ¹⁄₂ mile to join the **A296**. *Cross over the traffic circle 1 mile later, following signs to* **Rochester (A2)**. *About ³⁄₄ mile from the traffic circle the road joins the A2. Drive for 6 miles, past Singlewell services, and uphill through* **Shorne Wood**. *Four miles before Rochester you move into the left lane for the A2. At* **Strood**, *near Rochester, drive through a traffic light and down the hill. Pass a second traffic light by the Coach and Horses pub, go under a railroad bridge, then straight ahead through another traffic light until you join the one-way system. Keep right, following signs to* **Chatham (A2)**, *move into the left lane and cross the* **River Medway** *at Bridge Reach. When the road becomes a divided highway move into the right lane, then turn right at the third traffic light into* **Blue Boar Lane**. *The car park entrance is on your right.*

Having parked, turn right into Blue Boar Lane, then left onto **Eastgate**. *The* **Tourist Information Centre** *is on the left at Eastgate Cottage,* **High Street**. *(Tel: (0634) 43666. Open: Daily 10am-1pm, 2pm-5pm, Jul-Aug; Mon-Sat Sep-Jun.)*

For details on **Rochester** *see* **page 309**. *You are also very close to* **Leeds Castle**, *one of England's most enchanting castles. Refer to* **page 307** *for directions from the A2 and for details of the castle.*

ROCHESTER TO CHATHAM (about 1 mile)

*Exit left from the car park, turn right at the traffic light onto the divided highway and go on through the next traffic light before turning left for **Chatham**. Follow the **High Street** towards another traffic light at its end and bear left into **Medway Street**, entering the one-way system. Pass the Sun Wharf center on your left and follow the road until you pass a small green on your right at the end of the one-way system, then bear left up a hill signposted to **Chatham Docks**. With the **Medway Heritage Centre** on your left you'll see a signpost to the historic dockyard (entrance ½ mile). At the next traffic circle take the left exit for the dockyard, go down a hill to a second traffic circle and turn left into the dockyard. The car park is on your left, next to the **Visitors' Centre**.*

Chatham Maritime and Historic Dockyard
Open: Wed-Sun 10am-6pm, summer; Wed, Sat-Sun 10am-4:30pm
       (last entry 3:30pm) winter
Admission: Adults £1.75, children £1 (50p extra for guided tour)

The dockyard, established in the mid-1500s, played a major role in the building and maintenance of the British Royal Navy. Admiral Nelson started his naval service here. His famous flagship, **HMS Victory**, was built and launched at Chatham in 1759. In the 1860s, as the navy converted from sail to steam and from wood to iron, the dockyard was extended to the north. Much of it is unchanged since the days of sail.

In the **Visitors' Centre** you'll see a 25-minute audio-visual account of the dockyard's fascinating history as well as a small maritime museum. In an 18th-century **Ropery**, occupying one of Europe's longest buildings (1,140ft), you can watch rope being made in the traditional way, while in the **Ordnance Gallery** you'll see restoration work in progress on a variety of naval cannon and guns and the **Mews Craft Workshops** demonstrate traditional naval crafts.

CHATHAM TO CANTERBURY (about 29 miles)

*From the dockyard turn right at the traffic circle by the entrance, go back up the hill and down to another traffic circle, then turn left for **Gillingham (A231)**. Drive straight on, passing a sports stadium on your right. Follow the main route into **Gillingham town center** and bear left into **Arden Street**, then right into **Jeffrey Street**. Here keep left through another traffic light and pass Gillingham Station. Follow signs for Sittingbourne as the road winds through the town center. Go on through the outskirts of Gillingham and pass the bus depot on your left. At the third traffic light keep left to rejoin the **A2 (Watling***

*Street). Passing the Territorial Army Centre on your right, continue over two traffic circles (Canterbury 22 miles). You then drive through the village of **Rainham** and enter the Kent countryside.*

If you're driving this tour in summer you'll probably see the flourishing hop fields, with their wire cages supporting the top-heavy plants. Hops were introduced into England by Flemish immigrants in the 15th century. Until then British beer had been made from fermented barley infused with herbs. After a shaky start the flavorsome hops became a vital ingredient in local brewing and in some medicines. Look for the conical roofs and rotating wind cowls of the oast houses, kilns where the hops are dried and pressed.

*After 5 miles the A2 runs through **Newington**, then on to the tiny village of **Keycol**. Continue to follow signs for Sittingbourne. Drive through **Chalkwell**, a suburb of **Sittingbourne**, 2 miles on. When you approach the Sittingbourne one-way system, bear around to the left for **Canterbury (A2)** and follow this well-marked route out of Sittingbourne to **Bapchild** village, then on through **Teynham**, where the Archbishops of Canterbury once had a palace. As you cross the gentle hills past Teynham you'll see the **River Swale** on your left, then a view over the town of **Faversham**. The A2 loops around Faversham, then speeds along the course of the Roman road stretched out before you.*

*You'll approach a major traffic circle over the last intersection of the M2 motorway 2½ miles from Faversham. Drive straight across onto the fast highway for **Canterbury**, passing Boughton Street village on your left before heading uphill towards a service station. One mile on take a left turn onto the **A28**, which goes all the way to Canterbury. You'll have your first sight of the cathedral before you reach the ring road circling the city walls. Turn right at the second traffic circle, for the the **city center**. Drive straight over three more traffic circles, passing the Man of Kent pub at the first, keeping the city walls on your left. From the third traffic circle, drive down **Lower Bridge Street** into **Broad Street**, passing the Magistrates Court on your right. Turn left into the car park opposite **St Augustine's Abbey**.*

*Take the **Queningate** exit from the car park, through a doorway in the city walls, and walk through the cathedral grounds, past the **Cathedral Welcome Centre**. Turn left past the center, through **Christ Church Gate**, and go straight on down **St Margaret's Street**, crossing High Street, until you reach the **Tourist Information Centre** at 34 St Margaret's Street. (Tel: (0227) 766567. Open: Mon-Sat 9:30am-6pm, Sun 10am-4pm May-Sep; Mon-Sat 9:30am-5pm Oct-Apr.)*

CANTERBURY

The first recorded foreign visitors to Canterbury were the Romans; next came the Saxons. In 597 St Augustine arrived from Rome to convert the English to Christianity with the backing of King Ethelbert of Kent and his Christian wife Bertha. A ruined Roman building was restored to create the first cathedral at Canterbury and **St Augustine's Abbey** was founded at the same time.

The next major historic event occurred in the 12th century. Henry II, eager to establish a particular Royal edict, needed the Church's powerful backing and swiftly appointed his friend Thomas à Becket Archbishop of Canterbury. Unfortunately the king and the archbishop didn't always see eye to eye. Henry came to regret his decision and was heard to exclaim 'Will no one free me from this turbulent priest?'. Four knights departed posthaste to Canterbury, traveling too fast for a messenger sent after them to abort their mission. Becket was murdered in his cathedral on December 29, 1170. You can stand on the exact spot where he is thought to have been struck down by the knights. When Thomas à Becket was canonized by Rome a shrine was erected in his memory which became a focal point for thousands of medieval Christian pilgrims flocking to the city. They in turn featured in one of the great works of English literature, Chaucer's *Canterbury Tales*, which in 1988 celebrated 600 years in print.

Canterbury has retained an enviable proportion of its beautiful historic buildings and is also an ideal base for excursions into the rolling Kent countryside, fondly known as the Garden of England because of its fruit growing tradition, 'garden' being the old word for orchard. The ancient city walls still encircle half the city center, which is bisected by a pedestrianized main street. This runs east from the 13th-century West Gate to St George's Tower, where the poet and playwright Christopher Marlowe was baptized in 1546.

WHAT TO SEE

Canterbury Cathedral
Open: Daily 8:45am-6:30pm Easter-Sep; until 5pm Oct-Easter
Free admission, donation appreciated

The **Visitors' Centre** offers an excellent selection of informative guides, slides and postcards, so it's worth stopping there first.

Founded by St Augustine in a Roman ruin, the original cathedral was redesigned in the Saxon period, only to be destroyed by fire in 1067. It was rebuilt in the Romanesque style, then extended at the beginning of the 12th century with the addition of the Glorious Choir of Conrad. History repeated itself in 1174 when fire again devastated large areas of the building. It was then rebuilt by the celebrated French architect William of Sens. The pattern of

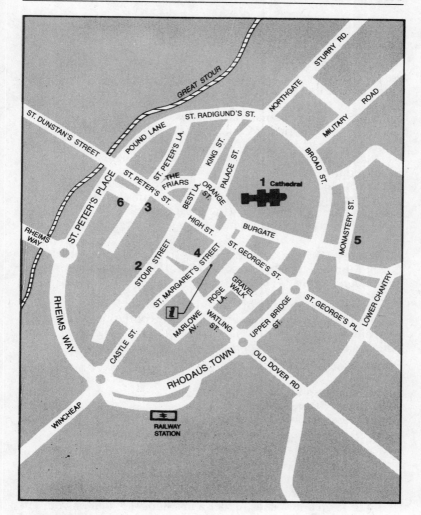

CANTERBURY

 Tourist Information Centre
1 Canterbury Cathedral
2 Canterbuy Heritage
3 Eastbridge Hospital
4 Pilgrims' Way Centre
5 St Augustine's Abbey
6 Weavers Cottages

rebuilding and extending continued through the 15th century, when the majestic central bell tower, **Bell Harry**, was completed in 1498.

Henry VIII's split with Rome in the 16th century saw the destruction of Becket's shrine and the dissolution of the monastery. Later the Puritan excesses of the Civil War in 1642 included the smashing of stained glass. Fortunately they were not too thorough, and much magnificent material remains.

The only king buried at Canterbury is Henry IV, who is interred here with his second wife, Joan of Navarre. The **tomb of Edward the Black Prince** is one of the great achievements of medieval British craftsmanship.

The sculpted prince is shown in full armor, while around the sides of the sarcophagus are shields, the prince's arms for war (lilies and lions) and his arms for peace (the ostrich plumes called the Prince of Wales' feathers). The **Norman crypt** is the largest in the world.

Canterbury Heritage, Poor Priests' Hospital, off Stour Street
Open: Mon-Sat 10:30am-4pm; also Sun 1:30pm-4pm Jun-Oct
Admission: Adults £1, children 50p

The center tells the story of Canterbury from its Roman origins to recent times. You can discover the treasures of the city displayed in a medieval building with a fine timbered roof. Holograms, computers and audio-visual presentations feature alongside ancient relics.

Eastbridge Hospital, St Peter's Street
Open: Daily 10am-5pm
Free admission, donations welcome

Dedicated to St Thomas the Martyr, the 'hospital' was founded in 1180 to accommodate pilgrims. It fell into decay, was refounded in 1342 by Archbishop Stratford and was probably at its peak when Geoffrey Chaucer was writing his *Canterbury Tales*. For the past 400 years it has cared for the elderly.

Enter down a few steps, under a low doorway, and on your left you'll see the **Chantry Chapel**. The **Undercroft** was the pilgrims' dormitory, with 12 beds 'kept in good order by a woman over 40 years of age' – in medieval times old enough to be considered a safe custodian of pilgrims' morals. Above the entrance hall there's a **chapel** which was extended to its present size in the 14th century. From 1584 to 1880 it was used as a schoolroom, then restored to its proper use in 1927.

Pilgrims' Way Centre, St Margaret's Street
Open: Daily 9:30am-5:30pm
Admission: Adults £3, children £1.50

Located in a medieval church, the center tells the story of Chaucer's pilgrims: a series of exhibits successfully bring the characters and conditions to life and offer intriguing insights into ancient Canterbury.

St Augustine's Abbey

Open: Mon-Sat 9:30am-6:30pm, Sun 2pm-6:30pm mid Mar-mid Oct; 9:30am-4pm, 2pm-4pm mid Oct-mid Mar
Admission: Adults 75p, children 35p

The original abbey, founded by St Augustine, was dedicated to St Peter and St Paul but was rededicated to St Augustine in 978. Today only the ruins of a Romanesque abbey built by Abbot Scotland and demolished in 1538 remain.

The abbey was the burial place for the royal household of Kent as well as for early archbishops. The separate **burial grounds** were linked to the main church by an octagonal Saxon building.

Weavers Cottages, 1 Kings Bridge

Open: Daily 9:30am-5:30pm summer; Mon-Sat 11am-3pm winter
Free admission

Opposite Eastbridge Hospital, you can stand on the bridge over the shallow River Stour as it flows past the Weavers Cottages and from there see a ducking stool once used for punishing offenders by ducking them in the water. During the 16th century many Flemish weavers fled to England from the religious wars raging on the Continent. They settled along Britain's east coast from Kent to The Wash, including Canterbury. Their cottages here have been transformed into a craft center.

Many traditional crafts have been revived: a shop on the ground floor offers hand-woven clothing and a range of quality gifts and souvenirs. On the upper floor visitors can try their hand at brass-rubbing.

West Gate, St Peter's Street

Open: Mon-Sat 10am-1pm, 2pm-5pm summer; until 4pm winter
Admission: Adults 30p, children 15p

The West Gate straddles the top end of St Peter's Street. This city gate dates from the 14th century, when Archbishop Simon of Sudbury (qv) tried to fortify the city during a period of peasant unrest. It didn't do him much good. In 1391 the unfortunate prelate was dragged from his refuge in the Tower of London by rebels from Canterbury and beheaded on Tower Hill.

Between the 15th and 19th centuries the West Gate was used as the city's prison. Now it houses a small museum of arms and armor. Climbing the spiral staircase out on to the battlements you'll be rewarded with a splendid panoramic view.

SHOPPING

Usual shopping hours are between 9am or 9:30am and 5:30pm. Many of the larger stores remain open until 8pm on Thursday. The city center provides all kinds of shopping facilities, from the modern chain stores of **Marlowe Arcade** to the antiques shops of **Palace Street**, where you'll find everything from bric-a-brac to beautiful Georgian silver. Antiques buffs should also check out the weekend antiques markets, particularly the one at the **Sidney Cooper Centre**. **St Peter's Street** and **High Street** offer plenty of opportunities for general shopping. On the corner of Buttermarket and Burgate you'll find a branch of **Laura Ashley**, with a good range of women's and children's clothes, plus the household fabric collection in soft, attractive designs. **Liberty**, at 44 Burgate, have a selection of gift items displayed alongside their classic printed fabrics. A little farther on, at 24 Burgate, you'll find a **National Trust Shop** that's great for gifts, cards and typically British country clothing. Walking back to the car park through the cathedral grounds, stop in at the **Cathedral Gift Shop**, just inside Christ Church Gate.

CANTERBURY RESTAURANTS

Along the **High Street, St Peter's Street** and **Burgate** are plenty of inexpensive tea shops and informal eating places. In the center of Canterbury you'll find many historic pubs that retain their old-fashioned ambience.

Caesar's Restaurant, 46 St Peter's Street   £
Tel: (0227) 456833
Open: Daily 11:30am-10:30pm
Credit cards: AE, DC, MC, V

Right in the town center, this modern, uncluttered American-style restaurant serves burgers, ribs and vegetarian dishes in a lively atmosphere. Service is efficient and the restaurant prides itself on offering 'more than you can eat for less than the price you would expect to pay'.

Queen Elizabeth Restaurant, 44-45 High Street   £
Tel: (0227) 464080
Open: Mon-Sat 9:30am-11:30am (morning coffee), noon-2:30pm
        (lunch), 2:30pm-6pm (tea)
No credit cards

Housed in a fine timber-framed building called **Queen Elizabeth's Guest Chamber** (though the Queen actually stayed at the abbey during her visit in 1573), this is a good place for a snack during your sightseeing. The richly embellished exterior of the building is matched by a fine decorative ceiling. Traditional roasts and lighter dishes are served for lunch, the afternoon menu includes cream teas with a selection of delicious cakes and pastries.

Waterfield's Restaurant, 5 Best Lane ££
Tel: (0227) 450276
Open: Mon-Sat noon-2pm, 7pm-10:30pm
Credit cards: AE, MC, V

Here's a sophisticated, attractively decorated restaurant housed in an old forge, ideal if you want to treat yourself to a special meal. The menu changes every two weeks and the set lunch is good value for money. A selection from the à la carte menu might include veal and herb terrine, salt beef with peppercorn sauce and an elderflower sorbet for dessert.

Westgate Restaurant & Take-Away, 5 St Dunstan's Street £
Tel: (0227) 464898
Open: Daily noon-3pm, 6pm-midnight; take-out open 11am-midnight
No credit cards

Just outside the Westgate, this simple eating house provides a variety of dishes from kebabs to chicken and fries. Don't be put off by the busy take-out in front; there's an attractive beamed restaurant in the back where you can select from an inexpensive menu of English, Turkish and Greek dishes.

CANTERBURY HOTELS

County Hotel, High Street ££
Tel: (0227) 66266
Amenities: ☎ ⬛ 🅿 🍴 🍸   Credit cards: AE, DC, MC, V

This attractive hotel is housed in a 16th-century building in the pedestrianized town center. First licensed in 1588 (the year of the Spanish Armada), the County Hotel has managed to retain its old-world charm while offering modern standards of comfort. All 74 rooms have bathroom, hairdryer, trouser-press and facilities to make hot drinks. There is also a selection of wonderful Tudor-style bedrooms with four-posters, and Georgian rooms with canopied beds. **Sully's Restaurant** serves traditional English specialties. For lighter meals you'll find a choice of snacks, tea and coffee in the Coffee Shop; drinks and cocktails in the Tudor Bar.

The Falstaff Hotel, St Dunstan's Street £
Tel: (0227) 462138
Amenities: ☎ ⬛ 🅿 🍴 🍸   Credit cards: AE, DC, MC, V

Standing just outside the Westgate, the Falstaff Hotel was built to accommodate pilgrims who arrived after nightfall when the city gate was closed. Later it became a coaching inn and the old-fashioned wooden beams are still an integral part of the decor. There are 25 well-furnished rooms with bath and hot drink-making facilities. Downstairs there's a friendly bar with an open fireplace where Kentish ales are served, an outdoor courtyard for the summer, and a rustic-style dining room with bare bricks and wood paneling where you can choose from a menu of hearty regional fare.

Route B: The Direct Return, CANTERBURY TO LONDON via Chilham   (about 66 miles)

CANTERBURY TO CHILHAM   (about 6 miles)

*Turn right from the car park and follow the loop road out of Canterbury, crossing straight over two traffic circles. At the third traffic circle take the left exit onto the **Ashford** road (**A28**). Follow it as it bears right to a traffic light and drive straight over the main London-Dover road (**A2**). On the right you'll see the **River Great Stour**, which sets the course for this winding road. Pass the sign to the village of Chartham and continue towards **Chilham** 1¾ miles ahead. Follow the road as it bears around to the right and you'll see a sign to **Chilham Castle**. Turn sharp left after the signpost. The car park is ahead on the right. Walk up the short hill to the village square.*

CHILHAM

The tiny center of Chilham is delightful, with the red brick Jacobean mansion known as **Chilham Castle** on the right and a few medieval cottages and shop fronts on the square. Opposite the castle there's **St Mary's Church**, with its 15th-century tower of flint and stone. At the **White Horse** pub, next to the church, you can get drinks, coffee or a meal.

WHAT TO SEE

Chilham Castle Gardens and **Rector Centre**
Open: Daily 11am-5pm (House not open to the public)
Admission: Mon-Sat: Adults £2, children £1; Sun: Adults £3, children £1.50

The lovely gardens surrounding Chilham Castle were designed by 'Capability' Brown, the famous 18th-century landscape gardener. They are home to the Rector Centre where birds of prey, including eagles, falcons and hawks, are on show from noon each day with falconry displays from 3:30pm, weather permitting. You'll also find a Battle of Britain museum, a gift shop and tea room.

CHILHAM TO LONDON   (about 60 miles)

*Turn out of the car park and back to the intersection, then turn right onto the A252 toward **Canterbury**. Four miles later turn left at the second sign for **Chartham Hatch**, a narrow country road called **Howfield Lane**. Pass **Howfield Manor** on your right, then a brick railroad bridge and drive on through the village of **Chartham Hatch**. Follow the winding road past an intersection and over the hills surrounding Chartham Hatch. Passing the oast houses you'll see the main A2 ahead in the distance. At the main road turn left for **Faversham (A2)** and continue on this fast road for 3½ miles to the M2 motorway for the quickest route back to London.*

*Just after passing Boughton Street village, on your right, you'll approach the intersection with the M2. Stay in the left lane, turning left for **London**, 52 miles ahead. Between Junctions 5 and 4 you'll pass the Farthing Corner services. Stay on the freeway for just over 26 miles, when it becomes the A2 at Junction 1. The road changes status but is still a major highway.*

*Sixteen miles on, when the road narrows, move into the center or right lane, following signs for **London**. Pass the intersection for Kidbrooke Station, just over 2 miles on before a traffic light. One and a half miles on from here keep to the left over the traffic lights, then bear off to the left, following signs for **London (A2)**, avoiding the Blackwall Tunnel. At a traffic circle with the Sun in the Sands pub on the far corner keep left for London (A2).*

*Stay in the center lane over two traffic lights, across **Blackheath** and another traffic circle. Follow the road off the heath, passing the Horse and Groom pub on the left, and drive on down the hill keeping straight on for 1½ miles into the **Deptford** one-way system by the Amersham Arms. Bear left, following the route into **Amersham Road**, then move to the right lane for **Central London (A2)**. At a traffic light opposite **Goldsmith's College**, follow the road round to the right and take the center lane for **Central London**.*

*Passing **New Cross Gate Station** on your right, keep straight on down to a traffic light. Stay in the right lane for **City of Westminster (A2)**, then bear right by the Montague Arms pub. At the end of the road turn left following signs for **City (A2)**. Drive through three traffic lights and then you'll pick up signs to **Tower Bridge** (1¼ miles). Keeping straight ahead, follow signs for **City/Westminster (A2)**. At a large traffic circle turn right under the overpass, taking the third exit for **Tower Bridge** (1 mile). This is Tower Bridge Road, which leads directly to the bridge.*

Route C: Continuing – CANTERBURY TO BRIGHTON
Via Sissinghurst Castle and Rye (about 97 miles)

CANTERBURY TO SISSINGHURST CASTLE (about 29 miles)

You now head for the Sussex coast. Turn right out of the car park opposite St Augustine's Abbey, Canterbury, follow the loop road, going straight over two traffic circles. At the third traffic circle take the left exit onto the A28 to Ashford. The road bears around to the right to a set of traffic lights where it crosses the main A2 London-Dover road. Go on 4½ miles, passing a turn to Chartham village on your left. To follow the A28 take the left turn at Chilham when the road ahead becomes the A252.

Follow the A28 for 8 miles, driving through the village of Godmersham and into Kennington, on the outskirts of Ashford. The road goes through typical Kentish farmland where for much of the year you may 'pick your own' fruit or vegetables. At weekends the area is busy with town dwellers doing just that. Try the delicious local honey that's for sale at many farms. Go through Kennington, cross the Folkestone-Dover freeway (M20) and at a set of traffic lights skirting round Ashford, take the right lane following the A28, signposted to Tenterden.

At a traffic circle about 1½ miles on take the right exit, signposted A28 to Tenterden. Drive onto a short stretch of divided highway, stay in the left lane and follow the A28 when it branches off left about 400 yards on. Drive nearly 1 mile, under a railroad bridge and up to a traffic circle, then take the second exit, turning right to follow the A28. In another ½ mile ahead turn right at a small traffic circle to follow the A28 for 4 more miles into the small village of Bethersden. Passing the picturesque, white-painted weather-board houses, you'll see on your right Stevenson Brothers Rocking Horse Makers (open: Mon-Fri 8:30am-5:30pm, Sat 8:30am-12:30pm). They make carousels and superb, traditional wooden rocking horses to order. Their clients include exalted Harrods, but individual orders are welcome. Each horse takes several months to complete. The workshop is open to the public, finished orders are displayed in the showroom.

Out of Bethersden the road takes you around to the left, then winds on for about 4½ miles through patchwork countryside and High Halden. Turn right onto the A262, signposted for Tunbridge Wells and Maidstone, then follow the road for 3 miles, turn left at the signpost for Sissinghurst and drive into the village of Biddenden.

In medieval and Tudor times this was a center for weavers. Today it's a picture-book village, timber-framed houses lining its main street with a small village green at its busy center. In the 12th century Siamese twins were born here. When they died they left 18 acres of land to the village, its earnings to feed the poor. At Easter special biscuits are baked in the village to commemorate the twins.

*From Biddenden drive 3 miles along the A262 towards Sissinghurst and turn right at the long narrow entrance to **Sissinghurst Castle**, an Elizabethan manor house. The car park is on the left at the end of the lane. The path to the ticket office is signposted.*

Sissinghurst Castle, Sissinghurst
Open: Tues-Fri 1pm-6:30pm, Sat-Sun 10am-6:30pm
Admission: Tues-Sat: Adults £3.00, children £1.50 Sun: Adults
£3.50, children £1.80

In 1930 author Vita Sackville-West and her writer husband Harold Nicolson bought Sissinghurst. It was the ramshackle remains of a Tudor mansion and garden once owned by Sir John 'Bloody' Baker, Mary Tudor's Chancellor, who had enthusiastically tortured Protestants and burned them at the stake.

During the mid-18th century the great house became camp for French prisoners of war, who badly vandalized it. Over the next 200 years house and grounds deteriorated even more, so that only the tower and bits of the main house used as outbuildings survived.

Today you'll see what many believe to be the finest garden in the British Isles. Designed by Nicolson as a series of 'outdoor rooms . . . with the strictest formality of design', and planted by Sackville-West with 'the maximum informality', this complex of squares and rectangles intersected by long walks enchants dedicated gardeners and those who simply revel in beauty spots. The rose garden has many magnificent specimens of both traditional and newer varieties, and their colors and textures make the beds masterful, painterly scenes, notably in the White Garden where silver and white blossoms prevail.

Set in the rolling Kentish Weald, the garden illustrates Nicolson's theory that proper garden design combines 'the element of expectation with the element of surprise'. Plantings are rotated through the year so the garden is worth a visit in any season. Whenever you go you'll find it even better than you expected. There is a National Trust shop for cards and gifts and an oast house tea room for light snacks.

*Drive back down the entrance lane from the castle and turn right onto the **A262**, through Sissinghurst village, less than a ½ mile ahead. A few small provisions shops make up the center of the village where you may like to visit **Sissinghurst Antiques**, The Street (open: Mon-Sat 9am-6pm, Sun as well Easter-Sep 30) run by Mr and Mrs Bisram. If you're interested in old books you could look in at the antiquarian bookshop just down the road, **Thornton Books**, The Street (open: Tues-Sat 11am-6pm).*

SISSINGHURST TO RYE   (about 19 miles)

*From Sissinghurst drive a ¹/₂ mile down the **A262** until the road forks into two lanes at the T-intersection with the **A229**. Turn left, following the signs to **Cranbrook**, then take the right lane and follow the **A229** to the right to **Hawkhurst** and **Hastings**. Follow the A229 for 5 miles, through **Hartley** and **Hawkhurst** (**Hawkhurst Castle** is on your left), then up a hill to the traffic lights at the square with the Royal Oak pub opposite. Turn left onto the **A268** to **Rye** and drive 5¹/₂ miles, passing the villages of Sandhurst and Newenden. The narrow road takes you through **Newenden**, across a bridge over the **River Rother** and into **East Sussex**. At the Rother Valley Inn turn left and follow the **A268** to **Rye**. Drive down the narrow, high-hedged road for 2¹/₂ miles to an ideal stopping point for younger members of the family.*

The Children's Farm, Great Knelle Farm, Beckley
Open: Tues-Sun 10am-5:30pm Apr-Oct
Admission: Adults £1.75, children £1.00

This is a working mixed farm with rare breeds, dairy animals, sheep, wheat and hops. There is fishing, an adventure playground and woodland walks with a picnic area beside a lake. Craft shops offer locally made items and souvenirs from the farm. There are snacks at the milk bar; lunches and farmhouse teas are served in the craft shop.

*From the Children's Farm, it's a 5¹/₂ mile drive to **Rye** through **Peasmarsh**, with its picturesque thatched cottages, and **Playden** before driving down the road into Rye. At **Deacons Corner** follow the signpost directing 'all traffic' around to the left, passing the Bedford Arms pub on your left and up to a traffic circle where you turn right. As you leave the traffic circle the car park is directly to your left.*

*Across the street from the car park entrance a steep path takes you onto Hilders Cliff and toward the center of the town. At the top turn right through the **Landgate**, then left down Tower Street. Continue along Tower Street, passing Rope Walk on your right. The **Tourist Information Centre**, Cinque Ports Street (Tel: (0797) 222293. Open: Mon-Fri 9am-1pm, 2pm-6:30pm, Sat and Sun 10:30am-1pm, 2pm-5:30pm May-mid Oct; Mon-Fri 9am-1pm, 2pm-5pm, Fri until 4:30pm mid Oct-end Apr) is on the right side of the street. You can pick up a map of the town, an historical guide and information on all the events and sights in the area.*

RYE

High on a sandstone rock above surrounding marshes, the historic town of Rye was once one of England's guardian ports, surrounded by the sea but for a narrow neck of land connecting it to the mainland towards the north. It was exposed to attack from both Danish and French invaders, and in 1377 the French burned it down and made off with the church bells. A year later the men of Rye and Winchelsea attacked Normandy and recovered them.

Much of the town dates from the 12th and 13th centuries and the wall, with its four gates, was built in the 14th. Parts of the wall can still be seen but the only remaining gate is the Landgate.

Notorious as a smuggling center, Rye grew in wealth and fame when it was attached to the **Cinque Ports**. The five original ports were Hastings, Romney, Hythe, Dover and Sandwich, but the date when the association was formed is unknown. A Henry II Charter (1155) referred to them, and the Confederation of Cinque Ports, legalized by a charter of Edward I in 1278, was intended to counter French attacks by providing ships and men. At that time there was no navy. The 'ship service' obliged the ports to supply 57 ships with crews for 15 days each year. In return the ports were made privileged towns and grew rich and powerful.

Rye and Winchelsea were attached to the port of Hastings and eventually became independent head ports. When the town's seamen were not battling for Britain they were smugglers. The harbors gradually silted up and the ports went into decline, never performing full ship service after 1445 but providing protection at certain perilous times such as 1588, when five ships from Rye sailed to fight the Spanish Armada.

One of Rye's most distinguished visitors was Elizabeth I, who bestowed the title of Rye Royal on the town. The town exudes an overwhelming sense of the past. To walk through its small, crowded center is to experience a rare awareness of history. Over the years Rye has attracted many artists and writers, among them the American author Henry James and the English writer E.F. Benson.

WHAT TO SEE

Landgate
Rye's remaining gate, with its two massive 40 foot drum towers, once had an iron portcullis. The chamber above the gateway originally housed machinery to operate a drawbridge but now contains the works of the Prince Albert Memorial Clock, which was restored in July 1981 to mark the wedding of the Prince and Princess of Wales.

Augustine Friary

Along **Hilders Cliff** from the Landgate (passing the path down to the car park on your left) you'll have a fine view over Romney Marsh – a view, it's said, of 53 parishes on a fine day. Follow the road into the **High Street** and turn right down **Conduit Hill**, where on your right you'll see the friary, now a pottery. The long, narrow building dates from 1378, when it was occupied by the Friars Heremites of St Augustine. It was closed during the Reformation and was later a refuge for French Huguenots, who came to Rye in large numbers from 1572 onwards. Since then it has been a warehouse, a Salvation Army barracks, a dance hall and a theater. Inside you'll find the **Cinque Ports Pottery** (open: daily 10am-7pm in summer, shorter hours in winter) offering a range of delicately glazed pottery – dishes, pots, bowls, plates, goblets and carafes.

The Parish Church of St Mary the Virgin

Along the **High Street**, on the left side walking from **Conduit Hill**, turn up **Lion Street**. Facing you right at the top you'll see this splendid parish church, built between 1150-1300. The chancel and nave date from about 1180 and the church clock is among the oldest and probably most famous in the country. Made by Lewis Billiard in 1561-62, it has an 18 foot-long pendulum and Quarter Boys that emerge to strike each quarter hour. The present clock face was installed in 1761. In fine weather the breathtaking view over the surrounding coast and country from the top of the tower makes clear why Rye had such a key defensive role.

Ypres Tower and Rye Museum

From the church turn right along **Market Street**, then right again in **Church Square** and down the hill to the Ypres Tower. It has a colorful history. Constructed in 1249 as a means of defense for the town, it was sold in 1430 to a private owner, John de Ypres, who lived in it. From 1518-1865 the tower was used as a prison and its lower floor served as a mortuary for over 60 years. The history of the whole town as well as the tower is outlined in the museum.

Rye Museum

Open: Mon-Sat 10:30am-1pm, 2:15pm-5pm, Sun 11:30am-1pm,
        2:15pm-5pm Easter-Oct
Admission: Adults 75p, children 60p

The museum covers the full history of Rye, including its connection with the Cinque ports, agricultural history, local crafts and industries as well as the social development of the town and surrounding area. Below the museum you'll find the **Gun Garden**, once a key defense point, now a pleasant area with ornamental cannons erected to mark the 80th birthday of the Queen Mother when she visited Rye in 1980.

Watchbell Street and **Mermaid Street**

From the Ypres Tower a walk along **Church Square** takes you to **Watchbell Street**, then through **Traders Passage** and into **Mermaid Street**. Note No 40, on the left in Church Square, a privately owned stone house with Gothic windows. It was here that the Friars of the Sack – thus named because they dressed in sack-like material – made their home in 1263. At the end of Watchbell Street you come to the **Look-out**, overlooking the quay, which was once a great ship-building and trading area. A bell hung in Watchbell Lane, just behind Watchbell Street, was rung in times of invasion to bring people outside the town walls scurrying in to safety.

Traders Passage brings you through to Mermaid Street, once a thoroughfare for smugglers coming from the Strand Gate with their contraband and the site of the famous **Mermaid Inn** (see page 239).

Lamb House, West Street
Open: Wed and Sat 2pm-6pm
Admission: Adults and children £1

This formal early Georgian townhouse was made famous by E.F. Benson in his Mapp and Lucia novels. It was rebuilt in 1722-23 by James Lamb, whose family lived here until 1832. One or another of Lamb's relatives was mayor of Rye for all but 19 years during this 109-year period. Henry James, the American author, rented the house in 1897, then bought it soon afterward. After James' death E.F. Benson lived here, writing his novels in the garden room, which sadly was destroyed in an air raid in 1940. The National Trust now looks after the house, where a fascinating collection of its famous occupants' possessions may be seen.

SHOPPING

Most stores open at 9am and close at 5pm or 5:30pm with many closing for the afternoon on Tuesday. We've indicated store hours only where they differ from the norm. To go shopping in many Rye stores is to step back in history as you enter their doors.

The Apothecary Shop, 104 High Street
Open: Sun 1:30pm-5pm   Closed: Tues and Sun in winter
Credit cards: MC, V

This has been an apothecary's shop for over 200 years. It now specializes in toiletries and related gifts. The ancient shop fittings inside were almost lost when an enthusiastic developer stripped the interior and was seen making off with them planning to sell them as antiques. The buildings and its contents are covered by a protection order, so the vandal was caught and the apothecary's old drawers and other fittings were restored to their rightful places.

The Linen Press, 105b High Street
Open: Wed-Sat 10:30am-4pm
No credit cards

This tiny shop overflows with beautiful examples of Victorian linen and lace, from delicate handkerchiefs to large tablecloths.

The Merrythought, Church Square
Credit cards: MC, V

Here you'll find a good selection of local Rye pottery as well as pottery and china from all over the country. A good place to purchase charming gifts and greetings cards.

Ye Olde Tuck Shoppe, Market Street
Open: Mon, Wed-Sat 8:30am-5pm, Sun 2pm-5pm
No credit cards

This ancient bakery still uses the original oven, which has been in continuous service since 1750. As well as the very best traditional breads and cakes there is a wide range of quality confectionery to tempt those with a sweet tooth or to take home as gifts.

Along almost every street in the town there are antique shops, some specializing in large items, others offering wonderful odds and ends. Whether you're buying or just browsing the following are worth a visit.

Grist Mill Pine, The Grist Mill, Strand Quay
Open: Sun 10am-5:30pm
Credit cards: MC, V

Lots of pine furniture, a selection of smaller antique items, basketware and a few gifts make this a good place to visit.

A Pocket Full of Rye, No 3 Warehouse, The Strand
Credit cards: MC, V

Here you'll find all sorts of fascinating old things, from bric-a-brac to large antiques. A great place for browsing.

'103', High Street
Open: Wed, Thurs and Sat 11am-5pm
No credit cards

A snug shop packed with small antiques – china, glassware, jewelry, cutlery, top hats, dishes and all kinds of collectables.

RYE RESTAURANTS

Whether you want a quick cup of coffee, a glass of chilled wine or a three-course meal there's lots of choice in Rye. Along the High Street alone you'll pass several establishments.

The Gatehouse Restaurant, 1 Tower Street   ££
Tel: (0797) 222327
Open: Wed-Sun noon-2:30pm, 6pm-10:30pm
Credit cards: DC, MC, V

Specializing in French cuisine, this small restaurant near the Landgate offers well-cooked food and a cosmopolitan range of wines.
The menu features such tempting specialties as scallops in champagne for an appetizer and a Grand Marnier soufflé for dessert.

Mrs Beeton's Restaurant, 36/38 Cinque Ports Street   £
Tel: (0797) 222262
Open: Daily 10am-9:45pm
Credit cards: MC, V

An inexpensive restaurant offering good British cooking and a
choice of imaginative vegetarian dishes. Ideal for coffee in the
morning or tea in the afternoon as well as main meals and light
dishes like omelettes and salads.

The Peacock Wine Bar, Lion Street   £
Tel: (0797) 223161
Open: Daily noon-3pm, 7pm-11pm summer; Mon, Wed-Sun
          noon-3pm, Fri-Sat 7pm-11pm winter
Credit cards: MC, V

This pleasant wine bar in a beamed 15th-century building offers
tempting home-cooked hot meals as well as light salads and snacks.
There are fifty wines to choose from, including several from local
vineyards, plus non-alcoholic drinks, including alcohol-free wine
and beer, for those who are driving.

Simon the Pieman, Lion Street   £
Tel: (0797) 222207
Open: Mon-Fri 10am-5pm, Sat 9:30am-5:30pm, Sun 2:30pm-6pm
No credit cards

Rye's oldest established tearoom is housed in all that remains of the
Red Lion Inn, which burned down in 1872. Its fireplace dates from
the 16th century. In these historic surroundings you can sample
homemade cakes, pies and light meals. Local artists display their
work on the walls. There's pottery, local honey, postcards, prints
and mouth-watering fudge in several flavors, for sale.

RYE HOTEL

Mermaid Inn, Mermaid Street   ££
Tel: (0797) 223065
Amenities: ☎ 🅿 ⊪ ⍦   Credit cards: AE, DC, MC, V

Though this is the largest medieval house in Rye it's famous for its more recent past as a haunt of smugglers. Now this intimate hotel enjoys a reputation for making its visitors welcome. The building has been lovingly restored; there's a great fireplace – 12½ feet wide by 4½ feet deep – in the bar and stunning wood beams throughout. Most of the 30 rooms have private baths; three have four-poster beds.

The pub serves good snacks and light meals while the restaurant features local seafood and Sussex beef.

RYE TO BRIGHTON (about 49 miles)

*From the car park turn left and follow the road around below the town to a traffic circle by the quay. Turn left, following the signposts for **Winchelsea**, with the Royal Military Canal on your left. In just over a mile you come to the outskirts of Winchelsea. Drive straight on, following the **A259** signposted **Hastings**. Hairpin bends take you around the outskirts of Winchelsea, avoiding the town center and giving passengers fine views over the marshes. A 5-mile drive along the A259 takes you into Hastings, with traffic lights 1 mile further on. Go straight ahead for another 1½ miles towards the sea front, then for a further ½ mile to a traffic circle with a fountain in its center. Take the left lane and drive along the promenade with the pebbly beach on your left and the holiday apartments and hotels on your right.*

*This typical British seaside scene bustles with visitors playing crazy golf, buying inexpensive gifts – or perhaps sheltering from rain and wind on the pier. Near the pier drive straight through traffic lights and continue beside the sea for a further 1½ miles. The road then takes you away from the sea, past flower gardens, and into **St Leonards** through a set of traffic lights. At a second set take the left lane and go on for 2 miles into **Bexhill-on-Sea**. At the double traffic lights stay on the **A259**, which becomes a short stretch of divided highway, to more traffic lights, then across onto a single-lane road, passing a cricket ground on your right. After almost 2 miles you reach a traffic circle where you go straight over, following signs to **Brighton** and heading into **Pevensey**, nearly 5 miles down the road. At the next traffic lights go straight on, now following the **A27** and passing the ruins of **Pevensey Castle** on your left. Drive for another 3 miles, going through **Westham**. The road takes you slightly inland for a little over 3 miles until you reach a T-intersection.*

*Turn left onto the **A22**, then take a right turn in just under ½ mile, following the **A27** signposted to **Lewes** and **Brighton**. Take this road for about 3 miles to the next traffic circle, alongside the rolling chalky downs. Cross right over the traffic circle, then drive for just under 7 miles, through **Selmeston** and **Beddingham** and crossing the **River Ouse**, to a traffic circle. Drive right over, following the A27 to Brighton and by-passing the center of Lewes on a divided highway* *for 2 miles. At another traffic circle continue across, following this fast road towards Brighton. After 2½ miles you'll pass the exit to* **Sussex University** *on the opposite side of the highway. The campus is on your right. The road runs beside Stanmore Park on your right to traffic lights at the intersection with the A23 London Road. Continue on the divided highway all the way into Brighton's center. Pass the large, unattractive, white building housing the Brighton Polytechnic, then continue for just over ½ mile through two sets of traffic lights. You'll see the steeple of* **St Peter's Church** *ahead. Drive through two further sets of traffic lights, pass St Peter's church on your right and go straight along* **Grand Parade** *beside* **Victoria Gardens**, *one of the many beautifully laid-out gardens that are features of Brighton. Take the right lane and drive straight through traffic lights. After the traffic lights bear right. At the immediate junction head across half right into* **Church Street** *following the blue Parking signs for Church Street parking lot. This you will see after 200 yards, on your left.*

For details on **Brighton** *see* **page 244**.

TOUR 2: SUSSEX AND THE COAST

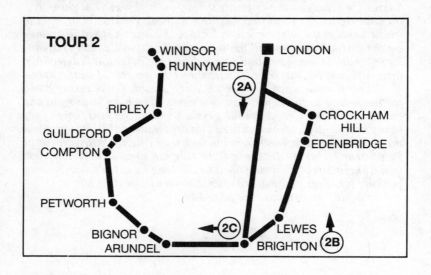

Route A: LONDON TO BRIGHTON   (about 60 miles)

*The journey starts by crossing **Vauxhall Bridge**, from north to south. Immediately over the bridge follow the signs for **A23 Brighton**, on the central-right lanes. You now go straight ahead under a vast railroad bridge. Just under the bridge is a set of traffic lights. Stay in one of the two right lanes and drive around to the right, then immediately change lanes to the left and follow the road around to the left at the next traffic lights (signposted **A23 Brighton**) onto **South Lambeth Road**. About a ½ mile down the road drive straight over more traffic lights following **South Lambeth Road**. A few yards on enter a one-way system, taking you around to the left, then follow the signs to **Brighton (A23)**, bearing right and left again onto **Stockwell Road**.*

*Drive ½ mile and around a one-way system to your left, then take the right lane to follow the A23. Follow the signs for the A23 under Brixton Railroad bridge. After ths follow the main road as it curves left. Then follow A23 signs right, and after this turn left onto **Brixton Hill**. Drive on for just over a mile, crossing five sets of lights, and onto **Streatham Hill**. Continue for just over 1 mile, through a set of lights, passing Streatham railroad station on the right, to traffic lights where the A23 forks left. Go down **Streatham High Road**, drive on for a ½ mile through two sets of lights with **Streatham Common** on your left.*

Drive through two more sets of lights. Continue for a little over 2 miles until you reach a traffic circle. Take the right lane and the second exit, following the A23 to Brighton. At the second traffic circle, in just over ½ mile, take the right lane and follow the third exit down the A23. Drive 1 mile, crossing three sets of lights, and up to a fourth set at a fork where the A23 bears left over a railroad bridge. Go over the lights on top of the bridge, then through another set about 200 yards ahead by the Propellor pub.

*Another 2 miles takes you to **Purley**, passing a large playing field area and parkland. As you drive downhill toward the shops take the right lane and go through three closely placed sets of lights and around to the right onto **Brighton Road**, Purley. Your last set of lights in the London area is ½ mile ahead. Just 2½ miles on, you'll see a signpost for the **M23** to **Brighton**. Take the slip road onto the M23 and go straight down the freeway, crossing the M25 orbital road about 1½ miles ahead.*

*Follow the M23 for about 26 miles, passing Gatwick Airport. The freeway ends at Junction 11 (signposted to **Pease Pottage**) and becomes the two-lane A23, which takes you on into Brighton. You'll come to the end of the divided highway after 7 miles, but it remains a fast drive, switching between one-lane and two. As you drive through green and woody Sussex you'll get your first glimpse of the rolling South Downs just before the end of a long, two-lane stretch. **Hickstead**, the home of the All England Show Jumping Club, comes up on your right; if an event is taking place you may be held up in traffic, with time to do more than just notice the club. At **Albourne** you come to traffic lights, with the impressive, bow-fronted green-domed King's Head pub on your right. Go straight on through the light for 3½ miles, then through the next set, and in just over a mile on you'll see two impressive pillars, one on either side of the road, marking the entrance to Brighton. A mile past the pillars you go straight on past traffic lights, passing **Patcham Park** on your right. The former manor house at the end of the Park now belongs to the Youth Hostel Association.*

*The outskirts of Brighton now rise up around you and you cross a mini traffic circle, heading toward the town center. Traffic lights may stop you beside **Preston Park**, which surrounds **Preston Manor** and the parish church of **St Peter**. As you drive straight on and alongside the park, note the beautifully laid-out gardens, in spring and summer filled with a dazzling display of plants. You may also see tags above the patches of garden bearing the names of towns or cities. The flower beds are products of a national horticultural competition with entries from cities all over Great Britain.*

*Just beyond the park, with its bowling greens and tennis courts, you enter the one-way system that takes you right into the town. Bear around to the left, then keep right, following the road towards the **town center**. You'll pass under an impressive railroad viaduct and come up to traffic lights at **Preston Circus**, the fire station on your left, the Standford Arms pub on your right and the Hare and Hounds* *opposite. Go straight on into the **London Road** shopping area and just under ½ mile from the traffic lights you'll pass impressive **St Peter's Church** on your left. Designed in 1824 by Sir Charles Barry, architect of the House of Commons, this is a superb example of Gothic Revival architecture. Follow the road around to the left, then immediately around to your right as you drive along **Grand Parade** with **Victoria Gardens** on your right. At the traffic lights, just beside **Queen Victoria's statue**, bear around to the right, moving immediately into the left lane at the intersection, where you give way. You'll see the blue-domed **Pavilion** across the road. Drive straight ahead onto **Church Street**, passing the **museum** and **library** on your left, and on up the hill. Two hundred yards ahead on your left you'll see the entrance to the car park.*

*From the car park walk down **Church Street**, then turn third right into **New Road**. At the end of New Road turn left onto **North Street** and go on straight down, along **Castle Square** and out onto **Old Steine**. Turn right and the Tourist Information Centre is on your right just past Steine Lane. They'll supply a street plan of Brighton and details of all events taking place during your visit. The center has up-to-date information on theater performances and other entertainment in town. You'll also find details of any antiques and crafts fairs in the area.*

*The **Tourist Information Centre** is in Marlborough House, 54 Old Steine. (Tel: (0273) 23755. Open: Mon-Sat 9am-6:00pm, Sun 10am-6pm Easter-Sep; Mon-Fri 9am-5pm, Sat 10am-5pm, Sun 11am-3pm Oct-Easter.)*

There is another TIC office on the Sea Front, Kings Road. (Tel: (0273) 29801, ext 550. Open: Tues 1pm-6pm, Wed-Sun 10am-6pm, Bank Holiday Mon (then closed following Tues and Wed am) Easter-Sep.)

BRIGHTON

Brighton as we know it today grew in the mid-18th century from a small fishing town called Brighthelmstone. By comparison with many towns and ports on England's south coast it has a short history, and that is centered on fashion and society instead of wars and victories.

Brighthelmstone had about 1,000 inhabitants at the height of its prosperity but fell into decline as the sea advanced to engulf walls and houses. The original walled and fortified town, with its four gates, arose on the site of an earlier Roman settlement. The English Channel now covers all traces of the original town, which was in the area of the Palace Pier. In the mid-19th century its name was shortened, to the disgust of the locals, to please its pleasure seeking visitors. A fashionable physician from Lewes, Dr Richard

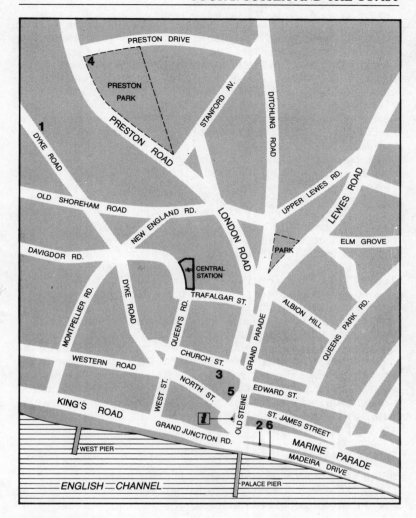

BRIGHTON

 Tourist Information Centre
1 Booth Museum of Natural History
2 Brighton Aquarium and Dolphinarium
3 Brighton Museum and Art Gallery
4 Preston Manor
5 The Royal Pavilion
6 Volk's Seafront Railway (station)

Russell, had moved to Brighton in the mid-18th century, indicating to Society that it was a town that would promote good health. The benefits of sea bathing and fine air were soon being applauded, though the real reason for the growth of this fashionable resort was royal influence. The Prince of Wales – later Prince Regent and then George IV – visited his uncle, the Duke of Cumberland, here in 1783. Impressed by the freedom and freshness of the seaside town, he rented and later purchased a respectable farmhouse on the Steine. On the site of this modest house the domed Pavilion now stands.

The Steine became a center of fashion and the resort a smart and wealthy playground for high society. In Jane Austen's *Pride and Prejudice*, with its great concern about marriage for young ladies, newly-married Lydia Bennett tells how her sisters may find husbands: 'They must all go to Brighton – that is the place to get husbands'. Later the town was graced with other royal visitors, notably Queen Victoria and the Prince Consort, who stayed at the Pavilion, then King Edward, who stayed in the Pavilion as a child but later, in 1908, chose a residence at the corner of Chichester Terrace and Lewes Crescent, at the east end of the promenade.

Among all its features Brighton's piers attest that it has always been a resort town. There have been three piers. **The West Pier**, opened in 1886 with a theater and concert hall along its 1,100 foot length, now stands closed and derelict. The **Palace Pier**, an elegant example of its type, opened in 1901, provides entertainment for the public today. The **Chain Pier**, opened in 1823, stood close to the site of the Palace Pier but in 1896, in a state of decay, was washed away by the sea. Brighton remains a fashionable center for relaxation and fun, a town to which young Londoners escape for weekends. All through its modern streets and ancient lanes the atmosphere is vibrant.

WHAT TO SEE

Booth Museum of Natural History, 194 Dyke Road
Open: Mon-Wed and Fri-Sat 10am-5pm, Sun 2pm-5pm
Free admission, donations welcome

From the Clock Tower near the Churchill Square shopping center Dyke Road runs 1½ miles inland and uphill to this museum, which houses a large collection of mounted British birds. There is also a gallery of the world's butterflies and an exhibition of skeletons illustrating vertebrate evolution.

Brighton Aquarium and Dolphinarium, Madeira Drive
Open: Daily 10am-6pm Apr-Sep; 10am-5pm Oct-Mar
Admission: Adults £2.60, children £1.70

There has been an aquarium in Brighton since 1872, and until the

London zoo aquarium opened, Brighton's collection of sea life was unrivaled in Europe. It is still Britain's largest, with marine, tropical and freshwater fish. There's also a **Pirate's Deep** children's playground and – surprisingly, for an aquarium – a simulator that allows visitors to experience the thrills of high-speed aerial combat.

Brighton Museum and Art Gallery, Church Street
Open: Tue-Sat 10am-5:45pm, Sun 2pm-5pm
Free admission

Just beside an imposing gateway to the Pavilion the museum and art gallery share the same building as the public library, which was once the site of Queen Adelaide's stables. Unlike many small town museums this one has fine displays of Art Deco and Art Nouveau furniture and decorative art, the famous Willett collection of pottery and porcelain illustrating British social history, and a collection of modern paintings and drawings. There is also a fascinating display of clothing in the Fashion Gallery that explores the reasons for various fashions and the development of styles since the 18th century. A coffee shop serves good coffee and snacks in peaceful surroundings; the museum shop sells cards and gifts.

The Palace Pier, Madeira Drive
Open: Mon-Fri 9am-11pm, Sat-Sun 9am-1am
Free admission

The pier, reaching over 2,500 feet out into the sea, was built in 1899 and is now a center for amusements, including a Ghost Train and Helter Skelter. You can walk out to the end of the pier for a superb view of Brighton's seafront, then stop at one of its two bars for a drink. The pier is undergoing long-term refurbishment and will eventually have a theater and several restaurants.

Preston Manor, Preston Park
Open: Tues-Sun 10am-5pm, public holiday Mon
Admission: Adults £1, children 60p

About 2 miles inland from the seafront, past the Pavilion and the London Road shopping area, you come to Preston Park. Its old manor house was built about 1250, rebuilt in 1738 and remodeled in 1905. The home of the Stanford family for 200 years, it is filled with wonderful antique furniture, silver, pictures and porcelain. Do visit the pets' cemetery in the walled garden and the 13th-century parish church of St Peter in the park.

The Royal Pavilion, Brighton
Open: Daily 10am-6pm Jun-Sept; 10am-5pm Oct-May
Admission: Adults £2.30, children £1.20

This dazzling royal seaside palace should be seen by every visitor to

Brighton. Built by Henry Holland on the site of a farmhouse as a simple classic villa, it was rebuilt from 1815-1822 by John Nash. George IV spared no expense in imaginatively creating and furnishing his south-coast retreat. Inside it is as lavish as its external façade suggests, though on a pleasantly small scale. Many areas are on display to the public and the sumptuous oriental decor is unforgettable.

Volk's Seafront Railway, Madeira Drive
Open: Daily 11:30am-6:30pm end May-beginning Sep; weekends only Apr, May, Sep, beginning Oct; every Sun and public holiday
Closed: Beginning Oct-Mar
Admission: Adults 60p, children 30p, one way fare

Britain's first public electric railroad, opened in 1883, runs along the seafront from the Palace Pier to Brighton Marina.

Brighton Marina, Marine Drive
Open: Daily from 9am-dusk
Admission: Pedestrian entry free

If you take a ride along the seafront on Volk's Railway you'll end up at Europe's largest marina, with mooring for about 2,000 yachts. Walk through the marina village, a new development with bars and specialty shops for the yachting community.

ENTERTAINMENT IN BRIGHTON

Brighton's nightlife encompasses a wide range of activities in summer. Check at the Tourist Centre for details of concerts, plays and sports events.

Brighton Centre, Kings Road, (tel: (0273) 203131). This is the south of England's biggest civic center, offering conference facilities, a venue for major sports events, exhibitions, shows, circuses and concerts.

Brighton Races, (tel: (0273) 603580). Brighton Racecourse, on the northern outskirts on top of the downs, is an excellent source of entertainment on a sunny afternoon. From April to October the day's racing usually starts around 2pm and six races are run. There are also occasional evening events.

The Dome, New Road, (tel: (0273) 674357). This historic concert hall is in the grounds of the Pavilion. Seating 2,100, it is the venue for pop concerts, variety shows, military bands and orchestral and symphony concerts.

Pavilion Theatre (tel: (0273) 674357). This small theater, seating 250, in the grounds of the Pavilion provides a stage for actors and playwrights who have not yet tasted national success. The program includes 'alternative comedy' and there are often late-night performances.

The Theatre Royal, New Road, (tel: (0273) 27480). Brighton's main theater was established in 1774 and has been in constant use since 1807. The standard of entertainment is first class, and includes many pre-London productions. Drama, comedies, thrillers, pantomime, musicals and ballet are all featured.

SHOPPING

There are two distinct sides to Brighton's shopping facilities. You'll find the latest and best of new goods in efficient new shops, but by way of contrast to this is a key antiques center. Visit the ancient shops in **The Lanes** or in the markets and antiques fairs that happen frequently. Shopping hours are generally from 9am or 9:30am to 5pm or 5:30pm. Some of the larger stores around the **Western Road** area are open until 8pm on Thursdays.

Churchill Square Shopping Centre
For chain stores, newsagents, pharmacies and all other everyday requirements this is the main shopping precinct but shops also stretch along Western Road.

Gardner Street Market
This is a magnet for those who love searching for bargains. Every Saturday morning the whole street is lined with traders offering an incredible variety of antiques, bric-a-brac and plain junk. Jewelry, silverware, coins, books, medals, china and glassware – you name it. There are also stands loaded with flowers, vegetables and fruit, clothes and 'odds and ends'. Trading is usually from 7am until about 1pm. Arrive early.

The Lanes
This maze of ancient buildings and narrow old streets offers a variety of shopping opportunities, notably for antiques and high-quality women's clothes. There are also shops offering unusual gifts and a lot of small coffee shops. Even those who hate shopping will love The Lanes for the sense of history pervading this paved warren.

London Road Shopping Area
More modern shops, not as good or as comprehensive as in the Churchill Square area but useful if you need a few necessities.

Brighton Square Antiques Gallery, 41 Meeting House Lane
Open: Mon-Sat 10am-5pm
Credit cards: Varies but most dealers accept AE, DC, MC, V

This center for large and small antiques has 30 traders selling everything from small items of bric-a-brac to furniture. If you don't want to walk around hundreds of different shops this is a good place to hunt for bargains and unusual gifts.

Casa Pupo, 8 Brighton Square
Credit cards: AE, DC, MC, V

Ceramics, lighting, rugs and gifts from Italy, Spain and Portugal are on offer. It's a good place to find an unusual gift.

Frocks, 12 Duke Street
Open: Mon-Sat 9:30am-6pm
Credit cards: AE, DC, MC, V

Elegant ladies' wear. You're almost bound to find a stunning outfit. Emphasis is on quality and individual attention – with prices to match.

The House of Antiques, 25 Meeting House Lane
Open: Mon-Sat 10am-5pm
Credit cards: AE, DC, MC, V

This is a place for high-quality antiques at prices to match.

Julian Chalcraft, 10 The Lanes
Open: Mon-Sat 9:30am-5:30pm; Sun 11:30am-5:30pm (closes on rainy days in winter)
Credit cards: AE, DC, MC, V

A fine place for a new dress or an attractive item of costume jewelry. Leading designer names fill the racks.

The Paper Weight Shop, 11 Brighton Square
Open: Mon-Sat 10am-5:30pm, Sun 11am-5pm
Credit cards: AE, DC, MC, V

Good for souvenirs and gifts. Over half the shop is devoted to paper weights; usually 300-400 to choose from, many made in Scotland with some from France.

Pecksniffs Perfumery, 45 Meeting House Lane
Open: Mon-Sat 9:30am-6pm, Sun 10am-6pm
Credit cards: AE, MC, V

Special toiletries may be bought at this unusual shop, which offers bespoke (custom made) perfumes and invites you to spend time experimenting until you decide on your ideal scent. There are also many perfume combinations already prepared. The assistants are charmingly dressed in Victorian-style dresses.

T. Barnes Jewellery, 24 Meeting House Lane
Open: Mon-Fri 11am-5pm
Credit cards: AE, DC, MC, V

The shop's specialties are vintage watches, antique jewelry, and decorative art (Art Deco and Art Nouveau).

BRIGHTON RESTAURANTS

Brighton's choice of places to eat is enormous and represents cuisines from all over the world. There are lots of Indian and Chinese restaurants, hamburger bars, sandwich bars and coffee bars, as well as many small vegetarian restaurants.

Buzz Bar, Churchill Square   £
Tel: (0273) 777998
Open: Daily 8am-6pm
No credit cards

This is a takeout, coffee bar and restaurant that's ideal for a quick late breakfast of croissants or Danish pastries and coffee, a tasty lunch or a refreshing afternoon snack. It's usually very busy but is inexpensive and provides salads, filled baked potatoes and a selection of hot dishes.

English's Oyster Bar & Seafood Restaurant, 29-31 East St £££
Tel: (0273) 27980/25661
Open: Mon-Sat noon-10:15pm; Sun 12:30pm-5:45pm
Credit cards: AE, DC, MC, V

This well-known restaurant specializes in fresh fish, seafood and oysters. You can sample all these cooked to perfection in various ways, whether plain, *à la meunière* or served in a delicate sauce. Traditional style and service make this a good place for a special meal or a pre-theater supper.

Food for Friends, 17 Prince Albert Street   £
Tel: (0273) 202310
Open: Daily 9am-10pm, weekends until 11pm
No credit cards

Here, in one of Brighton's better-known wholefood restaurants, you'll be served with good home cooking from an imaginative cosmopolitan menu. Whether you're gasping for the first coffee and croissant – wholemeal of course – or relaxing over an informal dinner you won't be disappointed by the food.

Muang Thai Restaurant, 77 St James's Street ££
Tel: (0273) 605223
Open: Mon-Tues, Thur-Sun noon-2pm, daily 6:30pm-11:30pm
Credit cards: AE, DC, MC, V

If you feel like an oriental meal but would prefer a change from Chinese cuisine try this excellent Thai restaurant. The menu features spicy dishes flavored with chillies and garlic, a selection of seafood specialties and vegetarian items.

The Orchard Restaurant, 33 Western Street £££
Tel: (0273) 776618
Open: Tues-Sat 7pm-10pm
Credit cards: AE, DC, MC, V

Situated just off the seafront in an 18th-century cottage, this restaurant offers meals for those who wish to sample traditional British food at its best as well as some light French-style cooking. The atmosphere is ideal for dining *à deux*.

BRIGHTON HOTELS

Beach Hotel, 2-4 Regency Square £
Tel: (0273) 23776
Amenities: ☎ ⌨ ⑧⑨ ⚱   Credit cards: AE, DC, MC, V

This modest and inexpensive hotel has all the essentials for a short stay and is handily placed in one of Brighton's loveliest old squares, 50 yards from the seafront, opposite the famous West Pier. There's no car park but there's public parking underground in the square.

The Grand, King's Road £££
Tel: (0273) 21188
Amenities: ☎ ⌨ 🅿 ⑧⑨ ⚱   Credit cards: AE, DC, MC, V

Though its Regency façade is typical of Brighton the Grand opened in 1864 and its interior is designed to the highest standards of Victorian elegance and luxury. Everything is on a grand scale: enormous rooms with lofty decorated ceilings, mighty marble pillars and, underfoot, polished marble or richly patterned carpeting. A vast central staircase sweeps around the foyer, serving 162 rooms on seven floors (there are, of course, elevators too). Since the hotel suffered an IRA bombing in 1984 it has been rebuilt and completely refurbished, keeping its original Victorian style but adding every modern luxury, including a health spa, the Midnight Blues nightclub and 'Romantic' bedrooms with double whirlpool baths. The Edwardian-style sea-view conservatory, complete with giant potted palms, serves the classiest teas in town.

King's Palace Hotel, 12-15 King's Road   £
Tel: (0273) 26848
Amenities: ⊑ ⦙⦙⦙ ♈   Credit cards: AE, DC, MC, V

This family-run hotel is an inexpensive and lively place with a wine bar/pub and steak house opening on to the street and its own disco. It is very central, close to the Palace Pier and backing onto that antique-hunter's paradise, The Lanes. There is no parking lot but public parking is close at hand.

The Portland House Hotel, 55 Regency Square   £
Tel: (0273) 820464
Amenities: ☎ ⊑ ♈   Credit cards: A, AE, DC, V

Occupying a Grade II protected Regency building in a seafront square, this quiet family hotel welcomes guests with a blazing open fire in winter. Though it has no formal restaurant, a home-cooked prix fixe evening meal is available upon prior request. Parking is in the public car park under the square.

Route B: BRIGHTON TO LONDON
Visiting Hever Castle And Chartwell   (about 63 miles)

BRIGHTON TO EDENBRIDGE   (about 35 miles)

---

*From the car park turn left, then first right onto **Spring Gardens**. At the end of the road turn right and go down the hill to the traffic lights. Take the left lane and follow the road signposted to **London A23**. At St Peter's Church keep to right fork following signs for **A27** to **Lewes**. Go right through one set of traffic lights and at the next set continue following the signs for A27 to Lewes. At the next set of lights follow the left lane, taking the A27 and moving onto a divided highway. Drive about 5½ miles to a traffic circle, passing through a set of lights with Stanmer Park on your left and the Sussex University campus just beyond the park. At the traffic circle take the left exit onto the **A275** to **Lewes** and drive 1 mile to traffic lights beside Lewes Prison, with its high brick walls and barred windows. Turn left at the lights, following the **A275** signposted to **East Grinstead** and **London**.*

    *After 7 miles you reach **Chailey**, then there's a T-intersection. Turn right here, then immediately left, following signs for **A275** to **Sheffield Park** and the **Bluebell Railway**. Drive along this country road for almost 2 miles to the town sign for Sheffield Park and, just beyond it, the entrance to the Bluebell Railway, Sheffield Park Station.*

Bluebell Railway, Sheffield Park Station, near Uckfield
Open: Daily Jun-Sep; Wed, Sat-Sun May and Oct; Sat-Sun Mar,
Apr and Nov; Sun only in Jan, Feb and Dec. Timetable
available on request (tel: (0825) 722370).
Admission: Adults 60p, children 30p
Fare: Adults £2.60, children £1.30 round trip

Steam trains run along a 5-mile track between Sheffield Park and
Horsted Keynes stations. The line was opened in 1882 but was little
used by the early 1900s. It was closed in 1958 but a length of track
was bought from British Rail by a keen local group, inspired by the
success of similar projects in Wales.

In 1960 a Light Railway Ordinance was granted, allowing renovation of the line for tourist and preservation purposes. Now it is
one of the most famous steam lines in the country, with frequent
services. Even if you don't travel, the engine sheds are fascinating.
You'll see the steam trains being repaired and cleaned. There are
occasional special events and you can even dine aboard the
Regency Belle if you book in advance. Full details of special
evening restaurant-train excursions are available on request.

*From the Bluebell Railway turn left and drive for 2 miles into the
attractive village of **Dane Hill**, passing Sheffield Park Vineyards on
your right. Another 3½ miles takes you through Chelwood Gate and
to an intersection where you turn left onto the **A22** (with the Roebuck
Hotel opposite) signposted **East Grinstead** and **London**. The drive
from Sheffield Park to East Grinstead takes you through parts of vast
Ashdown Forest, the setting for A.A. Milne's adventure stories about
Pooh Bear. Drive through the picturesque village of **Forest Row**,
around sweeping bends and out towards **East Grinstead**, a prosperous commuter town. At the next traffic circle take the left exit for the
town center. Drive along **Middle Row** to the attractive High Street and
another traffic circle where you turn right onto **London Road**. Go on
down London Road, following the one-way system around to the
right and past the train station on your left. Here you pick up signs
for **Tunbridge Wells (A264)**. Follow these to the small church, before
which you turn left. This winds along for about 1 mile to an
intersection where you turn left for **Edenbridge**. This wooded country
road goes through the village of **Dormansland** to a complex junction.
Here keep right for **Edenbridge (B2028)**. Drive for just over 1 mile to
Marsh Green, a simple country village, then to an intersection in
another mile where you turn left (B2026) and go on into **Edenbridge**.
The main car park, off the **High Street**, is well-signposted.*

EDENBRIDGE

This bustling country market town on the River Eden, the site of a

Roman road in 100AD, was probably some kind of settlement as early as the 10th century. The parish church dates from the 12th and 13th centuries and the town developed during the 15th and 16th centuries, when it became a center for the surrounding iron industry at Cowden, Hever, Chiddingstone and other parishes. After that early period of wealth, the decline of the iron industry and the fluctuating fortunes of agriculture produced a checkered history of alternating wealth and poverty for Edenbridge. A busy gathering place for local farmers, the High Street is punctuated with many pubs of great character, a variety of antiques shops and a fair selection of restaurants. This is a fine place to catch a glimpse of true British country-town lifestyle. As you explore the High Street you may like to visit **Bigwood Antiques**, 102 High Street (open: Mon-Sat 10:30am-5pm), which offers large and small items of antique furniture. Should you make a large purchase Bigwood helps with tax and shipping arrangements. **Chevertons of Edenbridge**, 67-69 High Street specialize in antique furniture and smaller items. The firm is experienced in shipping and happy to help with organizing transportaion of large items. **Interesting, Old and Unusual**, 71 High Street (closes Sat at 4:30pm) is packed with all kinds of bric-a-brac and small antiques and is a good place to browse for unusual gifts or odds and ends.

For light bar meals or snacks, including sandwiches, ploughman's lunch or hot food such as steak and kidney pie, try one of the old beamed pubs, among them **The Old Crown** and **The King and Queen**. If you prefer a formal meal, **Honours Mill**, 87 High Street (tel: (0732) 866757; open Tues-Fri 12:15pm-2pm, 7:15pm-10pm Sat dinner only, Sun lunch only), a restaurant in the 18th-century mill, is definitely worth a visit. Here an inspired choice of well-cooked dishes includes traditional specialties. Try chicken stuffed with nuts or a fish pâté perhaps followed by a luscious English trifle.

SIDE TRIP TO HEVER CASTLE   (about 2½ miles)

From the car park go back down the **High Street**. *The left turn to Hever is just past the bridge. Follow this road for almost 2 miles to a T-intersection, where you turn left. The castle is ¼ mile ahead on the right.*

Hever Castle, near Edenbridge
Open: Daily: Garden: 11am-6pm; Castle: noon-6pm (last entry
        5pm) Apr-Oct   Closed June 16
Admission: Castle and Gardens: Adults £3.40, children £1.70;
        Gardens only: Adults £2.20, children £1.90

Famous as the residence of the Bullen, or Boleyn, family and the childhood home of Anne Boleyn, second wife of Henry VIII, this moated castle dates from 1270, when the **Gatehouse** and outer walls were built. In 1470 the family created a comfortable Tudor dwelling within the walls. In 1903 the castle was bought by the American William Waldorf Astor, who spent a fortune on restoring it and filling it with the many treasures now on view to the public. Astor created the **Tudor Village**, gardens and lake. A wealth of rich carving characterizes the interior and the walls of the **Drawing Room** are lined with inlaid paneling. The original **Great Hall** is now a Dining Hall with an elaborately carved Minstrels' Gallery, and is the venue for '**King Henry VIII' banquets**. You can see Anne Boleyn's and Henry VIII's rooms. In the Long Gallery is an exhibition, '**Henry VIII and Anne Boleyn at Hever Castle**'. The **Oratory** is a charming chapel of around 1584. The extensive gardens include a fine maze and lake and an adventure playground for children. A shop sells gifts, souvenirs, postcards and slides. The restaurant offers snacks and hot meals, including traditional cream teas. The annual program of special events includes open air theater performances; full details can be obtained by calling (tel: (0732) 865224). Now retrace your steps to Edenbridge.

EDENBRIDGE TO LONDON Via Chartwell   (about 30 miles)

From Edenbridge it's a short distance to Sir Winston Churchill's famous home at **Chartwell**.

*The **B2026** takes you straight out of the town, passing Edenbridge British Rail Station on your left. The village of **Crockham Hill** is 1½ miles outside Edenbridge. As you drive out of it you turn right to continue along the **B2026**, signposted to **Westerham** and **Chartwell**. Follow the road for just over 2 miles across the wooded **Crockham Hill Common**, then turn right into **Mapleton Road**, following the signpost to **Chartwell**. About 200 yards down the road you'll see the house.*

Chartwell, Crockham Hill, near Edenbridge
Open: House and Garden: Tues-Thur noon-5pm, Sat-Sun & public holidays 11am-5pm (closed Tues after holiday Mon) Apr-Oct; House only: Wed, Sat-Sun 11am-4pm Mar & Nov
Closed: Dec-Feb
Admission: House and Garden: Adults £2.70, children £1.40
House only: Adults £1.40, children 60p

This unpretentious red brick Victorian house was bought by Sir (then Mr) Winston Churchill in 1922. It is filled with memorabilia of the war leader's paintings and many personal items. There are also uniforms and items relating to Churchill's political life. The house overlooks peaceful grounds with a lake and beautiful flower gardens.

*From Chartwell turn right out of the car park and follow **Mapleton Road** back to the **B2026**. Turn right, signposted **Westerham**, starting the trip back to London. A mile along the road you'll come into Westerham, going down a hill to a T-intersection where you turn left onto the A25, signposted to **Reigate**. Follow the A25 through Westerham and for a further 2 miles to traffic lights, then go straight on, bypassing the town of Oxted and heading for a traffic circle in a further 3 miles. Turn right at the circle, following the signs for **London, Croydon, M25**. Go straight over traffic circle at M25 interchange following signs for **London/A22**. At traffic circle, 3 miles later, keep on for **London**. The road then narrows in a residential area, and 1 mile on you come to traffic lights by the **Whyteleafe Tavern**. Take the left lane and go straight on, driving a further 2½ miles to a set of lights at **Purley**, where you take the center lane and go straight on. Follow road as it curves right at traffic lights, then get immediately into the left lane once around the corner and follow the signs taking you sharp left uphill toward **Central London** on the A23. Along **Purley Way**, passing the Purley Way Recreation Ground, you'll get a panoramic view of London ahead. At the third set of traffic lights, on a railroad bridge, take the right lane and follow the road around to the right towards Central London. Three more sets of lights take you through an industrial area, past a power station on your left and over a railroad bridge. From here in about ¾ of a mile you hit yet another traffic circle, where you take the second exit for **Central London** and continue for 1 mile to the next circle. Take the second exit, again well signposted, to Central London.*

*The rest of the journey into central London follows a straight course through a battery of traffic lights. Four miles and 8 sets of lights take you from the last traffic circle to **Brixton Hill**. Continue on across 11 more sets of lights, following the clear signs to Central London. At the next set of lights, turn left towards the **Oval** and continue on about 200 yards to yet more lights. Drive around the walled **Oval Cricket Ground** and beyond the Oval you'll reach traffic lights (just under ½ mile from the previous ones). You're now facing the vast railroad bridge at **Vauxhall**.*

*Follow the road as it bears left and take the right lane, driving first beside, then under the bridge and following the signs to the **West End** and **Ring Road**. Under the bridge take the right lane to bear right at traffic lights, then move immediately into the left lane as you cross onto **Bondway**. To your left you'll see **Vauxhall Bridge**. Take the left lane, follow the road around to the left at the traffic lights and cross the bridge to the starting point of the tour.*

Route C: Continuing On From BRIGHTON TO WINDSOR
Via Arundel Castle, Petworth House And Wisley Gardens
(about 78 miles)

BRIGHTON TO ARUNDEL CASTLE (about 19 miles)

*From the **Tourist Information Centre** in Old Steine bear right around a large fountain to the sea front. At the traffic circle in front of the **Palace Pier** turn right and drive 1½ miles along the sea front to **Hove**. Turn right into **Grand Avenue** around a statue of Queen Victoria, signposted **Lewes/A27**. Continue up Grand Avenue almost to its end turning left at the lights following the signs for **Worthing/A27**. Stay on the A27 past a large cemetery and past Lancing College to your right. You'll see its magnificent Great Chapel in a dramatic position at the top of the hill overlooking the water meadows of the Adur valley. Continue to follow A27 signs to **Chichester/Portsmouth** as you skirt Worthing. Just before **Arundel** turn right at a traffic circle below the town, keep going up to the **Castle**, turning right at the end of the approach road and then left through the Castle gates. After paying the entrance fee drive up through the grounds to the car park near the top. Parking costs 50p. (Should you wish to include Arundel town in your visit, use the car park opposite the entrance gates as you may find difficulty in parking in the town itself. You'll need to buy a parking ticket from the machine by the entrance: 70p for 2 hours.)*

Arundel Castle
Open: Sun-Fri 1pm-5pm Apr-Oct; noon-5pm Jun-Aug
Closed: Sat
Admission: Adults £2.80, children £1.70

This great castle stands in magnificent grounds overlooking the River Arun. Built at the end of the 11th century by Roger de Montgomery, Earl of Arundel, to defend the valley against sea raiders, it has been the seat of the Dukes of Norfolk and their ancestors for over seven hundred years. The castle was largely rebuilt in the 18th century, following extensive damage by Cromwellian troops during the Civil War. Among its treasures are fine furniture, tapestries, portraits by Van Dyck, Gainsborough and Reynolds and the tombs of the **Fitzalan Chapel**. The views from the 12th-century stone keep extend over the town to the river marshes beyond.

ARUNDEL

The **Tourist Information Centre**, 61 High Street (Tel: (0903)

882268. Open: Daily 9am-6pm June-Sep; Mon-Fri 9am-noon, 1pm-4pm Nov-Feb; Mon-Fri 9am-5:15pm Mar-May, Oct) is close to the top exit gates of the Castle, on your left as you walk down the High Street. The town is mostly Victorian, but there are a number of fine, 18th-century houses dotted around and both **Mount Pleasant** and **Bond Street** contain interesting, flint-walled cottages dating from the early 1800s. **The Museum and Heritage Centre** at 61 High Street (open: Sat, Sun 10:30am-12:30pm, 2pm-5pm Mar-May, Sept; daily Jun, July, Aug; admission: adults 50p, children 15p) tells the story of the town that grew up at the foot of the ancient castle. Flanking the castle walls are the late 14th-century parish church and the **Roman Catholic Cathedral** of St Philip Neri, which was built by the 15th Duke of Norfolk in 1868-9. The Cathedral was designed by Joseph Hansom, inventor of the Hansom cab.

SHOPPING

You'll find a great variety of antique and art shops in every street. They all open at normal hours, but many close for lunch between 1 and 2pm. In Tarrant Street, half way down the High Street, you'll find **Serendipity** at No 27 with an interesting collection of antiquarian maps, prints, and oil paintings. Opposite is the **Old Printing House Arcade** with a number of specialist shops including, at No 2, **William Morris**, a china specialist and **Arundel Antiques** which stocks period English furniture. From Tarrant Street there is a small passageway half way along on the left which takes you down into Crown Yard. At the far end, among the antique shops there, you'll find **Tarrant Gallery**, worth visiting for good quality pictures and furniture.

ARUNDEL RESTAURANTS

There is a good choice of pubs, cafés and restaurants within a short walk of the top gate or lower car park. Do remember, however, that once you leave the castle, you'll have to pay again to re-enter.

Dukes, 65 High Street   **££**
Tel: (0903) 883847
Open: Daily 5:30pm-9:15pm (9:30pm Sat)
Credit cards: MC, V

Opposite and to the left of the top Castle gates – your exit point. A small but sumptuous candle-lit interior boasts a ceiling from an Italian palace. The French menu is original and varied, especially on Friday, the gourmet evening. The smoked salmon starter or salmon steak and veal are particularly recommended.

ıngway's Diner, 33 High Street   £
.ı: (0903) 883378
Open: Mon-Fri 11:30am-2:30pm, 7pm-10:30pm, Sat 11:30am-
    10:30pm, Sun 1pm-7pm
Credit cards: DC, MC, V

Turn left from the castle exit, down the High Street and you'll find
Hemingway's at the bottom on the right. It is a new 'American
style' diner and wine bar. The open plan and colorful furnishings
give it a friendly, comfortable atmosphere. Suitable zest is added to
otherwise simple fare to enhance omelettes and burgers, or you
may prefer to try the jumbo prawns and Cajun chicken.

Swan Hotel, 27/29 High Street   £
Tel: (0903) 882374
Open: Daily 11am-11pm (food served noon-2pm, 6:30pm-9pm;
    Sun noon-3pm, 7pm-10:30pm)
Credit cards: AE, DC, MC, V

A traditional pub next door to Hemingway's on the High Street
corner. This oak beamed pub is quite spacious but can be crowded
at lunchtimes. The standard pub food has variations daily which are
displayed on blackboards. 'Appetizers' include homemade pâté
and rolled smoked salmon. Instead of hot or cold snacks you can
order a choice of half a dozen main courses including 8oz steaks and
fresh trout with almonds.

Belinda's Tea Shop, 13 Tarrant Street   £
Tel: (0903) 882977
Open: Tues-Sun 9:30am-5pm   Closed: Mon and 4 wks Jan
No credit cards

Belinda's is an enchanting, 16th-century coffee house in a traditional English style, serving homemade food with a variety of tempting
scones and cakes on display.

Castle Garden Café, adjacent to Castle car park   £
Open: During Castle opening hours
No credit cards

You can picnic or sit outside in the gardens behind the Cathedral.
This small café serves a wide variety of tasty sandwiches and cakes
as well as good coffee.

ARUNDEL TO BIGNOR ROMAN VILLA   (about 6 miles)

*Leave Arundel Castle through the top exit, turn left and first right
following the street straight out of Arundel to a traffic circle on the
Arundel by-pass. Take the fourth exit marked **London/A284**. The*

*Castle wall is on your right for 2 miles. At the next traffic circle take the second exit ahead signposted **London/A29**. As you climb the hill you'll have magnificent views across Sussex. After 1½ miles turn left for **Bignor Roman Villa** as signposted. Continue into the picturesque village of **West Burton**, with its well-tended thatched cottages. Turn left in the town center following the signs for Bignor Roman Villa which is 1 mile further in the heart of the Sussex countryside.*

Bignor Roman Villa, Bignor, Pulborough
Open: Daily 10am-5pm Mar-Oct
Admission: Adults £1.50, children 75p

The villa occupies a massive 4½ acre site. It was first excavated in 1811, after a section of floor showing a dancing girl was discovered during farm work. It contains some of the finest mosaics in the world, depicting, among others, Venus, Gladiators, Ganymede (Zeus's cup bearer), Medusa and Winter. The buildings are set around a large courtyard and were almost certainly the home of a rich man. It was probably occupied between the 2nd and 4th centuries AD.

BIGNOR TO PETWORTH HOUSE (about 6 miles)

*Turn right out of Bignor Roman Villa and right again in **Sutton**, following the signs for **Petworth**. Two miles on turn left for Petworth at a T-junction. Continue a further 1½ miles to the **A285**, turn right and keep straight on through Petworth. The gates to Petworth House are directly ahead of you. Drive through the gates and you'll find the parking lot 200 yards down on the right.*

Petworth House
Open: Tues-Thur, Sat-Sun 12:30pm-4:30pm Apr-Oct
Admission: Adults £2.50 (Tues: 'connoisseurs' day', £3), children £1.25

This 17th-century palatial mansion was built by the 6th Duke of Somerset and incorporates the 13th-century chapel of an earlier mansion. A later owner, Lord Egremont, was a friend of the artist J. W. Turner who painted Petworth House, its grounds and guests, while staying on the estate. The Petworth fine art collection now includes a number of paintings by Turner, as well as others by Holbein, Rembrandt, Hals, Van Dyck, Gainsborough and Reynolds. The house is richly decorated and sumptuously furnished, while outside you can admire the parkland laid out in 1752 by 'Capability' Brown.

PETWORTH

The small town of Petworth is every bit as charming as the great house. A short walk from the car park across the road and down the cobbled **Lombard Street** will take you to the heart of the town, **Market Square**. The arcaded town hall dates from the 18th century and in the narrow, winding streets around it you'll see several half-timbered Tudor houses. At the bottom end of Market Square, past the tiny, ancient chapel, look for **Sockets Wine Bar** (tel: (0798) 42576; open: Tues-Sat noon-2pm, 7pm-10:30pm; credit cards: AE, MC, V) which serves good French cuisine in a cozy, friendly atmosphere. They have additional dining space in an adjacent courtyard. There are 25 antique shops in Petworth with plenty of variety including one specializing in clocks, barometers and nautical instruments – **Baskerville Antiques** in Saddlers Row. This is to the right of Market Square if you're entering from Lombard Street.

PETWORTH TO LOSELEY PARK   (about 17 miles)

*Out of Petworth House keep in the left-hand lane and turn left at the main road junction, signposted to **Guildford/A283**. Follow the A283 for 11 miles through **Chiddingfold**. At 2nd Milford traffic circle follow sign for Guildford. The A283 ends 300 yards ahead; turn right at the lights for the **A3 to Guildford**. Veer left at next traffic lights. After 2 miles on the A3 turn right signposted **Loseley**. Keep going for 1 mile through **Compton** following signs left up a narrow road for 1/4 mile and left again to Loseley House.*

Loseley House
Open: Wed-Sat 2pm-5pm last Sat May-last Sat Sept
Admission: Adults £2.20, children £1.40

The fame of Loseley House has spread through the great British public on the lids of yoghurt pots. This is no joke . . . the highly successful farm attached to the lovely Elizabethan mansion produces and markets a wide range of high-quality dairy products. Once you've looked around the house, admired the paneling, ceilings, paintings and furniture, you can go on conducted farm tours (£1.40).

LOSELEY TO GUILDFORD   (about 3 miles)

*Turn left out of the Loseley Hall approach road to **Guildford** as signposted and follow the winding lane. At the end of this road (known as the **Pilgrims Way**) in the outskirts of Guildford turn left and follow the **Portsmouth Road (A3100)** for its last 1/2 mile to the traffic lights. As you cross the lights take care to get into the right lane. Follow the road round on the right side and at the next lights at* *the bottom of the road, turn right. Take the second turn left, then left again up the* **High Street** *(closed on Saturday). Parking is available at any of the parking places indicated or at the end of the High Street just behind the* **Civic Hall** *on the left. You are now very close to the* **Tourist Information Centre***, Civic Hall,* **London Road** *(Tel: (0483) 575857. Open: Mon-Fri 9:30am-5pm, Sat 9:30am-4:30pm. Closed Mon & Sat 12:30pm-1:30pm) but without our help you'd have to be a sharp-eyed sleuth to find it: it's actually in the entrance to the theater and marked 'Box Office'. We're not the only ones to encounter difficulties, and the TIC is due to move to new premises in the High Street during 1989, when it will occupy part of a medieval building. The current office and the new one will be open throughout the year; new times and days were not available as we went to press. If in doubt, telephone first.*

GUILDFORD

At first glance, Guildford could be any busy town within London's commuter belt, but look closer and you'll see surprising signs of antiquity. The town is known to have been a borough for nearly 900 years, but the presence of a royal mint here during the late Saxon period shows that it was an important place over 1,000 years ago.

WHAT TO SEE

The tower of **St Mary's Church**, in Quarry Street, dates from about 1050. By contrast, the town's largest place of worship, the **Cathedral**, on Stag Hill, was built less than 30 years ago to the design of Edward Maufe, and consecrated in 1961.

The invading Normans built a castle in Guildford. The **Keep** still stands (grounds open: daily sunrise to sunset, free admission; keep open: daily 10:30am-6pm Apr-Sep; admission: adults: 40p, children 20p). The castle was used by royalty as a palace, rather than a fortress, and as such was one of the most luxurious in England.

During the Middle Ages Guildford's prosperity grew with its thriving wool and cloth industry. It might well have declined in size and stature when the wool trade died out in the 17th century, but for the fact that the town lay halfway between London and the increasingly important south-coast port of Portsmouth. Since it was a day's ride between each town, the ancient High Street soon bustled with the trade of a growing number of large coaching inns. Of these, only the **Angel Hotel** (see page 264) remains.

The 16th-century **Guildhall**, in High Street, was built on the site of a medieval hall, and was refronted in 1683, when it acquired its very handsome projecting clock. Just a little way up the High Street you'll find **Abbots Hospital**, founded by George Abbot in 1619 for the elderly.

Both historic buildings are open to view by special arrangement –

enquire at the Tourist Information Centre for details. Between the two stands **Guildford House**, a fine, 17th-century building (open: Mon-Sat 10:30am-4:50pm, free admission). This mounts regularly changing exhibitions of paintings, prints, sculpture and crafts, with many original pieces on sale. The **Royal Grammar School**, further up the High Street on the right, was founded in 1507 and is open by arrangement only – but it's worth walking up to it just to admire its handsome 16th-century exterior.

Guildford Museum, Castle Arch in Quarry Street, (open: Mon-Sat 11am-5pm; closed: public holidays; free admission) contains exhibits relating to this part of Surrey dating from prehistoric time to the present day. It also contains memorabilia relating to Lewis Carroll, author of *Alice in Wonderland*, who lived nearby.

GUILDFORD RESTAURANTS

Angel Hotel, High Street   ££
Tel: (0483) 64555
Open: Daily 12:30pm-2:30pm, 7pm-9:45pm
Credit cards: AE, DC, MC, V

It's only a short walk up the High Street to this 13th-century coaching inn with an attractive cobbled courtyard and oak-beamed interior. The hotel has a wide selection of quality English fare and a well-stocked cellar. Fixed price menus are good value at £9.50 (lunch) and £11.50 (dinner). If you choose à la carte you could try the escalope of veal (£9.50) or fillet steak (£10.50).

Rat's Castle, 80 Sydenham Road   £
Tel: (0483) 572410
Open: Meals served: Mon-Sat noon-2:30pm, 7pm-10pm; Sun
      noon-2:30pm only
Credit cards: MC

This pub is in a back street the other side of the High Street from the Guildhall through Tunsgate. The Edwardian interior is stylish with tiles and marble complementing the rattan furniture. You'll be able to choose from a comprehensive list of traditional English dishes or sandwiches.

Rumwrong, 16 London Road   ££
Tel: (0483) 36092
Open: Tues-Sun noon-2:30pm, 6pm-11pm
Closed: Mon and first 2 wks Aug
Credit cards: MC, V

This Thai restaurant is at the top of the High Street opposite the Civic Hall. It could be your antidote to a surfeit of French cuisine: the colorful interior creates a happy atmosphere and you'll be able to choose from a variety of excellent dishes. The set dinners at £12 normally include spicy soups and barbequed beef *quenelles*, although specialties, such as roast duck, will cost a bit more.

GUILDFORD TO WISLEY GARDENS (about 9 miles)

The top end of Guildford High Street becomes the London Road as it forks to the left past the Civic Hall. Follow this road until it meets the A3, where you turn right towards London. After 6 miles you will see Wisley Gardens on the left off the A3 just before the M25 junction.

Wisley Gardens, Ripley, Surrey
Open: Mon-Sat 10am-7pm, Sun 2pm-7pm (or sunset if earlier)
      Feb-Oct; 10am-4:30pm (or sunset if earlier) Nov, Dec, Jan;
      Sun, members only
Admission: Adults £2.50, children 6-14 years £1, under 6 years free

All devoted horticulturalists stop here! These gardens are the headquarters of the Royal Horticultural Society, and form the training ground for its students. If you're inquisitive, you too can learn a lot in one visit, although most first-timers simply enjoy the acres of splendid and varied gardens. The 300-acre estate also includes experimental grounds where new varieties of fruit and vegetables are developed.

WISLEY GARDENS TO RUNNYMEDE (about 13 miles)

*Leave the gardens following signs for M25 and continue north. Follow the M25 as far as **exit 13** for **A30**. As you take the slip road off the motorway, look for signs to Windsor and follow these right round the traffic circle which is beneath the M25. Take the last exit off the traffic circle which confusingly brings you back alongside the M25. Stay in the left-hand lane which then circles left and takes you beneath the M25 again. At the next traffic circle take the third exit signposted to **Windsor/A308** and **Runnymede**.*

SIDE TRIP TO THORPE PARK (about ½ mile)

Thorpe Park
Open: Daily 10am-6pm end Mar-Sep
Admission: Adults and children £7 (includes all rides)

*Directions: Leave the M25 at Junction 12 (the M3 interchange) and follow the signs to **Thorpe** and **Thorpe Park** ½ mile ahead.*

This is a diversion that only those with kids in tow will want to take. An entertainment park loosely based on 'Our Heritage', it has joy rides and lots of fun activities.

*To get to **Runnymede** from Thorpe Park turn left at the Park exit and stay on the road (**A320**) to **Staines**. At the next traffic circle take the second exit marked **Windsor/A308** which takes you under the M25 to a traffic circle. Take the third exit signposted to **Windsor/Runnymede/A308**.*

RUNNYMEDE

In the broad meadow alongside the River Thames at Runnymede, King John signed the preliminary draft of **Magna Carta** in 1215. You'll find the memorial to Magna Carta, a domed classical temple, at the foot of Cooper's Hill, south of the road. The memorial was built by the American Bar Association. Halfway up the hill, the **John F. Kennedy Memorial** stands on an acre of ground given to the USA.

RUNNYMEDE TO WINDSOR   (about 5 miles)

*Keep going on the **A308** through the exit gates, right across the mini traffic circle. You drive through **Old Windsor** and after 1½ miles you reach an extended traffic circle where you turn left signposted **Windsor**. Before you reach the town of Windsor 1 mile away, you'll get a magnificent view of **Windsor Castle** to your right up the '**Long Walk**' (this walk continues to your left for a mile to the Copper Horse statue). At the next traffic circle, take the third exit to **Windsor town center**. At traffic lights turn left into **Victoria Street**, and at traffic circle turn right into **Charles Street**. At next traffic circle come back up **Charles Street** and turn left into parking lot.*

*For detailed information on **Windsor** see **page 313**; for information on **Eton** see **page 267**.*

TOUR 3: THE ROYAL TOUR

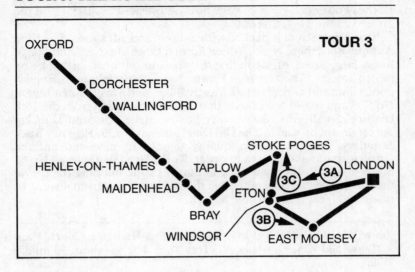

Route A: LONDON TO WINDSOR AND ETON (about 23 miles)

LONDON TO WINDSOR   (about 23 miles)

For **directions** see **page 312**; for details of **Windsor** see **page 313**.

WINDSOR TO ETON (about 100 yards by foot or 3 miles by car)

Since the bridge over the Thames at Windsor is closed to traffic, oyou'll find it easier to walk to Eton. If you prefer to drive, leave the King Edward Court car park and follow signs for Maidenhead/A308 at the immediate traffic circle. Cross two sets of lights to the overpass. At the traffic circle take exit for Slough/A332/(M4) up the slip road to the overpass. Stay in the left-hand lane. After ¾ mile take the slip road to the left marked Eton/Slough Central. Turn right at the traffic circle at the end of the road. Keep going through Eton as far as the bridge, turn right into the car park directly ahead of you.

ETON
Eton College was founded by Henry VI in 1440. The school has grown extensively since then, with the **Lower School** building, dating from 1443, being the sole survivor of that early period. Eton College dominates what is really little more than a village, with the

traditional local shops, like the stationers **Calladine's** on the High Street serving the needs of boys and their parents. You'll find Barnes Pool, with Eton College beyond Barnes Pool Bridge, at the far end of the High Street.

Eton High Street is packed with antique and gift shops. The **Eton Antique Bookshop**, No 88, (open normal times plus Sun 2pm-5pm), has a large stock of secondhand, rare and antiquarian books on most subjects. **The Heritage House**, No 53, specializes in English bone china and crystal, while **Mostly Boxes** and **Mostly Furniture** at No 52B and No 90 sell exactly that, with stock dating from the 16th century. Small gifts like jewelry boxes, cache pots and Dubarry porcelain are on sale in **The Old Dial House** at No 39. **Regency Buck Jewellery**, No 121, stocks quality diamonds, new and antique jewelry, and makes pieces to order. **Turks Head Antiques** at No 89 is worth a visit, if only for the antiquity of the building (medieval timbers inside and out), although the stock, ranging from jewelry to silver and lace, is interesting as well.

Route B: WINDSOR TO LONDON Visiting Hampton Court, Ham House and Kew Gardens, Via Day Tour 4   (about 35 miles)

WINDSOR TO HAMPTON COURT   (about 13 miles)

*From the **King Edward Court car park** turn left down **Charles Street** and left again at **Victoria Street** to the T-junction. Turn right, at the traffic circle take first left for **A308 Staines**. The **Long Walk** is on your left. Continue on this road to the traffic circle at **Old Windsor**. Turn right, staying on the **A308 to Staines**, through **Old Windsor** to a mini traffic circle, fork left here.*

*Continue through **Runnymede** to the large traffic circle at the road's end. Take the left turn over the **Thames** signposted **A30**. Stay in the left lane alongside the M25 until you reach the traffic circle below the motorway. Take the third exit off the traffic circle signposted **A30**. Get in the left lane before the next traffic circle, take the left slip road signposted **A308**. Follow signs for the **A308** to **Kingston** through the complex junction and traffic lights. You now begin to pick up signs for **Hampton/A308**. Continue on A308 straight across the next traffic circle, through **Sunbury** to the traffic circle beneath the M3. Take the third exit straight ahead, still on the **A308**, past **Kempton Park** race course, through the village of **Hampton** all the way to the traffic circle in front of **Hampton Court** (opposite you to the right). Go through main gate for car park. For details of **Hampton Court** see **page 279**; for details of Hampton Court to London via **Ham House** and **Kew Gardens** see page 282.*

Route C: Continuing On From WINDSOR AND ETON TO OXFORD Via Stoke Poges, Cliveden and Henley-On-Thames
(about 60 miles)

WINDSOR AND ETON TO STOKE POGES   (about 9 miles)

*Follow the driving instructions to Eton in **Route A** as far as the **overpass**. Stay on this road as it goes under the M4, then across another large traffic circle, and turn right at the next lights signposted **Slough Centre/A4**. (From **Eton** take the **Slough Road** back to the traffic circle, go straight across under the M4, turning left immediately – signposted **(M4)**. Follow the **(M4)** signs, turning left at the lights to the large traffic circle. Follow signs for **Slough** and turn right at the next lights signposted **Slough Centre/A4**.) After ¼ mile turn left at the traffic lights into **Stoke Poges Lane**, signposted to **Stoke Poges**. Stay on this road for 1¾ miles past the Horlicks Factory and across the next traffic lights. **Stoke Poges Church** is on the left before the village in two miles (the turning is a little concealed). At the end of the short drive you'll find a car park.*

STOKE POGES

The little village of Stoke Poges sprang to eternal fame with the publication of Thomas Gray's poem 'Elegy in a Country Churchyard'. You are now about to enter that same churchyard, where Gray is buried. Alongside it are beautiful, modern gardens, established in the 1920s as a memorial to the poet. They lead down to a lake, with a fountain and rose garden . . . every bit as tranquil as the very different 18th-century scene which Gray described.

STOKE POGES TO CLIVEDEN   (about 7 miles)

---

*Turn left out of the **church drive**, left again at the crossroads following the **B416** to **Farnham Royal**. At the next junction turn left and immediately right following signs to **Burnham Beeches**. After ½ mile turn right just beyond the right-hand bend signposted **Burnham Beeches**. Follow the road until you come to **Caldicote School** on your right. At the crossroads turn left for **Taplow** (2 miles). Take the next right then an immediate left, following signs for **Taplow**. Drive straight over the crossroads, turn left at the next T-junction and follow the road for ¼ mile. Now turn right into **Taplow Drive**, past the car park and pretty village green, and turn right at the junction. Follow the road uphill (about 3 miles). You'll see **Cliveden** on your left.*

Cliveden, Taplow
Open: Grounds: Daily 11am-5:30pm (or sunset if earlier) Mar-Dec
            House: Thur and Sun 3pm-5:30pm Apr-Oct
Admission: Adults £2.20, house 80p extra; children half price

---

Cliveden was once the home of Lady Nancy Astor, an American who became the first woman Member of Parliament in Britain. In more recent times, the estate achieved less desirable notoriety during the 'Profumo Affair' in 1963 which brought down the Government. The setting of the house 200 feet above the River Thames is particularly fine. The 375 acres of garden and woodland include a water garden, a magnificent parterre (formal turfed and bedded garden), temples by Giacomo Leoni and extensive woodland.

Cliveden is now a hotel with a restaurant open to non-residents. In the grounds, the **Orangerie Restaurant** (open Wed-Sun 11am-5pm Apr-Oct), occupies a delightful setting and has particularly good homemade teas. Cliveden marks the start of a gastronome's quandary, for this part of the tour is rich in opportunities for a good feast, or an overnight stop in considerable style.

Cliveden Hotel   £££
Tel: (062 86) 68561
Amenities: ☎ ⊒ 🅿 ⑊ 🍸 ≋ ✓ (arranged) ⌇ ◎
Credit cards: AE, DC, MC, V

'It's all right for you, your husband's a millionaire', heckled a bystander at a Nancy Astor political gathering.
'I should hope he is. That's why I married him', replied Cliveden's owner.

Given the prices that prevail at this, the only hotel in a stately home in England, it helps to have a million or two (doubles start at £170, suites at £280).

That said, the 25 rooms are sumptuous in the extreme – fireplaces feature in some bathrooms as well as all bedrooms. What's more the rooms themselves have historic associations with a vast panoply of Britain's past movers and shakers from Churchill and Kipling to Lawrence of Arabia and Lord Mountbatten. The paneling in the French Drawing Room is a Madame Pompadour retread. The Great Hall contains the famous Sargeant portrait of Nancy Astor, while the swimming pool evokes memories of Christine Keeler's ace backstroke.

Chef John Webber's creations are first-rate and feature delicious dishes such as terrine of *fois gras* with Sauterne and *bavarois* of smoked salmon with a tomato and basil sauce. Set lunch is £25.80, dinner £37.80.

Breakfast is included in the room's price. Clearly the management realize that *un oeuf* is enough.

If you are into self-indulgence this must be the place.

CLIVEDEN TO BRAY   (about 8 miles)

*Turn left out of **Cliveden gates**, left again after 400 yards following the signs for **Bourne End**. Slow down as you approach the Bourne End sign marking the beginning of the village and turn left immediately after it, signposted to **Cookham**. Follow the road to the junction, turn left to **Cookham**. As you drive over Cookham bridge and straight over the crossroads in the middle of the village, you'll glimpse the picturesque High Street to the right. Follow the **Maidenhead Road** all the way to Maidenhead bridge passing the famous Boulters Lock and following the **River Thames** on your left. Turn right at the traffic circle by the bridge, get in the left lane to turn left at the next turning signposted to **Bray/B3028**. Follow the road to Bray turning left just before the village and left again in the center for the **Waterside Inn** down by the river, or continuing straight through the 'narrowed' road to the **Crown Inn** on the right – the car park is on the right just before it.*

Bray's 17th-century vicar, Simon Alleyn, is famed in song for his ability to survive numerous changes of religion by reigning monarchs: 'That whatsoever king shall reign, I'll still be the Vicar of Bray, Sir.'

BRAY AND MAIDENHEAD RESTAURANTS

Waterside Inn, Ferry Road, Bray-on-Thames   £££
For details see page 318.

Crown Inn, High Street, Bray-on-Thames   £
Tel: (0628) 36725
Open: Bar snacks: Daily except Sat 12:30pm-2:30pm, no bar food
      evenings
Credit cards: AE, MC

Watch your head on the low beams in this charming old pub. It gets very crowded in the evenings but you'll usually find plenty of space at the table for lunchtime bar meals. The blackboard menu varies daily. Try the pâté, lamb or cottage pie; prices from £2 to £4.

Shoppenhangers Manor, Manor Lane, Maidenhead   £££
Tel: (0628) 23444
Open: Mon to Fri 12:30pm-2pm, Mon to Sat 7pm-10:30pm (reser-
      vations recommended)
Closed: Sat lunch, Sun, Christmas through New Year's Day
Credit cards: AE, DC, MC, V

Directions: see below.

The approach to this 16th-century manor is particularly beautiful and well matched by the elegant, stylish interior. The gourmet menu includes slices of smoked salmon (£13) and the fixed price menu (£24) offers a choice of six starters (such as baked fillet of sea bass and strips of salmon and sole) and six entrées (try the fillet of English lamb) as well as mouthwatering desserts (such as glazed fresh fruit or the rich chocolate slice).

BRAY TO HENLEY-ON-THAMES   (about 12 miles)

*Continue through **Bray** on the main road. At the T-junction turn right for **Maidenhead A308**. At the traffic circle take the second exit, following the blue 'M' sign for A308 in the direction of **Maidenhead**. At the next traffic circle take the third exit marked **Oxford/Henley A423 (M)**. You soon pass through the woods of **Maidenhead Thicket**. (If you wish to visit **Shoppenhangers Manor**, which you'll see up the hill to your right, take the next left signposted **White Waltham**. Turn right over the motorway then first right 400 yards up the hill just beyond the **Crest Hotel**. Shoppenhangers Manor is on the right a little further on. When leaving Shoppenhangers return to the **A308(M)** turning right for **Henley**.)*

The thicket was once notorious for highwaymen who could take advantage of the many stagecoaches to Bath and to the West which dispensed of their London escorts beyond Maidenhead. Despite the names of Robin Hood and Dick Turpin used locally, neither of these famous robbers is believed to have actually cried 'stand and deliver' here.

*Follow the **A423** for 1 mile to a traffic circle where you take the second exit straight ahead for **Henley**. Follow the road for 7 miles to the bridge into Henley. Just before the bridge are the rowing clubs and grounds which are the setting for the annual Henley regatta, held in the first week of July.*

*Drive straight across the lights to the other side of the bridge into **Hart Street** and straight over the next lights into the center of Henley. Ahead of you in the middle of **Market Place** is the imposing **Town Hall** which has the **Tourist Information Centre** (Tel: (0491) 578034. Open: Daily 9am-12:30pm, 2:15pm-4:30pm Easter to Sep) just inside the front door downstairs. Parking here can be difficult. If the car park is full, turn right behind the Town Hall, go straight down the **King's Road** one-way system for 200 yards and right as directed into another car park. To get back to the town hall walk to the exit end of the car park where you'll find an alley – this takes you into Market Place.*

HENLEY-ON-THAMES

Reputedly the oldest settlement in Oxfordshire, Henley is best known for its famous **Royal Regatta**, which has been held on the 'straight mile' just downstream from the bridge every year since 1829. It is now one of the high points of the social 'season'. The town is largely Georgian. It has over 300 listed buildings, including the parish church of **St Mary** with its distinctive tower of black and white checkered Chiltern flint and stone. Among Henley's many coaching inns is the **Red Lion**, Hart Street, whose guests have included Charles I and the Duke of Marlborough. The neighboring **Chantry** House dates from 1400 (open: Thur and Sat 10am-noon; free admission). Once a school, it is now used as the church hall.

SHOPPING

Henley's shopping area is centered around **Hart Street** (note the fine 18th-century houses), **Market Place**, **Bell Street** and **Duke Street**. **Carousel Fine China and Crystal** at 35 Hart Street and 17 Duke Street sells a wide range of just that. If you walk down to the river and turn left by the Red Lion Hotel into New Street you'll find the **Century** and **Thames Galleries** 100 yards along on the left. The Century has an extensive collection of contemporary paintings and three-dimensional art. The Thames Gallery stocks both 18th- and 19th-century paintings as well as Georgian and Victorian silver, including candlesticks, mugs, salts and peppers. The sweet-smelling gift shop **Saffron**, 28 Bell Street, has a courtyard herb garden (open in summer) which might entice you to buy some of their terracotta planters made in Sussex. **Eight of Harts**, 8 Hart Street, sells *very* seductive chocolates. If you arrive in Henley on a Thursday, the area behind the Town Hall will be packed with market stalls.

HENLEY RESTAURANTS

Chef Peking, 10 Market Place   ££
Tel: (0491) 578681
Open: Daily 12:30pm-2pm, 6pm-11pm
Credit cards: AE, DC, MC, V

From the Town Hall this Chinese restaurant is 50 yards down on the left. The well-lit interior creates a spacious feeling by the use of white walls and sparkling white tablecloths intermingled with greenery. You can order a set three course meal for £12.50 or select specialties such as Aromatic Crispy Duck (£9.25).

The Argyll, Market Place   £
Tel: (0491) 573400
Open: Daily 10am-2:30pm, 6pm-11pm (no food evenings)
No credit cards

Behind the black and white timbered exterior is an old world interior with stained-glass leaded windows and tartan carpet (not Argyll tartan which apparently would have been too dark). Friendly staff serve excellent traditional English fare, such as steak and kidney pie (£3.60) and sherry trifle (£1.50).

HENLEY TO WALLINGFORD   (about 12 miles)

*From **Market Place** turn left for **A423 Oxford**. From the car park in **King's Road** continue along the one-way system until you reach **Bell Street** and turn left. Fork left, following the road to **Oxford/A423** along the open 'fair mile', up the hill beyond and through **Nettlebed**. Keep going straight across two traffic circles into **Wallingford**. On the right you'll see a tiny antique shop, containing some odd curiosities, called **Penny Farthing** (named after a genuine penny farthing bicycle hanging over the door). Just over the **bridge** to the left is a **church** with an ornate spire where you turn left for a car park which you will soon see on your right. Walk back to the bridge and turn left to reach **Market Place** and the **Town Hall**. Part of this is occupied by the **Tourist Information Centre**. (Tel: (0491) 35351. Open: Mon-Fri 9:30am-1pm, 2pm-4:30pm Apr-Oct; 9:30am-1pm Nov-Mar.)*

WALLINGFORD

Wallingford has had a somewhat checkered history: destroyed by the Danes in 1006; decimated by the Plague in 1349 which left only 44 households; torn apart by the Civil War in 1652 and almost burnt to a cinder by a great fire in 1675. Perhaps it is appropriate that the castle, built in 1071, is now in ruins, mostly as a result of Cromwell's work in the Civil War when Wallingford was one of the last royalist castles to fall. Now a quiet market town, Wallingford is a pleasant place to browse. The **Market Place**, with its 17th-century Town Hall standing on stone pillars and its fine, Georgian houses, is at the heart of the central shopping area which still follows the medieval street pattern.

The **Lamb Arcade** in High Street occupies a former 17th-century coaching inn, housing over twenty antique dealers, a furniture restorer, craft gallery, coffee shop and wine bar in the vaults. **Anne Brooker**, in the Arcade (closed Wed), sells only British crafts, with the emphasis on the unusual and amusing (fun jewelry in titanium, flying animal mobiles, sports clocks, book-ends and so on). Call at **First Edition**, 9 The Market Place, for knitwear in natural yarns, some hand-dyed, spun and made locally.

WALLINGFORD TO DORCHESTER   (about 4 miles)

*Turn right from the car park and right again, followed by a sharp left turn. Take the first right after 200 yards and a left turn into a one-way system. Turn right shortly afterwards at a T-junction and drive right round a mini-roundabout picking up signs for **Oxford/Shillingford/ A329**. Drive straight up through the Market Place and cross straight over a set of traffic lights, continuing to follow signs for **Oxford/ Shillingford A329**.*

Shillingford Bridge Hotel   **££**
Tel: (086732) 8567
Open: Daily 11am-2:30pm, 6pm (7pm Sun)- midnight; restaurant
        12:30pm-2pm, 7:30pm-10pm (9:30pm Sun); no bar food
        evenings
Credit cards: AE, DC, MC, V

This hotel is beautifully situated on a lovely reach of the Thames.
The interior is well-appointed, comfortable and spacious. You can
choose high quality English fare from the bar where it is attractively
presented or from the restaurant looking directly on to the river.
The restaurant caters for those with particularly 'healthy' appetites
who might like to try the mixed grill (£11) or T-bone steak (£16).

*Cross over the bridge to the A423 ¹/₂ mile ahead where you turn left
for **Oxford**. After a further ¹/₂ mile on the two-way highway, turn left
as signposted for **Dorchester/Dorchester Abbey**. The car park is
immediately to the left after the bridge and you should park here
unless you wish to visit the **George Hotel** (see below). Cross the road
and walk up the path to the **Abbey Church** entrance. From the George
Hotel (further up the main road on the left) enter through the
Victorian lychgate past the tearooms and round the Abbey Church to
the right for the main entrance.*

DORCHESTER-ON-THAMES

The site of an ancient settlement dating back to 2500 BC, Dorchester sits on the River Thame near its junction with the River
Thames. The Romans built a substantial, walled town strategically
placed between their towns of Silchester and Alchester. Only a few
fragments of the Roman wall survive, but the cobbled **High Street**,
now no longer the main route through the town, follows the line of
the Roman road. Dorchester later became a powerful ecclesiastic
stronghold and the seat of the Anglo-Saxon bishops of Wessex,
effectively the largest and most important section of England in the
Middle Ages. The **Abbey** was founded by the Pope's envoy, Bishop
Birinus, in 635.

The **Abbey Church** that you see today, standing apart from the
town among the willows beside the River Thame, belongs to the
Norman period. It was enlarged in medieval times. Among its
treasures are a 12th-century lead font and glorious, 13th-century
glass windows, including the famous **Tree-of-Jesse** window.

DORCHESTER RESTAURANTS

The George Hotel, High Street   **££**
Tel: (0865) 340404
Open: Bar: Mon-Sat 11am-11pm, Sun noon-3pm, 7pm-10:30pm
    Meals served: Daily 12:15pm-1:40pm, 7:15pm-9:45pm
    (Sun until 9pm)
Credit cards: AE, DC, MC, V

This 500-year-old coaching inn has two restaurants, the first galleried with a high ceiling, and a new one overlooking a pleasant water garden. The cuisine is English with set price evening menus of £16 or £22; a businessman's lunch at £11.50. The menu changes frequently, but usually includes popular choices such as salmon, scotch beef, quail and Gressingham duck. The homemade soup of the day (£1.50) and beef and kidney pie (£3.50) followed by an excellent cheeseboard in the bar, may be the best option if time is limited.

The **Abbey Tea Rooms** just inside the lychgate are recommended for a quick snack if they are open – usually Wed, Thur, Sat 3pm-5pm, but this depends on voluntary labor.

Just across the road from the George Hotel you'll see **Hallidays Antique Shop** which has an extensive collection of English and Continental furniture on display.

DORCHESTER TO OXFORD   (about 8 miles)

*Follow the **High Street** through Dorchester, fork left just before its end and turn right at the junction 1 mile further on. Another ¼ mile takes you to the **A423** where you turn left for **Oxford**. At the main traffic circle take the exit for the two-lane highway signposted **Oxford**. At the second traffic circle take the first exit left for Oxford. At the next traffic circle take the second exit right for **Oxford** city center. If you're arriving at a busy time of day, especially in the summer, it is probably wise to leave your car in the **Redbridge 'Park and Ride' car park** a few hundred yards along on your left after the traffic circle. Parking is free and the frequent bus service into the center costs 50p. In order to park in Oxford cross the **River Thames** (known as the **Isis** in Oxford) over **Folly Bridge** and turn left immediately into **Thames Street**. Pass the next junction and get into the right-hand lane for the car park. Walk out the other end of the car park to the **Tourist Information Centre**, following the signs (up **Castle Street**, right into **Bonn Square** and **Queen Street** to **Carfax**). The Centre is a few yards down on your right.*

For details of the **City of Oxford** see **page 387**.

TOUR 4: PARKS, GARDENS AND ROYALTY

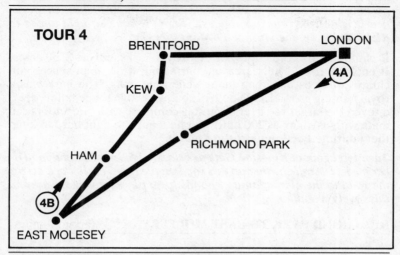

Route A: LONDON TO HAMPTON COURT
Via Richmond Park   (about 25 miles)

LONDON TO RICHMOND PARK   (about 11 miles)

*Head west on the **Cromwell Road**, the main road out to the M4 and Heathrow Airport. When the road broadens at Earls Court move over to the left lane. One mile further on take the slip road to the left of the Hammersmith overpass signposted for **Guildford/Portsmouth** and join the one-way system beneath the overpass. Follow round to the right, then take the third exit just after a church. Keep left, following signs for the A3. You cross **Hammersmith Bridge**, an ornately decorated iron suspension bridge built in 1887. Continue straight along **Castelnau Road** for 1 mile, following the main road as it bends to the left at a traffic light. Drive on across **Barnes Common** to a junction with the **South Circular Road** (A205) ¾ mile ahead. Straight ahead you'll see a thatched house – one of the few remaining in London. Turn right here then after 200 yards turn left following a sign to **Richmond Park**. Continue past playing fields and a golf course for 1 mile until you reach the park gate called **Roehampton Gate**.*

Richmond Park
Open: Gates close at dusk or at the time quoted on the notice to
       the left of the gate
Free admission

At the entrance you'll see a map of the park showing two routes to **Kingston Gate**, *your exit point at the far end 5 miles away. Car parking is restricted to marked parking areas (these include car parks near each of the four main gates). Take the road straight ahead to* **Richmond Gate**, *then turn left to* **Kingston Gate**.

Richmond Park, the largest of the Royal Parks, covers 2350 acres. It encloses a wild hilly area of contrasting wide open spaces and clumps of trees including many venerable oaks. The park was a royal hunting ground and you'll probably be able to see fallow deer, or even the larger red deer. One stag complete with fine antlers can mate with as many as 200 hinds but he'll have to fight hard to keep them during the autumn rutting season.

Turn left again at **Kingston Gate** *to visit the* **Isabella Plantation**. *The car park is ½ mile further up this road on the right. Walk back across the road to the plantation and ponds for a pleasant wander around this lovely woodland garden.*

RICHMOND PARK TO EAST MOLESEY   (about 9 miles)

Turn left out of the **car park** *back to* **Kingston Gate**. *Exit through the gate, straight down the road for ⅓ mile to a main road junction. Turn right following the road down to the traffic circle. Take the road straight ahead on the other side of the circle underneath a railroad bridge. Move over to the right-hand of the two central lanes following signs to* **Town Centre/Kingston Bridge** *(A308) which take you straight across a traffic light. At the next light take the right fork to* **Kingston Bridge**. *Keep going straight on through the shopping area to the bridge. Cross the bridge, turning left at the traffic circle on the other side.*

To your left is a long brick wall which borders **Hampton Court Palace**, *to the right is Bushy Park. After 1 mile the road bears left to a mini traffic circle. Go straight across the traffic circle then turn immediately left into Hampton Court Palace through enormous wroughtiron gates. These are* **Trophy Gates**, *hung between pillars supporting statues of a lion, a unicorn and trophies of arms. Turn left again into the car park which costs £1. Alternative parking is available over the bridge to the left in the railroad station car park which costs 60p (10p or 5p coins only). Before walking back across the bridge you'll have a good view of the Palace with the River Thames in the foreground. Free car parking is also available at the end of the green by the Palace. (Instead of turning left into the station car park, you'll need to turn around by taking the first right turn and continuing around the traffic circle to the right. Turn left back over the bridge. At the mini traffic circle turn left and park at the other end of the green on the right.)*

Hampton Court Palace, East Molesey
Open: Mon-Sat 9:30am-6pm (last entry 5:30pm), Sun 11am-6pm
Apr-Sep; 9:30am-5pm, 2pm-5pm Oct-Mar
Closed: Dec 24-26, New Year's Day
Admission: Adults £2.80, children £1.40; the Maze is 50p, the
gardens are free, both close at dusk or 9pm (whichever
is earlier)
Guided tours of State Apartments: Mon-Sat 11:15am and 2:15pm
May-Sep; free with Palace entrance ticket

Take the short walk from the main gate to the Palace entrance.
You'll see a most unusual skyline broken by numerous tall chimneys all of different designs and a variety of roofs covering the large
expanse of the Palace. You're approaching the western face of the
Palace. The buildings on this side were begun by Thomas Wolsey in
the reign of Henry VIII. Wolsey was a butcher's son who became
first a cardinal, then Lord Chancellor of England. As the most
powerful and wealthy subject in the kingdom his household numbered nearly 500. He could even afford to entertain and accommodate the French Ambassador with his retinue of 400. Eventually
he incurred the King's displeasure and attempted to regain favor by
presenting Hampton Court with its rich furnishings and plate to
Henry VIII. This didn't delay his fate for long. He was stripped of
all his wealth and power, then died while he was being brought to
London to be tried for high treason in 1530. Henry VIII enlarged
Hampton Court and lived in it with each of his five wives, after his
divorce from Catherine of Aragon.

During Henry VIII's time feudal lords were not allowed to
maintain private armies in defensive castles, so the moat at Hampton Court is only a token one and the windows are wider than the
usual slits. Over the main gateway are the Royal Arms and either
side are terracotta roundels with the heads of Roman emperors in
relief. Go through the gate into the first courtyard called **Base
Court** where you'll find the ticket office. On the far side is **Anne
Boleyn's Gateway**. There's a gift shop through the gateway arch on
the right where you can buy a comprehensive pictorial guide for
£3.50 or a booklet with more written detail for 95p.

As you go into the next courtyard, **Clock Court**, turn around and
look up at the famous astronomical clock above the entrance. This
was made by Nicholas Oursian in 1540 to indicate the hour, the day,
the month, the number of days since the beginning of the year, the
signs of the zodiac, the phases of the moon and its 'southing' which
allows high water at London Bridge to be calculated – this was
particularly important as the tide affected the principal means of
transport, namely river barges. You'll see that the sun is depicted as
revolving around the earth which is in the center of the clock –
Copernicus wasn't going to refute this theory for another 100 years.
Over on the right side of the court there's a colonnade with

rooms behind containing an exhibition which provides a useful guide to the design, construction and history of the Palace. This includes Sir Christopher Wren's ambitious plans for reconstruction in the early 18th century. As you emerge from the exhibition turn right along the colonnade to the **State Apartments** off the **King's Staircase**. You may prefer to dispense with your guide for this part of the tour as you'll find pictures and good descriptions in every room. The King's Staircase is made of elaborate wrought iron; the highly decorative walls and ceiling depict a Roman allegorical theme. At the top you enter the **King's Guard Chamber** which contains more than three thousand weapons. Turn immediately right through a small door into the **Wolsey Rooms**, stepping from the 18th century into Wolsey's 16th century. Follow the arrows round until you return to the Guard Chamber. Court etiquette required that access to the Royal Suites should be through a series of rooms, each more exclusive than the last.

After the King's Suite you enter the **Queen's Rooms** through the Guard Chamber with its monumental chimney pieces. There's a good view of the gardens from the last window of the Queen's Drawing Room before the Prince of Wales's three rooms. Then it's on to the **Haunted Gallery** where you might meet the ghost of Catherine Howard on your way to the Royal Chapel. Catherine, Henry VIII's fifth wife, was beheaded after her imprisonment at Hampton Court. When the arrows eventually lead you back to Base Court make sure you visit the **Great Kitchens** and offices including a pastry, confectionery, saucery, spicery and boiling-house, as well as larders and sculleries. You can also check out the King's Great Buttery, Beer Cellar and Wine Cellar beyond.

The Gardens
The fabulous formal gardens were designed to integrate with the East Front of the building in the classic Baroque style of the late 17th century. The principal element in the design are **Broad Walk** (across the front), the **Fountain Garden**, **Long Water** and three great **lime avenues** radiating out from the Palace. Turn right to walk along the eastern façade, then right again to the more intimate **Privy Gardens**. After this wealth of flowers and scents you'll find the **Vinery** and **Orangery**, where you turn left to visit the **Banqueting House** overlooking the river. Retrace your steps back to where you entered the gardens, at the eastern end of the Palace, and continue past the vestibule exit to the **Royal Tennis Court** in the next building to the left. Modern tennis was originally 'real tennis' played here since 1620 – and even earlier on a previous court. During Henry VIII's time only courtiers were allowed to play as the 'lower orders' would be distracted from their work and gamble on the results of matches. Turn left as you leave the Tennis Court, then left again at the end of the building into **The Wilderness**. Take the diagonal path to the 17th-century **Maze** with its 9-foot-high hedges.

A proficient Maze walker can get through in 15 minutes but the usual time spent inside is ½ to ¾ of an hour or longer if it's very crowded. Some have spent over two hours trying to get out so be sure to allow enough time. Alongside the Maze is the **Lion Gate**. Outside this gate you can choose to visit a traditional English pub or restaurant (see below). At the other end of The Wilderness you'll see a squat tower which overlooks the **Tiltyard** where jousting tournaments were held. Pass the teahouse here to return to the car park and main gate.

EAST MOLESEY

SHOPPING

A dozen antique shops crowd together in **Bridge Road** on the far side of the bridge. As you cross the bridge look off to the right and you'll see a corner pub called the **New Street of London**. This is at the end of Bridge Road (there's no road sign to guide you). **Martin Speed**, 5 Bridge Road, has quality Victorian furniture; **Irontiques**, 18 Bridge Road, has unusual architectural antiques made from metal; **Howard Hope**, 19 Bridge Road sells ancient gramophones and phonographs; and the **Antiques Centre** (closed Wed) at the end of the road offers two floors filled with antiques and collectables. In general, these shops are open Mon-Sat 10am-5pm, but these times are not strictly adhered to. (The gramophone shop only guarantees to be open Fri-Sat.) Some close Wednesday afternoons; most do not accept credit cards.

EAST MOLESEY RESTAURANTS

You have a reasonable choice of pubs, cafés and restaurants within a short walk of each gate.

Hampton Court Brasserie, 3 Palace Gate Parade   £
Tel: (01) 979 7891
Open: Daily noon-3pm, 7pm-11pm
Pianist at night, live jazz on Sunday
Credit cards: AE, MC, V

Opposite the Trophy Gates this restaurant operates a valet parking service. Behind the lightly-tinted windows you'll find a smart interior and welcoming, helpful staff. The color scheme is an attractive contrast of yellow tablecloths and bottle green decor with original art on the walls. The food is fresh, creative and well presented. There is an extensive wine list (although it tends to be on the expensive side).

Henekey's Restaurant, Hampton Court Road   £
Tel: (01) 977 8121
Open: Daily noon-2:30pm, 7pm-10pm, Sat until 11pm
Credit cards: AE, MC, V

Opposite the Lion Gate, go through the hotel entrance and up the stairs to the left. Tables on the left overlook Bushey Park with a fine view down the magnificent chestnut avenue. This restaurant is delightfully decorated and furnished – including a white mini grand piano. The cuisine is good and reasonably priced. A selection of starters includes seafood crêpe, *tortellini alla carbonara* and home-made soup. The main course varies from vegetable or beef stir-fry to chicken curry and the Coachman's Grill as well as the daily house specialties. They also have a good choice of desserts, cheeses and liqueur coffees.

King's Arms, Hampton Court Road   £
Tel: (01) 977 1729
Open: Bar: Daily 11am-11pm; Meals served: noon-10pm
Credit cards: AE, MC, V

A traditional pub just outside the Palace to the left of the Lion Gate. The cozy interior has wooden floors, brick walls and dark wooden beams. Real ale is served at the three bars; light meals are available in the left-hand bar downstairs and the main restaurant upstairs provides a selection of British dishes at reasonable prices.

Palace Tea Rooms, Palace Gate Parade   £
Tel: (01) 941 5988
Open: Daily 9am-8pm
No credit cards

These tearooms are directly opposite the main Trophy Gates and are particularly suitable for morning coffee, a quick snack at lunchtime or a leisurely tea. Space is limited, service prompt and attentive. A limited menu offers good value home-cooked snacks, hot and cold main dishes and a variety of pastries.

Route B: EAST MOLESEY TO LONDON Via Ham House and Kew Gardens (about 22 miles)

HAMPTON COURT TO HAM HOUSE (about 6 miles)

*From the traffic circle outside the front of Hampton Court take the route marked **A308 Kingston**. This follows the Palace walls around to the right again past the Lion Gates. After 1 mile turn right at the traffic circle, crossing **Kingston Bridge** to join the one-way system* *which leads you left beneath a building. Continue right around the one way system until left turn for **A307 Richmond** which leads beneath a railroad bridge. Follow A307 as it turns left into Richmond Road. Follow this road until just before the green, **Ham Common**, where you turn left signposted for **Ham House**. (If you miss this turn you can take either of the two next turns which lead you back across Ham Common to the first road.) At the end of the green, drive straight on through the village of **Ham** which has a quiet country atmosphere. Continue down this winding road for ³/₄ mile until you reach Ham House on your right. There's a free car park by the River Thames. Walk back down an avenue of trees to the main entrance.*

Ham House, Ham
Open: Tues-Sun 10am-6pm Closed: Over Christmas, Good Friday
Admission: Adults £2, children £1, grounds free

Ham House was built in 1610 by Sir Thomas Vavasour, Knight Marshall to James I. Designed in the traditional Jacobean H-shape, it was considerably altered by the Duke and Duchess of Lauderdale in 1670. Their descendants occupied the house until 1948 when it was given to the National Trust. It's one of the most complete examples of an English 17th-century mansion.

Numerous busts of Roman emperors are displayed on either side of the front door, as well as two English kings, James I and Charles II. The period front door opens into the Great Hall with its fine black and white marble floor. Take the first door to the right if you wish to buy a comprehensive guide and start your tour of the house in the Marble Dining Room which boasts leather wall hangings and a parquet floor dating from 1756. A right turn will take you through the Duke and Duchess's private apartments. The Chapel is off the Inner Hall at the bottom of the Great Staircase. This takes you up to the exotically named Yellow Satin Room with its separate dressing room. The Museum and Miniature Rooms are adjacent to the Round Gallery, then head on to the North Drawing Room and the Green Closet. The beautiful paneling in the Long Gallery dates from 1639 and you'll see a fine collection of portraits by Sir Peter Lely and artists of the School of Van Dyck. Turn right at the far end of the Gallery for a quick look at the Library before visiting the Queen's Bedchamber. The tapestries in the Bedchamber are based on pictures by Watteau portraying *The Dance, The Fountain, The Swing* and *The Fruitgatherer* in that order. As the Duchess suffered from gout she had a pair of 'sleeping chairs'. One of these is displayed in the end room, the Queen's Closet. Return downstairs the way you came to visit the domestic offices through the West Passage past the bookshop. Here you'll find the Gentleman's Dining Room, the Back Parlour with access to the Duchess's bathroom by the back stairs and the basement with other stairs leading to the buttery. As you leave the house turn left to visit the gardens which have been carefully restored to their full 17th-century glory.

HAM HOUSE TO KEW GARDENS (about 5 miles)

*Retrace your route along **Ham Street** and turn left before the **Royal Oak** pub along **Sandy Lane**, continue to the junction with **Petersham Road** where you turn left. Stay on this road as it winds through **Petersham** and ¾ mile beyond take the right fork up **Star & Garter Hill**, to **Richmond Hill (B353)**. Keep sharp left beyond the gate to **Richmond Park** at the top of the hill – you'll have an excellent view to the left with the River Thames below you. The road bears to the right at the end of the ridge. Follow the main road around the church. Stay on this main road to its end as it winds through Richmond crossing straight over traffic lights halfway down the hill. When you've found your way to the end of this road, turn right at the lights to another traffic light on an elongated traffic circle. Follow the signs to **Kew Gardens/Kew Bridge (A307)**, the second turning to the left off the traffic circle. Soon you see the ten-story pagoda in **Kew Gardens** across the open sports fields to the left but the main entrance to the Gardens is 1 mile further on at the far end of the long perimeter wall on your left. At the traffic lights turn left, then left again alongside **Kew Green**. The main gate to **Kew Gardens** is at the end of the green.*

Kew Gardens, Kew
Open: Gardens: Daily 9:30am-6:30pm May-Sep; to dusk Oct-Apr
Closed: Christmas Day, New Year's Day
Admission: Adults and children over 10 years 50p, under 10 free; free map and color brochure at entrance.

The origins of Kew go back to 1759 when Princess Augusta started a small botanic garden on her nine-acre Kew estate purely for her own amusement. The fact that this was a private enterprise explains why this world-famous garden is sited on sandy soil which is, in theory anyway, entirely unsuitable. In due course Princess Augusta's estate was joined up with the adjacent property known as Richmond Lodge which belonged to her son, George III. Hence the plural in the name.

While royalty have been associated with Kew and its buildings continuously, Sir Joseph Banks is undoubtedly the single towering figure in Kew's development. He accompanied Captain Cook on his famed 1768-1771 voyage and brought back thousands of exotic plants. During his 34-year stewardship he took on the massive task of recording and classifying all the world's plants, establishing a tradition that is carried on today.

The increased 300-acre site now contains many special collections such as rose, alpine, rhododendron and heather gardens. Hothouses and glasshouses have been built for tropical and subtropical species so Kew now boasts one of the most comprehensive plant collections and reference libraries in the world.

Of all the glasshouses, you may find the **Princess of Wales Conservatory** the most interesting as it divides into five sections, each having a sharp climatic variation from a hot humid atmosphere to a cool dry one. This glasshouse is located down the main path past the Orangery on the left and can just be seen from the entrance to the Palace. Kew Gardens really require a full day's visit to do them justice. They're one mile long and half a mile wide so that a walk round the garden features will take time.

Oranges were grown in the white **Orangery** from 1761. Now there's a gift shop where you'll find a selection of books about Kew, botanical publications, cards and very attractive souvenirs. Continue down **Broadwalk** to the pond, then turn right for the imposing **Palm House**. This renowned Victorian conservatory was completed in 1848, and conceals the **Rose Garden** which is laid out behind it. On your way to the Pagoda you can visit **King William's Temple** and the **Temperate House**, another mammoth Victorian glasshouse completed in 1899. It was the largest structure of its kind in the world. After the **Japanese Gateway** and the **Pagoda**, which dates from 1761, you walk through the **Ruined Arch** and the **Marianne North Gallery**. Here you'll find Victorian paintings, the tallest flagstaff in Britain and the **Temple of Bellona**. Continue to skirt the gardens and pond past the **Museum** and aquatic garden to the **Alpine House** and **Wood Museum**, a short walk from the main gates or Kew Palace.

Kew Palace (Dutch House)
Open: Daily 11am-5:30pm Apr-Sep   Closed: Oct-Mar
Admission: Adults 80p, children 40p

Kew Palace was originally a merchant's house built in 1631. The merchant's Dutch connections may well account for the attractive curved style of the gables and the unusual way the bricks were laid. When the house was acquired by George III it became his country retreat, the smallest and most intimate of the Royal Palaces in London. Some of the King's 15 children lived here, then the King himself when mental illness forced him to retire from public life. His wife, Queen Charlotte, died in her bedroom in November 1818.

The oak-paneled rooms downstairs contain an exhibition area. Upstairs the paneling is painted in a lighter and more decorative style. All the fabrics and wallpapers have been carefully chosen to blend in with the fashionable ideas of Queen Charlotte's day.

KEW RESTAURANTS

Jasper's Bun In The Oven, 9-11 Kew Green   £
Tel: (01) 940 3987
Open: Mon-Sat 12:30pm-3pm, 7pm-11pm   Closed: Sun
Credit cards: AE, DC, MC, V

From the main entrance to the gardens turn right and walk on past the church along Kew Green. The restaurant has three small cozy rooms decorated with French Impressionist drawings and pine dressers. The French flavor extends to the menu which offers an appetizing range of provincial style cuisine plus a good value three-course set menu. It's a popular restaurant so try and get there early. Dine in the garden in summer.

Pissaro's Bar Au Vin, 1-5 Kew Green   £
Tel: (01) 940 0286
Open: Daily 11:30am-3:30pm, 7pm-11pm
Credit cards: MC, V

The small interconnecting rooms of three houses combine to make this ground-floor restaurant, furnished with plain wooden tables and chairs. A rustic atmosphere prevails with a collection of rural antiques, farm implements and horseshoes surrounding the brick fireplaces. It's a busy, cheerful restaurant with hearty homemade main dishes, plus a range of good snacks, sandwiches and a salad bar. Friendly staff do their best to keep up with the orders, and you can wait for a table at the bar which offers a good choice of wines by the bottle or glass.

KEW TO KEW BRIDGE ENGINES   (about 2 miles)

*The engines are marked by a prominent 250 foot tower of grey-brown London brick. Take a left turn from **Kew Green** over **Kew Bridge**. Keep in the left lane up to the double traffic light where you turn left again, then immediately right into **Green Dragon Lane** signposted for the **Living Steam Museum** and **Kew Bridge Engines**.*

Kew Bridge Engines, Green Dragon Lane, Brentford
Tel: (01) 568 4757
Open: Daily 11am-5pm
Admission: Adults £1 (Sat-Sun £1.70), children 50p (Sat-Sun 80p)

This fine collection of giant pumping engines is best seen at weekends when they're 'in steam'. The world's first steam engine was the 'Beam Engine'. Its ability to drive machines (and replace water mills) was a vital factor in the English Industrial Revolution. The largest of these enormous engines has a beam of nearly 50 tons supported on 30-foot cast iron pillars and one 'stroke' can pump as much as 717 gallons of water. Of the four Beam Engines the earliest, built in 1820, ran for 123 years. The old boiler room off the main exhibition hall contains four later engines; the earliest, dating from 1867, supplied water to Lord Rothschild's country estate. You can also see two of the boiler engines supplying the steam and view the beam engines from the upstairs level before entering the passage to look at the large 90 to 100-inch engines. The **Diesel House** is open as well as the **Forge** and **Workshop** with a working steam hammer for on site repair jobs, dating from 1838.

KEW BRIDGE ENGINES TO LONDON   (about 9 miles)

*Return down **Green Dragon Lane** to the main road by **Kew Bridge**. Turn left, crossing straight over the traffic light to the extended traffic circle under the M4 overpass. Join the flow, moving over to the right-hand lane and keep right around the traffic circle, taking the third exit marked **Central London** (A4). Hammersmith is 2½ miles straight ahead on the A4 which continues into central London.*

> When booking accommodation be sure to check as to whether or not breakfast is included in the price of the room. We think it should be; ideally a proper British breakfast not one of those namby-pamby continental affairs.

TOUR 5: A PAINLESS OXFORD EDUCATION

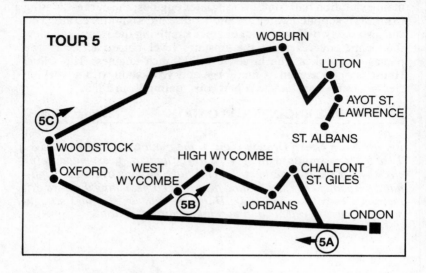

Route A: LONDON TO OXFORD (about 57 miles)

*This tour starts from **Marylebone Road** in London, at the north end of **Baker Street**. The journey to Oxford is direct and takes around an hour. From Marylebone Road follow the **M40** signs westward keeping to the right lanes as you approach the overpass near Paddington and drive up onto the **A40(M)** for **Oxford**. The motorway section changes to the **Western Avenue** two-way highway, eventually becoming, around 10 miles later, the **M40** at **Beaconsfield**. Stay on the M40 to its end where it becomes the **A40** 6 miles before the Oxford Ring Road.*

*If you're arriving in Oxford in the evening or during a quiet part of the day out of the tourist season, it's worth driving into the city center and looking for space to park. Otherwise, Oxford is notoriously difficult for motorists (all the better, once you're in there on foot, of course). Instead, use the free, out of town car parks and regular, 50p bus service. You'll find the **Thornhill 'Park and Ride' car park** on your left at the first set of traffic lights on the **Oxford Ring Road**. (Don't worry if you miss it: at the traffic circle turn back towards London, keeping in the right lane, and you'll be able to turn right into the car park.)*

*If you're driving into Oxford, go straight across the ring road traffic circle signposted to **Oxford/Headington/A420**. The road ends at a traffic circle just before **Magdalen Bridge** across the **River Cherwell**. Take the third exit across the bridge and continue up **Oxford***

High Street to the central crossroads, called Carfax. Turn left into St Aldate's noting the location of the Tourist Information Centre a few yards down on the right. Continue for ½ mile turning right just before the bridge into a one-way system (Thames Street). After the next junction get in the right lane turning right into the car park on the right. Walk out the other end of the car park to the Tourist Information Centre following signs (up Castle Street, right into Bonn Square, and Queen Street to Carfax. The Centre is a few yards down on your right).

For details of the **City of Oxford** see **page 387**.

Route B: OXFORD TO LONDON Visiting West Wycombe Park And Hughenden Manor　　　　　　　　　(about 53 miles)

OXFORD TO WEST WYCOMBE　　　　　　　(about 13 miles)

Turn right out of the car park and left at the traffic lights. At the next lights turn left to the central intersection called Carfax. Here turn right. At the traffic circle take the left road signposted to London/Headington/A40. Stay on this road through Headington to the Oxford Ring Road. Cross over the ring road following the signs for London/M40.

Just after joining the M40 you'll see an exit to the left signposted Thame/A418. If you have time, and the funds, for a gastronomic feast and perhaps an overnight stop in great luxury, this is the start of a diversion to Raymond Blanc's Le Manoir aux Quat' Saisons in Great Milton (tel: (0844) 278881; open: Wed-Sun 12:15pm-2:30pm, Tues-Sun 7:15pm-9:30pm; credit cards: AE, MC, V; £££). Take the Thame/A418 exit and follow the road round, turning left; just beyond the road crosses over the motorway. This left turn is signposted Great Milton. Continue for 2½ miles to Great Milton and straight through the village. The restaurant/hotel is on the left just beyond the church. The restaurant in this luxurious, elegant Elizabethan manor house features some of the best cooking in the British Isles. The French gourmet dishes change three times a year. The set meals are £18.20 (lunch) and £38 (dinner) and the excellent wines are appropriately expensive. Bedrooms are booked months ahead in the summer. You'll need to reserve far in advance for dinner, but lunches need less planning.

Return to the M40 by turning right out of the restaurant and following the road to its end where you turn right to the M40 and right again at the far side to join the M40 towards London.

Ten miles on, exit at Junction 5 signposted High Wycombe/A40 and turn left onto the A40 to West Wycombe, a pretty village with some quite extraordinary associations. Much of the village is now under the protection of the National Trust, which also looks after the neighboring stately home, West Wycombe Park. High on a hill above *the village is the **Church of St Laurence** with a massive golden ball perched 646 feet above sea level. As you enter the village you will see a signpost for free parking on your left.*

The village was on the main Oxford to London route for about 600 years before the freeway was built. **The George & Dragon** (tel: (0494) 23602) halfway down the main street on your right, is a coaching inn dating from the 17th century. There are plenty of bar snacks, or you could try a house specialty such as game pie (£3.60) or beef Wellington (£5.10).

West Wycombe Park
Open: Sun-Thurs 2pm-5pm Jun-Aug; grounds open Apr-Aug
Admission: Adults £2.20, children £1.10; grounds only £1.60

A Palladian mansion set in grounds skillfully landscaped by Humphrey Repton, West Wycombe Park is best known as the home of Sir Francis Dashwood, the 18th-century eccentric who founded the Hell Fire Club. Members of the club used to meet in the nearby caves, now open to the public (daily 11am-6pm Easter-Sep; Sat-Sun 1pm-5pm Oct-Easter; admission: adults £2, children £1). The caves are now fitted out with tableaux depicting the strange doings of the Hell Fire Club, whose members were drawn from the circle of friends revolving around Frederick, Prince of Wales.

WEST WYCOMBE TO HUGHENDEN MANOR   (about 5 miles)

*Continue on the A40 into **High Wycombe**, straight across the traffic lights and traffic circle signposted **Town Centre**. At the second traffic circle in the town center take the left turn signposted **Great Missenden/A4128** and then left again at the central square. As you leave High Wycombe, you'll see the lush green golf course and parkland on your left. Look for a left turn up a narrow open road which will lead you up to Hughenden Manor.*

Hughenden Manor
Open: Wed-Sat 2pm-5:30pm, Sun and public holiday Mon noon-
5:30pm Apr-Oct; Sat-Sun 2pm-5:30pm Mar
Closed: Good Friday
Admission: Adults £2 (Thur-Fri £1.60), children £1

This large mansion was the home of statesman Benjamin Disraeli, Prime Minister to Queen Victoria, with whom he enjoyed a good working relationship. Like so many great country houses, Hughenden became the victim of the Victorian penchant for the Gothic Revival style. The library is the only room to retain its 18th-century fireplace and plaster ceiling. Disraeli's study is laid out as it was during his lifetime, and contains letters from Queen Victoria. The

169-acre estate includes the country church where the statesman is buried. 'I have a passion for books and trees,' wrote Disraeli. 'When I come down to Hughenden I pass the first week in sauntering about my park and examining the trees, and then I saunter in the library and survey the books.' You can follow his practice during an afternoon's visit.

HUGHENDEN MANOR TO CHALFONT ST GILES Via Jordans
(about 12 miles)

*Turn right out of the **Manor road** and return to **High Wycombe**. Turn right at the end of the square, following the sign for **All Through Traffic** to a traffic circle. Turn left signposted **London/A40**. Stay on the A40 through **Beaconsfield**, a charming town with broad-timbered inns, and across the next traffic circle, following the signs to **Gerrards Cross/A40**. One mile down the A40 turn left to **Jordans**.*

Just before Jordans you'll see a building to the right and a sign **'Friends Meeting House'** (open: Mon 10am-1pm, Wed-Sat 10am-1pm, 2pm-6pm, closes at dusk in winter, free admission). Built in 1688, this was the Quaker Meeting House where William Penn, founder of Pennsylvania, and his friends gathered. Penn and his two wives, together with 10 of their 16 children, are buried in the local churchyard. Continue into the village where the 17th-century farm is now owned by the Society of Friends. The farm buildings include the **Mayflower Barn** whose timbers include wood from The Mayflower. Admission to the barn is free and it is open daily. If the door is locked, go to the office in the main house (clearly marked) and they'll let you in. The office is manned from 7am-10pm daily.

*Continue through Jordans, turning right at the junction, into **Chalfont St Giles**, a pretty village in which the poet Milton sought refuge from the plague in 1665. His cottage is now a museum. Before you leave the center of the village, spare time to look at the ancient cottages around the village green, and if you're planning a picnic, stop off at **Chalfont Foodhalls**, 122 High Street, which has a good delicatessen section. To reach **Milton's Cottage**, cross straight over the traffic circle in the center of the village and continue down the road ahead for ½ mile. Milton's cottage is beside the road on the right with a car park opposite.*

Milton's Cottage
Open: Tues-Sat 10am-1pm, 2pm-6pm Mar-Oct
Admission: Adults £1, children 40p

Old, lonely and almost blind, this is where Milton completed *Paradise Lost* and wrote its sequel, *Paradise Regained*. The cottage contains many personal and contemporary relics. In its library you'll find first editions of both his great works.

CHALFONT ST GILES TO LONDON (about 23 miles)

Turn left out of the Milton Cottage car park and continue down the road to the main crossroads where you turn right signposted London/ A413 and Chalfont St Peter. Stay on this road all the way, passing under the M25 until it joins the A40 where you follow the signs for Central London. This eventually takes you to Western Avenue, then the A40(M) which leads directly into Marylebone Road to the north of Baker Street in Central London.

Route C: Continuing On From OXFORD TO ST ALBANS Visiting Blenheim Palace, Woburn Abbey And Luton Hoo
(about 91 miles)

OXFORD TO BLENHEIM PALACE (about 9 miles)

From the car park turn right and right again at the first traffic lights. At the next traffic lights turn left and now follow the signs for 'North' as the road twists and turns through town. This eventually leads you left onto the broad street of St Giles. Two hundred yards down this street keep left at the fork for Woodstock/A4144. Three miles ahead at the traffic circle take the third exit signposted for Blenheim Palace and then straight ahead over a series of traffic circles for 6 miles to Woodstock. Blenheim Palace gates are on your left as you arrive at Woodstock.

For details of Blenheim Palace see page 399.

SIDE TRIP TO BLADON (about 2 miles)

You can take an energetic 20-minute walk from Blenheim to Bladon (signposted). To drive there leave by the exit gate (not the same as the entrance gate) and turn right for Bladon. In the churchyard of this small, gray stone village lies the grave of Sir Winston Churchill so Bladon has become something of a place of pilgrimage. You might like to stop at the White Horse pub on your right; you can reach the churchyard by the pathway opposite (to the left of the church beyond two cottages). Otherwise you will find the car park on the left at the other end of the village.

BLENHEIM PALACE TO WOBURN ABBEY (about 45 miles)

Turn left at main exit gate. Cross next traffic circle for A4095 to Bicester. Follow the A4095 signs as the route makes a quick left onto the A423 then right onto the A4095, ½ mile later at junction turn right on A4095. One mile later turn left to Kirtlington, with its many picturesque gray stone cottages. One mile from Kirtlington turn right to Bicester following the A4095, turning right then left across the A43. At the next T-junction turn right for Bicester. Turn left through Bicester on the A421 to Buckingham, taking the second exit straight across the traffic circle continuing on A421. Eight miles later at T-junction turn right. Buckingham is marked by a dominant church spire. Follow the main A421 as it skirts the town across two traffic circles, turning right at the third, signposted to Milton Keynes South/ Bletchley/A421. Stay on the main A421 crossing several traffic circles, then over a freeway. At the next traffic circle turn right for A5 south. Two miles further on at the traffic circle take left exit for Woburn Abbey. Half a mile later, turn right at a mini traffic circle, then right again at the next mini traffic circle in Woburn Sands and straight across the adjacent traffic circle. Continue for 2 miles to the village of Woburn. In the center, turn left as signposted for Woburn Abbey.

To spend time in Woburn, park 100 yards down on the left. Walk back to the main road, turn right and the Tourist Information Centre is across the road in the Heritage Centre (Open: Daily 2pm-4:30pm May-Sep). Before going to Woburn Abbey, you could visit Christopher Sykes Antique shop ('wine affiliated' and scientific antiques) next to the Tourist Centre or Atrium Antiques (lots that's genuine Georgian, some reproductions).

Woburn Abbey
Open: Daily 11am-5:00pm, Sun until 5:30pm (house), 10am-
    4:45pm, Sun until 5:45pm (garden) Apr-Oct; Sat-Sun 11am-4pm
    (house), 10:30am-3:45pm (garden) New Year's Day, Jan-Mar
    (times quoted are last entries to house and garden.)
Closed: Nov-Dec
Admission: Adults £4, children £1.50

Woburn Abbey has been the home of the Dukes of Bedford for over 300 years – it was given to the family by Henry VIII at the Dissolution of the Monasteries. The house was rebuilt by Henry Flitcroft in the mid 18th century, and added to by Henry Holland early in the 19th century. It is home to one of the finest private art collections in the world, with paintings by Canaletto, Van Dyck, Cuyp, Teniers, Rembrandt, Gainsborough, Reynolds and many more. Fine 18th-century English and French furniture, plus the unique Sèvres dinner service given to the 4th Duke by Louis XV, are among many treasures inside.

The three-thousand-acre deer park was landscaped by Repton. Some of the deer that now freely roam are unique. Descended from the Imperial Herd of China, they were saved from extinction at Woburn. In another part of the extensive parkland is the **Wild Animal Kingdom** (open: daily 10am-5pm mid Mar-Oct; admission:

adults £5, children £4), where anyone with a hard-topped car can drive through the monkey jungle, the lion and tiger reserves; or take a boat safari round the chimpanzees' island. Woburn has its own **Antiques Centre** (open: daily 11am-5pm Nov-Easter Sat; daily 10am-6pm Easter Sun-Oct; free admission). This occupies the South Stable block. Inside you'll find genuine shop façades rescued over the years from demolition or defacement and re-erected here to house 40 antique shops. Stock covers porcelain, glass, silver, prints and paintings.

WOBURN RESTAURANTS

Paris House, Woburn Park   ££
Tel: (0525) 290692
Open: Daily 12:30pm-2pm, 7pm-10pm
Closed:Sun eve, Mon, Feb
Credit cards: AE, DC, MC, V

This black and white timbered house was built in 1878 as a folly in Woburn Abbey Park. Particularly popular dishes include haddock in a flaky pastry case, suprême of duck followed by raspberry soufflé. Set meals are priced at £13.50 (lunch) and £18.50 (dinner).

Black Horse Inn   £
Tel: (0525) 290210
Open: Mon-Sat 11am-2:30pm, 6pm-11pm, Sun noon-3pm, 7pm-
        10:30pm; Meals served: Daily noon-2pm, 6pm-9:30pm
Credit cards: AE, DC, MC, V

Back in the center of Woburn – from the Abbey turn right and on your right you'll find this comfortable former coaching inn with an extensive, appetizing bar food menu. Popular choices include sirloin steaks (£5.20), American style burgers (£2.40) and savory cauliflower cheese (£2.25).

WOBURN TO LUTON HOO   (about 20 miles)

*From Woburn Abbey turn left in Woburn to **Hockliffe/A4012**. At the next traffic lights turn left as signposted to **London/A5**. Continue for 9 miles through **Dunstable** to a junction at Markyate. Turn left as signposted for **Luton/B4540**. Drive through **Slip End**, under the M1 freeway and turn right for **Luton**. After ½ mile turn left onto the **A1081** signposted to **Luton/Airport**. Another mile takes you up to a signposted to **Luton Hoo**. Follow the road down the steep hill for 1 mile. Turn right at the bottom of the hill for the Luton Hoo main gate.*

Luton Hoo

Open: Tues-Sun 2pm-5pm Easter, mid Apr-mid Oct
Closed: Mon except public holidays
traffic circle. Take the second exit, then right at the traffic lights
Admission: Adults £1, children 50p (gardens and Russian room);
Wernher Collection: Adults £1.50, children 75p

This palatial mansion, built by Robert Adam in 1768 and remodeled after a fire in 1843, is the home of the Wernher family. Their collection of pictures, tapestries, porcelain and other treasures is outstanding and includes Russian Fabergé jewels. Walking in the 1500-acre park landscaped by Capability Brown, you'll find it hard to believe that the industrial town of Luton is barely one mile away.

LUTON HOO TO AYOT ST LAWRENCE (about 11 miles)

*Retrace your route from Luton Hoo left up the hill and left again at the lights back to the traffic circle for the M1. Take the second exit back down the **A1081** signposted to **Harpenden/St Albans**. Just beyond the center of Harpenden, take the **Wheathampstead/B487** road to the left at the next traffic circle. Go straight on at the next traffic circle then left at the following one. Turn right for Wheathampstead at the next traffic circle. Then turn left and drive through the village. Turn right at the following traffic circle and first left to the **Ayots**. Follow the road to **Ayot St Lawrence/Shaw's Corner**, forking left at the crossroads.*

Shaw's Corner

Tel: (0483) 820307
Open: Wed-Sat 2pm-5:30pm, Sun noon-6pm Apr-Oct
Admission: Adults £1.60, children 80p

The isolation and general air of being removed from the late 20th century will give you some clues as to why the playwright George Bernard Shaw chose to live here. He read an epitaph in the local churchyard of a woman who died at the age of 70. 'Her Time was Short' went the inscription. Shaw concluded that the area must be healthy. The 20th-century house in which he lived for 44 years (dying there at the age of 94) is laid out almost exactly as it was in his lifetime, down to his famous hats hanging in the hall. Much of his work was done in the revolving summerhouse in the garden.

AYOT ST LAWRENCE TO ST ALBANS (about 7 miles)

*Retrace your steps from the corner by Shaw's house following signs to **Wheathampstead**. Fork right at the first junction and right again at the end traffic circle. Turn left at the next traffic circle into **Wheat-***

hampstead *on the B651 and follow the signs to St Albans/City Centre. A word of warning now: St Albans central one-way system is liable to change. Our suggestion is that you tour the one-way system, following the signs for city center. Turn off into one of the central parking lots, then walk to the Tourist Information Office, which is in the large white building by Market Place in the center of town.*

For details of St Albans see page 299.

If you find restaurants, hotels or shops which you think we should include let us know. For finds which find their way into further editions we're happy to give you credit.

TOUR 6: STATELY HOMES, ST ALBANS AND A FAIRY TALE CASTLE

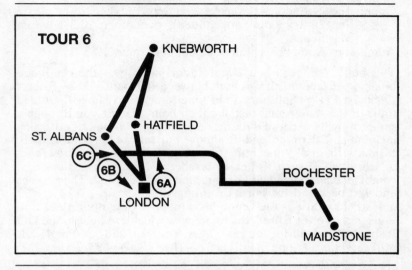

TOUR 6

KNEBWORTH

HATFIELD

ST. ALBANS

6C

6B

6A

LONDON

ROCHESTER

MAIDSTONE

Route A: LONDON TO ST ALBANS Visiting Hatfield House And Knebworth House (about 44 miles)

LONDON TO HATFIELD (about 21 miles)

*This tour starts at **Hyde Park Corner**. Head north up **Park Lane**, around **Marble Arch** and take the third exit into **Edgware Road**. Follow the signs for **North/M1**, through **Maida Vale**, **Kilburn** and **Cricklewood**. Five miles after leaving Hyde Park Corner, you approach an overpass as the road intersects with the North Circular (A406). Keep in the left lane and follow the road down underneath the overpass. Take the exit off the traffic circle under the overpass, signposted **M1**, and take the first exit on the left which brings you onto the M1. Leave the freeway at **Junction 2**, following signs for the **A1/ North**. After 2 miles take the second exit right at the traffic circle signposted **Welwyn Garden City/A1**. Follow this road for 3 miles as it takes you on to the A1(M) signposted to **Hatfield/Hatfield House**. Drive through the tunnel beyond **Hatfield**, take the left turn for **Hertford/A414**. Turn right at the traffic circle following signs for **Hatfield House**. At the next larger traffic circle take the second exit marked **Hertford/A414** and **Hatfield House**. In 1 mile take a left turn continuing to follow signs for Hatfield House. At the immediate junction turn right, at the traffic lights turn left as signposted. After 1½ miles you'll find the entrance to Hatfield House on the* *right, opposite Hatfield train station.*

Hatfield House and Old Palace
Open: Tues-Sat noon-4:15pm (guided tours only),
        Sun 2pm-5:30pm (not guided), park open 10:30am-8pm
        Mar-Sept
Admission: Adults £3, children £2.50, park only £1.50

This noble Jacobean house and Tudor palace was the childhood
home of Elizabeth I. It was built between 1607 and 1611 by Robert
Cecil, 1st Earl of Salisbury and Prime Minister to James I. Guided
tours of the state rooms last about an hour, trailing you through a
series of richly decorated rooms hung with world-famous portraits,
including the 'Ermine' and 'Rainbow' portraits of Queen Elizabeth
I. Fine 17th- and 19th-century furniture, Tudor treasures and relics
of Elizabeth I, such as her embroidered hat and silk stockings,
combine to leave you feeling somewhat overwhelmed. The gardens
and vast parkland are worth exploring.

Hatfield House is the venue for a number of temporary exhibitions and also for **Elizabethan banquets** which are held in the **Old
Bishop's Palace** during the year, Tues, Thur, Fri and Sat. For details
or reservations telephone (01) 837 3111 or (01) 930 2377.

HATFIELD TO KNEBWORTH   (about 10 miles)

*Turn right out of the main gates and at the lights 400 yards ahead,
turn right again signposted **Welwyn Garden City**. Take the next turn
left, following signs for the **A1(M)**. Get in the right lane to turn right
at the next traffic circle and drive up to the large traffic interchange.
Keep in the right lane, following signs for A1 (M) North through a
series of complicated traffic circles. At the final large traffic circle
continue to follow signs for A1 (M) North (i.e. NOT A1 (M)
London). Stay on the A1(M) freeway to **Exit 7**, signposted to
Knebworth House/Stevenage/A602. Now turn left into Knebworth
House.*

Knebworth House
Open: Tues-Sun: house noon-5pm, park 11am-5:30pm June-mid
        Sep; Sat-Sun, Bank Holidays and school holidays Apr-May
Admission: House and Gardens: Adults £3.30, children £2.80;
        Park only: Adults and children £1.80

The Lytton family have lived here since 1490, and the current
building actually dates from Tudor times, although only one wing of
Tudor Knebworth survives. The romantic Victorian novelist, Sir
Edward Bulwer-Lytton, was responsible for the high Gothic fantasy that swept away most of the older building early in the 19th

century. A magnificent **Jacobean Banqueting Hall** survived and is on view to the public. You can also see the 1843 **State Drawing Room** and the Edwardian **White Drawing Room** designed by Sir Edwin Lutyens. He also redesigned the beautiful formal gardens, which include a unique quincunx pattern herb garden designed by the celebrated gardener Gertrude Jekyll. This is the perfect place if you have children with you: the adventure playground is terrific.

KNEBWORTH TO ST ALBANS   (about 13 miles)

*Return to the A1(M) by crossing over the highway to join the A1(M) direction **London**. Drive through the tunnel at **Hatfield** and immediately after the tunnel turn left, following signs for **A414**. At the next traffic circle take the third exit marked **St Albans/A414**. Continue along the A414 until you reach a large traffic circle. Take the last exit signposted to **St Albans/A1081**. Continue to follow signs for **City Centre/A1081**. A word of warning now: St Albans central one-way system is liable to change. Our suggestion is that you follow signs for City Centre and park at one of the central parking lots. The **Tourist Information Centre** is a short walk away in the large white building by Market Place in the center of town (Tel: (0727) 64511. Open: Mon-Fri 10am-5pm, Sat 10am-4 pm).*

ST ALBANS

This Hertfordshire city dates back 2000 years when Belgic tribes settled here. The Romans later built Verulamium beside the River Ver, 1½ miles west of today's city center. In Roman times this was the only British city important enough to be given the status of municipium, which meant that its inhabitants were entitled to Roman citizenship. The site of the Roman city was not excavated until the 20th century when remains of a theater, hypocaust and several fine mosaic pavements were discovered.

WHAT TO SEE

Exhibits relating to both the Belgic and Roman periods in St Albans's history can be seen in the **Verulamium Museum** in St Michael's Street (open: Mon-Sat 10am-5:30pm, Sun 2pm-5:30pm, closing at 4pm in winter; admission: adults £1, children 50p, family ticket £2). The museum is about a 20-minute walk from the city center – there's space to park for those who prefer to drive.

From the grounds of the museum you get a good view of the

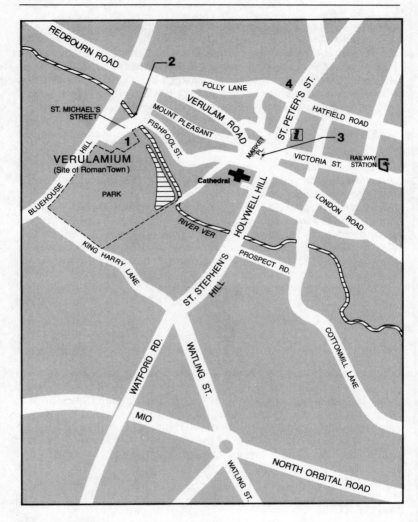

ST ALBANS

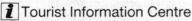 Tourist Information Centre
 1 Verulamium Museum
 2 Kingsbury Water Mill
 3 Clock Tower
 4 City Museum

cathedral, the huge **St Albans Abbey**. It sits on top of a hill incorporating the remains of an earlier, 11th century abbey. Alban, a Roman soldier executed outside Verulamium in AD 303, was the first Christian martyr in Britain. The Saxons built an abbey on the supposed site of his execution. This was rebuilt by the Normans and enlarged in the 13th century, becoming a cathedral in 1877 when the bishopric was created. The Victorians began to clean off the Puritan's whitewash in the Norman nave, and discovered fine medieval paintings on the piers of the long nave. More paintings have since come to light inside the abbey.

Also in St Michael's Street you'll find the **Kingsbury Water Mill**, a restored mill with working machinery and a good waffle house (both open: Wed-Sat 11am-6pm, Sun noon-6pm; closes one hour earlier Nov-Mar). To the south, in Chiswell Green Lane, are the gardens of the **Royal National Rose Society** (open: Mon-Sat 9am-5pm, Sun 10am-6pm mid June-mid Oct; admission: adults £1.50, children free).

In St Albans High Street stands a five-floor 15th-century flint and rubble **clock tower**. The Admiralty telegraph system operated from its roof during the 19th century. If you happen to be in St Albans on a weekend, you can climb up the clock tower (open: Sat, Sun, public holidays 10:30am-5pm; admission: adults 20p, children over five years 10p, under five years free). This gives a splendid view of the town, looking down onto the roofs of medieval houses in Fishpool Street and George Street and beyond to the Abbey. The **City Museum**, Hatfield Road (open: Mon-Sat 10am-5pm, free admission), houses an important collection of local craft tools displayed in reconstructed workshops.

SHOPPING

Normal shopping hours are from 9am or 9:30am until 5pm or 5:30pm. While Thursday is the early closing day many shops remain open throughout the afternoon.

St Albans has several shopping malls. **The Maltings** off Chequer Street has **Athena** for prints and posters, the ubiquitous **Body Shop**, **Benetton** and **Miss Selfridge** for women's fashions. Escalators lead up to the **In Shops** complex, a collection of tiny shops that aren't worth the ride. Within The Maltings there is an excellent **Arts Center** which presents a constant varied program of dance, theater, music and other entertainments at extremely reasonable prices. 'A Midsummer Night's Dream' was on during our visit for a mere £3.75.

Beyond the town hall (where you will find the Tourist Information Centre) Chequer Street becomes St Peter's Street where you'll find an excellent Marks & Spencer and a British Home Stores department store. Turn left coming out of the Tourist Information Centre and you'll come into **French Row**, (so named because the

Dauphin's troops were quartered here in 1216 and King John of France was detained in the Fleur de Lys Inn 1356). Another shopping complex, **Christopher Place**, runs off the Row. There's a **Bally** shoe store, **Dash** for leisurewear and a **Next B&G** for good children's togs. Summer concerts are given in the bandstand.

Classic at 14 Chequer Street features classic menswear, including Jekyll & Hyde, Boss and New Man clothes in appropriately handsome surroundings with William Morris wallpaper and elegant glass-fronted wooden cabinets.

Holywell Hill has some good shops. **Ashburton Garner** at No 9 has an impressive display of china and glass, including Belleek, Hummel and Waterford crystal. They offer a tax-free export scheme and duty-free mailing overseas. Further down at No 21 you'll find the **Quartet Gallery** which has an excellent selection of watercolors, oil paintings and limited edition prints. Delightful Bateman golf prints as well as some terrific tennis scenes were on offer during our visit. Virtually directly opposite at No 34 you'll see **Paton Books** which is everything a bookstore should be. The selection is comprehensive, notably on local guides; the staff friendly and knowledgeable.

George Street, the continuation of High Street, is another good shopping area. **Stuart Wharton**, a goldsmith and jewelry designer of exceptional skill is at No 1. His finely crafted silver bracelets and earrings are reasonably priced. We were particularly taken by his screaming eagle pendant. **Pitlochry Knitwear** at No 24 has a comprehensive reasonably priced selection of Scottish tartans, tweeds and knitwear.

ST ALBANS RESTAURANTS

Kyriakis, 30 Holywell Hill   £
Tel: (0727) 32841
Open: Daily noon-2:30pm, 6pm-11:30 pm
Credit cards: AE, DC, MC, V

Step into this low vaulted room with its bas-relief mosaic tiles, pottery and soft bouzouki music in the background and you could be in Athens. The food is equally authentic and extremely appetizing. Their three course 18 dish meze is an outstanding bargain at £8.95. Wash it down with the house retsina – under £6 a bottle.

Pastificio, 21 Chequer Street   £
Tel: (0727) 44264
Open: Daily noon-2:30pm, 6:30pm-11pm
Credit cards: AE, MC, V

The name translates as 'pasta factory' in Italian. That's appropriate as this is THE place to go for great made-on-the-premises pasta. We particularly like their spinach varieties. The decor is uncluttered and trendy, staff are equally 'with it'. Opposite is The Maltings so this is a good place to stop when shopping.

The Peahen Pub, corner Holywell Hill & London Road **£**
Tel: (0727) 53669
Open: Normal pub hours; meals served Mon-Sat 11:30am-2:30pm
No credit cards

The pub grub here is nothing to write home about but the decor is something else again. McMullens Brewery have created a museum-quality Victorian pub complete with one of the longest mahogany bars, including brass footrail, in England.

The walls are lined with china as well as some extraordinary display cases. One houses Victorian ladieswear ranging from ball gowns to mourning dress. Another concentrates on Victorian children's toys. There is even one that contains a stuffed tiger's head. The pictures are equally colorful. 'The Return of The Sword' is kitsch not Kitchener. 'The Long Bill' features a parliamentarian with a heron and will make you smile.

La Province, 13 George Street **££**
Tel: (0727) 52142
Open: Daily noon-2pm, 7pm-10pm
Credit cards: AE, MC, V

Just above Abbey Mill Lane this small French provincial restaurant, set on two levels, has much to commend it. The cooking is commendably good. Our halibut with almonds was beautifully prepared as were the duck's breasts with apples in a creamy sauce. Lighting is pleasantly subdued with candles on all tables. The decor is relatively nondescript with the odd modern print and painting. Spanish Maitre d', Raphael, is ultra attentive, but we found the French pop radio music in the background a genuinely bad and distracting idea.

St Michael's Manor Hotel Restaurant, Fishpool Street **££**
Tel: (0727) 64444
Open: Mon-Sat noon-1:45pm, 7pm-8:30pm (Sat until 9pm); Sun
        12:30pm-1:45pm, 7pm-8pm
Credit cards: AE, DC, MC, V

Their cuisine is Anglo-French, and the setting in a conservatory that would do credit to Alexandra Palace is delightful. There is a set price menu at £15 which during our stay included pheasant *chasseur* as an option or you can have such à la carte specialties as asparagus and oyster sweetbreads (£10). The wine list is extensive and good value for money.

Sally Lunn's Eating House, 17 St Michael's Street   **££**
Tel: (0727) 54405
Open: Mon-Thur 7:30pm-9:30pm, Fri-Sat 8pm (Feast – one sitting
      only), Sun lunch 12:30pm-2:30pm
Credit cards: DC, MC, V

*Directions: You may prefer to drive to Sally Lunn's. To do so turn right at the Tourist Information Centre down **Chequer Street** then right into the **High Street**, carry on into **George Street** (the Tudor Tavern will be on your right). This in turn becomes **Fishpool Street**, which is an education in the history of British architecture in and of itself. At the T-junction at the bottom turn left into **St Michael's Street**. Sally Lunn's is 200 yards down on the left between the Rose and Crown and the Six Bells pub across the street. You can park beyond the restaurant next to the Verulamium Museum.*

This restaurant has five Tudor dining rooms with original fireplaces and oak beams. It is a popular local choice for their outstanding set menu feasts. The three course feast which is on offer from Monday through Thursday costs just £12. On Friday and Saturday they have five courses for £16 while their delicious Sunday lunch of roast beef rib is £8.50. The fresh, traditional English fare, such as roast leg of lamb or pork and apple cider casserole, is excellent value for money.

Ye Olde Fighting Cocks Inn, Abbey Lane   **£**
Tel: (0727) 65830
Open: Normal pub hours; meals served daily noon-2pm
No credit cards

*Directions: From the **High Street** fork left down **George Street**, then left again at the triangle into **Abbey Mill Lane**, which goes through the **Abbey gateway**. The road forks and both branches lead to this inn which is located at the bottom of the hill. If you are driving take the right one since it goes to the main car park.*

The Fighting Cocks is the oldest inhabited licensed house in England. The interior consists of a series of small intimate rooms with beams at all angles. As its name would imply this was a renowned center for cock fighting. Today we recommend the Fighting Cock pie (£3.25) and the homemade soups (£1.00).
    Special note – this pub is best visited at lunchtime because in the evenings it can become raucous and extremely crowded.

ST ALBANS HOTELS

Noke Thistle Hotel, Watford Road   £££
Tel: (0727) 54252
Amenities: ☎ ⌨ 🅿 ⵗⵗ 🍸   Credit cards: AE, DC, MC, V

Directions: The hotel is on your left at the traffic circle where the A405, meets the B4630 (Watford Road). Alternatively from the Tourist Information Centre take the London Road down Holywell Hill. This becomes St Stephen's Hill after the traffic circle then the Watford Road after the next set of circles. Continue straight down this to Chiswell through Chiswell Green; at the next traffic circle you'll spot the Noke off to your right.

This large Victorian mansion has been extended and modernized. Its public rooms are comfortable with the feel of being in one's own elegant living room. The cocktail bar, with its Chinese ceramic lamps and floral patterned couch is particularly welcoming. All 57 bedrooms are en suite and include pleasant extra touches such as hair dryers, trouser presses and terry cloth bathrobes. Breakfast costs extra which we thought was a bit much.

St Michael's Manor Hotel, Fishpool Street   £££
Tel: (0727) 64444   Closed: Dec 27-29
Amenities: ☎ ⌨ 🅿 ⵗⵗ 🍸   Credit cards: AE, DC, MC, V

This handsome hotel is set in five verdant acres which slope down to a lovely large pond. Parts of the foundation are medieval while a portion of the main building dates from the 16th century. One wing (now somewhat obscured by a spectacular dining room conservatory) with its mansard roof and dormer windows is William and Mary. In contrast the central staircase is classic Edwardian.

All 26 bedrooms have a bath or shower and toilet en suite; four of the ten doubles have proper four posters. All of these overlook the gardens.

The rooms, tastefully decorated in pastels, incorporate thoughtful extra touches such as hair dryers and an intercom system which allows for baby sitting. We found the cocktail bar a bit of a jolt. See if the wood paneling reminds you of a Finnish sauna.

The hotel is run by the Newing Wards who clearly know their business. Newspapers with breakfast are a pleasant touch. The restaurant is excellent (see page 303).

The White Hart Inn, Holywell Hill   £
Tel: (0727) 53624
Amenities: ☎ ⌨ 🅿 ⵗⵗ 🍸   Credit cards: AE, MC, V

"Breakfast, madam. You tell us what you would like and we'll do our best to supply it", typifies the staff's attitude at this handsome late 15th-century coaching inn. Centrally located directly across from the walkway to the Cathedral their 11 rooms are spacious, furnished in a combination of modern pine and the odd piece from granny's attic.

Our room, No 10 under the eaves, was 24 feet by 30 feet and not for those inclined to sea sickness since the floor's tilt was such that keys kept falling off the bureau.

All bedrooms have adequate en suite bathrooms although towels are smallish. All rooms also have kettles for coffee or tea.

You enter the Inn via one of two wood paneled bars. The one on your left contains a copy of Hogarth's portrait of Jacobite rebel, Lord Lovat, drawn on the premises when he took ill here on his way to the hangman in London. The residents' lounge has a minstrels' gallery and beat up old sofas rubbing shoulders with Christie's quality antique.

Breakfasts in the pleasant dining room are what B&B breakfasts should be and all too often aren't. There is ample parking in the former stable yard.

Route B: ST ALBANS TO LONDON   (about 20 miles)

Follow the central one-way system round until you pick up the signs for London/Watford/(A405)/(M1 South) which lead you out of town. This road leads you over the M25, until you meet the M1 at Junction 6. Turn left onto the M1 for London. Stay on the M1 to its end, then bear right under the North Circular overpass and get in the left-hand lane for the next exit signposted London/A41. Keep going on this road through North London until it reaches Marble Arch.

Route C: Continuing – ST ALBANS TO ROCHESTER
Visiting Leeds Castle   (about 92 miles)

ST ALBANS TO LEEDS CASTLE   (about 80 miles)

At the outset it must be said that this drive is not scenic but is necessary to take you to one of Britain's most beautiful moated castles.

Follow the central one-way system until you pick up the signs for M25. These lead you out of town in the direction of London Colney.

*Join the **M25** at **junction 22** driving eastbound toward **Potters Bar**. Just after the M25 junction 31 you'll go through the **Dartford Tunnel**. This has a 70p toll: keep in the right lane if you have the exact money, which can be dropped into the automatic basket (no change given – you'll need coins value 5p and over). After 2 miles, move into the left lane for the **Rochester/A2** turn off at **Junction 2**. Continue down the A2 until you approach the M2 turning when you move into the right lanes which take you on to the **M2** for **Dover**. At **Junction 3**, signposted **Maidstone/A229**, leave the highway, turn left across the M2 and take the third exit at the traffic circle for the **Maidstone Road** (**A229**). Turn sharp left immediately after the traffic circle following signs for A229. In 2 miles turn left onto **M20** following signs for **M20/ Dover** and **Leeds Castle**. As you turn left onto the **M20** towards **Dover** you'll see the sign for **Leeds Castle**. At **Junction 8** where the M20 finishes, cross over the first traffic circle and turn right at the second signposted to **Leeds Castle**. The entrance to the Castle is 100 yards further on your left.*

Leeds Castle, near Maidstone
Open: Daily 11am-5pm Apr-Oct; Sat-Sun noon-4pm Nov-Mar
Admission: House and Grounds: Adults £4.50, children £3
Grounds only: Adults £3.50, children £2

Lord Conway described this as: 'The loveliest castle in the world'. It gets its name from Ledian or Leed, chief minister of the 9th-century King of Kent, Ethelbert IV. The castle dates back to the 9th century, but was rebuilt as a Norman fortress in 1119. It occupies two islands in a lake formed by the River Len. Leeds became known as the Ladies' Castle because of the number of queens who have lived here: two wives of Edward I, the wife of Edward III and Henry VIII's first wife, Catherine of Aragon. Elizabeth I was imprisoned here before she became queen. Henry VIII made it an official Royal Residence and it remained as such for over 300 years. The castle was restored in the 19th century. It houses a superb collection of medieval furnishings, tapestries and Impressionist paintings. There's also an extraordinary museum of medieval dog collars, a Culpeper flower garden, rare swans, geese and ducks, a picnic area, restaurant and nine-hole public golf course. Green fee £5.95, reserve ahead, tel: (0622) 65400).

HOTELS NEAR LEEDS CASTLE

Court Lodge, West Farleigh   **£**
Tel: (0622) 812222   Closed: Over Christmas, Jan
Amenities: ♉ **P** ♨♪ ✓ (nearby)   No credit cards

*Directions: Take the **A26** from Maidstone. After 4 miles turn left* *onto the B2163. Drive over a level (train) crossing and River Medway (medieval bridge). After ½ mile left at T-junction B2010. After another ¼ mile turn left before Lodge Cottage. House name on stone pillars.*

Mr and Mrs Morlock are welcoming hosts in their gracious Georgian country home set in two acres of grounds with gardens and a lake. The Lodge is a member of the Wolsey Lodges group of private home owners who share their splendid homes with a few guests. This is an excellent way to get to know the British. Facilities include a croquet lawn, horseback riding nearby and golf at the Leeds Castle course. One bedroom has en suite facilities, the other two share a bathroom. Dinner is reasonable at £15. Non-smokers preferred.

Great Danes Hotel, Ashford Road, Hollingbourne £££
Tel: (0622) 30022
Amenities: ☎ ⌨ 🅿 ⅋⅋⅋ ♈   Credit cards: AE, DC, MC, V

The Great Danes (named after the original owners' pets) is far from a dog of a hotel. For openers it's set in 20 acres of parkland which once belonged to its next door neighbor, Leeds Castle. The 128 bedrooms are extemely well done with pleasant modern furnishings, pretty patterned curtains and discreet lighting. All rooms have tea and coffee making equipment and hair dryers. Then there are the facilities – indoor pool, solarium, gym, tennis courts, pitch and putt golf course, fishing lake, snooker room – the list is near endless. Yes, Virginia, there is a helicopter pad. Prices for single rooms between £55-£72 and double rooms between £70-85, with deluxe suites at £90 and £110.

Tudor Park Hotel & Country Club, Ashford Road, Bearsted
£££
Tel: (0622) 34334
Amenities: ☎ ⌨ 🅿 ⅋⅋⅋ ♈ Credit cards: AE, DC, MC, V

Directions: 2 miles east of Maidstone on the A20 at Bearsted.

Facing out on its own 18-hole golf course this modern hotel also has remarkable facilities including a large indoor pool, two squash courts, two tennis courts, a sauna and steam room, a fitness studio and beauty salon. Rooms are pleasant if unoriginal. Singles run £50-£88, doubles £60-£110. These prices include temporary membership in their leisure club but golf, squash, snooker, sun beds and fitness studio are extra.

LEEDS CASTLE TO ROCHESTER (about 12 miles)

*From the castle turn right, returning to the **A20**. At the next intersection, turn left onto the **M20**. Drive to **Junction 6**, taking the slip road and bearing left for **Chatham/A229**. Continue all the way to the Chatham outskirts, where you fork left for **Rochester**. At the mini traffic circle turn left. Bear round to the right at the traffic lights, and after 200 yards turn left into the large open car park. The **High Street** is at the end of the car park, and the **Tourist Information Centre** occupies Eastgate Cottage in the High Street (Tel: (0634) 43666. Open: Daily 10am-1pm, 2pm-5pm Jul-Aug; Mon-Sat Sep-Jun).*

ROCHESTER

Strategically placed on the lower reaches of the River Medway, Rochester has been inhabited since pre-Roman times. The Romans built a walled city here, later re-fortified by the Saxons and much strengthened by William the Conqueror who ordered a castle to be built to defend the important crossing over the river on the route between London and Dover.

WHAT TO SEE

Cathedral, High Street
Open: Daily 8:30am-6pm, until 5pm in winter
Free admission, donations welcome

Rochester cathedral, begun in 1080, was designed by William the Conqueror's great architect, Bishop Gundulph. The original cathedral was founded by St Augustine and consecrated in 604, to become England's second bishopric. In the crypt you'll find particularly fine tombs of medieval bishops. The cathedral library houses several ancient manuscripts, including a copy of Miles Coverdale's English version of the Bible, printed in 1535. Outside there are peaceful, open lawns where the ruins of the chapter house, cloisters and the gateways of the monastery, all destroyed in the Reformation, can be seen.

Rochester's oldest buildings are clustered around the Cathedral and the High Street. Many of them feature in Dickens' novels. The novelist lived at Gad's Hill, just outside Rochester, for many years until his death in 1870.

The Charles Dickens Centre, Eastgate House, High Street
(next to the Tourist Information Centre)
Open: Daily 10am-5pm   Closed: Over Christmas
Admission: Adults £1.60, children £1, family ticket £4.40

The center contains reconstructions of scenarios from his books.

The house itself, which also features in Dickens' work as the Nun's House in *Edwin Drood* and Westgate House in *The Pickwick Papers*, is a fine, late Tudor building.

Rochester Castle, Castle Hill
Open: Mon-Sat 9:30am-6:30pm, Sun 2pm-4pm mid Mar-mid Oct;
        Mon-Sat 9:30am-4pm, Sun 2pm-4pm mid Oct-mid Mar
Admission: Adults £1, children 50p

The great square keep of Rochester Castle has resisted destruction for 900 years. Besieged many times, it held out in 1215 for two months against the attacking armies of King John. Battering the castle with huge, stone-throwing engines, the king finally weakened its defenses by mining under the castle and setting fire to the pit props with the fat of 40 pigs.

SHOPPING

Stores are open normal hours with small shops closing Wednesday afternoon. There are several fine food shops selling specialist teas, confectionery and delicatessen items. For a good choice visit **Casa Lina**, at 168-170 High Street. You'll also find a number of gift and antiques shops, including **Fagin's Alley**, 23 High Street, an indoor shopping mall offering a fascinating range of goods from antiques and bric-a-brac to fine quality craftwork.

ROCHESTER RESTAURANTS

Castle Restaurant, 151 High Street   **£**
Tel: (0634) 42812
Open: Mon to Sat 10:30am-5:30pm, Thur-Sat until 7:30pm, Sun
      noon-5pm
Credit cards: v

This is a good place for generous hot and cold home-style snacks. The full menu is available all day, the surroundings are comfortable and the service is friendly.

City Wall Wine Bar, 120-122 High Street   **£**
Tel: (0634) 406837
Open: Mon-Sat 11am-11pm, Sun noon-3pm, 7pm-10:30pm
Credit cards: AE, MC, v

This wine bar is just opposite the car park and is the most popular restaurant in the High Street. The recent substantial refurbishment has made this a smart spacious restaurant with friendly staff offering a range of English dishes.

Jolly Knight, 56 High Street   £
Tel: (0634) 830073
Open: Mon-Sat 11am-11pm; Sun noon-3pm, 7pm-10:30pm
No credit cards

An ancient pub standing on foundations dating from medieval times, the Jolly Knight has kept most of its original architectural character. In the wood-paneled lounge bar, armor and medieval weapons hang on the walls. Coffee is served in the lounge throughout the day; sandwiches and good-value meals are sold at the bar from noon-2pm. If you've worked up a thirst you'll find a selection of real ales on draft.

To continue on to **Canterbury** see **page 222**.

TOUR 1: GREAT CATHEDRAL CITIES
AND REGENCY BATH   (about 312 miles)

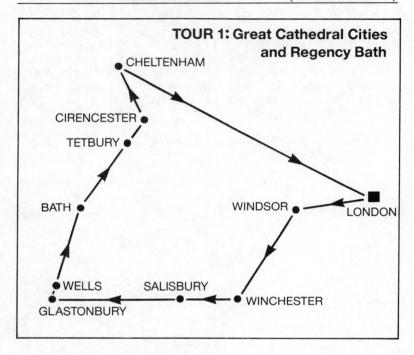

TOUR 1: Great Cathedral Cities and Regency Bath

CHELTENHAM
CIRENCESTER
TETBURY
BATH
WINDSOR
LONDON
WELLS   SALISBURY
GLASTONBURY   WINCHESTER

LONDON TO WINDSOR   (about 23 miles)

*Leave London on the **A4/M4** via Hammersmith, following signs for **The West** and **Heathrow Airport**. One mile after Hammersmith, at the Hogarth Roundabout (traffic circle), take the third turning signposted **A4/M4**. A few yards further on your left you'll pass **William Hogarth's** house (for which the traffic circle is named), a small brick villa where the famous painter lived from 1749 until 1764. Soon afterwards you'll come to **Chiswick House**, an 18th-century Palladian building in the grand style, contrasting with Hogarth's more humble residence.*

*One mile further get into the middle or right lane for the elevated section of the **M4** freeway, which becomes three lanes. Ten miles on you'll pass the Heathrow exit. You'll reach **Exit 6**, signposted **Windsor** and **Slough**, after another 7 miles.*

*Just before leaving the freeway at Exit 6 you'll see **Windsor Castle** and **Eton College Chapel** on the left. Take the first left at the traffic circle, the **A332 Windsor Road**, cross the River Thames, with a view* *of the castle behind the long arched bridge, and turn left, signposted* **A308** *to* **Windsor**. *At the next traffic circle turn left and follow the signs for the town center. This is* **Maidenhead Road**, *which becomes* **Arthur Road**. *At the traffic circle after the Duke of Connaught pub turn right, heading for* **King Edward Court car park**, *now on the left. Park on Level 4 for shops and the castle. Take your parking ticket with you, paying the appropriate fee at the machine outside Level 4 on your return.*

From Level 4 walk through the shopping complex, following the signs for the castle. This will lead you to the Central Station and the **Tourist Information Centre** *(Tel: (0753) 852010. Open: Mon-Sat 9:30am-6:30pm, Sun 10am-6:30pm Apr-Oct; Mon-Sat 9:30am-5pm, Sun 10am-4pm Nov-Mar), where you can pick up a map and more information about the town.*

WINDSOR

Royal Windsor lies on the River Thames and the famous castle has been a residence of English monarchs for over 850 years. The original fortress-castle was founded by William the Conqueror and the buildings now cover 13 acres, making Windsor one of the oldest and largest inhabited castles in the world.

WHAT TO SEE

Windsor Castle
Open: Castle precincts are generally open daily 10am-7pm summer, 10am-4pm winter; State Apartments daily 10:30am-5pm (last entry 4:30pm); Queen Mary's Dolls' House open at similar times. When the Queen is in residence the State Apartments and sometimes the Dolls' House are closed, usually 5 weeks at Easter and over Christmas. For exact times ask the Tourist Information Centre.
Admission: Castle precincts free
State Apartments: Adults £2, children £1
Queen Mary's Dolls' House: Adults £1, children 50p

The castle stands on a high, chalk ridge overlooking the River Thames, thus guarding the approaches to London. Henry III (1216-72), and later Edward III (1327-77), did most to extend and strengthen the fortifications and gave the castle its present shape. Elizabeth I built the North Terrace as a promenade, which has magnificent views over the Thames valley. She also commanded Shakespeare to write a play for the court: *The Merry Wives of Windsor*. During the whole of the Civil War, Cromwell's forces kept firm control of the castle, so that Windsor, unlike many other strongholds in England at that time, survived intact. The castle is

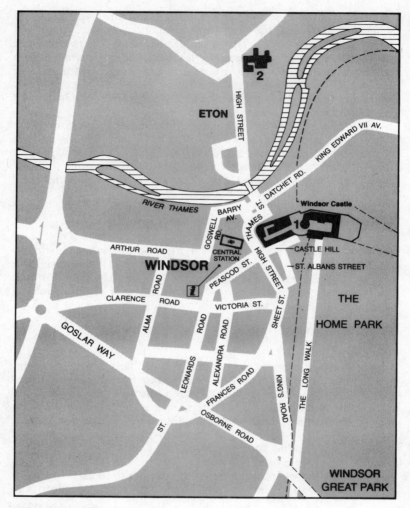

WINDSOR

 Tourist Information Centre
 1 Windsor Castle
 2 Eton College

the Queen's second home; entrance to some parts is restricted when the Royal Family is in residence.

The central **Round Tower** was built for Henry II, and gives a view over 12 counties, while the superb **St George's Chapel** in the Lower Ward, spiritual home of the Knights of the Garter, is one of the finest examples of English perpendicular architecture. The stately interiors, much altered in the 19th century, contain extensive collections of art, furniture, porcelain and memorabilia. Don't miss **Queen Mary's Dolls' House**, designed by Sir Edwin Lutyens, the famous architect, complete with minutely detailed and exquisitely crafted furnishings.

Parks and Gardens
To the south of the castle is the private **Home Park**, surrounded by the **Great Park**, together totaling 4,800 acres. The Great Park is bisected by **The Long Walk**, which leads to the Copper Horse equestrian statue of George III on Snow Hill, the park's highest point. Windsor Great Park also contains two special gardens open at different times. You'll almost certainly want to drive to these, unless you have an afternoon to spend walking across the Great Park.

The Valley Gardens
Open: Daily 8am-7pm or sunset when earlier
Admission: £1.50 per car, £2 Apr-May. Free to pedestrians. Pay
barrier at entrance accepts 10p, 50p and £1 coins

*Directions: From Windsor take the A332, driving across **Windsor Great Park**. The Gardens are signposted from here.*

Park your car and walk. These extensive woodland gardens are planted around the lake of **Virginia Water** and cover 400 acres in all. There's a large heather garden and glorious shrubberies cleverly planted to give marvelous color all year round.

The Savill Gardens
Open: Mon-Fri 10am-6pm, Sat-Sun 10am-7pm, or sunset if earlier
Closed: Dec 25-28
Admission: Adults £1.80, children under 16 free

*Directions: Leave Windsor on the **Osborne Road/A308** signposted **Staines**. Drive through **Old Windsor**. Just after you pass a large house called 'Bells of Ouzeley' make a right turn signposted **Englefield Green/A38**. Towards the top of the hill follow the signposts for the Savill Gardens. The gardens are about 5 miles from Windsor.*

This lies just north of the Valley Gardens, near **Englefield Green**, and is a remarkable 20th-century garden of 35 acres, with a huge variety of species, displayed *in situ*, of year-round interest to gardeners. Laid out by George VI, the present Queen's father, it has woodlands planted with dazzling azaleas and rhododendrons, scented rose gardens, rock screes designed for hardy alpines and many rare and unusual shrubs and other plants. A self-service restaurant is open from March 15 to mid December.

Eton College
It is a short hop across the Thames by footbridge from **Thames Avenue** to **Eton High Street** and that bastion of English educational superiority, Eton College. Founded by Henry VI in 1440, England's premier 'public' school opens its beautiful chapel, cloisters and school yard to visitors daily (afternoons only in term time). Famous old Etonians are too numerous to mention, but include 20 British prime ministers. Literary enthusiasts might like to combine their trip to Windsor with a visit to **Stoke Poges** (4 miles north of Windsor on the **B416**), where Old Etonian Thomas Gray composed his *Elegy in a Country Churchyard*. See **page 269**.

SHOPPING

Windsor's main shopping area is centered on **Peascod Street**, the **King Edward Court** Complex and **Guildhall Island**. Here you'll find all the classic British stores, such as **Jaeger, John Lewis** and **Scotch Corner**. The old-established perfumers, **Woods of Windsor**, at 50 High Street, can titillate your nostrils with all kinds of wonderful scents, pot pourri and fragrant drawer liners, while a stroll down **Leonards Road** will reveal seductive antiques and print shops offering both contemporary art and Victoriana. There's a Saturday market in **Sun Passage**, and no genuine antiques enthusiast should miss window-shopping in **Eton High Street**, with its antiques market and crop of craft shops. If you've plenty of time to spend in Eton, see **page 267** for more detailed information on shops there.

WINDSOR AND ETON RESTAURANTS

Angelo's Wine Bar, 5 St Leonard's Road, Windsor £
Tel: (0753) 864405
Open: Daily noon-2:30pm, 6:30pm-10:30pm
Credit cards: AE, DC, MC, V

There's a jolly Mediterranean atmosphere and bistro-style food, including pasta, a good daily selection of hot main dishes and generous salads.

Cope Oyster House, 6 Church Street, Windsor ££
Tel: (0753) 850929
Open: Mon-Sat noon-2:30pm, 7pm-10:30pm
Credit cards: AE, MC, V

Downstairs is a cool blue interior with barstools; a full restaurant above offers a mouthwatering selection of fish and game specialties in season. You can snack on Scottish smoked salmon washed down with dry white wine, and the more adventurous can try the skate wings with black butter.

Eton Wine Bar, 82 Eton High Street, Eton £
Tel: (0753) 854921
Open: Mon-Sat noon-2:30pm, 6pm-11pm; Sun noon-2pm,
    7pm-10pm
Credit cards: MC, V

The busy wine bar has a small but imaginative menu varied daily, with soups, casseroles, quiches and salads as delicious as they are good for you. Health fiends have the rare chance to indulge in good desserts too.

Windsor Chocolate House, 8 Church Street, Windsor £
Tel: (0753) 860157
Open: Daily 9:30am-5:15pm
Credit cards: AE, DC, MC, V

Tucked away in a cobbled street off Castle Hill, this is a tea house with everything: delicious pastries and lunchtime snacks plus a shop selling handmade chocolates and various English specialty packaged foods. There's a good value set menu.

WINDSOR HOTELS

Royal Adelaide Hotel, Kings Road ££
Tel: (0753) 863916
Amenities: ☎ ☐ P ⑂ ⑂   Credit cards: AE, DC, MC, V

In a quiet residential area, facing a perfect terrace of Georgian houses, it is a short walk from the town center with well-equipped rooms, restaurant and bar.

Sir Christopher Wren's House, Thames Street £££
Tel: (0753) 861354
Amenities: ☎ ☐ P ⑂ ⑂   Credit cards: AE, DC, MC, V

Designed, built and inhabited in the 17th century by the architect of St Paul's Cathedral, this is an exceptional hotel. Its 40 well-appointed rooms give views over the Thames or the castle and it has elegant reception rooms, a riverside dining room with an international menu, and private parking.

Ye Harte & Garter Hotel, High Street ££
Tel: (0753) 863426
Amenities: ☎ ☐ ⑂ ⑂   Credit cards: AE, DC, MC, V

A Berni Inn right opposite the castle, whose Victorian façade belies a history that includes several guest appearances in Shakespeare's *Merry Wives of Windsor*. It has well-equipped bedrooms, a Grill Room, olde worlde lounge and four bars. Public parking close by.

AROUND AND ABOUT

SIDE TRIP TO BRAY   (about 5 miles)

*Directions: retrace your route down Arthur Road, taking the **A308** for Maidenhead; after 4 miles drive under a freeway bridge and turn right onto the **B3028** to Bray.*

A meal at **Michel Roux's Waterside Inn** (see below) is the normal reason for a trip to Bray but this pretty riverside village also boasts attractive half-timbered houses in its High Street and picturesque almshouses founded in 1627 by William Goddard, whose likeness graces the gateway. The village secured a place in the national consciousness with a 17th-century ditty, *The Vicar of Bray*, reputedly based on the career of Simon Alleyn. This highly adaptable cleric switched his political allegiances so adroitly that he retained his sinecure through the reigns of four monarchs.

The Waterside Inn, Ferry Road   £££
Tel: (0628) 20691
Open: Tues 7pm-10pm, Wed-Sun noon-2pm, 7pm-10pm
Closed: Mon, Tues lunch; Dec 25-mid Feb
Credit cards: AE, DC, MC, V

This beautiful country restaurant hovers close to the English culinary stratosphere. It's worth treating yourself – but try not to worry about the check. Intriguing menus, created with enviable lightness of touch, are served by immaculate staff. For full appreciation of the mood and the situation you should go on a sunny, summer day. Reservations recommended.

WINDSOR TO WINCHESTER   (about 46 miles)

*From **King Edward Court car park** take the first left at the traffic circle, signposted **A332 Staines/Ascot**. At the next mini traffic circle turn left and drive along **Victoria Street**. Turn right at the stop lights at the junction with **Sheet Street**. Sheet Street becomes **Kings Road**, with the Great Park off to your left. At the traffic circle take the second exit for Ascot via Great Park (6 miles). After almost ½ mile you'll enter **Windsor Great Park** with a view of a distant equestrian statue on your left. This is an ideal place for a picnic, with its rolling grassland, mature trees and plenty of car-parking facilities. When you leave the park get into the right lane, signposted **A332 Ascot**, which bears* *sharply around to the right, and take the left turn to Ascot (3 miles). At the double traffic circle keep straight ahead. On your left you'll soon see **Ascot Race Course**, famous for its annual royal race meeting, instituted by Queen Anne in 1711 and held each June (see page 14). Avoid Ascot town center ꞇand follow the **A332** in the direction of **Bagshot/M3** for 3 miles, through the **Crown Estate** beech and fir woods, fronted by rhododendrons. Follow the signs for **Bagshot A322(A30)**, bearing around to the left at the major intersection (If you are short of time continue on the **A322**, taking the **M3** direct to Winchester to rejoin the main route.)*

*Pass under an overpass, then over another one, turning left for Bagshot and **Camberley**, and loop around to the left over the bridge and onto the **A30** in the direction of **Basingstoke** (21 miles).*

*The **A30** runs through the outskirts of Bagshot, over the Jolly Farmer traffic circle and into Camberley, home of the **British Army's Staff College**. At the first stop lights carry straight on, avoiding the town center, and carry straight over the traffic circle, following the signs for **Basingstoke/A30**, and heading for **Blackwater** village, where you'll enter the county of **Hampshire**. At the next traffic circle take the second exit, leading onto a divided highway and taking you into Hampshire heathland. After the Ely pub carry straight over the traffic circle, passing Blackbushe Airport on your right after a mile. Go right over the next traffic circle and through the village of **Hartley Wintney**. This has many charming old buildings, including the **Lamb Hotel** on your right, a good place to stop for lunch, though there are also many attractive pubs along this stretch of road with snack bars and restaurants. On your left you will see charming Victorian terraced cottages set around the village green.*

*After **Phoenix Green** and **Hook**, keep straight ahead on the A30 through a partially built-up area, past the Hatch pub on your left, and you'll soon see **Basingstoke** stretching out in front of you. This is an ugly dormitory town with an inscrutable one-way system, best avoided, so a mile after the Hatch take the Basingstoke by-pass, signposted as the **Ring Road**, **Alton** and **Alresford**, second left at the traffic circle. At the next traffic circle, soon afterward, turn first left for Alton and Alresford, **A339**, and straight over a third traffic circle, called the Venture Roundabout. You'll shortly pass under the M3 freeway, then turn right for **Alresford** (14 miles).*

*This country drive takes you through delightful villages of thatched cottages, such as **Cliddesden**. You're apt to spot pheasant and other game birds in the wooded countryside. After **Preston Candover** turn left for **Alresford** at the T-intersection, through rich Hampshire farmlands for a further 5 miles to **Old Alresford**.*

Once a medieval wool town, Alresford stands on the banks of the **River Alre**, a tributary of the **Itchen**. The chalk streams of Hampshire and Dorset provide not only ideal conditions for trout fishing and farming but also for cultivating watercress, and Alresford is one of Britain's main cress producers. You'll see **Alresford Watercress** on your right as you pass through the town.

An old railroad, the **Watercress Line**, which ran from the local station to Alton, has been rescued from obscurity and neglect by a group of steam-train enthusiasts. You can make the short round trip during the summer season. (Open: Sat, Sun and public holidays mid-March to end Oct, also weekdays from mid-July through August, and various dates out of season. Fare: Adults £4, children £2. Tel: (0962) 734200 or 733810 for more information.)

*Continue across the causeway bridge to one of Hampshire's prettiest small market towns, **New Alresford**. Drive up **Broad Street**, lined with lime trees and neat pastel-washed Georgian cottages, and turn right at its top for **Winchester**. If you feel like a break before seeing Winchester, **The Horse and Groom** pub at the top of Broad Street, bedecked with flower baskets, is a good place to stop; so are **The Tiffin Tearooms** at 50 West Street. Turn right a mile from Broad Street onto the **B3047** for **Kings Worthy**, through **Itchen Stoke** to **Itchen Abbas**, where Charles Kingsley wrote **The Water Babies**. Opposite The Plough Inn is the turning for Avington Park.*

Avington Park
Open: Sat-Sun and public holidays 2:30pm-5:30pm (last tour 5pm)
　　　May-Sep
Admission: Adults £1.50, children under 10 years 75p

Originally a Tudor building, Avington was greatly altered and extended in 1679 to include an impressive Doric portico in the style of Wren and a ballroom with a magnificent, painted ceiling. The house, set in lovely grounds, was visited by Charles II and George VI and once was owned by John Shelley, brother of the poet Percy Bysshe Shelley. Another owner, the Marquess of Caernarvon, added a delightful Georgian chapel, which is rich in carved mahogany. Light meals are available on Sundays and public holidays, making this a very pleasant spot for afternoon tea.

*Back on the **B3047** continue for 2 miles to a T-intersection where you turn left, then immediately right for **Winchester** on the **A3090** through **Kings Worthy**. Less than 3 miles further, after passing a modern housing tract, you'll descend a hill into the town. Bear left at the bottom of the hill into **Hyde Street** and ignore the signs for the long- and short-stay car parks straight ahead. At the traffic lights turn left and follow the one-way system right around to the long- and short-term car parks in the city center.*

*Leave your car and, using Marks & Spencer's green and gold motif as a landmark, you'll find an information booth on the sidewalk outside between the Post Office and the Kings Walk Shopping Arcade entrance, where you can pick up a map. The main **Tourist Information Centre** is in the **Guildhall**, on Broadway. (Tel:*

(0962) 840500. Open: Mon-Sat 9:30am-6pm, Sun 2pm-5pm May-Sep; Mon-Sat 9:30am-5pm, closed Sun, Oct-Apr.)

WINCHESTER

Home of the great **Round Table** of Arthurian legend, Winchester was the Saxon capital of the ancient kingdom of Wessex. King Alfred's statue can be seen at the bottom of Broadway. An enlightened king, Alfred translated the works of Pope Gregory the Great and commissioned the first English language history of England to educate his people. He united the population of southern England to counter the 9th-century Danish invasions, captured London and drove the Vikings north. After the Norman invasion of 1066, William the Conqueror made Winchester joint capital with London and was crowned King of England in the Great Hall of **Winchester Castle**. Here too, Sir Walter Raleigh, Elizabethan sailor and explorer, was sentenced to death in 1603, a sentence that took 15 years to be carried out under the weak and vacillating direction of James I.

Today Winchester is the administrative capital of Hampshire. There are many interesting old buildings, particularly around the dominating cathedral and **Winchester College**, as well as a good range of shops. The **Tourist Information Centre** organizes excellent walking tours, daily, Easter to October, which last 1½ hours for £1.25. Tours are less frequent in winter; check at the TIC office.

WHAT TO SEE

Winchester Cathedral, Cathedral Close
Open: Daily 8:30am-6:30pm (except during Sunday services at
      8am, 10:30am, 11:30am, 3:30pm)
Admission: Suggested donation £1

This beautiful Norman cathedral was founded in 1070 by William the Conqueror and Bishop Walkelyn. Remodeled by William of Wykeham in the 13th-century Perpendicular style, at 556 feet the cathedral is the longest in England. It contains some stunning carvings and one of the seven square black marble fonts from Tournai in Belgium. Looted and destroyed in 1538, St Swithin's shrine was a popular place of pilgrimage during the Middle Ages, second only to that of St Thomas à Becket's at Canterbury. St Swithin, a 9th-century bishop of Winchester, is reputed to have a say in British weather; should it rain on his feast day, July 15, it is said, it will go on raining for 'forty days and forty nights'. Painted Mortuary Chests containing the remains of several early English kings are placed in niches above the central nave. Novelist **Jane Austen**, who lived at nearby Chawton, and **Isaak Walton**, author of

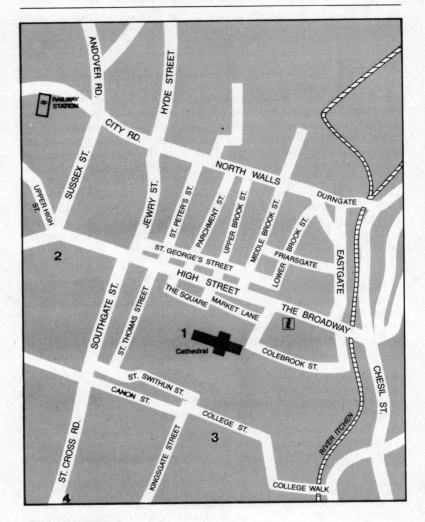

WINCHESTER

Tourist Information Centre
1 Winchester Cathedral
2 Great Hall and Round Table
3 Winchester College
4 St Cross Hospital

The Compleat Angler, are also buried here. The cathedral library boasts several treasures, including the first American Bible and the glorious, 12th-century illuminated **Winchester Bible**, with its illustrations and calligraphy, executed by at least six artists over many years.

Great Hall and Round Table, off the top of the High Street
Open: Daily 10am-5pm Oct-Mar; Mon-Fri 10am-5pm, Sat-Sun
     until 4pm Nov-Feb
Admission: Voluntary donation

Egbert the powerful King of Wessex, was crowned here in 827, while William the Conqueror, having made the town a joint capital with London, was crowned in both towns. Henry III was born here in 1207, and the various royal marriages celebrated within the building include those of Henry I in 1100, Henry V in 1402 and Mary and Philip of Spain in 1554. In the **Great Hall** are the remains of a royal dais – the alleged 'Round Table' of King Arthur, which is 18 feet in diameter.

Winchester College, College Street
Open: (chapel and chantry) Mon-Sat 10am-6pm, Sun 2pm-6pm
     Apr-Sep; Mon-Fri 10am-4pm, Sun 2pm-4pm Oct-Mar
Guided tours: Mon-Sat 11am, 2pm, 3:15pm; Sun 2pm, 3:15pm
     Apr-Sep; additional tour 4:30pm May-Aug. Price:
     Adults £1, children 75p

South of the cathedral is Winchester College, another famous 'public' school, founded in 1382, and noted for producing politicians – the school motto is 'Manners Mayketh Man'. Perhaps more suitable still is the Latin inscription to be found in 'school', a chantry chapel in the cloister of the graceful school chapel (copied by Henry VI at Eton), which translates to read 'Learn, leave or be licked'. Near the College you can take the footpath to the ancient **Hospital of St Cross**, Britain's oldest charitable foundation, where you can still claim the traditional Wayfarer's Dole of bread and a pitcher of beer from the Porter's Lodge.

SHOPPING

Stores generally open Monday-Saturday between 9am and 9:30am and shut at 5:30pm. Very few stores observe an early closing day. Only stores whose hours vary from the normal pattern have opening hours listed. Market days are Wednesday, Friday and Saturday.
    The pedestrianized **High Street** and **Broadway** contain a good selection of popular stores and boutiques, and **The Square** opposite the cathedral (left at the **Buttercross**) features some wonderful specialty shops.

Blazer, 10 The Square
Credit cards: AE, DC, MC, V   Open: until 6pm

Traditional menswear ranging from socks and cuff links to heavy winter coats, suits and the ubiquitous blazer under their own label. Good selection of men's toiletries.

Cadogan and Co., 30-31 The Square
Credit cards: AE, MC, V

This is a must stop if you're interested in the best of British casual country clothes for men and women, as well as Austrian Lodenwear. They also have some unusual items for the dedicated field and streamer from pocket flasks to binoculars and antique brass fishing reels at prices that will make you catch your breath. Beautifully laid out on four half floors; you'll be spoiled for choice. Staff are as splendidly understated as the clothes.

Carol Darby, 23 Little Minster Street
Credit cards: AE, MC, V

Ms Darby has been carefully crafting exquisite, one-of-a-kind silver and gold jewelry for over twenty years. Her small shop offers a wide selection of work ranging from pins and pendants to remarkable rings. Prices start at £10 with a variety of items at under £50. She is happy to design to your specification. Free gift wrapping.

The Chocolate Box, 23a Little Minster Street
Credit cards: AE, DC, MC, V   Open: 10am-6pm

Up an outside iron stairway, this tiny shop is a chocoholic's idea of paradise. Predominantly Belgian, German and locally made, you can buy them by the quarter pound for under £2 or splash out on one of their lovely silken-boxed gift assortments.

Design and Craft, 4 The Square
Credit cards: MC, V

Well-made modern furnishings and gifts. To the left as you enter you'll find their first-rate fabric department. Strong on glassware, china, soaps and scents. The upstairs gallery exhibits British artists on a rotating basis. Isle of Wight glassware is a specialty.

Doves, 152 High Street
Credit cards: MC, V   Open: until 6pm

A good choice for designer clothes at reasonable prices (including French Connection, Jeffrey Rogers, Mexx and Adini) in a high-tech store. They also have a reasonably priced selection of belts, bags and costume jewelry.

House of Tweed, 12 The Square
Credit cards: AE, DC, MC, V

If you're into tweed this has to be your day. The first floor features a huge range of kilts, sweaters and, somewhat incongruously, Gucci handbags. The smaller upstairs room has a superior collection of wool suits (£130 upwards), cashmere coats and capes. Irish and Scottish labels such as Viyella, Tulchan and Pringle predominate.

Magpie, 5 St Thomas Street
Credit cards: MC, V

Like the bird's nest, you'll find quite a collection here. The front of the store features super separates while at the back you'll find more formal finery including oh-so-chic cocktail dresses. Manageress Lindy Allerton and her staff couldn't be more helpful.

Mary Roof Antiques, 1 Stonemasons Court, 67 Parchment Street
No credit cards   Open: from 10am

Set in a small remodeled courtyard this excellent establishment is devoted to the artistry of the well-wrought antique box and they have them in their hundreds – boxed games, jewelry boxes, boxes with medical instruments, draughtsman's tools, writing boxes. Some are inlaid with rare woods, brass and ivory. All are gorgeous. They also sell antique clocks and the occasional exceptional item.

Monsoon, 143 High Street
Credit cards: AE, DC, MC, V   Open: Sat until 6pm

With its well-made, own-label clothes that are bound to appeal to the young and the young at heart, there's a heavy emphasis on separates in this shop. Lovely, scarves, handbags and jewelry.

The Rod Box, 52 St George Street
Credit cards: AE, DC, MC, V   Open: Sat until 5pm

If you're fly fishing for brown trout on the fabled Test or Itchen (where the sport began) be sure to start here. Owner Ian Hay and his sporting staff can arrange a beat for as little as £40 per day. Excellent assortment of flies and other fishing paraphernalia. Barbour coats, sturdy sweaters and boots, some handsome glassware and china featuring (what else?) sporting motifs.

St George's Antique Centre, off St George's Street
Credit cards: V   Open: Tues-Sat 10am-4:30pm

Tucked down the side of a little alleyway, the Centre is three crammed floors of china, jewelry, from the very old to art deco, twenties' lingerie, snakeskin bags, scientific instruments and paintings in constantly changing profusion. The stall holders are both knowledgeable and friendly.

The Silver Shop, 5 Stonemasons Court, 67 Parchment Street
Credit cards: MC, V

Family-run for generations, much of their silver is handmade on the premises using traditional tools – no machining here please. Excellent cutlery as well as some good antique pieces. They are shortly to bring out a handsome Winchester souvenir spoon featuring the city's coat of arms.

WINCHESTER RESTAURANTS

Branns, 9 Great Minster Street, The Square   £££
Tel: (0962) 64004
Open: Mon-Sat noon-3pm, 6pm-10:30pm
Closed: Restaurant: Mon lunch, first two wks Jan
Credit cards: AE, MC, V

One of Winchester's newest restaurants is also, in the judgement of many, its best as a successful exponent of the new wave of English cooking. They emphasize fresh ingredients cooked to perfection with sympathetic accompaniments. This means the ever-changing menu varies by season. Seafood is a specialty, as are lamb and duckling. There's always one vegetarian dish of the day. As you enter, a long bar dominates the left-hand wall. Delicious bar meals are available, such as their fish chowder and Covent Garden salad with hot salmon, Stilton and bacon. Trad jazz or classical music plays in the background.
There's a good view of the cathedral from the second floor restaurant with its comfortable beige interior. The prix fixe menus are £12.50 for lunches, £18.50 at night. In the evening reservations are advisable.

Minstrels, 2 Little Minster Street   £
Tel: (0962) 67212
Open: Mon-Sat 9:30am-5:30pm, Sun 11:30am-5pm
No credit cards

Tucked away from the High Street this counter-service counter-culture restaurant is a best bet for breakfast or a light lunch at a price that's light as well. Lots of potted plants, and a notice board that shows all that's on in the area. The house wine is excellent value.

Muswells, 8-9 Jewry Street   £
Tel: (0962) 842414
Open: Mon-Sat 11am-11pm, Sun from noon
Credit cards: AE, DC, MC, V

All bare wood and brass rails, with an understated, elegant, raised cocktail bar in the middle, this is Yuppie-chic come to a cathedral city. Good Cajun cooking, chicken wings and burgers in all sorts of guises. The staff are young, friendly and vaguely self-conscious. So are many of the customers.

The Old Vine, 8 Great Minster Street   £
Tel: (0962) 54616
Open: Mon-Sat 11am-11pm; Sun noon-3pm, 7pm-10:30pm
Meals served: Mon-Sat noon-2pm, 6:30pm-9pm; Sun noon-3pm, 7pm-9pm
Credit cards: MC, V

One of Winchester's most popular pubs. This large beamed room with its central bar and inglenook fireplace is normally crowded with a good cross-section of the local citizenry from students and local merchants to shoppers stopping for half a pint and a Yorkshire pudding sandwich. Good pub grub at reasonable prices plus a small restaurant at the back, **The Minster Room** (try their Hampshire Hog Platter – a thick slice of ham in a yummy peach sauce). Conveniently located just to the north of the Cathedral Close, which it overlooks.

Richoux, God Begot House, 101 High Street   £
Tel: (0962) 841790
Open: Mon-Sat 9am-9pm, Sun from 10am
Credit cards: AE, DC, MC, V

Started in London over sixty years ago, Richoux serves great breakfasts, such as the New Yorker which includes egg, bacon and a delicious waffle with maple syrup. But that's only part of the story. Other strong suits are their traditional British dinners (shepherd's pie, fish and chips, steak, kidney and mushroom pie etc.) and their English tea which includes two warm scones with freshly whipped cream and strawberry preserve. The limited wine list is reasonably priced. Service can be slow.

Waltons, 20-21 The Square   £
Tel: (0962) 62333
Open: Mon-Sat 10am-5:30pm
No credit cards

This bright, airy combined café, patisserie and ice cream parlor is a Winchester shopper's favorite for a quick delicious break – croissants, cappuccino, espresso, teas, succulent shortbread etc. Upstairs is a no-smoking area.

WINCHESTER HOTELS

The Royal Hotel, St Peter Street   **££**
Tel: (0962) 840840
Amenities: ☎ ⌨ 🅿 ⛾ ⚲   Credit cards: AE, DC, MC, V

Built in 1720 the building became a convent for Benedictine nuns
after the Reformation and only converted to hotel use in the 19th
century. The lobby is magnificently old fashioned as is the main
building, to which has been added a modern wing. All 59 rooms
have baths and rubber ducks (it's true), most have showers as well.
Other common facilities include not just remote-control TV but
free video plus coffee and tea makers. Breakfast is not included in
the room price. Parking, which can be a problem in Winchester, is
free. Some rooms are directly adjacent to the lots. With three
stories and no elevator you may wish to request one of these rooms.
There's a large patio garden area where meals can be taken on the
odd, clement day.

Wessex Hotel, Paternoster Row and Colebrook Street   **££**
Tel: (0962) 61611
Amenities: ☎ ⌨ 🅿 ⛾ ⚲   Credit cards: AE, DC, MC, V

This modern, four-star Trusthouse Forte hotel overlooks the Cathedral. It has well-equipped rooms and many facilities, including a
coffee shop, à la carte restaurant with stained glass by contemporary British artist, John Piper, and off-street parking.

The Wykeham Arms, 75 Kingsgate Street   **£**
Tel: (0962) 53834
Amenities: ☎ ⌨ 🅿 ⛾ ⚲ ◉   No credit cards

A cozy pub in a quiet area near the College, with log fires, draft
ales, pub grub in the bar, a good restaurant with a fine local
reputation and a sauna and lounge for residents.

AROUND AND ABOUT

Broadlands, Romsey
Open: Tues-Sun 10am-6pm (last entry 5pm) Apr 1-Sep 30; daily
        Jul-Aug
Admission: Adults £3, children 12-16 years £1.70, under 12 free

*Directions: At the top of **St George's Street** in Winchester follow the
well-signposted route to **Romsey** for 11 miles along the A33/A31.*

Broadlands was built in 1536 for Romsey Abbey and extensively
altered in the Palladian style of the 18th century. The house was
sold to Lord Palmerston in 1739, and inherited in 1936 by the
Mountbatten family who still live here. The Queen and Prince
Philip and the Prince and Princess of Wales spent parts of their

honeymoons in the mansion. You can visit the richly decorated interior, catch an audio-visual display of Admiral of the Fleet, Lord Mountbatten's life and career, and explore the beautiful grounds, landscaped by Capability Brown in 1767.

Mottisfont Abbey, Mottisfont, Nr Romsey
Open: Grounds: Mon-Thur, Sun 2pm-6pm (last entry 5pm) Apr-Sep
House: Wed 2pm-6pm Apr-Sep
Rose garden only: Tues-Thur, Sun 7pm-9pm during rose season (last entry 8:30pm)
Admission: Gardens £1.50, gardens and house £1.90

Directions: Off A3057 between Stockbridge and Romsey.

Originally a 12th-century Augustinian priory, Mottisfont is now a private house, partially owned by the National Trust and open to the public. It is famous for its rose gardens, which are at their peak in June and July. Inside you can see the cellarium of the old priory and a spectacular Gothic-style *trompe l'oeil* drawing room, designed by Rex Whistler in 1938-9 (guided tours only).

The Vyne, Sherborne St John, Basingstoke
Open: Tues-Thur, Sat-Sun, 2pm-6pm Apr-Oct; public holiday Mon 11am-6pm (closed following Tues)
Admission: Adults £2, children £1; garden only, £1 and 50p

*Directions: This architectural gem is well worth a detour from the A30 en route to Winchester. From the **Basingstoke Bypass**, take the third exit at the traffic circle and 2 miles later take the A340 (fourth exit) signposted to **The Vyne**. Two miles on turn right for **Sherborne St John** to a T-intersection, then turn left. Follow the country road through the attractive village and after 1 mile you'll see the red brick house set in parkland on your left.*

The Vyne, a superb 16th-century house, was built in 1515 for William, 1st Lord Sandys, later Lord Chamberlain, and host to Henry VIII and the luckless Anne Boleyn. The house was owned by the Chute family from the Civil War until 1956, when it was handed on to the National Trust. Both it and its furnishings have been carefully preserved. It has a theatrical Palladian staircase, beautiful linenfold paneling in the **Long Gallery**, and a Gothic Tudor chapel containing striking, Flemish stained glass and Italian floor tiles. Sweeping lawns lead away from a Classical portico (1650), the earliest – if slightly out-of-place – example in England, to an attractive lake and open countryside beyond.

*From the **central car parks** in Winchester follow the one-way system up **St George's Street**, turn right onto **Jewry Street**, then left onto **City Road** at the lights and, as you approach the station, get into the left lane. Go straight on for **Stockbridge** on the A272, with the station on your left, then over the St Paul's Hill traffic circle. The old Roman road whisks you across country to Stockbridge (10 miles), where the Romsey Road (A3057) joins from the south, and you follow the signs for **Salisbury** on the A30.*

STOCKBRIDGE

There's plenty of parking in the High Street and it's well worth stopping to stretch your legs in this attractive market town with a chance to admire the **River Test** – one of the finest and most picturesque trout-fishing rivers in Britain – running beside the High Street. Note the fish-topped weather vane on top of the old clock tower on your left. Stockbridge has more than its fair share of good antiques and craft shops, but real bargains are rare on this well-trodden route. However, two outstanding shops in the High Street are **Stockbridge Antiques** for museum-quality antique glass and **Broughton Crafts** for supple eelskin handbags, designer sweaters and jackets, stunning pottery and glass from several British design studios, as well as small, inexpensive gifts that will delight the under-tens. The tearooms here are notable. Try **For Goodness Sake**, or **Squirrels**, which has a coffee shop above a tempting array of fancy linen, exotic boxer shorts, cards and a delightful selection of children's clothes, toys and books.

*We can think of no pleasanter pub for lunch than the **May Fly** on the A3057 just 3 miles from the Stockbridge traffic circle at the western end of the town where you entered via the A272. Follow the **Andover** signs onto the A3057; you'll pass through the pretty village of **Leckford** in about 1½ miles. After approximately another 1½ miles you'll turn sharp left onto a bridge over the **River Test** (do not follow Chilbolton signs). Then turn left again into the parking lot.*

The **May Fly** has a selection of 12 salads (you help yourself at a fixed price per spoonful) and serves great home-cooked slabs of beef, ham or pork. Their smoked trout is worth a trip on its own. In addition there are usually three hot dishes and a huge selection of cheeses, not to mention the crunchy granary bread. Choose a picnic table beside the river and don't forget to save a bit of your bread for the trout.

STOCKBRIDGE TO SALISBURY (about 15 miles)

*Go through the village of Stockbridge and from here the **A30** heads for **Salisbury** (15 miles), with splendid views across rolling fields bordered by hedgerows and punctuated with copses of beech and oak. The villages of Over, Middle and Nether Wallop, known collectively as 'The Wallops' and as quaint as their names, lie to the north. After 5 miles you'll enter the county of **Wiltshire**. Soon after crossing the county boundary turn left at a traffic circle and continue on the **A30** towards the city of Salisbury. **Salisbury Plain**, off to your right, is edged with flagpoles, and red flags indicate army maneuvers. You'll pass the ancient hill fort of **Figsbury Ring** on the right (free parking) and if you feel like walking to its top you'll be rewarded by a splendid view of Salisbury. As you approach the city, the cathedral spire dominates the skyline. Almost 2 miles after entering the city's suburbs you'll reach a traffic circle with signs for the town center. Go around the circle following the signs for the **Cattle Market** and **Churchfields**. At the next traffic circle again follow **Cattle Market**, **Churchfields** and **City Centre** signs. The car park turning is about 50 yards further on your left. The central pay-and-display car park is well signposted. When you've parked and paid, make for its top left corner and Market Place. Walk through the covered walkway by the library which brings you out onto **Minster Street**. Cross over, turn right and walk toward the **Poultry Cross**. At the Cross turn left onto **Fish Row** for the **Tourist Information Centre**. (Tel: (0722) 334956. Open: Mon-Sat 9am-5pm.) Note the traditional half-timbered 15th-century building, **Ye House of John A'Port** opposite Fish Row, now an interesting shop selling china, glass and ornaments.*

SALISBURY

The city of Salisbury, or New Sarum, has grown up around its magnificent cathedral, but the original settlement of **Old Sarum** lies 2 miles north of the city center. A Roman hilltop garrison and trading center, commanding a panoramic – and strategic – view across the plain, the town was gradually abandoned during the 12th and 13th centuries as its growing population moved down to the fertile and more spacious valley. The **Cathedral Close** is lined with beautiful buildings including **Mompesson House**, a National Trust property, and the **Kings House** which hosts the **Salisbury and South Wiltshire Museum**.

WHAT TO SEE

Salisbury Cathedral, Cathedral Close
Open: Mon-Sat 8am-8pm, Sun 8am-6:30pm (closes 6pm in winter)
Admission: Suggested donation, adults £1, children 50p

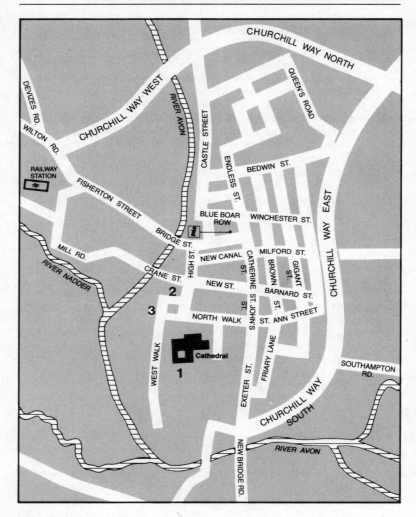

SALISBURY

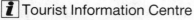 Tourist Information Centre
1 Salisbury Cathedral
2 Mompesson House
3 Salisbury and South Wiltshire Museum

This beautiful cathedral was begun in 1220 and finished less than 40 years later, giving it an exceptional uniformity in style. When it was decided to move the Bishop's see from Old Sarum to Salisbury, the present site of the cathedral, legend has it that the place was chosen by the random flight of an arrow. Today its breathtaking 404 foot spire, the tallest in England, dominates the landscape. Inside you can see a beautiful, 13th-century painted ceiling in the choir, the oldest clock in England (1386) in the North Transept, and one of the four original copies of the **Magna Carta** in the **Chapter House**.

Mompesson House, Cathedral Close
Open: Mon-Wed, Sat-Sun 12:30pm-6pm (or dusk if earlier)
      Apr-Oct
Closed: Good Friday
Admission: Adults £1.50, children 70p

This fine 18th-century Queen Anne town house has an elegant interior with period furniture, interesting plasterwork and an unusual collection of 18th-century drinking glasses.

Salisbury & South Wiltshire Museum, Kings House, 65 The Close
Open: Mon-Sat 10am-5pm, Apr-Sep; Sun 2pm-5pm Jul-Aug;
      Mon-Sat 10am-4pm Oct-Mar   Closed: Dec 25-27
Admission: Adults £1.50, students £1, children 50p

Housed in a Grade I Listed Building, the museum has a large collection of local historical artifacts, including finds from Old Sarum, Stonehenge and the many ancient settlements around Salisbury Plain.

SHOPPING

Branches of all the useful British chain stores can be found dotted around the **Market Square** (market days Tues and Sat), **New Street, High Street** and in the **Maltings** complex by the car park.

Stores are generally open from 9am or 9:30am until 5pm or 5:30pm Monday to Saturday. Many of the smaller shops still observe early closing on Wednesdays and shut at 1pm. Only shopping hours which deviate from the norm are shown below. Safeway, Sainsbury and other large food emporiums remain open Wednesday afternoon as well as staying open until 8pm most weekday evenings, with the exception of Saturday, when they tend to close at 6pm.

Antique and Flea Market, 37 Catherine Street
Credit cards: Varies with individual dealers but there is a central desk which will accept cards for larger purchases – AE, MC, V

Antiques and collectables galore on three floors. Thirty dealers sell mostly china, glass, small pieces of furniture, and some metal work. You'll find fine blue willow pattern plates, Victorian chamber pots, Sunderland lusterware jugs and 1930s Shorter & Son cheese dishes amongst the huge selection of china. In addition, there's a large section of vintage toys on the ground floor at the back. Mr Wells is particularly interested in clockworks, steam and electric items. He also carries lead soldiers, Dinky and Matchbox toys, along with transport ephemera. Wren Books on the first floor sells a combination of antiquarian and new books. Mr Care's books span centuries: the oldest 1550, the newest 1987. You'll also find old and reproduction prints and collectable records on this floor.

There are some Victorian linen items on the top floor along with more china. Save at least an hour for browsing through this emporium.

Confetti, Old George Mall
Credit cards: MC, V   Open: from 10am

This cheerful, candy-colored little shop sports 500 flavors in 200 different sweets. You simply pick up a bag and fill it with your favorites. Wash them down with one of the six varieties of slush puppies. Original recipe American ice cream, summer only.

Country Casuals, 53 New Canal
Credit cards: AE, DC, MC, V

Elegant, classic womens' shop concentrating on separates. The aim is to coordinate, so blouses, sweaters, and skirts all tone together. Bally shoes, particularly chosen to complement the clothes, are featured. You'll enjoy the calm, quiet atmosphere and the undivided attention of your salesperson.

Courcoux, 90-92 Crane Street
Credit cards: AE, DC, MC, V

Selected by the British Crafts Council as a gallery of outstanding quality, Courcoux represents many of Britain's leading contemporary artists, sculptors and ceramicists, whose works are displayed to maximum effect in this attractive, modern and well-lit gallery.

D.M. Beach, 52 High Street
Credit cards: AE, MC, V

A real find for lovers of antique books and prints. You could browse for hours amongst the huge and varied collection of second-hand classics and first editions, or choose from a selection of sporting prints, cartoons, maps and oil paintings.

Dash, 15 Old George Mall
Credit cards: AE, MC, V

This cheery shop sells casual and leisure wear for the three to thirteens. They have their own label clothes in delightful pastel colors. Black and navy make only a token appearance in the autumn and winter. White walls, floor and ceiling make an ideal backdrop for these nifty girls' outfits.

Note: There are men's and women's toilets (loos) off the covered walkway between Old George Mall and Catherine Street.

Greenfields, 21 Milford Street
Credit cards: MC, V   Closed: Wed

Mr Greenfield is as charming as he's knowledgeable with no less than 55 years in the gun trade. He specializes in quality second-hand guns. The quality translates as £1,000 to £12,000 for a Purdey, which is a bargain considering a new Purdey would set you back £20,000 or more. There's a good stock of Barbour jackets, waterproofs and sleeveless Puffas, along with boots, knives and other country equipment. Don't be fooled by the refurbished exterior – parts of this building go back to 1300.

Ian G. Hastie, 46 St Anne Street
No credit cards

Mr Hastie stocks a large general range of 17th-19th-century English and Continental furniture, silver, clocks and other items on his attractive listed premises.

John and Judith Head, Antiquarian booksellers, 88 Crane Street
Credit cards: AE, DC, MC, V   Closed: Sat

This is a treasure trove for the sporting enthusiast – over 3,000 books on fishing alone, some dating from the 16th century. Shooting, hunting and field sports figure prominently in their collection with less well-known sports also represented. Prints by Snaffles and Lionel Edwards.

Mace and Nairn, 89 Crane Street
No credit cards   Closed: Daily 1pm-2pm, Wed 12:30pm, Sat 4pm

Miss Nairn has this tiny shop chock full of supplies for all sorts of embroidery – everything from books on smocking to canvases for needlepoint. Besides plain and painted needlepoint canvases she carries trammé canvases. There are several Erica Wilson adaptations of William Morris designs as well as adaptations of tapestries from the Metropolitan Museum in New York. A wonderful supplier for those handy with a needle.

Magpie, 30 Milford Street
Credit cards: MC, V

Betty Barclay, Puccini and Parigi are some of the well-known designers this shop features. There's a good range of separates, along with some quite dressy clothes in this black and white building whose age is uncertain, but is at least several hundred years old. Magpie prides itself on making the customer happy whether this means ordering a dress specially or organizing alterations.

National Trust Shop, 41 High Street
Credit cards: AE, DC, MC, V

At the southern end of the High Street by the cathedral gates you'll find a great selection of clothes, gifts and general information on the Trust's many interests. The pleasing fragrance in this shop is the result of the scented pillows and pot pourri items on sale.

Rolands of Bath, 7 Fish Row
Credit cards: AE, DC, MC, V

An unusual building, once probably a private home; the working fireplace bears a date of 1649. Wood beamed and carpeted throughout, this store is a fine setting for its elegant, understated clothes for both sexes. Austrian Loden coats come in several styles for women, while the classic hunting Loden is carried for men. Do have a look through the dressy clothes, mostly silk, designed by 'Kanga' (The Lady Tryon). Supposedly nicknamed by Prince Charles, Kanga designs wonderfully feminine but wearable clothes in unique prints. Prices aren't bad for a designer of such talent: about £200 per outfit.

Next door is **A. Pritchett & Son** whose sign reads 'High Class English Meat only'. Take a minute to peruse this traditional butcher's shop with sawdust on the floor and meat displayed in the window in a picture-book, bow-windowed Elizabethan building.

SALISBURY RESTAURANTS

The Haunch of Venison, 1 Minster Street (opp Poultry Cross) £
Tel: (0722) 22024
Open: Mon-Sat 11am-11pm, Sun noon-3pm, 7pm-10:30pm. Meals
       served: Mon-Fri noon-2:30pm, 6:30pm-9:45pm, Sat noon-
       3pm, 7pm-10:30pm, Sun noon-2pm
Credit cards: AE, DC, MC, V

Over 600 years old, the Haunch is a Salisbury institution of great character and charm. You enter into a tiny room which has a black and white tiled floor and an ancient pewter bar with hand taps of great age. Here it's invariably crowded but equally, invariably friendly. Up the narrow stairs you'll find the dining room with its wooden sloping floors and excellent, simple pub food such as home-made soups and pies.

Mainly Salads, 18 Fisherton Street   £
Tel: (0722) 22134
Open: Mon-Sat 10am-5pm
No credit cards

Great vegetarian snack food is available here all day, and not just salads but delicious hot soups, quiches and pies. The home-baked scones and cakes go down well with morning coffee or afternoon tea. No smoking.

Mo's, 62 Milford Street   £
Tel: (0722) 331377
Open: Mon-Sat noon-2:30pm, 5:30pm-11:15pm, Sun 6pm-10:30pm
Credit cards: MC, V

The sign hanging over the door announces hamburgers, but Mo has plenty more up her culinary sleeve. A very pleasant, informal little restaurant-cum-wine bar with a mouthwatering range of inventive entrées, casseroles, salads and savories plus vegetarian specials and killer chocolate pudding desserts.

The Yew Tree Inn, Odstock, near Salisbury   ££
Tel: (0722) 29786
Open: Daily for meals: noon-2pm, 7pm-9:30pm, Sun until 9pm
Credit cards: AE, DC, MC, V

Directions: Take the A338 out of Salisbury following signs for the South Coast, Odstock, Harnham and Ringwood. Then take the A354 signposted Blandford and Odstock Hospital. Now just follow the Odstock Hospital signs, pass the hospital and shortly you'll see The Yew Tree directly in front of you.

Just 1½ miles from the heart of Salisbury, this inn has been a local favorite since the early 16th century. The low-ceilinged room has an enormous fireplace on the left-hand side as you enter, which is put to good use when it's chilly. The blackboard on its mantel spells out the daily specials such as lamb chops with rosemary butter. It's owned by local brewery Gibbs Mew; the charming manager and his wife have just done up two rooms for bed and breakfast (£18 single, £30 double). The trout pâté is out of this world. They do no less than 12 boozy coffees including monk's coffee which features Benedictine and cream.

SALISBURY HOTELS

The Red Lion, Milford Street   ££
Tel: (0722) 23334
Amenities: ☎ ➴ 🅿 ⑪ ⑨ ◎   Credit cards: AE, DC, MC, V

This 13th-century hostelry in the town center, with its long tradition
of hospitality, has been managed by the Thomas and Maidment
families for over 70 years. There's a lovely creeper-clad courtyard
with tables in the summer, comfortable rooms – some with four-
poster beds and most with own bath – bar snacks, a dining room
with a hearty British menu and private parking.

The Rose & Crown Hotel, Harnham Road   £££
Tel: (0722) 27908
Amenities: ☎ ➴ 🅿 ⑪ ⑨   Credit cards: AE, DC, MC, V

In a quiet position backing onto the **River Avon** (off St Nicholas
Road), and recommended by the American Tourist Council, this
hotel offers accommodation in four-posters under ancient oak
beams or in a brand-new modern wing. The **Club Restaurant**
specializes in 'olde English fayre' and there are lunchtime snacks in
the **Avon Bar**.

The White Hart, 1 St John Street   ££
Tel: (0722) 27476
Amenities: ☎ ➴ 🅿 ⑪ ⑨ ◎   Credit cards: AE, DC, MC, V

This Trusthouse Forte hotel in the city center, just by the Cathedral, is a Georgian building with an impressive pillared front. It
stands on the site of an ancient inn that was visited by Henry VII.
All 68 rooms have bath/shower. There's a scale model of Stonehenge in its comfortable lounge. The pleasant **Fountain Bar** overlooks a courtyard, and the restaurant serves both fixed-price and à
la carte menus.

AROUND AND ABOUT

Wilton House
Open: Tues-Sat and public holiday Mondays 11am-6pm, Sun 1pm-
      6pm (last entry 5:15pm) Apr-mid Oct
Admission: Adults £2.50, children under 16 years £1.25

Directions: Three miles west of Salisbury on A36.

The name Wiltshire derives from that of the small town of **Wilton**,
where King Alfred founded an abbey to celebrate his victory over
the Danes. The abbey was dissolved by Henry VIII, and its lands
given to the 1st Earl of Pembroke. When the original house was
destroyed by fire in 1647 the incumbent earl consulted the
renowned architect Inigo Jones, who created a masterpiece in the

Classical style. The highlight of the interior is the remarkable **Double Cube Room**, hung with portraits by Van Dyck. Other State Rooms contain superb collections of furniture by Chippendale and Kent, china, glass, fine art and massed ranks of model soldiers. The famous landscaped gardens are scattered with examples of Palladian architecture, including a splendid bridge built in 1737. There's also a model railway and an adventure playground.

SALISBURY TO GLASTONBURY (about 43 miles)

*Leave the **central car park** and follow the signs for **Old Sarum** and **Stonehenge**, which will take you back onto the ring road and a traffic circle where you turn left for **Amesbury** on the A345. Just as you leave Salisbury, opposite the Old Castle pub, you'll see the footpath to **Old Sarum**, with parking a little further on the left.*

Old Sarum
Open: Daily 9:30am-6pm Mar 15-Oct 15; Mon-Sat 9:30am-4pm,
      Sun 2pm-4pm Oct 16-Mar 14
Closed: Christmas and New Year
Admission: Adults 75p, children 35p

Old Sarum was successively an Iron Age camp, the Roman garrison of Sorbiodunum, and a Norman fortress town. You can trace the foundations of the castle and original cathedral, visit the small museum of local artifacts, and enjoy fine, open views across windswept Salisbury Plain.

*Continue on to **Amesbury** (8 miles) and drive through the town. Follow the signs for **Honiton** and turn left into **Countess Road**, then, approaching the traffic circle, take the first left, after an unusual walled gatehouse on your left. You are now on the A303. After a mile, from the brow of a hill, you'll see **Stonehenge** ahead. For a closer look bear right at the bottom of the hill for the free car park.*

Stonehenge
Open: Daily 9:30am-6:30pm Apr-Sep   Closes 4pm Oct-Mar
Admission: Adults £1.30, children 65p

One of Europe's most famous prehistoric monuments, this enigmatic circle of stone blocks is thought to have been an ancient ceremonial center and sanctuary. It was built in three phases between 2700BC and 1400BC. The inner bluestone circle was erected by Bronze Age man, the stones somehow transported from Pembrokeshire, in southwest Wales. Though the true reasons for its construction remain clouded in mystery and speculation, its powerful presence is indisputable, and at sunrise or sunset it's a spectacular subject for photographers.

Now go back to the intersection and turn right on the A303. Note the many ancient barrows (burial mounds) on both sides of the road. Go straight over the traffic circle 3 miles later, following the signs for **Exeter** *and* **Honiton, A303.** *Traffic on this road can be heavy, and there are few passing places, but the views of the open Wiltshire countryside are good and it's only 10 miles from Stonehenge to the* **Wylye** *exit for* **Warminster** *on the* **A36.** *Turn off here just after going under an overpass, then turn left at the intersection and left again, crossing over the A303.* **Wilton House** *is straight on down the* **A36** *in the opposite direction. A further 10 miles of green and pleasant valley road along the river bank will bring you to Warminster. At the traffic circle after Knook, the new Warminster bypass might be completed, in which case take it, turning left for the* **A362** *to* **Frome.** *If not follow the* **A36** *through Warminster, with its Georgian buildings, turning left at the first of two mini traffic circles on your way out of town, then straight over the second, following signs for* **Frome** *on the* **A362** *and keeping the Farmers Hotel on your left. At the stone urn memorial turn left up* **West Street,** *signposted for* **Frome** *and* **Longleat.** *After 2 miles you'll reach Longleat House and Safari Park.*

Longleat House and Safari Park

Open: House: Daily 10am-6pm Easter-Sep 30; until 4pm
        remainder of year   Closed: Christmas Day
        Safari Park: Daily until 6pm (last entry 5:30pm) mid Mar-
        end Oct only; convertible cars not admitted to Safari Park
Admission: House: Adults £2.80, children 4-14 years £1, under 4
        free; Safari Park: Adults £3.50, children £2.50

This great Elizabethan house, built between 1566-80, is the finest example of English Renaissance architecture in the country. The home of the Marquess of Bath, it was modernized at the start of the 19th century and lavishly decorated by Italian artists who added superb ornate ceilings to the State Rooms. The Victorian kitchens are fascinating examples of domestic history. In the gardens you can tackle the world's largest maze or sample darkest Africa from the privacy of your car with a drive through the ever-popular safari park. Lions and other big cats roam while the monkeys will try to make their escape by stowing away with you unless you keep your windows closed.

From Longleat, after passing ancient **Cley Hill** *on your right, the* **A362** *continues to* **Frome** *(5 miles) in the county of* **Somerset.** *Go straight through Frome, following the signs for* **Glastonbury** *up the hill, then follow the road around to the left at the first traffic lights. From the stop lights at the top of the hill, follow the signs for* **Nunney** *(3¹/₄ miles) and* **Shepton Mallet** *(11¹/₂ miles). Turn left at the traffic circle, signposted to Glastonbury, onto the Marston Road, which takes you out of Frome. Three miles from Frome there's a small traffic circle and a signpost for the little village of* **Nunney.** *If you feel* *like getting off the road for a pub lunch turn off here. Follow the lane down into the heart of the village and park opposite **The George**. You'll see the ruins of an old fortified house, built in 1373 by Sir John de la Mere and designed after the Bastille in Paris. Its three remaining walls have turrets at the corners and below them is one of the deepest moats in England. The George is a friendly country pub with a few simple rooms (one including a four-poster bed), a cozy bar and a restaurant serving substantial home-cooked meals with game dishes in season. The relaxed atmosphere is resonant with soft Somerset accents.*

*After passing through the Somerset countryside and its attractive villages, such as East Cranmore and Doulting, you'll reach **Shepton Mallet**. Turn left, heading for **Glastonbury**, rather than pass through the town, and a ½ mile further turn left again at the T-intersection opposite the Highwayman Inn, signposted to **Castle Cary (A371)**. A ¼ mile ahead turn right for **Yeovil, Exeter** and **Taunton**, then right again, following the sign to **Glastonbury (A361) (9 miles)**. In the village of **Pilton**, about 2 miles down the steep hill, passing the signposts for Pilton and North Wootton vineyards, you'll get your first glimpses of the great mound of **Glastonbury Tor** up ahead, dominating the landscape. Entering Glastonbury, 7 miles on, drive carefully down the steep **Coursingbatch Hill**.*

*Somerset is big on sheep, and as you go toward the town center you'll see several wholesale manufacturers of sheepskin and leather products, who welcome the public. Just past the **Hide Shop** turn left at the traffic circle **(A39)** and follow the signs to the car park, passing the **Tourist Information Centre** on your left in **Marchant's Buildings**. (Tel: (0458) 32954. Open: Mon-Sat 9:30am-5pm mid Mar-Oct. Closed: Nov-mid Mar.)*

GLASTONBURY

The mythical site of King Arthur's **Avalon** and a center of early Christian pilgrimage, Glastonbury continues to tantalize the imagination with its 'proofs' that legend may be history. The unusual Tor (hill) undoubtedly exists, but can it really be the spot where Joseph of Arimathea buried the Holy Grail, the chalice used at the Last Supper? A 10th-century abbey was built on the site where Joseph is said to have built a simple wattle-and-daub church and introduced Christianity to Britain. The abbey is now a ruin, though the Norman **Lady Chapel** remains, and this is where the monks claimed to have found the burial places of King Arthur and Queen Guinevere in 1191. The **Glastonbury thorn**, allegedly created when Joseph stuck his staff in the ground, and it miraculously took root, blossoms here in the winter. There's also recently discovered evidence of a great palace at **South Cadbury** dating from the correct period. None of this can be counted as conclusive proof of the legends, but the **Gothic Image Bookshop** at 7 High Street arranges 'mystical tours of ancient Avalon'. Also in the attractive High Street you'll find several good leather goods shops offering a wide range of sheepskin rugs, coats and gloves, plus leather luggage, wallets and other accessories.

GLASTONBURY RESTAURANT

Rainbow's End Café, 17a High Street £
Tel: (0458) 33896
Open: Mon-Tues, Thur-Sat 10am-4:30pm
No credit cards

This is a small, welcoming café in the **Flintlock Arcade** with a wide range of vegetarian and wholefood lunch dishes, offering delicious crumbly scones with butter and jam, and homemade cakes and snacks throughout the day.

GLASTONBURY HOTEL

The George & Pilgrims, High Street ££
Tel: (0458) 31146
Amenities: ☎ ⌨ 🅿 🍴 🍷   Credit cards: AE, DC, MC, V

This ancient inn has been catering to pilgrims and visitors to Glastonbury for over 500 years. Great care has been taken to preserve its antique surroundings and traditional atmosphere. It has 12 rooms with their own facilities, a coffee shop, a pleasant bar and an elegant Georgian Restaurant serving many local dishes and products.

This is the point in your tour where you can either continue to Bath or explore **Devon** and **Cornwall** (see **page 401**).

GLASTONBURY TO WELLS   (about 18 miles)

*From the **car park** turn left up **High Street** for **Wells** on the **A39** (5 miles). At Wells follow the one-way system to the city center car park and you'll see the **Tourist Information Centre** in the Town Hall at the top right corner of **Market Place**. (Tel: (0749) 72552. Open: Mon-Fri 9:30am-5pm, Sat-Sun 10am-4pm.)*

WELLS

Henry James wrote that 'it's always Sunday afternoon in Wells'. That's appropriate. Wells (named after springs near the cathedral) has had strong ecclesiastical connections since its earliest days. This smallest of cathedral cities (population circa 10,000) was the seat of a Bishopric for centuries, until this was transferred to Bath. As a result Wells became something of a medieval backwater. As you'll see, much of its medieval character remains. Indeed **Vicar's Close** is reputed to be the oldest inhabited street in Europe and many of the almshouses and medieval inns date from the early 15th century. From the window of one of these, the **Crown Inn**, William Penn preached before departing for what became Pennsylvania.

WHAT TO SEE

Wells Cathedral

Open: Daily 7:30am-8:30pm mid May-Aug; 7:30am-6pm Sep-mid
     May. Parts of the Cathedral are closed to visitors during
     services on Sunday 8am-8:30am, 10am-12:30pm and 3pm-
     4:30pm; weekdays 4:30pm-6pm
Admission: Suggested donation, adults £1, children 50p

Building continued in several stages from 1180 until the 14th century, when extraordinary inverted arches were constructed in the nave to support the tower with massive grace. The magnificent carved façade on the west front was commissioned by Bishop Jocelin in 1280, and contains nearly 400 statues, in decorative niches. The kaleidoscopic beauty of the stained glass is another highlight, as is the richly painted 14th-century astronomical clock inside, a marvel of medieval mechanics, with figurines performing every quarter of an hour except half an hour before and during services.

Bishop's Palace

Open: Thur, Sun and public holiday Mon 2pm-6pm Easter-Oct;
     also Wed 11am-6pm May, Jun, Jul, Sep; daily 2pm-6pm in
     Aug
Admission: Adults £1, children 30p

The early part of the palace, the Bishop's chapel and the ruins of the banqueting hall date from the 13th century and the undercroft has remained almost unchanged since then. The palace is ringed by fortifications and a moat, with access through a 14th-century gate-house. The wells in the gardens give the city its name. You'll see the well water on either side of the High Street as it pushes up from underground conduits, runs along the gutters and then disappears below ground again.

Perhaps the Oscar-winning performance is by the swans on the moat surrounding the palace, who ring a bell when they want to be fed. Another curio is the beautifully preserved **Vicars' Close**, Europe's oldest complete street, cobbled and lined with terraced houses decorated with ornate chimney pots and mullioned windows. It was built in 1348, to house a group of wayward young clergy whose night-time activities so concerned the bishop that he constructed a cul-de-sac with a gate that could be locked at night.

WELLS RESTAURANTS

The City Arms, corner High Street and Queen Street £
Tel: (0749) 73916
Open: Mon-Sat 10:30am-2pm, 6pm-11pm. Meals served: noon-
2pm, 7pm-9:30pm
No credit cards

Originally built as the city jail under special charter from Queen
Elizabeth I, the premises became a pub in 1841. The old cell blocks
still surround the courtyard, where you can eat outside in summer
in a riot of color from well-tended flower tubs. Chef David Milne
and restaurant manager John Turner took over in 1988 and hope to
repeat the success of their last pub, where they were awarded the
coveted 'Pub of the Year' award in 1986. Good, inexpensive snacks
in the bar (try Somerset Chicken – chicken in a tomato and cider
sauce, with red and green peppers, zucchini, egg-plant, mushrooms
and herbs, served with rice, salad and garlic bread – £3.85) with a
more extensive menu in the upstairs restaurant.

Cloister Restaurant, The Cathedral £
Tel: (0749) 76543
Open: Daily 10am-5pm Mar-Oct; 11am-4pm Nov-Feb
No credit cards

This handy self-service café is housed in a lovely cloister overlooking a green courtyard. Snacks and home-baked cakes and scones
are served through the day. At lunchtime the menu includes soups,
salads and hot meals.

WELLS HOTEL

Ston Easton Park, Ston Easton £££ (very)
Tel: (076 121) 631
Amenities: ☎ ⊑ Ⓟ ⦚ ℘
Credit cards: AE, DC, MC, V

*Directions: If you have a friendly bank manager, try this sumptuous
country house hotel, 1 mile off the main (A39) road from Wells to
Bath (13½ miles from Wells) and well situated for either city.*

Originally built in 1739 as a private house, it has been expensively
and sympathetically restored and furnished with 18th-century
pieces. Bedrooms are of magnificent proportions and individually,
tastefully furnished, including original Chippendale and Hepple-
white four-poster beds. Period paintings abound.
  Guests are encouraged to tour 'below stairs' where they'll see the
original kitchens (shortly to become a 18th-century kitchen
museum), servants' hall and wine cellars.
  The menu tends toward classic English and there's a strong

supporting wine list with particular strength in red Bordea
Burgundies. Excellent food – at a price!

There are facilities for landing hot-air balloons, if you hap
have brought one with you; otherwise take a trip in one of them.

AROUND AND ABOUT

Wookey Hole Caves
Open: Daily 9:30am-5:30pm in summer 10:30am-4:30pm in winter
Closed: Week before Christmas
Admission: Adults £3.70, children 4-16 years £2.60, under 4 free;
           family ticket £11.20 (2 adults and 2 children)

Directions: Take the A371 Cheddar road from Wells and after 2 miles turn right for Wookey Hole.

Wookey Hole, deep in the Mendip Hills, is one of Britain's largest cave complexes, so stout shoes and warm clothes are recommended. You can explore the subterranean chambers, ancient dwellings occupied from Palaeolithic times by both man and beast, as uncovered implements and the bones of hyenas and mammoths indicate. Other attractions include fairground rides, a waterwheel and an enormous Victorian papermill, once the largest in Europe, where you can see paper being made.

Cheddar Gorge and Caves
Open: Daily 9:30am-5:30pm in summer, 10:30am-4:30pm in
       winter   Closed: Over Christmas

Directions: Take the A371 Cheddar road from Wells.

Cheddar's famous gorge is the local equivalent of the Grand Canyon, with 450 foot-high limestone cliffs. The Cheddar Caves complex consists of several caves – the most beautiful being Gough's Cave – as well as rock pools, stalactites and stalagmites along a ½ mile of underground pasages. In the **Museum** you can see the 10,000-year-old skeleton of 'Cheddar Man', and many other interesting exhibits.

CHEDDAR RESTAURANT

The Wishing Well Tea Rooms, The Cliffs   **£**
Tel: (0934) 742142
Open: Daily 10am-6pm Apr-mid Oct; Sun only mid Oct-Nov, Feb-
       Mar   Closed: Dec-Jan
No credit cards

This friendly tearoom has plenty of homemade goodies: simple savory snacks, including generous sandwiches of delicious local Cheddar cheese, salad and baked potatoes, plus tempting teacakes and biscuits.

*From Wells, wind your way around the one-way system, following the signs for through traffic to **Bath** on the A39. From the hill out of town, edged by a low stone wall, there are splendid views across the valley before the landscape smoothes out, and 9 miles from Wells you turn right (on the **A39**) to the village of **Hallatrow**. The country-side becomes more hilly with the **Mendip Hills** off to the left, as you go on for a further 8 miles to the intersection with the **A4**. After ½ mile keep left on the **A4** and follow the **Upper Bristol Road** toward **Bath town center**. When the road divides keep left for **Charlotte Street** and (left again), park in the central car park. Re-emerge on **Charlotte Street** and turn left into **Queen Square**. Diagonally across the square is Wood Street, leading onto the busy shopping scene in Milsom Street. Turn right here and walk straight on down pedestrianized **Old Bond Street** and **Union Street** until you reach the **Abbey Church Yard** on your left, where you'll find the **Tourist Information Centre** (Tel: (0225) 462831. Open: Mon-Sat 9:30am-7pm, Sun 10am-4pm Easter-Sep; Mon-Sat 9:30am-5pm, closed Sun, Oct-Easter.)*

*If you find the car parks are full, there is an alternative. The County of Avon have introduced a '**Central Bath On-Street Parking Card**' system, which allows you to park on the street for one hour or two, depending on the area. You can obtain these cards at local newsagents or chemists which display this sign:* **C** *A single ticket costs 20p but if you plan to spend a few days in Bath it's probably worth buying a booklet of ten. They come with simple instructions, and a diagram of where, and for how long, they can be used.*

BATH

Bath is unique in Britain. Britain's only thermal waters gush in the heart of the city, an unvarying 260,000 gallons a day at a constant temperature of 120°F. The Celts reckoned the waters belonged to their goddess, Sulis. When the Romans moved in, they obligingly called the place Aquae Sulis, although they also brought their own goddess, Minerva. Her temple lies beneath what is now Stall Street.

Roman Bath flourished for nearly 400 years, then when the empire collapsed, the fortunes of Aquae Sulis declined. A marsh formed around the decaying Roman baths and temple. It was not long, however, before the curative powers of the thermal springs were rediscovered. Under Saxon rule, Christian monks built new baths around the springs, and a great Abbey nearby. Here, in 973, the first king of all England, Edgar, was crowned.

The present, smaller Abbey stands on the site of the original. It dates from the 15th century, when Bath was at the center of a flourishing cloth trade. Three hundred years were to pass before the city achieved real prominence. In 1705 a Welsh gambler called

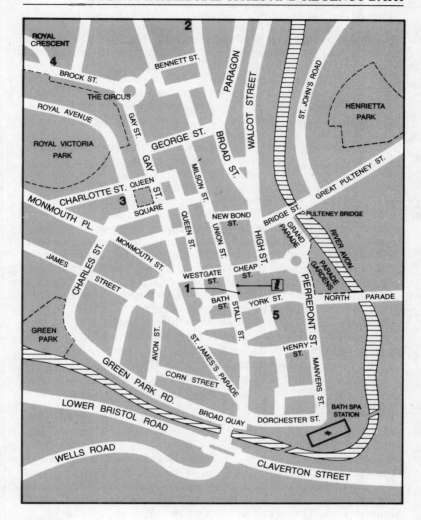

BATH

 Tourist Information Centre
 1 Roman Baths Museum
 2 Museum of English Naïve Art
 3 Geology Museum
 4 No 1 Royal Crescent
 5 Sally Lunn's Kitchen Museum

Beau Nash was appointed Master of Ceremonies and by dint of his personality, as much as anything else, quickly turned the modest spa town into a fashionable resort. Ralph Allen, who made a fortune from developing an improved mail service, opened up the Bath stone quarries. He employed a brilliant young architect, John Wood. Together they laid the foundations for a new, stunningly beautiful Georgian city, its elegant terraces and crescents climbing the hills that rise up from the River Avon and the spring waters below. Almost all of Georgian Bath remains.

Much of the city center around the Roman baths is now closed to traffic, so that there is an elaborate system of one-way streets in the surrounding area. We recommend that you park in one of the long-stay car parks on the outskirts – the one in Charlotte Street is well-sited – and walk. Bath is both compact and kind to pedestrians.

Turn right out of the Tourist Information Centre and left into Stall Street. Immediately on your left is the 18th-century **Pump Room**, so called because the thermal waters are pumped here. A fountain dispenses spa water for those eager to taste its supposedly curative tang. Considerably more palatable are the morning coffees, lunch and afternoon teas which are served daily in elegant surroundings. The Pump Room Trio plays during morning coffee all year and during afternoon tea in the summer.

Much the best way to explore in Bath is to join one of the free walking tours that leave regularly from outside the Pump Room (look for the board proclaiming 'Free Walks Here'). The walks take approximately two hours and are run by the Mayor's Corps of Honorary Guides, all of them knowledgeable volunteers. They will show you the exterior of the buildings and streets of historical and architectural interest. Times of tours are as follows: Mon and Thur 10:30am, Wed and Sun 10:30am and 2:30pm, Tues and Fri 10:30am and 7pm, Sat 7pm May to October; Mon-Fri 10:30am, Sun 10:30am and 2:30pm November to April.

Chief among Bath's most splendid architecture is the **Royal Crescent**, built by John Wood the Younger, between 1767 and 1774; the **Circus**, a complete circle of Georgian houses, each with an original stone frieze; and **Pulteney Bridge**, designed by Robert Adam in 1771. This is one of Bath's best surprises. Walk along it, and it seems just like a street lined with small shops. Walk to the back of one of these shops, peer out of the window and you look down on the River Avon: you are in fact standing on a bridge.

Bath Abbey is the last of the great English pre-Reformation churches. Look up at the west front and you'll see angels carved on the exterior, apparently climbing up and down a ladder. This sculpture is to commemorate a dream of Bishop King, who began building the present structure on the remains of the Norman church in 1499. In the dream he saw angels ascending and descending a ladder from heaven and heard a voice say 'Let a King restore the church'.

It's worth trying to find time to visit the **Theatre Royal** in Sawclose. It was recently restored to its former Georgian splendor and frequently has pre-West End London shows, plus its own productions. Public tours of the auditorium and backstage take place on Wednesdays and Fridays. Enquire at the Box Office.

WHAT TO SEE

Roman Baths Museum, Stall Street
Open: Daily 9am-6pm Mar-Oct; Mon-Sat 9am-5pm, Sun 10am-5pm Nov-Feb
Admission: Adults £2.50, children £1.25 (combined ticket for Roman Baths and Museum of Costume: Adults £3, children £1.50)

The remains of the Roman baths are remarkably complete, with the Great Bath, the Roman's swimming pool, standing almost exactly as it was 1900 years ago. You can see where the hot springs bubble up in a cloud of steam and where the Roman conduits fed a series of hot and cold baths. This was once a very sophisticated health center, with exercise rooms and an underarm hair plucker. The museum also displays Roman artifacts uncovered throughout centuries of later building work, including the gilt-bronze head of a statue of Minerva.

Museum of English Naïve Art, Huntingdon Centre, Paragon
Open: Mon-Sat 11am-6pm, Sun 2pm-6pm Apr-Oct
Closed: Nov-Mar
Admission: Adults £1.50, children 75p

The city's newest attraction occupies an 18th-century school house adjacent to the Countess of Huntingdon's Chapel. It's a friendly, unintimidating collection of folk painting by traveling artists of the 18th and 19th centuries that reveals a charming preoccupation with livestock, country sports and the market town.

Geology Museum, Reference Library, 18 Queen Square
Open: Mon-Fri 9:30am-6pm, Sat 9:30am-5pm
Free admission

The area around Bath has been called 'The Birthplace of English Geology'. This museum substantiates the claim, displaying fine examples of the minerals, rocks and fossils found in the region.

No 1 Royal Crescent
Open: Tues-Sat 11am-5pm, Sun 2pm-5pm
Closed: Mon and Jan-Feb
Admission: Adults £1.50, children 80p

The spectacular Royal Crescent is one of the architectural gems of the city. No 1 has been restored and furnished down to the finest detail as an 18th-century home. You really do get the feeling that you're a house guest 200 years ago: there's even real food laid out on the dining table.

Sally Lunn's Kitchen Museum, off Abbey Green
Open: Mon-Sat 10am-1pm
Free admission

Sally Lunn's House is the oldest in Bath, a tiny, narrow building in the lane between Abbey Green and the Fernley Hotel. It is famous for its bun, which is still baked on the premises to the original secret recipe made famous by Sally Lunn, who came to Bath in 1680. The museum is in the cellar (narrow, turning stairs), where you can see the original kitchen with its oven, Georgian range and old baking utensils. Adjoining is a cellar with stalactites and stalagmites. This shows the building's Roman and medieval foundations. You can sample the buns in the tea shop upstairs.

SHOPPING

Bath has attracted most of the major national chains of stores, and has a wealth of smaller, specialist shops and antique dealers. Normal shopping hours are 9am or 9:30am to 5:30pm or 6pm. Some of the smaller shops, especially antique dealers, may close for an hour's lunch break. Bath has no early closing day. Only the shopping hours which deviate from the norm are listed below.

George Bayntun, Manvers Street
Credit cards: MC, V   Open: Mon-Fri 9am-1pm, 2:15pm-5:30pm

Leading antiquarian bookshop with a bindery, where you can have books bound and restored, behind the shop.

Beaux Arts, York Street
Credit cards: AE, MC, V   Open: Mon-Sat 10am-5pm

This gallery regularly mounts exhibitions of the works of leading British painters, sculptors and ceramicists. You'll also find the work of talented young artists.

The China Doll, 31 Walcot Street
Credit cards: AE, MC, V   Open: Mon-Sat 10:30am-4:30pm

China dolls from all over Europe, soft toy animals and dolls' houses join Lynne and Michael Roche's own range of porcelain dolls for sale here.

General Trading Company, 10 Argyll Street, Pulteney Bridge
Credit cards: AE, DC, MC, V

This is the only branch of London's well-known treasure house for presents, selling china, glass, linen, cutlery, traditional, modern and oriental gifts plus some well-chosen antiques.

Great Western Antique Centre, Bartlett Street
Credit cards: varies from stall to stall

About 70 dealers, selling a wide range of antiques and collectables, have stalls in this vast emporium. The stock changes regularly.

Hitchcock's, 10 Chapel Row
Credit cards: MC, V   Open: Mon-Sat 10am-5:30pm

Fleur Hitchcock sells handwoven rugs in natural colors, clothes made from printed, painted and knitted textiles, charming hand-painted wooden toys, ceramics, etchings and contemporary jewelry. Some of the work is exclusive to her shop.

Papyrus, 25 Broad Street
Credit cards: AE, DC, MC, V

Michael and Lula Gibson sell hand-marbled books and albums, desk accessories and beautiful stationery. You can order your own printed paper here. There's a design studio offering traditional copperplate engraving for stationery, cards and bookplates, which can be shipped home for you.

Thomas Pink, 1 Queen Street
Credit cards: AE, DC, MC, V

In the 18th century Thomas Pink was a tailor in London's fashionable Mayfair. He made the best hunting coat of his time and such was the quality that the expression 'hunting pink' or 'in the pink' came to mean the very best in taste and style. Mr Pink probably never made a shirt, but his name, and high quality, live on in this tiny Georgian shop where you can choose from a wide range of men's and ladies' shirts.

Quiet Street Antiques, 3 Quiet Street
Credit cards: AE, DC, MC, V   Open: Mon-Sat 10am-6pm

Every piece, from a 19th-century grandfather clock to a silver tea caddy, has a price tag and descriptive label, which makes these extensive showrooms a comfortable place in which to browse.

The Tapestry Studio, 32 Broad Street
Credit cards: MC, V   Open: Mon-Fri 10am-5pm, Sat 10am-4pm

Patricia Hecquet sells her own handpainted tapestry designs plus all
the wools, tools and kits you could use in a decade of long winter
evenings.

BATH RESTAURANTS

The Circus Restaurant, 34 Brock Street   ££
Tel: (0225) 330208
Open: Tues-Sun noon-2:30pm, 7pm-10pm   Closed: Mon, Sun eve
Credit cards: AE, MC, V

Opened quite recently by amiable Chef-patron Matthew Sharp
(who used to be sous-chef at the nearby Royal Crescent Hotel), this
has a good choice of delightful English regional dishes, though
there are Continental overtones which give an interesting twist. A
fair wine list and a good selection of bottled beers.

Clos du Roy, Edgar Buildings, George Street   £££
Tel: (0225) 64356
Open: Tues-Sat noon-2pm, 7pm-10pm
Closed: Sun-Mon; 2 wks Aug, 2 wks Jan or Feb
Credit cards: AE, DC, MC, V

Pretty pink and white dining room run by Emma Roy, whose
husband, Philippe, creates the delicious and beautifully presented
dishes constantly emerging from the kitchens. Light, varied lunch
and dinner menus, plus the 'menu surprise', which you can accept
as just that, or ask for a run down. Excellent wine list.

The Grapes, Westgate Street   £
Tel: (0225) 310235
Open: Mon-Sat 11am-10:30pm, Sun noon-2:30pm, 7pm-10:30pm
        Meals served: Mon-Sat noon-2:30pm
No credit cards

A traditional, old-fashioned pub hung with flower baskets and
boasting a lamplit interior complete with fine Jacobean timbers and
a magnificent beamed ceiling on the first floor. Good place to stop
off for a pint and a bar snack at lunchtime.

The Moon and Sixpence, 6a Broad Street   ££
Tel: (0225) 60962
Open: Mon-Sat noon-2:30pm, 5:30pm-10:30pm, Sun noon-2pm,
        7pm-10:30pm
Credit cards: AE, MC, V

An attractive wine bar set in a pretty courtyard with outdoor
seating in summer, a bistro-type menu and a particularly good

value lunchtime buffet. The upstairs restaurant offers a broader and more interesting menu with daily specials.

Popjoys, Beau Nash House, Sawclose   £££
Tel: (0225) 460494
Open: Tues-Fri noon-2pm, Tues-Sat 6pm-10:30pm
Closed: Sat lunch, Sun, over Christmas
Credit cards: MC, V

Adjoining the Theatre Royal, through wrought iron gates to the right, you'll find a small, paved courtyard and a large, stripped pine door with a brass knocker which announces: 'Beau Nash House'. Until he died in 1761, at the age of 86, Beau Nash, the self-styled 'King of Bath', lived here with his mistress, Juliana Popjoy.

Something of the atmosphere still remains in the well-proportioned dining-room, furnished in Regency style, which now houses Popjoy's Restaurant. Chef Edgar Buhrs offers inventively prepared dishes. Start, perhaps, with pastry-wrapped parcels of baked salmon topped with a warm, mango sauce. Follow with crispy breast of goose with a pineapple and green pepper sauce, finish with a poppyseed parfait smothered with a coffee and Kahlua sauce. If all this sounds too much, or you're a calorie-counter, vegetarian dishes are always available, but they're not so much fun to write up. Juliana Popjoy's ghost, dressed in grey, is said to appear occasionally; nobody has yet claimed to see her serve at table.

The Theatre Vaults, Theatre Royal, Sawclose   £
Tel: (0225) 65074 (ask for Theatre Vaults)
Open: Mon-Sat 12:30pm-2:30pm, 6pm-11pm Closed: Sun; Mon if
        no theater performance
Credit cards: AE, MC, V

A pleasant little restaurant in the vaulted cellars below the theater. Good, freshly-cooked dishes or crisp, garden-fresh salads served by a friendly staff. Limited but adequate, inexpensive wine list.

Try, while you're here, to sneak a peek of the theater auditorium (if the doors are locked, look through the oval windows on your way to the john). Its three tiers, dominated by a massive chandelier, give an intimate, cozy feel. It's difficult to believe it holds almost 1,000 people. In 1982 the theater was beautifully restored for the second time since its opening in 1805; its ornate ceiling is breathtaking.

BATH HOTELS

Hunstrete House, Hunstrete, Chelwood £££
Tel: (07618) 578
Amenities: ☎ ⛁ 🅿 ⵵⵵ 🍷 ≋ 𝒫   Credit cards: AE, DC, MC, V

Directions: Less than 8 miles from Bath city center. Take the A4 towards Bristol for about 4 miles. Take the left turn marked A39/A368 Wells and Weston-super-Mare. At Marksbury keep on the A368 and take the first turning right.

A lovely 18th-century private house, converted by Thea and John Dupays into an hotel in 1978. Its attractive entrance, through a courtyard bursting with flowers around a statued fountain, is echoed by the wealth of flowers and plants within the house itself. Friendly small public rooms reflect the owners' interest in antiques; shelves and alcoves are filled with collections of porcelain and pottery, while the walls are liberally hung with paintings. Twenty-four bedrooms, named after British birds and all individually decorated and furnished with antiques, have effectively captured the feel of an elegant country home which takes in guests.

You'll eat well here, too. The menu is imaginative, the food beautifully cooked and presented, with a wine list that's impressive for its range and depth of vintages. The dining room is delightful and overlooks the Italianate courtyard; there's a separate dining room for smokers.

Paradise House, 86 Holloway £
Tel: (0225) 317723   Closed: Dec-Jan
Amenities: ☎ ⛁ 🅿   Credit cards: MC, V

Directions: Located off A367 south of the city

Located to the south of the city on a steep cul-de-sac this delightful 18th-century house is furnished in impeccable taste with a combination of antiques and the best of modern British design, such as Liberty fabrics. All eight en suite bedrooms are individually furnished to equal standards, and in them you're perched above Bath so you look down on the city as though on a stage. There's a lovely walled garden out back where killer croquet is practiced.

The Priory Hotel, Weston Road £££
Tel: (0225) 331922
Amenities: ☎ ⛁ 🅿 ⵵⵵ ≋ ◉   Credit cards: AE, DC, MC, V

Another delightful conversion, this time of an early Victorian property, with superb south-facing, flower-bordered lawns to the rear. An adjoining 18th-century property has been purchased and is being incorporated into this most friendly and welcoming hotel. It enjoys an excellent reputation for food and boasts a stunning range of red Bordeaux and Burgundy wines from £8.50 up.

The Royal Crescent Hotel, Royal Crescent   £££
Tel: (0225) 319090
Amenities: ☎ ⌨ 🅿 ⛽ 🍷 ℘   Credit cards: AE, DC, MC, V

The hotel comprises two adjoining houses right in the middle of this architectural masterpiece of 30 identical Georgian properties, whose façades form an elegant 530-foot crescent. A city ordinance prohibits the hotel from any outside identification and this enforced discretion seems to have set the tone for all else within the hotel. It's authentically furnished in Georgian style. You'll see oils in the style of Joshua Reynolds and Gainsborough, the two great English painters of the 18th century, as well as 'The Comforts of Bath' – the famous cartoon series penned by Rowlandson, whose wickedly observant, and sometimes coarse, caricatures brilliantly commented on Regency social life.

The elegant dining room in the newly-built Dower House overlooks the billiard-table lawns, and here, if you're adventurous, you may be tempted to try Chef Michael Croft's specialty, Pigeon Pithivier – breast of wild pigeon with a mousse of its legs, flavored with fresh herbs and cognac, wrapped in puff pastry and served with a Madeira sauce. Afterwards? How about easing it down in your own personal jacuzzi in a Dower House suite?

Somerset House, 35 Bathwick Hill
Tel: (0225) 66451
Amenities: ☎ 🅿 ⛽ No smoking   Credit cards: AE, MC, V

'Not so much an elegant B & B more a happy houseparty', is how one recent guest described her stay here. Malcolm and Jean Seymour are hosts par excellence in this classical Regency House. As a former tourist board official Malcolm is a mine of information on Bath and surroundings; while Jean's a cook of great ability, who's made a fetish out of finding super Somerset recipes. Their gardens are glorious, the views over Bath superb. All eight large en suite bedrooms are furnished like the elegant guest rooms in a private house – some have fireplaces. Small wonder that the British Tourist Authority has commended this establishment.

BATH TO TETBURY   (about 27 miles)

*Leaving the **Charlotte Street car park**, you'll turn left into **Queen's Square**. Take the next left (top left corner of the Square) into **Gay Street**, then immediately right onto **George Street**. After the pedestrian crossing lights, the road bears slightly left, at which point you'll fork right into the **Paragon**; this becomes London Street and is the old road to London. Keep on this road, following the signs for the **M4, A4 and A46**. It will bring you into **Batheaston**, on the outskirts of Bath. At a set of traffic lights in the middle of the village, just after the*

*White Lion pub, turn left onto **Bannerdown Road** for **Colerne**. You climb a hill out of the village and emerge on a plateau, with valleys to either side and open fields surrounded by dry stone walls. Keep right for Colerne and **Castle Combe**. Ignore the turning on the right to the village of Colerne, 1 mile on, and continue to **Ford**, where the fields slope so steeply the sheep appear to balance precariously. At the junction with the **A420**, turn right and almost immediately left for **Castle Combe** (2 miles).*

Clustered around the delightful parish church of St Andrew, Castle Combe is an exceptionally pretty village set in a wooded valley beside a stream known as Bye Brook. Soft Cotswold stone cottages and the odd half-timbered façade snooze peacefully beneath a jumble of tiled roofs and peep-eye windows, oblivious to the passage of Rex Harrison and the Great Pink Seasnail, who briefly invaded this rustic backwater during the filming of the children's classic 'Doctor Doolittle'. Inside the 14th-century church you'll find medieval wall paintings, the mighty tick of an ancient faceless clock and fresh flowers arranged by that great British village institution, the church flower ladies.

Another fine idea is to wander down the lane by **The Crown Hotel** (good bar snacks, morning coffee and some accommodation), past an immaculate row of terraced cottages, to **The Manor House Hotel** (tel: (0249) 782206). This is a beautiful country house set in 26 acres of parkland, with a trout stream and gardens where you can indulge in a Wiltshire cream tea by the croquet lawn, or dine on Devon lobster and locally-caught fish and game in the restaurant (open daily 12:30pm-2:30pm, 7:30pm-9:15pm; credit cards: AE, DC, MC, V). The interior of the manor boasts a superb, oak-paneled hall, an ornate, 18th-century frieze in the main lounge, and individually furnished rooms, some with four-poster beds.

*At the top of the village, turn left for **Acton Turville** (4 miles), and then left again onto the **B4039**. Just after Burton you cross a bridge over the M4, and turn right for **Badminton**. There are a couple of unusual little cottages on your left as you enter this picturesque village. The traditional muted hues of Cotswold stone have been interspersed here and there by soft ice-cream pinks and oranges. The road bears sharply left, by the entrance to **Badminton House**, the stately home setting for the annual **Badminton Horse Trials** (held in March). Follow the country road through **Little Badminton**, where only a couple of the cottages have opted for the revolutionary pastel shades so popular up the road, until you reach the junction with the A46. Turn right towards **Stroud** and almost immediately fork right on the **A433** towards **Cirencester**. Tetbury is signposted 7½ miles. Shortly you enter the county of **Gloucester**, proclaimed on a boundary sign, and the road takes you through the village of **Didmarton**; you are now heading for **Westonbirt**, which you reach 4½ miles after* *leaving the junction with the A46/A433.*

It's well worth your time to visit the **Westonbirt Arboretum**, clearly signposted to the left in the village, and open daily 10am-8pm or dusk, whichever is earlier. This splendid park, run by the Forestry Commission, has 17 miles of tracks and paths and identifies some 14,000 different trees and shrubs. Entrance is £1.20 for adults and 50p for children. The Visitors' Centre (open: daily 10am-5pm spring to autumn) offers maps, trail guides and teacher packs at nominal cost. Features change with the seasons but you'll be due for a special treat if you're there for the spring flowering shrubs (May) or the autumn foliage colors (October). Tea, coffee, soft drinks, and light snack foods are available, along with picnic area and toilets. There's ample car parking.

*Leaving the Arboretum, continue on the road to **Tetbury**. Almost immediately you'll pass on your right the imposing entrance to **Westonbirt School** (tel: (066 688) 333), where a variety of musical events are staged by the school throughout the year. It might be worth your while checking beforehand to see what's on. Tetbury is only 3 miles away but, en route, you'll pass the **Hare and Hounds** pub/hotel on your left, which is good for morning coffee or afternoon-tea. It also offers a reasonably priced lunch or evening meal; the hammer-beamed dining room overlooks an attractive garden. Just 1½ miles further along, in **Doughton**, you'll notice, on your left, a stretch of exceptional dry stone walling – a classic example of superb country skill. This is the boundary wall to **Highgrove House**, the country estate of Their Royal Highnesses The Prince and Princess of Wales. The park between the road and the house is heavily planted with trees ensuring privacy. The property commands a good view of the tall, slender steeple of Tetbury parish church – a view you have yourself, on your right, as you enter the town. It's the third highest steeple in England. The church was a victim of the Victorians' passion for reviving the Gothic style, but it's worth a visit if only for its very fine box pews.*

TETBURY

Tetbury is an Elizabethan market town with a stunning 17th-century town hall known as **Market House** built on three rows of pillars. You can't miss it: it's right in the middle of Market Place. Over the crossroads from here there's ample car parking in **The Chipping**, but beware if it's market day (Wednesday), when you'll have to park where you can. Chipping is from the Old English word for 'market' and it crops up in several place names in this region (see Chipping Camden, below).

*Come back to the **Market House** and turn right. Now you're in **Long Street** and three minutes' walk will bring you to a road junction. On* *your right you'll see the **Tourist Information Centre**, 63 Long Street. (Tel: (0666) 53552. Open: Mon-Sat 10:15am-4:15pm Apr-Oct. Closed: Nov-Mar.)*

The center occupies part of the old town police station, whose cells are now the home of a small Police Byegones Museum. As in many small British towns, the Tourist Information Centre is small and run by volunteers, whose expertise varies, but you'll be able to pick up local maps and information booklets.

It's easy to accept that Long Street, which you have just paced, has changed little in the last couple of hundred years or so. No 43 – the one with a wrought-iron bracket over the door – was built in the 17th century, as was the building on the other side of the road with a protruding two-story porch and named, adequately enough, The Porch House. The doorcase proclaims its origins in 1677.

SHOPPING

Normal trading hours are 9am to 5:30pm, with many shops closing at lunchtime on Thursday. You'll find almost 20 antique shops in Tetbury, most offering a range of furniture and some collectables. Of those in Long Street, these three are well worth a visit. **Malcolm Bristow** at No 28 is a specialist in antique long-case clocks and has a good selection of bracket and lantern clocks too, as well as mercurial barometers. Kinsman **Daniel Bristow** at 54 Long Street is another specialist – this time in stringed instruments and bows. If you enjoy oils or watercolors, do look in on Joy Simcock at **Colleton House Gallery**, 16 Long Street. She has a most appealing selection, cleverly broad in range, and reasonably priced. Back in the Market Place, and almost opposite the Post Office, the **Alyson Ager** boutique, at 18 Market Place, offers a small range of attractive hand-embroidered works which might well solve some of your gift headaches. Just a few yards away is the site of the ducking-pond, where 'scolding and unquiet women' were unceremoniously tied into the 'gumstool' and roughly pushed backwards into the water. Gumstool Hill is just around the corner and still boasts some attractive old Cotswold properties, while just a little way down on the left you can eat and drink well, but inexpensively, in the exceptionally friendly atmosphere of **The Crown Inn**, a 17th-century pub cheerily run by hosts Mr and Mrs Housam.

TETBURY HOTELS

The Close Hotel, Long Street   £££
Tel: (0666) 52272
Amenities: ☎ ⌨ 🅿 🍴 🍸   Credit cards: AE, MC, V

More than 400 years ago this was the home of a wealthy wool merchant. Today David Broadhead (with previous experience at the Savoy and Claridges) runs an exceptional country hotel, with

18 beautifully furnished en suite bedrooms. Classic English cuisine, with exceptional wines, is served in the elegant dining room, with its delicate Adam ceiling and fireplace. Try the suckling pig, stuffed with cabbage and fresh peaches, served with a light, garlic-scented gravy. Expensive, but if you're feeling flush or are prepared to spend the next night in the car . . .

Calcot Manor, near Beverston   £££
Tel: (066 689) 355
Amenities: ☎ 💻 🅿 ⛽ ⚲ 〰 (✓ and ✗ nearby)
Credit cards: AE, DC, MC, V

*Directions: No more than ten minutes' drive to the west of Tetbury on the **A4135**, just beyond **Beverston**, and just 50 yards from the junction with the **A46**.*

This is a real find. The Ball family has created an excellent little country hotel with seven bedrooms, and one of the best restaurants in Gloucestershire. Delicious contemporary dishes with just the right note of adventure but few pretensions; amazing and amazing-value salad lunches; cheerful and friendly staff, and an appealing informality. All in all, they should be awarded high marks indeed.

TETBURY TO CIRENCESTER   (about 10 miles)

*By now you'll be familiar with **Long Street**. Leave Tetbury along it, swinging right past the Tourist Information Centre along what is locally known as London Road but is signposted as the **A433** to **Cirencester**, just 10 miles away. Gently undulating, wooded country-side flattens for a while as you pass Kemble airfield on your right where, until recently, the RAF aerobatic team, known as 'The Red Arrows', trained. Soon the road straightens out. You've now joined the line of the old **Roman Fosse Way**. On your left you'll see the Thames Head Inn, a small, unimpressive roadside pub, which is only a short walk from the (equally unimpressive, at this point) source of the River Thames. It's difficult to believe that this will develop eventually into England's most famous waterway.*
*Shortly the A429 joins from the right while you carry straight on, over the traffic circle. You enter **Cirencester** via another large traffic circle; take the left exit, past the Black Horse pub, following the signposts to the **town center** and **car parks**. This brings you along **Castle Street** to the **Market Place**, in the center of the town. Although there's parking here, it's difficult. Continue a few more yards to the next right turn, by the Bear Inn, which leads into a large car park. Walk back to the main road, turn left, and on your left you'll find the **Tourist Information Centre**, **Market Place**. (Tel: (0285) 4180. Open: Daily 10am-5:30pm, 4:30pm in winter. Closed: Sun.) It occupies part of the Corn Hall, adjoining The King's Head Hotel.*

CIRENCESTER

The town name is a corruption of 'Corinium', given it by the Romans, and 'ceaster' whose Latin derivation means 'a Roman camp or town'. The town is one of the oldest in the country: there are references to it in the Domesday Book. The origins of Cirencester go back at least as far as the 2nd century AD when it was the second largest Roman town in Britain (London, or 'Londinium', was the largest).

WHAT TO SEE

The site of the old town has been excavated and most of the finds are exhibited in the excellent **Corinium Museum** in Park Street (open: Mon-Sat 10am-5:30pm, Sun 2pm-5:30pm; closed: Mon Oct-Apr; admission: adults 60p, children 30p). There are reconstructions of a Roman dining room, kitchen and craftsman's workshop. Among displays of local finds are some fine mosaic floors. In a small, internal courtyard a fountain plays. The flower beds are planted with herbs that were grown here in Roman times.

The wealth of all the medieval market towns in this area grew from wool. Cirencester is no exception. Its magnificent parish church of **St John the Baptist** much enlarged in the 15th and 16th centuries, is nearly as big as a cathedral. Inside you'll find many monuments and brasses commemorating the wealthy wool merchants who contributed to the church's prosperity. The peal of 12 bells is the oldest in Britain.

On the edge of town – and no more than 10 minutes' walk from the Tourist Information Centre, via Black Jack Street, Park Street and Cecily Hill – is **Cirencester Park**, home of The Earl of Bathurst. As you walk past the walls of the estate at the junction of Park Street and Park Lane, notice the 40-feet high yew hedge behind the wall, on your left: it was planted 170 years ago. Although the house is not open to the public, you can visit the park, which is one of the largest in England. The impressive entrance leads immediately into Broad Ride – an apt name for the straight, wide, drive which stretches for 1¼ miles between spreading chestnut trees. Alexander Pope composed many of his poems in these idyllic surroundings.

SHOPPING

Cirencester Market held on Monday and Friday each week, enhances the feeling you'll get that this is a typical, small country town, whose shops tend to be individually owned, rather than chain-controlled (though further planned development may change this situation shortly). Even further emphasizing this tradition, a number of craft workshops have opened in **Brewery Court**, just around the corner from the Tourist Information Centre and opposite Woolworths. Here you'll see traditional and new craft skills and there's a readiness to undertake individual commissions in most disciplines. So, if you're looking for gifts of jewelry, embroidery, ceramics, studio glass or leather, or if you simply want to watch the more traditional skills of blacksmith, weaver, saddler or bookbinder, among others, pay a visit.

The link with Cirencester's wooly past is maintained by the **Cotswold Sheepskin and Woollens** shop in Dyer Street, which offers a wide selection of skins and knits.

CIRENCESTER RESTAURANTS

Cirencester isn't blessed with notable restaurants but you'll find an adequate meal at **The Fleece Hotel** or, if a snack suffices, try **Shepherd's Wine Bar** (same building and owned by the hotel), where the food is good but the staff need prodding.

The King's Head, next to the Tourist Information Centre dates back to the 14th century, and serves good bar snacks in pleasant surroundings. Public rooms in this one-time coaching inn boast a wealth of beams and stone vaulting.

CIRENCESTER HOTEL

The Fleece Hotel, Market Place   **££**
Tel: (0285) 68507
Amenities: ☎ ⌨ 🅿 ⵘ 🍸   Credit cards: AE, DC, MC, V

At ground level, a small, open courtyard currently separates the Tudor and Georgian buildings which comprise this pleasant, country-town hotel, but it is being enclosed, improving facilities. Formerly a coaching inn, it has 25 rooms, individually decorated and comfortably furnished. Staff are friendly and competent.

CIRENCESTER TO CHELTENHAM   (about 15 miles)

*Leaving the **Tourist Information Centre** on your left, turn right at the first intersection, passsing the parish church on your right. This leads into **Gosditch Street** and then **Dollar Street**, a short stretch lined by charming 17th- and 18th-century stone-built gingerbread houses. About 1/4 mile on, you'll take the **A435** to the right, clearly signposted **Cheltenham**. Turn left at the next traffic lights onto a busy main road; then shortly, when the road splits, take the right fork clearly marked **A435** to **Cheltenham**, which is 15 miles from this point. **Cirencester Golf Club** (open to visitors) is just over 2 miles beyond, on your left, and you'll continue to follow this pleasant, but fairly busy, main road, which offers few opportunities for overtaking. It emerges into open, well-groomed farmland with gentle hills until, eventually, over the brow of a hill, you'll see Cheltenham laid out in a valley before* *you; from here you'll follow the hill down into the town, passing the* **Lilleybrook Golf Club** *(guests welcome) on your left, near the bottom, less than ½ mile from the outskirts of Cheltenham. Follow the signs towards the town center, past the turnings to the train station and the general hospital. Go straight over the traffic lights, leaving Stratford House Hotel on your left, into a tree-lined avenue with Georgian houses on either side. Don't miss those on your right with attractive wrought iron balconies and canopies.*

This road then becomes part of the **Inner Ring Road**, *which takes you around, rather than through, the city center. However, it's very well signposted for major points of interest and car parks, which are designated either short, or long stay (best for stays of more than four hours). Shortly after joining the Inner Ring Road – and after turning left into* **Bath Road** *and then right into* **Oriel Road** *– you'll see car parks signposted on your right. Take the one between* **Rodney Road** *and* **Regent Street**, *since you'll be within comfortable walking distance of the city center and the* **Tourist Information Centre**, *Municipal Offices,* **Promenade** *(Tel: (0242)522878. Open: Mon-Fri 9:30am-6pm, Sat 9:30am-5pm, Sun 10am-1pm June-Sept; Mon-Fri 9:45am-5:15pm, Sat 9:45am-5pm, closed: Sun Oct-May), which is virtually in the middle of the main shopping area.*

CHELTENHAM

Its Regency splendor rivaling Bath's, Cheltenham lies a short distance from the highest point of the Cotswolds at Cleeve Hill. Its spa, or mineral spring, was not discovered until the 18th century, but a visit by George III in 1788 put the town on the map. This was further underlined by a recommendation from the Duke of Wellington in 1816, who found the waters most effective in combating a liver complaint contracted during tropical service, which resulted in a steady stream of similarly afflicted Empire-builders flocking to take the cure – a rather more sedate clientele than that of fashion-conscious Bath. The town is also home to the very proper Cheltenham Ladies' College, established in 1853, and one of England's oldest private schools for girls.

WHAT TO SEE

To catch the essence of Georgian Cheltenham, promenade along **Promenade**, and admire its elegant façades sporting intricately wrought balconies, the formal flower gardens and the glittering Neptune fountain based on the famous Trevi Fountain in Rome. Visit the superb **Pump Room Museum** (open: Tues-Sat 10:30am-5pm; also Sun Apr-Oct; admission: 40p) in Pitville Park; a gem of restrained Greek Revivalist architecture set among the lawns and shaded walks of the park. The **Cheltenham Art Gallery and**

Museum in Clarence Road (open: Mon-Sat 9:30am-5pm; free admission) displays some fine collections of art, porcelain, furniture and costume, plus exhibitions of local history and crafts. Music lovers might like to drop in at the birthplace of **Gustav Holst** (composer of *The Planets* suite), also in Clarence Road (open: Tues-Sat 10am-5pm; free admission), a beautifully preserved Victorian town house with period furnishings, musical instruments, photographs and memorabilia from the composer's life. Racing fans should check out the **Racecourse**, which holds the world-renowned Cheltenham Gold Cup steeplechase in March, the highlight of a season which runs from October to May.

SHOPPING

While most shop hours are from 9am to 5pm or 5:30pm, the larger stores remain open until 8pm on Thursday. Only the smaller shops observe the early closing on Wednesday afternoon.

An excellent range of quality stores occupies prime sites in **Promenade**, and also in the stylish new **Regent Arcade**. For the pick of the bunch in the Arcade, head upstairs where you'll find wonderfully glitzy costume jewelry at **Diamanté**, delectable Belgian chocolates at **Bellina**, and a choice of cheerful gift ideas and children's toys at **Planks**, and **Leapfrog**.

South of Promenade, and fronted by a 'regiment of monstrous women' (caryatids in this case, built to the original Greek recipe), is **Montpellier Walk**. Sadly, it retains little of its original cachet, save for two interesting antique shops – **Gladys Green** at No 15, and **Joy Turner** at No 22 – but you can gain access to both of these via the eminently chic Montpellier Street. Here you'll find a bevy of bijou boutiques, antiques and the entrancing **Design Craftsman Shop**, loaded with jewelry, ceramics, printed silk and much, much more. Also, a couple of handy watering-holes in the well of the courtyard: **The Shambles** for healthy salads and snacks; and **Stone's**, a modern brasserie for the less cholesterol-conscious.

CHELTENHAM RESTAURANTS

Beaujolais Restaurant, 15 Montpellier Street **££**
Tel: (0242) 525230
Open: Daily noon-2pm, 7pm-10:30pm
Credit cards: AE, DC, MC, V

Friendly little French restaurant with bistro-style decor and a cozy atmosphere. Light, classic menu including plenty of fresh fish and game in season.

Forrest Wine Bar, Imperial Lane (off Promenade)   £
Tel: (0242) 238001
Open: Mon-Sat 12:30pm-2:15pm, 6:30pm-10:30pm
Credit cards: MC, V

Jolly basement wine bar with truly international flavor – from traditional British steak and kidney pud to German Bratwurst to Maryland Chicken from 'over the pond'. Good snacks and starters as well.

CHELTENHAM HOTELS

Eton House, Wellington Street   £
Tel: (0242) 523272
Amenities: ⚏ 🅿 ᐈᐈᐈ, No smoking   Credit cards: MC, V

This lovely four-story late Regency terraced house with wrought iron railing and veranda is located centrally yet in a quiet street. Rooms are tastefully done and have coffee/tea makers. Meals are excellent and as reasonably priced as the rooms.

The Queen's Hotel, Imperial Square   £££
Tel: (0242) 514724
Amenities: ☎ ⚏ ᐈᐈᐈ ♈   Credit cards: AE, DC, MC, V

Lovely Georgian hotel with an imposing colonnaded façade, right in the town center and overlooking the Imperial Gardens. Elegantly furnished rooms with their own facilities; gracious reception rooms and restaurant with à la carte or fixed price menus. This is a popular conference venue, so do check ahead.

If you'd like to continue your tour through the **Cotswolds** to **Stratford** and **Oxford** see **page 365**. Otherwise, follow the directions below for a quick return to London.

CHELTENHAM TO LONDON   (about 97 miles)

*From the **Tourist Information Center** go to the end of the **Promenade** towards **Montpellier Walk**. Turn right at the end into **St George's Road**. Follow this round to its end; then turn left into **Gloucester Road**. Travel down this road past the industrial estate to its end. You'll see the **A40** (Lansdowne Road), signposted **Oxford** and **London**. Stay on the **A40** around **Oxford**, until it joins the **M40** at junction 7 signposted **London/High Wycombe**.*

TOUR 2: THE COTSWOLDS, MARKET TOWNS, OXFORD AND SHAKESPEARE (about 146 miles)

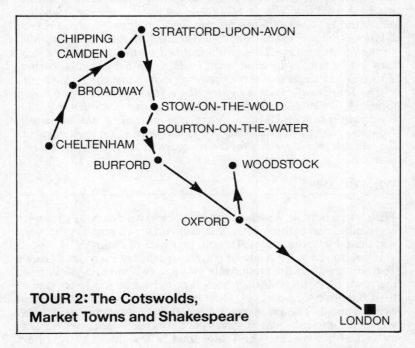

TOUR 2: The Cotswolds, Market Towns and Shakespeare

This tour continues on from Longer Tour 1: **Great Cathedral Cities and Regency Bath** (see **page 312**).

CHELTENHAM TO WINCHCOMBE   (about 18 miles)

*From **Rodney Road**, join the **Inner Ring Road** again near the Town Hall, follow across The Promenade, and then turn right at the traffic lights into **Royal Well Road**, passing the bus station on your left. This takes you along **North Street**, where, at the junction with Albion Street, you again turn right with the main traffic flow but after the turn keep in the left-hand lane because you immediately turn left up **Portland Street**, which has two-way traffic, so exercise caution. Pass the short stay car park on your left and keep in the right-hand lane, for, at the traffic lights at the junction with **Clarence Road**, you'll turn right. At the next junction with Winchcombe Street there's a traffic circle: take the second exit, marked **Winchcombe**. This is the **A4632** and is also the road to **Broadway** (17 miles) and **Stratford-upon-Avon**, but be careful, for from now on the road may be numbered either*

A4632 or A46 (the old road number which is being changed and some signs have yet to be altered).

*Go straight over the next traffic circle; then the A4632 bears hard left and is clearly marked. From now on it's plain sailing and the road takes you up Cleeve Hill (note the rocky crest on your right above the tree line) with spectacular views on your left of the Vale of Gloucester. Just 7 miles from Cheltenham, you enter Winchcombe. In the center of the village, and identified by the protruding clock, turn left by the town hall, a small building on the left-hand corner. This is **North Street** and there's parking a little way up on the right.*

*The **Tourist Information Centre**, **High Street** (Tel: (0242) 602925. Open: Mon-Sat 10am-5pm Mar-Oct) is in the small Town Hall – identified by the clock – as are the minute Folk and Police museums. Note that the stocks have holes for seven limbs – the story goes that the odd one was especially for a one-legged local who was constantly in trouble.*

WINCHCOMBE

The church here at Winchcombe is adorned with curious gargoyles and contains an embroidered altar cloth on which much of the work was done by Catherine of Aragon, first wife of Henry VIII.

If you're ready for a cup of coffee, or tea, try **Lady Jane Grey's Teashop**, back on the main route and just two minutes' walk from the town hall; the tempting smell may persuade you to try one of their freshly-baked pastries. Otherwise, if it's time for lunch, or an evening meal, **The Plaisterer's Arms** (which was on your right as you drove into the village) serves good food in its cellar restaurant, as well as bar snacks. **The White Hart**, a few doors away, offers similar fare.

Shopping is very limited but there's a first-class gallery in a lovely old half-timbered building opposite the Tourist Information Centre: **Kenulf Gallery**, where Eric Ford offers a range of 19th-century and early 20th-century oils, watercolors, prints and drawings by acknowledged artists. As a sideline, he also has cottages for rent in the village.

Sudeley Castle
Open: Daily: House: noon-5pm; Grounds: 11am-5:30pm Apr-Oct
Admission: Adults £3.25, children £1.75

Directions: You'll find the castle on the southeastern edge of the village – and no more than 10 minutes' walk from the town center past what seems like stone dolls' houses. There's ample parking if you prefer to drive.

Sudeley is a 'must' for history buffs. Now the home of Lord and Lady Ashcombe, whose family have had connections with it since

1367, the property has had a checkered history since it was built almost a thousand years ago. Best known, perhaps, as the home (and resting place) of Queen Katherine Parr, widowed sixth wife of Henry VIII, who then married Thomas Seymour, Lord High Admiral and Baron of Sudeley, the house has hosted at least six Kings and Queens of England. Elizabeth I spent some of her time here as a child.

Sudeley Castle houses works by Turner, Constable, Rubens and Van Dyck. Also on display are many relics of the past, including a fascinating collection of toys and playthings, arranged in several rooms in the ancient dungeon tower. There are falconry displays in the summer.

WINCHCOMBE TO BROADWAY (about 8 miles)

*Continue northeast on the **A4632**. At the traffic circle, cross straight over and **Broadway** is signposted 5 miles. You're now driving through pleasant but unremarkable countryside, although you'll see the occasional gem of a property. Almost 8 miles after leaving Winchcombe you'll reach the outskirts of Broadway: at the T-junction turn right onto the **A44** signposted **Oxford/Stratford** and within moments you are in the town center.*

Parking is exceptionally difficult in Broadway so, rather than fight for a roadside place, go to the far end of the village and turn left at the car park sign. Just 200 yards up on the right there is ample space, with rest rooms.

*You'll have passed the **Tourist Information Centre** in Cotswold Court (Tel: (0386) 852937. Open: Daily 10am-5pm, Easter-Oct) on your right, in a small shopping arcade in the High Street. The center is run by volunteers and may sometimes be closed at lunchtime.*

BROADWAY

Many regard this as the crown jewel among Cotswold villages. Tudor, Jacobean and Georgian homes all use varying shades of the honeyed local stone to stunning effect. These tones are offset by the village green, well-tended trees and window boxes of the residents. What makes the scene doubly appealing is the higgledy-piggledy juxtaposition of roof lines and façades.

SHOPPING

There's good general shopping, but, inevitably the nature of the town focuses attention on the antique shops, of which there are several. In the High Steet, **Gavina Ewart**, at No 60, specializes in silver cutlery, tea sets, and other general silverware, though she also has porcelain, maps, prints and oils. **Picton House Gallery**, also in High Street, has a large stock of 19th-century and 20th-century oils and watercolors, as well as general antiques, mostly small items and furniture. **H.W. Keil Ltd**, Tudor House, Broad Close, has a magnificent range of 17th- and 18th-century furniture in oak, walnut and mahogany.

BROADWAY RESTAURANT

Hunter's Lodge, High Street ££
Tel: (0386) 853247
Open: Tues-Sun 12:30pm-2pm, 7:30pm-9:45pm
Closed: Sun eve, Mon, 2 wks Feb, 2 wks Aug
Credit cards: AE, DC, MC, V

A happy combination of traditional English and French cuisine has been the secret of the success of owner-managers, the Friedlis. The vegetables are always reliable – surely the mark of any good restaurant. Separate menus for lunch and dinner. The wine list is fair and reasonably-priced if you don't go for the exotics.

BROADWAY HOTELS

Collin House, Collin Lane ££
Tel: (0386) 858354
Amenities: ⌨ (on request), **P** ⵀ⵬ ⵉ ≈ ⵝ (nearby)
Credit cards: MC, V

Small (only seven bedrooms) but a friendly and cheerful hotel, in an old stone house dating from the 1600s and in a very peaceful setting. Run by owner-managers John and Judy Mills (she's an excellent cook), their period dining room is open to non-residents. With a set menu, there are no pretensions and food is of a high quality. Good wine list for such a small place.

Dormy House, Willersey Hill £££
Tel: (0386) 852711
Amenities: ☎ ⌨ **P** ⵀ⵬ ⵉ ⵝ   Credit cards: AE, DC, MC, V

Directions: Follow the A44 towards Oxford, up Fish Hill, then first left and it's just under a mile from there.

The modernization and extension of this one-time 17th-century farmhouse has been cleverly achieved. It's next door to Broadway Golf Club (open to guests) and many of the 50 rooms have beamed ceilings and exposed stone walls, retaining the original character, while there are also banqueting and conference facilities in the modern wings. The food is good and beautifully cooked. If the à la carte menu seems a little lacking in imagination, Chef John Sanderson introduces some exciting dishes in the daily table d'hôte menus (lunch £11.50, dinner £18.50). First-class light meals are served in the Cotswold Bar. The wine list offers good choice and price range.

The Lygon Arms £££
Tel: (0386) 852255
Amenities: ☎ ⬛ 🅿 ⅷ ⏱ ✓ (nearby), ⚲
Credit cards: AE, DC, MC, V

This centuries-old, luxurious hotel was taken over by the Savoy Group in 1986, and, if it were possible, the standards have improved. With the heavily-beamed ceilings, oak paneling and period pieces it's easy to realize that King Charles I knew the place and that Cromwell slept here; both have rooms named after them. The modern Garden and Orchard wings have been tastefully and cleverly combined with the old, giving, in all, more than 60 rooms and suites. Some of the most magnificent are at the front and inclined to be a little noisy during the day, despite the double glazing. Even if you can't stay in them, try to see the Great Bedchamber and the Charles I Suite, which has its own secret stairwell.

The paneled and barrel-vaulted Great Hall, with its 17th-century minstrels' gallery and heraldic friezes makes a marvelous setting for the restaurant where the choice is wide. Perhaps you'll be tempted by the classic, succulent English dishes such as jugged steak, venison with game sausages, or a combination of grilled red mullet fillets with rosemary cutlets of local lamb. Expensive, but worth it.

AROUND AND ABOUT

Broadway Tower Country Park
Open: Daily 10am-6pm Apr-Oct
Admission: Adults £1.75, children £1

*Directions: Take the **A44** road towards **Stowe** and **Oxford**. The entrance to the Park is about 1½ miles out of Broadway, on your right.*

Broadway Hill, which rises up to about 1000 feet above sea level, is topped by a folly built by the Earl of Coventry in 1799. The surrounding parkland contains excellent picnic sites, but most spectacular are the views obtained from the tower – climb to the top of the folly and you have a view over 12 counties.

Snowshill Manor
Open: Sat and Sun 11am-1pm, 2pm-5pm Apr and Oct; Wed-Sun
11am-1pm, 2pm-6pm May-Sep   Closed: Nov-Mar
Admission: Adults, £2.60, children £1.30

*Directions: Take the **minor road** to the right of the Tourist Information Centre and then follow the signs to **Snowshill**, 3 miles on.*

This is a splendid Tudor house, with a 17th-century façade, in a delightful setting, sculpted into small, formal gardens with lovely views across the valley. It houses what can only be described as an eccentric collection of artifacts, embracing musical instruments, clocks, toys, an incredible display of Japanese samurai armor, bicycles, craft instruments and much more. The collections were put together by Charles Paget Wade. The National Trust are now the stewards of this remarkable exhibition. Note the roof timbers over the bicycle display.

BROADWAY TO STRATFORD   (about 15 miles)

Leave Broadway on the A44 towards Oxford but, after climbing Fish Hill and leaving the Broadway Tower on your right, turn left, after ¹/₂ mile onto the B4081. Almost immediately the road starts the drop into Chipping Camden, about 1 mile distant, and the lovely Vale of Evesham unfolds on your right. Your entry to this pretty village is past entrancing, thatched sugarloaf cottages and immaculate small stone houses. Bear left around a bend into Sheep Street (signposted Stratford) and at the top you'll turn right into High Street (signposted Mickleton, Stratford and Tourist Office). Park as soon as you find space, either in the High Street or in one of the side streets.

CHIPPING CAMDEN

By way of contrast with Broadway (qv) many of the village's High Street buildings date from the reign of King James I (1603-1625) and thus form a remarkably harmonious scene. The town is set like a stage with hills all around.

The small, volunteer-staffed **Tourist Information Centre** (Tel: (0386) 840289. Open: Daily 11am-6pm, Apr-Oct) is at the far end of the **High Street**. It occupies part of the **Woolstaplers' Hall**, which was built in 1340 and was a wool exchange for many centuries; the Hall also houses a little country museum. The **Jacobean Market Hall**, with its pointed gables and open arcade was built in 1627.

CHIPPING CAMDEN HOTELS

Cotswold House Hotel and Restaurant, The Square   **££**
Tel: (0386) 840330
Amenities: ☎ ⬛ 🅿 ⑾ ⓨ   Credit cards: AE, MC, V

Located in a handsome Regency house on the Market Square, this small hotel has much to commend it. Public areas with fresh flowers, comfortable sofas and a mix of antiques make it seem like visiting a friend with particularly good taste, which carries over into the individually appointed bedrooms – more like bedsitting rooms – useful if after a long day you crave a quiet drink away from the madding crowds. Some rooms and the dining room face into the pretty main courtyard-garden.

The Kings Arms Hotel, High Street   £
Tel: (0386) 840256
Amenities: 🅿 ⵙⵖ ⵧ   Credit cards: MC, V

This is a modest 16th-century country hotel, with simple furnishings and a few en suite rooms. Dinner is moderately priced at about £10.

Noel Arms Hotel, High Street   ££
Tel: (0386) 840317
Amenities: ⬛ 🅿 ⵙⵖ ⵧ   Credit cards: MC, V

This hotel offers much the same level of comfort as its competitor across the street, except that all rooms are en suite and you'll have the chance to reserve their one massive, heavily-carved, four-poster, engraved 1657. Room prices are just fractionally more expensive.

*Continue on the Stratford Road towards **Mickleton** and after ¾ mile you'll fork right, staying on the **B4081**, and this brings you into Mickleton, where, just ½ mile to the southeast, you'll find Hidcote Manor Gardens.*

Hidcote Manor Gardens, Hidcote Bartrim
Open: Daily 11am-8pm except Tues and Fri (last entry 7pm or
         sunset if earlier) Apr-Oct   Closed: Good Friday
Admission: Adults £2.70, children £1.35; £3 and £1.50 on Sun

These gardens, created between 1908 and 1948 by horticulturalist Major Lawrence Johnson, are some of the most delightful in England. They contain many rare trees, shrubs, plants and bulbs. Be sure to pick up the 40p brochure as you enter; without it you'll go in circles.

   Artfully segmented into a series of small, self-contained gardens, each has a different theme or concept. You're led from one to the next through walls and hedges of differing species, occasionally catching glimpses of one of the corps of six full-time gardeners, who tend the rare shrubs, herbaceous borders and trees, and make sure that all exhibits are clearly marked. Formal gardens, country gardens, wild gardens . . . when you've had enough, there's a tea-room with very pleasant and helpful staff, who serve freshly-baked scones with sinfully rich clotted cream.

*The road through Mickleton to Stratford bears hard left at the end of the village and then ½ mile later, sharp right, signposted **Stratford**. For the next few miles the countryside is flat and dull. Just over 7 miles from Mickleton there's a junction with the **A34 Oxford/Stratford** road, at which you'll turn left, and you'll find you're almost in **Stratford-upon-Avon**. After ¾ mile bear left at the traffic circle, following the **town center** signs. Immediately before the river bridge, by the Swan's Nest Hotel, turn left into a large public car park. You're now separated from the town only by the River Avon, which* *you cross by a footbridge, bringing you to the far end of **Bridge Foot**, at the bottom of the main road through the town. On your right you'll see a **Tourist Information boutique**, but this has limited opening hours (Mon-Sat 11am-4pm May-Sep). To reach the main **Tourist Information Centre**, at 1 High Street (Tel: (0789) 293127. Open: Mon-Sat 9am-5:30pm, Sun 2pm-5pm mid Mar-Oct; 10:30am-4:30pm, closed Sun, Nov-mid Mar) go straight up **Bridge Street**, ahead of you. The Centre is on the left-hand corner of **High Street**. This office is well-run by extremely helpful professionals, who have a wealth of local information, booklets, etc.*

STRATFORD-UPON-AVON

A monastery is known to have occupied the site of the present parish church in 691. An agricultural and cattle-raising community grew up around this, and as early as the 12th century, what is now Stratford became the site of an important local market. The **Mop Fair**, held annually on October 12, derives from the medieval statute fair at which workers were hired. The Guild of the Holy Cross, a tradesmen's society fostering crafts and industries, was also founded in the 12th century. The increasing prosperity of Stratford as a market town was fostered by the generosity of Sir Hugh Clopton, a local man who later became the Lord Mayor of London. The 15th-century bridge over the River Avon, built by Clopton, bears his name and still stands. The happy coincidence of Stratford being Shakespeare's birthplace has ensured the survival of many of the town's oldest buildings. Tourists first visited the town in 1623, after the first folio of Shakespeare's plays was published.

You won't be surprised to learn that there is much to see. The **River Avon** still has its swans, as it did in Shakespeare's time, and a walk along the riverside meadows is a pleasant interlude in the inevitable bustle of sightseeing. **Holy Trinity Church**, Trinity Street, dates from the 13th century. Shakespeare and members of his family were baptized, worshipped and are buried here. **The Royal Shakespeare Theatre** in Waterside (Tel: (0789) 295623 for bookings; (0789) 69191 for 24-hour booking information) has regular seasons of both matinée and evening performances.

WHAT TO SEE

The following five places of interest are known as **The Shakespeare Properties** and share the same opening times. You can visit them individually or buy a combined ticket which gives access to all five. During the summer there is a regular, guided bus tour service connecting the properties in town with those in the surrounding countryside. Details are available from the Tourist Information Centre.

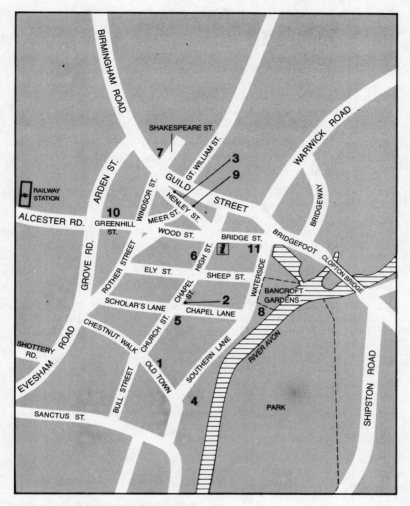

STRATFORD UPON AVON

[i] Tourist Information Centre
1 Hall's Croft
2 New Place/Nash's House
3 Shakespeare's Birthplace
4 Brass Rubbing Centre
5 Grammar School and Guild Chapel
6 Harvard House
7 Motor Museum
8 Royal Shakespeare Theatre Museum and Picture Gallery
9 Shakespeare Centre
10 The Teddy Bear Museum
11 The World of Shakespeare

The Shakespeare Properties (details below)
Open: Mon-Sat 9am-6pm, Sun 10am-6pm Apr-Oct (closes at 5pm
    Oct); Mon-Sat 9am-4:30pm, Sun 1:30pm-4:30pm Nov-Mar
Admission (combined ticket): Adults £4.50, children £2. This also
    covers entrance to the costume exhibition in Shakespeare's
    birthplace

Anne Hathaway's Cottage, Shottery
Admission: Adults £1.60, children 50p

Directions: The cottage is signposted from the town center. Take the
Evesham Road (A439) and after ¼ mile take the turning right to
Shottery and Anne Hathaway's Cottage.

This lovely old thatched cottage was the home of Shakespeare's
wife before her marriage. The Hathaways were a substantial farming family and in their time the cottage was a twelve-room farmhouse. The kitchen contains the original bread oven and the dairy is
very much as it was in the 16th century.

Hall's Croft, Old Town (name of street)
Admission: Adults £1, children 40p

Home of Shakespeare's daughter, Susanna, and her husband Dr
John Hall, this house contains some exceptionally fine Elizabethan
and Jacobean furniture. Hall was a very successful medical practi-
tioner and among the exhibits here are the apothecary jars, herbs
and surgical instruments which he, and other doctors of his time,
would have used. The beautiful walled garden is justly famous, and
worth a visit in its own right.

Mary Arden's House and Shakespeare Countryside Museum,
    Wilmcote
Admission: Adults £1.50, children 50p

Directions: Wilmcote is 3 miles from the town center. Take the A34
road signposted Birmingham, after 2¼ miles turn left to Wilmcote
and Mary Arden's House.

This Tudor farmstead, with its old stone dovecote and farm buildings, was the home of Shakespeare's mother and contains rare
pieces of country furniture. In the outbuildings and the neighboring
Glebe Farm you can see a substantial collection of farming
implements.

New Place/Nash's House, corner Chapel Street and Chapel Lane
Admission: Adults £1, children 40p

The site and foundations of New Place, a handsome house where
Shakespeare spent his retirement and where he died in 1616, are

preserved in the setting of an Elizabethan garden. The entrance is through the adjoining Nash's House which belonged to Thomas Nash, the first husband of Shakespeare's granddaughter, Elizabeth Hall. The house is furnished in period styles and also contains a museum of local history.

Shakespeare's Birthplace, Henley Street
Admission: Adults £1.80, children 70p (includes costume
    exhibition)

The house where Shakespeare was born and spent his early years is a half-timbered building of a type common in Elizabethan Stratford. In the playwright's time, part of the family home was used by his father in his trade as a glover. Part of the house today is authentically furnished to recreate the atmosphere of a middle-class home in 16th-century England. Also in the building is an exhibition illustrating the life and work of the dramatist.

OTHER PLACES TO SEE:

Brass Rubbing Centre, The Royal Shakespeare Theatre Summer
   House, Avonbank Gardens, Southern Lane
Open: Daily 10am-6pm Apr-Sep, 11am-4pm Oct
Closed: Nov-Mar
Free admission, but rubbing charges range from 50p to £6 (includes materials and instruction)

Pop in here to try your hand at rubbing brasses. Even first-timers usually leave with an impressive souvenir.

Grammar School and Guild Chapel, Church Street
Open: During school holidays; check with the Tourist Information
    Centre or the school (Tel: (0789) 293351) for specific dates

Present-day schoolboys will show you around the half-timbered Guildhall (built in 1417) which includes the school and classroom which Shakespeare attended. The school is known to have been in existence at least 200 years before Shakespeare's birth.

Harvard House, High Street
Open: Mon-Sat 10am-noon, 2pm-4pm Sun 2pm-4pm, Jul-Sep
Admission: Adults £1, children 50p

Built in 1596, this was once the home of the grandfather of John Harvard, who gave his name to Harvard.

Motor Museum, Shakespeare Street
Open: Daily 9:30am-6pm, Apr-Oct; 10am-4pm Nov-Mar
Admission: Adults £1.40, teenagers 90p, children 70p

This houses a large collection of vintage cars, motor cycles and motoring accessories, including cars ordered specially by the Maharajahs of India. Only one minute's walk from Shakespeare's Birthplace, the museum has a picnic garden.

Royal Shakespeare Theatre Museum and Picture Gallery, The Swan Theatre, Waterside
Open: Mon-Sat 9:15am-8pm, Sun noon-5pm
Admission: Adults £1.50, children £1

A museum for theater buffs, containing the relics of distinguished theater personalities, paintings of stage scenes and portraits of Shakespeare and his contemporaries in the picture gallery.

Shakespeare Centre, Henley Street
Open: Mon-Fri 9am-5pm, Sat 9am-12:30pm
Admission: Adults 15p, children 5p (small exhibition area)

Much used by students of Shakespeare, this contains a museum as well as a library packed with literary data belonging to the Shakespeare Birthplace Trust.

The Teddy Bear Museum, 19 Greenhill Street
Open: Daily 9:30am-6pm
Admission: Adults £1.50, children 14 and under 75p

Teddy bear madness recently hit Stratford when Gyles and Michelle Brandreth opened this museum. It has an extraordinary range of bears, from the oldest and most famous to mechanical bears, miniature bears and well, frankly, very odd bears. The museum occupies an Elizabethan building. Bears are also on sale.

World of Shakespeare, 13 Waterside
Open: Daily 9:30am-5:30pm (shows every half hour)
Admission: Adults £2.25, children £1.75

Half-hourly performances of an audio-visual presentation which begins in the summer of 1575 when William Shakespeare was a young boy of eleven and takes you through the life and times of the dramatist.

SHOPPING

Shopping hours are normally 9am or 9:30am until 5:30pm; late night opening is Thursday until 8pm.

There's a wealth of good, small shops in Stratford. If you're looking for small, easily-packed gifts, the **Little Gallery**, 30 Bridge Street (shipping facilities) specializes in small dolls, pendants, and brooches containing old British coins embellished with gold on silver. If you fancy larger dolls, some exotically dressed, or if you'd prefer a range of gifts of lace from various parts of the world, try **Pretty Presies**, a small shop in The Minories – the lane between Meer Street and Henley Street. If woolens are on your list, you must visit **The Tradition of Wales**, 22 Henley Street for a good selection of designer knits and other craft work in clay and wood (a wooden 'love-spoon' makes an inexpensive, but different, gift). **The House of Tweed**, 2 Bridge Street, also has fashionable woolens.

Antique-hunters will have fun in Stratford. The Antique Market is at the top of Ely Street, near the junction with High Street. You can browse through a range of bric-a-brac, bogus and genuine antiques. If you're searching for quality collectables, cross over the junction with High and Chapel Streets, and visit the boutique stalls of 14 dealers in **The Antique Arcade** (closed Mon), in Sheep Street, just past the Town Hall, on the right. At 31 Sheep Street, at the bottom on the left, **Diana Chambers** has a well-displayed range of antique jewelry and silver.

STRATFORD-UPON-AVON RESTAURANTS

Blue Boar Inn, Temple Grafton   £
Tel: (0789) 750010
Open: Mon-Sat noon-2pm, 6:30pm-10pm, Sun noon-2pm,
      7pm-9:30pm
Credit cards: MC, V

*Directions: Just 5 miles from Stratford, off the A422 to Alcester, very near **Billesley Manor** (see page 378).*

If you've seen enough other tourists for one day, try this little, ordinary country pub where landlord Ponzi puts on an inexpensive, broad selection of good food. His fish soup with cognac and cream is alone worth the trip.

Café Natural, Greenhill Street   £
Tel: (0789) 415741
Open: Mon-Sat 9am-5:30pm, Thur-Fri until 7:30pm
Credit cards: MC, V

This offers, as the name suggests, vegetarian and wholefood dishes in a warm, friendly atmosphere with a cheerful staff.

Shepherd's Restaurant, Sheep Street (associated with the Stratford
      House Hotel)   ££
Tel: (0789) 68288
Open: Tues-Sat noon-2pm, 6pm-11pm   Closed: Public holidays
Credit cards: AE, DC, MC, V

A light, cheerful restaurant, overlooking a courtyard, where Nigel Lambert, the chef-partner, rotates the mainly English menu weekly, and has the reputation of running the best independent eating place in town. A slender, but well-chosen, wine list, starting at about £6.

The Slug and Lettuce, 38 Guild Street   £
Tel: (0789) 299700
Open: Mon-Sat noon-2pm, 6pm-10pm, Sun noon-1:30pm,
    7pm-9:30pm

This is a frenetic restaurant/wine bar with outdoor dining, if the weather's up to it. If you can stand the lively pace, it's fun and the food's of a good standard, with innovative dishes.

The Swan's Nest, Bridge Foot (over the bridge, where it was
    suggested you leave your car)   ££
Tel: (0789) 66761
Open: Daily 12:30pm-2pm, 6:15pm-9:30pm
Closed: Christmas Day and New Year's Day to non-residents
Credit cards: AE, DC, MC, V

This hotel has a modern hotel restaurant, overlooking the river, which would be unexceptional but for the fact that the chef was a 'Chef of the Year' finalist in 1988. Book a window table and try his fillet of lamb, wrapped in puff pastry, with orange zest and served on a thyme sauce. Good wine list.

STRATFORD-UPON-AVON HOTELS

Billesley Manor, Billesley, Alcester, near Stratford   £££
Tel: (0789) 400888
Amenities: ☎ ⌨ 🅿 ⑴⑴⑴ ⑴ ≈ ✓ ⑴   Credit cards: AE, DC, MC, V

If you're looking for somewhere away from the hustle and bustle (and sometimes noisy rooms) of Stratford, this luxurious hotel is just 3 miles away, off the **A422**. It has been expensively refurbished, modern comforts blending discreetly with the dignified old building, which Shakespeare is said to have visited. You'll find the young staff exceptionally friendly and helpful. Well-prepared, largely traditional English food is served in the oak-paneled restaurant; the wine list is well-balanced, if expensive.

The Glenavon Hotel, 6 Chestnut Walk   £
Tel: (0789) 292588   Closed: Over Christmas
Amenities: 🅿   No credit cards

We hate to publicize this reasonably priced small hotel. Perched on the corner of Chestnut Walk and West Street it is an easy five minute stroll past Hall's Croft to the Royal Shakespeare Theatre. The bedrooms are plain but spotlessly clean (our favorites are at the back of the hotel on the ground floor running along West

Street). There are no en suite facilities but they are generally only a door or two away. Mr and Mrs Wilson are friendly, casual hosts. Breakfasts served off the kitchen are hearty and cooked to order. Finally there is ample public parking directly across the street.

The Shakespeare Hotel, Chapel Street   **£££**
Tel: (0789) 294771
Amenities: ☎ ⌨ 🅿 ⑪ ⏰   Credit cards: AE, DC, MC, V

Its heavily-timbered, gabled façade, beamed and flagstone-floored public rooms make it easy to accept that you're in the Bard's home town. Dating from the early 17th century (there's evidence that the central section may be 100 years older still), some of the front bedrooms are equally appealing, but you need to reserve them well in advance.

White Swan Hotel, Rother Street   **£££**
Tel: (0789) 297022
Amenities: ☎ ⌨ 🅿 ⑪ ⏰   Credit cards: AE, DC, MC, V

Owned by the same 'group' as The Shakespeare, this hotel, too, is central and dates from the late 1600s. The lounge is a magnificent room, heavily beamed, with old stone fireplace, carved overmantel and, opposite, you'll see wall paintings which it's believed date from 1550. The old bedrooms, at the front, are just as attractive.

STRATFORD TO OXFORD   (about 40 miles)

*This route will take you through some Cotswold towns which are gems. From Stratford, leave the car park by The Swan's Nest Hotel. Turn right, exercising great care, since, in crossing to the far lane, you tend to get stranded in the middle of the road, alongside the brick edifice, by the stream of traffic coming at you from over the bridge – a stream which you have to join. Almost immediately, there's a traffic circle, where you'll exit right, leaving the Shell gas station on your left, following the A34 signs to Oxford. After 7½ miles you'll pass a 'Little Chef' coffee shop on your right and 100 yards beyond is a traffic circle. Turn right onto the A429, signposted **Moreton-in-the-Marsh/Stow**. It's 8 miles from here to Moreton, through farming land, of no special beauty; you may notice fewer trees than in some of the earlier scenery.*

*Park where you can in the wide, sweeping main street and walk to the **Tourist Information Centre**, Council Offices, **High Street**. The Centre is halfway through the village on the left-hand side in the offices of the North Cotswold Rural District Council, near the pedestrian-controlled traffic lights. This is a very small office, not always manned. For information call the TIC at Stow-in-the-Wold (Tel: (0451) 31082).*

Although Moreton's not a major tourist center, it has one or two old coaching inns. The **Redesdale Arms Hotel** (tel: (0608) 50308; credit cards: AE, MC, V; **££**) is one of the best. A large heraldic coat of arms on the wall above the entrance proclaims: 'God careth for Us'. It might have added: 'so do Michael Elvis and Patricia Seedhouse' – the genial resident proprietors. Bedrooms are prettily and warmly furnished, and the bars, beamed and paneled, are friendly spots.

Perhaps a little more sophisticated – denoted by the extra star rating awarded by the AA and RAC – is the 16th-century **Manor House Hotel** (tel: (0608) 50501; credit cards: AE, MC, V; **££**) further up the village on the left-hand side of the High Street. Cheerful public rooms with comfortable armchairs and a pleasant dining room reflect the nature of the owners and their dedication to the comfort and well-being of guests. Bedrooms are equally welcoming, whether in the main house or in the modern extension.

If your needs demand no more than a quiet cup of tea, or coffee, yummy pastries or a light snack, then try the **Market House**, 4 High Street, 200 yards beyond the Tourist Information Centre, on the opposite side.

Next stop is **Stow-on-the-Wold** *but, while in Moreton-in-the-Marsh, you may want to take in the* **Batsford Arboretum** *(open: daily 10am-5pm Apr-Nov; admission: adults £1.50, children 75p). If so, as you leave Moreton, turn right on the A44, signposted* **Bourton-on-the-Hill**. *A short way along this road is a turning to the right to* **Batsford Park**.

The notable oriental influence in the Arboretum results from the love Lord Redesdale (who originated the plantings 100 years ago) developed for Japanese trees while at the British Embassy in Tokyo. Many species from other parts of the world have been added by Lord Dulverton in post-war years.

Leaving the gardens, drive back to the main road and turn right on the **A44** *to the junction with the* **A424** *(3 miles from Moreton) where you turn left.* **Stow-on-the-Wold** *is 5 miles from here, and, were you able to see it on your right, Snowshill Manor, with its eccentric collections, would be no more than a mile distant.*

The **A424** *rejoins the* **A429** *just as you enter Stow, and you'll 'dog-leg' over the traffic lights and turn left immediately into the* **High Street**. *At once you're in the wide town square, where you should park, and pass either side of St Edward's Hall, which is in the middle, to reach the Tourist Information Centre which is in* **Talbot Court**, *a narrow passage at the far end of the square, between the Talbot Hotel (built 1714) and Lloyds Bank. The* **Tourist Information Centre** *(Tel: (0451) 31082. Open: Mon-Sat 10am-5:30pm Apr-Oct.*

Closed: lunchtime Nov-Mar), is down on the left, just before you enter Sheep Street.

STOW-ON-THE-WOLD

Of all the medieval Cotswold wool towns, Stow was the busiest and richest, for no other reason than that it lay at the junction of eight roads. The buildings which huddle irregularly around the market square are said to reflect the local maxim 'Stow-on-the-Wold where the wind blows cold'. Here you're 800 feet above sea level; on a chill winter's eve any protection from the prevailing wind is more than welcome. Within the church, which dates from Norman times, Oliver Cromwell imprisoned 1500 Royalist captives during the Civil War.

SHOPPING

Stow is a mecca for antique collectors – and is an entirely appropriate setting – it's difficult to walk far without passing a dealer. Small, but different, is the shop run by **Lilian Middleton**, in Sheep Street. She specializes in antique dolls. If you want to buy, mend, dress or generally refurbish one of your own, she's the girl to see. She sells modern dolls, too, and will ship anywhere. **Huntingdon Antiques Ltd** in Church Street has few small pieces, but the range of period oak, walnut and country furniture, from medieval times to 1740, both English and continental, is staggering. If you buy, you may need a mortgage – one medieval table was £32,000. On the other hand, **Stow Antiques** on the corner of the square, tucked behind the town stocks, has a good, broad range of collectables, especially small silver and porcelain pieces. Owners John and Hazel Hutton-Clarke are only too happy to show the lot. There are two rooms behind those you see through the windows, so go inside and browse.

STOW-ON-THE-WOLD HOTELS

There is no shortage of hotels, at differing price levels in and around this charming little town.

Stow Lodge Hotel, The Square   **££**
Tel: (0451) 30485   Closed: Mid Dec-Jan
Amenities: 🖵 🅿 🍴 🍷   Credit cards: AE, DC

Tucked in a quiet position, off the main square, in its own gardens, this is a modest, unaffected 17th-century hotel, with a welcoming, warm staff. The lounge, which once boasted its own secret priest-hole, has an open stone central fireplace. En suite bedrooms are pleasantly simple and comfortable.

Unicorn Hotel, Sheep Street ££
Tel: (0451) 30257
Amenities: ☎ ⌨ 🅿 ⚒ ⚱   Credit cards: AE, DC, MC, V

A pleasing 17th-century building, with a heavily-beamed lounge and stone fireplace; comfortable, well-appointed bedrooms, with matching covers, drapes, etc. The restaurant, which enjoys a good local reputation, majors in classical English cuisine, but is moderately expensive. The wine list has good range.

Wyck Hill House, Burford Road £££
Tel: (0451) 31936
Amenities: ☎ ⌨ 🅿 ⚒ ⚱   Credit cards: AE, DC, MC, V

*Directions: Take the A424 out of Stow towards **Burford**. The hotel is 2 miles from Stow, on the right.*

This distinctly charming country house hotel was built in 1722 and claims to stand on the remains of a Roman villa. From 1984 until March, 1988, the hotel was owned by three Texans; the new owners have lavished money upon renovation and refurbishment and the result is a gloriously luxurious hotel of impeccable standards. These standards follow through into the lovely dining room and the kitchens – under the able control of well-respected Chef Ian Smith – and are reflected in the traditional menus, though more innovative and exciting dishes are often featured. The wine list is exceptionally good and has depth in red Bordeaux and Burgundy wines, and, nice to see, a very good representation from Beaujolais.

*To pick up the route again for **Bourton-on-the-Water**, your next destination, come out of **Stow Square** to the main road, and turn left. Just ¾ mile after leaving Stow, the road forks, and you take the right-hand road, the **A429** towards **Cirencester**. This follows the line of the old Roman road and is as straight as a die to Bourton, where, 3 miles after leaving Stow, you take a clearly signposted left turn into the town. However, just before reaching this point you will pass a turning to the right for **Lower and Upper Slaughter**. If you have time, do take the short side trip to see those idyllic villages; they're totally unspoiled. You'll come back to the main road at the same point and continue into Bourton-on-the-Water, as before.*

*As you come into the town, the road bends hard left and just beyond the bend, on the left, is a car park. It is easier to leave your car here than to fight for space in the High Street. Walk back to the bend and then turn left into the **High Street**. The River Windrush runs alongside, not more than an attractive stream at this point, transversed by several pretty little footbridges.*

There isn't a Tourist Information Centre in Bourton, but the TIC in Stow-on-the-Wold will be able to help with questions on this village.

BOURTON-ON-THE-WATER

This lovely small village with its six bridges over the Windrush is often called the Venice of the Cotswolds. The Windrush has played a vital role in the town's development. The road from Stow-on-the-Wold was the Roman Fosse Way and at the precise point where you turned to come into the village the Romans had a posting house and a bridge over the river.

By the 12th Century there were three mills in the village and it's possible that the Windrush was diverted to its present course then to provide power for these.

Most of the solidly built houses with their honeyed sandstone exteriors date from the 17th century. When the railroad came to town (1862) Bourton became a popular retirement retreat for the well-to-do. With the advent of the car after WWI the town became what it is today – a favorite day trip for British and overseas visitors alike.

SHOPPING

This is inevitably limited in a small town of this size but you should pay a visit to the **Cotswold Perfumery** in Victoria Street, near the river. They make all their own perfumes. It's fun to see it being done, and to see them tending the flowers they use. There's also an exhibition, which will probably have special interest for the ladies. They ship worldwide.

Close to the perfumery is **Studio Antiques**, housed in what used to be an old pub – it still has a minstrels' gallery. Some very good pieces among a broad range of furniture, collectables and odds and ends: this is a place that's fun to browse through.

BOURTON-ON-THE-WATER RESTAURANTS

You may want no more than a bolstering cup of coffee, or – that great reviver of the British – a pot of tea. There's no better spot than the **Small Talk Tea Room** (tel: (0451) 21596; no credit cards; **£**) which is in the High Street, but almost hidden, near the War Memorial. A good range of homemade pastries, supplemented by imaginative light lunchtime snacks, served in a tiny little beamed room, with clean, fresh lace tablecloths and chunky country crockery.

If it's dinner you want, you won't better the **Rose Tree Restaurant** (tel: (0541) 20635; credit cards: AE, DC, MC, V; **££**) run by Ann and John Hicks, on the other side of the river and virtually on its bank. Small, with no claims to magnificence, it offers a choice of two very good set menus and a wine list that would put many sophisticated restaurants to shame. Good to see Wente whites from the Napa Valley, and at least one super Coonawarra Estate red from Australia, as well as a remarkable selection from English vineyards. Incidentally, there's a wine shop at the back, so if you like what you drank, take a bottle home with you. If you happen to be here in the evening, when the village is lit up, it's a little like fairyland with the reflections in the water.

*You now aim for **Northleach**, so drive back the ¾ mile to the **A429** and turn left at the T-junction (signposted **Cirencester**). Again, you're on the old Roman route (ignore the right-hand fork to Cheltenham) and the straight road undulates its way through rich farmland, the soil picking up a reddish color as you travel southwest. Soon you cross the main **A40** Oxford/Cheltenham road and, shortly after, you follow a gentle hill down into Northleach. At the bottom is a set of traffic lights (the only ones you'll meet) and immediately before these, on the right, is the entrance to the **Cotswold Countryside Collection** (open: Mon-Sat 10am-5:30pm, Sun 2pm-5:30pm Apr-Oct; admission: adults 60p, children 30p). This is a rural life museum and well worth an hour. The staff also run the **Tourist Information Centre** (Tel: (0451) 60715. Open: Mon-Sat 10am-5:30pm, Sun 2pm-5:30pm Apr-Oct) from the same counter.*

Immediately beyond the lights, turn left into Northleach (leaving the Amoco gas station on your left) and in a ¼ mile, you'll be in the center of the village.

Park in the **Market Place**, and walk on the few yards to Keith Harding's **World of Mechanical Music** (open: daily 10am-6pm; admission: adults £1.50, children £1). There's a small shop on the left, with an equally small museum in back. Keith adores what is both hobby and work and he'll be delighted to tell you about the antique clocks, musical boxes, automata and musical instruments he has on show and for sale. He sells a neat little musical gift box for only £3.50.

*For **Burford**, your next stop, follow the road straight through Northleach; after 1¼ miles the road swings very sharply left and you then join the main **A40**, where you turn right towards **Oxford**. Five miles along, through pleasing open, rolling country, you'll pass the **Inn for all Seasons** on your left. This pub, run by amiable John Sharp and his wife, makes a welcome stop for coffee, pub lunch, or, indeed, a reasonably-priced evening meal. Another 3 miles and you'll enter Burford, where, at the traffic circle, the left exit will take you down the hill into the town center. At the far end, on the right, and clearly signposted, is a car park, the entrance to which winds past the lovely old parish church. In the car park is a dispensing machine for local tourist information (50p); it's wise to take one, since the **Tourist Information Centre**, The Brewery, **Sheep Street** (Tel: (099382) 3558. Open: Mon-Fri 9:30am-1pm, 2pm-4:45pm, Sat 9:30am-12:45pm, Apr-Oct. Opening times vary Nov-Mar) quaintly located in a wine merchant's shop at the top end of Sheep Street, is manned on a casual basis and closes for lunch.*

BURFORD

Most of Burford lies on the long High Street. Walk up the hill away from the church and car park. On left and right Tudor houses intermingle with Georgian façades. Among the oldest are the **Bear Inn** and the **Grammar School**, both 15th-century, and the **Crown Inn** and **Bull Inn**, dating from the 16th century. The town is thought to have been the scene of a church assembly in 683, attended by the King of Mercia. The present church dates from Norman times and is one of the largest in the county of Oxfordshire. Standing apart from the town, beside the water meadows, the church has been flooded several times by a swollen River Windrush.

SHOPPING

As with many Cotswold towns, antique shops dominate. There are several in the High Street of a general nature but, for those of you with sporting bent, **Crypt Antiques** offer fishing tackle and golf collectables, while **Peter Norden** specializes in period firearms (especially blunderbusses) and armor. At the top of the town, on the traffic circle, the **Burford Antiques Centre**, housed, somewhat paradoxically, in a modern building, has several dealers who offer a wide range, from collectables to furniture of various periods.

BURFORD RESTAURANTS

Burford is not a gourmet center and, apart from the **Bay Tree Hotel**, food tends to be of average standard. That is not to say you can't eat well at this level at the pubs in the High Street, but **The Lamb**, in Sheep Street, might have the edge, because it's reputed to serve the best pint in town of 6X (Wadworths Brewery's much admired brew).

BURFORD HOTEL

Bay Tree Hotel, Sheep Street ££
Tel: (0993) 823137
Amenities: ☎ ⌨ 🅿 🍴 🍷   Credit cards: AE, DC, MC, V

This exceptional Tudor building, dating from 1580, and the home of Sir Lawrence Tanfield, Queen Elizabeth I's despised Lord Chief Baron of the Exchequer, has recently been sold. The new owners are bent upon improving it even further. Apart from the appealing, beamed rooms in the main building, there are delightful suites in converted adjoining premises – Stable Cottage, 1580; Miller's Cottage, 1750. Public rooms are heavily beamed, with period antiques. Chef Paul Evans provides interesting variations on traditional themes (roast brace of quail, cooked with honey and a cider sauce, for example) and at moderate prices. Good wine list.

AROUND AND ABOUT

The Cotswold Wildlife Park
Open: Daily 10am-6pm (or dusk if earlier)
Admission: Adults £2.70, children £1.60

Directions: The park is just under 2 miles from Burford, crossing over the traffic circle at the top of the town, onto the A361. It's a simple, straight journey and the entrance is just beyond the hospital, to your right. After turning right, the gates are about 100 yards along on your left.

Arranged around a manor house, there are 120 acres of enclosures (for the dangerous animals, such as tigers, leopards), paddocks (rhinos, zebras, ostriches) and a walled garden housing aviaries and some of the smaller animals. Tropical, reptile and butterfly houses, as well as an aquarium, complete the wildlife picture. There are also extensive gardens. Try your hand at brass rubbing in the manor house itself. There's a basic restaurant, bar and refreshment facilities.

*To continue, come back to the traffic island at **Burford** and take the **A40** to **Oxford**. After a few miles, the road becomes two-lane, but, 9 miles from Burford, narrows again to single lane. As you enter Oxford, exactly 15 miles after leaving Burford, there's a traffic circle, where you turn right into **Woodstock Road** and you'll follow signs for the **city center**, 2½ miles on. Note that from here the left-hand lane is for city buses and taxis only. You'll pass Radcliffe Infirmary on the right, and immediately the road will widen out into a stretch known as **St Giles**.*

*You'll see the **Randolph Hotel** up on the right; turn right here, leaving the hotel on your left and the **Ashmolean Museum** on your right. This is **Beaumont Street**, and immediately past the hotel on the left is parking (under the bus station). If this is full, continue to the end of the street and, at the junction with **Worcester Street**, turn left, and there's parking at the end of the street, on the right. Either car park leaves you within a few minutes' walk of St Aldate's, where, opposite the Town Hall, you'll see the **Tourist Information Centre** at **Carfax** (Tel: (0865) 726871. Open: Mon-Sat 9am (Tues 9:30am)-5:30pm; Sun and Bank Holidays as well in summer 10:30am-1pm, 1:30pm-4pm). This is run by very professional and helpful staff.*

*Although we have given you directions on parking in the city center, you may have difficulty finding space, especially if you arrive mid-afternoon, mid-season. Oxford operates a flat-rate (50p) bus service from four '**park and ride**' free car parks on the edge of the city. The buses run Mon-Fri 7:30am-6:30pm, Sat 8:30am-6:30pm; accompanied children under 16 ride free. Arriving from Burford on the A40, the nearest 'park and ride' is at **Pear Tree Car Park**. As you* *approach the outskirts of Oxford, you come to a traffic circle signposted left to **Woodstock** and **Stratford** (**A43**, then **A34**). Take this road; the car park is less than half a mile along on the right.*

OXFORD

Oxford is the oldest seat of learning in Britain. The city began in the 8th century with the foundation of a nunnery. By 1214 a university had been established – but don't go looking for it. It is not any one place or building but a collection of colleges: 40 of them in all. Enquire after the University and you may get withering looks. Almost all of the colleges allow visitors to wander around their quadrangles, chapels, halls and gardens. Catch them out of term and out of high tourist season and you can often stand silent in a quad, a distant bell ringing, and imagine yourself 400 years back in time. Full details of opening times (mostly in the afternoon) for all colleges are to be found in *Welcome to Oxford*, a leaflet which you can buy for 40p from the Tourist Information Centre.

The city has something of interest, something of beauty at almost every corner. Hundreds of famous artists, writers, scientists and politicians have studied here. If you want to follow in the footsteps of literary giants, pick up a free booklet, ***Blackwell's Literary Heritage Trails***, at Blackwell's Bookshop in Broad Street. Some of Oxford's 'watering-holes' trade as much on their literary connections as their beer. **The Lamb & Flag** in St Giles is where C.S. Lewis and J.R. Tolkien met regularly in the 1950s and 60s. You ought not to miss the **Turf Tavern**, just off Bath Place, which is famous for its steak sandwiches and mixed clientele of town and gown.

There are 653 listed buildings (that means that they're of sufficient historic interest to merit protection from change), so you'll appreciate that to 'do' Oxford in full would take around a year. Choosing which colleges to visit is probably a matter of personal taste, but there are the 'greats' which appear on almost everyone's list.

Christ Church is one of these. Strictly speaking, it is not Christ Church College, but the House of Christ. In 1523 Cardinal Wolsey, then the most powerful man in England, dissolved 22 monasteries in order to fund the foundation of a college at Oxford. It was to be the greatest and the grandest, something of which remains in **Tom Quad**, the largest in Oxford. In the 16th century the priory church adjoining the college became the city's **Cathedral**. It was restored in 1870, with a new entrance from the east side of Tom Quad. As cathedrals go, it is tiny, but seems large because of the great height of soaring arches capping the narrow nave. Christ Church has a second, smaller quad, the exquisite **Peckwater Quad**, a perfect example of early 18th-century Palladian architecture. Listen at five minutes past nine each evening for the bell of **Tom Tower**, which rings 101 times, calling what was the original complement of Christ

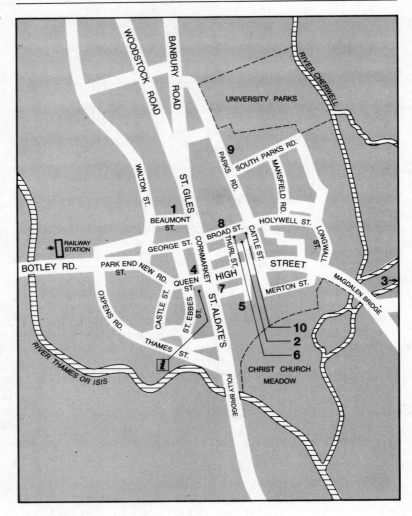

OXFORD

 Tourist Information Centre
1 Ashmolean Museum
2 Bodleian Library and
Divinity School
3 Botanic Gardens
4 Carfax Tower
5 Christ Church
Picture Gallery

6 Museum of the History
of Science
7 Museum of Oxford
8 The Oxford Story
9 Oxford University
Museum
10 Sheldonian Theatre

Church students back to college before the doors were shut.

Alongside Christ Church and its cathedral is **Christ Church Meadow** (open: daily 7am-dusk), a piece of countryside in the city center, its two main walks leading through avenues of trees to the Rivers Isis and Cherwell. Nearby is **Merton College**, whose statute was approved in 1264, which makes it the oldest foundation in Oxford to have 'collegiate form and stature'. Merton has one of the oldest libraries in England, dating from 1370. The library, along with the rooms used by celebrated Merton undergraduate, Max Beerbohm, is open to the public, as are the quadrangles (the 14th-century **Mob Quad** is the oldest in Oxford) and chapel, where music recitals are often held.

Across High Street, **New College** (not at all new, but founded in 1379) has the grimmest, and most purely medieval approach of any in Oxford. Past towering walls, you emerge through the gatehouse into the largely 14th-century **Great Quad**. Move on to the **Cloister Quad**, arguably the loveliest in Oxford, its northern wall part of the ancient city wall. Both the hall and chapel date from 1386, and the gardens are stunning.

WHAT TO SEE

Ashmolean Museum, Beaumont Street
Open: Tues-Sat 10am-4pm, Sun 2pm-4pm
Free admission

This is Britain's oldest public museum. It opened in 1683, sixty years before the British Museum, to display the collection of Elias Ashmole. Gradually the collection grew to include great treasures and relics belonging to the University. The present building, a massive, classical affair of the 1840s, now houses a remarkably rich hoard: a major collection of Michelangelo drawings, Italian, Dutch, Flemish, French and English oil paintings, sculptures and bronzes, a collection of European silver and, among the many British antiquities, the celebrated ninth-century Alfred Jewel . . . all just a small part of the treasures inside.

Bodleian Library and Divinity School, Catte Street
Open: Mon-Fri 9am-5pm, Sat 9am-12:30pm
Admission: Tours: Adults and children over 14 years £2; younger
          children not admitted

This ancient group of buildings includes the Duke of Humphrey's Library, the Divinity School, built between 1420 and 1490, and the old schools, whose names are painted above the wooden doors in the Schools Quadrangle. Tours of their interior take place Mon-Fri 10:30am, 11:30am, 2:00pm and 3:00pm; Sat 10:30am and 11:30am only.

Botanic Garden, High Street
Open: Mon-Sat 8:30am-5pm, Sun 10am-noon, 2pm-6pm, Apr-Oct;
      Mon-Sat 8am-4:30pm, Sun 2pm-4:30pm Nov-Mar. Glass-
      houses open daily 2pm-4pm
Free admission

Originally known as the Physic Gardens, these were laid out in 1621, in order to grow medicinal herbs. They no longer fulfill that role, but the basic design is the same, with extensions that lead to grassy paths along the River Cherwell. This is a good place to take a rest from sightseeing. You can sit on the riverbank and gaze up at Magdalen Tower from which the choir sings at dawn on May Day morning.

Carfax Tower, Carfax
Open: Daily 10am-6pm Mar 18-Oct 22; Daily 10am-4pm Oct 23-
      Nov 19   Closed: Nov 20-Mar 17
Free admission

Climb to the top of Carfax Tower for stunning views of the city's spires and rooftops.

Christ Church Picture Gallery, (entrance in Oriel Square)
Open: Mon-Sat 10:30am-1pm, 2pm-5:30pm, Sun 2pm-5:30pm
      (closes at 4:30pm Oct-Mar)
Admission: Adults 40p, children 20p

If you have only a short time free to stand and gaze at beautiful paintings, this is the place to be. Among the important Old Master paintings are Van Dyck's 'Continents of Scipio' and Carracci's 'The Butcher's Shop'.

Museum of the History of Science, Broad Street
Open: Mon-Fri 10:30am-1pm, 2:30pm-4pm
Free admission

Remarkable collection of early scientific instruments housed in the original building (1678-83) for the Ashmolean collection.

Museum of Oxford, St Aldates
Open: Tues-Sat 10am-5pm
Free admission

Directly opposite the Tourist Information Centre, this museum occupies part of the Town Hall and provides a good, free introduction to the city's history.

The Oxford Story, Broad Street
Open: Daily 9am-5:30pm
Admission: Adults £2, children £1

Oxford's newest tourist attraction combines full-scale models and audio-visual technology to give you a lively look at eight centuries of university life. This is a good way to get some historical perspective of events in Oxford.

Oxford University Museum, Parks Road
Open: Mon-Sat noon-5pm
Free admission

This is off the beaten track, on the way towards the University Parks, but you can't miss it; the museum occupies a massive, Victorian Gothic building. The collections are all related to natural history.

Sheldonian Theatre, Catte Street
Open: Mon-Sat 10am-12:45pm, 2pm-4:45pm (closes at 3:45pm
    Dec-Feb)
Free admission

This is not a proper theater but a large assembly hall where many of the University ceremonies take place, including the granting of degrees. It was built in 1663 and is one of the earliest and best works of Sir Christopher Wren. The building is often used for musical recitals. For details contact **Music of Oxford** (Tel: (0865) 864056) and **Oxford Pro Musica** (Tel: (0865) 240358).

SHOPPING

Oxford offers a wide range of shops, many of them branches of nationwide multiples (for example **Debenhams** and **Jaeger**, in Magdalen – pronounced 'Mawdlen' – Street), but there are also plenty of highly individual shops. There's no early closing day in Oxford, although, as elsewhere, some of the antique dealers may close for lunch. Major stores, including **Marks & Spencer**, 13-18 Queen Street, and **Selfridges**, 27 Westgate Centre, stay open late (until around 8 or 8:30pm) in December, but at other times of the year hours are normally 9am to 5:30 or 6pm. Only shopping hours that deviate from the norm are listed below.

If books fascinate you, or you're unable to find a title elsewhere, search out either **Blackwell's**, 50 Broad Street, the traditional homing place for literati, with 200,000 titles in 16 departments on three floors, or Oxford-newcomer, **Dillons**, on the corner of Broad Street and Cornmarket Street. Both bookstores stay open until 9pm on weekdays and open on Sundays 10am to 5pm.

Not far away, off Cornmarket Street, is the **Golden Cross Shopping Arcade**, a group of boutique shops offering men's and women's wear, leather goods, gifts etc., in a converted complex of medieval, 15th- and 17th-century buildings. This leads into the **Covered Market** (open: Mon-Sat 8am-5:30pm) where more than

40 traders offer a wide range of game, meats, pies, fruits, vegetables, flowers and so on. The market hall was built in 1774 to provide a permanent home for Oxford's untidy market stalls. It is surprisingly light and airy, with what are now permanent shops divided into four avenues. Visit **Next to Nothing** for trendy womenswear. Look for **Ben's Cookies** in Avenue 3: freshly baked throughout the day, they're hard to resist. If you're after a proper lunch, try **Le Bistro du Marché** or **Casa Blanca**, see page 395.

Alice's Shop, 85 St Aldates
Open: Mon-Sat 9:30am-5pm, Sun 10am-3pm summer; Mon-Sat
        10am-4:30pm winter
Credit cards: v

In one of the oldest buildings in Oxford (it dates back to the 15th century), the shop is linked with *Alice in Wonderland*, the fabulous tale by Lewis Carroll, because the real Alice, daughter of the Dean of Christ Church, used to buy her barley-sugars (candy) here. Carroll wove the shop into his story, transforming the old lady who kept it into the old sheep knitting with a multitude of needles. Now you can buy 'Alice in Wonderland' memorabilia, including dolls, T-shirts, china and collectors' plates and chess sets.

Chico, 136 High Street and 16 Golden Cross Walk
Credit cards: AE, DC, MC, V

Top quality casual wear for men and women from both British and European designers, including Fair Isle sweaters, co-ordinated separates from Golf Club and Parks, and ties by Ticky Tack.

Crabtree & Evelyn, 45 Queen Street
Credit cards: AE, MC, V

The same fruits, herbs and flowers that have been used for centuries in the stillrooms of English country houses form the base of this collection of toiletries and comestibles. The fragrance inside this little store is compelling. Everything comes direct from nature, including the English rose pot-pourri, the jams, preserves and sweet-smelling soaps. Pretty packaging.

House of Tweed, 90 High Street
Open: also Sun 10am-5.30pm summer only
Credit cards: AE, DC, MC, V

This is one of a chain of stores (other branches at 2 Woodstock Road and 18 Broad Street) selling high quality kilts, skirts, cashmere, lambswool, Shetland, Aran, Icelandic, Scottish and designer knitwear. They also stock some Burberry coats and accessories, lambswool and cashmere scarves and gloves. The High Street store incorporates **Raffles Tea Rooms**, serving hot and cold dishes, gâteaux, pastries and traditional cream teas. No smoking.

Oxford Antiques Omnibus, George Street
Open: Wed-Sat 10:30am-4:30pm
Credit cards: Varies with dealer

An underground treasure trove (it occupies the basement of Omni Store), this is the place to browse. There's a wide range of stalls selling everything from antique jewelry to period costumes, antiquarian books, paintings, china and glass.

Oxford Gallery, 23 High Street
Open: Mon-Sat 10am-5pm
Credit cards: AE, DC, MC, V

Exciting showcase for the work of British craftsmen, including jewelers, textile designers and graphic artists. New exhibitions every month, plus an international collection of limited edition prints. They'll ship worldwide.

Oxford Print Shop, 46c Richmond Road (off Walton Street)
Open: Tues-Sat 10:30am-5pm, Sun 11am-5pm
No credit cards

Good range of paintings and prints of Oxford.

Payne & Son (Goldsmiths), 131 High Street
Open: Mon-Sat 8:30am-1pm, 2pm-5pm
Credit cards: AE, DC, MC, V

Founded in 1790, this family-run business sells a wide range of antique and modern silver. They also specialize in rare and unusual gemstones such as tourmaline, pink and yellow sapphires and golden beryl.

Rainbow & Spoon, 22 Park End Street
Open: Mon-Sat 10am-5:30pm
Credit cards: MC, V

Lively fashion store with young British designers' wear, casual and formal clothes, including a large selection of ball gowns, many of which are hand-painted.

Shepherd & Woodward, 109-114 High Street
Open: Mon-Fri 8:30am-5:30pm, Sat 8:45am-5:30pm
Credit cards: AE, MC, V

This privately-owned store supplies the University with robes, gowns, college ties and so on. There's a huge selection of good quality British menswear, plus University T-shirts and sweatshirts for those who have been 'up at Oxford' for only a day or so.

OXFORD RESTAURANTS

As in many university towns, Oxford has an abundance of inexpensive and moderately priced restaurants, wine bars and pubs. Four of our favorites are **Baedekers, Browns** and the twin restaurants, **Casa Blanca** and **Le Bistro du Marché**, in the covered market. For really splendid meals we've also listed three restaurants which are our best bets.

Baedekers, 43A Connaught Street   £
Tel: (0865) 242063
Open: Mon-Sat noon-11pm, Sun noon-2:30pm, 7pm-10:30pm
Credit cards: MC, V

Ascend the modern stairs to the sound of modern (but modulated) jazz to find this second story oasis of outstanding food in the heart of town. Off to your left there's a modern circular bar while to your right there's a two-level floor plan designed like the decks of a yacht – steel railings, canvas panels, brass fittings and hardwood floor. Tables, each with a single flower, tulips when we were there, are well spaced. The muted, modern decor has track spotlights for constantly changed art exhibits.

The choice of dishes is equally eclectic. Starters include *nachos* (£2.15), chicken *satay* and sublime crispy Peking duck (£4.75 per quarter). While main courses include Cajun baked shark steak (£6.95) and 'The Best Hamburger Ever' (a ½lb of great ground round for £4.95).

For something lighter their soup and salads are delicious, their pastrami on rye (£2.95) and tuna melt (£3.95) generous in the extreme. Super selection of beers, including Dos Equis, and reasonably priced wines including some unusual finds such as Cousiño Macul Chardonnay '86, a lovely dry white from Chile. Service is efficient and very friendly. Baedekers is, as its namesake guides would put it, not to be missed.

Browns, 5 Woodstock Road   £
Tel: (0865) 511995
Open: Daily 11am-11:30pm, Sun from noon   Closed: Dec 24-26
No credit cards

This is what the new 'theme' restaurant chains try to accomplish and never do. This large, airy restaurant is loaded with leafy ferns and funky wall decorations. The food is fresh, simply prepared and delicious. Portions are more than ample as befits the partly student clientele but the restaurant is equally popular with all walks of local life – including moms with toddlers in tow taking tea while a pianist tickles the ivories in the background. This is also a best bet for lunch. Their house wines are excellent value for money.

Le Bistro du Marché, 9A High Street, 1st Floor in Covered Market
£

Tel: (0865) 723342
Open: Daily 9:30am-11pm
Credit cards: AE, DC, MC, V

Ideal for morning café au lait and a croissant or one of their delicious pastries, this charming bistro also serves delicious crêpes, pasta dishes (such as their *tagliatelle aux 4 formages* – tagliatelle pasta with spinach, cream and four cheeses) and a great *cassoulet* at lunch. In the evening French provincial cooking is the order of the bill. For shoppers its location, right in the covered market, is ideal.

Casa Blanca, 2nd Floor, Market Avenue 1 in the Covered Market
(Cornmarket Street and High Street)   ££
Tel: (0865) 791198
Open: Daily noon-2:30pm, 7pm-10:30pm
Credit cards: AE, DC, MC, V

Rather more refined than its downstairs sister, the emphasis here is on oriental and classic French cuisine in whitewashed surroundings. We recommend their *soupe de poisson du marché* (fresh fish soup with ingredients from the nearby market) and their *suprême de volaille à l'Indienne* – chicken in a creamy curry sauce with apples and bananas.

Le Petit Blanc, 61A Banbury Road, Summertown   £££
Tel: (0865) 53540
Open: Daily 12:15pm-2:15pm, 7:15pm-10:30pm   Closed: Tues
Credit cards: MC, V

In the unusual setting of a Victorian conservatory, this exceptionally good restaurant is 100 per cent French, from Chef-patron Bruno Loubet to the formally-dressed young staff. Inspired variations of classical French dishes combine simplicity with ingenious invention, so as to make selection a nail-biting, difficult exercise, but whatever you choose the probability is you won't be disappointed. As one might expect, the wine list betrays Gallic prejudice, but it's superb – if expensive beyond the bottom range.

Restaurant Elizabeth, 85 St Aldates   £££
Tel: (0865) 242230
Open: Daily 12:30pm-2:30pm, 6:30pm-11pm (Sun 7pm-10:30pm)
Closed: Mon
Credit cards: AE, DC, V

Not far beyond the Tourist Information Centre, on the same side of the road and opposite the end of Christ Church College, up on the second floor, Antonio Lopez has stamped his warm personality on this intimate restaurant since 1958. The conspiratorial, dark-paneled restaurant and adjoining bar with ornate ceiling and marble fireplace provide a rich setting for the consistent, traditional cuisine – *piperade* or salmon *quenelles* to start, perhaps, and then partridge or grouse, if the season's right, with delectable candied chestnuts in kirsch to close – or, if you're adapting to that great European custom – a selection from the tempting cheese board. The wine list is exceptionally good in parts.

La Sorbonne, 130A High Street (in the side passage) £££
Tel: (0865) 241320
Open: Mon-Sat noon-2:15pm, 6pm-10:30pm; Sun noon-2pm,
    6pm-10pm   Closed: Public holidays, 2 wks Aug
Credit cards: MC, V

This restaurant is in Kemp House, also known as Boswell's House – built in 1637 and one of the best-preserved examples of its type in Oxford. Allowing for the mildly-irritating, Gallic self-congratulation of Chef-patron André Chavagnon, who opened the restaurant in 1966, the standard of classic French cuisine is good and specialties include an enticing *rable de lièvre, sauce poivrade*, and the soufflé Rothschild is exquisite. The wine list is good. For name-droppers, there's no shortage of distinguished previous guests – HRH The Princess Royal, HRH King Hussein, Fonteyn, Nureyev, etc., etc., etc.

OXFORD HOTELS

There are fine country hotels in villages around the city, most of them a good half-hour's drive from the center of Oxford. Two hotels to the northeast of Oxford, plus those in Woodstock, can be reached in rather less than 30 minutes. Details of these follow the Oxford hotels.

Ladbroke Linton Lodge Hotel, Linton Road £££
Tel: (0865) 53461
Amenities: ☎ ⬜ 🅿 ⁇ ⏛   Credit cards: AE, DC, MC, V

Directions: Leave the city center via St Giles. Keep right, and as St Giles divides into two roads, take the right-hand route onto the Banbury Road (A4165). Linton Road is a right-hand turn off the Banbury Road, less than 1 mile on.

This busy hotel has been refurbished to the standards required by businessmen, who number heavily among its guests. What it may lack in charm is certainly compensated for by the friendly staff.

Oxford Moat House, Wolvercote Roundabout ££
Tel: (0865) 59933
Amenities: ☎ ⬜ 🅿 ⁇ ⏛ ≋   Credit cards: AE, DC, MC, V

*Directions: At the northern end of **St Giles**, keep left and take the **Woodstock Road (A4144)** until the next traffic circle.*

This is a fairly large, bright, open-plan, modern hotel where the more active can take advantage of their many indoor and outdoor leisure facilities. Rooms are fair-sized and light and the staff mainly young and helpful. Coffee shop.

Randolph Hotel, Beaumont Street   **£££**
Tel: (0865) 247184
Amenities: ☎ ⌨ 🅿 ⛏ 🍷 ◉ (some)   Credit cards: AE, DC, MC, V

This Victorian Gothic hotel has for years had an old-fashioned, as opposed to traditional, image, and has tended to be more popular with parents than students. However, large sums of money have been, and are being, spent on updating the public rooms. These improvements, with a more helpful attitude from the staff, are making the best of the great deal that this splendid building has to offer.

HOTELS OUTSIDE OXFORD

Studley Priory Hotel, Horton-cum-Studley   **£££**
Tel: (086 735) 203
Amenities: ☎ ⌨ 🅿 ⛏ 🍷   Credit cards: AE, DC, MC, V

*Directions: At the northern end of **St Giles**, keep right and take the **Banbury Road (A4165)**. At the next traffic circle turn right on to the **A40**, signposted **London**. Continue for 2 miles and at the next traffic circle (the Headington Roundabout) take the first left. This is a minor road, the houses dwindling fast as you move out into country-side. At the crossroads with the **B4027** continue straight ahead and follow the signs to **Horton-cum-Studley**. The hotel is on your right just before the village.*

This Elizabethan manor house was converted from a Benedictine nunnery in 1540 and was then a family home for 300 years. It is now a family owned and run hotel, the ancient rooms, some lined with Jacobean paneling, dotted with antiques. The restaurant special-izes in *cuisine moderne* and has an extensive wine list.

Weston Manor Hotel, Weston-on-the-Green   **£££**
Tel: (0869) 50621
Amenities: ☎ ⌨ 🅿 ⛏ 🍷 ≈   Credit cards: AE, DC, MC, V

*Directions: At the northern end of **St Giles**, keep right and take the **Banbury Road (A4165)**. At the first traffic circle (intersecting with the **A40**) continue straight ahead. About 1 mile on, turn right at the next traffic circle, signposted **Bicester (A43)**. After 3 miles you come to another traffic circle. Continue straight ahead towards Bicester on what is now the **A421**. The entrance to the hotel drive is about 500* yards on, to your left.

This has all the atmosphere of a country house, although the building is part ancient Priory, part manor and once the property of Henry VIII. The oak-paneled restaurant has a minstrels' gallery. Stylish, very individual bedrooms, with lots of character.

See also hotels in **Woodstock**, page 400.

OXFORD TO WOODSTOCK (about 9 miles)

*Leave Oxford by forking left at the top of **St Giles**, by the church, onto the **Woodstock Road** (i.e. the same route as you entered). After 2¹/₂ miles you'll come to the Wolvercote traffic circle (by the Oxford Moat House Hotel); cross straight over, following the signpost **Woodstock 5 miles (A34)**. **Blenheim Palace** is also clearly indicated. About ¹/₂ mile on, at the next traffic circle, take the second exit (**A34**) and at the next traffic circle, 1 mile on, with the Grapes pub on your right, go straight on to Woodstock. After ¹/₂ mile there's another traffic circle; again go straight over. The road now becomes two-lane and traffic speeds up a little; after ¹/₂ mile, at **Begbroke**, there is another traffic circle which you'll cross straight over (there's a Texaco gas station on your right). Continue on past Kidlington airport, on your right, and at the traffic circle, cross straight over (Woodstock and Blenheim Palace clearly signposted). The road now narrows to single lane again and ¹/₂ mile further on you'll enter Woodstock and a sign will tell you that Blenheim Palace is 300 yards further along on the left. For the village, continue on past the main gate to the traffic lights, where you turn right into **Hensington Road**, at the end of which, by the fire station, is a car park and the **Tourist Information Centre** (Tel: (0993) 811038. Open: Mon-Sat 9:30am-1pm, 2pm-5:30pm). Walk back to the traffic lights and cross straight over into the village center.*

WOODSTOCK

Rather belatedly, since so many of the fine Georgian buildings now have modern, uglier neighbors, the center of Woodstock has been designated a Conservation Area. Its origins go back to the 12th century when Henry I created the town to rehouse people he had evicted from a nearby hunting park. The **Marlborough Hotel** conceals what remains of Woodstock's 18th-century Assembly Rooms, but the **Town Hall**, built in Palladian Style in 1766, is there for all to see. Dotted among the honey-colored stone houses are many antique and crafts shops, but Woodstock's greatest attraction is Blenheim Palace. The entrance to the grounds and palace is right in the center of the town.

WHAT TO SEE

Blenheim Palace

Open: Daily 10:30am-6pm (last entry 5pm) mid Mar-Oct
Admission: Adults £4.25, children £2, covers park, palace, exhibition, butterfly house and car parking

The Palace is Britain's largest house. Designed by Sir John Vanbrugh, it was a gift from Queen Anne on behalf of a 'grateful nation' to the first Duke of Marlborough after his victory over the French and Bavarians at Blenheim in 1704. Today it is the home of the 11th Duke of Marlborough. The Palace contains a very fine collection of furniture, tapestries and paintings as well as a permanent exhibition devoted to the life and times of Sir Winston Churchill, who was born here. The two thousand acre gardens were landscaped in the late 18th century by 'Capability Brown'.

Oxfordshire County Museum, Park Street

Open: Mon-Fri 10am-5pm, Sat 10am-6pm, Sun 2pm-6pm May-Sep; Tues-Fri 10am-4pm, Sat 10am-5pm, Sun 2pm-5pm Oct-Apr
Free admission

This collection shows the crafts, industry and domestic life of the Oxford region since Neolithic times, and is housed in the 16th-century Fletchers House. On your way in, notice the curious, five-hole stocks.

SHOPPING

Inevitably, there are antique shops, but you may be 'antiqued out' by now. If you want to get togged up with good English country clothes, however, visit Mr D.J. Connelly at **Country Flair**, 2 Market Street. Up-market clothes, Barbours, etc. which you can also buy on Sundays, 2:15pm-6pm.

WOODSTOCK RESTAURANTS

The Feathers Restaurant, £££ (see page 400) offers excellent lunch and dinner set menus. An excursion into the à la carte section is tempting, though many dishes find their way onto the set menu, perhaps in different form, as it changes daily. Parcels of wild mushrooms and English brie (why isn't that name protected?) wrapped in filo pastry with a cream sorrel sauce is a good way to start and who cares what follows, even if it is no less tempting? The wine list is extensive and expensive, though there are one or two very drinkable bottles at less than £10.

If you want something more modest, try **Brothertons Brasserie** (tel: (0993) 811 114; credit cards: AE, MC, V; £), 1 High Street, which specializes in unusual, and very tasty, light meals, but they keep eccentric hours: 10:30am-noon for coffee, 12:30pm-2:30pm lunch, 3:30pm-5:30pm afternoon teas, 7pm-10:30pm supper. **Ye Anciente House** (tel: (0993) 811 231; no credit cards; **£**) is a traditional tea and coffee shop, with delectable pastries, fresh jellies and honey. It's somewhat bizarrely named, even for a building built in 1627, but it's clean, fresh and welcoming (open: Mon-Sat 8am-5pm).

WOODSTOCK HOTELS

The Feathers Hotel, Market Street   **££**
Tel: (0993) 812291
Amenities: ☎ ⛁ ⴹⵎ ♉   Credit cards: AE, DC, MC, V

All the signs of a well-run, family controlled, establishment, right from the initial warm welcome. There are two lounges – one with the personal intimacy of a comfortable private sitting room, the other, beamed and paneled, reminding you of its 17th-century origins. Bedrooms have individual style, are delightfully furnished, and have luxurious bathrooms.

The Bear Hotel, Park Street   **£££**
Tel: (0993) 811511
Amenities: ☎ ⛁ 🅿 ⴹⵎ ♉ ◎   Credit cards: AE, DC, MC, V

It's difficult not to be overwhelmed by the well-preserved antiquity of this lovely building – manifested in the flagstone entrance, beamed bars, restaurants and public areas – a scene repeated in many of the bedrooms, of which some of the more expensive have four-posters and cathedral ceilings. Antiques and opulence abound, but, lovely though it is, there's a lack of the intimacy found at The Feathers.

If you'd like to continue your tour to **St Albans** visiting **Woburn Abbey** and **Luton Hoo** see **page 292**. Or, if you prefer to return to London follow the directions below.

WOODSTOCK TO LONDON   (about 66 miles)

*From the **Hensington Road car park** go out past the public toilets on the right and the police station on the left and at the top turn right into **Hensington Road**. Go to the end and turn left by the Punch Bowl Inn. This is the A34. Take the A34 through Woodstock southerly to the A40 then the A40 joins with the **M40** signposted **London**.*

TOUR 3: EXPLORING DEVON AND CORNWALL
(about 430 miles)

This tour continues on from Longer Tour 1: **Great Cathedral Cities and Regency Bath** (see **page 312**).

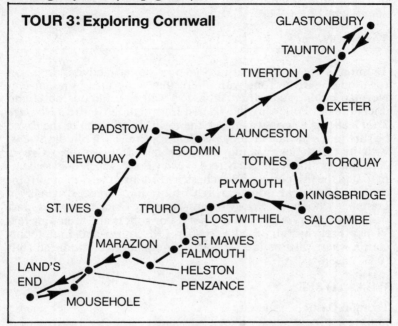

TOUR 3: Exploring Cornwall

GLASTONBURY
TAUNTON
TIVERTON
EXETER
PADSTOW
LAUNCESTON
BODMIN
NEWQUAY
TOTNES
TORQUAY
PLYMOUTH
ST. IVES
KINGSBRIDGE
TRURO
LOSTWITHIEL
SALCOMBE
MARAZION
ST. MAWES
FALMOUTH
LAND'S END
HELSTON
PENZANCE
MOUSEHOLE

GLASTONBURY TO TAUNTON
(about 20 miles)

*From the **car park** turn left and go down **Fisher's Hill**, then left again at the traffic circle for **Taunton (A39)**. In a ¼ mile you'll pass Moorlands factory shop and then cross the **River Brue**. At the traffic circle get into the right lane and go straight on, signposted **Taunton** (22 miles), the first major town you come to being **Street** in about 2 miles. In Othery a pub called the London Inn reminds you of what you've left behind. This is rather flat land with several rivers crossing it, the only high ground being the **Polden Hills**, which you cross at **Pedwell** and **Greinton**. This lowland region is the **Somerset Levels** and was once under water. You can still see drainage ditches in the fields. Just before **Durston** you'll cross the **Bridgewater and Taunton Canal** and then the M5 freeway, going straight on to Taunton. At the T-intersection turn left onto the divided highway (A38), and after crossing the **Bathpool Bridge** over the **River Tone** turn right for **Taunton**. At the Creech Castle traffic circle, in just under a mile, turn left for the **town center**, into **Victoria Park Way**, following the road* *around at the traffic lights. In less than a ½ mile the road becomes* **East Reach***, then* **East Street***, bringing you to the larger traffic circle in the town center. Taunton is a busy town: its car parks fill up quickly, so you may have to try a few before you're successful, but they're well signposted. Best bets are the* **Wood Street** *and* **Castle Street car parks***. The Tourist Information Centre is in the public library on* **Corporation Street***. (Tel: (0823) 274785. Open: Mon-Sat 10am-4pm.)*

TAUNTON

Taunton is the county seat of Somerset, an attractive old market town on the River Tone with interesting sites, such as an ancient Norman castle, and varied shops, as well as a famous hotel and cricket team. Following the Tourist Information Centre's **Heritage Trail** leaflet is a good way to see the town. In addition to the castle be sure to see the late medieval **St James's Church** in Middle Street, with its almshouses dating from the late 18th century; **Gray's Almshouses** (1635) in East Street; **Vivary Park**, which once accommodated the fish ponds of Winchester's bishops; the 15th- and 16th-century **Municipal Buildings** in Corporation Street, originally a grammar school; and **Priory Barn**, within the Cricket Ground, part of a 12th-century Augustinian priory. For golfers and tennis players **Vivary Park** has an 18-hole, 63-par golf course and four tennis courts where visitors are welcome. Equipment can be hired (tel: (0832) 333875).

WHAT TO SEE

Taunton Castle, Castle Green
(Somerset County and Military Museums)
Open: Mon-Sat 10am-5pm
Admission: Adults 70p, children 20p (free on Fridays)

A castle built by the Saxon king Ine around 710 as a stronghold against the Celts may originally may have stood on the site, but the present castle's surviving buildings are largely 12th-century or later. They date from the civil war between King Stephen and his sister, the Empress Matilda, which led to six castles being built in the 1130s and 1140s, of which Taunton was one, part of the Winchester bishops' great estate. The castle has played a part in many important historic English periods, such as the Wars of the Roses and the 15th-century rebellions against Henry VII. During the Civil War the town was pro-Parliamentarian; the castle unsuccessfully besieged by a royalist army. The people suffered cruelly at the hands of the infamous 'hanging' Judge Jeffreys, who in 1685 held one of his Bloody Assizes in the castle, condemning 200 men to the gallows and hundreds more to slavery in the West Indies. The castle's **Great Hall** now houses an exceptional County and Military

Museum with finds from one of the early lake villages at Glastonbury and a fine Roman mosaic floor circa 350AD.

SHOPPING

As well as its lively Saturday market Taunton has several good
shopping streets: **Bath Place, Riverside, Fore Street, East Street,
High Street, Bridge Street, North Street** and **Station Road**, with
large covered shopping malls at **County Walk** and the **Old Market
Centre**. Here you'll find **Debenhams** department store and **Marks
and Spencer, Next** for fashionable men's and women's clothing,
Laura Ashley for women's and girl's fashions, and many other top
stores. The local department store is **The County Stores**, 52 North
Street, selling ranges of china, glass, fashion accessories, perfume
and food. For antiques try **William Morley Antiques** at Musgrave's
Old Farm, West Monkton, Taunton. Established in a 14th-century
house, the shop deals in fine 17th- and 18th-century period English
furniture, with some needlework, early metalware, china, glass and
decorative items for the country house.

TAUNTON RESTAURANTS

The County Stores – Gallery Restaurant, 52 North Street   £
Tel: (0823) 272235
Open: Mon-Sat 9am-5pm
No credit cards

This bustling second-floor restaurant, in a large store on a main
Taunton shopping street, is an ideal stop for morning coffee, lunch
or tea. It serves standard English food with varying dishes of the
day and wine by the glass. Local and national newspapers are on
hand if you want to catch up on the news.

Winchester Arms, Castle Green   £
Open: Daily 11:30am-2:30pm, 7pm-11pm (no food Sunday eve)
No credit cards

The lively Winchester Arms pub on Castle Green serves an excellent range of hot food and salads at lunchtime. Specials of the day
might include chicken in white wine sauce, *carbonnade* of beef, or
steak-and-kidney pie, priced under £5. It's an attractive old building with Gothic-style windows and roses climbing its walls. From
the benches and tables outside you can relax and watch the world
go by. The pub also offers moderately priced accommodation with
one single and three double rooms (no private facilities).

TAUNTON HOTELS

The Castle Hotel, Castle Green   £££
Tel: (0823) 272671
Amenities: ☎ ⚏ 🅿 ⚎ 🍸 ◉   Credit cards: AE, DC, MC, V

Perhaps the best hotel in the West Country, The Castle is celebrated far and wide as a place to stay and for its restaurant. Once
part of ancient Taunton Castle, it's an attractive, wisteria-clad
building. Part of the interior is medieval and there are Norman
walls in the garden. Despite its location in the town center it's all
peace and quiet within. Its comfort is legendary, decor beautiful
and antiques interesting. Try the restaurant (open also to non-
residents) and see why it's been awarded a Michelin star. Besides
delicious food there's an international wine list of over 150 items,
with many rare vintages, and a cheeseboard of up to 16 cheeses,
including many English varieties. The hotel will happily arrange
local sports and other activities for you, including Exmoor safaris,
hot air balloon trips, golf, clay pigeon (skeet) shooting and fishing.

The County Hotel, East Street   £££
Tel: (0823) 87651
Amenities: ☎ ⚏ 🅿 ⚎ 🍸 ◉   Credit cards: AE, DC, MC, V

Originally a coaching inn, this large Trusthouse Forte hotel in the
town center was recently modernized and has good public rooms,
attractive bedrooms (all 67 with bath and shower) and several
restaurants and snack bars specializing in local dishes. Staff will
help arrange golf, fishing, pony trekking, riding, swimming, bowls
or local tours to help you enjoy your stay in Taunton.

Old Manor Farm House, Norton Fitzwarren   £
Tel: (0823) 289801   Closed: Over Christmas
Amenities: ⚏ 🅿 ⚎ 🍸   Credit cards: DC, MC, V

The building is Edwardian (so not very old) and it's no longer a
farmhouse. These are the only surprises you will find at this
excellent establishment, three miles from Taunton off the A361.
Rooms are modern, spacious and most have en suite facilities.
Breakfast and other meals feature good local produce. Dinners are
very reasonable. Drinks are available.

AROUND AND ABOUT

Hatch Court, Hatch Beauchamp
Open: Thur only 2:30pm-5:30pm early Jul-mid Sep; also open
          August Bank Holiday Monday afternoon
Admission: Adults £2, children under 12 free
Eating facilities: Teas available: 3:30pm-5:30pm

*Directions: From Taunton take the A358 to **Ilminster**. **Hatch Beau-***

champ *village is 6 miles southeast of Taunton.*

Hatch Court was built in 1755 by Thomas Prowse of Axbridge. It is a Palladian-style Georgian house with curved wings, a magnificent stone staircase, a good collection of pictures, 17th- and 18th-century furniture, and an unusual semi-circular china room. A small Canadian military museum and a medieval parish church are nearby.

Sheppy's Cider,, Three Bridges, Bradford-on-Tone
Tel: (0823) 461233
Open: Mon-Sat 8:30am-7pm Apr-Sep; 8:30am-6pm Oct-Mar; Sun, Easter and Christmas Day noon-2pm
Free admission

*Directions: Sheppy's Cider is 3½ miles along the **A38** from Taunton to **Wellington**.*

Somerset is famous for its cider, and here's your chance to see how the ancient drink is made. The Sheppy family have been making cider since the early 1800s. You can see their award-winning **Farm and Cider Museum** as well as their 42-acre orchards, the press room where the apple crop is processed, and their shop.

TAUNTON TO EXETER   (about 35 miles)

*Leaving Taunton, take the **M5** southward to **Exeter** and the first left from the Creech Castle traffic circle, following the signs. After a ½ mile take the third turn for **Exeter/M5**, which takes you onto the freeway, with a good view of Taunton town on the right and the hills beyond. In about 8 miles you'll see a huge monument on a hill to your left. This obelisk, high on the **Black Down Hills**, commemorates the Duke of Wellington, who won the Battle of Waterloo in 1815. He took his title from the nearby town of Wellington.*

In 15 miles you cross the county border into the interesting landscape of Devon, rich dairy country with checkerboard fields. It is an agricultural area, but famous also for two large stretches of moorland, Dartmoor and Exmoor, the beautiful cathedral city of Exeter and an interesting coastline making it a favorite holiday area.

*At **Junction 30** take the **A379** exit for **Exeter** and at the traffic circle take the third turn left for the **A379**. After about a mile of divided highway the road is joined by the **B3181**. Turn left at the Countess Wear traffic circle and about a ¼ mile further take the third turn for the city center, about 2 miles along **Topsham Road**, which becomes **Holloway Street**. Continue up **South Street** past the White Hart Inn on your left and turn left at the traffic lights into **Fore Street**, where there* *is a car park on the left. Alternatively at the traffic lights go right over into **North Street**, then take the first right into **Paul Street** for the **Paul Street** or **Guildhall car parks**. **The Tourist Information Centre** is in the Civic Centre, Dix's Field, **Paris Street**. (Tel: (0392) 265700. Open: Mon-Fri 9am-5pm, Sat 9am-1pm, 2pm-5pm.)*

EXETER

Exeter is a cathedral and university city with excellent shops (including several pedestrian precincts), many attractive old buildings and a **Maritime Museum**. One of the major cities of southwest England, its rich history stretches back to the Celts of the 3rd and 2nd centuries BC, and the Romans, who called the town Isca Dumnoniorum and surrounded it with a 10 foot-thick stone wall, three quarters of which remains.

Despite a World War II German bombing raid which destroyed much of Exeter, there is still lots to see. The **Cathedral Close** is at the city's heart, with interesting stores, houses and cafés. Devon's most famous seafarers, Drake and Hawkins, are said to have visited **Mol's Coffee House**, now an art gallery. Other interesting buildings include the **Bishop of Crediton's residence**; the 14th-century **Guildhall**, which is the oldest municipal hall and criminal court in the country; the 15th-century **Tuckers Hall**; and the 17th-century **Custom House. St Mary Arches Church**, in the street of the same name, has a 12th-century double Norman arcade, and **St Mary Steps Church** has a famous clock with 17th- and 18th-century striking jacks.

WHAT TO SEE

Exeter Cathedral, Cathedral Close
Open: Daily 7:15am-6pm
Admission: Donation requested from adult visitors

Originally built in the 11th century on the site of an earlier monastery, then added to in Norman times, most of the present cathedral dates from the 13th and 14th centuries. The front entrance door is in the richly decorated West Front. The impressive interior features a long vaulted nave with marble pillars and a 14th-century carved minstrels' gallery; fine carved wooden misericords and a bishop's throne; side chapels; interesting old monuments and tombs and some 14th-century stained glass. The store sells souvenirs and postcards.

Exeter Cathedral Library has a 900-year history. Leofric, the first Bishop of Exeter in 1050-1072, donated several books, including **The Exeter Book**, the largest collection of Saxon poems, and the **Exeter Domesday Book**.

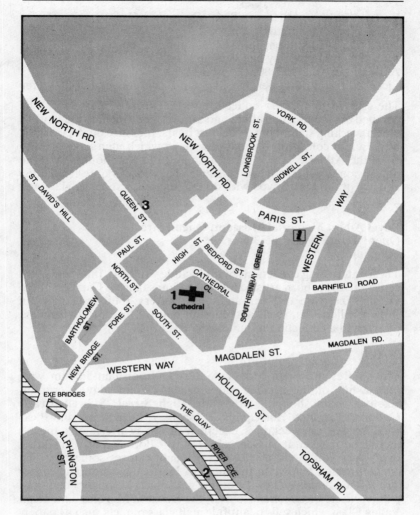

EXETER

 Tourist Information Centre
1 Exeter Cathedral
2 Exeter Maritime Museum
3 Royal Albert Memorial Museum

Exeter Maritime Museum, Town Quay and Canal Basin, Haven
   Road, off Alphington Street
Open: Daily 10am-6pm Jul-Aug; 10am-5pm Sep-Jun
Closed: Christmas Day and Boxing Day
Admission: Adults £2.80, children £1.50
Licensed restaurant open Jun-Sep and Easter; snack bar in winter

The craft in this largest collection of the world's boats can all be
climbed on and touched afloat and ashore. They include the world's
oldest working steamboat, specialist boats, pleasure boats, working
boats and a collection of small vessels in which men have tried to
cross the Atlantic. There are also quays, old warehouses, and the
oldest pound lock canal in England. These locks date from 1563
and are of the Dutch type with double top gates and a single lower
gate.

Royal Albert Memorial Museum, Queen Street
Open: Tues-Sat 10am-5:30pm
Free admission

These interesting collections of art include works by 18th- and 19th-
century Devon-born artists and by London's famous Camden Town
Group. There are also local and studio pottery, Inuit and American
Indian collections, local and foreign natural history and archaeology, and a collection of handsome Exeter silver.

SHOPPING

Most stores are open Monday-Saturday from 9am-5:30pm with
only a few of the smaller shops closing Wednesday afternoon.
Exeter's main shopping areas are **High Street, Sidwell Street,
Guildhall Precinct, Harlequins, Princeshay, Fore Street** and **Pickwick Arcade**. On weekdays, except Wednesday afternoons, there's
a covered market at **St George's Hall**, off Fore Street. On **Cathedral Close** you'll find a selection of quality stores some of which
we've profiled below. In the modern Harlequins shopping center
you'll find **Chandri Chowk's** ethnic gifts, such as Indian boxes and
papier mâché ornaments, **Habitat**, the **House of Marbles**, and **Teign
Valley Glass** which sells beautiful small glass objects such as paperweights. The **Cookshop** has good quality French porcelain, knives
and other utensils, **Ann Chocolatier** (in the food hall downstairs)
sells handmade Royal Belgian chocolates. The **Body Shop** plus
several men's and women's fashion stores can be found in the
adjacent Guildhall precinct.
   In the pedestrianized town center there are several well-known
national stores. On the High Street you'll find **Marks & Spencer**
(open: Thur until 8pm), **Laura Ashley, Austin Reed** (men's clothing), **Sherratt & Hughes** (books), **Benetton, Russell & Bromley**

(shoes), **Champion Sport** (sportswear), and **Dingles** and **Debenhams** department stores, both with restaurants open all day.

The Tourist Information Centre will supply antiques hunters with a helpful collector's guide to the city.

Antartex, Cathedral Close
Credit cards: MC, V

This is the place for classic sweaters, handmade rugs, woolen slippers plus traditional country sportswear, with a heavy emphasis on Hunter boots, Barbour jackets and their own-label goods. They'll ship for you and offer a tax rebate scheme on purchases over £60.

Antique Centre, on the Quay
Credit cards: Varies with each proprietor

As you might expect, everything from china, brass, and linen to jewelry, postcards and other collectables can be found in this medium-sized market. A fun place to browse.

Du Barry, Cathedral Close
Credit cards: MC, V

A large selection of stunning imported shoes and accessories from Italy and elsewhere including labels like Bandolino, Gina and Charles Jourdan in an elegant small shop where furniture is as tastefully matched as the wares.

The **Well House** wine bar nearby is a pleasant place for a drink.

Fred Keetch Gallery, Cathedral Close
Credit cards: DC, MC, V

Good range of original paintings plus limited edition prints and other art plus glassware, including Dartington, and china, such as Llandro figures, and glass paperweights. For those who practice as well as purchase there's a fine array of artist's supplies downstairs.

Hay Fever, Cathedral Close
Credit cards: MC, V

Flower power in aromatic abundance (dried flowers even festoon the ceiling) in this rustic stone-floored shop. Potpourri and pottery, dried bouquets and baskets, stencils and stationery, make this the ideal place to pick up something special for the hard-to-please.

Nottingham and Walsh, Cathedral Close
Credit cards: AE, MC, V

Specialists in Exeter silver and flatware, this store also carries a collection of their own hand-crafted jewelry in unusual designs.

Pirouette, 5 West Street
Credit cards: MC, V

This tiny shop tucked away at the bottom of the town is perfection if you're out to snare Bertie Wooster at a 20s' country house party. Great beaded flapper frocks and other frippery including Edwardian blouses for as little as £25 plus loads of antique lace, linen and 20s' accessories.

Priory Antiques, 19-20 Friernhay Street
No credit cards

On a tiny lane off Fore Street and located in one of the oldest brick buildings in Exeter (it dates from 1690) they specialize in board and table games, tribal art and artifacts, oak and other country furniture. Two tiger cats greet you warmly as you enter.

EXETER RESTAURANTS

Hanson's, 2 Cathedral Close   £
Tel: (0392) 76913
Open: Mon-Sat 9am-7pm   Closed: Over Christmas
Credit cards: MC, V

Close to Exeter's beautiful cathedral, this friendly restaurant serves snacks and meals throughout the day. Try for one of the window seats with an incomparable view of the Cathedral Close's comings and goings while you enjoy such fairly traditional food as egg mayonnaise, roast beef and Yorkshire pudding or a liver-and-bacon broil. Tasty pancakes are among the desserts. You can also have breakfast, morning coffee or a Devon cream tea. The restaurant serves alcoholic drinks.

Jakarta Brasserie, 77-78 South Street   £
Tel: (0392) 210503
Open: Mon-Fri noon-2pm, daily 6:15pm-11:30pm
Closed: Christmas Day and Boxing Day
Credit cards: AE, DC, MC, V

For unusual meals try this batik-decorated restaurant's Indonesian, Singaporean and Malaysian food. Its specialty is a *Rijstafel* which will amply replace the calories you've burned up while sightseeing. The à la carte menu offers unusual dishes such as *satay* sticks and duck stir-fried with cabbage, all at reasonable prices.

King Tandoori Restaurant, 94-95 South Street   £
Tel: (0392) 56992
Open: Daily noon-3pm, 6pm-11:30pm
Credit cards: AE, DC, MC, V

Here you'll find high-quality Indian and *Tandoori* dishes made with fresh herbs and spices. Try the delicious lamb *Peshawari*. House specialties include *Tandoori* Chicken King cooked in homemade tomato sauce with cream, nuts and special oriental spices, and *Jeera* chicken cooked in butter with cumin seed and peppers. The menu also features traditional Indian desserts.

Tinley's, 2 Broadgates, Cathedral Close   £
Tel: (0392) 72865
Open: Mon-Sat 8:30am-6pm (restaurant from noon)
Credit cards: MC, V

This preserved building on the site of Exeter's old city walls is an attractive tea room and restaurant, ideal for morning coffee, lunch or afternoon tea – though it does get crowded. Hot and cold dishes include Japanese chicken sticks, Welsh rarebit, various pies, grills, cakes, toasts and teabreads, with a choice of many different teas.

Turk's Head, High Street   £
Tel: (0392) 56680
Open: Mon-Sat noon-2pm, 5pm-10pm, Sun noon-2pm, 7pm-10pm
Credit cards: AE, DC, MC, V

This historic building, with its fine façade, is now a Beefeater Steak House, appealing to a youngish clientele, but if you fancy a reasonably priced steak it's worth sampling. Note the decor in the downstairs bars, with their stags' heads, books, pictures, old bottles, prints and other memorabilia, before moving upstairs to the cozy beamed restaurant.
    See also **The White Hart Hotel** and **St Olaves Court Hotel** below.

EXETER HOTELS

St Olave's Court, St Mary Arches Street   ££
Tel: (0392) 217736   Closed: Over Christmas
Amenities: ☎ ⌨ 🅿 ⛏ 🍸 ◎   Credit cards: AE, DC, MC, V

Built by a local merchant in 1827, this attractive, privately owned hotel is 300 yards from Exeter Cathedral. It has a pleasant walled garden with a pond and a fountain, and inside a delightfully decorated cocktail bar and dining rooms, with delicious *nouvelle cuisine*, à la carte and table d'hôte lunch and dinner menus. The 17 bedrooms are comfortable. Guests have the use of a jacuzzi, solarium, swimming pool and sauna facilities at a nearby health center.

The Rougemont Hotel, Queen Street   ££
Tel: (0392) 54982
Amenities: ☎ ⌨ 🅿 ⛏ 🍸 ◎   Credit cards: AE, DC, V

It's hard to believe that a debtors' prison once stood on the site of this imposing and spacious hotel. Built in 1876, it has every modern comfort, including a hairdresser and even a chiropodist for those aching feet. It has recently been refurbished throughout. There's a restaurant with reasonable prices, à la carte and prix-fixe menus, and an attractive residents' cocktail bar. Facing the hotel are the Rougemont Gardens, first laid out in the 18th century in the outer bailey of the castle.

The White Hart Hotel, South Street   **££**
Tel: (0392) 79897   Closed: Dec 24-26
Amenities: ☎ ⬛ 🅿 ⵞⵞ ⏋   Credit cards: AE, DC, MC, V

Only a short walk from the city center, this 14th-century inn is thought to have been originally a monks' rest house. Its most notable rooms are on the first floor, and include the 15th-century **Wine Room** and the **Reception**, once the stables where Oliver Cromwell rested his horses during the Civil War. The bars, with flagstone floors, are full of old oak furniture. The attractive dining room serves a good range of food and wine with attentive service, and there are comfortable residents' sitting rooms. Even if you're not staying here it's a good place to stop for a drink, a snack or a meal.

EXETER TO TORQUAY   (about 22 miles)

*From **Exeter Guildhall car park** turn right into **Paul Street**, go over the traffic lights and take the first left into **St Mary Arches Street**. Turn right at the end into **Fore Street**, which takes you to the large Exe Bridge traffic circle. Following the signs to **Okehampton, Plymouth** and **Torquay**, get into the left lane over Exe Bridge South and turn left into **Alphington Street (A377)**, with Sainsbury's and the Leisure Centre on your right. In a ½ mile you'll pass the livestock market on the left, then in a ¼ mile, at the large traffic circle, turn left to **Plymouth (A38)** and out into the countryside. The first left at the next traffic circle, in just over a ¼ mile, takes you onto the divided highway A30. Two miles on the road divides – left lane for Taunton, right lane for **Plymouth** and **Torquay** – and in another 2½ miles you take the A380 for the 'English Riviera' as **Torquay, Torbay** and **Paignton** are known. Just past the Exeter Court Hotel stay in one of the two left lanes for **Torquay (A380)**. The two right lanes go on to Plymouth (A38). To your left a ¼ mile on you'll glimpse the sea; in another mile you'll see the far-off tors and peaks of **Dartmoor** on the right. The road here is flanked by thick woods. Thirteen miles from Exeter the road skirts around **Kingsteignton**, with views of the **River Teign** to the left, and you enter **Newton Abbot** via **Besigheim Way**.*

Keen antiques collectors may like to stop here at the **Newton Abbot Antiques Centre**, 55 East Street (open: Tues 9am-4pm). Every

Tuesday over 50 dealers offer a wide range of goods for sale. *From the Newton Abbot bypass traffic circle follow Besigheim Way for the town center. The third left at the Penn Inn traffic circle takes you into* **Torquay Road**, *then East Street.*

From the traffic circle on the **A380** *at Newton Abbot take the second turn,* **Torquay Road**, *for* **Torquay**. *Two miles on, at* **Kingkerswell**, *you'll see palm trees thriving in this mild climate. At the traffic circle 3 miles further, at* **Kerswell Gardens**, *keep in the left lane and go right over and along* **Newton Road** *2 miles for Torquay town center. Shortly after Torre Station you'll enter the one-way system. Follow signs for the* **town center**, *turning right into* **South Street**, *which becomes* **Belgrave Road**. *The town center car parks fill up quickly in high summer so your best bet is the* **Sea Front car park**, *off Belgrave Road on the right. If this is full follow the signs for the several other car parks.*

The Tourist Information Centre *is on* **Vaughan Parade**, *near the Old Harbour and Marina. (Tel: (0803) 27428. Open: Mon-Sat 9am-7pm, Sun 10am-5pm Aug; Mon-Sat 9am-5:15pm, Sun 10am-5pm Sep-Jul.) At the Tourist Information Centre you'll find a* **Town Trail** *leaflet which gives you an interesting guided tour around historic Torquay.*

Overlooking beautiful **Tor Bay**, Torquay is Devon's biggest beach resort. You'll understand its 'English Riviera' title when you see the wooded hills and painted villas among the trees, the curving bay, mild climate, sub-tropical gardens, and big hotels along the sea front. There are good beaches here and nearby **Babbacombe** is famous for its golden sands.

TORQUAY

WHAT TO SEE

Torquay Museum, 529 Babbacombe Road
Open: Mon-Fri 10am-4:45pm; Sat as well Easter-Sep; Sun too
        mid July-mid Sep
Closed: Christmas, New Year's Day, Good Friday.
Admission: Adults £1, children 50p

This is worth a visit for its impressive natural history gallery, collections from Kents Cavern and other local caves, the archaeology of South Devon, rural life, local pottery and Victoriana.

Torre Abbey, Abbey Park, Torquay Seafront
Open: Daily 10am-5pm (last entry 4:30pm) Apr-Oct
Admission: Adults 65p, children free

Surrounded by extensive gardens, opposite Abbey Sands, Torre

Abbey is Torbay's oldest historic building. Originally a 12th-century monastery, it was converted into a residential house in the 16th century and remained as such until 1930. You can see the ruins of the monastery as well as the Cary family chapel, beautifully furnished period rooms, collections of silver and glass, art galleries, an Agatha Christie memorial room, and a restored Victorian kitchen serving light refreshments.

SHOPPING

Torquay has a good shopping center with many large stores such as Marks & Spencer and Debenhams. The main shopping streets are near the **Old Harbour** between **Fleet Street** and **Strand**. Antiques enthusiasts should try Colin Stodgell's **Devonshire Gallery**, 45 Abbey Road, specializing in paintings, also **Birbeck Antiques**, 219 Union Street, oriental specialists. Slightly further afield are **Francis Peter**, on South Street, and **The Attic, Old and New**, off Laburnum Row, Tor Hill Road, where you can browse through all manner of secondhand goods and may even find a treasure.

TORQUAY RESTAURANTS

Bianco's, 38 Torwood Street ££
Tel: (0803) 23430
Open: Daily noon-2:30pm, 6pm-11pm Jul-end Sep; daily 6pm-
    11pm, Sun noon-2:30pm Oct-Jun   Closed: 2 wks Jan
Credit cards: MC, V

A small cheerful Italian restaurant serving such dishes as mozzarella and tomato salad, pasta starters or main courses, *Tournedos Rossini*, and *Saltimbocca alla Romana* as well as steaks grilled over charcoal, salads and fresh local fish, including salmon. Try the 'Best of Italy' menu – *Gnocchi Gorgonzola* followed by *Tournedos Marco Polo* or *Veal alla Cesare* – for the authentic flavor of Italy.

Boulevards, The Pavilion, Vaughan Road £
Tel: (0803) 211801
Open: Mon-Sun 9:30am-late   Closed: Over Christmas
Credit cards: AE, DC, MC, V

On the second-floor terrace of a new shopping center, Boulevards is a lively café, bar and restaurant serving various menus to suit the time of day. There's a daytime menu until 5:30pm, an interesting evening menu of American-style food from 6:30pm until late; a Sunday buffet menu; a wine list with cocktails, beers, spirits and a reasonably priced house champagne; plus a mouthwatering dessert menu. The friendly staff serve tea, coffee and cakes all day long.

Skippers, Vaughan Road,   **££**
Tel: (0803) 24767
Open: Daily noon-2pm, 7pm-10pm Easter-end Sep; until 9:30pm
      in winter   Closed: Sun Oct-Easter
Credit cards: MC, V

Conveniently situated overlooking the Marina, opposite the Tourist Information Centre, this modern restaurant has nautical decor, with bare wood, beams and brass. The menu is varied, with lots of fresh local fish, light lunchtime meals, and daily specials in the evening such as carrot and orange soup, fresh crab bisque, *bouillabaisse* and poached salmon steak as well as poultry, steaks, and two vegetarian dishes.

TORQUAY HOTELS

The Corbyn Head Hotel, Sea Front   **£££**
Tel: (0803) 213611
Amenities: ☎ 🖥 🅿 🍴 🍷 ≈ ◉   Credit cards: AE, DC, MC, V

A reasonably priced, well-kept hotel with good facilities and superb views over Tor Bay, the Corbyn Head has recently been redecorated throughout to a high standard. Situated half a mile south of the town center, near Corbyn's Head, it has a pleasant sundeck beside a heated outdoor swimming pool. Some bedrooms have balconies and most have sea views. Sailing, water-skiing and windsurfing can be arranged nearby.

The Grand Hotel, The Seafront   **£££**
Tel: (0803) 296677
Amenities: ☎ 🖥 🅿 🍴 🍷 ≈ 𝒫 ◉   Credit cards: AE, DC, MC, V

Mystery writer Agatha Christie spent her honeymoon at the Grand, an imposing four-star hotel on the sea front with excellent views of Tor Bay and superb amenities. There are several restaurants and bars; luxurious sitting rooms; indoor and outdoor heated swimming pools; a new leisure complex with jacuzzi, gym, sauna and sunbeds; a hairdressing salon, snooker and table tennis. The attractive bedrooms and suites have every modern facility, most have sea views.

Livermead Cliff Hotel, Sea Front   **££**
Tel: (0803) 22881
Amenities: ☎ 🖥 🅿 🍴 🍷 ≈ ✔ ◉   Credit cards: AE, MC, V

This is a traditional, family-owned and operated hotel where friendly staff make you welcome. It's on Livermead Cliff, beside Livermead Sands, half a mile from the bustling town center. There are good facilities for relaxing, including a nine-hole putting green, hairdresser and – in conjunction with its nearby sister hotel –

squash, sauna, a solarium, mini-gym, and games room. Many rooms have spectacular sea views.

If this hotel is full try its sister, the **Livermead House Hotel**, 200 yards further in toward Torquay town center (tel: (0803) 24361).

SIDE TRIP TO BRIXHAM Via Paignton   (about 7½ miles)

*From Torquay take **Torbay Road (A379)** south along the sea front and on into Torbay's **Torquay Road**. Follow the signs for **Brixham** and sea front and after 1¼ miles turn left into **Seaway Road** under a railroad overpass, then right into **Marine Drive** beside Paignton's sandy sea front and colorful beach huts, and past the Royal Festival Hall on the left in ¾ of a mile. Turn right into **Sands Road**, signposted **Brixham**, then left at the mini traffic circle and up **Whitstone Road** past Sharon House. At the next mini traffic circle take the first left into **Dartmouth Road (A379)** and continue along here for Brixham. Three and a half miles after leaving Torquay you'll have excellent views of Tor Bay.*

*Brixham car parks get crowded in peak season so if you're there in August try the **park-and-ride** facilities: from a car park 5½ miles outside Torquay and 2 miles from Brixham frequent buses will take you into the village (Mon-Fri 10am-6pm). You enter Brixham on **New Road (A3022)** and follow the signs for the **town center**, harbor and car parks. In the town center this will take you left, passing a museum and theater on the left. Turn left at the traffic lights into **Market Street**, then into **Middle Street**, where there's a multi-story car park on the right.*

Brixham, at the southern end of Tor Bay, is a delightful old hillside fishing village with a busy working harbor full of fishing boats and other craft. In Victorian times its fishing fleet was among Devon's largest; hence the early 19th-century character of much of the village. It's still an important commercial fishing center with lots to see, including a **British Fisheries Museum** (open: daily 9am-6pm Apr-Oct; admission: adults 30p, children free) on Quayside and a replica of Sir Francis Drake's **Golden Hind** in the harbor (open: daily 10am-5pm mid May-end Oct approx; admission: adults 80p, children 40p).

Return to Torquay to continue your tour westward.

TORQUAY TO TOTNES   (about 16 miles)

*From Torquay take the **Torbay Road (A379)** south along the seafront, following signs for **Totnes** and **Paignton**, into **Torbay** (2½ miles). In the one-way system at Lloyds Bank follow the signs for the **town center**, then **Totnes**, which leads you back onto the **Torquay***

Road. In a ½ mile get into the right lane and turn right at the traffic lights signposted **Totnes**, *into* **Cecil Road**, *in front of the Longcombe Dairy, avoiding Paignton town center. The road becomes hilly* **Colley End Road**, *passing quaint thatched cottages. In 1 mile turn left into* **King's Ash Road** *for Totnes. At the traffic lights and major intersection a ½ mile on turn right into* **Totnes Road** *for Totnes (4½ miles) and Plymouth. Two miles further you'll see a stunning part of the Devon landscape. A sign welcomes you to the* **South Hams**, *as the area between Plymouth and Torbay is known.*

Five miles from Paignton you come into **Totnes***. Go down* **Bridgetown Hill** *and follow the signs for the* **town center**, **Steamer Quay** *and* **Tourist Information***, crossing the* **River Dart** *by the Brutus Bridge. At the traffic circle take the first left along* **Coronation Road***, crossing over Fore Street after 200 yards and into* **The Plains***, which becomes* **New Walk***; follow the road around, then turn left for the car park.*

The Tourist Information Centre *is on* **The Plains***. (Tel: (0803) 863168. Open: Mon-Sat 9:30am-1pm, 2:15pm-5:30pm Easter-Oct.)*

TOTNES

Totnes is a delightful old town set in a beautiful part of the Devon countryside beside the River Dart. There are the remains of a 13th-century castle keep and walls overlooking the town, interesting old houses and part of a 16th-century **Guildhall**, now a museum. Crossing Fore Street you'll see the 15th-century **Eastgate** with its clock and tower, one of the town's old gates.

WHAT TO SEE

Totnes Castle, Castle Street
Open: Mon-Sat 9:30am-6:30pm, Sun 2pm-6:30pm mid Mar-mid
      Oct; Mon-Sat 9:30am-4pm, Sun 2pm-4pm mid Oct-mid
      Mar
Admission: Adults 75p, children 35p

High on a commanding hill, overlooking the town and the surrounding countryside, are the remains of Totnes Castle. The mound is 12th-century, the remaining ruins mainly 14th-century.

Totnes Motor Museum, Steamer Quay
Open: Daily 10am-5:30pm Easter-Oct
Admission: Adults £2, children £1

Vintage, sports and racing cars, with showcases of old instruments, books, engines, motorbikes and toy cars are on display. All the cars are kept in running order, some have fascinating histories.

SHOPPING

General shopping hours are from 9am-5:30pm with many stores closing between 1pm-2pm for lunch and at 1pm Thursday for the afternoon.

Elizabethan England is relived every Tuesday (May-Sep) with a costumed charity market on the **Civic Hall** forecourt, 9am-1pm and an antiques market in the Civic Hall. Each Friday there's a lively pannier (general) market in the forecourt and antiques in the Hall.

Totnes is famous for its many new and secondhand bookshops: the Tourist Information Centre supplies leaflets listing these.

Among the many bookshops try **Pedlar's Pack Books**, 4 The Plains, for a range of good quality secondhand and antiquarian books as well as old postcards, sheet music and maps. **Ken Parnell**, 72 Fore Street, has a general stock of out-of-print and secondhand books, plus lots of paperbacks.

For general shopping **Fore Street, High Street** and **The Narrows** are best. For antiques, James Sturges of **Past and Present**, 94 High Street, sells such collectables as china, stuffed fish, swords and aeronautica. There are many jewelry, craft and gift shops such as **Galahad Crafts**, 36 High Street, plus those selling local products and confectionery – Devon clotted cream, toffees, fudge and so on.

TOTNES RESTAURANTS

Planters, 82 High Street, The Narrows   £
Tel: (0803) 865522
Open: Daily 10:15am-2:15pm, Thur-Sat 6:30pm-9pm May, Jun
         and Sep; Mon-Sat 6:30pm-9pm Jul-Aug
Closed: 2 wks at Christmas
Credit cards: DC, V

This highly commended little restaurant is cheerful and friendly, with excellent views over the Devon countryside from the garden terrace at the rear. The Planters theme continues inside with a green color scheme and lots of plants. The menu consists of teas, coffees, cakes and snack meals as well as such main-course dishes as pork fillet with whiskey, chicken mornay, and a delicious *boeuf bourguignon*.

Willow, 87 High Street, The Narrows   £
Tel: (0803) 862605
Open: Mon-Sat 9am-5pm, Tues-Sat 6:30pm-11:30pm Jul-Sep;
         Mon-Sat 10am-5pm, Wed, Fri, Sat 6:30pm-10pm Oct-Jun
No credit cards

A casual, arty, vegetarian wholefood café-restaurant with large stripped-pine tables, comfortable easy chairs in the family room and an attractive garden. On Wednesday nights there's an Indian menu, on Friday nights live music. The menu, chalked on a blackboard, offers soups, *couscous*, nut roasts, quiches and salads, plus various teas and other drinks.

TOTNES AND DARTINGTON HOTELS

The Cott Inn, Cott, near Dartington £
Tel: (0803) 863777
Amenities: **P** ⌘ ⌾ ◎   Credit cards: AE, DC, MC, V

A picture-postcard thatched cottage, built in 1320 and retaining immense olde-worlde charm, this small inn has beamed walls and ceilings, flagstone floors, interesting bars with antique furniture and, perhaps best of all, a superb little restaurant with a high standard of cooking that's patronized by locals as well as visitors. Staying here is a delightful experience.

The Royal Seven Stars Hotel, Totnes £
Tel: (0803) 862125
Amenities: ☎ ⌷ **P** ⌘ ⌾ ◎   Credit cards: DC, MC, V

Dated 1660, this traditional English hotel in the center of Totnes once was a coaching inn. Its impressive pillared front entrance leads through to a covered interior courtyard-style hall. Daniel Defoe, the author of *Robinson Crusoe*, once stayed here and fished for salmon in the nearby River Dart. A dinner dance and cabaret show is held most Saturday evenings. There are light lunches, evening bar meals and full à la carte menu in the **Brutus Room Restaurant**.

AROUND AND ABOUT

Bowden House
Open: Tues-Thur noon-5pm Apr-Sep; Sun-Thur Jul-Aug; tours of
         house 2pm-4:30pm
Admission: House and museum: Adults £3, children £1.50;
                 House only: Adults £2, children £1

Directions: Take the A381/Kingsbridge Road from Totnes and you'll find Bowden House 1½ miles ahead on the left.

Part Tudor, with a Queen Anne façade, Bowden House contains collections of antique weaponry, furniture and paintings, and has the **British Photographic Museum** in its grounds. You'll be given a guided tour by the family, who wear Georgian costumes. A licensed café serves light meals.

Dartington Hall
Open: All year
Admission: Donation requested

Directions: From Totnes take the A385 towards Plymouth for about 1 *mile. At Shinner's Bridge traffic circle take the third exit on your left, signposted **Dartington Hall (A384)**, then turn right onto a narrow road in about 200 yards and drive down it for about 1 mile to the Hall.*

Dartington Hall, 14th-century palace of the Duke of Exeter, is now home to the **Dartington Hall Trust**. Founded over 50 years ago by American heiress Dorothy Elmhirst and her English husband Leonard, the organization runs many different ventures, including a College of Arts, a school, a film theater, such businesses as glass-blowing and farming, and charities, all based in the local community.

The Hall's gardens are open all year, and concerts and other functions are put on in the magnificent medieval **Great Hall**. You'll see the beautiful courtyard as you walk through to the gardens. An art gallery and restaurant are also part of the complex. For details of events tel: (0803) 863073.

Dartington Cider Press Centre, Shinner's Bridge, Dartington
Open: Mon-Sat 9:30am-5:30pm; Sun as well Jul-Sep

This is a group of twelve shops, two restaurants and a picnic area just off the Shinner's Bridge traffic circle on the **A384** to **Buckfast-leigh**. These interesting shops include a pottery, a cobbler's bench, cookshop, farm foods, Dartington crystal glassware, craft show-rooms, unusual gifts, a wood-turning workshop, a toyshop, and designer knitwear. There are bargain items such as slightly imper-fect Dartington glassware at reduced prices. Some exquisite pottery.

Cranks restaurant serves delicious vegetarian food, which can be eaten in the gardens on a fine day. If you'd like to stretch your legs there's an attractive riverside walk from the Centre.

TOTNES TO SALCOMBE   (about 16 miles)

*From the **Station Road/Coronation Road traffic circle** turn left into **Station Road** with the Brutus Bridge behind you. In 200 yards at the traffic lights turn left into **Western Bypass (A381)** for **Kingsbridge (12 miles)**, crossing the railroad bridge in another 100 yards. Look left for a departing glimpse of the castle. This is a winding hilly road with good views of the **South Hams'** rounded hills and steep-sided valleys, though you may find cloud descending onto the road, reducing visibility. In the village of **Harbertonford** you cross the **River Har-bourne**, which joins the River Dart toward the estuary.*

*You enter **Kingsbridge** down a steep hill past New Parks Farm on your left, then down **Belle Hill** and past Dodbrooke Church. At the intersection with Church Street turn left at the phone booth down*

*Bridge Street (ignoring Ebrington Street on the left) into **Prince of Wales Road**, with the river estuary on your left, then left again into the car park beside the water.*

*The **Tourist Information Centre** is on **The Quay** by the car park, off Prince of Wales Road. (Tel: (0548) 3195. Open: Mon-Sat 9am-5:30pm mid Mar-Oct; 9am-1pm Nov-mid Mar.)*

KINGSBRIDGE

This is a quaint market town at the head of a tidal estuary, with interesting stores around **Bridge Street, Church Street, Mill Street** and **Fore Street** and many intriguing little alleys and passageways. Every Tuesday a crafts market is held in the **Town Hall** foyer, selling work produced by local people.

The **Cookworthy Museum** at 108 Fore Street, (open: Mon-Sat 10am-5pm Easter-Sep; Mon-Fri 10am-4:30pm Oct; closed Nov-Easter; free admission) details the rural life and history of the area, with interesting displays of costumes, school life, a Victorian pharmacy and so on.

*From **Kingsbridge car park** turn left into **Prince of Wales Road** and **Ilbert Road**. At the traffic circle take the first left, into **West Alvington Hill**, for Salcombe (A381). Watch out as you enter **Marlborough**, 4 miles on, for a sudden narrow 'pinch' in the road, followed by a sharp bend to the left. Just 1½ miles further on, past an Esso gas station on your right, you'll enter Salcombe on **Main Road**. Turn left into **Onslow Road** by the swimming pool, and follow the signs for the **town center**. This will lead you into **Knowle Road**, at the end of which you'll come to a junction of three roads, at the top of Church Street (the church is ahead, on your left). Turn left here, into **Shadycombe Road**. There's a car park immediately on your right. If this is full, follow the road on around to the right, past the gasometer, to the very large car and boat parks on the quay.*

*The five-minute walk back into town, along **Island Street**, and then keeping left along the water's edge, is so attractive that you'll undoubtedly dawdle en route to take it all in.*

*There's a small car park in the center of town, in **Fore Street**, on the left-hand side, but it's almost always full, since it accommodates so few cars. If there's no room, you'll have to follow the one-way system around town again, so it's a gamble not worth taking. It's best to take one of the car parks mentioned above.*

*As we go to press there is doubt about the future of the TIC in Salcombe. However, the **Tourist Information Centre** in Kingsbridge will be able to assist you with information on Salcombe.*

SALCOMBE

One of the most beautiful towns in South Devon, Salcombe lies at the mouth of the large estuary that has Kingsbridge at its head. It's a well-known sailing center but its southerly position, dramatic views, sandy beaches and interesting old town center make it a favorite vacation spot for non-sailors too. The headlands, **Bolt Head** and **Bolt Tail**, south and west of Salcombe, are owned by the National Trust and offer excellent walks and chances to observe wildlife. Visit the **Maritime and Local History Museum** in Cook's Boat Store, at Custom House Quay (open: daily 10:30am-12:30pm, 2:30pm-4:30pm end May-end Sep; admission: 50p), for maritime exhibitions about wrecks, lifeboat rescues etc. with interesting old photographs. The stores are situated around **Fore Street** and **Cliff Road**. In the many alleyways off the main streets you'll find local craft shops, ships' chandlers, boutiques and jewelers.

SALCOMBE AND KINGSBRIDGE RESTAURANTS

Buckland-Tout-Saints, Goveton, near Kingsbridge   **£££**
(see page 424)

Dusters Bistro, 50 Fore Street, Salcombe   **£**
Tel: (054 884) 2634
Open: Daily 7pm-10:30pm Easter-Oct   Closed: Nov-Easter
Credit cards: MC, V

Cheerfully decorated in red, white and blue, this friendly restaurant is up a small flight of steps. On Friday and Saturday evenings in the season you can hear live piano music while you dine. The varied menu offers some interesting salads – chicken liver, Caesar, or salade niçoise – plus a range of pasta and vegetarian dishes, fish such as *scampi anisette*, monkfish and crab mornay as well as steaks, poultry and other meat dishes.

Lavinia's, Loddiswell, near Kingsbridge   **££**
Tel: (0548) 550306
Open: Wed-Sat 7:30pm-9:30pm Easter-Oct
Credit cards: MC, V

*Directions: From **Loddiswell** take the **B3196** for about a mile and turn left at the restaurant sign.*

This is one of the most highly regarded restaurants in the area, run by a husband-and-wife team with Lavinia, the wife, doing the cooking. Her imaginative French-style dishes might include hot watercress soup with fresh lime, a cold salmon mousse garnished with smoked salmon, and a terrine of vegetables accompanied by home-baked bread and followed by a chocolate roulade with orange and brandy sauce. Dinner is leisurely, perfectly suiting the delightful rural surroundings. You can wander in the circular walled garden before or after your meal.

The Marine Hotel, Cliff Road, Salcombe   £££
(see page 424)

The Wardroom, 19 Fore Street, Salcombe (thru Chandlery) £
Tel: (054 884) 2620
Open: Mon-Sat 10am-5:30pm; and from 7pm Aug only
Closed: Jan-Feb
Credit cards: AE, DC, MC, V

This small café-restaurant has a truly magnificent sea-level view of Salcombe harbor across water a couple of feet from its terrace, with boats sailing past just outside. A favorite haunt of the local sailing fraternity, it's an ideal place for morning coffee, a snack lunch or tea. All the food is homemade or from local suppliers. Delicious specials of the day include chicken provençale or seafood mornay. The cakes and desserts are irresistible.

Wellingtons, 84-86 Fore Street, Salcombe   £
Tel: (054 884) 3385
Open: Daily from 7pm-late Easter-Oct   Closed: Nov-Easter
Credit cards: AE, DC, MC, V

This attractive restaurant near Custom House Quay is so popular that you may have to book a table for a Friday or Saturday evening in the peak season. The specialty is fish, such as delicious Salcombe crab or lobster. Specials of the day may include baked local cod and prawns in chervil butter, salmon, brill or bass, as well as many meat and poultry dishes such as rack of lamb and chicken suprême, or prime Devon steak. There's a reasonably priced three-course prix fixe menu.

SALCOMBE AND KINGSBRIDGE HOTELS

The Bolt Head Hotel, Bolt Head, Salcombe   £££
Tel: (054 884) 3751   Closed: Mid Nov-late Mar
Amenities: ☎ 🖳 🅿 ⑪ ⚱ ≈ ◎   Credit cards: AE, DC, MC, V

This friendly hotel overlooks the sea and the Salcombe Estuary from 140 feet above sea level, with fine views from most rooms. It's near Bolt Head, about a mile south of Salcombe, convenient for walks in the National Trust-owned countryside of the Head and on the nearby Coastal Path. There's a heated outdoor swimming pool, private moorings, sun terrace, badminton court, and games room. In the attractive restaurant you can enjoy traditional British and French food from a prix fixe menu, with many local specialties.

Buckland-Tout-Saints, Goveton (off **A381**), near Kingsbridge
£££

Tel: (0548) 3055   Closed: Jan
Amenities: ☎ ⌨ 🅿 🍴 ⌄ ✓ ◎   Credit cards: AE, DC, MC, V

Directions: The hotel is signposted from the A381. In Goveton village (2 miles) turn right up the steep hill, taking care along the very narrow road, and in a ¼ mile you'll come to the hotel's white wrought-iron gates and long drive on your right.

A magnificent country hotel, this historic Queen Anne mansion was built in 1690. It's an elegant building, beautifully decorated and furnished throughout, with an original Adam fireplace in the lounge and a paneled dining room. It's set in immaculate grounds with a croquet lawn and putting green. There's fishing, sailing and riding nearby. A delightful, peaceful spot. The restaurant has an excellent reputation and on the menu you may find sea bass with basil and orange hollandaise sauce, or steamed breast of chicken with pistachio stuffing. The desserts and cheeseboard are incredible.

The Marine, Cliff Road, Salcombe   £££
Tel: (054 884) 2251
Amenities: ☎ ⌨ 🅿 🍴 ⌄ ≋ ◎   Credit cards: AE, DC, MC, V

There are superb views of Salcombe estuary from this splendid hotel, so relaxing in its lounges, bar and library is that much more pleasurable. It's a tiered white building, right at the water's edge, just minutes from the town center. Most bedrooms have estuary views. The facilities include jacuzzi, sauna, plunge pool and solarium, a hairdressing salon, beauty treatments, games room, sundeck, and the hotel's own small boats. As well as interesting lounge bar meals there are superb restaurant menus; both *carte du jour* and a special 'Estuary menu' feature fresh local seafood.

The Tides Reach, South Sands, Salcombe   £££ (incl dinner)
Tel: (054 884) 3466   Closed: Mid Nov-mid Mar
Amenities: ☎ ⌨ 🅿 🍴 ⌄ ≋ ◎   Credit cards: AE, DC, MC, V

Facing the beach at South Sands, about a mile south of Salcombe, this delightful hotel has superb facilities. With its own boathouse and moorings it offers windsurfing, waterskiing and sailing. In its modern leisure complex you'll find a swimming pool, sauna, solarium, hair and beauty salon, squash court, multi-gym and games room. There are magnificent views of the sea and estuary, specially enjoyable from the restaurant, where you can choose from wide-ranging à la carte and prix fixe menus.

Wood Grange Hotel, Devon Road, Salcombe   £
Tel: (054 884) 2439
Amenities: 🖵 🅿 ⑪ 🍸   Credit cards: AE, DC, MC, V

This cheery small hotel is ideally perched above the town so many rooms have a lovely view of Salcombe's famous estuary. All rooms have en suite facilities and tea/coffee makers, as well as radios which is a nice extra touch. Mary and Peter Fleig are considerate hosts.

*From Salcombe return to Totnes via **A381**.*

TOTNES TO PLYMOUTH   (about 24 miles)

*From **Totnes town center** take the **A385** towards **Dartington** and **Buckfastleigh**. At the Shinner's Bridge traffic circle in 1 mile take the second left (**A385**) for **Plymouth**, passing through **Tigley** and **Culverlane** before you reach a major traffic circle about 4½ miles on. Take the first left (**A38**) for **Plymouth**, a major divided highway which has superb views of Dartmoor's hills and tors to the right.*

*   ***Dartmoor** is one of the wildest and most unspoilt areas of Britain. It's a National Park, 365 square miles in size, with craggy heights, bleak moorland, picturesque villages in sheltered valleys ('combes'), and beautiful countryside. It's covered with antiquities – mostly dating back 3,000 years to the Bronze Age Beaker People – such as groups of huts, cairns (marking graves), burial chambers and stone rows.*

*   *Having passed **Ivybridge** and **Plympton** you'll arrive at the outskirts of **Plymouth**. At the major traffic circle, Marsh Mills, follow signs for the **city center** (**A374**), which is the first left. In a ¼ mile get into the middle or right lane for the city center with the **River Plym** on the left Then just over 1½ miles on, join the left lane as you branch left along **Gdynia Way**. After ¾ of a mile turn left at the traffic circle down **Exeter Street**, shortly passing the First and Last pub. If you want **The Barbican** or **The Hoe** turn left in about a ½ mile and carry on for the city center, arriving at the Charles Cross traffic circle in just under a ¼ of a mile (note the ruined church in the middle). Turn first left down **Exeter Street**, with the bus station on your left, to St Andrew's Cross traffic circle, with fountains in the middle. Take the third left onto **Royal Parade** and you'll find the **Guildhall shoppers' car park** immediately on the left.*

Tourist Information Centres:

Civic Centre, Royal Parade *(nearest the car park)*
Tel: (0752) 264849/264851
Open: Mon-Thur 9am-5pm, Fri 9am-4:30pm, Sat 9am-4pm May-
    Sep; Mon-Fri only Sep-May

12 The Barbican
Tel: (0752) 223806
Open: Mon-Sat 9:30am-5pm, Sun 10am-3pm May-Sep
Closed: Oct-Apr.

*Pick up the **Historic Plymouth Trail** leaflet and other city guides at these Information Centres.*

PLYMOUTH

The largest town in Devon and a major port, Plymouth lies at the mouths of the Rivers Plym, Tavy, Tamar and St Germans. Much of the town was destroyed by World War II bombs so while the buildings are modern the city boasts a long seafaring history. This is the town where Sir Francis Drake played his famous game of bowls while awaiting the Spanish Armada in 1588. He's commemorated by a statue on **Plymouth Hoe**. Drake left Plymouth in 1577 on his great voyage of circumnavigation, and in 1583 Sir Humphrey Gilbert sailed to America from this harbor. In 1620 the Pilgrim Fathers made it their last stop before setting sail for the New World. At the entrance to **Sutton Harbour** the **Mayflower Stone and Steps** celebrate their voyage.

Despite the Blitz, there are still many old houses in the narrow streets surrounding the Barbican. The **Royal Citadel**, overlooking the harbor, was built by Charles II in 1666.

WHAT TO SEE

City Museum and Art Gallery, Drake Circus
Open: Mon-Fri 10am-5:30pm, Sat 10am-5pm
Free admission

There is a large collection of paintings here, including one by Sir Joshua Reynolds, ceramics, Old Master drawings, locally-made porcelain, and a silver-gilt cup presented to Sir Francis Drake by Queen Elizabeth I on his return from his famous voyage; also natural history, archaeology and mineral exhibits.

Elizabethan House, 32 New Street, The Barbican
Open: Mon-Fri 10am-5:30pm, Sat 10am-5pm, Sun 3pm-5pm
Admission: Adults 50p, children 10p

This Elizabethan sea-captain's house has been beautifully restored and furnished with period items.

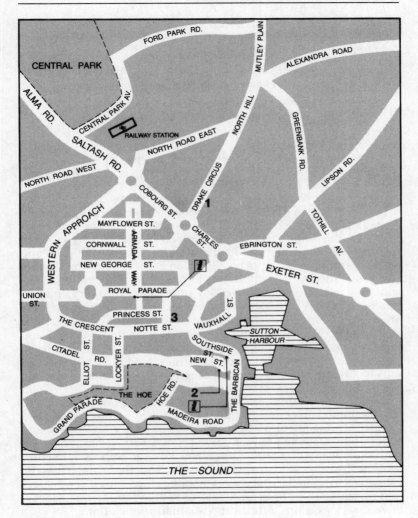

PLYMOUTH

Tourist Information Centre
1 City Museum and Art Gallery
2 Elizabeth House
3 Merchant's House

Merchant's House, 33 St Andrew's Street
Open: Mon-Fri 10am-5:30pm, Sat 10am-5pm, Sun 3pm-5pm
Admission: Adults 50p, children 10p

The largest merchant's house of the 16th and 17th centuries left in the City is now a museum on early Plymouth.

SHOPPING

Stores are open Monday-Saturday 9am-5:30pm with many open until 8pm on Thursday.

You'll find two distinct shopping areas in Plymouth. Among the **Barbican's** narrow streets there are interesting craft, antiques and souvenir shops; in the city's modern pedestrianized zones and shopping malls you'll find the large national stores.

In old Plymouth's **New Street Antique Market** there is a variety of stalls selling books, curios, clocks, jewelry, militaria, prints and brass. In **Barbican Craft Workshops** on White Lane you'll see weaving, wood-turning and leatherworking. Dartington glass and pottery are also on display. Back on New Street the **Janner Sheepskin Shop** sells leatherwear, knitwear and sheepskin jackets and rugs, while **Scruples** (No 44) offers silver jewelry, picture frames, brooches and rings in unusual designs. The **Barbican China Shop** (No 45) has good quality china, such as Royal Doulton. **A. & D. Clement** (No 46) sell old prints and secondhand books, and **Plethora** has a good range of hand-loomed rugs, Indian bags, Celtic-style jewelry and enameled earrings. On Pin Lane **Westcraft** sells hand-knitted sweaters, including Arans, and there's also the **Three Rivers Pottery Workshop. Wm E. Fox-Smith** and **Colin Rhodes**, 53 New Street, sell interesting pictures, original prints of old Plymouth, silver and antiques. New Street's **Craft Arcade** and **Pannier Market** are also worth a quick browse, for bric-a-brac and collectables. **Dolls and Miniatures**, 54 New Street, sells antique and reproduction dolls, dolls' houses and kits, as well as miniature furniture, fittings and toy soldiers. On The Barbican, **Chas R. Cload**, yacht chandlers, is a workmanlike store with a good selection of fishing rods, lines and reels, as well as barometers, clocks, brass key rings, ships' fittings and weatherproof clothing.

In the new shopping center, **Armada Way**, on New George Street you'll find **Principles, Top Shop** and **Next** (ladies clothing), **Hornes** (menswear), **Debenhams** (department store) and **Sherratt & Hughes** (bookshop). There's also **Edinburgh Woollen Mills** for a great range of sweaters, scarves, slippers and hats, **Country Casuals** for classic women's clothes, and **Fagin's Bookshop**.

PLYMOUTH RESTAURANTS

Chez Nous, 13 Frankfort Gate   £££
Tel: (0752) 266793
Open: Daily 12:30pm-2pm, 7pm-10:30pm   Closed: Sep
Credit cards: AE, DC, MC, V

Standards are high in this excellent little French restaurant behind slatted wooden blinds in the modern shopping center. The food is varied and interesting, with dishes such as French onion soup, medallions of monkfish with saffron and Devon lamb with herbs. The prix fixe and à la carte menus are chalked up on a blackboard. The flavor of the place – in the decor, music, and friendly professional service – is very French. The extensive wine list features some interesting rare vintages and bin ends.

The Distillery, Southside Street, The Barbican   £
Tel: (0752) 224305
Open: Daily noon-2pm, 6pm-10:30pm
Credit cards: AE, DC, MC, V

If you'd like to dine where the Pilgrim Fathers are said to have spent the night before setting out for the New World, visit The Distillery and ask for a table in the **Refectory Room**. It has a magnificent timbered roof and dates back to the 15th century, when it was the refectory of a Dominican monastery. The building has been a gin distillery for the past 200 years and you can see its machinery. The second-floor restaurant, now a Beefeater Steak House, serves a variety of dishes such as chicken *cordon bleu* and rack of spring lamb as well as steaks. The downstairs bar offers lunchtime snacks and a hot dish of the day.

Green Lanterns, 31 New Street, The Barbican   £
Tel: (0752) 660852
Open: Mon-Sat 10am-2:15pm, 6:30pm-10:45pm
Credit cards: AE, DC, MC, V

This half-timbered, 16th-century eating house in old Plymouth is full of nooks and crannies, wooden beams, old stone walls and lots of interesting pictures and ornaments; an open spring trickles water beside the bar. The food is interesting and unusual though traditionally English, with many Devonian and Cornish dishes such as Cornish crabbers pie, cockerel pudding (a steamed suet pudding of chopped chicken and pork), and mock goose (stuffed pork fillet). There are delicious desserts such as cider apple tart and a good cheeseboard with many English varieties.

Hosteria Romana, 58 Southside Street, The Barbican   £££
Tel: (0752) 668827
Open: Mon-Thurs, Sun, noon-2pm, 7pm-11pm, Fri-Sat
      7pm-midnight
Credit cards: AE, DC, MC, V

This is a lively Italian restaurant in the interesting old heart of
Plymouth. On a sunny day you can eat at outdoor courtyard tables,
surrounded by climbing roses and honeysuckle, but you'll enjoy the
extensive menu just as much indoors. The dishes are typically
Italian; with lots of pasta, fresh fish Italian style, several veal
dishes, steak, chicken, interesting vegetables and a lengthy wine
list.

PLYMOUTH HOTELS

The Astor Hotel, Elliott Street, The Hoe   ££
Tel: (0752) 225511
Amenities: ☎ ⌨ 🅿 🍴 🍷 ◉   Credit cards: AE, DC, MC, V

This pleasant hotel is in a quiet street a short walk from the sea yet
convenient to the town center. In Victorian times it was a sea
captain's home. It's a comfortable, friendly place with a good
restaurant and rooms with every modern facility.

The Copthorne, The Armada Centre, Armada Way   £££
Tel: (0752) 224161
Amenities: ☎ ⌨ 🅿 🍴 🍷 ≈ ◉   Credit cards: AE, DC, MC, V

This attractive new hotel is on the main Plymouth inner ring road,
Western Approach, and is an ideal choice for drivers, yet the
Armada Centre pedestrianized shopping precinct is only minutes
away. The hotel's excellent facilities include an indoor pool with
jetstream, solarium, sauna, exercise equipment and indoor games
area, plus two restaurants – one brasserie-style and one with a full à
la carte menu – and a galleried cocktail bar where there's live piano
music twice a week in the evenings.

The Grand Hotel, Elliott Street, The Hoe   ££
Tel: (0752) 661195
Amenities: ☎ ⌨ 🅿 🍴 🍷 ◉   Credit cards: AE, DC, MC, V

The Grand is in a quiet part of Plymouth near the famous Hoe, with
a splendid view over Plymouth Sound, making it a favorite for
those who like peace. You can stroll along Cliff Road, overlooking
the sea, while the town center is also within your easy reach. Built
in 1879 the building retains many original architectural features,
such as the fine staircase. There's a delightful restaurant, with live
piano music on most nights, serving traditional English cuisine that
includes lots of fresh seafood. The young, enthusiastic staff will do

everything they can to ensure that you enjoy your stay.

AROUND AND ABOUT

Antony House, Torpoint
Open: Tues-Thur and public holiday Mon 2pm-6pm Apr-Oct; Sun
2pm-6pm as well Jun-Aug (last entry 5:30pm)
Admission: Adults £2.20, children £1.10

*Directions: This stately Queen Anne house of gray stone and brick is
reached by ferry from Plymouth or the A38/A374 to Torpoint.*

Built between 1711 and 1721 for Sir William Carew on the Cornwall
side of Plymouth Sound it has a most interesting collection of
period furniture, porcelain and family portraits displayed in fine
oak- or pine-paneled rooms. Wander through the splendid gardens
or relax by the River Lynher.

Buckland Abbey, Yelverton
Open: Daily 11am-6pm (last entry 5:30pm) Apr-Oct
Admission: Adults £2.80, children £1.40

*Directions: Drive via A386 north of Plymouth; turn off a ¼ mile
south of Yelverton (signposted).*

This 13th-century Cistercian monastery became a house in the 16th
century and was home to Sir Francis Drake and his family. You can
see the monks' guesthouse, 18th-century farm buildings and an
exhibition illustrating the Abbey's history.

Mount Edgcumbe House and Country Park
Open: Gardens: Daily 8am-dusk; House: Wed-Sun 11am-5:30pm
Good Friday-Oct
Admission: Gardens: Free; House: Adults £2, children £1

*Directions: Take the ferry from Plymouth, or drive via the A38/A374
to Torpoint and B3247 to Millbrook.*

Spectacularly positioned to face Plymouth across the sound, this
restored Tudor mansion in rolling parkland offers walks along 10
miles of coast with superb views. Home of the 7th Earl of Mount
Edgcumbe, it has formal gardens, containing the only Grade I
Historic Garden in Devon and Cornwall, and a deer park.

Saltram House, Plympton
Open: House: Sun-Thur 12:30pm-6pm plus Good Friday and Sat
of public holiday weekends Apr-Oct; Garden: 11am-6pm
all year round
Admission: House: Adults £3, children £1.50; Garden only: £1

Directions: Off A38 before reaching Plymouth.

This mid 18th-century house has an extraordinarily beautiful interior, with ornate plasterwork and wallpaper, a dining room and a salon designed by Robert Adam, a grand ballroom, 14 paintings by Sir Joshua Reynolds, and some fine furniture.

PLYMOUTH TO LOSTWITHIEL   (about 30 miles)

From the Guildhall car park turn left into Royal Parade, and go 200 yards to Derrys Cross traffic circle, just after the Theatre Royal on the left. Following signs to Torpoint, Saltash and Liskeard (A38), take the third turn, along Union Street, moving into the right lane almost immediately to turn right into Western Approach at the traffic lights 50 yards away. Passing the new shopping center and Copthorne Hotel on the right, you'll reach North Cross traffic circle in almost a ½ mile. Take the first left for Saltash, Liskeard and Tavistock, along Saltash Road. At another traffic circle just over a ¼ mile past Plymouth station on the right, take the second left up the hill (Alma Road, A386) for Liskeard. In just over a ½ mile go straight through the traffic lights at the Britannia pub and down Wolseley Road. At another traffic circle 300 yards on go straight over. After a mile, following signs for Cornwall, take the middle or right lane and turn right at the traffic lights (the St Budeaux bypass). A mile later filter left off this road for Cornwall to join a major divided highway (A38).

In 1½ miles you'll see the magnificent Tamar Suspension Bridge, built in 1961, with its 250 foot towers, spanning the river before you. This is the gateway to Cornwall. Take the second left at the traffic circle and cross the bridge. There is no toll going into Cornwall but you have to pay to leave this way. On the left is Brunel's interestingly shaped railroad bridge, the Royal Albert Bridge, built in 1859, with wonderful views beyond. In Saltash go through the new tunnel for Cornwall.

Cornwall is an immensely varied county at the southwestern tip of Great Britain. Its southern coast is a series of wooded estuaries and small fishing villages and towns while its northern Atlantic coast has miles of beautiful sandy beaches and dramatic cliffs. Nowhere in Cornwall are you more than 20 miles from the sea. It is also a farming county, with rich soil and pasture that make possible the famous Cornish clotted cream and pure ice cream.

On **Bodmin Moor** and towards the far west you'll find rugged moorland with ancient stones and the remains of Neolithic settlements, for this part of Britain was inhabited from prehistoric times. The Cornish today are an independent people with their own language, a Celtic one similar to Irish, Welsh and Breton – though many residents are newcomers. Tin-mining used to be one of Cornwall's main industries but nowadays china-clay works are more in evidence, especially around St Austell. The clay is exported worldwide to be used in making porcelain and china.

Cornwall is a very popular vacation area, partly because it enjoys one of Britain's mildest climates.

*At Trerulefoot traffic circle, 13 miles out of Plymouth, take the second left for **Liskeard** (A38). After about 6 miles take the **Liskeard** **bypass**, following signs for **Bodmin**, then after a further 4½ miles, just past the village of **Dobwalls**, turn left for St Austell (A390). You'll now catch glimpses of Bodmin Moor on your right, and to the left small fields and rounded hills. Note the strange names of many Cornish villages, in particular many beginning with Tre-, Pen-, Pol- or Porth. In Cornish Tre means home or town, Pen means hill, Pol means pond or pool, and Porth means cove.*

*As you enter **Lostwithiel** the A390 bends to right and left across two bridges, first over the railroad, then over the **River Fowey**. Immediately after this follow the sign on your left for the car park (free), a rough-surfaced area in front of Lostwithiel Community Centre, which is also the **Tourist Information Centre**. (Tel: (0208) 872207. Open: Mon-Sat 10am-5pm.) Alternatively, carry on along the main road and take the second turn on the left into **Fore Street**, turning right at the bottom for the free car parking.*

LOSTWITHIEL

Lostwithiel was the medieval capital of Cornwall. It's an ancient stannary town where the Duchy of Cornwall Parliament opened in 1272 for assaying the metal tin, and where the Stannary Court settled local disputes. The town's importance as a port declined as the river silted up. Today it's a charming place to wander around, especially if you collect antiques, for there seem to be antique shops everywhere you look.

From the main street, **Queen Street**, walk down **North Street** to the narrow nine-arched **Tudor bridge** over the River Fowey; it has alcoves for pedestrians to retreat from the traffic. Return up North Street and turn right past 13th-century **St Bartholomew's Church**, named after the patron saint of tanners, then turn right into **Fore Street**, where you'll find the museum and the old town jail.

WHAT TO SEE

Museum and Town Jail, Fore Street
Open: Mon 2:30pm-4:30pm, Tues-Fri 10:30am-12:30pm, 2:30pm-
       4:30pm Easter, end May-Sep
Free admission

The small museum is full of such local relics as cooking utensils, irons, kettles and a Georgian cooking range. Walk through to the old prison, a dark 12 foot-by-12 foot room with an iron grating over its small window, where prisoners were kept in crowded and unsanitary conditions with heavy blocks attached to their ankles.

SHOPPING

Most stores are open Monday to Saturday from 9am or 9:30am to 5pm or 5:30pm. Many shops close for the day at 1pm on Wednesday.

Lostwithiel is known for its antique and craft shops, which can be found on **Queen Street, Fore Street, South Street** and **Quay Street**. Starting on Queen Street, at No 7, is **Treval Fine Art**, for original oil paintings and watercolors, and **Collectables**, for antique furniture, stripped pine, and decorative items and trivia, like small brass objects and tea sets. **The Higgins Press**, on South Street, sells antiques, bric-a-brac and curios, copper objects, pictures and the blue and white china known as Cornish ware.

Fore Street is the most interesting shopping street, with **Ann's Gallery**, Nos 15 and 24, a good place for quality gifts – original paintings, unframed prints, potpourri, greeting cards, stationery, mugs, and scented candles. **The Spinner's Web**, No 9, is a delightful shop selling spinning wheels, various fleeces such as Merino and Corriedale, looms, handspun and weaving yarns, handmade sweaters and sheepskin toys. **John Bragg Antiques** sells furniture and plates, and on North Street you'll find **The Old Malt House Antiques**, for plates, china and vases. There's a working blacksmith's forge to the right of the shop.

On Quay Street **The Old Palace Antiques** sell small objects, including copper and brassware, china, old pressing irons and furniture, while **Quay Street Traders** stock secondhand furniture, collectors' items and curios. On Parade Square you'll find **Riverside Antiques,** with a selection of furniture and china.

LOSTWITHIEL RESTAURANTS

Tawny Owl Restaurant & Tea Rooms, 19 North Street   £
Tel: (0208) 872045
Open: Mon-Sat 9am-5pm, Sun 12:30pm-2pm
No credit cards

These cheerful tearooms and restaurant are ideal for morning coffee, a light lunch or afternoon tea. You can choose from Cornish pasties, flans, hot-pots and salads, as well as sample the delicious cakes and pastries, all made on the premises to an extremely high standard. The traditional Sunday lunches are excellent – it's advisable to reserve a table. The restaurant serves wines and spirits.

Lanhydrock House Restaurants, near Bodmin   £
(see page 435)

Trewithen Restaurant, 3 Lower Fore Street   ££
Tel: (0208) 872373
Open: Tues-Sat from 7pm; also Mon in summer
Closed: Dec 26-Jan 3, 3 wks May
Credit cards: DC, MC, V

This charming little restaurant is decorated cottage-style with checked gingham café curtains, corn dollies, antiques, and an old Cornish cooking range in the hallway. The food, imaginative but unpretentious, includes seafood pancakes, double pork chop with scrumpy (cider) sauce, and braised crab claws. Specials such as lobster are chalked up on a blackboard. The wine list consists of an album of bottle-labels from which you choose. Reserve in advance.

AROUND AND ABOUT

Lanhydrock House
Open: Daily 11am-6pm (last entry: 5:30pm) Apr-Oct; garden only
         during daylight hours Nov-Mar
Admission: Adults £3.50, children £1.60; garden and grounds
         only, adults £1.60, children 80p

Directions: Take the A390 out of Lostwithiel towards St Austell. After 1½ miles turn right at the ancient cross signposted Lanhydrock House. From the car park you'll have a pleasant 600-yard walk through parkland to the mansion.

This fine gray stone 17th-century house, largely rebuilt after a fire in 1881, stands in rolling parkland with views across Cornwall to the hills beyond. Note the granite gatehouse, completed in 1651, where guidebooks may be bought, the fine avenue of trees leading away from it, and the small church tucked behind the house. Identical squat obelisk shapes are found on the gatehouse, on the house itself, and at the lodge gates.

Walk through the formal gardens to the house. Be sure to see the 116-foot gallery with its fine plaster ceiling, finished just before the outbreak of the Civil War in 1642.

The superb 25-acre garden, laid out in the mid 19th century, contains many beautiful plants, especially magnolias and rhododendrons.

The **Lanhydrock House Restaurants** serve delicious meals. The Servants Hall Restaurant is open for lunch from noon to 2:15 pm. Try the homemade soup, home-cooked ham, salads and the banana and walnut syllabub. From 3pm to 5:30pm you can indulge in luscious Cornish cream teas.

In the Housemaid's and Housekeeper's Room from noon to 3pm light meals are served – for example savory flan with salads – as is high tea, 3pm to 5pm, with cakes, soups, flans and cold meats. Each restaurant has table service by waitresses dressed in old-fashioned servant-style costumes, with lace caps and frilled floral aprons.

Restormel Castle
Open: Mon-Sat 9:30am-6:30pm, Sun 2pm-6:30pm Mar 15-Oct 15;
Mon-Sat 9:30am-4pm, Sun 2pm-4pm Oct 16-Mar 14; also
open Sun from 9:30am Apr 1-Sep 30
Closed: All day Tues and Wed am in winter
Admission: Adults 75p, children 35p

*Directions: From **Lostwithiel Community Centre car park** turn left
onto the main road (**A390**) then immediately right, signposted for the
Castle, which is a mile up the road.*

Restormel Castle is the oldest and best preserved Norman castle of
its type in Cornwall, overlooking the Cornish countryside from a
high circular mound within a deep moat. The **Gate Tower** dates
from the 12th century but was built on the site of an earlier
earthwork. The castle was completed in the 13th century. It was
twice visited by Edward the Black Prince in the 14th century and
was a ruin by the 16th. Its atmosphere is redolent of its dramatic
past.

LOSTWITHIEL TO TRURO   (about 22 miles)

*From **Lostwithiel car park** turn left onto **Queen Street** (**A390**), which
quickly takes you out of the town and up a wooded hill towards **St
Austell**. In 2 miles you'll have views over St Austell Bay to your left,
the town stretching in front of you. Five miles out of Lostwithiel
you'll enter **St Blazey**, crossing the railroad line, then it's 4 miles more
to St Austell, center of the Cornish china-clay industry.*

You'll notice huge white pyramids and mounds of quartz and sand
to the right as you loop around the town. The clay is transported
from Par Docks and nearby Fowey. An excellent small hotel in the
area is Boscundle Manor.

ST AUSTELL HOTELS

Boscundle Manor, Tregrehan   **£££**
Tel: (072681) 3557   Open: Easter-Oct
Amenities: ☎ ⬚ 🅿 ⑪ ⏃ ≋ ⋰   Credit cards: AE, MC, V

Walk in the door of this country-house hotel and at once you'll be
made to feel at home by its lively owners, Andrew and Mary Flint.
They've furnished and decorated this historic part-18th-century
building with enormous flair and they do all the cooking and tend its
10-acre garden. There is an area set aside for practice golf holes
while regulation courses are nearby. The daily changing prix fixe
menu has interesting dishes made with absolutely fresh ingredients,
and there's a varied wine list. This is one of Cornwall's best
hotel/restaurants.

SIDE TRIP TO CHARLESTOWN (about 2 miles)

Directions: Before driving on to Truro make a detour to see the picturesque port of Charlestown. Less than ¼ mile into St Austell take the left turn at the traffic lights, signposted **Charlestown**. *At the mini traffic circle turn first left, onto* **Church Lane**, *and after passing* **St Paul's Church** *turn left onto* **Charlestown Road**. *As you descend into Charlestown (½ mile) you'll have a good sea view. Follow the signs for the car park on the left, then walk down the hill for the port and museum.*

Charlestown is an old fishing village and still a working port. In the harbor you can see ships loading as they have since the 1790s. Originally shipments of china clay, coal, timber, tin, lime and pilchards were handled here. Now you'll most likely see china clay being loaded.

Charlestown's unspoilt character has made it a favorite location among TV and film directors. At either side of the harbor are pebbly beaches. There's a fine view of the coastline from the harbor wall.

WHAT TO SEE

The Heritage Centre
Open: Mon-Fri 10am-4pm, Sat and Sun 10am-6pm Easter-end
        May; 10am-late end May-Oct.
Admission: Adults £1.30, children 65p

The Heritage Centre records the history of the china clay industry, past village life in Charlestown, and local crafts. There's a pilchard packing room with an original pilchard press. The Museum boasts Britain's biggest collection of shipwreck memorabilia. Nautical relics, an ancient wooden diving barrel, figureheads, and ships' instruments illustrate the melancholy history of the many shipwrecks on the rocky Cornish coast over the centuries.

The Rashleigh Arms, next to the car park, (open: daily noon-2pm, 7pm-9:30pm) is a pleasant place to stop for a light lunch. The lunchtime bar snacks menu includes such dishes as cauliflower cheese and fries or crab and prawn sandwiches. Coffee is always available, as are tea and cakes in the afternoon. The flower-filled garden, with wooden benches and tables, is a pleasant spot in fine weather.

Beside the harbor, with a fine view over the bay, the **Pier House Hotel** serves breakfast (Mon-Sat 8am-9:15am, Sun 8:30am-9:15am), lunch and dinner, with a choice selection of seafood dishes such as crab au gratin or prawn salad.

Retrace your steps toward **St Austell** *via* **Charlestown Road**. *At the first traffic circle follow the signs for* **Truro** *and the* **town center**, *turn* *first left into* **Polmear Road**. *Go straight across the next traffic circle, after a ¼ mile, then over the double mini traffic circle, ¾ mile after that, then turn left for* **Truro**.

The road out of St Austell takes you through rich dairy farmland with occasional derelict tin mines high on the hills. Watch out for cattle crossings; this is still a very rural area. As well as the traditional black and white Friesian cows you may see other interesting breeds such as brown Jerseys and white Charolais.

As you pass through **Grampound**, 7 miles out of St Austell, note the attractive bell tower with its weather vane. Here you cross the **River Fal**, passing **Trewithen Gardens** in 2½ miles, then the **Probus Demonstration Garden** and the village of **Tresillian** on River Tresillian River. **Manor Cottage**, on your right as you leave the village, serves very good teas (open: daily 2:30pm-6pm). Truro is 3 miles along a twisting, narrow, wooded stretch of road. As you approach it you'll glimpse the cathedral's three spires, which dominate the city. Half a mile after entering Truro, **Tregolls Road (A39)** becomes a two-lane highway. At the traffic circle take the third turn to cross over the **River Truro**, then a ¼ mile on, at the next traffic circle, take the middle lane and follow the signs for the **short-stay car park**, the third turn left. Immediately you enter **Fairmantle Street** turn right into the pay-and-display car park.

From the car park walk up **Fairmantle Street** and turn right into **Lemon Street** – note the fine yellowstone Georgian houses – then right into the delightful cobbled **Boscawen Street** and the **Tourist Information Centre** is on the right in the City Hall. (Tel: (0872) 74555. Open: Mon-Fri 9am-5pm, Sat 10am-1pm May-Sep; Mon-Fri 10am-1pm, 2pm-5pm Oct-Apr; Fri until 4:45pm all year.)

TRURO

Cathedral city and administrative center of Cornwall, Truro is a place of cobbled streets, old houses, a museum, varied stores and sights. All in all it's an interesting town to explore.

WHAT TO SEE

Truro Cathedral, High Cross
Open: Daily until dusk
Admission: Donation appreciated

For eight centuries Cornwall and Devon shared a cathedral. Then Truro cathedral was completed in 1910 on the site of the 16th-century parish church of St Mary, the first Anglican cathedral built since St Paul's, London, in 1666. Like many French cathedrals it is surrounded by the narrow streets and old houses of the city center.

As you enter its front doors and look toward the altar note the sharp bend in the nave, incorporated to make the cathedral fit into the surrounding streets. The architecture, inside and out, is very beautiful. Note, too, the carved pulpit, the alabaster-and-marble memorial to the Robartes family, the teak Bishop's throne, the ancient stone statue of Saint Nicholas, the 14th-century carved Breton pietà, and the carved Baptistery.

Coffee is served in the **Chapter House** 10am to noon, afternoon tea 2pm to 4pm. The cathedral shop sells souvenirs and postcards.

The County Museum and Art Gallery, River Street
Open: Mon-Sat 9am-1pm, 2pm-5pm   Closed: Public holidays
Admission: 50p

At **Victoria Square**, leading on from **Boscawen Street**, turn right into **River Street** for the museum. It is well worth a visit, particularly for the first-floor display of ancient Cornish gold jewelry, such as the beautiful early Bronze Age beaten gold collars found at Harlyn Bay, near Padstow, and the twisted gold 'armilla', or bracelet, which would still look fabulous if worn today. There are displays of Cornish archeology and history, a world-famous collection of minerals, English ceramics and pewter, Japanese ivories and lacquer-work, paintings and a natural history collection that includes local sea shells, birds and insects.

SHOPPING

Stores are generally open from 9am to 5:30pm. Early closing is on Thursday, when the smaller stores shut at 1pm. **Lemon Street, Boscawen Street, Victoria Square, Kenwyn Street, River Street, High Cross** and **St Mary Street** are best for shops. The indoor **Truro Pannier Market** is held Monday to Saturday on **Back Quay**, opposite the bus and coach depot, and there's a **Flea Market** in the City Hall, Boscawen Street, on Fridays and Saturdays. At **The Old Grammar School Hall** every Wednesday there's an **Antiques Market** for Georgian and Victorian silver, porcelain, glass, brass and copper. The **Craft Market** in the same place each Thursday has handmade jewelry, local knitwear and other interesting items.

The Tourist Centre staff will mark the locations of antiques and other interesting shops on your map. **Alan Bennett Antiques** at 15 and 16 St Mary's Street has friendly staff who will arrange shipments to the USA. The shop sells fine furniture, antique jewelry, framed prints and pictures, interesting old copper, brass candlesticks and old wooden boxes. St Mary's Street also has several jewelry shops.

At 35 River Street you'll find **City Bookshop**, for local-interest books. Note the interesting window displays. Opposite, at No 2, there's **The Body and Face Place** for a range of natural skin preparations, plus basketware and dried flowers which make unusual gifts. **Velvet Crystal**, No 8, sells ladies' fashions and exotic jewelry (open: 10am) and at the **National Trust Shop**, No 9, you'll find local preserves and mustards, honey, candles, scented pillows and cushions, cards and books. **Casa Fina Interiors**, No 29, sells modern Italian china bowls, jugs, large plates, serving dishes, lamps and modern glassware. **Mounts Bay Trading Company**, Nos 12-13, sells kitchenware, china, basketware and such curios as carved wooden ducks. **Roberts** department store, back on St Nicholas Street, has a wide range of clothes, cosmetics, perfumes and other goods. **Michael Spiers**, 82 Lemon Street, offers a wide range of antiques, secondhand and modern jewelry in exclusive designs, many incorporating precious or semi-precious stones, and silverware.

TRURO RESTAURANTS

Chimes Coffee House, High Cross   £
  (opposite the cathedral entrance)
Open: Mon-Sat 10am-5:30pm
No credit cards

An ideal spot for a break when visiting the cathedral, this coffee house has beamed ceilings, pretty pink tablecloths over its small round tables, cane chairs, and a spiral staircase to the second floor. A seat near the window gives you an unbeatable view of the sculptures on the side of the cathedral. The menu offers coffee, tea, hot chocolate, sandwiches, and toasted sandwiches as well as light snacks such as homemade soup, quiches and salads. Homemade cakes such as iced ginger cake will boost your flagging energy.

Pearce's Grill, The Royal Hotel, Lemon Street   £
(see page 441)

Roberts (in the department store), Boscawen Street   £
Open: Mon-Sat 9:15am-5pm
Credit cards: MC, V

There's coffee, a range of teas including Earl Grey, hot chocolate, open sandwiches, salads, jacket potatoes, a specialty of the day, desserts and Cornish cream teas. Just the spot for a quick snack.

TRURO HOTELS

The Marcorrie Hotel, 20 Falmouth Road   £
Tel: (0872) 77374/77761
Amenities: ☎ ⌨ 🅿 ⚒ ⌙ ◉   Credit cards: MC, V

This family-owned hotel is within walking distance of the city center. There's car parking in front of the attractive stone building, with its window-boxes full of flowers. The bedrooms are cheerful, each with tea and coffee making facilities, though be sure to insist on one that has an en suite bathroom. Box lunches and evening snacks are available. Special diets can be catered for by arrangement. A three-course dinner is served at 7pm.

The Royal Hotel, Lemon Street   **£**
Tel: (0872) 70345
Amenities: ☎ 😐 🅿 ⚒ 🍷 ◎   Credit cards: MC, V

You can't get much closer to the center of Truro than the Royal Hotel, at the top of Lemon Street. Established in the 19th century and considerably modernized subsequently, it's cheerful and comfortable rather than luxurious. The rooms are pleasantly furnished, each with a radio, tea and coffee making facilities and a writing desk. All 34 rooms have private bath or shower. Have a drink in the **Cellar Bar** with its traditional slate floor, natural granite and exposed timbers. **Pearce's Bar and Grill** offers a reasonably priced à la carte menu of English dishes and a table d'hôte menu which may include main courses of sirloin steak, cod in parsley sauce or ham salad.

AROUND AND ABOUT

Probus Demonstration Gardens, Probus
Open: Mon-Fri 10am-5pm, Sun 2pm-6pm May-Sep; Mon-Fri
     10am-4:30pm Oct-Apr
Admission: Adults 60p, children free

Directions: Off A390, 3¾ miles outside Truro, next to Trewithen House.

A fascinating place for keen gardeners, these 7½ acres contain displays of many kinds of plants and examples of design for small and large gardens. Modern techniques in vegetable and fruit growing are featured along with wild flowers and a collection of Cornish plants. The culinary and herb gardens are but two of the many specialized gardens. There are conducted tours and demonstrations.

Trewithen House and Gardens, near Probus
Open: Gardens: Mon-Sat 10am-4:30pm Mar-Sep; House Tours:
     Mon and Tues 2pm-4:30pm Apr-Jul
Admission: Gardens, Adults £1.20, children under 15 years 75p;
         house £2 per person

Directions: Off A390, 4 miles outside Truro, between Probus and Grampound (next to Probus Demonstation Gardens).

This impressive 18th-century gray stone house, overlooking a lake and parkland, has been owned and occupied by the same family since 1720. It contains fine porcelain, paintings and period furniture. The gardens, covering about 30 acres, are some of the most beautiful in Cornwall. Created early this century, they contain a fine collection of camellias, rhododendrons, magnolias and many trees and shrubs that are rare in Britain. Your first view is of a water lily pond and fountains in a charming walled garden with immaculate lawns, herbaceous borders, rose beds and herbs. Note the wisteria trained over the pergola near the eagle statues at the far end before you pass through the gateway into the rest of the garden.

Trelissick Garden, Feock, near Truro
Open: Mon-Sat 11am-6pm (or sunset if earlier), Sun 1pm-6pm
   (garden and shop) Mar-Oct
Admission: Adults £1.80 children 90p

*Directions: Off **A39**, signposted at traffic circle 2 miles southwest of Truro; left 1 mile after **Come-to-Good** village.*

Here is another beautiful Cornish garden full of rare shrubs and plants. It's in a dramatic position above the River Fal, with wonderful views and woodland walks. The 20 acres are divided into areas devoted to hardy plants, tree ferns, figs, fuschias, ivies, camellias, rhododendrons and so on. There's an excellent restaurant (open: Mon-Sat 11am-6pm, Sun noon-6pm when the garden is open), and a shop selling National Trust gifts, books and souvenirs. The house isn't open to the public.

SIDE TRIP TO ST MAWES   (about 22 miles)

*About 2 miles from Probus on the **Truro Road** you'll see a sign to **St Mawes** (15 miles) on your left (**A3078**). This road winds between high hedges through the hilly Cornish countryside, and in 4 miles, at **Tregony**, crosses a narrow stone bridge over the **River Fal**. Don't now be tempted to take the left turn but go on around to the right, and on to St Mawes. After Ruan High Lanes glimpses of the sea become ever more frequent along with fine views of the patchwork Cornish fields. As you enter the parish of **St Just-in-Roseland** you'll see the **River Percuil** on your left just before a steep hill and sharp bend. Entering the village you'll see a sign for Truro via the King Harry Ferry on the right; it's another 2¼ miles to St Mawes. As you enter the town go on to the left for the town car park (or take the right turn if you just want to see the castle). Come down hilly **Tredenham Road**, following the line of the bay, with a view of the castle and prettily colored houses; in ¼ mile turn right into the car park. There isn't a Tourist Information Centre in St Mawes but the Falmouth and Truro TIC's will be able to offer advice on this area.*

ST MAWES

First the site of a religious retreat, St Mawes then assumed importance because the peninsula, once fortified in combination with Pendennis Castle, provided ideal protection from French entry via the intervening Carrick Roads water to the Fal estuary. The town's terraced houses look down on the water below, a perfect picture of what a Cornish coastal village should be.

Turn right out of the car park onto **Marine Parade** to walk along the picturesque harbor. The bay is busy with boats: ferries ply between here and Falmouth, and there are cruises up the **River Fal**, the **River Helford** and **Frenchman's Creek** (made famous by Daphne du Maurier's novel of that name). There are boats for rent and a fine-pebbled beach.

WHAT TO SEE

St Mawes Castle
Open: Daily 9:30am-6:30pm (closed between 1pm-2pm) mid Mar-mid Oct; 9:30am-4pm (closed between 1pm-2pm), Sun 2pm-4pm mid Oct-mid Mar
Closed: Christmas Day, Boxing Day and New Year's Day
Admission: Adults 75p, children 35p

Henry VIII built this castle in the mid 16th century, the age of gunpowder and cannon, along with Pendennis Castle at Falmouth, as part of his coastal defences against the French. The cloverleaf-shaped castle was never seriously attacked, so it's still in good condition. You can see the circular central towers (so designed to deflect cannonballs) and bastions with gun slits covering every possible approach.

ST MAWES HOTELS AND RESTAURANTS

Braganza, Grove Hill   £
Tel: (0326) 270281   Closed: Oct 1–April 15
Amenities: **P**   No credit cards

This delightful small, antique-filled guest house features wonderful views over the village. Rooms are well decorated with the added pleasant touch of fresh flowers and tea/coffee makers. They all have en suite facilities. Your hostess, Mrs Moseley, is a fund of knowledge on St Mawes and its surroundings.

The Rising Sun   £££
Tel: (0326) 270233
Amenities: ☎ ⌨ **P** ⑪ ♈ ◎   Credit cards: AE, DC, MC, V

Set by the St Mawes seafront, beside the car park, this white-

washed inn has a flower-filled garden with tables and chairs.
Antique maps, prints and furniture are in the entrance hall. The
pretty bedrooms have floral curtains and interesting pictures. The
charming little restaurant has an appetizing fixed price dinner menu
based on fresh local produce, which might include fish and dishes
such as a suprême of duck and strawberries. Bar snacks (served
noon-2pm) include filled baked potatoes, salads, sandwiches, or
dishes such as 'creamy hake bake'.

Hotel Tresanton   **£££ (incl dinner)**
Tel: (0326) 270544   Closed: Nov 1-Dec 20, Jan 1-Mar 1
Amenities: ☎ ⌨ 🅿 ⑂⑂ ⑂ ◎   Credit cards: AE, DC, MC, V

The Tresanton's attractive whitewashed façade with blue paint-
work, decorated with red geraniums, hides a deceptively spacious
hotel and terraced gardens. The hotel overlooks the bay and every
room has a sea view. The decor in this family-run hotel is tasteful
and charming, featuring many antiques and paintings. The dining
room serves an interesting selection of local meat and vegetables,
with fish a specialty. You could start with local scallops, followed by
pan-fried red and grey mullet with dill and orange salad. Bar snacks
are served at lunchtime.

TRURO TO FALMOUTH   (about 11 miles)

*On leaving Truro from the **Fairmantle Street car park** turn right, then
left into **Lemon Street** at the top of the road. Lemon Street becomes
the **Falmouth Road** in about a 1/4 mile, then in another 1/4 mile you'll
come to a double traffic circle. Take the second major left up **Arch
Hill (A39)**, following the signs for **Falmouth** and **Helston**. At the
village of **Playing Place**, 2 miles on, is another double traffic circle.
Go straight over both. At **Carnon Downs**, in 1 mile, you'll have wide-
ranging views before crossing the **River Carnon** in another mile. Two
and a half miles further you'll cross a railroad bridge, then another
double traffic circle where you go over the first and turn left at the
second for **Falmouth (A394)**, bypassing Penryn.*

*Beware of heavy traffic from now on since there's only one main
road in and out of Falmouth which does get congested. After Penryn
the road follows **River Penryn**. The many ships' chandlers, sail-
makers, dinghy centers and yacht and boat showrooms attest to
Falmouth's importance as a port and sailing center. Pass the first
traffic lights on the Falmouth Road, with the river on your left as you
cross the bridge. After a further 1/2 mile go straight over the traffic
circle and bear right up **Dracaena Avenue**, following the signs for the
town center, docks and beaches. At the next traffic lights turn left for
the town center, into **Kimberley Park Road**, with a beautiful flower-
filled park on your right. Turn left at the intersection just before **The***

*Moor for the short stay car park in the square. Alternatively the long stay pay-and-display car park is signposted on your left, up **Quarry Hill**.*
*The **Tourist Information Centre** is in front of you, in the Town Hall on **The Moor**. (Tel: (0326) 312300. Open: Mon-Thur 8:45am-5:15pm, Fri 8:45am-4:45pm, Sat 9am-5pm mid May-mid Sep; closed for lunch 1pm-2pm and Sat mid Sep-mid May.)*

FALMOUTH

Falmouth is a leading Cornish port and holiday resort. It's on the 'Carrick Roads', where several rivers, including the Fal, come down to the sea, and is claimed to be the third largest natural harbor in the world. The wide sweep of **Falmouth Bay** is commanded by another of Henry VIII's castles, at **Pendennis Point**, opposite St Mawes. The town is still a busy port, harbor and sailing center. Fishing boats, tankers and ferries go from here to St Mawes and up the Fal and Helford rivers. Fishing and other water sports can all be arranged.

For vacationers there are superb sandy beaches, good hotels, and a lively shopping center in the old town near the harbor.

WHAT TO SEE

Maritime Museum, Bell's Court (opposite Marks & Spencer), Market Street
Open: Museum and Steam tug: Mon-Sat 10am-4pm Easter-Oct; may stay open later July-Aug
Free admission, donation appreciated.

You'll get a good idea of the maritime history of southwest Cornwall by visiting this interesting museum. It occupies a historic protected building and was started a few years ago by local enthusiasts. There are models and displays of the famous **Falmouth Packet** (a model of an 1806 packet ship), nautical paintings, ships' instruments and sailors' belongings. Visitors may go aboard the steam tug **St Denys**, moored at **Custom House Quay**, near the museum.

Pendennis Castle, Pendennis Head
Open: Mon-Sat 9:30am-6:30pm, Sun 2pm-6:30pm Mar 15-Oct 15; Sun 9:30am-6:30pm Apr-Sep; Mon-Sat 9:30am-4pm, Sun 2pm-4pm Oct 16-Mar 14
Admission: Adults £1.00, children 50p

Completed in 1546, three years after St Mawes, the castle continued to guard Britain's coast for a remarkable 399 years (it only came out of active service at the end of World War II). The inner keep and curtain wall were built during Henry VIII's reign, while the outer wall was added during that of Elizabeth I.

Pendennis, with its commanding position, held out against Cromwell's forces for over five months, surrendering only when both food and ammunition ran out.

By way of contrast sister castle, St Mawes, surrendered after one day without a shot being fired. The St Mawes commander reasoned that his role was to defend from the sea. Attack from the land at the back simply wasn't part of his brief.

SHOPPING

Most shops are open Monday through Saturday 9am-5:30pm. Very few observe the early closing on Wednesday and you'll find some stores open until 8pm during the season.

Falmouth has a lively shopping center, busy in high season. Going toward the harbor the main shopping streets are between **The Moor** and **High Street** to the left, **Market Street, Church Street** and **Arwenack Street** to the right.

You'll find **Marks & Spencer** at 44 Market Street. There are several good bookshops: **The Falmouth Bookshop**, 21 Church Street, has local books and maps; **M. & P. Miller**, 15 Arwenack Street, **Insights**, 55 Killigrew Street; and a branch of **W.H. Smith** at 17 Church Street. **John Maggs**, 54 Church Street, has a good selection of antiquarian maps and prints, covering many areas and subjects. **The Cornish Stone Co. Ltd**, 4 Market Street, offers a selection of unusual jewelry incorporating semi-precious and precious stones, and at the **Gold and Silver Jewelry Workshop**, 27 Church Street, unique earrings, rings, bracelets and brooches are very reasonably priced. For antiques try **E. Cunningham**, 5 Webber Street, **Marilyns** in St George's Arcade for Victorian to 1950s clothes, linen and costume jewelry, **Old Country Antiques**, 26a Market Street; **Rosina's**, 4 High Street, and the **Waterfront Antiques Market**, 4 Quay Street, where you'll find a wide range of decorative and collectors' items such as books, clocks, metalware, old kitchen equipment, silver and jewelry.

FALMOUTH RESTAURANTS

Cornish Kitchen, 28 Arwenack Street   £
Tel: (0326) 316509
Open: Daily noon-2pm, 6pm-10:30pm in summer
Closed: Mon in winter, Christmas Day
Credit cards: DC, MC, V

There's a bistro feel to this small cheerful restaurant, with its red tablecloths, green wooden seats and lace curtains. Fresh fish is the specialty and the menu includes homemade crab soup, monkfish and giant prawn kebabs followed by homemade treacle tart with clotted cream, then port and Stilton cheese.

De Wynn's Coffee and Tea House, Church Street £
Tel: (0326) 319529
Open: Daily 10am-5pm

This attractive 19th-century tea and coffee house has an olde-worlde feel to it, with oak paneling on the walls, old signs and posters and interesting lamps. They are licensed for alcoholic drinks and serve morning coffee, light snacks like delicious Cornish pasties and specials of the day like bobotie (spicy minced lamb pie) or seafood pie. At teatime try the delicious homemade meringues or the tempting cakes. A warning – the place gets crowded, especially at lunchtime.

FALMOUTH HOTELS

The Bay Hotel, Cliff Road, Seafront ££
Tel: (0326) 312094 Open: Mar-Nov
Amenities: ☎ ⬛ 🅿 ⅋ ⅋ ◎ Credit cards: AE, DC, MC, V

Sister hotel to the nearby Falmouth, this is a similarly comfortable establishment in the traditional mold, also on the seafront. It's an impressive building with attractive terraced gardens and a large restaurant. It has its own sauna and solarium but shares the Falmouth's swimming pool, ballroom and some other facilities, though the views are so splendid you may not want to stir from the hotel.

Falmouth Hotel, Castle Beach £££
Tel: (0326) 312671 Closed: Over Christmas
Amenities: ☎ ⬛ 🅿 ⅋ ⅋ ≈ ◎ Credit cards: AE, DC, MC, V

This large and impressive hotel provides hospitality in the grand old style and is a haven of tranquility after Falmouth's bustling town center. With its own grounds just a few yards from Castle Beach it enjoys superb panoramic views of Falmouth Bay yet is an easy walk from the town. Facilities include a heated outdoor swimming pool, a croquet lawn, a games room and a full-size pool table. There are comfortable lounges and bars and a large restaurant with à la carte and prix fixe menus.

The Royal Duchy Hotel, Cliff Road ££
Tel: (0326) 313042
Amenities: ☎ ⬛ 🅿 ⅋ ⅋ ≈ ◎ Credit cards: AE, DC, MC, V

In a superb position overlooking Falmouth Bay, with a sandy beach only minutes' walk away, this hotel offers a high standard of comfort, with such amenities as a sauna and solarium, gym, table tennis and pool. Weekly dinner dances are held in the ballroom during the summer. Box lunches may be ordered.

FALMOUTH TO HELSTON   (about 10 miles)

*From the car park follow the one-way system around the town center, watching out for the crowds of pedestrians in high summer. You'll come up **Dracaena Avenue**, then return to **Falmouth Road**, with glimpses of the river to your right. One mile on get into the right lane to cross the bridge at the traffic lights, following signs for **Helston** and **Truro**. The road becomes **Commercial Road**. After 1 mile, at the traffic circle, take the first left (**A394**) for Helston, 8 miles away. In a ½ mile you'll have sea views to the left; in another ¼ mile turn right at the T-intersection.*

If you're interested in military vehicles the **Lamanva Museum** (open: daily 10:15am-5pm June-Sep; admission: adults £2, children £1), on the left immediately after the intersection, has a great display of American, British and German ones.

For the next couple of miles the road is exposed and windswept, with views across miles of open country punctuated by disused tin mines.

*Six miles out of Falmouth the aerial dishes of **Goonhilly Satellite Earth Station** can be seen on the left. Their satellites, 22,000 miles out in space, provide instant global communication. The dishes are on an outcrop of land called the **Lizard Peninsula**, a place of dramatic cliffs, old villages, beaches, and bays that once were the haunts of smugglers. It's an unspoilt area, rich in wildlife.*

*Entering **Helston** take the first left into **Clodgey Lane** at the double traffic circle, signposted for the **town center;** 200 yards later take the first major right into **Trengrouse Way**. The car park is 200 yards on the right by the Gateway supermarket. The town center is signposted.*

*There are tourist information brochures in the **Town Library**, a modern stucco-and-glass building in the back of the car park. (Open: Mon, Tues, Thur 9:30am-5pm, Fri 9:30am-7pm, Sat 9:30am-12:30pm. Closed: Wed and Sun.)*

HELSTON

Helston is a hilly little market town, not much changed in the past 100 years. At the **Angel Inn**, an old coaching inn on Coinagehall Street, it's easy to imagine the stagecoaches changing their horses. Until a wide bank of sand and shingle finally silted up the harbor mouth in the 13th century, Helston was a leading port. However, it continued to play an important role as a stannary town, where locally-mined tin was brought to be weighed and taxed.

Helston is famous for its annual Furry Dance on Flora Day, May 8, when costumed dancers weave through the streets, in and out of the houses. Five processional dances are performed, at 7am, 8:30am, 10am, noon and 5pm. The most spectacular of these is at

10am when about 800 children, dressed in white, dance through the streets.

WHAT TO SEE

Helston Folk Museum, The Old Butter Market, Church Street
Open: Mon, Tues, Thur-Sat 10:30am-1pm, 2pm-4:30pm; Wed
  10:30am-noon
Free admission, donations welcome

*Directions: Cross **Coinagehall Street** from **Meneage Street** and go down the cobbled way to the right of the **Guildhall**. The museum, with early 19th-century ships' guns outside, is on the right in the old butter, egg and meat market halls.*

Concentrating on the crafts and industries that flourished in and around Helston during the 19th and early 20th centuries, the museum has a good collection of farming tools and machinery, a large wooden cider press *circa* 1750, clothes, photographs, dolls, toys, a large box wringer, a Victorian swing cradle, a threshing machine, a printing press, a buttermaker and, not for the squeamish, a parish bier and old coffin. The museum also pays tribute to Henry Trengrouse (1771-1854), who invented the ship-to-shore rocket life-saving apparatus used by lifeboatmen and coast-guards. His tomb lies in the churchyard.

SHOPPING

Shopping hours are from 9am-5:30pm Monday to Saturday with many closing at about 1pm on Wednesday. Market days are Monday for cattle and Saturday for food and general goods.

Go down Church Street from the museum for an antiques shop with a very friendly owner – **Tudor Antiques**, at No 20 – and ring the bell if the door is locked. You'll find early silverware – sets of spoons, knives, cruets – and wooden boxes, china and some furniture. Mondays there's a small market on **Coinagehall Street**. The main shops are on this street too, as well as on **Meneage Street**, where **Gallery Arts**, No 55, sells local pictures and prints and artists' materials. **Crafty's**, at No 3, has traditional country craft items: different mixes of potpourri, scented gifts like lavender bags, embroidered cushions, patchwork baby carriage quilts, and children's pinafores and padded jackets.

The **Flower Seller Coffee Shop** in the basement offers tea, coffee, salads, sandwiches and cakes and **The Cornish Candy Shoppe**, with branches in St Mawes, Padstow and St Ives, has a mouthwatering selection of traditional fudges plus other Cornish specialties. They'll box fudge and mail it for you.

HELSTON RESTAURANTS

Nansloe Manor, Meneage Road ££
(see below)

The New Inn, Wendron, near Helston £
Tel: (0326) 572683
Open: Mon-Sat 11am-2:30pm, 7pm-11pm (but last food orders
9:30pm); Sun noon-2:30pm, 7pm-10:30pm
No credit cards

An attractive stone building facing the church, with shuttered
windows and outside bench seats for fine days, this is a cheerful inn,
decorated inside with horse brasses, old cartwheels and saddlery.
Bar snacks include turkey pie and cheese flan. The small, homey
restaurant, with red-checked tablecloths, specializes in steak, trout
and gammon grills as well as such daily specialties as smoked
salmon pâté and beef casserole.

The Yard Bistro, Trelowarren House, Mawgan-in-Meneage,
near Helston £
Tel: (032622) 595/224
Open: Mon-Sat noon-2pm, 7pm-9pm; Sun lunch Mar-Dec
No credit cards

A part of the old carriage house on the Trelowarren House estate,
this delightful bistro-style restaurant serves lunchtime snacks and a
more adventurous, French influenced menu in the evenings. This
includes fresh local seafood as available and such seasonal specialties as pheasant or guinea fowl, all at reasonable prices.

HELSTON HOTEL

Nansloe Manor, Meneage Road ££
Tel: (0326) 574691 Closed: Over Christmas
Amenities: ☎ ⊑ 🅿 ⑪ ⏛ Credit cards: MC, V

Nansloe Manor's long treelined driveway prepares you for a pretty
special place. This hotel, with an excellent restaurant, was built
between 1735 and 1900. It's an elegant, creeper-clad manor house,
tastefully decorated and furnished to a high standard, with fine old
fireplaces, a Georgian dining room, and well-kept gardens that
include a croquet lawn. The imaginative menu might include crab
fritters with cucumber mayonnaise followed by roast breast of duck
with lime and ginger sauce, or baked fillet of sea bream.

AROUND AND ABOUT

Godolphin House, Godolphin Cross, near Helston
Open: Thur 2pm-5pm May and Jun; Tues, Thur 2pm-5pm Jul and
Sep; Tues 2pm-5pm, Thur 10am-1pm and 2pm-5pm Aug;
public holiday Mondays
Admission: Adults £1.50, children 50p

*Directions: Take the **A394** out of Helston then turn right onto the **B3302** heading NW toward **Hayle**. In about 4 miles turn left for **Godolphin Cross** village, then follow signs for **Townshend**. Godolphin House is between the two villages, on the left.*

Formerly the home of the Earls of Godolphin, the largely 16th-century house has 17th-century and later additions, including an impressive colonnaded front which was built over an Elizabethan gateway. The Godolphins were local squires, prominent during Henry VIII's reign, and the future King Charles II is said to have stayed in the fine 'King's Room' after his escape from Pendennis Castle.

Poldark Mine, Wendron, near Helston
Open: Daily 10am-5pm Apr-Oct; 10am-8pm (last mine tour at
7pm) Aug
Admission: Adults £3.30, children £2

*Directions: Take the **B3297** from Helston to **Redruth** and the mine is on your right about 3 miles out, just past Wendron village.*

At this 18th-century Cornish tin mine there are guided underground tours every 15-20 minutes in peak season (hard hats provided). There are two routes of different lengths through the mine and you can see pumping engines, an old locomotive and other machinery. There's an ice cream parlor, a snack bar and cafeteria, souvenir shops and children's play areas.

Trelowarren House, Mawgan-in-Meneage, near Helston
Open: Wed and Sun 2:30pm-5pm end Jul-beg Sep; Wed only Sep,
Oct, Apr, Jul; all public holiday Mondays. No private
viewing; guided tours only
Admission: Adults £1, children over 12 years 50p, under 12 free

*Directions: From **Trengrouse Way car park** turn right into **Trengrouse Way**, then take the first left into **Meneage Street**, going straight over the first traffic circle, 100 yards on, into **Meneage Road**. At the next traffic circle, in just under a ½ mile, take the third turn, **The Furry**, signposted **The Lizard (A3083)**, just past the hospital. You immediately begin looping around the Royal Naval Air Station Culdrose, where you may see helicopter activity. On the left, 3½ miles out of Helston, you'll see a sign to **Trelowarren**. Turn left at the traffic circle, signposted **St Keverne (B3293)**, drive for a mile and at the next small* *traffic circle take the second left, signposted **Trelowarren**. Turn left about 700 yards afterward. You'll find the house and gardens in about 1½ miles, along the narrow winding road.*

Home of the Vyvyan family since 1427, the weathered yellow stone house is mainly early 16th-century, a reconstruction of a medieval manor. Surrounded by lawns and woodland, the pleasing house, with its buttressed sides, has an air of tranquility. There's a grand staircase inside, notable paintings and interesting antique furniture. Don't miss the splendidly decorated neo-Gothic chapel, rebuilt in the 18th century, where classical music is played Thursday evenings (8pm end Jun-early Sep). The Vyvyan family now live in the north wing only; the rest of the house is leased to a Church charity.

HELSTON TO PENZANCE, Via St Michael's Mount
(about 16½ miles)

*From **Trengrouse Way car park** turn right into **Trengrouse Way** itself, then take the first left into **Meneage Street**, and at the traffic circle take the second turn, down the **Helston Relief Road Hill**. At the double circle at the bottom take the first left at the first circle, then the second left at the second circle, following signs for **Penzance (A394)** with Helston cattle market on your left. You're now on the **Penzance Road** and soon crossing the **River Cober**. Two miles on you'll reach **Breage** village and a further 2 miles brings you to **Praa Sands**, on your left, where visitors are welcome at the golf club. Two more miles and you'll get fine views of Mount's Bay all the way to Penzance and Newlyn. A parking bay on the left, just past Bertie Wooster's Restaurant, is a good vantage point for photographing St Michael's Mount. Three and a half miles on go straight over the traffic circle for **Penzance**, crossing a bridge over the railroad and the **River Red**. In a ½ mile, at a traffic circle, take the first left for **Marazion, St Michael's Mount**, car parks and magificent views of the castle. Turn left at the T-intersection at the end of the road and drive along to the car parks.*

St Michael's Mount, Marazion, near Penzance
Open: Mon-Fri 10:30am-5:45pm Jun-Oct; Mon, Wed and Fri only
        Nov-May; tours 11am, noon, 2pm and 3pm
Admission: Adults £2.30, children £1.15

Access can be on foot over a cobbled causeway at low tide, but in summer a ferry crosses at high water. The numbers of people allowed in are restricted because of the castle's narrow passages, but once inside you can go around 'free-flow' or on a guided tour, according to the time of year.

    A spectacular rock, rising out of the sea and crowned with a castle, St Michael's Mount strikingly resembles the French Mont St

Michel, which belonged to the same Benedictine order of monks. Local lore has it that the island was a part of the legendary King Arthur's lost realm.

It was probably Ictis (the ancient name for this island), where Mediterranean merchants bought tin in the 1st century BC. From the 12th century on the Mount's potential as a fortress attracted both English kings and rebellious nobles; in 1425 the Crown seized it and evicted the monks from their chapel here.

The present castle on the Mount dates from the 14th century. In 1657 the St Aubyn family bought it and still live here. Be sure to see the **Monks' Refectory**, the 15th-century **Chapel** with its fine north door, west window and roof, and the **Armory**.

MARAZION RESTAURANT

Sail Loft Restaurant, St Michael's Mount £
Tel: (0736) 710748
Open: Daily 10:30am-5:30pm Easter-Oct   Closed: Nov-Easter
Credit cards: AE, DC, MC, V

Once a boathouse on St Michael's Mount, and now run by the National Trust, with their usual high standards of cooking, this restaurant does morning coffee, light lunches and traditional teas. The lunchtime menu includes local fish, with daily hot dishes and a choice of three desserts. The cakes at teatime are gorgeous. As you eat you can enjoy a splendid view of the harbor and the sea beyond.

MARAZION HOTEL

Mount Haven Hotel and Restaurant, Turnpike Road   £
Tel: (0736) 710249   Closed: Over Christmas
Amenities: ☎ ⛐ P ⸾⸾ ⸾ ✓ (nearby) ◎   Credit cards: AE, DC, MC, V

There's a magnificent view of the Mount from this hotel and most windows give a panoramic sweep of Mount's Bay. Formerly a coaching house, the hotel is in a peaceful spot a short distance from Marazion village. It has terraced gardens, comfortable rooms, a galleried restaurant with prix fixe and extensive à la carte menus and wine list. Free golf is available for residents at nearby **Praa Sands** golf course.

*Now retrace your steps from Marazion to the **A394** for **Penzance**.*

*At the traffic circle take the second left (**A30**) and continue into **Penzance** (2 miles), passing **British International Helicopters** heliport on the right – where you can take a pleasure flight for about £10 or a day trip to the **Scilly Isles** for £27. The road loops around the bay, with fine views of all the sailing activity as you enter Penzance along **Chyandour Cliff**, passing the train station on the left. After the station turn left down **Station Road**, keeping in the left lane; signposted for*

Newlyn and the car park, then follow the road around to the right into
Wharf Road*. The car park is on your left.*

The **Tourist Information Centre** *at the* **train station** *(Tel: (0736)*
62207. Open: Mon-Sat 9am-6pm, Sun 10am-1pm Jun-Sep; Mon-Fri
9am-5:30pm, Sat 10am-1pm Oct-May. Centre closes 5pm on Fri)
will provide an interesting **Town Trail** *brochure and map for 20p.*

PENZANCE

Penzance, with its busy harbor, is a popular resort overlooking
Mount's Bay and St Michael's Mount. Its mild climate, caused by
the warm waters of the Gulf Stream, encourages palms and other
sub-tropical plants to flourish in its gardens.

From the **Wharf Road car park** walk up **Albert Street** or **New
Town Lane**, turning left into **Market Jew Street**, with its raised
sidewalk. The town's most interesting streets are **New Street,
Chapel Street** and **Abbey Street** on the left and **Old Bakehouse
Lane**, with its attractive 17th- and 18th-century houses. Note in
particular Nos 6 and 7 Chapel Street, the **Egyptian House** (built
about 1835) – now housing a National Trust shop – with its unusual
windows, columns and statues. **Number 25** was once the home of
Maria Branwell, mother of Charlotte, Emily, Anne and Branwell
Brontë. **The Regent** is one of the town's oldest buildings, believed
to be more than 400 years old, and **No 53** is actually a 17th-century
house behind a Georgian façade. The **Admiral Benbow Inn** is also
more than 400 years old. It was a smugglers' meeting place, now
named after the 18th-century band, the Benbow Brandy Men,
whose second in command clambered onto the roof during a raid
and fired off his pistols to create a diversion. The revenue men shot
him down, but the inn and the band were saved – and Benbow
himself recovered. The **Turk's Head Inn** is probably the oldest
building in Penzance; behind its 'new' front, added after a Spanish
raid in 1595, lies a 13th-century building.

WHAT TO SEE

The Museum of Nautical Art, 19 Chapel Street
Open: Mon-Sat 10am-5pm Apr-Oct
Admission: Adults £1, children 50p

On display are a full-size four-decked section of an 18th-century
man-o'-war, showing the cramped conditions in which seamen
lived, hundreds of items salvaged from local sunken wrecks, model
ships, and other nautical memorabilia.

The Morrab Gardens (morrab being the Cornish word for sea-
shore) in the center of town provide a peaceful three-acre oasis with
interesting plants, many tropical.

SHOPPING

Normal shopping hours are 9am-5:30pm, Monday-Saturday with no early closing day. **Chapel Street** is packed with shops offering a wide selection of antiques, including porcelain, jewelry, militaria, silver, glassware and clocks. Try **Peter Mansfield**, No 61, **The Old Posthouse**, No 9, **Chapel Antiques**, No 10, **Peter Dalwood**, No 57, (antiquarian books), **Castle Books and Curios** and **Antron House Antiques**, No 55, **Tony Sanders New Gallery and Antiques**, No 14, **Daphne's Antiques**, No 17 and **Kitt's Corner**, at the corner of **Kitt's Court**, which also has a small tea garden.

Other recommended shops are **Zodiac Sports**, 11 Market Place, for a wide range of sports equipment, **The Penzance Bookshop**, 5 Chapel Street, for new and secondhand books on all subjects, including local interest, **Egyptian House**, Nos 6 and 7, for unusual and interesting gifts such as antiquarian maps and prints of southwest Cornwall, **Spinning Jennie**, on Old Bakehouse Lane, for high-quality local crafts such as knitwear and smocks, and **Medals and Militaria**, 1 Old Bakehouse Lane, with items ranging from medals to military chests, including books, helmets, swords and coins.

PENZANCE AND LAMORNA RESTAURANTS

The Abbey Hotel, Abbey Street   ££
(see page 456)

Harris's, 46 New Street   ££
Tel: (0736) 64408
Open: Mon 7pm-10pm, Tues-Sat noon-2pm, 7pm-10pm
Closed: 2 wks Nov
Credit cards: AE, DC, MC, V

Be sure to book in advance at this popular little restaurant a stone's throw from the sea down a narrow cobbled street. On its varied menu first courses might include avocado pear, fresh crab and mango, or king prawns, hot or cold; typical main dishes are suprême of chicken stuffed with Stilton and bacon in a cream and sherry sauce, English spring lamb, or the freshest of fish in season. The decor is darkish and atmospheric, with an unusual reddish-pink molded plaster ceiling and interesting antiques. Highly recommended.

The Lamorna Cove Hotel, Lamorna   ££
(see page 460)

Richmond's Restaurant and Patisserie, 12-13 Chapel Street £
Tel: (0736) 63540
Open: Mon-Sat 10:30am-5pm, 7pm-10:30pm; Sun 7pm-10:30pm
Closed: Christmas Day and Boxing Day
Credit cards: MC, V

A light, airy restaurant with a good-value, wide-ranging menu, the Richmond's Chapel Street position makes it a convenient stop while browsing around nearby sites and antiques shops. All the food, including the exceptional patisserie, is prepared and cooked on the premises. There are different lunchtime and evening menus, which might include first courses of shellfish or mussel soup, duck liver and marsala pâté; a selection of *plats du jour* chalked on a blackboard, such as *cassoulet* or baked halibut; desserts like strawberry sabayon or hot apple tart. It's best to reserve a table for the evenings. Richmond's is deservedly popular with locals and vacationers.

PENZANCE AND NEWLYN HOTELS

The Abbey, Abbey Street, Penzance £££
Tel: (0736) 66906   Closed: Jan-Feb
Amenities: 🖵 🅿 ⑂⑂ ⑂ ◎   No credit cards

Built in 1660, this small hotel is one of Penzance's oldest buildings. It is also one of the most delightful places to stay in Cornwall. It has a country-house atmosphere and each room is beautifully decorated in an individual style, with splendid antiques – furniture, rugs, ornaments and mirrors. There are real fires in the dining and drawing rooms. Five rooms have sea views. The interesting menu of traditional English food changes daily.

Higher Faugan Country House Hotel, Newlyn £££
Tel: (0736) 62076
Amenities: ☎ 🖵 🅿 ⑂⑂ ⑂ ≈ ⚲   Credit cards: AE, DC, MC, V

Admirers of the Newlyn School of painting will love this hotel, built at the turn of the century and lived in by Stanhope Forbes RA, the leader of the movement, who held his painting school here. A gray stone, gabled building set in ten acres of gardens 300 feet above sea level overlooking Penzance and Mount's Bay, it is a peaceful spot, with excellent facilities, good cooking and friendly owners and staff.

Kimberley House, 10 Morrab Road, Penzance £
Tel: (0736) 62727   Closed: Dec-Jan
Amenities: 🖵 🅿 ⑂⑂ ⑂   Credit cards: AE, MC

This nine-bedroom Victorian hotel is pleasantly furnished but none of the rooms has en suite facilities. The hotel is located in a residential area which is a 10-minute walk from the center of town.

See also **The Lamorna Cove Hotel** (page 460) and **The State House Hotel**, Lands End, (page 459).

AROUND AND ABOUT

Chysauster Ancient Village, near Badger's Cross, Penzance
Open: Mon-Sat 9:30am-6:30pm, Sun 2pm-6pm Mar 15-Oct 15;
       Mon-Sat 9:30am-4pm, Sun 2pm-4pm Oct 16-Mar 14
Closed: Thur 4pm, all day Fri, Dec 24-26, New Year's Day
Admission: Adults 70p, children 35p

Directions: Coming out of Penzance on the A30 toward Redruth take the first left after Chyandour Lane to Gulval, then the third right (Green Lane Hill, B3311), a sharp left, then another right, passing Gulval Cross. About a mile past Gulval, at Badger's Cross, turn left to Chysauster (1¾ miles), and go on through the village, following the signs to Chysauster Ancient Village, a ¼ mile on. Park on the left. There's a seven-minute walk up a steep narrow path to the village.

In an isolated, windswept spot, the village comprises eight ruined stone houses, dated between the 2nd or 1st centuries BC and the 3rd century AD. Each round house is built around a central courtyard with small rooms leading off it, and was probably roofed with stone or thatch. Many of the walls still stand, giving a good idea of the village's layout. There are remains of gardens and terraced fields further down the hillside.

Trengwainton Gardens, near Tremethick Cross and Madron, Penzance
Open: Wed-Sat 11am-6pm Mar-Oct, public holiday Mondays and
       Good Friday
Admission: Adults £1.40, children 70p

Directions: Leave Penzance by Madron Road (B3312); the gardens are about 2 miles on.

These beautiful gardens, with their lovely view over Mount's Bay, cover 16 acres. Dating from 1867, they contain many rare and exotic plants, some grown outside nowhere else in England. There's also a large shrub garden with a stream, a bog garden containing many specialties, a series of walled gardens at the foot of the drive and some splendid magnolias, rhododendrons and hydrangeas.

PENZANCE TO NEWLYN   (about 2 miles)

From the Wharf Road car park follow the road past the harbor, with its superb views of Mount's Bay, and cross the water by the Ross

*Swing Bridge. Pass the docks, then at the traffic circle almost a mile further go straight on for **Newlyn** (A3077). The Barbican (a good vantage point in past centuries) and a Memorial are on the right. Sandy beaches line the Promenade and Esplanade, and after **Bolitho Gardens**, open to the public, you'll see the famous **Newlyn Art Gallery** on the left (open: Mon-Sat 10am-5pm). Pass it, turn left at the major intersection and follow the sign for **Mousehole** (pronounced Mowsal) and car parking just before the Fish Market on the left.*

NEWLYN

Newlyn's pleasant hilly center is interesting to wander around. The town is still a working port with fish sold and shipped from the market. The celebrated **Newlyn School of Painters** working here in the late 19th and early 20th centuries included Stanhope Forbes, Lamorna Birch and Laura Knight.

NEWLYN TO LAND'S END   (about 9 miles)

*At the major intersection at the corner of the harbor take **The Combe** (keeping the harbor to your rear) signposted **Land's End** and **St Just** (A30/A3071). About a mile on turn left at the large traffic circle onto a road that passes many neolithic standing stones, stone circles and quoits, relics of the area's ancient past. The countryside here is bare and windswept, so you'll probably feel your car being buffeted. If you want some aerial sightseeing **Land's End Airfield** offers coastal flights. About 8 miles out of Newlyn are **Sennen Village** and **Cove**. Turn right, following the signs for the Cove (½ mile), for one of Cornwall's longest sandy beaches, ideal for picnicking and swimming, with a clear turquoise-blue sea in summer. Use one of the car parks a ¼ mile down the hill from the A30 since there's very little parking at the beach. The pub on the seafront is a good place for a short stop.*

Way to Success Inn, Seafront, Sennen Cove   £
Open: Daily, lunchtimes and evenings

Established in 1691, this independently-owned pub has a splendid view over the Cove, both from inside and from its seats outside. Its ship's rigging, beams, pine paneling and old photographs give it a nautical air. The good basic food might include cottage pie or roast beef as well as snacks and sandwiches.

Return to the main route.

*From Sennen Cove **Land's End** is about 1½ miles on, through **Sennen Village**. There are ample car parks before you reach the complex, which gets very crowded in high season.*

WHAT TO SEE

Land's End

Open: Daily 9:30am-5:30pm
Admission: Car park and exhibits: adults £3, children £2; car park
    only: £2 per car

Land's End was recently bought by financier Peter de Savary, who
built a new, very commercialized tourist center here. Nevertheless,
it is worth a visit for its exhibitions – **Man Against the Sea** (ships,
wrecks and rescues) and **The Spirit of Cornwall** (how people make
their living from the land and the sea); for its **crafts center**, with
crafts-people working; souvenir shops; train making regular circular tours; and children's play areas, restaurant and cafés – not to
mention the actual rocks of Land's End itself. If you prefer not to
visit the attractions, you just pay for car parking, then wander
freely over the surrounding headland and enjoy the magnificent
ocean view in peace.

LAND'S END HOTEL

The State House Hotel, Land's End   **£££ (incl dinner)**
Tel: (0736) 871844
Amenities: ☎ ⊑ 🅿 ᵇᵘᵘ ⊊ ◎   Credit cards: AE, DC, MC, V

Sited on the cliff-top in the Land's End tourist complex, the State
House has been beautifully refurbished and is now a luxury hotel
with deluxe individually designed bedrooms, some with four-poster
beds and many with sea views. There's a conservatory-style restaurant and bar, also giving superb views of sea and sky. When the day
visitors have gone the hotel guests have Land's End, a wonderfully
peaceful spot, to themselves.

LAND'S END TO ST IVES Via Penzance (including Lamorna
    Valley and Mousehole)   (about 19 miles)

*This scenic route takes you via **Porthcurno**, **Lamorna Cove** and
Mousehole. If you are in a hurry take the **A30** back to Penzance, then
the **B3311** or **A3074** to **St Ives**.*

*About 200 yards from Land's End turn right (**B3315**) for **Porthcurno** and the **Minack Open-Air Theatre**. The narrow road winds for
³/₄ mile through hedges full of wild flowers and stunted trees. Turn
right for the village and theater. Drive through the village to the
theater car park at the bottom on the right, or alternatively use the
public car park in Porthcurno valley, from this the theater is a 20-
minute uphill walk.*

The Minack Open-Air Theatre, Porthcurno
Box office: Tel: (0736) 810471 (9am–noon, Easter–Oct)
All seats: Adults £3, children under 14 years £1.50 (unreserved, on sale at the theater box office from 1¾ hours before performance begins); some matinées (about 2pm) and evening performances (8pm) from end May to mid Sep

This spectacular theater on the cliffs above the sea was built in this century, though it looks like a classical Greek theater. A wide selection of plays is staged against an ever-changing backdrop of the Atlantic Ocean. One recent season included *Tartuffe* (Molière), *All's Well That Ends Well* (Shakespeare), *Under Milk Wood* (Dylan Thomas), *The Marriage of Figaro* (Mozart), *Patience* (Gilbert and Sullivan) and *The Threepenny Opera* (Brecht/Weill). Performances are rarely canceled. Do take warm clothing; cushions are for rent and hot drinks are available.

*From Porthcurno turn right onto the **B3315**, taking care at the very sharp bends about a mile on. About ½ mile after this, turn right for **Newlyn (B3315)** in front of the phone box. Just under 2 miles on you'll see an ancient cross in the shoulder on the right and standing stones in fields on either side. You'll soon see the **Merry Maidens** stone circle on your right, legendary maidens turned to stone for dancing on Sunday. Wind down into the secluded **Lamorna Valley**, turning right at the sign for **Lamorna Cove**, about a mile past the Merry Maidens. Use the village car park by the cove about a ¼ mile past the Wink pub.*

Wooded Lamorna Valley, its rocky cove and turquoise-blue sea are a wildlife haven nurturing interesting flowers, birds and animals, including woodpeckers and naturalized mink. Until the 1920s Lamorna granite was quarried here; some of it was used to build the London Embankment.

LAMORNA VALLEY HOTEL AND RESTAURANT

The Lamorna Cove Hotel, Lamorna   **£££ (incl dinner)**
Tel: (0736) 731411
Amenities: ☎ ⌨ 🅿 🍴 ⅄ ≋   Credit cards: AE, MC, V

This comfortable and tranquil hotel with attractive gardens overlooks the secluded Lamorna Valley and the sea beyond. Nothing is too much trouble for the staff, who will even wash your car in the morning if you have parked it under the rooks' nests in the trees beside the car park. Some rooms are in an unusual old building with a bell tower; others are in a modern extension. To sit on the terrace by the swimming pool, enjoying lunch or a drink, is to have found heaven.

The hotel's restaurant is one of the best in the area (open: daily

12:30pm-2pm, 7pm-9:15pm), offering an interesting three-course menu with coffee and mints for £13.50. All produce is fresh and from local suppliers. The hotel also serves morning coffee, cream teas and bar snacks to non-residents.

LAMORNA VALLEY TO PENZANCE Via Mousehole
(about 7 miles)

Return to B3315, crossing a small bridge; note the unusual dog weather vane on your right 200 yards on. After 1¼ miles turn right for Mousehole, a delightful old fishing village whose steep, narrow streets and harbor give you the true flavor of old Cornwall.

When the village was sacked by the Spanish in 1595 Squire Keigwin slew six Spaniards while defending his home, a famous Mousehole event that's celebrated in the village on July 22 each year. Villagers like to believe that the Spanish Armada was first sighted from here.

Parking is at the bottom of the hill and, when you're tired of exploring, you'll find lots of places in which to have a spoiling Cornish cream tea.

Return to Newlyn and Penzance, with far-reaching views of Mount's Bay as you enter the built-up areas.

PENZANCE TO ST IVES
(about 10 miles)

Leave Penzance, past the station and along Chyandour Cliff following signs for Redruth (A30). You'll see Penzance Helicopters on the left, then a traffic circle where you take the second left to St Ives. At the next traffic circle, about a mile on, take the first left to St Ives and Redruth (A30 – 8 miles). You're now heading for Cornwall's north coast. Five and a half miles out of Penzance, at a major traffic circle, take the first left for St Ives (A3074). This road takes you through Carbis Bay, with its beautiful beach, to St Ives, which you will enter on Trelyon Avenue. In the town center turn left at Tregenna Hill onto Gabriel Street and go up the Stennack and Stennack Gardens to Trenwith Bridge car park on the left. The five-minute pedestrian route to the town center and Tourist Information Centre is clearly sign-posted from the car park. Alternatively, in high season buses leave the car park every five minutes and will drop you at the Royal Cinema, Royal Square.

Tourist Information Centre, is in The Guildhall, Street-an-Pol (Tel: (0736) 797600. Open: Mon-Sat 9am-6pm, Sun 10am-1pm mid May-mid Sep; Mon-Thur 9am-5:30pm, Fri 9am-5pm mid Sep-mid May).

ST IVES

St Ives is one of Cornwall's most picturesque villages, so it's very popular with visitors, especially in the summer. Yet the town has so much charm that it can stand the invasion. Once a small fishing village and now a sizeable town, the center of St Ives is still a maze of narrow cobbled streets, pretty houses, hidden alleyways and glimpses of the sea with summer flowers everywhere. The sandy beaches around the town are magnificent – St Ives' own beaches as well as **Porthmear** to the west and **Carbis Bay** and **Hayle** to the east. The area's natural beauty and clear light have long attracted artists to the area, and in Victorian times a famous art colony grew up here. James McNeill Whistler and Walter Sickert visited. More recently, Ben Nicholson, sculptor Barbara Hepworth and the potter Bernard Leach lived and worked in St Ives. Today the **St Ives School of Painting** (Back Road West) holds daily classes, open to visitors from April to October. There are numerous art galleries and craft shops.

Allow plenty of time for strolling through the town and for sitting by the bustling harbor, enjoying the incomparable view over the wide sweep of St Ives bay.

WHAT TO SEE

Barbara Hepworth Museum and Sculpture Garden, off Back Street
Open: Mon-Sat 10am-5:30pm Apr-Jun and Sep; 10am-6:30pm, Sun 2pm-6pm Jul-Aug; 10am-4:30pm Oct-Mar
Admission: Adults 60p, children 30p

*Directions: The gallery is signposted from **Fore Street**, on the left up **Ayr Lane** and left into **Back Street**.*

Barbara Hepworth, the renowned sculptor, lived and worked here in **Trewyn Studio** from 1949 until her death in 1975. It's now a fascinating little museum with personal photographs, documents and other memorabilia as well as 40 Hepworth sculptures in wood, stone and bronze, both indoors and in an atmospheric garden, Barbara Hepworth's own creation. Her plaster and stone-carving workshops have been left almost exactly as they were on her death; her smocks still hang on the wall and unfinished works can be seen.

Leach Pottery Showroom, Upper Stennack
Open: Mon-Fri 10am-5pm plus Sat & public holidays in summer
Free admission

*Directions: The showroom is off the **B3306/B3311**.*

Handmade stoneware and porcelain by Janet Leach and Trevor

Corser is on sale. There's a small display of work by Bernard Leach, best known of British potters, who spent many years learning his craft in Japan and Korea.

Penwith Gallery, Back Road West
Open: Tues-Sat 10am-5pm
Admission: Adults 20p, children free

An interesting exhibition of works by notable 20th-century artists, including Barbara Hepworth, Ben Nicholson and Bernard Leach.

St Ives Society of Artists Gallery, in Old Mariners Church, off
Church Place and Norway Lane
Open: Mon-Fri 10am-12:30pm, 2pm-4pm, Sat 10am-12:30pm
Mar-Oct
Admission: 20p

A fine collection of oil paintings and wood carvings.

Trewyn Sub-Tropical Gardens, off Market Place
Open: Daily

Immaculate lawns and delightful floral displays for those who want to sit in the sun and listen to the gulls. Ideal for a picnic.

SHOPPING

Shopping hours change with the season. Though most shops are open from 9:30am until 5pm all year you'll find many open until 9pm in summer, particularly around Fore Street. In winter shops tend to close either all day Thursday or at 1pm. We've listed below only the unusual opening times.

St Ives town center has a wide variety of shops, mainly on **Tregenna Hill, High Street** and **Fore Street**. As you walk down Tregenna Hill into the town you'll find **J.C. Williams** on Fern Lea Terrace for small brass objects, Portmeirion china and modern glassware. **Sports and Leisure**, No 4 (closes Thur 1pm), offers fishing rods, reels and sportswear and will arrange deep-sea shark fishing or wreck and reef angling, tackle supplied. On Tregenna Terrace the **Cornish Stone Co.** (open: Mon-Fri 7:30pm-10pm in summer) sells beautiful silver and gold jewelry incorporating many precious and unusual semi-precious stones – such as cornelian, blue agate, rose quartz and moss agate – in brooches, rings, earrings and necklaces; also unusual designs in Celtic silver. The shop has been owned by the same family for all of its 110 years. **Spalls**, next door, offers small statues, jewelry and Celtic brooches, while **The Cat's Whiskers**, opposite, stocks small ornaments and glass figures, miniature country cottages and jewelry.

The attractively designed **Edinburgh Woollen Mills** on High Street (open: Mon-Fri until 9pm and Sun noon-4pm in summer) sells traditional Scottish Aran and Guernsey sweaters for children and grownups, country hats and gloves, ties, kilts, scarves, sheepskin hats, gloves and slippers.

Still on High Street, **A Family Affair** (closed: 1pm-2pm and Thur at 1pm) is full of kitchenware, basketware, scented and novelty gifts, Indian scarves and unusual cards.

On **Fore Street** try **The Country Goodness** (open: daily 10am-10pm in summer) for a gorgeous choice of fudge, honey, cream toffees, West Country cookies and other edible gifts. **White's Furnishers** (open: Mon-Fri 7:30pm-9pm in summer) stocks Cornwall's biggest collection of tea towels decorated with local motifs as well as tea cozies, coasters, table mats, aprons and finely embroidered gifts. **D. & M. John**, No 18, (closes: 1pm-2:15pm, all day Thur) sells quality British china and glass such as Royal Worcester, Dartington glass, handmade Caithness crystal and paperweights.

The New Craftsman, No 24, (open: Mon-Sat from 10am, Sun 11am-6pm in summer) is worth a visit to see local artists' work, including interesting original pottery, gold and silver jewelry, sculptures, watercolors and oil paintings, original signed prints, framed and unframed, and, upstairs, more expensive works by local painters from earlier in this century. Staff are very knowledgeable and helpful.

Opposite, **The African Connection** sells unusual jewelry, paintings and basketware in lovely colors and shapes. **St Ives Model Railway and Shop**, 44-6 Fore Street (open: 10:30am-late pm in high season), caters for model railroad freaks. There are seven working layouts in different settings plus copies of fine old railroad posters, postcards, souvenirs and other railroad items.

The Sloop Lane Craft Market (walk through the car park) is full of small booths run by craftspeople, most of whom you can see at work, whether wood turning, dressmaking, potting, painting on wood, casting pewter or making jewelry, enamelware, mirrors or embroidery. Stop here for a quick bite at **Pudding Bag Lane Restaurant** (open: Mon-Sat 10am-6pm). Sit on the terrace overlooking old St Ives and the coast.

On and off St Ives' main streets you'll find a wealth of small art galleries and other interesting shops.

ST IVES HOTELS AND RESTAURANTS

Boskerris Hotel, Boskerris Road, Carbis Bay   **££ (incl dinner)**
Tel: (0736) 795295
Amenities: ▣ ♨️ ♀ ≈   Credit cards: DC

This is a moderately priced but comfortable hotel run by a very professional mother-and-son team in a quiet road in Carbis Bay, 1¾ miles from St Ives. There are good views over the wide bay from most parts of the hotel and the sandy beach is only a seven-minute walk down a steep footpath. Facilities and decor at the hotel are good. The standard of cuisine is high. Light bar lunches are served in the cocktail bar overlooking the sea. The room price per person includes a four-course dinner and coffee.

Garrack Hotel, Burthallan Lane, Higher Ayr　　　　£
Tel: (0736) 796199
Amenities: ☎ 🅿 ♨ ⚱ ≈　　　Credit cards: AE, DC, MC, V

First impressions of this hotel are of an attractive old creeper-clad building with a long case clock ticking slowly in reception. If peace and calm are what you want this is the place. This family-run hotel is set high above St Ives, about 1½ miles from town, in two acres of grounds with magnificent views. The comfortable bedrooms are in the original old building and in a tasteful modern extension. There's a splendid modern leisure center that includes a swimming pool, sauna and solarium. The restaurant's à la carte menu is superb and reasonably priced; the table d'hôte offers four courses and coffee for a remarkable £10. Many of the fruits and vegetables are grown in the hotel's garden. The lengthy wine list has a fixed price mark-up, which makes normally expensive bottles worth sampling here. If you have Cornish connections and want to trace relatives, Mrs Kirby will do what she can to help.

The Porthminster Hotel, Porthminster Terrace　**££ (incl dinner)**
Tel: (0736) 795221
Amenities: ☎ 🖵 🅿 ♨ ⚱ ≈ ✓ (nearby) Credit cards: AE, DC, MC, V

This large, centrally-placed three-star hotel is right on St Ives Bay, with fine views and its own access to the sandy beach below. Almost 100 years old, it is a grand building, with fine gardens and excellent facilities. The attractively decorated rooms are large and spacious. There are both à la carte and table d'hôte menus in the restaurant overlooking the bay, with a 40-bottle wine list. There's a golf course nearby and the hotel can arrange other sports for you. During the high season there are regular events, dances and entertainments in the public rooms. The staff go out of their way to be helpful.

AROUND AND ABOUT

Hayle Towans, Hayle
Open: Daily through the year

*Directions: Take the A3074 and A30 from St Ives to **Hayle**.*

Hayle has been a port and industrial center since Phoenician times. The estuary and bay sweep around 3 miles of golden sandy beach to reveal **Godrevy Lighthouse**, the inspiration of Virginia Woolf's *To the Lighthouse*. Hayle recurs often in Cornish and industrial/ mercantile literature, as tin is said to have been traded here to foreigners since before the time of Christ. From Hayle Towans (dunes) you can look across to the pristine outline of the lighthouse. Walk the rocky promontories for an even deeper idea of Virginia Woolf's dream location for a daytrip. The film of her novel was shot on Hayle Beach.

ST IVES TO NEWQUAY   (about 27 miles)

*From **St Ives harbor** drive up **Tregenna Hill** and **Trelyon Avenue**, which becomes **St Ives Road** (A3074). Four miles out from St Ives town center, at the major traffic circle, take the second turn (A30) signposted to **Camborne** and **Redruth**. The road soon becomes a two-lane highway. You'll see warnings of cross winds on its high, exposed sections. You'll also see many ruined tin mines on both sides; for centuries clay and tin were mined in these parts. It's said that in pre-Christian times the Phoenicians sailed from the Eastern Mediterranean to Cornwall, such was the fame of its mining industry. Stay on this road, looping around to **Camborne**, for 15½ miles to the big traffic circle just after **Three Burrows**. Now take the third left for **Newquay** (A3075). The A30 goes on to **Bodmin**, and if you're in a hurry you can rejoin the main route there. Eight miles on, at the traffic circle after crossing the **River Gannel**, take the first left for **Newquay town center** (Trevemper Road, A3075), which runs beside the river, turn right about ¾ of a mile on at the boating lake on the left and in 200 yards you'll come to a traffic circle. Take the second left, **Edgcumbe Avenue**, passing under a railroad bridge, then bearing left, still on Edgcumbe Avenue, until in about 200 yards you'll see Newquay Bay in front of you. Turn left into **Cliff Road**, then left again into **Oakleigh Terrace** opposite the Penthouse Coffee Lounge, immediately right into **Springfield Road**, then immediately left into **Pargolla Road** for a car park that's handy for the Tourist Information Centre.*

*   **Tourist Information Centre, Cliff Road**, is opposite the train station. (Tel: (0637) 871345. Open: Mon-Sat 9:15am-7pm, Sun 10am-1pm, 5pm-7pm mid May-mid Sep; Mon-Fri 9:15am-1pm, 2:15pm-5pm, Sat 9:15am-1pm mid Sep-mid May.)*

NEWQUAY

Newquay is remarkable for its long sandy beaches, and is a busy holiday town that attracts young people with its surfing, probably the best in Cornwall. It has little else of interest. Tourism arrived with the railroad which was opened in 1876. For more than 400 years before that the town relied on pilchards for its prosperity. Men called 'huers' watched for shoals of fish from little huts built on the cliffs: Huers House on Towan Head survives today. Beaches to the south are **Perran Beach** with **Penhale Sands** and extensive dunes (where you can see the celtic **St Piran's Church**, which was buried under the sand from the 11th to the 19th century), **Holywell Beach, Crantock Beach** and **Fistral Beach**; to the north of Newquay Bay there's **Watergate Beach**. At the town's attractive 17th-century harbor you can see the 19th-century pilot gigs that used to help guide in cargo ships.

NEWQUAY RESTAURANT

Cairn Cottage Tea Garden, Gannel Road   £
Open: Daily 11am-5pm Apr-Oct

*Directions: About 300 yards along **Gannel Road** after turning right at the end of the boating lake.*

In this 400-year-old cottage with a flower-filled garden, overlooking the River Gannel, you can enjoy morning coffee, light lunches like Welsh rarebit, or Cornish cream teas in very pleasant surroundings.

NEWQUAY HOTEL

Corisande Manor Hotel, Riverside Avenue (off Pentire Crescent),
    Pentire, near Newquay   **£ (incl dinner)**
Tel: (0637) 872042   Open: early May-early Oct
Amenities: **P** ⛄ ♆ ✓ (19-hole putting green)
Credit cards: MC, V

The friendly owners of this quiet hotel, Mr and Mrs Painter, have run it for more than 20 years. It's an unusual turreted building, built in 1900 on a magnificent site high above the Gannel estuary, west of Newquay. Its three-acre grounds include a croquet lawn sloping down to the river and a private foreshore for swimming, fishing and rowing.
    Mr Painter, a trained cook, devises interesting daily menus and delights in telling the history of the 300-year-old timbers of the fine staircase and dining-room's panels and beams. Surfing, horse riding, golf, and sea-fishing can all be arranged.
    Reserve well ahead of time; it's very popular.

AROUND AND ABOUT

Bedruthan Steps
Open: Daily 10:30am-6pm Apr-Oct
Free admission

*Directions: Off **B3276**, between Newquay and Padstow.*

The giant Bedruthan stepping stones are large granite rocks standing on their own on the shore. You reach the beach they're on by a steep staircase set in the cliffs. Alternatively you can get a good view from above, where the National Trust has a car park, shop and café.

Trerice, St Newlyn East
Open: Daily 11am-6pm Apr-Oct
Admission: Adults £2.40, children £1.20

*Directions: Take either the **A3075** or **A392** out of Newquay and at the traffic circle take the first left or third right respectively. The turn for **Trerice** is signposted on the right or left, and is by the converted chapel in **Lane** (Trerice is about 4 miles from Newquay). Drive past the house; the car park is immediately on the right.*

This charming little Elizabethan manor house, rebuilt in 1571, is set in attractive, well-tended gardens. Its beautiful rooms contain fine furniture of various periods. Note in particular the **Hall**, with its Minstrels' Gallery, molded plaster ceiling and 20-foot-long oak table; the **Drawing Room**, with its plastered barrel ceiling and overmantel, dated 1573; and the **Gallery** running across the central part of the house. The gardens are notable for some unusual plants. There is an orchard of Cornish fruit trees. You may visit what is perhaps the world's only lawn-mower museum.

There is a National Trust shop for books, postcards and quality souvenirs and an excellent restaurant in a massive old barn with special screens to keep out inquisitive chaffinches (open: 11am-5:30pm). Morning coffee, lunch and afternoon tea are available (counter service).

NEWQUAY TO PADSTOW (about 15 miles)

*From Newquay town center go along **Cliff Road**, past the train station, with the beach to your left, onto **Narrowcliff**. At the traffic circle in about 200 yards go right over, bearing right soon afterwards along **Henver Road**, away from the sea. At the double traffic circle in about 350 yards turn left into **Porth Way (B3276)** for the coastal route to **Padstow** along one of Cornwall's most attractive stretches of coast. The roads here are narrow and winding. About 3 miles on you'll come to Watergate Beach, with St Mawgan Airfield to the right, then the attractive village of **Mawgan Porth**, with its pretty beach, and, 7 miles out of Newquay, **Bedruthan Steps** (see page 467).*

*Drive 2 miles to **Porthcothan**, where the road turns inland through **St Merryn**, and you'll enter Padstow on the **Newquay Road**. A sign for the church points left down Church Street; ignore this, and 200 yards past it turn left into the car park. Padstow's narrow streets become crowded, so it's best to park here and walk down unless you're staying in one of the Padstow hotels. **The Metropole** has its own parking lot; for the others park on the **Quay**.*

Padstow doesn't have a Tourist Information Centre but the New-

quay office (open all year) or the Wadebridge TIC (open summer) should be able to help.

PADSTOW

Padstow's a pleasant old town with narrow winding streets clustered around a picturesque harbor. Its position on the River Camel estuary gives excellent views across to Rock and out to Padstow Bay. A passenger ferry runs to Rock from the harbor except at low tide, when passengers should take the low-tide landing stage, reached by a footpath from the harbor through **Chapel Stile Field**.

The silting up of the estuary led to the town's decline as a fishing port but it's now a favorite vacation spot with interesting shops and good restaurants. On May Day you can see the ancient **Hobby Horse Dance Festival**, in which a masked man and hobby horse dance through the streets to welcome summer.

Boat trips leave **North Quay** ferry steps daily. There are luxury cruises around the offshore islands as well as fishing expeditions.

WHAT TO SEE

Prideaux Place, 2 Fentonluna Lane
Open: Sun-Thur 1:30pm-5pm Spring Bank Holiday-early Sep
Admission: House and grounds: Adults £2, children 5-14 years £1;
            Grounds only: Adults £1, children 50p

This attractive, creeper-clad Elizabethan house is the home of the Prideaux-Brune family. It's set in well-kept gardens and overlooks a 22-acre deer park that's believed to be the oldest in Britain. Inside you'll see much decorative plasterwork, a fine cantilevered staircase in the hall and a magnificent ceiling with bible-scene tableaux in the **Great Chamber**. There are also porcelain, paintings, antique furniture and rare books. The tearoom sells local pottery, guidebooks and postcards.

SHOPPING

Shops are generally open Monday-Saturday 9am-5:30pm with some shops closing at lunchtime on Wednesday. During the summer many shops are open until 9pm.

The streets around the harbor – **Duke Street, Market Square, The Strand, The Drang, Broad Street, New Street, South Quay, Mill Street, Lanadwell Street** and **Middle Street** – have the best shops.

The Cat's Whiskers, 4-6 Broad Street, sells novelty clocks and handknit sweaters. At **Bagend Leatherwork**, on Lanadwell Street, you can see craftsmen at work while you choose from a selection of belts, bags and purses. At **Padstow Pottery**, you can buy vases, mugs, traditional Cornish milk pitchers and small vases that were made on the premises. **Upsteps**, 24 Duke Street, has a good range of souvenirs and gifts: unusual modern pottery, small mirrors with Art Deco-style frames, puppets and mobiles, and at No 20 there's **Virginia Antiques**, for old lace dresses, linen and fans. The **Studio**, on Market Square, sells Cornish pewter; on the harbor **Rigmarine Leisurewear** offers deck-shoes, espadrilles and waterproof clothing; **Sport and Leisure** sells fishing tackle and nets, sports gear and smocks, and will organize fishing trips (deep sea, shark or mackerel).

RESTAURANTS IN PADSTOW

The London Inn Pub, Lanadwell Street   £
Tel: (0841) 532554
Open: Meals served: Daily noon-2:30pm, 7pm-9:30pm
Closed: Over Christmas
No credit cards

This is an attractive old stone inn, bedecked with flower baskets in summer, where you'll find traditional local beers and such bar snacks as Ploughman's lunch and sandwiches.

The Old Custom House Inn, South Quay   ££
(see page 472)

The Old Grain Store, The Harbour   £
Tel: (0841) 532934
Open: Daily 10:30am-5:45pm, 6:30pm-9:30pm summer
Closed: Winter
No credit cards

This attractive café-cum-restaurant offers a range of such light meals as salads, filled baked potatoes, lasagne and curry as well as sandwiches, cakes, ice cream, tea and coffee. It's licensed for alcohol and has a good view over the harbor.

The Pilot Tea Room, 32 Duke Street   £
Open: Daily in summer
No credit cards

You'll spot this pretty tearoom up the hill from the harbor by the climbing roses growing in the old chimney pots outside the door. It's a small friendly place decorated with old pictures and mirrors where you can enjoy a traditional Cornish cream tea with a view of the flower-filled back garden.

Rosano's Restaurant, 9 Mill Square   ££
Tel: (0841) 532796
Open: Daily 10am-2pm, 3pm-10pm   Closed: Public holidays
Credit cards: MC, V

Tucked away just off Padstow harbor you'll find this lively, welcoming restaurant where you can lunch or dine outside on the terrace in fine weather. There's a reasonably priced prix fixe menu as well as full à la carte, with dishes such as smoked salmon cornets, *escargots*, fine lemon sole fillets cooked in various ways, steaks, pheasant, duck, a cold buffet and a trolley groaning with homemade desserts.

The Seafood Restaurant, Riverside ££££
Tel: (0841) 532485
Open: Mon-Fri lunch (by advance booking only), Mon-Sat 7pm-
10pm   Closed: Jan-Feb
Credit cards: AE, DC, MC, V

Superb fish has earned this restaurant a deservedly high reputation and diners come from far away. There's a reasonably priced prix fixe meal that changes daily and an exciting à la carte menu that includes steamed crab claws, brill, John Dory, skate, porbeagle shark, hot lobster and *fruits de mer* served in their shells on ice. A book of recipes by the chef, Richard Stein, is on sale in the restaurant. The decor is light and airy with the harbor just outside.

PADSTOW HOTELS

The Dower House, Fentonluna Lane £
Tel: (0841) 532317
Amenities: 💻 (if booked) 🅿 🍴 🍷 ◎   Credit cards: MC

This delightful, reasonably priced little hotel was built in 1858 as the Dower House to the nearby Elizabethan manor, Prideaux Place. It's a protected building, decorated and furnished with style by its enthusiastic present owner, Mrs Christine Thomas, who will be having her fourth season in 1989. She does all the cooking for the menu of the day and à la carte, and will happily provide picnic lunches, bar snacks, cream teas and high teas. The setting is peaceful and quiet, yet the town is five minutes' walk away. If you're lucky enough to catch any fish on a local fishing trip Mrs Thomas will happily cook them for you.

The Metropole, Station Road £££
Tel: (0841) 532486
Amenities: ☎ 💻 🅿 🍴 🍷 〰 ✓ (putting green) ◎
Credit cards: AE, DC, MC, V

Situated right on the waterfront near the harbor and pier, this large Trusthouse Forte hotel overlooks the River Camel estuary, with a view of the distant hills. It was built at the turn of the century and has spacious rooms, many with fine views, and attractive gardens. Facilities are good, the staff friendly. In addition to the large **Harbour Restaurant** with its à la carte and table d'hôte menus there's the **Verandah Bar**, where snacks are available from 10am-6pm.

The Old Custom House Inn, South Quay   £
Tel: (0841) 532359   Closed: mid Dec-end Feb
Amenities: ☎ ⌨ ⅋ ⍟ ◎   Credit cards: DC, MC, V

Padstow's bustling harbor is only steps from the front door of this hotel. With its white, creeper-clad walls, green awnings and attractive leaded windows it looks friendly and welcoming, and the staff soon make you feel at home. Parking is in the town car park (pay and display) on the quay.

The standard of cuisine in the attractive low-beamed restaurant is high, with such dishes as locally caught crab lovingly served with several dips or ice cream made the old-fashioned way on a Cornish farm. Fishing, sailing and golf are all near at hand.

The Seafood Restaurant, Riverside   ££
Tel: (0841) 532485   Closed: Jan-Feb
Amenities: ☎ ⌨ ⅋ ⍟ ◎   Credit cards: AE, DC, MC, V

This notable restaurant (see above) also has comfortable bedrooms decorated in light colors with good facilities and superb views. Breakfast is served in an airy, plant-filled conservatory. A reservation automatically books you a table in the restaurant if you want one.

AROUND AND ABOUT

Tintagel Castle
Open: Mon-Sat 9:30am-6:30pm, Sun 2pm-6:30pm Mar 15-Oct 15;
          9:30am-4pm, Sun 2pm-4pm Oct 16-Mar 14
Admission: Adults £1, children 50p

*Directions: From Padstow take the A389, signposted for **Wadebridge**, by turning left out of the car park. About 5 miles on turn left onto the **A39** at the T-intersection and drive through **Wadebridge** (2 miles) where you cross the **River Camel**, then turn left at the traffic circle immediately afterwards for **Bude** (A39), up **Gonvena Hill**. Wadebridge is an intersection of three major roads and can get very crowded in high season. Along this road you'll get views of moorland to your right. Just 18 miles out of Padstow, 150 yards after the Shell garage, at **Valley Truckle**, turn left for **Tintagel** (B3266). Two miles on turn left at the crossroads for Tintagel, then right after about 50 yards (B3263) and follow the winding road past some slate quarries.*
*   Entering Tintagel ignore the first car park signs you see. There's a better car park nearer the Castle. Turn left for the **Castle** and **car park** at the T-intersection; the **Old Post Office** is on the left about a ¼ mile*

on and you'll see the Castle parking lot just past the **Castle Pottery** *on your left. The Castle is signposted from the parking lot where you can see its brooding bulk against the backdrop of the sea.*

This ruined castle is associated in legend with King Arthur and his Knights of the Round Table. The infant Arthur was supposedly thrown by waves onto the beach beside Merlin's cave and later had his castle here before the present one. Whatever the truth, it's an atmospheric spot, well worth the ⅓ mile walk from the village.

The Old Post Office, Tintagel
Open: Daily 11am-6pm Apr-Oct
Admission: Adults 90p, children 45p

The building was a post office in Victorian times but it's really a 14th-century manor house, built of local slate, a rare surviving example of the period. It's in good condition despite its uneven-looking roof, and inside you can see the parlor – probably originally the kitchen – bedroom and hall, with interesting old furniture. There's a Victorian village post box in the original post room.

TINTAGEL RESTAURANT

The Cornishman, Fore Street   **£**
Tel: (0840) 770238
Open: Meals served: Mon-Sat 11am-2:30pm, 6pm-9:30pm, Sun
      noon-2:30pm, 7pm-9:30pm
No credit cards

Walk along the main shopping street from the car park and you'll see this old pub on your right. The bar serves local ales and a good range of light meals such as a farmhouse ham lunch, pâté Cornish-man, open sandwiches, *spaghetti alla bolognese*, Cornish pasties, deep-fried snacks like scampi and a seafood platter. It's cozy, with a low-beamed ceiling and much copper and brassware. Wooden trestle tables outside at the back overlook the countryside.

PADSTOW TO BODMIN   (about 14 miles)

From Padstow take the **A389**, *signposted to* **Wadebridge**, *by turning left out of the car park. About 5 miles on turn left onto the* **A39** *at the T-intersection and you'll get to Wadebridge in 2 miles. At the traffic circle after you've crossed the* **River Camel** *turn right for* **Bodmin** **(A389)** *along* **Egloshayle Road**, *passing a sports ground and bowling green 300 yards further on your left. The river is on your right until you leave the town, after which you have good views of wooded, hilly countryside on both sides. Cross the river again 6 miles later, after* **Mount Charles** *and some steep bends. You'll soon enter Bodmin along* **Dunmere Road** *with St Lawrence's Hospital on your right.*

*One mile into the town there's a traffic circle; take the second left for the **town center**, along **Town End**, which becomes **Higher Bore Street**. After a ¼ mile enter the town center one-way system, turning left down **Cardell Road**, then right after 100 yards into **Burnards Lane**, which becomes **Dennison Road**. Car parks are indicated on both your right and left.*

*   **Tourist Information Centre**, Shire House, **Mount Folly Square** (Tel: (0208) 76616. Open: Mon-Fri 9:30am-1pm, 2pm-4:30pm, Sat as well 9:30am-1pm, 2pm-5pm May-Aug).*

BODMIN

Bodmin, on the edge of **Bodmin Moor**, is now the county town of Cornwall, having taken over from Launceston. It's a traditional market town with a large open-air Saturday market on **Mount Folly** in the town center, and boasts Cornwall's biggest church, the interesting **St Petroc's**, which was rebuilt in the 15th century. Bodmin's history is time-shrouded. It was the only Cornish town recorded in the Domesday Book in the 11th century.

    Bodmin Moor, about 12 square miles, is smaller than Dartmoor. It is wild and high, with marshy ground, streams, standing stones and rocky outcrops, notably **Brown Willy** (1377ft) and **Brown Gelly** (1112ft).

WHAT TO SEE

Bodmin Museum, Mount Folly
Open: Mon-Sat 10am-12 noon, 2pm-4pm
Free admission

This is one of Cornwall's most varied museum collections, with medieval tiles, old bottles and jars, militaria, town stocks capable of holding six offenders at once, Bodmin's old fire engine, domestic exhibits from local cottages and houses, archaeological remains and a collection of stuffed birds.

SHOPPING

You'll find more unusual shops elsewhere, but worth browsing in are **Whitell's**, 34 Fore Street, for kitchenware and small gifts, **Wendy's Bookroom**, 82 Fore Street, for new, antiquarian and secondhand books and cards, **The Bookshop**, 13 Honey Street, for a good selection of new books, and **Bunts** the newspaper store, opposite the museum, for local maps and artistic postcards.

BODMIN RESTAURANTS

Barry's in The Old Guildhall, Fore Street   £
Open: Mon-Sat 9am-5:30pm
No credit cards

In the unusual surroundings of the Old Council Chamber, with its high ceiling and bare beams, you can enjoy morning coffee, snacks, summer salads, afternoon tea with confections and pastries from the local bakery, toasted teacakes and scones and a selection of hot savories.

Golden Vine Restaurant, 6 Lower Bore Street   ££
Tel: (0208) 72593
Open: Daily noon-2pm, 6pm-10:30pm in summer
Credit cards: DC, MC, V

This is the best restaurant in Bodmin, with a choice of formal restaurant fare, perfect for dinner, or bistro-style meals served in a bright conservatory at the rear of the building, great for lunch or early supper. There's a range of grills, such as ham or T-bone steaks with french fries, and a large selection of local seafood, meat and poultry dishes, with good desserts. The extensive wine list includes rare armagnacs, cognacs and whiskies, and about 40 vintage ports.

Pots, 55 Fore Street   £
Tel: (0208) 74601
Open: Mon-Sat 9am-5:30pm, Fri and Sat 7:30pm-9:30pm
Closed: Public holidays
Credit cards: MC, V

This is a cheerful café that becomes a bistro-style restaurant two evenings a week, serving a varied fixed price menu. The coffee shop offers baked potatoes with a choice of 30 fillings such as ratatouille or cheese and tomato, plus a good selection of sandwiches and homemade cakes.

The Weavers, Honey Street   £
Tel: (0208) 74511
Open: Meals served: Mon-Sat noon-2pm, Tues-Sat 7:30pm-10pm
Credit cards: DC, MC, V

This attractive black and white pub, hung with flower baskets in summer, is a good place for morning coffee, bar snacks or sandwiches. There's a beer garden for fine days.

AROUND AND ABOUT

Pencarrow House, Washaway
Open: Sun-Thur 1:30pm-5:30pm Easter-mid Oct; public holiday
       Mon and June-mid Sep from 11am. Gardens open daily
       during season
Admission: Adults £1.90, children 95p; gardens only adults 50p,
       children 25p

Directions: Off A389 between Bodmin and Wadebridge.

This beautiful Georgian mansion was built in about 1776 by Sir John Molesworth and is still owned and occupied by the Moles-worth-St-Aubyn family. Things to see include a paneled music room and library, a cantilevered staircase, notable and rare paint-ings, including some portraits by Sir Joshua Reynolds, and fine furniture and china. The 50-acre grounds comprise an Italian garden, granite rockery, bog garden, palm house, lake and wood-land gardens. There are tearooms and a picnic area.

BODMIN TO LAUNCESTON   (about 22 miles)

*From the **Dennison Road car park** turn left and continue along the town's one-way system, following signs for **Launceston (A30)**. At the traffic circle about 200 yards on, at the Duke of Cornwall pub, take the first left up hilly **Priory Road** with the church on your left. In another 200 yards take the left fork up steep **Launceston Road (A389)**. Two miles out of Bodmin you'll join the major A30 two-lane highway, which cuts across **Bodmin Moor** to Launceston. Three miles further you'll start seeing rocky outcrops and have magnificent views over Cornwall, with Colliford Reservoir on your right in 1½ miles.*

At **Bolventor**, 11 miles out of Bodmin, the **Jamaica Inn** is on the left. Immortalized by the Cornish writer, Daphne du Maurier, in her novel of the same name, this old coaching inn remains an atmospheric place despite its souvenir shops and large car park. Lunchtimes and evenings it serves soups, ploughman's lunch, quiche and salads.

*At **Polyphant**, 8 miles further, note the ancient cross beside the road on your left. The countryside is tamer as you approach Launceston, and you have views across to Dartmoor in Devon. At the major crossroads on the outskirts of the town turn left for **Launceston** (the A30 goes straight on for Okehampton) up **Western Road (A388)**. After a ½ mile you'll see a sign for the car park on the right – the town center is signposted straight on – up **Westgate Street**.*

*The **Tourist Information Centre** is in the Market House Arcade on **Market Street** (Tel: (0566) 2321. Open: Mon-Thur 8:45am-1pm, 1:45pm-5pm, Fri 8:45am-1pm, 1:45pm-4:30pm), where you can get a **Town Trail** leaflet to guide you around the noteworthy buildings.*

LAUNCESTON

The capital of Cornwall until 1838, Launceston is almost on the county's boundary with Devon, placed between Bodmin Moor and Dartmoor. It's a pleasant little market town on a hill with interest-ing old streets, medieval, Tudor and Georgian houses, the ruins of a once imposing castle from which there are splendid views over the countryside, and one of the original city gates, built in the time of Edward VI, son of Henry VIII.

The 16th-century **Church of St Mary Magdalene**, on Tower Street, is particularly fine. Its granite walls are ornately carved and at the east end you'll see a statue of Mary reclining with the pot of ointment beside her. Be sure to see the **Guildhall Clock (Western Road)**, whose bells are struck by two figures called quarterjacks.

A pannier market is held on Tuesdays and Saturdays.

WHAT TO SEE

Launceston Castle, Castle Dyke
Open: Mon-Sat 9:30am-6:30pm Sun 2pm-6:30pm mid Mar-mid Oct; Mon-Sat 9:30am-4pm, Sun 2pm-4pm mid Oct-mid Mar
Closed: Tues and Wed am in winter
Admission: Adults 75p, children 35p

Ruined Launceston Castle dominates the town and the surrounding countryside. The first Norman Earl of Cornwall lived here before it became the property of William the Conqueror's half-brother. It was augmented and strengthened over the years but since it was never besieged or captured it's still in relatively good condition. In 1973 Prince Charles, the present Duke of Cornwall, came to the castle to receive the feudal dues owed him.

Launceston Museum, Lawrence House, 9 Castle Street
Open: Mon-Fri 10:30am-12:30pm, 2:30pm-4:30pm Apr-Sep
Closed: Public holidays
Free admission, donations welcomed

Named for the man who built it in 1753, this Georgian building, of special architectural and historical interest, houses the town's local history museum. Its two thousand exhibits include a collection of the flora of Cornwall and Devon, man-traps, clocks, Victorian gadgets and costumes.

SHOPPING

Launceston has no large shopping center. Try **The Bookshop**, 10 Church Street, for a good choice of new books; **Tony Kennedy**, 6-8 Church Street, for fishing tackle, guns, Barbour jackets, outdoor sweaters, boots and walking sticks. **The Tamar Gallery**, 5 Church Street, has a good selection of blue and white china, lusterware, old glass and watercolor paintings. At No 22 (**the National Provincial Building Society**) look up and you'll see it was once **Hayman's Pianoforte Warehouse**. On **Western Road**, opposite the castle, **Reels** sells hand-embroidered gifts, cushion kits, panels for quilting and embroidery and stenciling kits.

LAUNCESTON AND OKEHAMPTON RESTAURANTS

The Arundell Arms, Lifton   ££
(see below)

The Greenhouse, Mudford Lane, Launceston   £
Tel: (0566) 3670
Open: Mon-Sat 10am-4pm
No credit cards

This inviting green and white wholefood vegetarian restaurant is
most welcome in the center of a town that appears to be a foodies'
desert. It serves morning coffee and cakes, an interesting and
healthy lunchtime menu – daily specials are chalked on the blackboard – and afternoon teas. The restaurant faces the castle.

Lewtrenchard Manor, Lewdown, near Okehampton   £££
(see page 479)

The Oxenham Arms, South Zeal, near Okehampton   £
Tel: (0837) 840244
Open: Mon-Sat 11am-2pm, 5:30pm-10:30pm, Sun 11am-2pm,
     7pm-10:30pm
Credit cards: AE, DC, MC, V

This delightful 15th-century village inn is justifiably popular with
the locals for its good beer, delicious bar snacks, such as homemade
soup, and excellent restaurant. It also has eight bedrooms, six with
bath/shower.

The White Hart Hotel, Launceston   £
Tel: (0566) 2013
Open: Daily noon-2pm, 7pm-9:30pm, Fri-Sat until 10pm
Credit cards: AE, DC, MC, V

This hotel in Launceston's central square has a beautiful granite
doorframe, taken from Newport's Augustinian priory. As well as
bar snacks you'll find a full à la carte and prix fixe menu in the
restaurant with such dishes as *escargots*, corn on the cob, rack of
lamb and T-bone steak.

LAUNCESTON AND OKEHAMPTON HOTELS

The Arundell Arms, Lifton   ££
Tel: (0566) 84666   Closed: Over Christmas
Amenities: ☎ ⛁ 🅿 ⦚ 🍷 Fishing   Credit cards: AE, DC, MC, V

The Arundell Arms has been a premier English fishing hotel for
more than half a century, with 20 miles of its own water on the
River Tamar and four tributaries where wild brown trout, salmon
and sea trout swarm. The hotel's skilled staff teach fishing for

beginners and experts alike. Tackle is available to rent or buy. It's a haven for fishermen but enthusiasts for other country pursuits – shooting, horse riding, walking, golf and birdwatching – will also love it. Beside superb facilities there are other pluses: a warm welcome, comfort, beautiful decor and deservedly famous food.

Lewtrenchard Manor, Lewdown, near Okehampton   **£££**
Tel: (056 683) 256   Closed: One month in winter
Amenities: ☎ 🖥 🅿 🍽 ♀ Croquet Lawn, Lake
Credit cards: DC, MC, V

If you'd like to taste the life of Britain's landed gentry stay here. From the moment you pass through the stone gates, up the long driveway to the magnificent old house, you're in another world. Built in 1620, the Manor was the home of the Baring-Gould family (Sabine Baring-Gould wrote *Onward Christian Soldiers* in the 19th century). The house is in the baronial style, with ornate ceilings, wood paneling, fine carvings and stained-glass windows. The gardens are superb, and the whole is set in a lush little valley just off the northwest corner of Dartmoor, an ideal base for exploring. The present owners are relaxed and friendly and the restaurant menu is superb. Try their special *Menu Gourmande* if you're really hungry.

LAUNCESTON TO TIVERTON   (about 50 miles)

*From Launceston **town center car park** follow the signs for **Okehampton (A30)** going back along **Western Road (A388)** about a ½ mile to rejoin the A30. In just under 2 miles you cross the Cornwall-Devon border, which runs along the **River Tamar**, via Dunkered Bridge. After another 2 miles, in **Lifton** village, you'll see the **Arundell Arms** on your left. This is a good place to stop for morning coffee, lunch, afternoon tea or dinner – or to stay (see page 478). **Dartmoor** is on the right, its tors and peaks rising distantly beyond the patchwork green fields and hedges. About 14 miles after leaving Launceston you'll catch glimpses of **Yes Tor** and **High Willhays** on the right. In 17 miles the A30 bypasses **Okehampton**, a pleasant market town with the ruins of Devon's largest castle. Take the **B3260** into Okehampton, turning first left at the traffic circle then left again at the T-intersection. (**Okehampton Castle** is open Mon-Sat 9:30am-6:30pm, Sun 2pm-6:30pm Mar 15-Oct 15; Mon-Sat 9:30am-4pm, Sun 2pm-4pm Oct 16-Mar 14; closed: Tues and Wed am in winter; admission: adults 75p, children 35p.)*

    *Take the **New Road** into Okehampton town center; it bears sharply right as you cross the river, becoming **West Street**, then **Fore Street**, then crossing the river a second time and becoming **East Street**. After **North Street**, on the left, fork left up **Crediton Road (B3215)**, leaving the town in about a ¼ mile and going up **Appledore Hill**. This attractive countryside is rich farming country.*

After passing under a railroad bridge 5½ miles out of Okehampton you'll come to an intersection with the *A3072*. Follow this, signposted to **Crediton** (12 miles). Rounded Devon hills and typical Devon villages line this road to right and left.

Crediton is a busy market town, with a large church in the town center. Pass through the town, turning first left after the church and Church Lane signposted for **Tiverton** (*A3072*). This takes you into **Mill Street**, which becomes **Exhibition Road**, then **Old Tiverton Road**. Tiverton lies 12 miles away along a winding hilly road that passes Cadbury and **Cadbury Castle**, an old hill fort, on the right. Two miles on you'll see **Bickleigh Castle** on your right, just before you cross the **River Exe**. The castle (open: Wed, Sun and public holiday Mondays 2pm-5pm Apr and May; Mon-Fri 2pm-5pm Jun-mid Oct; admission: adults £2, children £1) is 15th-century and stands on the site of a Norman castle. It's worth stopping to see the **Great Hall** over the arch with its minstrels' gallery, the 11th-century **Chapel**, the 17th-century **farmhouse wing**, the **medieval towers** and **gatehouse**, and the **Chapel of St Francis**, dedicated to the welfare of animals.

Continue along the **A3072** into Bickleigh village. **Bickleigh Mill Farm and Craft Centre** (open: daily 10am-6pm Apr-Dec; daily 2pm-5pm Jan-Mar) is on the right at the **A396** traffic circle. Here you can see a restored water mill and a craft center with working craftsmen, as well as a farm life museum and some rare breeds of animals.

From Bickleigh take the **A396** to **Tiverton** (5 miles), a major Devon town on the River Exe and the site of another fine castle. (**Tiverton Castle** open: Sun-Thur 2:30pm-5:30pm Good Friday-last Sun in Sep, admission: adults £1.80, children £1.) It was built in 1106 by command of Henry I and subsequently owned by the Courtenays, Earls of Devon. Do look at the superb clock collection in the round tower and the Joan of Arc exhibition.

You'll enter Tiverton on the **Exeter Road**, running beside the river. Turn right over the bridge and go straight on up **Angel Hill**, passing the town hall on the right. In about 300 yards, at the traffic circle, turn first left onto **Blundells Road** (*A373*), signposted to **Taunton and M5** freeway. There's a second traffic circle another 300 yards on; take the second left here on up **Blundells Road**, which becomes a divided highway out of the town. Seven miles out is **Junction 27** of the M5. Drive up the freeway to **Taunton** and rejoin the main route.

TOUR 4: CAMBRIDGE AND ELIZABETHAN EAST ANGLIA (about 186 miles)

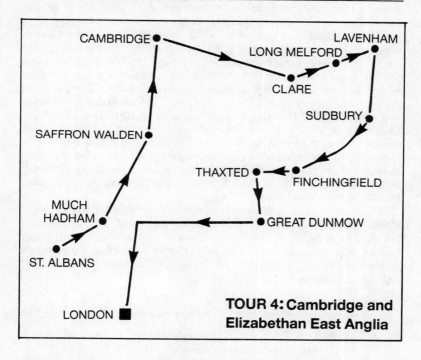

TOUR 4: Cambridge and Elizabethan East Anglia

This tour begins in St Albans. For directions from **London**, see **page 297**; for details of **St Albans** see **page 299**.

ST ALBANS TO MUCH HADHAM (about 27 miles)

*Follow the central one-way system round until you pick up the signs for **Hatfield (A1057)**. Stay on the Hatfield Road passing three sets of traffic lights and one traffic circle. After 2 miles of suburbs you'll emerge into countryside. Four miles from St Albans you'll begin to spot the grounds of **British Aerospace** on the left; Concorde was born here. Another ½ mile brings you to a traffic circle where you turn left onto the **A1001 (Hertford)** with the main entrance to British Aerospace Commercial Aviation on your left.*

*At the next traffic circle take the third exit off it, signposted **Hertford (A1001)**. At the following traffic circle take the fourth exit off it for **Hertford (A414)**. **Hatfield House** is ½ a mile from this traffic* *circle; follow the Hatfield signs and see page 298 for details should you wish to make a detour.*

For the most part, you'll be on a good divided highway for the next 3 miles, then the road alternates between a divided highway and single lane traffic. Drive through two traffic circles following signs for Hertford (A414). At the third circle follow signs for **Town Centre**. *Go straight across the next traffic circle but at the following traffic circle, with the central car park on your left, follow signs for* **Ware** *(A119). Follow signs for Ware through the next traffic circle and a set of lights. Turn left at the following traffic circle (about 2 miles from the Hatfield House traffic circle) signposted* **Much Hadham (B1004)** *and* **Cambridge (A10)**. *Drive right round the following traffic circle following signs for Much Hadham (B1004). This road is fairly narrow running through rolling countryside with farms nestling in the valleys on either side. Keep following the B1004. After a bit less than 2½ miles you'll enter the rather unattractive village of* **Wareside** *with its box-like houses. You'll pass* **Widford** *in another 1½ miles with its green spired church.*

At the crossroads after Widford turn left, following signs for the **B1004 (Bishop's Stortford)**. *Continue on this road. In a mile you'll see the* **Much Hadham** *town sign. Do not stop at the first group of houses, the most attractive part of the town is about a mile or two further on. You'll know when you've arrived at the best part of town – the* **Bull Inn** *will be on your left.*

MUCH HADHAM

Before reaching the pub you'll have noticed the remarkable diversity of the domestic architecture on both sides of the High Street. Medieval houses with their marvelous timbering nestle next to Georgian buildings, Regency façades face those with Edwardian and Victorian fronts. It's easy to see why eminent architectural historian Nicholas Pevsner wrote that, 'Much Hadham is visually probably the most successful village in the country'. It's also well worth exploring on foot. But first it's been a long, boring drive – you deserve a drink and, possibly, a bite to eat. **The Bull**, with ample parking alongside, can provide just that.

Coming in from the parking lot you'll be in the upper level bar. This features an extensive collection of pictures of the village taken during the early days of this century. That's a pleasant nostalgic note. Another is apt to strike you quickly – or should we say notes? Could that possibly be Glen Miller playing in the background? Indeed it is. The publican is a devotee of the big band sound. He plays masses of tapes from the 30s and 40s (with the odd bit of John Denver thrown in). The Bull serves real ale and scrumptious food – their Bullwich steak sandwich (£3.95) is Texan-sized and delicious. Ditto their smoked haddock in creamy parsley sauce (£3.25). But the menu stretches well beyond pub grub with such items as venison (reared locally) in a port and red currant sauce (£6.95 including all the trimmings). For clement weather there's a pleasant garden out back. Don't miss the N.A.S.A. aerial photograph of the whole county. It hangs in the passageway between the two bars.

Coming back down to earth it's time to take a walk through the village. Just to the left of the pub across the street you'll spot **The Hall** which dates from 1728 and was home to famed poet Walter de la Mare (1873-1956).

The village post office sells a good small guide to the village, *A Walk in Much Hadham*, by resident Mr S. Ruff (£3.50) which we highly recommend.

SIDE TRIP TO PERRY GREEN (about 1½ miles)

*Across the street ten yards to the right of the pub you'll spot a tiny lane – drive down this single-track road and you'll shortly come to a ford (the ideal way to clean the car). Cross this then take a right up a hill. This will bring you into **Perry Green**. At the intersection you'll see St Thomas's Church on the green. Turn right and shortly you'll see **The Hoops** pub on your left; park just beyond it in the large car park.*

Noted sculptor Henry Moore (1898-1986) lived in this tiny village from 1941, when his London studio was bombed out, until his death. The **Henry Moore Foundation** is based here. Opportunities to visit this are confined to selected afternoons during the summer and must be applied for well in advance in writing. To do so write to The Henry Moore Foundation, Dane Tree House, Perry Green, Much Hadham, Herts. If this sounds daunting we'll show you some Moores in a mile and three quarters.

The Hoops is an extraordinarily pleasant pub. The landlord, Duncan Campbell, long ago abandoned a job at the Bank of England to play mine host, a role he fills admirably. The food here is both good and reasonable (fresh skate at £3.50, lasagne at £2.80). There are no starters or desserts, they put their all into main dishes and it shows.

*Now return the 1½ miles to the **High Street** in Much Hadham and turn right. If you haven't visited it before, **Careless Cottage Antiques** on your right has exquisite items at prices to match.*

*Almost at once you'll come to a road off to your right signposted **Bishop's Stortford**. You're going to take this road in a minute but for now carry straight on and immediately off to your right you'll see **The Lordship**. Built in 1740 this nine bay house is everyone's dream of the elegant Georgian country manor. Next to it there's a magnificent stable block surmounted by a clock cupola as well as a number of other outbuildings from the 17th and 18th centuries. Now execute a*

U-turn and turn left for Bishop's Stortford. Off to your right a lane leads to **St Andrew's Church**. Parts of this building date from the 12th- and 13th-centuries, but most of what you'll see is from the 14 and 15 hundreds.

Notice the inscription above the doorway, 'This is the gate to heaven', and the king and queen head stops carved by Henry Moore and given to the church in 1953.

The scale and grandeur of many Much Hadham residences are connected with the presence in the village of a palace for the Bishop of London at least since the 10th century. The latest of these is at the north end of the churchyard. It's been converted into apartments. Hard to believe but true.

MUCH HADHAM TO SAFFRON WALDEN   (about 15½ miles)

*Turn right as you come out of the churchyard and follow the signs for **Bishop's Stortford**. Go over the bridge and continue on the **B1004** for 4½ miles to the traffic circle. Go straight down **Bell's Hill**. At the T-junction at the bottom turn right for the **Town Centre**. At the next traffic circle (about a ¼ mile) turn left for the **B1383** signposted Newport. Follow the B1383 at the next traffic circle where it's signposted **Stansted Mountfitchet/Saffron Walden**. Just after the Stansted Mountfitchet town sign on your left do look for the **windmill** on the left. Built in 1787 and still with much of its original machinery, it's the finest example of a tower mill in Essex (open first Sun in the month, public holiday Sun and Mon 2:30pm-6:30pm Apr-Oct; every Sun in Aug; admission: adults 50p children: 25p). There are also several enticing antiques shops along this stretch of road.*

*Stay on the B1383, and drive through **Newport**. At the intersection turn onto the **B1052** signposted **Saffron Walden**. You'll enter Saffron Walden 2 miles from the intersection. Turn right onto the **London Road** which becomes **High Street South** for the town center.*

SAFFRON WALDEN

Bronze and Iron Age tribes settled in this area but it's the Saxons who had a permanent impact on this intriguing town. As you enter the High Street you're traversing the previous site of Saxon palisades. In the 8th century they fortified this location and erected a castle and a church made of wood.

*Turn right off the High Street into **George Street** following the **Car Park** signs. One block later this becomes **Hill Street**. The road now forks. Take the left branch (again there's a Parking sign). The car park is on your right at the edge of the vast common.*

Once parked, cross the street called **Common Hill**. Directly in front of you you'll see a modern arched walkway with a sign pointing to the Tourist Information Centre. To your left is the Town Hall on the market square as you emerge from the short walkway. The **Tourist Information Centre** is at **1 Market Place**. (Tel: (0799) 24282. Open: Mon-Sat 9:30-4:30pm Apr-Oct; 10am-4pm Nov-Mar.) Guided walking tours with Blue Badge Guides originate at the Centre, daily at 2:30pm Apr-Oct. Tours last one-and-a-half hours and cost £1 for adults, children under 14 years are free. For specialist tours (e.g. Medieval Walden, Victorian Walden, Inns and Hostelries, etc.) telephone (0799) 27735.

There's been a market here since 1141 and, unusually, the small lanes where different trades sold their wares have survived as Butcher, Market and Mercer Rows.

The **Town Hall** with its imposing Tudor timbered front is a bit of an imposter. Most of the present structure dates from the 1820s.

The modern **Boots Chemist** (drug store) stands on the site of the 17th-century Rose and Crown Hotel which, sadly, burned down in 1969. Next to it is **Barclays Bank** neo-Tudor extravaganza built in 1874. While off to your left the classic-Italianate **Corn Exchange** occupies the site where the Woolstaplers' Hall stood for centuries.

Different agricultural commodities have dominated the town's commercial life during different centuries, wool in the 15th, saffron in the 16th and 17th, and malt in the 18th and early 19th.

The malt was destined for London's many breweries but as these grew they began to cultivate their own supplies elsewhere. What's more, when the railway first came to this part of the country it passed Saffron Walden by. These former economic misfortunes turned out to be a blessing in disguise since much of the town has retained its original character and buildings which are a history of its venerable past.

The Tourist Information Centre sells two excellent publications: *Saffron Walden Pocket Directory* (15p) which includes a map and two historic walking tours and, one of the best historic and architectural guides we've encountered, *Saffron Walden – Portrait of a Merchant Town*, which is a great bargain at £1.25.

Saffron was first brought back from Turkey and Greece by returning crusaders. Local soil conditions proved to be ideal for these purple crocuses which were prized as a dye, medicine, condiment, perfume and, some maintained, as an aphrodisiac.

The Walden of the town's name comes from the valley of the Britons (Wheala den). Essex with its six streams, of which the Cam is most famous, is characterized by hills (dons) and river valleys (dens) and these names are much in evidence throughout the region.

WHAT TO SEE

The parish church of **Saint Mary the Virgin**, at close to 200 feet long and 80 feet wide, is the largest church in Essex. The carved structure was built between 1450 and 1525 but parts are older, such as the chapel and the crypt. The carved tie beams of the roof are magnificent and the South Chapel contains a black marble monument to Sir Thomas Audley, Lord Chancellor and the namesake for nearby Audley End (qv). This dates from 1544. The 193 foot spire (1832) dominates the skyline of the town.

Across Museum Street from the church you'll find the **Saffron Walden Museum** (open: Mon-Sat 11am-5pm Apr-Sep; 11am-4pm Oct-Mar; Sun and public holiday Mon 2.30pm-5pm; closed: Good Friday, Dec 24-25; free admission). This contains a series of excellent exhibits on the town's history and its buildings, a new Great Hall Gallery which has a recreated Iron Age hut, Roman potter's workshop and a simply stunning Viking pendant. We were also particularly taken with the collection of dolls and toys from the 17th through the 19th century and by the Staffordshire pottery.

Directly behind the Museum you'll spot the **Castle Ruins** which are just that. Built in 1125, by the 14th century it was an abandoned shell.

The Castle Ruins overlook the **Common** which is bordered by a number of lovely Georgian houses as well as **The Priory**, just up the street from the car park. This was built in the 16th century, extended in the 17th, with a Venetian window above the main entrance added in the 18th.

At the far (western) end of the Common, just off Chater's Hill Road you'll find the **Maze** – a mile of narrow winding pathways within a 100 foot diameter. Its age is as puzzling as its purpose. The earliest record concerning it is 1699 when it was recut.

The **Old Sun Inn** at the corner of Church Street and Market Hill, which leads out of Market Place, is an outstanding example of pargetting, a regional form of exterior ornamentation consisting of plaster mixed with lime and oxblood. Some maintain that these figures represent a giant and a local carter and that the circle is the cartwheel, others maintain that it's the sun itself. You decide. What's unquestionable is the loveliness of these four interconnected medieval buildings. They now house **Lankester Antiques and Books**, which is great on the latter and not particularly impressive on the former.

Other buildings you really shouldn't miss are the 15th-century house, **The Close**, with its spectacular windows. Note particularly the unusual oval 'spider' window. This is located at the corner of High and Castle Streets. Diagonally across the street you'll spot the early 16th-century **Malt House**, which is now a youth hostel.

Head down **High Street** which now becomes **Bridge End** and just past Number 41 at the corner of Myddylton Place, a 15th-century timbered house, you'll spot a tiny lane. This leads down to the **Fry Art Gallery**, (open: Sat-Sun, public holiday Mon 2:30pm-5:30pm Easter Sun – last Sun Oct; free admission). This houses a collection by artists from the area, many well known, such as John Aldridge and Michael Rothenstein, who played an active role in the artistic community in and around the nearby village of Great Bardfield before and after World War II. From time to time they hold excellent exhibitions of local artists' very reasonably priced work. You'll be knocked out by the marbleized Italian entrance hall.

Just beyond this, further down the lane you'll come to the entrance to Victorian **Bridge End Gardens**, (open: daily 9.00am-sundown; free admission). As you explore the circular Rose Garden, what remains of a maze (currently being replanted after being vandalized some years ago) the statuary and the Dutch Garden, you're invited to take part in a Mystery Trail crossword puzzle. Just off to the right of the Gardens you'll see the **Anglo-American Memorial Playing Fields**, created as a war memorial by the town and the 65th Fighter Wing of the US Air Force.

SHOPPING

Roundhill Antiques, 14 Market Row, specializes in handsome small items such as silver boxes, perfume bottles, silver jewelry – including some real treasures from the 1920s and 30s.

Bush Antiques, Church Street at the corner of Museum Street, is our best bet for antiques. Four rooms of fine furniture and reasonably priced brass and copper items (we picked up a super brass trivet for £19.50). Jewelry designer Hilary Webb has a case of her lovely silver and gold creations on display here.

Weavers, across the street, has a good assortment of china and glasswear by well-known makers.

Antiques, just off Market Place up Market Street at the corner of Emson Close, features everything from a handsome linen press (£2600) and silver spoons to a pair of Queen Anne candlesticks (£220).

Hoops, 15 King Street, is a storehouse of good gift ideas. We loved their laundry bags which show sheep at washboards (£8.50). Other best bets are the Maggie White sweaters, terrific ties and Tate Gallery jigsaw puzzles such as 'A Couple of Foxhounds' by George Stubbs.

For a way out gift check out **PJT Telephones**, 1 George Street. AT&T would have a heart attack if they spotted the instruments here – buried inside teddy bears (£149), inside red telephone kiosks (£139), camouflaged as ladybugs (£29.95) are just a few of their offerings.

For something more traditional, **Lay's Tea and Coffee Shop** just down George Street at the corner of Market Walk has Mrs Bridge's strawberry preserves in attractive pottery jars with strawberries on the lid (£5.95) as well as tons of tea pots, cheerful china and tea in tin caddies.

SAFFRON WALDEN RESTAURANTS

The Old Hoops Restaurant, 15 King Street ££
Tel: (0799) 22813
Open: Tue-Sat noon-2:30pm, 7pm-10:30pm
Credit cards: AE, DC, V

After visiting Audley End (qv) Samuel Pepys stayed in the 400+ year-old inn that now houses this restaurant and 'stole a kiss from the landlord's daughter'. The interior beams were once part of a man-of-war, the green walls are decorated with menus from around the world. The two chef patrons have a decidedly delicate touch. We thought their Musselcress Soup (watercress and fresh mussels) at £2.45 was excellent, their Venison Steak *Lochaish* (served with a raspberry liqueur sauce) sublime (£7.50). Service though was somewhat less than friendly.

The Eight Bells Tudor Beam Restaurant, Bridge Street ££
Tel: (0799) 22790
Open: Mon-Sat noon-2pm, 6pm-9.30pm, Sun noon-2pm
Credit cards: AE, DC, MC, V

Located in a late 15th-century barn which retains its hay loft and straw ricks, this is a first-rate restaurant on several counts. Surroundings are lovely (plaster and frame red walls, settles, flowers on all tables) and there's plenty of space between tables as well as some partitioning. The prix fixe dinner at £14 was excellent, including for starters choice Cromer crab or smoked haddock bake topped with Wensleydale cheese and tomatoes; for main courses half a local pheasant braised in cider and cream or Lowestoft seafood pie – which included cod, prawns, scallops and salmon cooked in white wine with a pastry crust; the chocolate pot with brandy is a sinfully delicious way to close. But the biggest news of all is the extensive, excellent wine list at remarkably reasonable prices. For a rare treat try their Lebanese red, Château Musar (£9.95). Another recommendation, their 1983 Lacoste Borie, a Pauillac Bordeaux of distinction at the distinctly reasonable price of £13.50. Staff are young, amiable, attentive.

SAFFRON WALDEN HOTELS

The Eight Bells, Bridge Street　　　　　　　　　　　£
Tel: (0799) 26237
Amenities: ⬛ 🅿 ⁏⁏⁏⁏ ⚲
Credit cards: MC, V

Some locals believe this 16th-century inn derives its name from bell ringers who used to practice here, others believe it comes from the bells in the nearby belfry; all agree that this inn is a national treasure. Oaken beams, great, reasonably priced bar food, local ales kept in pristine condition are just some of the reasons.

What the locals won't know is that they do an outstanding bed and breakfast. Rooms are above the pub, but ultra quiet as well as ultra spacious – big enough in our case to have a separate TV area and a modern dining room set. The bathroom is just outside the door. Breakfast is served in the rooms – it's croissants, juice, butter, jam and coffee or tea. For an extra £2.50 you can get two eggs, bacon, and grilled tomatoes. All this and the price is right. Keep an eye out for the owners' two cats – Crazy and Lazy – they steal socks. Parking is in the pub's lot.

The Saffron Hotel, High Street　　　　　　　　　££
Tel: (0799) 24282
Amenities: ☎ ⬛ 🅿 (limited) ⁏⁏⁏⁏ ⚲
Credit cards: MC, V

Housed in three 16th-century buildings, there are 22 bedrooms, 16 of which have shower or bath and toilet en suite. This can best be described as like staying in someone's second best guest room. The large roaring fire in winter is welcoming – so are the staff. Limited parking is through the arch in their own small lot, otherwise it's on the fairly busy High Street, right at a knoll which worried us.

SAFFRON WALDEN TO CAMBRIDGE　　　(about 15 miles)

*Drive out of the **Common Hill parking lot** (by the village green). Turn right, go up the hill, take your first left onto **Church Street**. At the bottom of Church Street turn left into the **High Street**. Follow the road around with the War Memorial on your left onto the **London Road**. After about half a mile drive straight over the traffic circle following signs for **Audley End**. Almost immediately you'll begin to see the estate's brick boundary wall on the right which will give you an idea of the extent of the property. About a mile from the traffic circle you'll see the great manor gates on your right, the parking lot is across the street.*

Audley End, London Road (B1383), Saffron Walden
Open: Tues-Sun 1pm-5pm (park from noon)
Closed: Mon (except public holiday Mon)
Admission: Adults £2.50, children £1.25

Audley End owes its site to a conniving opportunist, its construction to a convicted embezzler and its current condition to an early minimalist (he felt less was more) and the devotion of one family who tried to keep it together for close to two hundred years.

As Speaker of the House of Commons, Thomas Audley (1488-1544) presided over the Black Parliament (1529) which abolished papel authority in England, the first in a series of errands he performed for Henry VIII in his attack on the clergy and the established order. Others, as Lord Chancellor, included assistance in Henry's divorce from Catherine of Aragon (1533), the imprisonment of Anne Boleyn (1536) and the annulment of Henry's marriage to Anne of Cleves (1540). These efforts did not go unrewarded. At the Dissolution of the Monasteries a number of estates were given to him including Walden Abbey erected on this site in 1190.

His grandson, Thomas Howard, First Earl of Suffolk, razed the Abbey to the ground and started construction of Audley End in 1603, the year in which James I appointed him Lord Chancellor of the royal household, the work being completed in 1616, two years after he became Lord High Treasurer.

These two positions allowed him to amass great wealth to spend on the project. And spend it he did. The cost was over £200,000, a staggering amount for the time. (Upon seeing it King James is reputed to have said that it was much too grand for a King but might suffice for a Lord High Treasurer.)

In 1618 Suffolk was stripped of office on a charge of misappropriating funds, tried in the Star Chamber, convicted and heavily fined.

During the Civil War various royal palaces had been sacked so after the Restoration Charles II was delighted to buy the place, which he dubbed the 'New Palace', for £50,000 in 1669.

As you enter the lobby you'll see Henry Winstanley's 1676 engraving of the royal palace, a veritable city in itself. The sole surviving architectural royal relics are the James II and William and Mary rainwater heads off the guttering.

In 1701, having never fully paid off the purchase price, the Crown returned Audley End to the 5th Earl of Suffolk (perhaps even royalty found the prospect of paying for the upkeep daunting).

In any event subsequent owners brought in Sir John Van Burgh and between 1721 and 1730 he oversaw the demolition of fully two thirds of the building.

Your visit will bring you in via the 18th-century **Lion Gate**. Once parked you'll note that today Audley Hall consists of its one great hall with three-story wings on either side, with mullioned windows beneath a profusion of turrets, chimneys and gables.

The Hall is, without a doubt, Audley End's most imposing room. The great Jacobean wooden screen at the northern end is positively Baroque in its decorative richness and in stark contrast to the serene stone screen at the southern end with its two fine staircases. The plaster ceiling is divided by wooden beams into panels, each of which bears a Howard family crest.

The **Little Drawing Room** (1776) is one of three Adam's decorated rooms. He was also responsible for the buildings in the garden and the bridge over the River Cam. By contrast, the **Chapel** is a lovely example of late 18th-century Gothic style.

Throughout the building you'll find noteworthy French and English furniture as well as some exquisite pictures including Canaletto's picture of the Campanili and the Doges Palace in Venice and a series of portraits of those associated with the building throughout the centuries.

The grounds are another demonstration of Capability Brown's genius. The handsome early 17th-century stables now house a museum of agricultural implements.

*To continue the drive to Cambridge, turn left out of the **Audley End parking lot** and at the end of the estate's grounds turn right following the **B1383** signposted **Cambridge**. Stay on this road following signs for Cambridge through the outskirts of **Great Chesterford**. About 5 miles from Audley End you'll come to the M11 interchange. Get on the **A1301** signposted **Cambridge/Sawston**. The landscape is flat which is typical of this area close to the East Anglia fens. Ignore signs for Cambridge 2 miles further on, stay on the A1301 signposted Sawston. Drive past the village of Stapleford. At the traffic lights go straight into **Tunwells Road**. After a short rather boring drive through uninspiring suburbs and 12½ miles from Audley End you'll see the 'entering **Cambridgeshire** county' stone on your left. You're still quite a distance from the heart of Cambridge. At the traffic lights turn right for **Cambridge** through the village of **Trumpington**. You're now on **Trumpington Road**. You'll see several prep schools on the right. At the lights go straight on with a village green on your left, this is now the **A134**. At the traffic circle drive straight over following signs for **City Centre/Short Stay Parking**. The road is now called **Trumpington Street**. Pass Brown's restaurant on your right and the Fitzwilliam Museum on your left. Following signs for **Little Lion Car Park** turn right into **Pembroke Street**, then left into **Corn Exchange Street** and enter the multi-story car park.*

From the car park, exit into **Corn Exchange Street** with the side of the Victorian Corn Exchange in front of you. Walk down to the side walk, cross the street, turn right and walk towards **Wheeler Street**. At Wheeler Street turn left, walk about 200 yards and cross the street to the **Tourist Information Centre**, Wheeler Street. (Tel: (0223) 322640. Open: Mon-Fri 9am-5:30pm (until 6pm Jul, until 7pm Aug-Sep); Sat 9am-5pm.) Do make the TIC your first stop. They have an enormous amount of information on what to see and what's playing at the theaters and musical venues.

GETTING AROUND

Cambridge Traffic – A Word of Warning
The city's center can get horribly congested on Saturdays and city center parking can be woefully inadequate. If you're heading for Cambridge on a Saturday and don't have an inner city hotel reservation we recommend you consider Park and Ride.

Park and Ride
There are two park and ride points. One is situated on the **Cowley Road**, off the **Milton Road**, and serves the north side of the city as well as the town center.

The second on **Cherry Hinton Road** at the **Cattle Market** serves the south side of Cambridge as well as the town center, stopping at Emmanuel College and the Grafton Centre.

They operate from 9am-6pm. The car park is free, cost of the bus ride is 45p. This service operates December 6-January 6 and on Saturdays only the rest of the year.

Bike Hire
You'll quickly see that the preferred means of travel in downtown Cambridge is the bicycle. It's fast, it's fun, it's carefully controlled with separate bike lanes; finally it's an easy way to cover the substantial distances between some of the colleges and other attractions.

The Tourist Information Centre in Wheeler Street (tel: (0223) 322640) has a free leaflet that lists ten local cycle hire companies. Rates per day vary from £2 to £3, per week from £2.50 (winter rate) to £10. Howes Cycles, 104 Regent Street (tel: (0223) 350350) is fairly centrally located and has good rates – £2.50 a day, £5 per week. There's a £25 returnable deposit.

Punt Hire In Cambridge
There is basically one main company to hire from but they have several hire points along the river (listed below). The company's name is **Scudamores**, Granta Place at the bottom of Mill Lane (tel: (0223) 359750). In summer students get together and hire out punts on a casual basis but Scudamores are the main bona fide professionals at it.

The hire charge for a punt (which will take up to six people) is £4 per hour and a £30 returnable deposit. They also have chauffeur punts which are on hire for approximately £12 for 45 minutes (this is the current rate and may go up slightly next year).

Rental points:
1. Magdalene Bridge
2. Near the Anchor Pub
3. The Stepps, near the Anchor Pub (lower river along the Backs)
4. Upper river, takes you to Grantchester

CAMBRIDGE

Cambridge stands on the site of ancient Celtic settlements that grew up around a ford on the River Cam. When the Romans came, they built a bridge and established an outpost here at the meeting point of a network of roads and navigable rivers. A well-established settlement by the time of the Norman Conquest in 1066, Cambridge saw the foundation of several small monastic houses during the 11th century. Some of these were later to evolve into colleges.

A group of students, in trouble with the authorities in Oxford, came to Cambridge in 1209. At that time there were no colleges: students were attached to the schools of cathedrals and monasteries, lodging where they could in the town. Relationships between local residents and students were hostile. Brawls became an everyday occurrence and in 1231 Henry III decreed that all students should be under the control of a Master.

WHAT TO SEE

It was not until 1281 that the first college, **Peterhouse** was founded by the Bishop of Ely. By 1284, it was established in its own buildings. Cambridge now has 23 colleges, the majority of them dating from the 14th, 15th and 16th centuries. Choosing which to visit is not an easy task, but for those for whom time is short, there are of course the 'greats', and we'll point you in their direction. You might decide, however, to join a guided tour of both the colleges and the historic parts of the city. Tickets for the **official tours** are available no more than 24 hours in advance from the **Tourist Information Centre** in Wheeler Street, price £2.50, with no reduction for children. Times of tours are as follows: Mon-Sat 11am, 2pm Oct, Easter-May; 11am, 1pm, 2pm June; 11am, noon, 1pm, 2pm, 3pm, 6:30pm July & Aug; 11am, 1pm, 2pm, 3pm Sept; 2pm Nov-Easter; Sun 11:15am June-Aug. Be warned – groups are limited to 20 and in the summer tours are very quickly filled.

The oldest colleges and University buildings are all within easy walking distance. As with Oxford, there is no University building. 'University' refers to the group of colleges that together make up

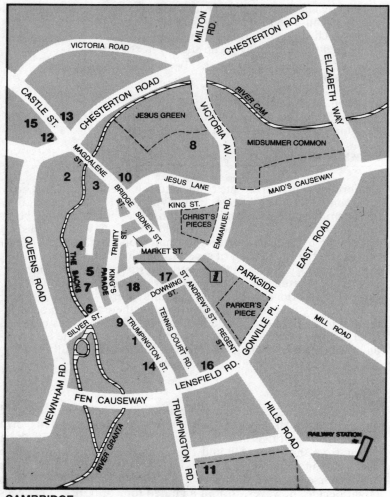

CAMBRIDGE

i Tourist Information Centre
 1 Peterhouse
 2 St John's College
 3 Trinity College
 4 Clare College
 5 King's College
 6 Queen's College
 7 Corpus Christi College
 8 Jesus College
 9 Little St Mary's Church
10 The Church of the Holy Sepulchre
11 Botanic Gardens

12 Cambridge and County Folk Museum
13 Cambridge Medieval Brass Rubbing Centre
14 Fitzwilliam Museum
15 Kettle Yard
16 Scott Polar Research Institute
17 University Museum of Archaeology and Anthropology
18 Whipple Museum of the History of Science

this center of learning. Colleges are generally open to view during daylight hours. You can visit the Courts (equivalent to Oxford's quadrangles), gardens and sometimes the chapel, hall and library. Halls are normally closed at lunchtime during term. The Tourist Information Centre will be able to advise you on individual opening hours.

Undoubtedly the best time to be in Cambridge is at the end of the academic year, during **May Week**, which is actually the first half of June. (It's not, however, the best time to visit colleges, many of which are closed to the public for part of this period.) Festivities, concerts and May Balls lend a carnival air to the city, and the inter-collegiate rowing races, **The Bumps**, provide good spectator sport. This is also the time when the **Footlights Revue**, traditionally the spawning ground for a large percentage of Britain's theatrical talent, takes place.

If you miss June, at least you'll be spared the crowds. The green, riverside lawns, known as **The Backs**, are even lovelier in the fall, and the echo of footsteps in some ancient courtyard twice as evocative when you've got the place to yourself one wintry day. If you must have a shortlist of colleges we suggest these: **St John's, Trinity, Clare, King's, Queens', Corpus Christi** and **Jesus.**

St John's was founded in 1511 by Lady Margaret Beaufort, mother of Henry VII, on the site of a hospital dating from the 13th century. It has an impressive **Tudor gateway**, an early 16th-century First Court, an Elizabethan Second Court, and a third square which leads to the 19th-century **Bridge of Sighs**. The bridge spans the River Cam and links the older buildings with New Court (new in the 1830s), getting its name from the Bridge of Sighs in Venice, whose style it reflects.

Next door to St John's is **Trinity College**, the largest in Cambridge. Henry VIII joined two 14th-century foundations to create Trinity and it is the only college to have a Master appointed by the Crown. It boasts the largest court in either Oxford or Cambridge. Here Isaac Newton worked on his Laws of Motion and budding literary stars like Byron, Thackeray and Tennyson studied. **The Hall** has a splendid hammerbeam roof and the library, built by Sir Christopher Wren, fine carving and statuary.

South of Trinity Hall lies **Clare College**, founded in 1326. The present 17th-century buildings replace the original ones destroyed by fire. Clare College boasts the oldest bridge in Cambridge, dating from 1640. By far the prettiest bridge over the River Cam is to be found in **Queens' College**. Built in 1749 on mathematical principles that obviated the need for nails, it was later reconstructed. Walk through the porter's lodge off Silver Street to reach the bridge, from which there are good views of the college, the Backs and the river. The college is named after two queens: Henry VI's wife Margaret of Anjou who founded it in 1448, and Edward IV's wife Elizabeth, who refounded and endowed it in 1465.

Although ancient college founders were drawn mostly from royalty, nobility or the church, there were exceptions. **Corpus Christi College**, dating from 1352, owes its existence to two of the town guilds, and has the best-preserved medieval court in Oxford and Cambridge. A little lane leads from the Old Court to **St Bene't's Church**, where students would worship before the college was endowed with a chapel. St Bene't's (short for St Benedict's) is believed to date from the reign of King Cnut.

Jesus College is set a little away from the others, built on the site of the suppressed Benedictine nunnery of St Radegond. It was founded in 1496. The chapel has a mid-13th century chancel and other parts of the old nunnery, notably the cloisters and chapter-house, have also been incorporated into the college buildings. Jesus is well-known for the crocuses in the **Fellows' Garden**. In spring the door to Jesus Lane is left ajar so that passers-by can glimpse the show of flowers.

Probably top of everyone's Cambridge list is **King's College**. Founded by Henry VI in 1440, its **Chapel** is spectacular. Built between 1446 and 1515, the Chapel is the city's crowning glory – a superb example of Perpendicular architecture, the soaring stone roof decorated with fan tracery. Rubens's **'The Adoration of the Magi'**, presented to the college in 1962, forms the altarpiece.

When you've 'done' the colleges, look for **Little St Mary's Church**, in Little St Mary's Lane, off Trumpington Street. It was rebuilt between 1340-50 and on its north wall bears a memorial to the **Rev. Godfrey Washington**, a Fellow of Peterhouse in the 18th century. The memorial shows the Washington coat of arms, from which the **Stars and Stripes** evolved. **The Church of the Holy Sepulchre**, in Bridge Street, is also worth a visit. One of only five round churches remaining in England (note: only part is round), it was founded in 1130 by the Knights Templar on the model of the Church of the Holy Sepulchre at Jerusalem. Now when you're dizzy with architectural splendor, slope off to the **Botanic Gardens**, 40 acres of gardens and glasshouses at the junction of Trumpington Street and Bateman Street.

Cambridge & County Folk Museum, Castle Street
Open: Mon-Sat 10:30am -5pm, Sun 2:30pm-4:30pm
Admission: Adults 80p, children 40p

The museum occupies the former White Horse Inn. Through exhibits ranging from domestic and agricultural bygones to toys and pictures, it charts the lifestyles of the Cambridgeshire people over three centuries.

Cambridge Medieval Brass Rubbing Centre, St Giles Church, Castle Street
Open: Wed-Sat 10am-5pm, also Mon-Tues Jun-Sept
Admission: Adults £2.50, children £2 (includes materials)

Ninety facsimile tombstones to rub, with figures dating from 1300 to 1650.

Fitzwilliam Museum, Trumpington Street
Open: Tues-Sat: Lower Galleries 10am-2pm, Upper Galleries 2pm-5pm; Sun all galleries 2:15pm-5pm
Closed: Mon, Good Fri, Dec 24-Jan 1
Free admission

Founded in 1816 with the bequest of the 17th Viscount Fitzwilliam, this is one of the oldest public museums in Britain. It houses a remarkable collection of fine and applied arts, including paintings by Titian, Rembrandt, Gainsborough, Hogarth and Turner, plus Greek and Egyptian antiquities, textiles, Chinese and European ceramics, pottery, historical and medieval manuscripts.

Kettle Yard, Castle Street
Open: House: Daily 2pm-4pm
       Gallery: Tues-Sat 12:30pm-5:30pm (until 7pm Thur), Sun 2pm-5:30pm
Free admission

House owned by the Universtiy of Cambridge with a permanent collection of early 20th-century art hung in a domestic setting. The gallery has an ever-changing series of exhibitions of modern and contemporary art.

Scott Polar Research Institute, Lensfield Road
Open: Mon-Sat 2:30pm-4pm
Free admission

Intriguing exhibits of expedition relics and equipment, plus Eskimo and general polar art collection.

University Museum of Archaeology and Anthropology, Downing Street
Open: Mon-Fri 2pm-4pm, Sat 10am-12:30pm
Free admission

Archaeological collections show world pre-history and Britain from the earliest period until post-medieval times.

Whipple Museum of the History of Science, Free School Lane
Open: Mon-Fri 2pm-4pm
Closed: Sat & Sun and also occasionally during university vacations
Free admission

Collection of historic scientific instruments, dating from the 16th to 19th century.

SHOPPING

If you were born to shop this cradle of learning is for you. The main shopping district is bordered on one side by the colleges off King's Parade which in turn becomes Trinity Street, and St John's Street and the parks known as Christ's Pieces and Parker's Piece. **Sydney Street** and the streets and lanes between it and **King's Parade/ Trinity Street** are where most good shops are concentrated.

There's a large **Marks & Spencer** on Sydney, a good **Liberty** on Trinity. Others include **Laura Ashley**, **French Connection**, **Jaeger** and **Monsoon**. There is no half day closing in Cambridge. Most shops are open from 9am or 9:30am-5:30pm or 6pm Monday-Saturday. Many stay open 'till 8pm on Wednesday evenings.

Heffer's, various locations
Credit cards: MC, V

Appropriately Cambridge abounds in good book stores and here Heffer's rules the roost as well as seeming to appear on every other block, but then they've been on the scene since 1876. Their **main branch** at 20 Trinity Street must be seen to be believed. This multi-level complex carries 200,000 books on two and a half miles of shelves. Records, tapes and compact discs are also on sale here. Their **Children's Bookshop**, 30 Trinity, is also extraordinarily well stocked while **Deighton & Bell**, 13 Trinity, offers second-hand and antiquarian books from recently restored 18th-century premises.

One of the charms of the city is shopping in the small pedestrian passages such as **Petty Cury**, **St Edward's Passage** and **Rose Crescent** which runs between Market and Trinity Streets.

Silks, 12 Rose Crescent
Credit cards: AE, MC, V

They have a fantastic array of sexy slinky lingerie in designer colors and slate gray including a nightgown cut on the bias that looks like it's heading off to a dinner dance at the Ritz, rather than the boudoir. Further along, the **Peppercorn Deli** has great picnic makings. Across the way and a bit further towards Trinity Street, **Marr's Leather Shop's** two bow windows display great leather wear for men and women. Belts start at £27 while an ultra chic Italian woman's bomber jacket will set you back £215.

Anna Rowena, 4 Trinity Street
Credit cards: AE, DC, MC, V

They have a stunning collection of their own handknits starting at £60 and boast the largest selection of designer sweaters in town. For knitters they have their own range of mohair yarns, Jaeger alpaca, angora and cashmere plus Kilcarra Donegal Tweeds.

Book-Shelf, 62-64 King Street
Credit cards: AE

This store has a split personality. On the one hand they offer beautifully bound blank books. On the other they have a simply smashing selection of small antique silver items – bracelets, clocks, napkin rings, perfume bottles, salters and serving spoons feature.

Cable & Company, corner Sydney Street and Petty Cury
Credit cards: AE, MC, V

This is a lovely, modern shoe store with super attentive staff. Surroundings are as elegantly understated as the shoes and boots themselves. Sold under their own label but sourced mostly in Spain or Italy, prices are understated as well; women's casual shoes start at just £30, men's at £35.

Gordon Lowes, 16 King's Parade
Credit cards: AE, DC, MC, V

Worth visiting if you're in the market for elegant, casual men's sportswear. They also stock Austrian Loden coats and capes and Barbour jackets.

House of Tweed, 3 Peas Hill
Credit cards: AE, DC, MC, V

Just around the corner from the Tourist Information Centre this small shop is, as its name implies, decidedly tweedy. Lovely ladies' woolen capes for £110; great lap rugs for granny (£12.75).

My Auntie Had One But She Threw It Away, 10 King Street
No credit cards

With a name like that who could resist a visit? If you do you'll find the odd excellent antique – a terrific 14-drawer pine chest when we were there – combined with smaller pieces and lots that my auntie had etc.

Pastimes Bead Shop, 7 Cobble Yard
No credit cards

Beads, bone, bobbins, books, brooch fasteners, ceramics, chains, clasps, cloisonné and everything to assist in making bracelets, earrings, necklaces and rings. They also have knockout finished jewelry at knocked down prices. Special note: closes at 3:45pm Monday-Friday.

Quints of Cambridge, 34 Trinity Street
Credit cards: AE, DC, MC, V

They have a wonderful selection of prints, on two levels with knowledgeable, friendly staff.

Ryder & Amies, corner of King's Parade and St Mary's Passage
Credit cards: AE, DC, MC, V

'Hosiers and Shirtmakers, Club Outfitters' their signs proclaim, and with justification. This is the home of the club tie, school crest cuff link and college gown. Good selection of rugby shirts, turtle necks and pukka umbrellas.

CAMBRIDGE RESTAURANTS

Cambridge has a large number of reasonable restaurants, wine bars and pubs to cater for the college population. We've included several of our favorites such as Browns, as popular in Oxford as they are here. What Cambridge has lacked is a really outstanding restaurant. That's just been corrected and complete details on Midsummer House are listed below.

Browns, 23 Trumpington Street   £
Tel: (0223) 461655
Open: Mon-Sat 11am-11:30pm, Sun from noon
Closed: Dec 24-26
No credit cards

This is where town and gown congregate for first-rate food and drink in friendly surroundings. There's nothing fancy about the decor (cream walls, ceiling fans, bentwood chairs at wooden tables, palms aplenty along with ivy sprawling out of high windowboxes); nor is the food fussy. Rather it consists of good fresh ingredients which are well prepared. Some of our favorites: crab and avocado salad (£5.65), Ruben's corned beef sandwich (£4.15), steak, mushroom and Guinness pie (£4.95). The house claret (£6.85) is eminently drinkable, cocktails exorbitantly priced.

Arts Theatre Restaurant, 6 St Edward's Passage   £
Tel: (0223) 355246
Open: Mon-Sat: Pentagon (self-service) 9:30pm-2:15pm, 7pm-
      8pm – snacks only; Roof Garden noon-2:15pm, 6pm-10pm
Closed: Sun, Christmas Day, New Year's Day
Credit cards: AE, DC, MC, V

Fortunately the food here is far less complicated than the opening hours. Pentagon is self-service, good for breakfast and does a good value make-your-own-salad from a buffet table. This including half a pint of lager or a glass of wine costs £6.50.

The waitress-service Roof Garden restaurant opens onto flowered terraces in good weather. They offer a good three course dinner menu for just £7.50; for example, prawn cocktail, *coq au vin*, and stilton cheese. Coffee and mints are 75p extra.

Don Pasquale, 12a Market Hill £
Tel: (0223) 67063
Open: Pizzeria: Daily 8am-1am; Restaurant: Daily noon-3pm, 5:45-midnight
Credit cards: AE, DC, MC, V

Located at the corner of Market Street, this modern eatery describes itself as a pizzeria and gellateria (a pizza and ice cream joint). But describing their Pizza San Valentino as just 'a pizza' is like describing Placido Domingo as 'a singer'; this wonderful concoction includes tuna, ham, salami, onions, mushrooms, mozzarella, olives, prawns, peppers and frankfurters. It costs £8.40 and they suggest it's for two. The pizzeria is in the basement.

Hard to believe they also do great light meals in the restaurant upstairs (cheese omelette £3.95, *Insalata di Arrosto Misto*, cold cuts with a side salad, £3.95). Their home-made pasta is similarly priced. Italian house wine is £5.90 the bottle. Small wonder that they're always packed.

Midsummer House Restaurant, Midsummer Common £££
Tel: (0223) 69299
Open: Tues-Fri noon-2pm, 6:30pm-9:30pm, Sat 6:30pm-9:30pm, Sun noon-1:30pm
Closed: Christmas Day, following three days, New Year's Day
Credit cards: MC, DC, V

*Directions: Go down **Chesterton Road** until you get into the one-way system at Mitcham's Corner. Follow one-way system and you'll see a sign for **Chesterton** and the **Ring Road**. Turn right onto **Ferrypath** (on the corner you'll see the Ashley Hotel and a bicycle shop). Go down Ferrypath to **Pretoria Road**. Park at the end of Pretoria Road. Cross the footbridge over the River Cam, the restaurant is on your left.*

We can hear you muttering 'after that kind of a fuss to get to the restaurant it better be worth it'. Well it is.

The food here is simply sublime. Chef Hans Schweitzer describes his set price menus as 'based on good French cuisine' but it goes well beyond that. Schweitzer trained in Munich, was executive chef at the Teheran Sheraton during the Shah's era, then cooked in the Caribbean. At each step of the way he picked up enough delicate tricks of the trade to win several culinary gold medals; then a Michelin star during his first year in Bad Hamburg.

The decor is that of a glorious country house with Cambridge blue the prevailing color. A double vaulted conservatory dining area leads off the main Victorian building. This is surrounded on three sides by a lovely garden with two tables for dining alfresco when weather permits. The prix fixe menu is £17.50 for three courses, £25 for six; while at lunch there's a £9.80 two course special.

Starters might be sauté of foie gras and quail on an autumn salad or fresh noodles with shrimps and sweetbreads in a light cream sauce. Main courses during our visit included filet of hare in orange and ginger sauce and pheasant pie with dark and white morels. Desserts are to die for. The house wine is an excellent California Chardonnay.

So it's a drive and a walk. It's worth it.

CAMBRIDGE HOTELS

Cambridge has a plentitude of hotels, a paucity of those one would consider first-rate. American translation – there isn't a really good hotel in the place. That said we've concentrated on three hotels which are perfectly nice if unmemorable and are decent value-for-money.

Regent Hotel, 41 Regent Street   ££
Tel: (0223) 351470   Closed: Christmas Eve - Jan 3
Amenities: ☎ ⌨ ⛾ ⚱   Credit cards: AE, DC, MC, V

This pleasant, small (19 rooms) hotel is ideally situated so that a five minute walk brings you to the town center. Fifteen of the rooms have en suite bathrooms, doubles with bath go for £48. Back rooms overlook peaceful Parker's Piece, a 25 acre open park. There is no parking and this can be a problem, Regent Street is busy. Breakfast is included in the price.

Royal Cambridge Hotel, Trumpington Street   ££
Tel: (0223) 351631
Amenities: ☎ ⌨ P ⚱ ⛾   Credit cards: AE, DC, MC, V

Special note: the address notwithstanding the hotel's entrance and parking lot are 50 yards down on the right off the Fen Causeway once you've turned off Trumpington Street.

When we checked rooms were sort of Scandinavian modern circa 1960 but we're assured they're in the midst of redecorating all 65 rooms, 47 of which have bathrooms en suite. Doubles with bathroom are £65 per night including full English breakfast.

University Arms Hotel, Regent Street **£££**
Tel: (0223) 351241
Amenities: ☎ ⌨ 🅿 ᛃ ♀   Credit cards: AE, DC, MC, V

This small skyscraper hotel features parking directly beneath it. It's one block up from the Regent Hotel and thus that bit closer to the city center. It's also been run by the same family, the Bradfords, for close to 100 years. Singles with bath are £44.50, doubles £60, so it just tips onto our expensive category. There are 115 pleasant albeit a bit dowdy rooms. There's 24-hour food and beverage service – a nice touch this. The partially stained-glass dining room windows overlook Parker's Piece park – so do some rooms. Their **Whisky Galore Bar** lives up to its name with 100+ to offer. The whole place is plush rather than posh.

An alternative:
Duxford Lodge Hotel, Ickleton Road, Duxford **££**
Tel: (0223) 836444
Amenities: ☎ ⌨ 🅿 ᛃ ♀   Credit cards: AE, DC, MC, V

Directions: Get off M11 at exit 10. Take A505 heading east to Duxford. Take first right into the village and the Lodge is on the junction in the center of town.

This pleasant country house hotel, a mere 20 minutes by car from Cambridge, has much to commend it (which is why it's a British Tourist Authority Commended Hotel). The 16 bedrooms are tastefully furnished with some antiques, all have bathrooms en suite. The building is Georgian, the grounds most pleasing. The French food is supposed to be excellent – reports please.

AROUND AND ABOUT

Anglesey Abbey
Open: House and Garden: Wed-Sun, Bank (public) Holiday Mon
1:30pm-5:30pm Apr-mid Oct
Garden only: as above plus daily 1:30pm-5:30pm early Jul-mid Oct
Admission: Adults £2.50, children £1.25

Directions: From the Tourist Information Centre in Wheeler Street go down St Bene't's Street, turn left into Trumpington Street, then first left into Pembroke Street. At the end of Pembroke Street turn left into St Andrew's Street and immediately right into Emmanuel Street. At the end of Emmanuel, turn right into Drummer Street (by the Bus Station). Take the first left into Emmanuel Road to the first traffic circle. Turn right into Newmarket Road (A1303) and follow signs to Angelsey Abbey (6 miles).

An Augustinian priory was founded on this 100 acre site in 1135.

This was largely destroyed during the Dissolution of the Monasteries and the present building is 16th-century, though the Chapter House and Canon's Parlour (now the dining room) date from the 13th-century.

Two notable former owners were Cambridge stablekeeper Thomas Hobson (when asked for a mount he'd say 'this horse or none' pointing to the mare nearest the door – hence Hobson's Choice) and Sir George Downing, founder of Downing College, Cambridge and grandson of the builder of Downing Street who was, amazingly, Harvard's second graduate.

That briefly is the past. The real interest here is very much the result of the present and relates specifically to what large amounts of American money can accomplish when judiciously spent by someone with a connoisseur's eye. That someone was Lord Fairhaven who bought the property in 1926. His father had made a fortune in the U.S.A. then compounded it by marrying a New York heiress. As a result Fairhaven was what is termed seriously rich. Happily he was also a serious student of art, furniture, porcelain, landscaping and much more.

Anglesey Abbey houses his priceless collection. This includes tapestries, paintings by Canaletto, Claudes, Constable, (his famed 'View of Waterloo Bridge' is here), Gainsborough and many other illustrious artists. There's a fascinating 350-year-old visual history of Windsor executed in oils, watercolors and engravings. The furniture collection includes English, Continental and Chinese treasures (the latter late Ming). Other collections include bronzes, arms, clocks and porcelain – all are shown in restful surroundings with muted light from stained-glass windows which is reminiscent of New York's Cloisters.

To complement the interior Anglesey boasts one of England's most magnificent gardens. It looks ancient, it's just under 50 years old. This features other Fairhaven finds such as the 12 marble imperial busts of the Emperor's Walk and the copy of Bernini's Boy David, but that's but some of many enchanting features. Many of the trees and other plants are rare – so it's like a visit to Kew. All are beautifully arranged to provide an unforgettable contrast between ordered symmetry and skillfully sculptured natural foliage effects. If you're a gardener you'll want to stay for days. The **Visitors' Centre** in the car park sells an excellent walking guide called *Discovery Trail*; it costs just 20p. You'll also find a good display here showing how the gardens were developed, as well as a shop and a restaurant.

Should you wish to end your tour at this point you can speedily reach London (about one and a half hours) by following the directions on **page 505**.

CAMBRIDGE TO LONDON (about 58 miles)

Drive down St Andrew's Street which becomes Regent Street. At the end of Regent Street there are traffic lights at the crossroads. Turn right into Lensfield Road (church on your left). Continue to the traffic circle, turn left into Trumpington Road. Follow signs for M11 (London).

CAMBRIDGE TO CLARE (about 26 miles)

Exit from Lion Yard Car Park into Downing Street (a continuation of Pembroke Street), turn left. At the T-junction turn right onto St Andrew's Street. Follow this road while it becomes Regent Street, then Hills Road, then the A604, signposted Colchester. Soon you'll see the signs read A1307/604 Colchester. You'll stay on this road for about 23 miles driving through flat fen country and a few nondescript towns like Haverhill. Be sure to come to a full stop just before the viaduct outside Haverhill. Shortly, you re-enter the county of Essex. At the next intersection (about 3 miles from Haverhill) turn left signposted Clare (A1092). Drive through the small village of Stoke by Clare. Note the attractive parish church and tempting antiques shop, both on your right. Just a few miles further and a total of 26 from Cambridge you enter the charming, sleepy village of Clare.

CLARE

Important since Saxon and Norman times, the latter built a 20 acre castle here. Clare today is a charming reminder of the wealth that once attached to the wool trade in this part of the world.

As you enter the village the **A1092** becomes **Nethergate Street** which is lined with a series of fine Georgian wool merchants houses – some with overhanging gables and pargetting. **Cloth House** on your right is one good example with a dramatic chimney at its core.

William I awarded Clare and its surroundings to Richard Fitzgilbert for his help at the Battle of Hastings. When his heirs failed to sire a male heir the estate was split between three sisters, one of whom endowed, Clare, the second oldest college at Cambridge.

WHAT TO SEE

As you enter the town you'll see a sign on your right pointing down a road to your left marked 'Priory'. Take this and after about 100 yards you'll pass through a metal gate into the Priory's grounds.

Clare first hosted a Benedictine Priory in the 12th century. The one you can visit dates from 1248 but was dissolved in 1338 and not re-established by the Augustinian order until 1953. Most of the buildings date from the 14th century (open: daily 10am-6pm; closed Jan 1-2; free admission though donations are welcome).

It's best to phone ahead – especially if it's out of season. To do so telephone (0787) 277326. If there is no reply at the front entrance, they suggest that you try the side door.

*Head down **Malting Lane** and you'll quickly come to a free car park for **Clare Castle Country Park**. The castle ruins are off to your left on a 60 foot mound. Little of the building remains but enough does as earthworks to amaze one at the sheer scope of the enterprise.*

Walk down the little **alleyway** at the northwest of the town square and you'll come to the churchyard of **Saint Peter and Saint Paul Church**. The lane turns left here and at its end (High Street) on your left you'll find an ancient house (1473) with magnificent pargetting. This now houses the **Ancient House Museum** (open: Wed-Sat 2.30pm-4.30pm; Sunday and public holidays 11am-12.30pm, 2:30pm-4:30pm Easter-Oct; admission: adults 40p, children 20p). The collection includes local archaeology, tools and crafts, domestic articles, costumes and toys.

Across from it the church with its perpendicular exterior is mostly 15th-century though the West Tower is 13th. As you'll see its spacious interior reflects the town's former importance. The 17th-century gallery and enormous bell ringers' beer jug are two notable features, so is the 1790 porch with sundial inscribed rather ominously 'Go About Your Business'.

SHOPPING

Granny's Attic, 22 Church Street, opposite the village church is, as its name implies, a great place to browse for memorabilia from the turn of the century onwards, dresses from the 20s and 1930s' bedspreads, and colorful crockery are all here.

Clare Jug and Bottle shop, High Street, is the place for Nethergate Bitter and some stoneware jugs from the brewery on its doorstep. Just down from this don't miss the oldest pub sign in England. Mounted on the wall above the door to the Swan Pub, it's over 400 years old.

The Clare Collector, 1 Nethergate Street, at the corner of Malting Lane, has some knockout antique Normandy farmhouse tables in cherrywood and elm at prices that won't have you reeling.

Market Hill Antiques, in the Market Square, has a great collection of china, including chamber pots, brass candlesticks and other decorative items. We coveted a fabulous brass bird cage when we visited.

Suffolk Sales Auctioneers, Church Street, holds regular 11am Saturday auctions which include antiques. These can be viewed on

Friday from 5pm to 9pm and on the day of the sale from 9am onwards. For details telephone (0787) 277993.

CLARE RESTAURANT

The Bell Hotel, The Square   **££**
Tel: (0787) 277741
Open: Daily noon-1:45pm, 7:30pm-9.30pm. Main restaurant
      closed Sunday evenings
Credit cards: AE, DC, MC, V

The 16th-century timbered inn offers the visitor two dining choices. The lovely long dining room with its brick fireplace, plaster and wooden beamed walls and ceilings, serves excellent meals with emphasis on all that's fresh and seasonal in the surroundings. The wine list is extensive and reasonably priced. Alternatively, you can eat in the Wine Bar which faces onto the Square. They specialize in pasta (such as *tagliatelli carbonara*, £1.95) and fish (our grilled haddock (£3.50) was beautifully tender), as well as excellent steaks. These two rooms contain the landlady's remarkable collection of teapots in every imaginable shape – as clocks, pigs, cottages, couples dancing, etc.

CLARE HOTELS

The Seafarer Inn, 18 Nethergate Street.   **£**
Tel: (0787) 277449
Amenities: 💻 🍴 🍷   Credit cards: AE, DC, MC, V

This 17th-century inn, on your left as you enter the village, has five attractive bedrooms, three of which have bathrooms en suite. All have color television and tea/coffee making facilities. There's a lovely beer garden out back enclosed by ancient flint walls. Saturday barbecues are held here throughout the summer. Parking is in front of the hotel.

The Bell Hotel, The Square   **££**
Tel: (0787) 277741
Amenities: ☎ 💻 🍴 🍷   Credit cards: AE, DC, MC, V

This hotel has 21 rooms which are all pleasantly furnished with tea/coffee machines, clock radios, TVs and direct dial phones. The ten new rooms in the Dickensian Courtyard out back all have en suite facilities and hair dryers. The rooms are exceptionally quiet. Numbers 14, 15, 17 and 19 all have proper four-posters and are particularly romantically furnished. Parking is just in front of the hotel.

*Turn right alongside the **Bell Hotel** into the **A1092 (Cavendish Road)**. In just 2½ miles you'll come into **Cavendish** with its green on your left and pink thatched **almshouses** nestling before the Norman **St Mary the Virgin Church**. These cottages won the West Suffolk architectural restoration award in 1973. A step or two from the cottages is **Cavendish Antiques**. Note the rare Victorian posting box in the side wall of the shop, facing the cottages.*

Cavendish Antiques (open: daily 2pm-6pm) has an interesting selection of metalware, china, glass and some furniture. Certainly worth a stop to browse. If it's closed but you've spotted something you like through the window knock on the door of the adjoining cottage. In the driveway a sign of the times: 'Please Keep Garage Access Clear' translated into French, German and – Japanese.

*Continue straight through the village staying on the **A1092**. You'll pass the left turning for **Clemsford** village before entering **Long Melford**. The first of the village's 32 antiques shops is on the right as you come into town, **Country Antiques** (lots of wood and copper items). Parking is plentiful along **Hall Street**. There is no Tourist Information Centre in town but the informative Long Melford, Official Guide, can be purchased at bookstores or newsagents.*

LONG MELFORD

There has been a town here since ancient times and Long Melford is mentioned in the Doomsday Book as 'Melaforda', old English for mill by the ford. The 'Long' is a very much more recent version and no doubt refers to the fact that the main street runs for over three miles.

If you love antiques the mile which constitutes the town's center is Valhalla. There are 32 antique stores in this stretch, as well as several other fashionable shops.

The town's name may derive from long-gone mills but the wool trade made it prosperous in the 15th and 16th centuries. As you come in from the north you'll cross the enormous village green which slopes down to the village. For centuries one of East Anglia's largest wool fairs was held here as well as an important cattle market. This trade created enormous local fortunes. Indeed the town's wealth was such that a large soft purse was known as a 'Long Melford'.

WHAT TO SEE

As you enter the town via the green off to your left you will spy a magnificent Tudor building which stands in front of the Church of the Holy Trinity. This is the **Hospital of the Holy and Blessed Trinity**, built and endowed by Sir William Cordell in 1573 as an old peoples' home – a role it performs to this very day.

The Hospital effectively blocks the Church's view of Long Melford. Opinion as to why this is so is split to this very day. The clergy maintain that the building is so placed simply because it was the end of Cordell's property and he wanted it to be as close to the Church as possible to gain proper credit from the Powers That Be.

On the other hand many villagers maintain that Cordell had a falling out with the Church and accordingly placed it here to block their view (it's known locally as a 'spite building').

Directly behind the Hospital you will find the **Church of the Holy Trinity**. There has been a Christian church on this site since 1050 but its religious associations may go back to a much earlier time. In 1914 the Vicar found relics which appear to come from an earlier Roman temple within the grounds.

Built in 1484 the Holy Trinity represents late Perpendicular architecture in all its glories, with its tall windows and stone and dressed flint exterior. The 118 foot tower encases bits of the original structure which was struck by lightning. The current tower only dates from the early years of this century and was designed by architect G. F. Bodley, a descendant of the creator of Oxford's Bodleian Library. It reminds many of Oxford. If you've been, see if you agree.

The Church itself is 180 feet long but the Lady Chapel extension which adjoins it, once clearly a separate building, takes its length to 250 feet in total.

You'll enter by the porch on the south side. Once inside you will see that the interior is rather cold and barren but it does hold some wonderful surprises. Not least amongst these are the **north aisle windows** which you can reach by crossing the nave. Our favorite amongst these is above the north door. This remaining fragment of a larger scene shows three rabbits as the Trinity. Notice that between the three they only have three ears, though each has two, (no mean feat this).

Most of the windows provide a remarkably accurate depiction of 15th-century costumes and the likenesses are thought to represent actual notables of the time. Just down to the right embedded in the wall is a remarkable bas relief of the **'Adoration of the Magi'** thought to date from the 14th century. Notice Joseph at the foot of the bed clutching his crook and the oxen and the ass peeping out from under the bed. The Virgin's elongated hands clearly suggest a Far Eastern influence.

Clopton's Chantry Chapel contains the famous **Lily Crucifix Window**, also ancient carved scrollwork thought to be the work of a medieval monk of Bury.

Virtually cheek by jowl with the altar to its right is the **Founder's**

Tomb of Sir William Cordell, who died in 1581. While he was a solicitor in life, he is dressed as a knight and his feet rest on the mythical bird which adorns his crest, a cockatrice. The gabled **Lady Chapel** was used as a school from 1670-1800 and you can still see a multiplication table on the wall from that period.

Kentwell Hall

Open: Good Fri, Tues-Thur 2pm-6pm, Sat-Mon 11am-6pm Good Friday-following Thur; Wed and Sun 2pm-6pm Apr-mid June; Sat-Sun 11am-6pm mid Jun-mid Jul (historic re-creations only, see below); Wed-Sun 2pm-6pm, public holiday weekends 11am-6pm, mid Jul-Sep

Admission: Adults £2.40, children £1.40

*Directions: coming down **Church Walk** from **Holy Trinity Church** make your first left onto **West Gate** and then turn left again (signposted A134). The brick entrance for Kentwell Hall is immediately on your left.*

You'll approach the Hall down a one mile long, 300-year-old avenue of majestic lime trees. There has been a building on this site at least since Norman times when Frodo, brother of the Abbot of Bury St Edmunds, lived here, while the Abbot occupied Melford Hall. The Clopton family settled here in the 14th century and the present elegant Tudor structure was built by Thomas Clopton in 1555. (He died in 1597, his tomb is in the church.) The house has an E-plan exterior and while the wings appear to be symmetrical, they're not. There are two fine two-story Elizabethan bay windows, one on either side of the three-story central porch. The house and its immediate garden are completely surrounded by moats, as is the walled garden. Many of the walls date from the 17th century and hold decorative espalier fruit trees.

The grounds contain a magnificent dovecote, a brick paved maze and unusual farm animals bred on the property.

Much of the present building was designed by Thomas Hopper in 1827 who renovated Melford Hall as well (qv).

Kentwell is, in many ways, a present day miracle. Over the years the building had been extensively bastardized with Georgian, then Victorian additions and 'improvements'. By this century it was a real hodgepodge and by the 60s it was also a virtual wreck surrounded by a jungle.

The current owners bought the property in 1971 and have worked steadily since to restore it to its former grandeur.

The **Great Hall**, one and a half stories high, has a delightful minstrels' gallery and a chimney-piece which dates from 1720, while the **main staircase** is late 17th century. The main **dining room** is also one and a half stories tall; its walls have recently been restored to reveal lovely marquetry. Where possible furniture of the period has been used.

In 1989 the historical re-creation centers on the year 1605 and how it impacted on the life of a Tudor household. This runs from June 19 to July 10.

Melford Hall
Open: Wed, Thur, Sun and public holidays 2:30pm-6pm Apr-Sep
Admission: Adults £2, children £1

*Directions: Coming out of **Kentwell Hall**, turn right on the **A134**. Shortly on your left you'll see the entrance to magnificent Melford Hall at the edge of the green.*

This moated Tudor mansion occupies the site of a previous manor house used by the Abbots of Bury St Edmunds until the Dissolution of the Monasteries. It was built by Sir Thomas Cordell to a Tudor, rather than an Elizabethan, design in 1554. Sir Thomas was Solicitor General under Henry VIII, then Queen Mary, followed by Elizabeth – a deft trick. Clearly he was excellent at taking clients' instructions.

The exterior features some delightful pepper-pot roofs as well as a series of harmonious chimneys. There is a central porch with projecting wings on each side. The exterior decoration is somewhat Italianate, much like Kentwell.

Cordell entertained Queen Elizabeth here in 1578 which must have cost him an arm and a leg. Contemporary records indicate that he had no fewer than 500 young men in attendance (200 attired in white velvet, 300 in black) and 1500 servants to look after the Queen and her retinue.

Later, during the Civil War, widowed Lady Rivers lived here after being thrown out of her other stately home which was ransacked, only to have the same thing happen at Melford Hall. She died in a pauper's prison.

In 1786 Sir Henry Parker bought the house, along with most of its contents. Subsequently he commissioned Thomas Hopper to design the stunning Regency library with its lovely inlaid woods. This is strongly nautical and that's not surprising. Sir Henry's uncle, brother and son were all noted British admirals.

You will see the handsome Romsey painting of Sir Hyde Parker on the 19th-century staircase. Sir Hyde was the admiral Nelson 'turned his blind eye to' at the Battle of Copenhagen. In more recent years Beatrix Potter was a regular guest.

The house contains much of interest in the way of furnishings and paintings. There is some exquisite Chinese porcelain brought back by Sir Hugh Parker when he captured a Spanish galleon, loaded with gifts from the Emperor of Peking to the Spanish King, in 1762. The two-story **Banqueting Hall** is particularly impressive. In the **main hall** you'll see a number of shields in stained glass. One is of John Winthrop, first Governor of Massachusetts. The **Blue Drawing Room** has a great rococo fireplace, the work of (department of silly names) Sir Cordell Firebrace.

The grounds have some wonderfully whimsical topiary and contain an unusual Tudor garden pavilion.

SHOPPING

Long Melford could best be described as 'Antique City'. What's more the shops are all conveniently located in the high street called **Hall Street**. Virtually all are open from 9:30am or 10am until 5pm, Monday through Saturday. On Wednesday many stores close at 1pm for the day.

We are starting our shopping tour at the **Bull Hotel** just over Chad Brook on your left as you enter the village. Unless otherwise noted all of our shopping choices are on **Hall Street**.

Denzil Grant Antiques – if you are looking for quality items at prices to match this shop is a must. They specialize in 17th- and 18th-century walnut and oak country furniture and tapestries. When we visited they had an enchanting *trompe l'oeil* 1906 watercolor by L. B. Smith at £585, a Regency dining room table and some matching chairs that wouldn't go amiss in a stately home and a museum quality oak jointed stool, circa 1660 for £1,390.

Bodilys – If boots and sensible country shoes appeal then step in here. They have some extremely well made attractive leather boots – a snip at £49.95.

Country Life has an extremely good collection of casual country wear including Pringle and Breton sweaters and super striped and checked women's shirts with ruffled collars (£37.50). They also have a good assortment of fly fishing gear and some handsome small gifts, pocket hip flasks, etc.

Sun House Antiques is a cracking good idea for those who like great antique glassware. They had some lovely Cranberry glass when we visited. Sun House also have some stunning old embroidered pieces, notably a Georgian cat in a handsome birds-eye maple surround (£785).

Seabrook Antiques' strength is in 18th- and 19th-century furniture with a heavy sideline in whimsy – metal lions' heads, Brigadier Pickman's brass-studded leather traveling case, etc.

On the opposite side of the street is Coconut House, which houses Tessa Sinclair's **Decorative Antiques** which is another good but unusual and amusing antique shop. (We loved her Regency sofa with Japanese print fabric upholstery.)

Also in Coconut House is **Roger Carling Antiques** which has an extensive collection of brass and copper, which included at the time of our visit a magnificent 2 foot diameter Georgian copper basin (£170).

Ward Antiques offers rather more elegant, ornate and formal artifacts. That's in keeping with their storefront which features cameos of Victoria and Albert under the windows. We particularly fancied their Chinese and Japanese ceramics.

Bruno Cooper Antiques, Saint Mary Street, the extension of Hall Street, specializes in 18th-century English furniture. Bruno Cooper is a Californian who has lived in England for 25 years and is a former Oxford don.

LONG MELFORD RESTAURANTS

Canes Bistro and Wine Bar, Hall Street £
Tel: (0787) 78213
Open: Tue-Sat noon-2pm, Mon-Sat 7pm-10pm
Closed: Sun and Mon lunch
Credit cards: MC, V

A cheery storefront spot with brick walls, wooden bar in the center, plants and a large blackboard with the specials of the day created by owner-chef Ernst Zips. He hails from Austria, so does much of the cooking. Fresh Hungarian Goulash £6.25.

Black Lion on the Green ££
Tel: (0787) 312356
Open: Meals served: Daily noon-2:30pm, 7pm-9:30pm; no food
        Sun eve
Credit cards: MC, V

This very pretty airy room has the feel of a lovely country cottage and that's appropriate because they work wonders with the local ingredients – lamb that melts in your mouth, marvelous monkfish, super salads. The wine list is excellent. Luke Brady, the proprietor, used to be in the trade. We were delighted to see Essencia, a Californian Muscat that beats Beaume de Venise.

LONG MELFORD HOTELS

The Crown Inn, Hall Street £
Tel: (0787) 77666
Amenities: ⌨ 🅿 🍴 🍷   Credit cards: AE, DC, MC, V

The entryway and guests' lounge can best be described as 'raffish', a wall coat rack full of picture hats, shelves full of books guests are welcome to borrow, an illuminated stained-glass window showing a courting couple from Shakespeare's 'A Midsummer Night's Dream'. Off to your right there's a plain bar with a wall hanging showing dogs playing poker. Brenda, the barmaid, knows the village like the back of her hand.

Rooms in the modern annex out back are extremely well

appointed with coffee/tea makers, hair dryers and guests' toiletries. Those in the main building (all with bathroom en suite) are more homey – the lovely wooden four poster room is worth the extra £5.50.

Cock and Bell, Hall Street £
Tel: (0787) 79807
Amenities: 🖵 🅿 ⑂⑂ ⑂   Credit cards: v

Cockfights used to take place here with the winning owner awarded a brass bell – hence the name. Three lovely double bedrooms (including a fourposter) share one large bathroom. The cock-a-hoop price: £15 for a single, £30 for a double including full English breakfast. New owner, Roy Woolston couldn't be more charming.

The Bull, Hall Street £££
Tel: (0787) 78494
Amenities: ☎ 🖵 🅿 ⑂⑂ ⑂   Credit cards: AE, DC, MC, V

Though this handsome ancient building started life as a wool merchant's house it's been an inn for over 400 years. As a result it's a Suffolk institution and it's the rare local art show that doesn't feature at least one painting of The Bull. The interior has been tastefully done (not always the case with Trusthouse Forte) with ancient rafters, open fireplaces and the odd grandfather clock.

Rooms are equally tasteful – some have enchanting nooks holding anything from the bed to coffee tables. All have coffee/tea makers. There's a pleasant interior courtyard for drinks and snacks in summer.

LONG MELFORD TO LAVENHAM   (about 9 miles)

*Leave town on **Hall Street** with the Bull Hotel on your right going toward **Long Melford Hall**. Hall Street becomes the **A134** for **Bury St Edmunds**. At the village called **Bridge Street**, 2 miles from Long Melford, turn right at the Rose and Crown pub, signposted **Lavenham**. After about a mile on this very narrow single-track road you'll see the tower of Lavenham's church of St Peter and St Paul. In another 1½ miles bear left passing the church on your left. Shortly thereafter you'll come down into Lavenham's **High Street** with the Swan Hotel on your right. Take the next right turn into **Lane** (street) which leads directly into the **Market Place**. Park here and visit the **Tourist Information Centre** in the Guildhall on the left of the main entrance. (Tel: (0787) 248207. Open: Mon-Sat 10am-5pm Easter-Oct.)*

LAVENHAM

A number of towns on this tour have buildings of great interest but Lavenham is in a class of its own. The site has been occupied at least since Saxon times (Lafa's home = Lavenham) but it's the medieval wool trade that makes Lavenham so special.

There has been a market here since 1257 but by the 14th century this was a different kind of market town, one devoted to trading in wool and weaving. Flemish weavers arrived during the 14th century, (you can see some of their cottages in **Water Street**) and no fewer than 300 buildings were erected between 1450 and 1500 to supply the clothiers' trade or as a result of the riches generated by the woven cloth.

Unusually the **Market Square** occupies the high point in the village as opposed to being on the high street. As a result there is a truly medieval street pattern here and one can imagine all of these houses filled with the families weaving away. Daughters were trained at an early age and could seldom escape the confines of the house to go courting; that's how the word 'spinster' entered our language.

Lavenham's citizens have been meticulous in preserving their movie-like surroundings, so much so that back in the 60s they had all electricity and telephone lines resettled under ground.

WHAT TO SEE

Pride of place here must go to the magnificent **Guildhall**, in our view the best half-timbered Tudor building in the country (open: daily 11am-1pm, 2pm-5:30pm end Mar-Mid Nov; admission: adults £1.50, children 50p).

Built in the early 1500s to house the 'Guild of Corpus Christi', you'll spot a full length statue of one of the key founders, the 15th Lord de Vere, Earl of Oxford. His descendant the 17th Lord de Vere is reputed by a minority to be the true author of Shakespeare's plays – a theory somewhat damaged by the fact that 14 of Shakespeare's plays were first staged after Oxford's death.

Corpus Christi was one of the three Lavenham Guilds founded by wool clothiers to regulate the woolen trade, to provide secure employment and for religious purposes such as the performance of religious plays. The guild was dissolved soon after the monastries were under Henry VIII and the building subsequently has housed everything from a prison and almshouse to the town hall and a nursery school.

Today its nine rooms have some stunning linenfold paneling, fabulous fireplaces and a complete history of the Lavenham wool industry and other items of local historical interest are on display. There's also a good National Trust shop.

The **Wool Hall**, now part of the Swan Hotel (qv), is on your right down Lady Street, to the left of the Guildhall as you emerge. Built even earlier, 1414, this once housed the Religious Guild of the Blessed Virgin (hence the name Lady Street when times turned secular). In the present century the building was dismantled and in the process of being shipped to Princess Louise's Ascot estate when the locals raised such a fuss that it was returned and restored.

The **Church of St Peter and St Paul** was endowed by the de Vere family and wealthy merchant Thomas Spring at the end of the Wars of the Roses in part to celebrate John de Vere's safe return after his distinguished service fighting for Henry VII at the Battle of Bosworth.

The church, built between 1483 and 1525, is 192 feet long by 68 feet wide and its lofty nave soars up to 43 feet. The 141 foot tower holds the famed Lavenham bells, reputed to be the finest eight ring set in the country.

The screen surrounding Thomas Spring's tomb, called the Spring Parclose, features enchanting carvings by Flemish renaissance craftsmen while the lower part of the Chancel Screen, which dates from the 1340s, is notably less ornamental than the upper half. That's because for a time it was used by a church warden as part of his pig pen.

We think you'll be particularly taken with the primitive carvings which feature in the miserere seats such as a man playing a pig like a bagpipe, and the Ibis and Spoonbill feasting on a man's head.

SHOPPING

Shopping hours in Lavenham are generally 9:30am-5pm. Many shops close at 1pm on Wednesdays during the winter.

Martin Hogg, High Street, directly across from the Swan Hotel, offers excellent Scottish knitwear, ranging from lambswool to cashmere. His other shop, right next door, has a comprehensive range of china and glass featuring such household names as Aynsley, Coalport, Royal Doulton, Royal Worcester, Waterford and Wedgwood. We were particularly taken by his china-handled bread, cake and pie knives.

Just up the street on the same side, **J & J Baker Antiques** has really fine pieces – barrel chests banded in brass, some lovely porcelain, 18th-century paintings at appropriate prices. They also have a second shop a block down from the Swan in Water Street (there's a pleasant bookstore next to this).

Next, at the corner of Hall Street, **Hingston's Gift Shop** is not your normal ticky-tacky soak the tourist set-up. Brixton Spongeware pottery from Ireland, whimsical address books with T-shirt covers, well-made wool ties are but a few of the items on sale. This shop is a good place to pick up small, inexpensive gifts.

Further up the High Street, **Gable End Antiques** has a tasteful selection of period pieces and country furniture at reasonable rates.

Finally don't overlook the shop in the Guildhall.

LAVENHAM RESTAURANTS

The Great House Restaurant, Market Place   **££**
Tel: (0787) 247431
Open: Daily noon-2:30pm, 7pm-10:30pm
Credit cards: AE, MC, V

The building's old (14th-century) but has a decidedly Georgian façade, as does the warm interior of this American owned establishment, with its lovely inglenook fireplace. The pork saddle in Dijon mustard sauce is to die for. Their traditional Sunday lunch at a prix fixe of £8.75 is great traditional food at a great price. This is the best food in town. Also has three lovely bedrooms.

Timbers Restaurant, High Street   **£**
Tel: (0787) 247218
Open: Tues-Sun noon-2pm; Wed, Fri-Sat 7:30pm-9:30pm
Credit cards: MC, V.

This simple restaurant (quarry tiled floors, wooden tables and cushioned chairs, terra cotta colored walls) serves excellent simple meals such as English rack of lamb with rosemary (£8.75) or homemade steak and kidney pie (£6.75).

Tickle Manor Tea Shop, High Street (**£**) is a good bet for a delicious tea or light meal. In spite of the twee name (after all 'twinkle, twinkle little star' was penned in the village), the food's not twee. Try the Slap and Tickle – layers of apple, potato and sausage with a lovely creamy cheese topping. Including a side salad it's just £3.75.

LAVENHAM HOTELS

The Angel Inn, Market Place   **£**
Tel: (0787) 247388
Amenities: 🖵 🅿 🍴 🍸 No credit cards

This is a bed and breakfast best bet. Four pleasant rooms upstairs. No facilities en suite but two bathrooms with separate loos are convenient to your door. Owners, David and Margaret Graves, are a pleasant couple, though their dog's a bit standoffish.
The all in price at £15 for a single occupancy, £28 for double is terrific.

The Swan Inn, High Street, Water Street, Lady Street   **£££**
Tel: (0787) 247477
Amenities: ☎ ➘ **P** ⁙ ℚ   Credit cards: AE, DC, MC, V

Going to Lavenham and giving the Swan a miss is as unthinkable as going to Windsor and leaving out the castle. Originally it was formed from three 15th-century medieval half-gabled lath and plaster buildings as a center for the wool trade and lodging house for wool traders. By the 18th century it had become an important coach house with thrice weekly service to London. The carriageway was converted into a courtyard and there was stabling for 50 horses. The entrance to this is now the entrance hall to the hotel. Today you can take light meals or a drink in the **Courtyard Garden Bar**, though we think £3.75 for a smoked salmon sandwich is highway robbery.

The **Old Bar** is another matter. Flying Fortress crews and their support staff called this their local during World War II. You'll see their service badges, roll of honor, and names – all perfectly preserved. See if you can beat their record for downing a half gallon out of the glass boot – it's 22 seconds.

The interior reeks of history and they have terrific concerts and gastronomic weekends – not to mention a harpsichordist at tea-time, a pianist for cocktails. Rooms are tasteful – pretty quilted comforters, handsome side lamps, tea and coffee makers etc., but at £79 for a standard double room with bathroom but no breakfast, it approaches London rates.

LAVENHAM TO SUDBURY   (about 6½ miles)

*Leave the **Market Square parking lot** turning left down **Lady Street**. At the bottom you'll see the Priory in front of you to the left. Turn right into **Water Street**. At the T-junction turn left into **Church Street** signposted **Sudbury** (6½ miles). The church of St Peter and St Paul is on your right as you head out of town. This road becomes the **B1071**. After 3 miles you'll join the **B1115** at the curve in the road. The tower of Waldingfield's Church of St Lawrence is in the distance. Drive through **Great Waldingfield**. At the fork in the road bear right around for **Sudbury**, you'll see signs for **Town Centre** at the next traffic circle. Follow town center signs into town passing rows of gloomy terraced houses on either side of the street. You'll have to turn left off **East Street** into **Girling Street** following the one-way system. Get into the right lane; follow signs for **Town Centre**. Turn right, then bear left. St Peter's Church is now on your right. Park on **Market Hill** or one of the streets close by. The **Tourist Information Centre** is in the Library (the old Corn Exchange Building) on Market Hill. (Tel: (0787) 72092). Open: Tue-Sat 9.30am-5pm. Closed: Sun-Mon.)*

SUDBURY

From the Tourist Information Centre look off to your right and you'll see a statue of famed painter Thomas Gainsborough in front of **St Peter's Church** – which confusingly looks like a town hall. Cross Market Hill and to your left you'll find Gainsborough Street running out of it.

Gainsborough Bookshop, No 48a, has an extensive collection of books on the area including a walking tour called *See Sudbury*.

Just down Gainsborough Street at **No 46** you'll find – surprise, surprise, where Gainsborough was born in 1727. This 16th-century building is now Georgian fronted. Gainsborough's father was in the wool trade, but at the age of thirteen Thomas persuaded his dad to let him escape to London (it's a feeling we share). He later moved to Ipswich in Suffolk and painted a number of small groups in landscapes as well as his better known portraits while there. Of fellow painter Joshua Reynolds he remarked, 'Damn him, how various he is'. Appropriately the house is now a contemporary arts and crafts center and a museum dedicated to Thomas Gainsborough's life (open: Tues-Sat 10am-5pm, Sun 2pm-5pm; closed: 4pm Oct-Easter; Mon, Good Friday, Dec 24-Jan 2; admission: adults £1, children 50p).

Across the street at No 11 **Pickwick's** serves good teas and has a delicious selection of small gifts including Crabtree & Evelyn toiletries and soap.

Further down the street, at the corner of Gregory Street, **Windsor Antiques** has the odd good find amongst a mass of bric-a-brac.

Turn up Gregory Street and shortly on your right you'll come to a large silk factory, **Venner's Silks**. They have a factory outlet shop, **Gregory Mills** (open: Mon-Fri 9am-12:30pm, 1:30pm-4pm) which sells seconds at rock bottom prices (ties and scarves start at £1). The perfect place to pick up a regimental tie to wear back home.

Further up the road and across the street you'll see **St Gregory's Church**. The hapless Simon Tebaud, former Archbishop of Canterbury, was beheaded during the Peasants' Revolt (1381). His head now resides in the vestry. Clearly it's time for a drink.

Fortunately one is readily to hand. Turn right off **Gregory Street** onto **Weaver's Lane** and you'll spot the **Waggon and Horses** pub on your left. It's a laid back Easy Rider sort of place – old Guinness ads on the wall with a pleasant outdoor terrace and good omelettes for under £2.

Continue down **Weaver's Lane** and you'll arrive back at **Market Hill** across from the Tourist Information Centre.

SUDBURY TO FINCHINGFIELD (about 14 miles)

*Head out of town on **Gainsborough Street**. Follow the street as it* *winds through town changing names as it goes. Follow the sign for the **A131** (**Chelmsford**). About 1½ miles from town you enter **Essex County** and shortly thereafter the village of **Bulmer Tye**. At the junction just out of town turn right onto the **B1058** signposted **Hedinghams**. Follow this road and signs for Hedinghams. About 3½ miles from the junction you'll see **Castle Hedingham** in front of you across the fields. Shortly, you'll see signs for **Hedingham Castle and Steam Trains**. Turn right into **Bailey Street**. The Castle entrance is 150 yards down the road on the right.*

Castle Hedingham, near Halstead on the B1058
Open: Daily 10am-5pm Easter weekend and May-Oct
Admission: Adults £2, children £1

The 850-year-old Norman Castle was built by Aubrey de Vere, son of one of William the Conqueror's most influential nobles. The powerful de Vere family became the Earls of Oxford maintaining their castle for 550 years. Today only the well-preserved **Norman Keep** remains intact. You're able to visit the **Garrison Chamber** and the **Banqueting Hall** with its Minstrels' Gallery and what many think is the finest Norman arch in England. Take note of the variety of decorative stonework within the building. Much of this was the work of talented Norman stone masons.

You'll approach the Keep via a **Tudor bridge** spanning the moat. Do plan to picnic on the pleasant grounds of the **Inner Bailey**.

*To continue the drive to **Finchingfield** turn right out of the castle drive onto the **B1058** signposted **Halstead/Braintree**. Turn right again and go through town on **Queen Street**. Note the superb 6 window Georgian façade on your left. Follow the road out of town, cross the river and after ½ mile you'll enter the village of **Sible Hedingham**. At the T-junction turn left onto the **A604** and take the next right by the Sugar Loaves pub signposted **Wethersfield** (4 miles). Follow the road around to the right with St Peter's Church on the right. Turn left just after the church into **Wethersfield Road** (also marked for **Finchingfield**). Off to the right you'll see the US Airforce Base. Patrick Brönte, the father of Branwell, Emily, Anne and Charlotte, was a curate in St Mary Magdalene Church (on your left) from 1806-9. Signs for Finchingfield point straight ahead on the **B1053**. In just under 2 miles you'll come to the outskirts of Finchingfield which look rather boring. However, in a few minutes you'll see a curious round house in the field on your right and just beyond it **'The Windmill'**. For a closer look pull into the **Red Lion** pub parking lot on your right. Otherwise, continue down the hill into the center of town with its glorious pond and ancient houses. Bear to the right and park in the lot near **Ye Olde Nosebag Restaurant**.*

There isn't a Tourist Information Centre in this small village but an informative town guide may be purchased at the post office (on road leading away from the pond opposite the Fox on the Green pub).

FINCHINGFIELD

We could tell you about 400+ year-old St John the Baptist Church, the Guildhall, the former almshouses, the nearby windmill, but all of these attractions you can find to a greater or lesser degree elsewhere.

What you'd be pushed to find is a village that better defines the term 'picture postcard'. Chosen as one of Britain's most pictures-que places during the Festival of Britain it has featured in countless calendars, brochures and booklets ever since. Now you know why. Happily it's just that bit off the beaten track so that it's seldom overrun with tourists. Uncase your camera and fire away.

When you've done so **The Fox on the Green** pub, alongside the bridge, is a cheery place to have a pint. The bar's beaten copper, in winter the free standing fireplace is aglow. There's even a mounted Louisville slugger baseball bat behind the bar in case you've had it with your traveling companions.

Ye Olde Nosebag Restaurant, next door, (open: Tues-Sun noon-2pm, Tues-Sat 7pm-10pm; credit cards: MC, V) serves good food – try the wild boar cooked in mead and juniper berry sauce (£12.75) – in horsey surroundings (nosebags on the wall as you enter, ingle-nook fireplaces with horse brasses etc.). In summer they do cream teas on the terrace out front.

FINCHINGFIELD TO THAXTED   (about 6 miles)

*Facing the War Memorial turn right out of the **parking lot** onto the **B1053** to **Little Sampford**. Drive through this hamlet passing Forest Nursery on your left. At the telephone box about 2 miles from Finchingfield turn left signposted **Thaxted**. Drive along this tree-lined road for about ½ mile, then turn left following signs for **Thaxted/ Great Dunmow**. Three miles down this single-track lane brings you to the outskirts of Thaxted with its church steeple and windmill off to the right. At the T-junction turn right signposted **B184/Saffron Walden**. In front of you you'll see the 14th-century Guildhall.*

THAXTED

Thaxted (Old English for 'the place where the thatch grows') goes back to Roman times but really came into its own in the 14th century. The Earls of Clare (qv) brought the cutlery trade to the town and by 1381 tax records show that about 40% of the 247 tradesmen listed were cutlers or in related fields such as blacksmiths.

In 1390 they built the beautiful double gabled **Guildhall** (open: Sun 2pm-3pm; free admission) which now houses a collection of local documents from the 17th century onwards as well as a small museum in the cellar.

The ground floor of the building – open on three sides – was a covered market. Inside an 18th-century staircase leads to the second floor which was also open but probably could be screened in during bad weather while the Cutlers met and (perhaps) the Warden lived on the second floor. Today the Parish Council meets here.

Turn left coming out of the Guildhall and this will bring you into the appropriately named **Stoney Lane**. On your left at No 4 you'll find **Turpin's Antiques** which is a real find. They have a glorious assortment of copper and brass (a great brass chestnut roaster when we were there, plus elegant pieces of 18th- and 19th-century furniture, porcelain and glass.

Carry on up the lane and you'll come to the **Church of St John the Baptist**, begun in 1340, completed 170 years (and 10 reigns) later in 1510. Both church and town benefit from an extraordinary legacy of endowments which do everything from help pay the vicar to give funds to prospective brides, other apprentices, and mothers of three or more children. To the far side of the churchyard you'll see the **Almshouses** and the **Chantry**, both heavily restored. Between these runs **Mill Row Lane**. Take this and after passing the **New Churchyard** on your right you'll come to the town **windmill** which dates from 1804. Today it's a rural museum, complete with 1835 fire engine (open: Sat-Sun, Bank Holiday Mon 2pm-6pm May, June, July and September; admission: adults 40p, children 15p).

Retrace your steps to the first right-hand lane (you'll spot a great **cat and mouse weathervane**). This unnamed lane leads into **Fishmarket Street** which leads back to the **Guildhall**.

THAXTED TO GREAT DUNMOW (about 5½ miles)

*Retrace your steps back the way you came into town. Follow the road around signposted **B184 Great Dunmow**. Note the little farm pond on your left just before you enter the village of **Great Easton**. Pass the turning for the village of **Butcher's Pasture** and 5½ miles from Thaxted you'll enter **Great Dunmow**. Follow the road to the town center with the village pond on your right just before the shops begin. You'll pass **The Star, Restaurant With Rooms** (see page 523) on your right as you come up the hill into **Market Place**. At the T-junction with Saracen's Head Hotel facing you, turn left into **High Street** then left again into an alleyway (**White Street**) by the Boar Pub which brings you into the parking lot (which has toilets). Walk back down **White Street**, turn left onto the **High Street**. Just behind the War Memorial and across the street you'll find the **Tourist Information Centre** in the Council Office Building near the post office. (Tel: (0371) 4533. Open: Mon-Fri 8:30am-12:30pm, 1:30pm-5pm (Fri until 4:30pm) all year; Sat 9:30am-12:30pm May-Sep.)*

GREAT DUNMOW

There's been a settlement here since the Iron Age. The Saxons named it (Dun-Mow=Meadow Mill). Though its basic street plan is largely Tudor some streets are even older – New Street dates from 1380.

Dunmow is synonymous with the ceremony of the **'Dunmow Flitch'** (it's referred to in Chaucer's *Canterbury Tales*). Couples married for a year and a day appear before a jury to swear that they've not only not quarreled during the period but that they've not 'since the parish clerk said amen, wished ourselves unmarried again'. Those who succeed in this outrageous prevarication are awarded a flitch of bacon and paraded through the village in a double chair which can be seen in the priory church.

All the buildings in **Market Square** date from the Tudor era but the one we suggest you concentrate on is The Star.

The Star, Restaurant With Rooms, Market Place   **£££**
Tel: (0371) 4231
Open: Mon-Fri noon-2pm, 7pm-9:30pm; Sat 7pm-10pm, Sun
       noon-2pm
Credit cards: DC, MC, V

Built in the 15th century, the only reminder of those times are the beams in the bar to the left of the entrance and the cellar which holds a spectacular array of wine. The low beamed dining room with its light green walls and lovely prints is welcoming. The prix fixe menu is outstandingly good. For lunch there are three or four starters, two or three main dishes to choose from plus a choice of desserts and coffee for £13.50 (£16.50 on Sunday). Crab mousse and smoked turkey with mangoes were delicious openers, so were the gorgeous brill and roast mallard which followed. At dinner both choice and price roughly double.

They've recently converted an old stable block out back into eight lovely individually decorated en suite bedrooms. These really are enchanting. Singles go for £50, doubles for £75 including a first-rate breakfast.

GREAT DUNMOW TO LONDON   (about 55 miles)

*Since you can't leave the **parking lot** the way you came in follow the exit signs turning left into the one-way system. You'll come out alongside the Town Hall. Turn left and immediately right with Saracen's Head Hotel on your left as you drive out of town. At the traffic circle follow signs for **Bishop's Stortford (A120)**. Drive along this road for about 7¼ miles passing the turning for **Bacon End*** *village on the left. Then you'll see a major traffic circle. Take the first left marked **M11 London/Harlow**.*

*Now you can drive either directly back to London or pick up the **M25** at the **M11 Exit 6 (M25 Exit 27)** for **Leeds Castle** and **Rochester** (**M25 Exit 2**) see **page 307**. Or, if you prefer, go directly on to **Canterbury** (**M25 Exit 2** to the **A2/M2**), see **page 224**.*

FURTHER READING

HOTELS/RESTAURANTS/PUBS

BTA Commended Country Hotels, Guesthouses and Restaurants, British Tourist Authority

Egon Ronay's *Cellnet Guide Hotels & Restaurants,* Automobile Association (UK) Publishing Division

Wolsey Lodges, available from the British Travel Centre, 12 Regent Street, London SW1 or Wolsey Lodges, 14 Museum Street, Ipswich

Good Hotel Guide, Britain and Western Europe, edited by Hilary Rubenstein, Consumers' Association

Staying off the Beaten Track, Elizabeth Gundrey, Arrow Books

The Good Food Guide, edited by Drew Smith, Consumers' Association

The Good Pub Guide, edited by Alisdair Aird, Consumers' Association

SHOPPING

Guide to the Antique Shops of Britain, compiled by Carol Adams, Antique Collectors' Club Ltd

The Serious Shopper's Guide to London, Beth Reiber, Prentice Hall Press

BUILDINGS

Treasures of Britain, Automobile Association (UK), Drive Publications

Beastly Buildings, Lucinda Lambton, Jonathan Cape Ltd

The National Trust Book of *Great Houses of Britain,* Nigel Nicolson, Weidenfeld and Nicolson

Historic Houses, Castles & Gardens (Open to the Public), edited by Sheila Alcock, British Leisure Publications

Country House Treasures, Arthur Foss, The National Trust

Museums & Galleries in Great Britain and Ireland, edited by Sheila Alcock, British Leisure Publications

PLACES

Village England, Peter Cookston, Hutchinson & Co Ltd

Great Gardens, Reader's Digest Association Ltd

Timpson's England (A Look Beyond The Obvious), John Timpson Jarrold Colour Publications

AA Book of British Villages, Drive Publications Ltd

London, The Biography of a City, Christopher Hibbert, Longmans Green & Co Ltd

A Literary Pilgrim (An Illustrated Guide to Britain's Literary Heritage), Edward Thomas, Webb & Bower Ltd

The National Trust Handbook, The National Trust

The Michelin Tourist Guide to The West Country, Michelin & Cie

The Sunday Times Book of the Countryside, Macdonald General Books

MAPS

Superscale Atlas of Great Britain, Ordnance Survey, Temple Press

100 Miles Around London – Primary Route Map, Geographia Ltd

Red Book Series, Estate Publications (individual town plans and books containing maps for all major towns in a particular county)

INDEX

All prices were accurate at time of going to press. Sadly inflation is a way of life.

Make AAA Your All-In-One Travel Center... Home And Abroad

Travel Services

- Complete travel agency services, including expert travel planning and reservations
- Passport photos and International Driving Permits
- American Express® Travelers Cheques with *no service charge*
- TourBooks®, CitiBooks® and CampBooks® packed with valuable information
- Discounts on Avis and Hertz car rentals here and abroad
- Discounts at AAA-approved hotels and motels
- Helpful Triptiks® prepared just for you, free of charge

Emergency Services

- AAA's dependable 24-hour Emergency Road Service
- National toll-free SUPERNUMBER for emergency service away from home
- Emergency check-cashing privileges at over 1000 AAA offices
- Check acceptance at AAA contract garages nationwide
- Guaranteed Bail and Arrest Bonds
- Personal accident insurance

Available at most AAA offices in the USA and Canada

🅰🅰🅰 MEMBERSHIP APPLICATION

Detach and mail in postage-paid reply card.
Or just call 1-800-AAA-HELP. (1-800-222-4357).

☐ **Yes, I want AAA to be my All-In-One Travel Center! Rush me my membership card so I can begin to enjoy my many membership benefits.**

☐ Charge my VISA ☐ Charge my MasterCard
☐ Charge my American Express ☐ Bill me

Credit Card Number _____ Exp. Date _____

Bank # (MC only) _____

Signature (for charges) _____

☐ Please send me more information about AAA membership. (Membership is available only to residents of the United States and Canada).

NAME _____

ADDRESS _____

CITY _____ STATE _____ ZIP _____

TELEPHONE: Home (_____) _____ Office (_____) _____

AOG-90

Discover the Benefits of Membership BEFORE You Take Your Next Trip.

Complete the postage-paid reply card TODAY.